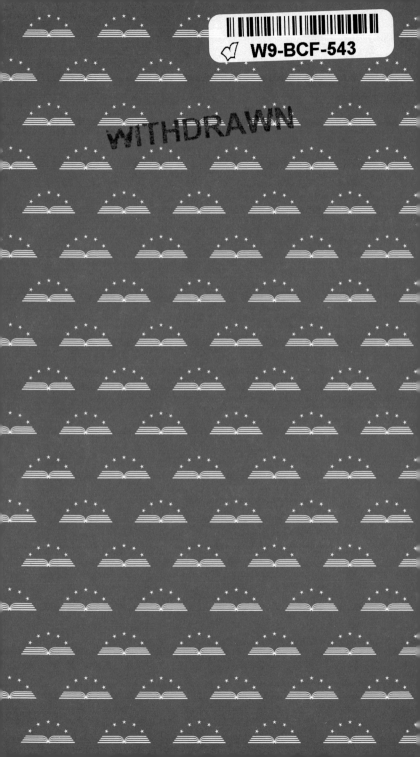

H. L. MENCKEN

H. L. MENCKEN

THE DAYS TRILOGY, EXPANDED EDITION

Marion Elizabeth Rodgers, *editor*

THE LIBRARY OF AMERICA

Manufactured in the United States of America

Contents

HAPPY DAYS
1880–1892

OCTOBER 8, 1888

Preface

THESE CASUAL and somewhat chaotic memoirs of days long past are not offered to the nobility and gentry as coldly objective history. They are, on the contrary, excessively subjective, and the record of an event is no doubt often bedizened and adulterated by my response to it. I have made a reasonably honest effort to stick to the cardinal facts, however disgraceful to either the quick or the dead, but no one is better aware than I am of the fallibility of human recollection. Fortunately, I have been able to resort, at many points, to contemporary inscriptions, for my people have lived in one house in Baltimore since 1883, and when I returned to it in 1936, after five years of absence, and began to explore it systematically, I found its cupboards and odd corners full of family memorabilia. My mother, who died in 1925, was one of those old-fashioned housewives who never threw anything away, and in the years following her death my sister apparently made only slow progress in excavating and carting off her interminable accumulations. Moreover, I found that my father, ordinarily no cherisher of archives, had nevertheless preserved, for some reason unknown, a file of household bills running from the year of his marriage to the early nineties—not a complete file, by any means, but still one showing many well-chosen and instructive specimens.

I have mined this file diligently, and found a number of surprises in it. One is the discovery that my memory was grossly at fault, for nearly half a century, on a salient point of my education. For all those years I boasted that I could read music at the age of six at the latest—indeed, I boasted that I could read it so far back in my nonage that it was impossible for me to recall the time when I couldn't. These boasts turned out, on reference to the bill file, to be mere sound and hooey, signifying nothing. Therein, as plain as day, was a receipt showing beyond cavil that there was no piano in the house until my *eighth* year—or, to be precise, until I was seven years, four months and one day old. This disconcerting experience caused me to check and re-check the whole saga of my infant recollections, partly by the same bill file, partly by the countless other

3

documents, glyphs and cave-drawings in the house, and partly by the memories of surviving contemporaries. I unearthed many other errors, but none so gross as the one about my genesis as a *Tonkünstler*, and on the whole I made a pretty good average score. As Huck Finn said of "Tom Sawyer," there are no doubt some stretchers in this book, but mainly it is fact.

It has, so far as I can make out, no psychological, sociological or politico-economic significance. My early life was placid, secure, uneventful and happy. I remember, of course, some griefs and alarms, but they were all trivial, and vanished quickly. There was never an instant in my childhood when I doubted my father's capacity to resolve any difficulty that menaced me, or to beat off any danger. He was always the center of his small world, and in my eyes a man of illimitable puissance and resourcefulness. If we needed anything he got it forthwith, and usually he threw in something that we didn't really need, but only wanted. I never heard of him being ill-treated by a wicked sweat shop owner, or underpaid, or pursued by rent-collectors, or exploited by the Interests, or badgered by the police. My mother, like any normal woman, formulated a large programme of desirable improvements in him, and not infrequently labored it at the family hearth, but on the whole their marriage, which had been a love match, was a marked and durable success, and neither of them ever neglected for an instant their duties to their children. We were encapsulated in affection, and kept fat, saucy and contented. Thus I got through my nonage without acquiring an inferiority complex, and the present chronicle, both in its materials and in its point of view, must needs fall out of the current fashion, which seems to favor tales of dirty tenements, wage cuts, lay-offs, lockouts, voracious landlords, mine police, foreclosed mortgages, evictions, rickets, prostitution, larceny, grafting cops, anti-Semitism, Bryanism, Hell-fire, droughts, xenophobia, and other such horrors. I was a larva of the comfortable and complacent bourgeoisie, though I was quite unaware of the fact until I was along in my teens, and had begun to read indignant books. To belong to that great order of mankind is vaguely discreditable today, but I still maintain my dues-paying membership in it, and continue to believe that it was and is authentically human, and therefore worthy of the attention of philosophers, at least to the extent that the Mayans, Hittites, Kallikuks and so on are worthy of it.

How, on one of its levels, it lived and had its being in a great American city in the penultimate decade of the last century is my theme, in so far as there is any theme here at all. I shut down my narrative with the year 1892, which saw my twelfth birthday. I was then at the brink of the terrible teens, and existence began inevitably to take on a new and more sinister aspect. It may be that I'll resume the story later on, but that is not certain, for on the whole I am more interested in what is going on now than in what befell me (or anyone else) in the past. My days of work have been mainly spent, in fact, in recording the current scene, usually in a far from acquiescent spirit. But I must confess, with sixty only around the corner, that I have found existence on this meanest of planets extremely amusing, and, taking one day with another, perfectly satisfactory. If I had my life to live over again I don't think I'd change it in any particular of the slightest consequence. I'd choose the same parents, the same birthplace, the same education (with maybe a few improvements here, chiefly in the direction of foreign languages), the same trade, the same jobs, the same income, the same politics, the same metaphysic, the same wife, the same friends, and (even though it may sound like a mere effort to shock humanity), the same relatives to the last known degree of consanguinity, including those in-law. The Gaseous Vertebrata who own, operate and afflict the universe have treated me with excessive politeness, and when I mount the gallows at last I may well say with the Psalmist (putting it, of course, into the prudent past tense): The lines have fallen unto me in pleasant places.

Roaring Gap, N. C., 1939.   H. L. M.

Table of Contents

I.

Introduction to the Universe

A T THE instant I first became aware of the cosmos we all infest I was sitting in my mother's lap and blinking at a great burst of lights, some of them red and others green, but most of them only the bright yellow of flaring gas. The time: the evening of Thursday, September 13, 1883, which was the day after my third birthday. The place: a ledge outside the second-story front windows of my father's cigar factory at 368 Baltimore street, Baltimore, Maryland, U. S. A., fenced off from space and disaster by a sign bearing the majestic legend: AUG. MENCKEN & BRO. The occasion: the third and last annual Summer Nights' Carnival of the Order of Orioles, a society that adjourned *sine die*, with a thumping deficit, the very next morning, and has since been forgotten by the whole human race.

At that larval stage of my life, of course, I knew nothing whatever about the Order of Orioles, just as I knew nothing whatever about the United States, though I had been born to their liberties, and was entitled to the protection of their army and navy. All I was aware of, emerging from the unfathomable abyss of nonentity, was the fact that the world I had just burst into seemed to be very brilliant, and that peeping at it over my father's sign was somewhat hard on my still gelatinous bones. So I made signals of distress to my mother and was duly hauled into her lap, where I first dozed and then snored away until the lights went out, and the family buggy wafted me home, still asleep.

The latter details, you will understand, I learned subsequently from historians, but I remember the lights with great clarity, and entirely on my own. They constitute not only the earliest of all my earthly recollections, but also one of my most vivid, and I take no stock in the theories of psychologists who teach that events experienced so early in life are never really recalled, but only reconstructed from family gossip. To be sure, there is a dead line beyond which even the most grasping memory does not reach, but I am sure that in my own case it must have run with my third birthday. Ask me if I recall the occasion, probably before my second, when I was initiated into the game of I-spy by a neighbor boy, and went to hide behind a wire screen, and was astonished when he detected me—ask me about that, and I'll admit freely that I recall nothing of it whatever, but only the ensuing anecdote, which my poor mother was so fond of telling that in the end I hid in the cellar every time she started it. Nor do I remember anything on my own about my baptism (at which ceremonial my father, so I have heard, made efforts to get the rector tight, and was hoist by his own petard), for I was then but a few months old. But not all the psychologists on earth, working in shifts like coal-miners, will ever convince me that I don't remember those lights, and wholly under my own steam.

They made their flash and then went out, and the fog again closed down. I don't recall moving to the new house in Hollins street that was to be my home for so many years, though we took possession of it only a few weeks later. I don't recall going into pants at about a quarter to four years, though it must have been a colossal experience, full of pride and glory. But gradually, as my consciousness jelled, my days began to be speckled with other events that, for one reason or another, stuck. I recall, though only somewhat vaguely, the deck of an excursion-boat, *circa* 1885, its deafening siren, and the wide, gray waters of Chesapeake Bay. I recall very clearly being taken by my father to a clothing-store bright with arc-lights, then a novelty in the world, and seeing great piles of elegant Sunday suits, and coming home with one that was tight across the stern. I recall a straw hat with flowing ribbons, a cat named Pinkie, and my brother Charlie, then still a brat in long clothes, howling like a catamount one hot Summer night, while my mother dosed him with the whole pharmacopoeia of the house, and frisked him for outlaw pins. I recall, again, my introduction to the wonderland of science, with an earthworm (*Lumbricus terrestris*) as my first subject, and the experiment directed toward finding out how long it would take him, laid out in the sun on the backyard walk, to fry to death. And I recall my mother reading to me, on a dark Winter afternoon, out of a book describing the adventures of the Simple Simon who went to a fair, the while she sipped a cup of tea that smelled very cheerful, and I glued my nose to the frosty window pane, watching a lamplighter light the lamps in Union Square across the street and wondering what a fair might be. It was a charming, colorful, Kate Greenaway world that her reading took me into, and to this day I can shut my eyes and still see its little timbered houses, its boys and girls gamboling on village greens, and its unclouded skies of pale blue.

I was on the fattish side as an infant, with a scow-like beam and noticeable jowls. Dr. C. L. Buddenbohn, who fetched me into * sentience at 9 P.M., precisely, of Sunday, September 12, 1880, apparently made a good (though, as I hear, somewhat rough) job of it, despite the fact that his surviving bill, dated October 2, shows that all he charged "to one confinement" was ten dollars. The science of infant feeding, in those days, was as rudimentary as bacteriology or social justice, but there can be no doubt that I got plenty of calories and vitamins, and probably even an overdose. There is a photograph of me at eighteen months which looks like the pictures the milk companies print in the rotogravure sections of the Sunday papers, whooping up the zeal of their cows. If cannibalism had not been abolished in Maryland some years before my birth I'd have butchered beautifully.

My mother used to tell me years afterward that my bulk often attracted public notice, especially when it was set off dramatically against her own lack of it, for she was of slight frame and less than average height, and looked, in her blue-eyed blondness, to be even younger than she actually was. Once, hauling me somewhere by horse-car, she was confronted by an old man who gaped at her and me for a while with senile impertinence, and then burst out: "Good God, girl, is that baby *yours*?" This adiposity passed off as I began to run about, and from the age of six onward I was rather skinny, but toward the end of my twenties my cross-section again became a circle, and at thirty I was taking one of the first of the anti-fat cures, and beating it by sly resorts to malt liquor.

My gradually accumulating and clarifying memories of infancy have to do chiefly with the backyard in Hollins street, * which had the unusual length, for a yard in a city block, of a hundred feet. Along with my brother Charlie, who followed

*Asterisks refer to notes by Mencken in "Days Revisited," pages 597–795 in this volume.

me into this vale when I was but twenty months old, I spent most of my pre-school leisure in it, and found it a strange, wild land of endless discoveries and enchantments. Even in the dead of Winter we were pastured in it almost daily, bundled up in the thick, scratchy coats, overcoats, mittens, leggings, caps, shirts, over-shirts and under-drawers that the young then wore. We wallowed in the snow whenever there was any to wallow in, and piled it up into crude houses, forts and snow-men, and inscribed it with wavering scrolls and devices by the method followed by infant males since the Würm Glaciation. In Spring we dug worms and watched for robins, in Summer we chased butterflies and stoned sparrows, and in Autumn we made bonfires of the falling leaves. At all times from March to October we made a Dust Bowl of my mother's garden.

The Hollins street neighborhood, in the eighties, was still almost rural, for there were plenty of vacant lots nearby, and the open country began only a few blocks away. Across the street from our house was the wide green of Union Square, with a fishpond, a cast-iron Greek temple housing a drinking-fountain, and a little brick office and tool-house for the square-keeper, looking almost small enough to have been designed by Chic Sale. A block to the westward, and well within range of our upstairs windows, was the vast, mysterious compound of the House of the Good Shepherd, with nuns in flapping habits flitting along its paths and alleys, and a high stone wall shutting it in from the world. In our backyard itself there were a peach tree, a cherry tree, a plum tree, and a pear tree. The pear tree survives to this day, and is still as lush and vigorous as it was in 1883, beside being thirty feet higher and so large around the waist that its branches bulge into the neighboring yards. My brother and I used to begin on the cherries when they were still only pellets of hard green, and had got through three or four powerful bellyaches before the earliest of them was ripe. The peaches, pears and plums came later in the year, but while we were waiting for them we chewed the gum that oozed from the peach-tree trunk, and practised spitting the imbedded flies and June bugs at Pinkie the cat.

There was also a grape-arbor arching the brick walk, with six vines that flourished amazingly, and produced in the Autumn a huge crop of sweet Concord grapes. My brother and I applied ourselves to them diligently from the moment the first blush of color showed on them, and all the sparrows of West Baltimore helped, but there was always enough in the end to fill a couple of large dishpans, and my mother and the hired girl spent a hot afternoon boiling them down, and storing them away in glass tumblers with tin tops. My brother and I, for some reason or other, had no fancy for the grape jelly thus produced with so much travail, but we had to eat it all Winter, for it was supposed, like camomile tea, to be good for us. I don't recall any like embalming of the peaches, plums and pears; in all probability we got them all down before there were any ripe enough to preserve. The grapes escaped simply because some of them hung high, as in the fable of the fox. In later years we collared these high ones by steeple-jacking, and so paid for escape from the jelly with a few additional bellyaches.

But the show-piece of the yard was not the grape-arbor, nor even the fruit-trees; it was the Summer-house, a rococo structure ten feet by ten in area, with a high, pointed roof covered with tin, a wooden floor, an ornate railing, and jig-saw spirals wherever two of its members came together. This Summer-house had been designed and executed by my mother's father, our Grandfather Abhau, who was a very skillful cabinet-maker, and ＊ had also made some of the furniture of the house. Everything of his construction was built to last, and when, far on in the Twentieth Century, I hired a gang of house-wreckers to demolish the Summer-house, they sweated half a day with their crowbars and pickaxes. In the eighties it was the throne-room and justice-seat of the household, at least in Summer. There, on fair Sunday mornings, my father and his brother Henry, who lived next door, met to drink beer, try out new combinations of tobacco for their cigar factory, and discuss the credit of customers and the infamies of labor agitators. And there, on his periodical visitations as head of the family, my Grandfather Mencken sat to determine all the delicate questions within his jurisdiction.

My mother was an active gardener, and during her forty-two ＊ years in Hollins street must have pulled at least a million weeds. For this business, as I first recall her, she had a uniform consisting of a long gingham apron and an old-time slat-bonnet—a head-dress that went out with the Nineteenth Century. Apron and slat-bonnet hung on nails behind the kitchen door, and on a shelf adjoining were her trowels, shears and other such tools, including always a huge ball of twine. My brother Charlie and I, as we got on toward school age, were drafted to help with the weeding, but neither of us could ever make out any difference between weeds and non-weeds, so we were presently transferred to the front of the house, where every plant that came up between the cobblestones of Hollins street was indubitably verminous. The crop there was always large, and keeping it within bounds was not an easy job. We usually tackled it with broken kitchen knives, and often cut our hands. We disliked it so much that it finally became convict labor. That is to say, it was saved up for use as punishment. I recall only that the maximum penalty was one hour, and that this was reserved for such grave offenses as stealing ginger-snaps, climbing in the pear-tree, hanging up the cat by its hind leg, or telling lies in a gross and obvious manner.

Charlie was somewhat sturdier than I, and a good deal fiercer. During most of our childhood he could lick me in anything approximating a fair fight, or, at all events, stall me. Civil war was forbidden in Hollins street, but my Grandfather Mencken, who lived in Fayette street, only three blocks away, had no apparent objection to it, save of course when he was taking his afternoon nap. I remember a glorious day when eight or ten head of his grandchildren called on him at once, and began raising hell at once. The affair started as a more or less decorous pillow-fight, but proceeded quickly to much more formidable weapons, including even bed-slats. It ranged all over the house, and must have done a considerable damage to the bric-a-brac, which was all in the Middle Bismarck mode. My grandmother and Aunt Pauline, fixed by my grandfather's pale blue eye, pretended to be amused by it for a while, but when a large china thunder-mug came bouncing down the third-story stairs and a black hair-cloth sofa in the parlor lost a leg they horned in with loud shrieks and lengths of stove-wood, and my grandfather called time.

*   Charlie and I were very fond of Aunt Pauline, who was immensely hospitable, and the best doughnut cook in all the

Baltimores. When the creative urge seized her, which was pretty often, she would make enough doughnuts to fill a large tin wash-boiler, and then send word down to Hollins street that there was a surprise waiting in Fayette street. It was uphill all the way, but Charlie and I always took it on the run, holding hands and pretending that we were miraculously dashing car-horses. We returned home an hour or so later much more slowly, and never had any appetite for supper. The immemorial tendency of mankind to concoct rituals showed itself in these feasts. After Charlie had got down his first half dozen doughnuts, and was taking time out to catch his breath and scrape the grease and sugar off his face, Aunt Pauline would always ask "How do they taste?" and he would always answer "They taste like more." Whether this catechism was original with the high contracting parties or had been borrowed from some patent-medicine almanac or other reference-work I don't know, but it never varied and it was never forgotten.

There were no kindergartens, playgrounds or other such Devil's Islands for infants in those innocent days, and my brother and I roved and rampaged at will until we were ready for school. Hollins street was quite safe for children, for there was little traffic on it, and that little was slow-moving, and a cart approaching over the cobblestones could be heard a block away. The backyard was enough for us during our earliest years, with the cellar in reserve for rainy days, but we gradually worked our way into the street and then across it to Union Square, and there we picked up all the games then prevailing. A few years ago, happening to cross the square, I encountered a ma'm in horn-rimmed spectacles teaching a gang of little girls ring-around-a-rosy. The sight filled me suddenly with so black an indignation that I was tempted to grab the ma'm and heave her into the goldfish pond. In the days of my own youth no bossy female on the public payroll was needed to teach games to little girls. They taught one another—as they had *
been doing since the days of Neanderthal Man.

Nevertheless, there was a constant accretion of novelty, at least in detail. When we boys chased Indians we were only following the Sumerian boys who chased Akkadians, but the use of hatchets was certainly new, and so was the ceremony of scalping; moreover, our fiends in human form, Sitting Bull and

Rain-in-the-Face, had been as unknown and unimagined to
the Sumerian boys as Henry Ward Beecher or John L. Sullivan.
The group songs we sang were mainly of English provenance,
but they had all degenerated with the years. Here, precisely, is
what we made of "King William" in Hollins street, *circa* 1885:

> King William was King James's son;
> Upon a ri' a race he won;
> Upon his breast he wore a star,
> The which was called the life of war.

What a *ri'* was we never knew and never inquired, nor did
we attach any rational concept to *the life of war*. A favorite
boys' game, called "Playing Se*bast*apool" (with a heavy accent
on the *bast*), must have been no older in its outward form than
the Crimean War, for Sebastapool was plainly Sevastopol, but
in its essence it no doubt came down from Roman times. It
could be played only when building or paving was going on in
the neighborhood, and a pile of sand lay conveniently near. We
would fashion this sand into circular ramparts in some friendly
gutter, and then bristle the ramparts with gaudy tissue-paper
flags, always home-made. Their poles were slivers of firewood,
and their tissue-paper came from Newton's toy-store at Baltimore and Calhoun streets, which served the boys and girls of
West Baltimore for seventy years, and did not shut down at last
until the Spring of 1939. The hired girls of the block cooked
flour paste to fasten the paper to the poles.

To the garrison of a Sebastapool all the smaller boys contributed tin soldiers, including Indians. These soldiers stood in
close and peaceful ranks, for there was never any attempt at
attack or defense. They were taken in at night by their owners,
but the flags remained until rain washed the Sebastapool away,
or the milkman's early morning horse squashed it. There were
sometimes two or three in a block. Girls took a hand in making
the flags, but they were not allowed to pat the ramparts into
shape, or to touch the tin soldiers. Indeed, for a little girl of that
era to show any interest in military affairs would have been as
indecorous as for her to play leap-frog or chew tobacco. The
older boys also kept rather aloof, though they stood ready to
defend a Sebastapool against raiders. Tin soldiers were only for
the very young. The more elderly were beyond such inert and

puerile simulacra, which ranked with rag dolls and paper boats. These elders fought in person, and went armed.

In the sacred rubbish of the family there is a specimen of my handwriting dated 1883—two signatures on a sheet of paper now turned a dismal brown, the one small and rather neat and the other large and ornamented with flourishes. They seem somehow fraudulent, for I was then but three years old, but there they are, and the date, which is in my mother's hand, is very clear. Maybe she guided my stubby fingers. In the same collection there is another specimen dated January 1, 1887. It shows a beginning ease with the pen, though hardly much elegance. My mother also taught me many other humble crafts—for example, how to drive a nail, how to make paper boats, and how to sharpen a lead pencil. She even taught me how to thread a needle, and for a time I hoped to take over darning my own stockings and patching the seats of my own pants, but I never managed to master the use of the thimble, and so I had to give up. Tying knots was another art that stumped me. To this day I can't tie a bow tie, though I have taken lessons over and over again from eminent masters, including such wizards as Joe Hergesheimer and Paul Patterson. When I go to a party someone has to tie my tie for me. Not infrequently I arrive with the ends hanging, and must appeal to my hostess.

This incapacity for minor dexterities has pursued me all my life, often to my considerable embarrassment. In school I could never learn to hold a pen in the orthodox manner: my handwriting satisfied the professors, but my stance outraged them, and I suffered some rough handling until they finally resigned me to my own devices. In later life I learned bricklaying, and also got some fluency in rough carpentering, but I could never do anything verging upon cabinet-work. Thus I inherited nothing of the skill of my Grandfather Abhau. All my genes in that field came from my father, who was probably the most incompetent man with his hands ever seen on earth. I can't recall him teaching me anything in my infancy, not even marbles. He would sometimes brag of his youthful virtuosity at all the customary boys' games, but he always added that he had grown so old (he was thirty-one when I was six) and suffered so much from dead beats, noisy children and ungrateful cigarmakers, drummers and bookkeepers that he had lost it. Nor could he match the endless stories that my mother told me in the years before I could read, or the many songs. The only song I ever heard him sing was this one:

> Rain forty days,
> Rain forty nights,
> Sauerkraut sticking out the smokestack.

Apparently there were additional words, but if so he never sang them. The only *Märchen* in his répertoire had to do with a man who built a tin bridge. I recall nothing of this tale save the fact that the bridge was of tin, which astonished my brother and me all over again every time we heard of it. We tried to figure out how such a thing was possible, for the mention of tin naturally made us think of tomato-cans. But we never learned.

II.

The Caves of Learning

M<small>Y FIRST</small> day in school I have forgotten as I have forgotten my first day on earth, but my second I remember very well, for I etched it on my cortex by getting lost, along with my cousin Pauline, who lived next door in Hollins * street.

Pauline and I were of an age, and hence entered the caves of learning together. They were situate in the very heart of old Baltimore, a good mile and a half from Hollins street, and the business of getting to them involved a long journey by the Baltimore-street horse-car, with a two-block walk to follow. * On the first day we were taken over the route by Pauline's father, my uncle Henry, who gave us careful sailing directions along the way, pointing out all salient lights and landfalls—the City Hall dome, the *Sun* Iron Building, Oehm's Acme Hall (which specialized in boys' pants with double seats), and so on. On the second day, launched on our own, we recalled enough of this instruction to board the horse-car going in the right direction, and even enough to get off correctly at Holliday street, but after that our faculties failed us, and we set out afoot toward the right instead of the left.

The result was that we presently found ourselves in Pratt street, an inferno of carts and trucks, with the sluggish Back Basin, which smelled like the canals of Venice, confronting us on the far side. The Basin looked immense to us, and unmistakably sinister. Over its dark, greasy waters a score of Chesapeake Bay packets were in motion, churning up the slime with their paddles and blowing their sirens ferociously. It was a fascinating spectacle, but terrifying, and in a little while we began to blubber, and a crowd of Aframerican dock-wallopers gathered around us, and a cop was soon pushing his way through it, inquiring belligerently what in hell the trouble was now. We must have managed to tell him the name of our school, though that part of it is a blank, for he delivered us only a few minutes late to the principal and proprietor thereof, Professor Friedrich Knapp, and got a shot of Boonekamp bitters for his pains.

This was my introduction (barring that obliterated first day) to F. Knapp's Institute, a seminary that catered to the boys and girls of the Baltimore bourgeoisie for more than sixty years. It was already beginning, in 1886, to feel the competition of the public schools, but Professor Knapp was not alarmed, for he believed firmly, and often predicted, that the public schools would collapse soon or late under the weight of their own inherent and incurable infamy. They were fit, he argued freely, only for dealing with boys too stupid, too lazy, too sassy or too dirty to be admitted to such academies as his own, and it was their well-deserved destiny to be shut down eventually by the police, if not by actual public violence. As for sending girls to them, he simply could not imagine it; as well shame and degrade the poor little angels by cutting off their pigtails or putting them into pants.

The professor discoursed on the obscene subject very often, and with special heat whenever another boy left him to tackle the new and cheaper learning. He always hinted that he had really kicked the traitor out, and sometimes he followed with a homily on parents who neglected the upbringing of their children, and so bred forgers, footpads and assassins. The worst punishment he ever threatened against a boy who came to school with his hair uncombed, or supernormal shadows behind his ears, was expulsion with a certificate so unfavorable that only the public schools would take him. Every time there was a hanging at the city jail (which was pretty often in those days when psychiatrists still confined themselves to running madhouses), he referred to the departed, not by his crime but by his education, which was invariably in the public schools. No authentic graduate of F. Knapp's Institute, he let it be known, had ever finished on the gallows.

Otherwise, the professor was a very mild and even amiable man, and much more diligent at praise than at blame. He was a Suabian who had come to Baltimore in 1850, and he still wore, nearly forty years afterward, the classical uniform of a German schoolmaster—a long-tailed coat of black alpaca, a boiled shirt with somewhat fringey cuffs, and a white lawn necktie. The front of his coat was dusty with chalk, and his hands were so caked with it that he had to blow it off every time he took snuff. He was of small stature but large diameter, and wore closely-clipped mutton-chop whiskers. His hands had the curious softness so often observed in pedagogues, barbers, and Y.M.C.A. secretaries. This impressed itself on me the first time he noticed me wiggling a loose milk-tooth with my tongue, and called me up to have it out. He watched for such manifestations sharply, and pulled, I should say, an average of six teeth a week. It was etiquette in the school for boys to bear this barbarity in silence. The girls could yell, but not the boys. Both, however, were free to howl under the bastinado, which was naturally applied to the girls much more lightly and less often than to the boys.

The professor viewed the pedagogical art with great pride, and was a man of some eminence in the town. He was on easy terms with the Mayor, General Ferdinand C. Latrobe, who once got us an hour's release from learning by dropping in from the City Hall across the street to harangue us darkly on civic virtue. The old professor, in the days when I knew him, had begun to restrict his personal teaching to a few extra abstruse subjects, *e.g.*, fractions, but he always lined up all the boys for inspection in the morning, and he led both boys and girls in the singing that opened every day's session. For this last purpose all hands crowded into the largest classroom. The professor conducted with his violin, and his daughter Bertha helped out at a parlor organ. The songs, as I recall them, were chiefly German favorites of his youth—"Goldene Abend Sonne," "Winter, Adieu!," "Fuchs, du hast die Gans gestohlen," "Hurrah, Hurrah, Hurra-la-la-la-la!," and so on. Most of the pupils knew very little German, though they were taught it fiercely, but they all managed to sing the songs.   *

As I have said, the institute had already begun to wither around the edges when I first knew it. In 1879 (so I gather from a faded announcement in an old Baltimore directory) it had had a teaching staff of twelve savants, and offered instruction in French, Latin and Hebrew, not to mention German and English, but by my time the staff had evaporated down to six or seven, and French and Latin had been abandoned. There was still, however, a class in Hebrew for the accommodation of a dozen or more Jewish boys, and I sat in on its proceedings (which went on in the same classroom with less exotic proceedings) long enough to learn the Hebrew alphabet. This must have been in my ninth year. By the time I left Knapp's for the Polytechnic the class had been shut down, and I had forgotten all the letters save *aleph, beth, vav, yodh* and *resh*. These I retain more or less to the present day, and whenever I find myself in the society of an orthodox rabbi I always show them off. On other Jews I do not waste them, for other Jews seldom recognize them.

There was no enmity between the Chosen and the *Goyim* in the old professor's establishment, and no sense of difference in his treatment of them, though he was in the habit, on bursting into a classroom that was disorderly, to denounce it violently as a *Judenschule*. He used this word, not because it was invidious, but simply because it described precisely the thing he complained of, and was sound colloquial German. He was also fond of using a number of Hebrew loan-words, for example, *tokos* (backside), *schlemihl* (oaf), *kosher* (clean) and *mashuggah* (crazy), most of which have since come into American. The Jewish boys of Baltimore, in that innocent era, were still palpably and unashamedly Jews, with Hittite noses, curly hair, and such given names as Aaron, Leon, Samuel and Isaac. I never encountered one named Irving, Sidney, Malcolm or Wesley, nor even Charles or William. The old professor and his aides labored hard to teach these reluctant Yiddo-Americans the principles of their sacred tongue, but apparently with very little success, for the only textbook I ever saw in use was an elementary *Fibel*, with letters almost as large as those in the top line of an oculist's chart. All its victims were of German-Jewish origin, and came of well-to-do families, for in those days Eastern Jews were still rare in Baltimore, and whenever we boys passed one on the street we went Bzzzzzzzz in satirical homage to his beard. I must add in sorrow that the Jewish boys at Knapp's were unanimously *Chazirfresser*.

There was also in the school a group of students, all male, from Latin America, chiefly Cubans and Demerarans. I recall that their handkerchiefs were always well doused with perfume, and that they willingly paid tops, marbles and slate-pencils for the seats nearest the stove in Winter. There was one Cuban whose father had been captured by brigands and carved in a dreadful manner: his detailed description of the paternal wounds was very graphic, and made him something of a hero. For the rest, the student-body included German-Americans, Irish-Americans, French-Americans, Italian- * Americans and even a few American-Americans. There was never any centrifugence on racial lines, and the only pupil I can remember who had a nickname hinting at anything of the sort was a husky German girl, lately arrived in the Republic, who went under the style or appellation of Germany-On-Wheels. She had a fist like a pig's foot and was not above clouting any boy who annoyed her. Moreover, she was a mistress of all the German declensions, and hence unpopular. The old professor treated these diverse tribes and species with uniform but benevolent suspicion—all, that is, save the American-Americans, whom he plainly regarded as intellectually underprivileged, to say the least. I also heard him hint more than once that their fathers were behind with their tuition fees.

The Institute, in its heyday, had specialized in German, but by my time all its teaching was in English. I must have learned some German in it, for to this day I can rattle off the German alphabet in par, and reading the Gothic type of a German newspaper is almost as easy to me as reading the Lateinisch. Also, I retain a few declensions in poll-parrot fashion, and can recite them with fearful fluency, especially under malt-and-hops power. Again, I can still write a very fair German script, though reading the script of actual Germans often stumps me. Yet again, I always get the curious feeling, hearing German spoken, that it is not really a foreign language, for all its sounds seem quite natural to me, including even the *ch* of *ich*. But the professor and his goons certainly never taught me to speak German, or even to read it with any ease. They tried to ram it into their pupils as they rammed in the multiplication table—by endless repetition, usually in chorus. To this day I know the conjugation of *haben* down to *Sie würden gehabt haben*, though I couldn't write even a brief note in Hoch Deutsch without resort to a grammar and a dictionary. What little of the language I actually acquired in my youth I picked up

mainly from the German hired girls who traipsed through the
Hollins street kitchen during the eighties—corralled at the
Norddeutscher-Lloyd pier at Locust Point by my father (who
spoke next to no German, but knew the chief inspector of immigrants), and then snatched away, after a year or so, by some
amorous ice-man, beer-man or ash-man. One actually married
* a saloonkeeper, learned bartending, survived him, and died
rich. My mother complained bitterly that these husky Kunigun-
das, Käthes, Ottilies and Charlöttchens were hardly house-
broken before they flitted away, but some of them, and especially
the Bavarians, were prime cooks, and all of them were ready to
feed my brother Charlie and me at any moment, and to lie us
out of scrapes.

My father, whose mother had been British-born, had a firm
grasp upon only the more indecorous expletives of German, so
the language was not used in the house. But my mother knew
it well enough to palaver with the hired girls, and with the
German marketmen, plumbers, tinners, beermen and grocery
* boys who were always in and out. When her father dropped in
he would speak to her in German, but she would usually talk
back, for some reason that I never learned, in English. Such
bilingual dialogues sometimes went on for hours, to the fascination of my brother and me. We tried to figure out what the
old man had said on the basis of what my mother answered.
Maybe this taught us some German, but probably not much.
One of the family anecdotes has to do with my efforts as a
small child to dredge out of this grandfather an explanation
of the puzzling differences between his language and ours.
"Grandpa," I asked him, "if the German for *kiss* is *Kuss*, why isn't
the German for *fish Fush*?" He knew English well enough, but
this mystery he could not explain. My brother and I concocted a
dreadful dialect for communicating with the German hired girls
in their pre-English stages. Its groundwork was a crudely simpli-
fied English, but it included many pseudo-German words based
on such false analogies as the one I have just mentioned, for
example, *Monig* for *money* (from *Honig-honey*) and *Ratz* for
rat (from *Katz-cat*). How we arrived at *Roch* for *(cock)roach*
(pronounced in the German manner, to rhyme with *Loch*) I
can't tell you: it must have been a sheer inspiration. To this
day, alas, my German is dreadful (though not quite as bad as

my Sanskrit and Old Church Slavonic), and it always amuses me to encounter the assumption that I am a master of it, and even a scholar.

Professor Knapp, to return to him, spent most of his day moseying in and out of his classrooms at the institute, observing the technic of his agents and doing drum-head justice on boys of an evil nature. He was a virtuoso with the rattan, and chose his tool for a given caning with apparent care. He had an arsenal as large as a golfer's bag of clubs, and carried it with him from class to class. But the routine of the operation was always the same, and every boy knew it as familiarly as he knew the rules of run-a-mile or catty. The condemned would be beckoned politely to the place of execution beside the teacher's desk, and at the word *Eins* from the professor he would hold up his hands. At *Zwei* he would lower them until they stuck out straight from his shoulders, and at *Drei* he would bend over until his finger-tips touched his ankles. The punitive swooshes *a posteriori* would follow—sometimes two, three or even four, but more often only one. As I have said, it was etiquette for the condemned to make an outcry. He was also allowed and even expected to massage his *gluteus maximus* violently as he pranced back to his bench. This always led the professor to remark sagely: "You can't rub it out." Criminal girls were punished more gently, with smacks from a ruler on the open palm. They consoled themselves by hugging the insulted hand under the opposite arm.

The professor showed very little moral indignation when he carried on such exercises, and I never heard of a victim denouncing them as unjust. Whenever they took place the whole class seemed to be convinced that they were sound in law and equity, and necessary to peace and civilization. No doubt this was because the professor always took much more visible delight in rewards than in punishments. When, listening in on a recitation, he noted a boy or girl who did well, he grinned like a Santa Claus, and halted the proceedings long enough to give the worthy one a "merit." A merit was simply a card inscribed with the date and the recipient's name, and signed by the professor. Teachers could also award them, but we naturally liked the professor's best. A pupil who accumulated fifty in the course of a year received a book at the close of school, with his parents present to swell with pride. I received my first on June 28, 1888. It was a copy of Grimms' Fairy Tales, horribly translated by a lady of the name of Mrs. H. B. Paull. I got it, as the inscription notifies, "for industry and good deportment." I have it still, and would not part with it for gold and frankincense.

These merits were not plain cards, but works of art in the *Gartenlaube* manner, and very elegant in our eyes. They were lithographed in full color, and commonly showed a spray of flowers, a cat playing with a ball of wool, or a Winter scene in the Black Forest, with the snow represented by powdered mica. Sometimes the art took the form of a separate hand, embossed as well as colored. The hand was anchored to the card at the cuff, which was always laced, and one got at the inscription by turning back the fingers. Merits with hands were especially esteemed, though they had no greater exchange value than the plain ones. One of them still survives as a bookmark in the copy of Grimms' Fairy Tales aforesaid. On my withdrawal from these scenes it will go to the League of Nations.

There were teachers at the institute who came and went mysteriously and have been forgotten, but I remember very clearly all the members of the permanent staff—the old professor's daughter, Miss Bertha; his niece, Miss Elvina; his son, Mr. Willie; his chief-of-staff, Mr. Fox; and his slave, Mr. Paul. Mr. Paul was a tall, smooth-shaven, saturnine German who always wore a long black coat, and was greatly given to scenting himself with *Kölnischwasser*. There was no science of ventilation in those days, and schoolrooms were kept hermetically sealed. Mr. Paul's powerful aroma thus served admirably as a disinfectant, but toward the end of a laborious day it sometimes made us more or less giddy. He lived at the school, taking part of his emolument in board and lodging, and I heard years later, from a fellow pupil who was a great hand at the keyhole, that his maximum salary in cash was never above $10 a week.

This fact was no doubt responsible for his generally subversive frame of mind, which led him to an unhappy false step in 1888 or thereabout, almost fatal to his career. It took the form of an address to his class advocating the eight-hour day, then an anarchistic novelty in the world, and almost as alarming to the bourgeoisie as the downright confiscation of tax-free

securities would be today. Worse, he recited a slogan in support
of it, running as follows:

> Eight hours for work;
> Eight hours for sleep;
> Eight hours for what you will.

The boys could make nothing of his argument, but quickly
learned the slogan. I did so myself and one evening recited it
proudly to my father, looking confidently for his applause. Instead, he leaped from his chair, turned pale, and began to
swear and splutter in a fearful manner. I made off in alarm, and
it was years afterward before I learned from him why he was so
indignant, and what followed from his dudgeon.

It appeared then that he had been convinced in conscience,
and was still convinced in conscience, that the eight-hour day
was a project of foreign nihilists to undermine and wreck the
American Republic. In his own cigar factory nearly all work
was piece-work, so he really didn't care how long his men kept
at it, but he conceived it to be his duty to holler against the
heresy in the interest of other employers. This he did, it appeared, on the very next day, and to Professor Knapp. The
professor, who had also heard from other fathers, was much
upset, and had Mr. Paul on the carpet. From that time on we
heard nothing more of the subject. Mr. Paul applied himself
with undivided diligence to his chosen branches—penmanship,
free-hand drawing, mathematics up to the multiplication table,
and deportment—and discreetly avoided all politico-economic
speculations.

He was a kindly man, with some gifts as a draftsman. He
taught me to draw complicated, fantastic, incredible flowers
with both pen and pencil, and on lazy afternoons he would
often suspend his teaching and entertain the boys and girls by
covering the blackboard with images of birds carrying letters
in their bills, and their plumage bulging out into elaborate
curlicues. This art, now in decay, was greatly esteemed in those
days. In penmanship Mr. Paul followed classical models. Every
downstroke had to be good and thick, and every upstroke as
thin as a spider's web.

At Christmas time all the boys and girls were put to writing
canned letters of filial duty to their parents. Fancy four-page

blanks were provided for this purpose, with the first page lithographed in full color. The text was written on the blackboard,
all inkwells were cleaned and refilled, and new pens of great
fineness were provided. The first boy who made a blot tasted
the rattan, and after that everyone was very careful. As I recall
it, the business of concocting these letters occupied the better
part of a day. The professor himself dropped in from time to
time to praise the young penmen who were doing well, and to
pull the ears of those who were making messes. When an error
was detected his son, Mr. Willie, was sent for to scratch it out
with a sharp penknife. Too many errors caused the whole blank
to be condemned and torn up, and the offender had to buy
another at a cost of ten cents. We were always glad when this
agony was over.

Mr. Willie, when I first knew him, was in his middle thirties.
He was short and stocky, wore the silky mustache of the period, and combed his hair in oyster-shell style. He was much
more worldly than Mr. Paul, and often entertained us with
tales of his adventures. One of his favorite stories recounted his
observations and sensations on seeing a surgeon cut off a man's
leg. This happened somewhere in the West, where he had
served for a year or two as a disbursing agent of the General
Land Office. The boys liked the story, and encouraged him to
improve its horrors, but the girls clapped their hands over their
ears whenever he began it, and professed to shiver. He was also
fond of telling about the hazards of navigating the Missouri
river, which he had traversed during the seventies to the southern frontier of what is now South Dakota. In one of his stories
he told how the river-packets of the time, when they ran
aground on a sandbar, put out stilts operated by steam, and
lifted themselves over it. Not a boy in the school believed this
story, and I myself was nearly forty years old before I discovered that it was really true. But one of Mr. Willie's actual
stretchers I swallowed without a shadow of doubt. He was
discoursing one day on the immense number of books in the
world, and their infinite variety. "On the single subject of the
eye of the dog," he said, "enough has been written to fill this
classroom." We all believed that one.

The dean or first mate of F. Knapp's Institute was Mr. Fox, a
tall Pennsylvanian with a goatish beard, greatly resembling the

late Admiral Winfield Scott Schley. He ran the school store, and carried it about with him in a large black dispatch-box. The boys believed that he made a large income selling them pens, slate-pencils, pads of scratch-paper, and other such supplies. They also believed that he made a great deal of additional money by serving as the secretary of a lodge of Freemasons. The business of this lodge occupied him on dull afternoons, when recitations degenerated into singsong, and there was no rattaning to be done. He would spend hours addressing postcards to the members, notifying them of initiations, oyster-roasts, funerals, and the like. While he plugged away he would solemnly chew his beard. We boys marvelled that it never grew any shorter.

Mr. Fox assisted the old professor as lord high executioner, and did most of the minor fanning of the wicked. He employed a frayed rattan of small percussive powers, and was but little feared. One day in 1889 I saw demonstrated before him the truth of Oscar Wilde's saying that nature always imitates art. The comic papers of the time had among their stock characters a boy who put a slate, a shingle or a book in his pants to protect himself from justice. This was actually done in my sight by a very small boy whose name, as I recall it, was Johnnie Horlamus. When Mr. Fox turned him over, the seat of his pants bulged out into an incredible square, and Mr. Fox halted the proceedings to investigate. His search produced a third grade geography-book. When he pulled it out the whole class roared, and he had to bite his beard hard to keep from roaring himself. He let Johnnie off with a single very gentle clout.

Mr. Fox was no virtuoso like the professor. He rattaned conscientiously, but without any noticeable style. The professor not only adorned the science, but made a notable contribution to it. This was the invention of mass caning, the use of which was confined to his morning inspection in the schoolyard. It often happened that he would detect three, four or even five boys with unshined shoes or unwashed ears. He would order them to step forward a few paces, and then line them up very precisely. When they had all got into the position called for by his command of *Drei* he would try to fetch their fundaments simultaneously with one swoop of an extra-long rattan. Sometimes he succeeded, and sometimes he failed. The favorite spot in the line was naturally the one nearest him, for the boy who had it got the thick part of the rattan, swinging through a small arc, and was hence but little hurt. The boy at the far end got the thin and poisonous tip, swinging over an orbit long enough to give it the speed of a baseball and the bite of an adder's fang.

The professor believed that he was responsible for the policing and sanitation of his pupils from the time they left home in the morning until they returned there safely in the afternoon. It was a felony by the school code for a boy to hook a ride on a horse-truck. Culprits were detected by the simple fact that such trucks, being dirty, commonly left marks on the knees of stockings or seats of pants or both, but the boys preferred to believe that they were betrayed by stooges among the girls. Many an innocent girl had her pigtail severely yanked on that charge. This yanking was itself a felony, but the victim seldom complained, for if she did so her pigtail would be surely yanked again, and with a yo-heave-ho so hearty that it just fell short of scalping her.

The most serious of all crimes, of course, was fighting on the streets. When detected, it not only brought a Class A rattaning, but also a formal threat of banishment to the Gehenna of the public schools. But the institute's statutes, like the canon law of Holy Church, always provided for exceptions and dispensations. In this case the pummeling, clubbing and even (if it could be imaginably achieved) strangling and dismemberment of a boy from Scheib's School was dismissed as venial. Scheib's was so close to F. Knapp's that the two were separated only by the narrow channel of Orange alley. Professor Knapp and Pastor Scheib were ostensibly on the most fraternal footing, and always spoke of each other in flattering terms, but there was a great deal of pupil-snatching to and fro, and deep down in their chalky pedagogical hearts they were a Guelph and a Ghibelline.

III.

Recollections of Academic Orgies

S OME TIME ago I read in the New York papers about the
death of an Irishman who had been esteemed and honored
in life as the inventor of the hot-dog. The papers themselves
appeared to believe that he had deserved this veneration, for
they gave his peaceful exitus almost as much space as they
commonly give to the terminal deliriums of a movie star or
United States Senator. They said that he had made his epochal
invention in the year 1900 or thereabout, and that it had been
first marketed as consumers' goods at the Polo Grounds.

All this made me smile in a sly way, for I devoured hot-dogs
in Baltimore 'way back in 1886, and they were then very far
from new-fangled. They differed from the hot-dogs of today in
one detail only, and that one was hardly of statistical significance. They contained precisely the same rubbery, indigestible
pseudo-sausages that millions of Americans now eat, and they
leaked the same flabby, puerile mustard. Their single point of
difference lay in the fact that their covers were honest German
Wecke made of wheat-flour baked to crispness, and not the
soggy rolls prevailing today, of ground acorns, plaster-of-Paris,
flecks of bath-sponge, and atmospheric air all compact.

The name hot-dog, of course, was then still buried in the
womb of time: we called them *Weckers*, being ignorant that the
true plural of *Weck* was *Wecke*, or in one of the exceptional situations so common in German grammar, *Wecken*. They were
on sale at the Baltimore baseball-grounds in the primeval days
before even Muggsy McGraw had come to town, and they
were also sold at all picnics. In particular, I recall wolfing them
at the annual picnic of F. Knapp's Institute. One year I got
down six in a row, and suffered a considerable bellyache thereafter, which five bottles of sarsaparilla did not cure. My brother
Charlie did even better. He knocked off eight *Wecke*, and then
went strutting about with no bellyache at all. But Charlie, in
those days, had a gizzard like a concrete-mixer, and I well recall the morning when he ate eighteen buckwheat cakes for

breakfast, and gave up even then only because the hired girl had run out of batter.

The annual picnic of F. Knapp's Institute, always holden in early June, was the great event of the school year, and the older pupils began chattering about it soon after Christmas. Tickets were twenty-five cents each, but every pupil could buy them at five for a dollar, and the extra quarter was his profit. It was clearly understood that the money thus amassed was undividedly his own, and that the way he spent it was nobody's damned business. It was not etiquette for the teachers of the institute, or even his parents, to molest him when he set out to clean up the *Wecke*, pretzels, doughnuts and other delicatessen that were on sale on the grounds, or tried to stretch his skin over ten or a dozen bottles of sarsaparilla. If he collapsed there were benches for him to lie on, and a bottle of paregoric to medicate him.

The picnic was always held at Darley Park, a pleasant grove adjoining a suburban brewery. It was outfitted in the stark, Philistine style of the period, with all the trees whitewashed up to a height of six feet. Scattered about were a couple of dozen plain board tables, each outfitted with hard benches. In the middle of the grove was a small pavilion, with a senile excursion-boat piano in the center of it. Along one boundary ran a long brick building, and somewhere within it was a bar. The *Weck*, crab-cake, pretzel, doughnut and sarsaparilla vendors circled about, howling their wares. In a far corner was a portable carrousel with four horses, operated by what was then always called jackass-power. That is to say, it was kept going by a sweating Aframerican turning a crank. He turned it steadily from 10 A.M. to 4 P.M., and there were always plenty of girls and baby-class boys waiting in line. We more elderly roués spent all our money on food and drink. Sarsaparilla had a sharp bite, and, like opium, produced an appetite for itself. So did *Wecke*.

When the great day arrived all the pupils of the institute piled into a string of Gay-street horse-cars and proceeded to Darley Park at high speed. Professor Knapp always traveled by the first car, and took up at once the police duties of the day. He never carried his battery of rattans along, but he had sharp eyes and a good memory, and any boy who pulled too many of the girls' pigtails, or engaged in fisticuffs with another boy, or indulged himself in sassing a teacher was sure to go on trial the next morning, with two or three swooshes to rearward following. But crime was relatively rare at those picnics, and I remember one (I should add in frankness that it was considered exceptional) which didn't produce a single culprit. We played the immemorial games of the schoolyard, but mainly we played follow-your-leader. Sometimes as many as forty boys would be in line, and the course would include hurdles over all the benches in the park, and even up into the pavilion and over the excursion-boat piano. One year the leader, a large, gaunt boy who was generally regarded as feebleminded, led the gang out of the park and into an adjoining brickyard, and there took it through a series of puddles bottomed with red clay. When the procession returned and the professor saw the boys' shoes, he got into a dreadful lather, and soon after sunrise the next morning he broke a rattan over the half-wit's caboose.

At noon or thereabout parents began to arrive, usually in buggies. They were received formally by the whole faculty of the school, and the mothers proceeded at once to track down and inspect their offspring, looking (in the case of boys) for dirty hands, holes in stockings and skinned shins, and (in the case of girls) for torn skirts and lost hair-ribbons. Sometimes a black-hearted boy would sneak into the adjacent brickyard, which was covered in large part with Jimson weeds, plantains and other such vegetable outlaws, and return with a large ball of nigger-lice.[1] One of these nigger-lice, on being thrown at a girl, would stick to her dress. If it hit her hair, getting it out would be a tedious and even painful business. Indeed, it was generally believed by the boys of Baltimore that a nigger-louse lodged in the wool of an actual Negro girl could not be removed without shaving her head. When nigger-lice began to fly about at a school picnic the whole faculty would mobilize instantly, and in a little while the marksmen would be detected and disarmed, and next morning they would get hearty fannings from the professor.

While the mothers of the pupils were inspecting them, their fathers, following custom, would invite the male pedagogues

[1] The burrs of the common burdock (*Arctium minus*).

to the bar, and there ply them with beer. My father always had a low opinion of the Baltimore beers, and complained bitterly whenever he had to drink them. He concocted an elaborate
* legend about one of the worst of them, to the effect that it was made of the ammoniacal liquor discharged from the Baltimore gasworks, with mill-feed for malt and picric acid for hops. Once, when I was still a small boy, I was riding proudly with him on the platform of a horse-car, when he encountered a *Todsäufer*[2] belonging to the brewery that made it, and proceeded to warn him solemnly that drinking his own goods would wreck his kidneys and bring him to an early grave. To my astonishment, the *Todsäufer* admitted it freely, but explained that he owed $2000 to a building association on a house he had bought, and wanted to work off the debt before returning to his former and less remunerative trade of soft-drink drummer. My father thereupon offered him a job as a cigar salesman, but they couldn't come to terms. He must have actually died soon afterward, for I remember my father citing him as a tragic example of what men will do and suffer for money.

But the pedagogues appeared to stand the Darley Park beer very well, and indeed plainly liked it. As father after father dropped in, and schooner after schooner was dispatched, the gogues apparently gave glowing accounts of the diligence and scholarship of their pupils, for it was not uncommon for a father, coming out for air, to give his boy an extra ten cents. Mr. Fox, a man of quasi-military bearing, usually swayed ever so gently as the session in the bar ended, and he made his way to the pavilion for the closing ceremonies of the day. As for Mr. Paul, he emerged mopping his face solemnly with his

---

[2]A *Todsäufer* (literally, dead-drinker) was, and is a sort of brewer's customers' man. He is commonly called a collector, but his duties go far beyond collecting the bills owed to breweries by saloonkeepers. He is supposed to stand a general treat in the bar whenever he calls, to go to all weddings, birthday parties and funerals in the families of saloonkeepers, and to cultivate their wives and children with frequent presents. When a saloonkeeper himself dies the *Todsäufer* is the principal mourner *ex officio*, and is expected to weep copiously. He is also one of the brewery's political agents, and must handle all the license difficulties of his clients. He belongs to all the clubs and societies that will admit him, including always, if there is one, the town press-club.

cologne-scented handkerchief, and burping surreptitiously under it. I never detected any such signs in Mr. Willie, but that was probably because he was something of an *eleganto*, and always called for small beers. His hair was plastered down with plenty of soap, and not a strand of it was ever out of place. The old professor, being a Suabian, was immune to all the ordinary effects of alcohol. Toward the close of the ceremonies in the pavilion he always fell into a doze, but he did the same thing every afternoon of his life, whether he had been consuming malt liquor or well water.

The ceremonies themselves tended to be banal, for everybody was tired by then. They began with some songs by the massed pupils, accompanied by Miss Bertha on the excursion-boat piano, and they moved through the classical répertoire of recitations. I was once chosen to do "The Wreck of the Hesperus," but blew up in the second stanza. Elocution, indeed, has always been a closed art to me, for I have never been able to memorize even the shortest piece, whether in prose or verse. At the time of my first and only appearance as an actor on the public stage (it was after I had left F. Knapp's Institute) I forgot both of my two lines. My brother Charlie was called for to pinch hit for me when "The Wreck of the Hesperus" went phooey, but he did not respond, and a quick and quiet search found him hiding under the pavilion. There was always a little girl with a piano solo, but she was invariably drowned out by a freight-train of the B. & O. Railroad, which ran only a few blocks away.

If there were any politicoes present, which was usually the case, they arose to expound the issues of the hour. General Ferdinand C. Latrobe, Mayor of Baltimore for seven terms, always showed up, and always made a speech. Inasmuch as the professor was a German, the general devoted himself courteously to whooping up the unparalleled scientific, aesthetic and moral gifts of the German people, and to revealing all over again the fact that he was partly of German blood himself, despite his French-sounding name. He made exactly similar speeches at all gatherings of predominantly non-Anglo-Saxon Baltimoreans, omitting only the Aframericans and the Chinese. In his later years (I had by then become a newspaper reporter) I heard him claim not only Irish, Scotch, Welsh, Dutch and

other such relatively plausible bloods, but also Polish, Bohemian, Italian, Lithuanian, Swedish, Danish, Greek, Spanish
and even Jewish. Once I actually heard him hint that he was
remotely an Armenian. Unable by the current *mores* to boast
of African ancestry, he consoled his colored customers by
speaking in high terms of Abraham Lincoln, whom he described as a Republican with a Democratic heart. The best he
could do for the Chinese, who were then very few in Baltimore, was to quote some passages from the Analects of Confucius, which he had studied through the medium of a
secretary.

When the last politico shut down the professor called off
the proceedings, and we all started home. My father drove
the family buggy, and I sat between him and my mother, with
my brother roosting on a hassock on the floor. We kept to the
horse-car tracks as much as possible, for the cobblestones of
Baltimore, in those days, were world-famous for their rough-
ness. Whenever we had to turn out on them my brother
bounced off his hassock, and had to be derricked back. He and
I were pretty well used up by the time we got home, and after
a meager supper were ordered to bed. We slept as profoundly
as convicts in the death-house, for it was not until the next
morning that the chigger-bites picked up in the brickyard
began to make themselves manifest. Half the boys scratched
violently for three or four days thereafter, but none of the girls.
The old professor always dropped in to point the moral. The
boys, being naturally vicious, had disobeyed orders and explored the brickyard, which was a resort of noxious insects
and human desperadoes, but the girls, being virtuous and
law-abiding, had stayed on the right side of the fence. Hence
their immunity.

There were plenty of other gala days during the school year,
but none so stupendous as the day of the annual picnic, save
maybe the day of the circus parade. All parades in Baltimore
passed within hearing of F. Knapp's Institute, for the City Hall
was only across the street, and its portico was the customary
reviewing-stand. The most brutal punishment that could be
imagined by a Knapp boy, or indeed any Baltimore schoolboy,
was to be confined to barracks when a circus parade was under
way. So far as I can recall, it never actually happened in our

school, though it was often threatened. We always turned out in command of Mr. Fox and Mr. Paul, each of them armed with a rattan, and the cops made room for us along the curb. If any of the loafers who hung about the City Hall refused to move, the cops fell upon them with fists and night-sticks, at the same time denouncing them as low characters, fit only for penal servitude.

I remember of these circus parades only the patient tramp of the elephants, the loudness of the music, and the unearthly beauty of the lady bareback-riders, with their yellow wigs, dazzling spangles and pink tights. They seemed to us boys to be even more beautiful than Miss Bertha and Miss Elvina, who were our everyday paragons of female loveliness. The parade consumed most of the morning, and those boys whose fathers were taking them to the actual circus also escaped for the afternoon. They returned next day full of astounding tales and in a low state of health, for pink lemonade in that era was actually pink, and four or five glasses of it left the gall-bladder considerably fevered. There was a memorable year when two circuses came to town, and another when the circus was followed by Buffalo Bill's Wild West Show. We admired Buffalo Bill and shivered at the sight of his bloodthirsty Indians, but the general feeling was that the circus was better. Certainly the lady sharpshooters and Indian squaws had nothing on the bareback riders.

Now and then the old professor and his staff would shepherd the whole student body to some other public show, usually of a painfully cultural character. I remember clearly only one such expedition. It was an exhibit of Mexican arts and handicrafts at a hall in Charles street. The squat pottery, gaudy blankets, crude jewelry and other such stuff left me cold; indeed, I dislike all Mexican fancy-goods to this day, and regard even the masterpieces of Diego Rivera as trash. But I remember very brilliantly a sort of side-show, for it consisted of two human skeletons, the first I had ever seen. One was the skeleton of a peon who had been shot by a bandit, with the bullet hole plainly visible in the center of his forehead. The other was the skeleton of the bandit who had shot him, with one of the cervical vertebrae dislocated to show the effect of the rope that had punished the crime.

These ghastly relics were displayed in two long boxes covered with black cloth, and set up at an angle of sixty degrees. My brother and I, at first sight of them, turned quickly and slunk away, but things that are horrible are always fascinating to boys, and so we came back every now and then for another look, and by the end of the afternoon we had got massive eyefuls. That night (we slept together) we pulled the quilt over our heads and dreamed dreadful dreams of shootings, stabbings, scalpings, hangings, graveyards and dissecting-rooms, with herds of bleeding ghosts all over the place. I have encountered a great many skeletons since, and got upon easy terms with some of them, but whenever I shut my eyes and ponder upon mortality I always see the poor bones of those forlorn and anonymous Mexicans, bounced into Heaven in a far country and so long ago.

The crown and consummation of the year at Knapp's was the annual exhibition in June, following soon after the picnic. For this sombre event the largest schoolroom was chosen, and chairs for the parents of the pupils were arranged on the two sides of the teacher's desk. The programme followed classical models, stretching back, I suppose, to the times of Tiglath-pileser. First the whole school would sing, with Miss Bertha at the organ and the old professor leading with his violin; then the prizes (always books) won by diligent and docile pupils would be presented to them by Mr. Fox, who was an eminent Freemason and hence accustomed to public speaking; and then Mr. Willie would call up, one by one, all those who were not downright idiotic, and show off their learning. Some recited, some spelled hard words, some bounded Caroline county, Maryland, or Ohio, or Spain, some parsed all the components of such sentences as "The dog ate the bone," and some read in high-pitched, staccato, somewhat panicky voices out of the McGuffey Readers.

My own contribution to this symposium never took the form of a recitation, for, as I have said, I was born incapable of remembering anything longer than a limerick. Once, in term, Mr. Paul gave me a German poem of two brief stanzas to memorize, and I made such heavy weather of trying to get it that my father had to rescue me with a note to the old professor, desiring him to instruct Mr. Paul to lay off such infernal nonsense. (In those days, parents who patronized private schools had some voice in what their children were taught. On another occasion my father was full of indignation when I brought home the news that Mr. Paul believed and was teaching that the first *a* in *national* should be pronounced exactly like the first *a* in *nation*. Indeed, he was so upset that he made a call on the old professor the next morning, and was closeted with him for an hour. Mr. Paul, so far as I know, never formally recanted, but he at least went so far as to avoid the word thereafter.)

My own contribution to the annual exhibition usually took the form of a mathematical demonstration at the blackboard, say the multiplication of 75.876593 by 1129.654, or the division of 17/39ths by 71/163rds. I had no interest whatever in figures, but my father was a violent fan for them, so it gave him a great kick if I came out with an error of no more than plus-or-minus ten per cent., and when we got home he handed me a nickel, which in those days would buy a grab-bag containing at least half a pound of broken taffy and a ring or stickpin set with a large ruby.

My cousin Pauline, who was a very good reader, went through McGuffey at high speed, and my brother Charlie usually gave a more or less creditable performance at spelling, especially when the words lined out happened to be of less than two syllables. The other boys and girls displayed their various gifts one by one, and so the long morning wore on, with Mr. Willie sweating away doggedly, the boys scraping their feet on the floor and squirming in their chairs, and the parents (save when their own progeny were up) yawning dismally and rubbing themselves. As for the old professor, he invariably fell into a quiet doze, with his gold-rimmed spectacles shoved up on his forehead. When the City Hall bell struck twelve and the noon whistles began to blow he awoke suddenly and half rose to his feet.

"Villie," he would say, "daash ish genook."

At all events, that is how it sounded to me, and how I recall it today. He was, as I have noted, a Suabian, and reverted to the dialect of his native *Dorf* whenever his faculties were dimmed. Mr. Willie understood him to say "Das ist genug," which, in English, is "That's enough," and so the proceedings terminated.

The boys always piled out leaping and howling like early Christian martyrs delivered by angels from the stake, for next * day was the beginning of the Summer vacation.

IV.
The Baltimore of the Eighties   *

THE CITY into which I was born in 1880 had a reputation all over for what the English, in their real-estate advertising, are fond of calling the amenities. So far as I have been able to discover by a labored search of contemporary travel-books, no literary tourist, however waspish he may have been about Washington, Niagara Falls, the prairies of the West, or even Boston and New York, ever gave Baltimore a bad notice. They all agreed, often with lubricious gloats and gurgles, (*a*) that its indigenous victualry was unsurpassed in the Republic, (*b*) that its native Caucasian females of all ages up to thirty-five were of incomparable pulchritude, and as amiable as they were lovely, and (*c*) that its home-life was spacious, charming, full of creature comforts, and highly conducive to the facile and orderly propagation of the species.

There was some truth in all these articles, but not, I regret to have to add, too much. Perhaps the one that came closest to meeting scientific tests was the first. Baltimore lay very near the immense protein factory of Chesapeake Bay, and out of the bay it ate divinely. I well recall the time when prime hard crabs of the channel species, blue in color, at least eight inches in length along the shell, and with snow-white meat almost as firm as soap, were hawked in Hollins street of Summer mornings at ten cents a dozen. The supply seemed to be almost unlimited, even in the polluted waters of the Patapsco river, which stretched up fourteen miles from the bay to engulf the slops of the Baltimore canneries and fertilizer factories. Any poor man could go down to the banks of the river, armed with no more than a length of stout cord, a home-made net on a pole, and a chunk of cat's meat, and come home in a couple of hours with enough crabs to feed his family for two days. Soft crabs, of course, were scarcer and harder to snare, and hence higher in price, but not much. More than once, hiding behind my mother's apron, I helped her to buy them at the door for two-and-a-twelfth cents apiece. And there blazes in my

memory like a comet the day when she came home from
* Hollins market complaining with strange and bitter indignation that the fishmongers there—including old Harris, her
favorite—had begun to *sell* shad roe. Hitherto, stretching
back to the first settlement of Baltimore Town, they had always
thrown it in with the fish. Worse, she reported that they had
now entered upon an illegal combination to lift the price of
the standard shad of twenty inches—enough for the average
family, and to spare—from forty cents to half a dollar. When
my father came home for lunch and heard this incredible news,
he predicted formally that the Republic would never survive
the Nineteenth Century.

Terrapin was not common eating in those days, any more
than it is in these, but that was mainly because few women
liked it, just as few like it today. It was then assumed that their
distaste was due to the fact that its consumption involved a
considerable lavage with fortified wines, but they still show no
honest enthusiasm for it, though Prohibition converted many
of them into very adept and eager boozers. It was not, in my
infancy, within the reach of the proletariat, but it was certainly
not beyond the bourgeoisie. My mother, until well past the
turn of the century, used to buy pint jars of the picked meat in
Hollins market, with plenty of rich, golden eggs scattered
through it, for a dollar a jar. For the same price it was possible
to obtain *two* wild ducks of respectable if not royal species—and
the open season ran gloriously from the instant the first birds
wandered in from Labrador to the time the last stragglers set
sail for Brazil. So far as I can remember, my mother never
bought any of these ducks, but that was only because the guns,
dogs and eagle eye of my uncle Henry, who lived next door,
kept us oversupplied all Winter.

Garden-truck was correspondingly cheap, and so was fruit
in season. Out of season we seldom saw it at all. Oranges,
which cost sixty cents a dozen, came in at Christmas, and not
before. We had to wait until May for strawberries, asparagus,
fresh peas, carrots, and even radishes. But when the huge,
fragrant strawberries of Anne Arundel county (pronounced
Ann'ran'l) appeared at last they went for only five cents a box.
All Spring the streets swarmed with hucksters selling such
things: they called themselves, not hucksters, but Arabs (with

the first *a* as in *day*), and announced their wares with loud, raucous, unintelligible cries, much worn down by phonetic decay. In Winter the principal howling was done by colored men selling shucked oysters out of huge cans. In the dark backward and abysm of time their cry must have been simply "Oysters!", but generations of Aframerican larynxes had debased it to "Awn-eeeeeee!", with the final *e*'s prolonged until the vendor got out of breath. He always wore a blue-and-white checked apron, and that apron was also the uniform of the colored butlers of the Baltimore gentry when engaged upon their morning work—sweeping the sidewalk, scouring the white marble front steps, polishing up the handle of the big front door, and bragging about their white folks to their colleagues to port and starboard.

Oysters were not too much esteemed in the Baltimore of my *
youth, nor are they in the Baltimore of today. They were eaten, of course, but not often, for serving them raw at the table was beyond the usual domestic technic of the time, and it was difficult to cook them in any fashion that made them consonant with contemporary ideas of elegance. Fried, they were fit only to be devoured at church oyster-suppers, or gobbled in oyster-bays by drunks wandering home from scenes of revelry. The more celebrated oyster-houses of Baltimore—for example, Kelly's in Eutaw street—were patronized largely by such lamentable characters. It was their playful custom to challenge foolish-looking strangers to wash down a dozen raw Chincoteagues with half a tumbler of Maryland rye: the town belief was that this combination was so deleterious as to be equal to the kick of a mule. If the stranger survived, they tried to inveigle him into eating another dozen with sugar sprinkled on them: this dose was supposed to be almost certainly fatal. I grew up believing that the only man in history who had ever actually swallowed it and lived was John L. Sullivan.

There is a saying in Baltimore that crabs may be prepared in fifty ways and that all of them are good. The range of oyster dishes is much narrower, and they are much less attractive. Fried oysters I have just mentioned. Stewed, they are undoubtedly edible, but only in the sorry sense that oatmeal or boiled rice is edible. Certainly no Baltimorean not insane would argue that an oyster stew has any of the noble qualities of the two

great crab soups—shore style (with vegetables) and bisque (with
* cream). Both of these masterpieces were on tap in the old Rennert Hotel when I lunched there daily (years after the term of
the present narrative) and both were magnificent. The Rennert
also offered an oyster pot-pie that had its points, but the late Jeff
Davis, manager of the hotel (and the last public virtuoso of
Maryland cookery), once confessed to me that its flavor was
really due to a sly use of garlic. Such concoctions as panned and
scalloped oysters have never been eaten in my time by connoisseurs, and oyster fritters (always called flitters in Baltimore) are
to be had only at free-for-all oyster-roasts and along the wharves.
A roasted oyster, if it be hauled off the fire at the exact instant
the shell opens, is not to be sniffed at, but getting it down is a
troublesome business, for the shell is too hot to be handled
without mittens. Despite this inconvenience, there are still
oyster-roasts in Baltimore on Winter Sunday afternoons, and
since the collapse of Prohibition they have been drawing pretty
good houses. When the Elks give one they hire a militia armory,
lay in a thousand kegs of beer, engage 200 waiters, and prepare
for a mob. But the mob is not attracted by the oysters alone; it
comes mainly to eat hot-dogs, barbecued beef and sauerkraut
and to wash down these lowly victuals with the beer.

The greatest crab cook of the days I remember was Tom
McNulty, originally a whiskey drummer but in the end sheriff
of Baltimore, and the most venerated oyster cook was a cop
named Fred. Tom's specialty was made by spearing a slice of
bacon on a large fork, jamming a soft crab down on it, holding
the two over a charcoal brazier until the bacon had melted
over the crab, and then slapping both upon a slice of hot toast.
This titbit had its points, I assure you, and I never think of it
without deploring Tom's too early translation to bliss eternal.
Fred devoted himself mainly to oyster flitters. The other cops
rolled and snuffled in his masterpieces like cats in catnip, but I
never could see much virtue in them. It was always my impression, perhaps in error, that he fried them in curve grease borrowed from the street railways. He was an old-time Model T
flat-foot, not much taller than a fire-plug, but as big around
the middle as a load of hay. At the end of a busy afternoon he
would be spattered from head to foot with blobs of flitter
batter and wild grease.

It was the opinion of my father, as I have recorded, that all the Baltimore beers were poisonous, but he nevertheless kept a supply of them in the house for visiting plumbers, tinners, cellar-inspectors, tax-assessors and so on, and for Class D social callers. I find by his bill file that he paid $1.20 for a case of twenty-four bottles. His own favorite malt liquor was Anheuser-Busch, but he also made occasional experiments with the other brands that were then beginning to find a national market: some of them to survive to this day, but the most perished under Prohibition. His same bill file shows that on December 27, 1883, he paid Courtney, Fairall & Company, then the favorite fancy grocers of Baltimore, $4 for a gallon of Monticello whiskey. It retails now for from $3 to $3.50 a *quart*. In those days it was always straight, for the old-time Baltimoreans regarded blends with great suspicion, though many of the widely-advertised brands of Maryland rye were of that character. They drank straight whiskey straight, disdaining both diluents and chasers. I don't recall ever seeing my father drink a high-ball; the thing must have existed in his day, for he lived on to 1899, but he probably regarded its use as unmanly and ignoble. Before every meal, including breakfast, he ducked into the cupboard ✱ in the dining-room and poured out a substantial hooker of rye, and when he emerged he was always sucking in a great whiff of air to cool off his tonsils. He regarded this appetizer as necessary to his well-being. He said that it was the best medicine he had ever found for toning up his stomach.

How the stomachs of Baltimore survived at all in those days is a pathological mystery. The standard evening meal tended to be light, but the other two were terrific. The répertoire for breakfast, beside all the known varieties of pancake and porridge, included such things as ham and eggs, broiled mackerel, fried smelts, beef hash, pork chops, country sausage, and even—God help us all!—what would now be called Welsh rabbit. My father, save when we were in the country, usually came home for lunch, and on Saturdays, with no school, my brother Charlie and I sat in. Our favorite Winter lunch was typical of the time. Its main dishes were a huge platter of Norfolk spots or other pan-fish, and a Himalaya of corn-cakes. Along with this combination went succotash, buttered beets, baked potatoes, string beans, and other such hearty vegetables. When

oranges and bananas were obtainable they followed for dessert
—sliced, and with a heavy dressing of grated cocoanut. The
calorie content of two or three helpings of such powerful ali-
ments probably ran to 3000. We'd all be somewhat subdued
afterward, and my father always stretched out on the dining-
room lounge for a nap. In the evening he seldom had much
appetite, and would usually complain that cooking was fast
going downhill in Baltimore, in accord with the general
decay of human society. Worse, he would warn Charlie and
me against eating too much, and often he undertook to ration us. We beat this sanitary policing by laying in a sufficiency
in the kitchen before sitting down to table. As a reserve
against emergencies we kept a supply of ginger snaps, mush-
room crackers, all-day suckers, dried apricots and solferino
taffy in a cigar-box in our bedroom. In fear that it might
spoil, or that mice might sneak up from the cellar to raid it,
we devoured this stock at frequent intervals, and it had to be
renewed.

The Baltimoreans of those days were complacent beyond
the ordinary, and agreed with their envious visitors that life in
their town was swell. I can't recall ever hearing anyone complain of the fact that there was a great epidemic of typhoid
fever every Summer, and a wave of malaria every Autumn, and
more than a scattering of smallpox, especially among the colored folk in the alleys, every Winter. Spring, indeed, was the
only season free from serious pestilence, and in Spring the
communal laying off of heavy woolen underwear was always
followed by an epidemic of colds. Our house in Hollins street,
as I first remember it, was heated by Latrobe stoves, the invention of a Baltimore engineer. They had mica windows (always
called isinglass) that made a cheery glow, but though it was
warm enough within the range of that glow on even the cold-
est Winter days, their flues had little heat to spare for the
rooms upstairs. My brother and I slept in Canton-flannel
night-drawers with feathers above us and underneath, but that
didn't help us much on January mornings when all the windows were so heavily frosted that we couldn't see outside. My
father put in a steam-heating plant toward the end of the
eighties—the first ever seen in Hollins street—, but such things
were rare until well into the new century. The favorite central

heating device for many years was a hot-air furnace that was even more inefficient than the Latrobe stove. The only heat in our bathroom was supplied from the kitchen, which meant that there was none at all until the hired girl began to function below. Thus my brother and I were never harassed by suggestions of morning baths, at least in Winter. Whenever it was decided that we had reached an intolerable degree of grime, and measures were taken to hound us to the bathroom, we went into the vast old zinc-lined tub together, and beguiled the pains of getting clean by taking toy boats along. Once we also took a couple of goldfish, but the soap killed them almost instantly.

At intervals of not more than a month in Winter a water-pipe froze and burst, and the whole house was cold and clammy until the plumbers got through their slow-moving hocus-pocus. Nothing, in those days, seemed to work. All the house machinery was constantly out of order. The roof sprang a leak at least three times a year, and I recall a day when the cellar was flooded by a broken water-main in Hollins street, and my brother and I had a grand time navigating it in wooden wash-tubs. No one, up to that time, had ever thought of outfitting windows with fly-screens. Flies over-ran and devoured us in Summer, immense swarms of mosquitoes were often blown in from the swamps to the southwest, and a miscellany of fantastic moths, gnats, June-bugs, beetles, and other insects, some of them of formidable size and pugnacity, buzzed around the gas-lights at night.

We slept under mosquito canopies, but they were of flimsy netting and there were always holes in them, so that when a mosquito or fly once got in he had us all to himself, and made the most of it. It was not uncommon, in Summer, for a bat to follow the procession. When this happened my brother and I turned out with brooms, baseball bats and other weapons, and pursued the hunt to a kill. The carcass was always nailed to the backyard fence the next morning, with the wings stretched out as far as possible, and boys would come from blocks around to measure and admire it. Whenever an insect of unfamiliar species showed up we tried to capture it, and if we succeeded we kept it alive in a pill-box or baking-powder can. Our favorite among pill-boxes was the one that held Wright's Indian

Vegetable Pills (which my father swallowed every time he got
into a low state), for it was made of thin sheets of wood veneer,
and was thus more durable than the druggists' usual cardboard
boxes.

Every public place in Baltimore was so furiously beset by
bugs of all sorts that communal gatherings were impossible on
hot nights. The very cops on the street corners spent a large
part of their time slapping mosquitoes and catching flies. Our
pony Frank had a fly-net, but it operated only when he was in
motion; in his leisure he was as badly used as the cops. When
arc-lights began to light the streets, along about 1885, they attracted so many beetles of gigantic size that their glare was
actually obscured. These beetles at once acquired the name of
electric-light bugs, and it was believed that the arc carbons
produced them by a kind of spontaneous generation, and that
their bite was as dangerous as that of a tarantula. But no Baltimorean would ever admit categorically that this Congo-like
plague of flying things, taking one day with another, was really
serious, or indeed a plague at all. Many a time I have seen my
mother leap up from the dinner-table to engage the swarming
flies with an improvised punkah, and heard her rejoice and
give humble thanks simultaneously that Baltimore was not the
sinkhole that Washington was.

These flies gave no concern to my brother Charlie and me;
they seemed to be innocuous and even friendly compared to
the chiggers, bumble-bees and hornets that occasionally beset
us. Indeed, they were a source of pleasant recreation to us, for
very often, on hot Summer evenings, we would retire to the
kitchen, stretch out flat on our backs on the table, and pop away
at them with sling-shots as they roosted in dense clumps upon
the ceiling. Our favorite projectile was a square of lemon-peel,
roasted by the hired girl. Thus prepared, it was tough enough
to shoot straight and kill certainly, but when it bounced back it
did not hurt us. The hired girl, when she was in an amiable
mood, prepared us enough of these missiles for an hour's brisk
shooting, and in the morning she had the Red Cross job of
sweeping the dead flies off the ceiling. Sometimes there were
hundreds of them, lying dead in sticky windrows. When
there were horse-flies from the back alley among them, which
was not infrequently, they leaked red mammalian blood, which

was an extra satisfaction to us. The stables that lined the far side of the alley were vast hatcheries of such flies, some of which reached a gigantic size. When we caught one we pulled off its wings and watched it try idiotically to escape on foot, or removed its legs and listened while it buzzed in a loud and futile manner. The theory taught in those days was that creatures below the warm-blooded level had no feelings whatever, and in fact rather enjoyed being mutilated. Thus it was an innocent and instructive matter to cut a worm into two halves, and watch them wriggle off in opposite directions. Once my brother and I caught a turtle, chopped off its head, and were amazed to see it march away headless. That experience, in truth, was so astonishing as to be alarming, and we never monkeyed with turtles thereafter. But we got a good deal of pleasure, first and last, out of chasing and butchering toads, though we were always careful to avoid taking them in our hands, for the juice of their kidneys was supposed to cause warts.

At the first smell of hot weather there was a tremendous revolution in Hollins street. All the Brussels carpets in the house were jimmied up and replaced by sleazy Chinese matting, all the hair-cloth furniture was covered with linen covers, and every picture, mirror, gas bracket and Rogers group was draped in fly netting. The carpets were wheelbarrowed out to Steuart's hill by professional carpet beaters of the African race, and there flogged and flayed until the heaviest lick yielded no more dust. Before the mattings could be laid all the floors had to be scrubbed, and every picture and mirror had to be taken down and polished. Also, the lace curtains had to come down, and the ivory-colored Holland shades that hung in Winter had to be changed to blue ones, to filter out the Summer sun. The lace curtains were always laundered before being put away— a formidable operation involving stretching them on huge frameworks set up on trestles in the backyard. All this uproar was repeated in reverse at the ides of September. The mattings *
came up, the carpets went down, the furniture was stripped of its covers, the pictures, mirrors and gas brackets lost their netting, and the blue Holland shades were displaced by the ivory ones. It always turned out, of course, that the flies of Summer had got through the nettings with ease, and left every picture

peppered with their calling cards. The large pier mirror between the two windows of the parlor usually got a double
dose, and it took the hired girl half a day to renovate it, climbing up and down a ladder in the clumsy manner of a policeman
getting over a fence, and dropping soap, washrags, hairpins
and other gear on the floor.

The legend seems to prevail that there were no sewers in
Baltimore until after the World War, but that is something of
an exaggeration. Our house in Hollins street was connected
with a private sewer down the alley in the rear as early as I have
any recollection of it, and so were many other houses, especially in the newer parts of the town. But I should add that we
also had a powder-room in the backyard for the accommodation of laundresses, whitewashers and other visiting members
of the domestic faculty, and that there was a shallow sink under
it that inspired my brother and me with considerable dread.
Every now and then some child in West Baltimore fell into
such a sink, and had to be hauled out, besmeared and howling,
by the cops. The one in our yard was pumped out and fumi-
gated every Spring by a gang of colored men who arrived on a
wagon that was called an O.E.A.—*i.e.*, odorless excavating
apparatus. They discharged this social-minded duty with great
fervor and dispatch, and achieved non-odoriferousness, in the
innocent Aframerican way, by burning buckets of rosin and tar.
The whole neighborhood choked on the black, greasy, pungent smoke for hours afterward. It was thought to be an effective preventive of cholera, smallpox and tuberculosis.

All the sewers of Baltimore, whether private or public, emp-
tied into the Back Basin in those days, just as all those of
Manhattan empty into the North and East rivers to this day.
But I should add that there was a difference, for the North and
East rivers have swift tidal currents, whereas the Back Basin,
distant 170 miles from the Chesapeake capes, had only the
most lethargic. As a result it began to acquire a powerful aroma
every Spring, and by August smelled like a billion polecats.
This stench radiated all over downtown Baltimore, though in
Hollins street we hardly ever detected it. Perhaps that was due
to the fact that West Baltimore had rival perfumes of its
own—for example, the emanation from the Wilkins hair factory in the Frederick road, a mile or so from Union Square.

When a breeze from the southwest, bouncing its way over the Wilkins factory, reached Hollins street the effect was almost that of poison gas. It happened only seldom, but when it happened it was surely memorable. The householders of the vicinage always swarmed down to the City Hall the next day and raised blue hell, but they never got anything save promises. In fact, it was not until the Wilkinses went into the red and shut down their factory that the abomination abated—and its place was then taken, for an unhappy year or two, by the degenerate cosmic rays projected from a glue factory lying in the same general direction. No one, so far as I know, ever argued that these mephitic blasts were salubrious, but it is a sober fact that town opinion held that the bouquet of the Back Basin was. In proof thereof it was pointed out that the clerks who sweated all Summer in the little coops of offices along the Light street and Pratt street wharves were so remarkably long-lived that many of them appeared to be at least 100 years old, and that the colored stevedores who loaded and unloaded the Bay packets were the strongest, toughest, drunkenest and most thieving in the whole port.

The Baltimore of the eighties was a noisy town, for the impact of iron wagon tires on hard cobblestone was almost like that of a hammer on an anvil. To be sure, there was a dirt road down the middle of every street, kept in repair by the accumulated sweepings of the sidewalks, but this cushioned track was patronized only by hay-wagons from the country and like occasional traffic: milk-men, grocery deliverymen and other such regulars kept to the areas where the cobbles were naked, and so made a fearful clatter. In every way, in fact, city life was much noisier then than it is now. Children at play were not incarcerated in playgrounds and policed by hired ma'ms, but roved the open streets, and most of their games involved singing or yelling. At Christmas time they began to blow horns at least a week before the great day, and kept it up until all the horns were disabled, and in Summer they began celebrating the Fourth far back in June and were still exploding fire-crackers at the end of July. Nearly every house had a dog in it, and nearly all the dogs barked more or less continuously from 4 A.M. until after midnight. It was still lawful to keep chickens in backyards, and many householders did so. All within ear range

of Hollins street appeared to divide them as to sex in the proportion of a hundred crowing roosters to one clucking hen.
My grandfather Mencken once laid in a coop of Guineas, unquestionably the noisiest species of *Aves* known to science. But
his wife, my step-grandmother, had got in a colored clergyman
to steal them before the neighbors arrived with the police.

In retired by-streets grass grew between the cobblestones to
almost incredible heights, and it was not uncommon for colored rag-and-bone men to pasture their undernourished horses
on it. On the steep hill making eastward from the Washington
Monument, in the very heart of Baltimore, some comedian
once sowed wheat, and it kept on coming up for years thereafter. Every Spring the Baltimore newspapers would report on
the prospects of the crop, and visitors to the city were taken to
see it. Most Baltimoreans of that era, in fact, took a fierce, defiant pride in the bucolic aspects of their city. They would
boast that it was the only great seaport on earth in which
dandelions grew in the streets in Spring. They believed that all
such vegetation was healthful, and kept down chills and fever.
I myself once had proof that the excess of litter in the streets
was not without its value to mankind. I was riding the pony
Frank when a wild thought suddenly seized him, and he
bucked me out of the saddle in the best manner of a Buffalo
Bill bronco. Unfortunately, my left foot was stuck in the stirrup, and so I was dragged behind him as he galloped off. He
had gone at least a block before a couple of colored boys
stopped him. If the cobblestones of Stricker street had been
bare I'd not be with you today. As it was, I got no worse damage than a series of harsh scourings running from my neck to
my heels. The colored boys took me to Reveille's livery-stable,
and stopped the bloodshed with large gobs of spider web. It
was the hemostatic of choice in Baltimore when I was young.
If, perchance, it spread a little tetanus, then the Baltimoreans
blamed the mercies of God.

V.
Rural Delights

THOUGH THE bourgeoisie of Baltimore, in the days I write of, always denied fiercely that the town was an inferno in Summer, they nevertheless cleared out whenever they could— and usually they could. The nether moiety of them—mainly bachelors and young married couples—went to boarding houses in the hills that fenced in the town to westward and northward, the middle section rented cottages in the same cool and sanitary regions, and the relatively well-heeled bought or built Summer homes of their own. Some of these Summer homes still stand as monuments to the unearthly taste of the Chester A. Arthur or Cast Iron era, though most of them have lost the towers and cupolas that were once their chief flaunts of elegance, and nearly all the jig-saw rails and braces of their wide-flung porches have been replaced by less elaborate millinery.

People now live in them the year round, shuttling in and out of town by motor-car. Efficient oil-heaters keep them snug in Winter, and the telephone and radio bring them all the great boons and usufructs of our Christian civilization. In the days I write of they were vastly more remote; in fact, they were so remote that the women and children in them, having once undergone the ordeal of being moved out, stayed put for the rest of the Summer. The head of each house, of course, had to come to town every day to look after his business, for it was not usual, at that time, for males with any sense of responsibility to take holidays, but no one ever mistook this round trip for a pleasure jaunt; on the contrary, it was regarded as heroic, and mentioned with praise. The only feasible way to get to our first Summer retreat in Howard county, Maryland, was by Baltimore & Ohio train to the ancient village of Ellicott City, and then up a steep zigzag road in the village hack. My father and my uncle Henry, whose family shared the house with us, made the round trip every day, but its second half always left them hot, dusty and worn-out, and I doubt that they could have endured it if the ground rules had not allowed them a couple of mint juleps when they finally reached the front porch. The luxurious day-coaches that now distinguish the Baltimore & Ohio were unheard of in those primitive days. The Main Line local to Ellicott City was made up of creaky wooden cars that had all seen heroic service in the Civil War, and in the fifteen-mile run (it took nearly an hour) they shipped enough cinders to set all their passengers to strangling.

From our house in Hollins street to Ellicott City was but ten miles by the old National pike, but the road had no surface save bare rock and there were four or five toll-gates and six or seven immense hills along the way, so no one ever drove it if the business could be avoided. One of the hills was so steep and so full of hair-pin bends that it was called the Devil's Elbow. A hay-wagon coming up would take half a day to cover the mile and a half from bottom to top, and sometimes a Conestoga wagon from Western Maryland (there were still plenty of them left in the eighties) got stuck altogether, and had to be rescued by the plow-horses of the adjacent farmers. At intervals of a mile or so along the road there were old-time coaching inns, and they were still doing a brisk trade in 25-cent country dinners and 5-cent whiskey.

The one nearest to town, kept by a German named Adam Dietrich, actually survived until the great catastrophe of Prohibition. Its ancient wagon-yard hugged the townward side of Loudon Park Cemetery, and in my youth it was believed that all experienced hack horses, on starting home from a funeral, turned in automatically to give the pallbearers a whack at old Adam's beer, which sold for five cents, came in glasses as large as gas masks, and carried a crab-cake or two fried oysters as *lagniappe*. It was no fun in those days to go to a funeral in Loudon Park. The outward trip, at the solemn pace funerals then affected, took a full hour. But the trip homeward, once the pallbearers had wiped their mustaches, was naturally much quicker, for most of it was downhill and the hack horses knew that oats were ahead. The hay-wagon drivers who made the long and arduous trek from Howard and Frederick counties did not patronize Adam, but preferred the specialists in 5-cent whiskey. Having imbibed, they would take their seats on boards which jutted out from the sides of their lumbering wagons, between the fore and hind wheels, and from that perch they undertook to work the brakes. Very often a jolt knocked one of them off, and the hind wheels converted him into an angel, or into the two halves of an angel. For many years this mishap was one of the principal causes of death among Maryland farmers, and it was not until hay-wagons began to disappear that anyone thought of putting the driver's seat in a safer place.

The house above Ellicott City was a double one, with a hall down the middle. We occupied one side, and the family of my uncle Henry had the other. It had been built by a German named Reus, a wine-grower from the Rhineland, and he had chosen the site because the hillside that swept down to the upper Patapsco, there a placid country stream, seemed perfect for vineyards. In the eighties his terraces were still visible, but their vines were in a sad state of decay, for Mr. Reus had discovered too late that Americans were not wine drinkers. He was now dead, and the place, which was still called the Vineyard, was owned by his widow, whose elder son had married my father's half-sister. She had two more sons, somewhat older than my brother Charlie and I, but still young enough to be polite to us. They were very pleasant fellows, and the two Summers that we spent with them were full of delight. When the big house was rented they lived with their mother and a sister in a tenant-house, and on the place there was also a farmhouse inhabited by a German *Bauer* named Darsch, of whom more anon. From the big house there was a superb view of the valley of the Patapsco—a winding gorge with wooded heights on both sides. Many years later, standing on the hill at Richmond in England and enjoying the famous prospect of the Thames, I was struck by the fact that it was completely familiar. Suddenly I recalled that the view from the Vineyard was almost precisely the same, though on a smaller scale.

The impact of such lovely country upon a city boy barely eight years old was really stupendous. Nothing in this life has ever given me a more thrilling series of surprises and felicities. Everything was new to me, and not only new but romantic, for the most I had learned of green things was what was to be discovered in our backyard in Hollins street, and here was everything from wide and smiling fields to deep, dense woods of ancient trees, and from the turbulent and exciting life of the

barnyard to the hidden peace of woodland brooks. The whole
panorama of nature seemed to take on a new and larger scale.
The sky stretched further in every direction, and was full of
stately, piled up clouds that I had never seen before, and on
every side there were trees and flowers that were as strange to
me as the flora of the Coal Age. When a thunder-storm rolled
over the hills it was incomparably grander and more violent
than any city storm. The clouds were blacker and towered
higher, the thunder was louder, and the lightning was ten
times as blinding. I made acquaintance with cows, pigs and all
the fowl of the barnyard. I followed, like a spectator at a play,
the immemorial drama of plowing, harrowing, planting and
* reaping. Guided by the Reus boys, who had been born on the
place, I learned the names of dozens of strange trees and stranger
birds. With them I roved the woods day after day, enchanted
by the huge aisles between the oaks, the spookish, Grimms'
Fairy Tale thickets, and the cool and singing little streams.
There was something new every minute, and that something
was always amazing and beautiful.

    I recall with special vividness the charm of early morning in
the country. We all turned out at an hour that would have
seemed unearthly in the city, for my father and my uncle had
to stagger down the crooked road to Ellicott City and catch
the eight o'clock train for Baltimore. After breakfast, and
sometimes before, I would go for a walk in the fields, still wet
with the dew. They radiated a fragrance that far surpassed that
of Mr. Paul's cologne water, and even that of the Jockey Club
and New-Mown Hay of our hired girls. I'd lie on my belly
watching the grasshoppers, crickets and other such saucy fellows at work around the roots of the grass—and picking up a
supply of chiggers that was renewed daily, and kept me
scratching all Summer. I also liked the hot calm of July and
August afternoons. The whole country would pass into a sort
of cataleptic state, with no sound breaking the silence save the
drone of bees along the hedge-rows and the far-off clang of
the blacksmith's hammer down in the village. The cows, clearing out of the fields, drowsed under the trees, the barnyard
fowl dozed in the shadows of straw-stack and manure-pile, and
the wild birds all seemed to vanish. Darsch the farmer was always busy somewhere along the slope, but he was a silent man,

and seldom spoke to the laborious son at his side, or even to his horse.

There was a brook down in the woods, called the Sucker branch, that seemed to me to encompass the whole substance and diameter of romantic adventure. My brother and I waded in it, dammed it, leaped over it, and searched under its stones for crayfish and worms. It rose in a distant field, ran down through the deepest part of the Vineyard woods, and disappeared toward the Patapsco in a thicket so dense and forbidding that my brother and I never ventured into it. Where the path from the house came to the brook there were the ruins of an old grist-mill, dating back to the first years of the century and maybe even beyond, but with its dam and the better part of its wooden wheel still surviving. Under the wheel there was a little pool that seemed infinitely deep to my brother and me: we would heave stones into it, and were always sure that we could never hear them strike the bottom. My father and uncle once undertook, on a Summer afternoon, to go swimming in it, but it was too small to give them elbow-room, and they quickly clambered out, shivering with the cold of the spring water. The Reus boys preferred a swimming-hole in the Patapsco itself, at the foot of the long hill stretching down from our house. They reported it to be full of bottomless pits and treacherous undertows, and refused loftily to let my brother and me come along.

The trees along the brook belonged to the original forest, and some of them were immense. Great vines clung to their trunks, and between them was a jungle of saplings and shrubs. There we made acquaintance with brambles and poison oak, and learned to detect the tracks of possums, coons and foxes, though we never saw any in the flesh. The Reus boys, inspired by our willingness to learn, also showed us the tracks of wolves, mountain lions, bears, and even tigers and elephants, but here we remained skeptical. This region was our Wild West, our Darkest Africa, our Ultima Thule. It even had its anthropophagus—a half-grown yahoo who was supposed to   * hunt little boys over the countryside, and to inflict mysterious indignities upon them when captured. What these indignities were we could never make out, and the Reus boys also appeared to be uncertain, but whenever there was a noise in the underbrush across Sucker branch one of them would shriek the yahoo's name, and all of us would make for home at a gallop. Our cousin John Henry was always a member of these expeditions. He was somewhat older than my brother Charlie and somewhat younger than I, and he was commonly called Little Harry to distinguish him from me, though in later years he grew tall enough to look over my head.

I had caught butterflies in the backyard at Hollins street, but at the Vineyard they were enormously more numerous. My mother made me a new net, and in a few weeks I had a fine collection, all of them poniarded to cards with pins. My brother and I also captured a great many lizards, and often came home of a late afternoon with a bird fallen from the nest, or a can of minnows from the brook, or a grasshopper leaking his tobacco-juice all over our hands, or maybe the skull of a rabbit come to death and dissolution in the woods. The Reus boys taught us many of the ancient arts and crafts of country boys—how to make whistles of willow twigs, how to climb trees, how to detect poison-oak, how to cut off a chicken's head, and so on. They even tried to teach us how to milk a cow, but the switching of the creature's tail disturbed us so much that we were unable to concentrate. One day they announced proudly that they were squiring the family cow to a farm up Merrick's lane for a necessary biological purpose, and we pleaded to be taken along. They were willing enough and promised an instructive exhibition, but the project was overruled by higher authority.

My uncle Henry, unable to go out for ducks in Summer, kept his eagle eye in trim by shooting such chickens as were needed for the table. He would go down to the barnyard on Sunday morning, draw a bead upon a strutting cockerel, and lift off its head with the ease of a laryngologist fetching an adenoid. We boys greatly admired his technic, and so did Darsch the farmer. At dawn one Sunday morning there was a loud explosion in the direction of the barnyard, followed by a series of grisly, despairing yells, as of an archbishop collared by Satan. My father and uncle turned out in their night-shirts, and made for the scene with slippers flapping. They returned in a few moments with Darsch, and my mother and aunt spent the next half hour bandaging him with strips of bedsheet. Never in this life have I seen a more luxuriant hemorrhage, though I have sat at the ringside through many a high-toned exhibition of scientific boxing. It appeared that Darsch, panting to emulate my uncle, had unearthed a fowling-piece brought from Germany in 1857, loaded it to the muzzle, and loosed it at an old rooster. When the barrel exploded the rooster suffered nothing worse than shock, but Darsch himself was dreadfully chewed up. But it is almost impossible to kill a German *Bauer* with anything short of siege artillery, and in a week he was back at the plow and seeing out of both eyes.

Some time after this, on a Sunday afternoon, while my father and his brother were sitting on the verandah drinking mint juleps, Darsch passed along the roadway in front of the big house, driving a calf. My uncle stopped him to inquire how his wounds were getting on, and then offered him the hospitality of a julep. The drink was a new one to Darsch, who had been to Baltimore only twice in nine years, and it appeared at once that he regarded it with approbation. Indeed, he not only liked it, but said so with unprecedented loquacity, and was soon chattering in a care-free and aimless manner, with swinging gestures. This exhilaration suggested something to my uncle, who was a man, like my father, of predominantly anti-social humor. Reaching for an old-time tin shaker that stood on the table, he poured three or four fingers of rye into it, and then offered to give Darsch's julep another shake. This, he explained, was a necessary process, designed to keep the julep from going flat. Darsch handed up his glass, got it back reinforced, took a long pull of it, and began babbling louder and faster than ever before. His calf wandered off, but he did not notice it. The second time my uncle made it five or six fingers, and the third time he emptied what was left of the bottle. Suddenly Darsch drained the glass with a great gulp, mint and all, leaped high into the air, let off a single explosive whoop, and started down the roadway at a gallop. My uncle and father set out after him, hoping to capture and calm him before he could do himself any harm, but he was too fast for them, and by the time they got to the barnyard he was disappearing through the door of the old bank-barn. They found him presently in the stable below, threshing around in the litter behind the cow. He had taken a header through the hatchway. They hauled him home and his wife put him to bed, and the next day he was down with what was described as malaria. I recall my uncle observing afterward that it was an agreeable and instructive episode, but that it had pretty well emptied a prime bottle of Maryland rye, and was thus rather expensive.

Housekeeping at the Vineyard must have been something of an ordeal for my mother and my aunt, who fed their flocks separately. The best cookstoves available were poor things that burned kerosene, and they were set out in a sort of arbor behind the house. Down in the village there was a butcher whose family had carried on in one of the old stone houses along the main (and only) street for the better part of a century, but I can recall no baker, and all the bread we ate was baked at home. Vegetables and fruits, such as they were, came from Darsch's market-garden, and fowl came from his barnyard. There must have been ice in the house, for I can't imagine my father drinking warm beer without alarming symptoms, and he and his brother often made mint juleps, especially when company took the long trail out from the city of a Sunday. But there were times when ice ran short, for I recall a Sunday afternoon when, after an overdose of Seckel pears, filched from Darsch's sclerotic trees, I developed a case of 1000-volt cholera morbus, and a colored boy had to be dispatched to the village on horseback to fetch a cake. When he arrived he had it in a gunnysack lashed to his horse. My father cracked it with a hatchet that he found in the cellar, cutting himself two or three times, and my mother fed it to me with a kitchen spoon. It seemed to work, for by Tuesday I was back at the Seckel pears.

The road down to the village was steep and rough, and the trip up was full of tribulation. It started off the main street at what must have been at least a ten per cent. grade, passed the county jail (bowered in flowers, and always showing a sad blackamoor or two at its barred windows), skirted a curious old house called the Château (it had towers and battlements, and clung to a steep crag overhanging the Patapsco), went by the columned portico of the Patapsco Female Institute, and finally brought up at our gate. One day my mother sent me down to the village for a can of lard and a sack of flour, and on my painful way home I was overtaken by a colored man driving a large, empty wagon. I accepted his offer of a lift with sincere thanks, and climbed in with my burden. Unhappily, he had but lately delivered a load of coal, and his wagon was still black with its remains, so when his horses started up the rough road and the wagon began to jolt and bounce, the dust almost smothered me. I got home with my face and hands black, my clothes ruined, the lard covered with a foul, bituminous scum, and the flour turned to a depressing gray. I was washed with kitchen soap, arrayed in a fresh outfit, and sent back to the village for another cargo, and this time I toted it home on foot.

We were at the Vineyard only two Summers, but it made so powerful an impression on me that I remember every detail of the place to this day—the wonderful adventures in the woods and along the brook, the fascinating life of beasts and birds, the daily miracles of the farm, and above all, the gay songs of the Reus boys of an evening, to the accompaniment of their sister Carrie's pre-Beethoven piano. If I am able today to distinguish between an oak tree and a locust, a goose and a duck, a potato vine and a tomato plant, it is because I acquired those valuable knacks on that happy hill. Some time ago my brother August and I drove up to it on a Sunday morning, and found Carrie and her husband living in the big house. The main terraces of the vineyard had been converted into roads, the roads were lined with bungalows, and in the field that I roved for butterflies there were more bungalows and worse ones, but the woods down by the brook had not changed at all, save that the trees were now almost as large in fact as they seemed to me as a boy. The old barnyard was also still there, with a sow and her pigs snuffling about. But Darsch the farmer was gone, and so was his diligent son, and the last Seckel-pear tree had long since yielded to human progress.

Early in 1892, at the close of the period covered by this record, my father bought a country house of his own at Mt. Washington, to the north of Baltimore, and at the same time my uncle Henry bought one at Relay, half way to Ellicott City. Mt. Washington was then a remote and beautiful place, and in Spring and Autumn I went to school in the city by train, but it was already mainly given over to the Summer homes of city people, and in a little while it began to attract the malignant

notice of real-estate developers. We lived there every Summer
until my father's death, but Baltimore was creeping out block
by block, year by year. First a trolley line penetrated to Roland
Park, half a mile or more away, and then another thrust itself
along the Falls road, only a few hundred feet from our house.
Today that southern part of Mt. Washington is only a shabby
suburb of the city, with a filling-station where a one-room
country school used to be, and traffic lights at every corner.

Nevertheless, a part of it has been fortuitously preserved,
and remains today substantially as it was in 1892. This is a
stretch of perhaps half a mile of wild woodland, running up a
steep hill from the east bank of Jones' falls, south of Belvedere
avenue. The land there is too steep to encourage realtors, and
so it continues almost untouched. Even hikers from the city
avoid it, for the old mill-road that used to lead into it has long
since washed away, and there are no other paths. My brother
Charlie and I roved it for many happy Summers, setting traps
for rabbits in the woods (and never catching any), fishing and
gigging eels in the stream, and trying to dam it at every shallow. An old carp of huge size lived in a pool under the Belvedere avenue bridge, and we used to spend hours throwing
stones at him as he basked just under the surface, and never
hitting him. He was finally fetched by a wicked boy who lifted
a stick of dynamite from a trolley construction camp, and let
him have it from the bridge. The roar brought a rush of game
wardens from all directions, but by that time we were safe in
the woods. The carp either made off for Europe or was blown
to bits, for no sign of him was ever seen thereafter.

This bridge, which still stands, was also the scene of my own
first experience as a target. The line of the Northern Central
Railway ran along the west bank of Jones' falls, and the freight
trains that came down from the north began to slow up there
for the entrance to the Baltimore yards. The same wicked boy
who assassinated the carp invented the game of dropping horse
apples and other such waggish missiles upon the brakemen
who rode on top of the box-cars, working the old hand brakes.
The trick was to fire the shot just as the car emerged below the
bridge, and then hide behind the heavy wooden stringpiece.
Unfortunately, the brakemen, in their dudgeon and alarm,
mistook the horse apples for rocks, and conceived the theory

that they were being beset by homicidal tramps. On a memorable afternoon one of them was waiting for us, and as the first
apples fell he yanked out his revolver and let go. I can still hear
the whistle of that lead. Some of it came so near to my head
that I could actually feel its heat.

VI.

The Head of the House

* **M**Y GRANDFATHER Mencken, in the days when I first became aware of him, was approaching sixty, and hence
seemed to me to be a very old man. But there was certainly
nothing decrepit about him, even though a broken leg dating
from the Civil War era had left him with a slight limp, for he
threw back his shoulders in a quasi-military fashion, he had a
piercing eye of a peculiarly vivid blue, and he presented to the
world what I can only describe as a generally confident and
even somewhat cocky aspect. His bald head rose in a Shakespearean dome, and the hair that survived over his ears was
brushed forward stiffly. His cheeks were shaven down to the
neck, but he wore a mustache of no particular kind, and allowed his beard to sprout and hang down within the meridians
of longitude marked off by his eyes. Whiskers of such irrational
* design were not uncommon in that age, which was immensely
more hairy than the present glorious day. Many of the extant
generals of the Civil War had sets of them, and so did many
German forty-eighters. My grandfather, in a way of speaking,
was a forty-eighter himself, for he shoved off for these shores
from his native Saxony at almost the precise moment the German Vorparlament met at Frankfort-on-Main. But that was as
far as his connection with democratic idealism ever went. In
his later life he used to hint that he had left Germany, not to
embrace the boons of democracy in this great Republic, but to
escape a threatened overdose at home. In world affairs he was
a faithful customer of Bismarck, and in his capacity of patriotic
* American he inclined toward the ironically misnamed Democratic party, which had fought a long war to save slavery and
was still generally disreputable. His two sons, who were high
tariff Republicans, finally managed, I believe, to induce him to
vote against Grover Cleveland in 1884, but my father told me
years later that they viewed his politics with some distrust to
the end of his days.

I recall him best on his visitations to our house in Hollins street, which, though not very frequent, were carried out with considerable ceremonial. He lived in Fayette street, only a few blocks away, and usually arrived on foot. When the stomp-stomp of his tremendous shillelagh of a cane was heard, and he heaved into sight in his long-tailed black coat, his Gladstonian collar and his old-fashioned black cravat, a hush fell upon the house, my mother and father put on their best party manners, and my brother Charlie and I were given a last nervous inspection and cautioned to be good on penalty of the knout. Arrived, he deposited his hat on the floor beside his chair, mopped his dome meditatively, and let it be known that he was ready for the business of the day, whatever it might turn out to be, and however difficult and onerous. It covered, first and last, an immense range, running from infant feeding and the choice of wallpaper at one extreme to marriage settlements and the intricacies of dogmatic theology at the other. No man on this earth ever believed more innocently and passionately in the importance of the family as the basic unit of human society, or had a higher sense of duty to his own. As undisputed head of the American branch of the Menckenii he took jurisdiction over all its thirty members—his two sons, his three daughters, his two daughters-in-law, his three sons-in-law, and his twenty grandchildren—with his wife, my step-grandmother, thrown in as a sort of friendly alien. There was never, so far as I could learn afterward, any serious challenge of his authority, nor, I must add, did he ever exercise it in a harsh and offensive manner. He simply assumed as a matter of course—indeed, as an axiom so self-evident that the human mind could not conceive a caveat to it—that he was charged by virtue of his status and office with a long list of responsibilities, and he met them in the amiable and assured fashion of a man who knew his work in the world, and was ready to do it though the heavens fell.

My mother, in the years after his death, always defended the justice of his decisions, or, at all events, their strict legality, though more than once, by her own account, they went counter to her own judgment and desire. There was, for example, the matter of the christening of my younger brother, born in 1889. For some reason that I never learned she wanted to call him Albert, and for months that was actually his studio or stable name. Even my father, who was prejudiced against the

name because the only Albert he knew was a dead-beat who owed him a bill of $135, nevertheless acquiesced, and all the cups, rattles, knitted jackets, belly-bands and velvet caps that came in for the baby were so engraved or embroidered. But my father yet hesitated strangely to send for a clergyman and have the business over, and one day the reason therefor appeared. It was a beautiful Sunday in early Spring and my grandfather chose it to set up his Court of King's Bench in the Summer-house in our backyard. Without any time-consuming prelimi-naries, he announced simply that the baby would have to be
* called August—plain August and nothing else, with no com-promise on a second name that might convert him eventually into A. Albert, A. Bernard, A. Clarence . . . . . . or A. Zoroaster. August had been the name of his own father, and was the name of his first-born son, my father. It was a proud and (to his ears) mellifluous name, ancient in the Mencken family and going back, in one form or other, to the dawn of civilization. Since this erstwhile Albert was my mother's fourth child, and in all human probability would be her last, it was of paramount necessity, as a matter of family decency and decorum, that he should be August. And August he was, and is.

Why the name hadn't been given to me I don't know, and the fact that it wasn't shows a touch of the mysterious, for I was the *Stammhalter* and hence the object of my grandfather's special concern and solicitude. As the eldest son of his eldest son I'd someday enjoy, in the course of nature, the high digni-ties of head of the family, and it goes without saying that he must have given a great deal of consideration to my labeling. His reasons for deciding that I was to be named after his sec-ond son, my uncle Henry, I have never been able to discover, and for many years I wondered what source had provided my incongruous middle name of Louis. Then I learned that my grandfather's first wife and my own grandmother, Harriet McClellan, had borne and lost a son in 1862, and died herself a few months later, and that this ill-starred and forgotten infant had been named Louis after one of her uncles. The old man never ceased to mourn his poor Harriet. They had married when she was but sixteen, and had been happy together in years of hard struggle. My mother once told me that he used to make surreptitious afternoon visits to Hollins street in his

declining years, to talk about his lost love. His undying thought
of her greatly touched my mother, and was probably mainly
responsible for the affection and respect that she always seemed
to have for him. His judicial decisions as head of the house had
more than once gone against her, but she was nevertheless
staunchly for him, and liked to tell me about him.

One of his judgments I recall very clearly, though it must
have been handed down not later than 1886. It had to do with
the hairdressing of my brother Charlie and me. We had been
patronizing a neighborhood barber of the name of Lehnert, and
we liked him very much, for he cut our hair in not more than
three minutes by the clock, and always gave us a horse-doctor's
dose of highly perfumed hair-oil. When we got back from his
atelier we let the admiring hired girl smell our heads, which
continued to radiate a suffocating scent for days afterward. But
my grandfather objected to Lehnert's free and far from well-
considered use of the clippers, and one day issued an order
that he was to be notified the next time our hair needed cutting. When the time came word was duly sent to him, and he
appeared in Hollins street the following Sunday morning. My
father vanished discreetly but my mother stood by for the operation, which was carried out in the sideyard. What I chiefly
recall of it is that Charlie and I sat in a kitchen chair and were
swathed in a bed-sheet, and that it seemed to us to take a
dreadfully long while. Lehnert could have clipped a whole
herd of boys in the same time. When the job was done at last
my mother professed politely to admire the result, but there
was very little enthusiasm in her tone. The next day my father
took us both downtown, and had my grandfather's zig-zag
shear marks smoothed out by the head barber at the Eutaw *
House, a majestic man of color who claimed to have serviced
not only all the principal generals of the Civil War, but also
every Governor of Maryland back to colonial days. But when
the time came to return to Lehnert for another clip he was
warned to follow the model before him, and this he always did
thereafter, to the relief and satisfaction of all concerned.

My grandfather, as I have said, wore a Gladstonian collar
and a stock-like cravat of archaic design. Both had disappeared
from the marts of commerce before my time, but my aunt
Pauline had plans and specifications for them, and so enjoyed

the honor of making them. She was the *châtelaine* of my
grandfather's big house in Fayette street, for his wife, my
step-grandmother, was in indifferent health. Aunt Pauline was
already married, with two children of her own, but she never
forgot her filial duty to her father, nor did he. When he arrived
home for dinner, which was at about 2 P.M., the soup had to
be ready to go on the table at the precise instant he hung up
his hat in the hall. He had copious and complicated ideas
about cooking and household management, as he had about
medicine, law, moral theology, economics, interior decoration
and the use of the spheres, and his public spirit, though it was
not strong, nevertheless forbade him to keep them to himself.
In his backyard in Fayette street he carried on extensive horti-
cultural experiments, virtually all of which, I believe, failed.
What I chiefly remember of them is his recurrent reports that
cats had rolled in and ruined his strawberries, or that a storm
had blown down his lima-beans, or that some other act of God
had wrecked his effort to produce a strain of tobacco resistant
to worms, high winds, and the irrational fluctuations of the
market. But he seems to have had some luck with the *Cucurbi-*
taceae, for every year he presented all his daughters and
daughters-in-law with gourds for use in darning stockings.
Inasmuch as these gourds, though very light, had surfaces as
hard as iron, they did not wear out, and so my mother, who
never threw anything away if room could be found for it in the
house, accumulated a large battery. Sometimes, when she was
out shopping, my brother Charlie and I fought with them in
the cellar, for when one of them collided with a human skull it
made a loud, hollow, satisfying report, and yet did not cause
death or even unconsciousness.

There is a document in the family archives, headed grandly
"Halte im Gedächtniss Jesum Christum!", which certifies that
my grandfather submitted to the rite of confirmation as a
Christian of the Protestant sub-species in the church at Borna,
Saxony, on March 20, 1842, but he had apparently lost his
confidence in Jahveh by the time I became acquainted with
him. Indeed, it would not be going too far to say that he was
an outright infidel, though he always got on well with the rev.
clergy, and permitted his three daughters to commune freely
with the Protestant Episcopal Church, the American agency of

his first wife's Church of England. It was in his character of
skeptic that he subscribed toward the Baltimore crematorium *
in 1889, and ordered his two sons to subscribe too—so far as I
know, the only example of overt social-mindedness that he *
ever showed. He belonged to no organization save a lodge of
Freemasons, and held himself diligently aloof from the Ger- *
man societies that swarmed in Baltimore in the eighties. Their
singing he regarded as a public disturbance, and their *Turnerei*
as insane. Most of the German business men of Baltimore, in
those days, had come from the Hansa towns, and as a Saxon he
was compelled to disdain them as *Plattdeutschen*, though his
own remote forbears had been traders in Oldenburg. I somehow gathered the impression, even as a boy, that he was a
rather lonely man, and my mother told me years later that she
was of the same opinion. Left a widower at thirty-four, with
four small children to care for and his roots in America still
shaky, he had seen some hard and bitter years, and they had
left their marks upon him. He showed none of the expansive
amiability of his two sons, but was extremely reserved.

By the time I knew him his days of struggle were over and
he was in easy waters, but he still kept a good deal to himself,
and when he took me of an afternoon, as a small boy, on one
of his headlong buggy-rides, he seldom paid a visit to anyone
save the Xaverian Brothers at St. Mary's Industrial School, a
bastile for problem boys about two miles from Hollins street.
These holy men tried to teach their charges trades, and one of
the trades they offered was that of the cigarmaker. My grandfather, who dealt in Pennsylvania leaf tobacco, sold them their
raw materials, and my father and uncle undertook to market
their output—in the end, an impossible matter, for the cheroots that the boys made were as hard as so many railroad
spikes, and no one could smoke them. When my grandfather
called upon the Xaverians the tobacco business was quickly
disposed of, and he and they sat down to drink beer and debate
theology. These discussions, as I recall them, seemed to last for
hours, and while they were going on I had to sit in a gloomy
hallway hung with gory religious paintings—saints being
burned, broken on the wheel and disemboweled, the Flood
drowning scores of cows, horses, camels and sheep, the Cruci-
fixion against a background of hair-raising lightnings, and so

on. I was too young, of course, to follow the argument; more-over, it was often carried on in German. Nevertheless, I gath-ered that it neither resulted in agreement nor left any hard feelings. The Xaverians must have put in two or three years trying to rescue my grandfather from his lamentable heresies, but they made no more impression upon him than if they had addressed a clothing-store dummy, though it was plain that he respected and enjoyed their effort. On his part, he failed just as dismally to seduce them from their oaths of chastity, poverty and obedience. I met some of them years afterward, and found that they still remembered him with affection, though he had turned their pastoral teeth.

The buggy that he used for his movements about town was an extraordinarily stout vehicle, and it had need to be, for when he got under way he paid no attention to the fact that the cobblestones of Baltimore were very rough. Where we went when I was aboard I didn't always know, for the top was always up and we elder grandchildren rode standing in the space between the seat and the back curtain. Sometimes he would jam in four or five of us, with a couple of juniors on the seat beside him and two or three more on hassocks on the floor. When, in his wild career over the cobbles, he struck one of the stepping-stones that used to run across the roadway at street corners, we all took a leap into the air, and came down somewhat mixed up. But somehow it never hurt us, and in the end we got so used to it that we rather liked it. In the last years of his life, after my brother Charlie and I had acquired a pony, my grandfather would drive out with us of an afternoon—he in his caterpillar-tread buggy and we in our cart. Once, pro-ceeding out the Franklin road, we came in sight of a tollgate, and he ordered us to drive ahead of him. When the tollkeeper asked for his money we were to point to the buggy following, and say that the old man in it would pay for us. We did so as ordered, but when he came up he denied that he knew us. By that time, of course, we were out of the tollkeeper's reach. The old man thought it was a swell joke, and told my father and uncle about it as if expecting applause, but they failed to be amused. The next time we drove out the Franklin road the tollkeeper charged ten cents instead of five, and he kept on charging us ten cents instead of five until his professional wounds were healed.

My grandfather made frequent trips to Pennsylvania to buy *
tobacco, and was full of anecdotes of the singular innocence of the Pennsylvania Germans, whose ghastly dialect he had picked up. His favorite tale concerned a yokel of Lancaster county from whom he had bought a crop of tobacco for future delivery, offering a three-months' note in payment. The yokel declined the note on the ground that he needed nothing to help his memory: he would be on hand without fail when the time came to settle. "Keep it yourself," he said, "so you won't forget to pay me." My grandfather traded with these ill-assimilated *Bauern* for many years in complete amity, and had a high regard for them. He sold their tobacco all over. Some of it actually went to Key West, which was then assumed by most Americans to be foreign territory, using only Havana leaf in its celebrated cigars. In deference to the visitors who sometimes dropped in at the factories, the Pennsylvania leaf sent to them was repacked in empty Havana tobacco bales. My grandfather, as a moral theologian, admitted that there was something irregular about this transaction, but he consoled himself by saying that Key West was full of swindlers escaped from Cuba and points south, and that it was impossible to do any business with them at all without yielding something to their peculiar ethics.

The house in Fayette street was a wonderland to us youngsters of Hollins street, for grandchildren are always indulged more than children, and we had privileges in it that were unknown at home. I have described in Chapter I a pillow-fight that almost wrecked it. We always made a formal call on Christmas morning—my brother Charlie and I representing the Augustine line of the family, and my cousins Pauline and John Henry representing the Henrician. Ostensibly, of course, our mission was to offer our duty to our grandparents, but actually, we glowed with other expectations. They were never disappointed. The parlor in Fayette street had a much higher ceiling than those in Hollins street, and so the Christmas tree that flamed and coruscated there was larger and more splendid. At its foot were piles of toys, and among them there was always an express-wagon—to haul the other things home. One year this wagon was for my cousin John Henry, the next it was for Charlie, the next it was for me, and so *da capo*. After taking aboard a suitable refreshment of *Pfeffernüsse, Springele, Lebkuchen* and other carbohydrates, and stuffing our pockets with almonds, butternuts, walnuts, candy and fruit, we loaded our cargo and started home at a run, yelling and cavorting along the way. Christmas in those days was a gaudy festival, and my Grandmother Mencken (or maybe it was my Aunt Pauline) had a singular facility for choosing good Christmas presents. Down to the middle of my teens she always managed to find something for me that really delighted me, and many of the books that provided my earliest reading were her selections— including the "Chatterbox" that took me through my first full-length story. But of this, more hereafter.

VII.
Memorials of Gormandizing

M Y BROTHER Charlie and I, in the days of our nonage, were allowed officially to eat all that we could hold but twice a year. The first of our two debauches came in the early Spring, the occasion being the annual picnic of F. Knapp's Institute, already described in Chapter III; the second was at Christmas, beginning for the same on the morning of the great day itself and continuing doggedly until our gizzards gave out at last, and Dr. Z. K. Wiley, the family doctor, arrived to look at our tongues and ply us with *oleum ricini*.

Our running time, in the average year, was about thirty-six hours, with eight hours out for uneasy sleep, making a net of twenty-eight. When we came leaping downstairs in our flannel night-drawers on Christmas morning there was not only a * blazing tree to dazzle us, and a pile of gifts to surprise us (of course only in theory, for we knew the cupboard where such things were kept, and always investigated it in advance and at length), but also a table loaded with candies, cakes, raisins, citrons and other refreshments of the season, on all of which, and to any amount we could endure, we were free to work our wicked will.

At other times things of that sort were doled out to us in a very cautious and almost niggardly way, for the medical science of the era taught that an excess of sweets would ruin the teeth. But at Christmas, under the prevailing booziness and goodwill to men, this danger was ignored, and we were permitted to proceed *ad libitum*, not only at home, but also on our morning visit to our Grandfather Mencken's house in Fayette street. Thus we worked away all of Christmas day, keeping our pockets full and grabbing another load every time we came within arm-reach of the reserves. When we were ordered to bed at last, for a night of pathological dreams, we went only reluctantly, and immediately after breakfast on Christmas Monday we resumed operations. It was in the early evening of that day that Dr. Wiley drove up in his buggy, hitched his horse to the ring in the marble horse-block out front, and came in to do his duty.

He was a tall, spare Georgian with a close-cropped head and a military goatee. He had been a surgeon in the Confederate army, and was thus appreciably older than my father, who was a boy of seven when the Civil War began, but the two were nevertheless very good friends, and whenever the doctor made one of his regular calls he and my father investigated the demi-johns parked in the dining-room cupboard, and discussed at length the evils of the times. The doctor was a humane and understanding man, and so he never introduced the subject of succoring my brother and me until we had had a dozen or more last whacks at the stuff on the table. Then he would suddenly fix us with his cold gray eye, call for a tablespoon, and proceed to view our tongues. His verdict, of course, was always the same. Indeed, my mother invariably anticipated it by fetching the castor-oil bottle while he pondered it. Two horrible doses from the same spoon, and we were packed off to bed. Christmas was over, though the tree still stood, and some of the toys were yet unbroken. We never had much appetite the day following.

Dr. Wiley had a low opinion of the Yankees, and was full of anecdotes of their treachery in the war. His accounts of surgical practice in the Confederate army were so gruesome that my mother always retired when he introduced them, but my brother and I enjoyed them, as boys always enjoy tales that raise the hair. But his best stories had to do with his professional exploits as dean of one of the Baltimore medical colleges in the seventies. There was then no Anatomy Act in Maryland, and in consequence the students suffered a dearth of cadavers. The only way to get a supply was to lift them from colored graveyards, and in this scientific *Arbeit* Dr. Wiley, by virtue of his office, necessarily had some hand, though not, of course, as an actual field worker.

He liked to tell how he had figured out a way to beat the Baltimore cops when they took to searching wagons driving in the Annapolis road late at night. His scheme, he said, was to prop up the carcass between the two students who manned every wagon. When a cop heaved in sight, they would steady the late lamented, and if he wobbled nevertheless they would

explain to the cop that he was a friend in his cups. The Baltimore police, of course, were eager to stretch every probability
in favor of the young doctors, and so they usually overlooked
the singularity of a pair of Caucasians taking so much trouble
with a drunken Aframerican and the even greater unusualness
of an Aframerican going on a jag in his best Sunday clothes
and a white choker collar.

Whether or not Dr. Wiley really invented this device to liberate anatomy from the imbecility of the law I don't know: it
was claimed, as I learned much later, by every dean of a Baltimore medical school, and in those days there were eight or ten
of them. But he liked to tell the story, and my brother and I
never got tired of it, though our delight in it was always punished by fearful dreams. We greatly admired the doctor, despite
the fact that his standard treatment for a sore throat was mop-   *
ping it with *tinctura ferri chloridi*, which had a taste like a
mixture of stove polish and tabasco. I am informed that medicine has made considerable progress since his day, but all the
same he had a great deal of natural talent for his trade, and his
clinical experience was so enormous that he was seldom at a
loss.

Twice, with scarlet fever in the house, he pulled the patients
through, and somehow managed to quarantine the rest of us.
Of the four Mencken children, he eased three into this slough
of misery, all of them sound and howling, and from time to time
he dealt successfully with such universal pests as chicken-pox,
measles, whooping-cough, quinsy and cholera morbus. He
cured me, in my teens, of malaria, and his instruction that the
milk used in the house be boiled probably saved us all from
typhoid. When he performed the rite of vaccination there was
a scar like a volcanic crater to show for it. In her old age my
mother gave him at least five per cent. of the credit for the fact
that all her children had reached maturity with straight limbs,
powerful digestions, and no cross-eyes.

His order that the household milk be boiled was a source of
minor but continuous gustatory delight to my brother and
me. The milk was brought in the morning by a milkman who   *
had it in a huge can with a shiny brass spigot, and when he
rang his bell the hired girl went out to his wagon, and fetched
it in in a pitcher. In its raw state it foamed like beer, and was

full of cow hairs, small twigs and other such adulterations. She got rid of them by straining it through a cloth, and then boiled it in a large saucepan. The smell of the boiling always reached my brother and me, and we waited impatiently until it was over. Then the hired girl poured the milk back into the pitcher, and made a mark with a knife across the bottom of the saucepan, which was covered with a gummy precipitate, brown underneath and reeking with incomparable flavors. One side of the mark was my brother's territory, and the other was mine. We fell to with spoons, and had the saucepan clean in a minute.

In those days ice-cream was still something of a novelty in the world, and the nearest store that sold it, an old-fashioned confectioner's, was six or eight blocks from Hollins street. Thus getting it in was a nuisance, and sometimes also a vanity, for on a hot Summer day it would melt on the way. My father accordingly bought a freezer, and announced grandly that we could now feast like Belshazzar whenever the mood was on us. But that was as far as he ever went in the matter, for his gusto for physical labor was even less than his skill at the mechanic arts, so he always avoided diligently the usual chores of a householder. This left the operation of the freezer to the hired girl, with such help as my mother and my brother and I could give her. It was not much. The first time we tackled the job it took nearly an hour, and all of us were worn out. Worse, the ice-cream came out of the machine in large, irregular hunks, frozen solid in their middles and slushy at their edges. Yet worse, some of the crushed rock-salt that was mixed with the ice had got into the cream.

My father ordered it condemned as probably poisonous, but my brother and I followed it back to the kitchen, and devoured it there during the afternoon. Dr. Wiley came that night, looked at our tongues as usual, and prescribed his standard remedy. For a month or so thereafter nothing was heard about the ice-cream freezer, but then it began to appear that the hired girl had been experimenting with it on the sly, and mastering its technic. One Sunday the first fruits of her researches came upon the table—a very passable imitation of boughten ice-cream, with large segments of peach (including slivers of kernel) imbedded in it. After that we had ice-cream every Sunday, and then twice a week, and then three times, and then almost every day; indeed, we had it so often that even my brother and I began to sicken of it, and to this day I always think of it as next door in unappetizingness to chain-store bread and fruit salad, and seldom eat it save in politeness.

The only member of the family who never got enough was the pony Frank, who had been acquired in 1890 or thereabout, and lived in a tiny stable at the lower end of the backyard. One Sunday he broke out of his imprisonment and trotted up to the sideyard that ran along the dining-room. The window being open, he stuck in his head in his usual blarneying manner and began to sniff. It occurred to someone that he smelled the ice-cream, and a gob of it in a kitchen pan was set on the sill, to see what he would make of it. He downed it with happy snuffles, and whinnied for more. After that he got his share whenever ice-cream was on the bill-of-fare, and eventually he was eating as much as all the rest of us put together. My father made an end to this by issuing a formal injunction, supported by an oral opinion. Feeding ice-cream to horses, he declared, was as insane a waste of money as shooting at clay pigeons or contributing to foreign missions. Frank repined somewhat, but was placated with an occasional half-peck of raw carrots, which he liked even better than ice-cream. So, in fact, did I—and so I do now.

There was another delicacy that delighted my brother and me almost as much as the rubbery lining of the milk saucepan, but we could enjoy it, unfortunately, only in Summer, when we were in the country. It consisted of stewed blackberries, spread while still warm on home-made bread, also still warm. To this day I can taste it at the moments when an aging man's memory searches through his lost youth for bursts of complete felicity. It had a heavenly flavor, and an even more heavenly smell. My brother and I would start out of an afternoon with a couple of lard pails and pluck the berries along the edge of some nearby wood. If there was a shortage of ripe ones we'd turn to the adjacent fields and hunt for dewberries. The job cost us a good many chigger bites and now and then a bee sting, but who cared?

When the cans were full we hurried back to the house, and emptied them on a newspaper spread out on the kitchen table. The hired girl would then go through the crop, rejecting the

contaminating gravel, twigs, dead grasshoppers and wild flowers, and when the cleaning was done it would be raked into a
saucepan along with a handful of sugar. The stewing took only
a little while, but it seemed pretty long to my brother and me.
When it was finished the fragrant berries were spread upon
large slices of the home-made bread, and we fell to. The hired
girl had strict orders to give us no more than two slices apiece,
but we had ways of blackmailing her. One was to agree to return the copy of the *Fireside Companion* that we had lifted and
hidden as a device of pressure politics. Another was to promise
to pull harder the next time she had a day off, and needed
help with the lacing of her stays. The hired girls of those days
were built like airplane-carriers, but always bought corsets
designed for Marguerite Gautier. I recall one, of Irish ex-
traction and heavily muscle-bound, who squeezed and pulled
herself into such brief compass that she fainted dead away, and
had to be revived with a stiff shot of Monticello. The whiskey
made her dizzy and set her to weeping, and in a little while
she had a full-fledged and alarming attack of what were then
called hystics.

This gobbling of stewed blackberries was policed only defectively, but nevertheless it was policed. The house statutes, as
I have said, limited us to two slices of bread, and there was a
rider to the effect that they must not be too thick. If law enforcement was knowingly slack—and I have no doubt that my
mother knew of and condoned our violations, for hired girls
always blabbed—it was because there was a theory in those
days that all stewed fruits were good for children. In the raw
state even apples were regarded with suspicion, but when
stewed they took on all the virtues of spinach, rhubarb and
sulphur-and-molasses. At F. Knapp's Institute the boarding
pupils were fed apple-butter every day, not only because it was
cheap, but also because it was supposed to tone up the system,
inure them to the perfect Baltimore climate, and prevent boils.

But my brother and I had no fancy for stewed apples, nor
for stewed pears, peaches, cherries, plums, apricots, bananas,
grapes, pineapples, oranges or what not. Our sole passion was
for stewed blackberries (including, of course, dewberries,
which are their brothers); we even excluded stewed raspberries, huckleberries and strawberries. But for all raw fruits, since

they were regarded as deleterious, we naturally had a great liking, and stuffed them down at every chance. On the hilltop above Ellicott City where we spent two Summers there were the remains of a large orchard. The fruit had not been sprayed for thirty years, and was thus in a state of extreme senescence. I recall especially that the Seckel (always pronounced *sickle*) pears had skins of the thickness and consistency of tin-foil, and were almost coal black. We were warned that they were dangerous to life and limb, and had even floored hogs, but the warning only urged us to follow the suicidal pattern of boys by eating more and more. Nothing happened save an occasional bellyache, sometimes rising to the virulence of cholera morbus. We ate until the compulsion wore off, and then simply stopped.

Many other eatables, in those days, were thought to be injurious to the young, or even fatal. One of them was cheese. When a boy was allowed to eat it at all it was a sign that he was almost well enough along to be intrusted with horses, edged tools and firearms, and even so he was always introduced to it by slow stages, with many cautious halts. His first dose was a very thin slice, and he was watched carefully for symptoms of spasms. If he appeared to turn a shade pale he was at once given a jigger of ipecac and put to bed, with the blankets piled a foot high, Winter or Summer. My brother and I had little confidence in such notions, and one day we made off with a heel of cheese that had been laid aside by the hired girl for her mouse-traps. We divided it evenly and ate it boldly, defying Jahveh, Dr. Wiley or anyone else it might concern to do his worst. Once more, nothing much happened. The taste was dreadful—indeed, so dreadful that we pitied the poor mice. But apart from a few sharp twinges in the gastric region, maybe of psychic origin, we suffered no damage.

Pork was another article of diet that was thought in that age to be unfriendly to the young. We were never permitted to eat it at night, for at night all foods, including even such generally salubrious things as raw carrots, were believed to take on virulence. My brother and I, ever eager for scientific experiment, dispatched at least a pound of cold roast pork one night when our parents were at the theatre, and suffered no evil that we could detect with the crude methods then available. If we slept a little uneasily, it was probably only conscience, for even boys of six and eight are afflicted by that curse of mankind. Another night we ate the better part of a prime *Cervelatwurst*, and heard the hired girl accused the next morning of feeding it to a suitor who had waited on her before our raid. She was stupid beyond the general, and defended herself by declaring that she had given him only four or five ham sandwiches, half a pie, a cup of coffee, and six bottles of Class D Baltimore beer. Under cover of the ensuing uproar we slipped off to school.

Thus we gradually accumulated a profound distrust of the dietetic science of the day, and ate anything we could collar, and in any amount, whenever constabulary backs were turned. There were plenty of days when, though we radiated innocence, we actually got down almost as many calories as we were allowed on the glorious day of F. Knapp's annual picnic. But such licentiousness, of course, gradually diminished as we gathered years and wisdom, and we got a boost along the road every time Dr. Wiley dropped in to do his dismal duty. It was not really the castor oil that alarmed us, for every boy of ordinary vanity, in those days, liked to boast that he could swallow it in any quantity, and without gagging. What scared us was the doctor's inspection of our tongues—always long drawn out, and done in sinister silence. We trembled lest he discover signs of sore throat, and get out his dreadful bottle of chloride of iron and his ancient and scratchy mop.

VIII.
The Training of a Gangster

THE BALTIMORE of the eighties had lately got over an evil (but proud) name for what the insurance policies call civil commotion. Down to the Civil War and even beyond its gangs were of such enterprise and ferocity that many connoisseurs ranked them as the professional equals, if not actually the superiors, of the gangs of New York, Marseilles and Port Said. It was nothing for them to kidnap a police sergeant, scuttle a tugboat in the harbor, or set fire to a church, an orphan asylum or a brewery. Once a mob made up of the massed gangs of the town broke into the jail and undertook to butcher a party of military gentlemen who had sought refuge there after a vain effort to save an unpopular newspaper from pillage. One of these gentlemen, a doddering veteran of the Revolution named General James M. Lingan, was done to death with great barbarity, and another, General Light Horse Harry Lee, father of the immortal Robert E. Lee, was so badly used that he was never the same again.

At the opening of the Civil War, as every schoolboy knows, another Baltimore mob attacked a Massachusetts regiment passing through the city on its way to save democracy at Bull Run, and gave it such a lacing that what it got in that battle three months later seemed almost voluptuous by comparison. This was in April, 1861. Before the end of the year the town proletariat had switched from the Confederate theology to the Federal, and devoted itself to tarring and feathering Southern sympathizers, and wrecking their houses. The war over, it continued its idealistic exercises until the seventies, and at the time I was born Baltimore was still often called Mob Town, though by then the honorific had begun to be only retrospective.

Thus it was necessary for every self-respecting boy of my generation to belong to a gang. No one, in fact, ever asked him if he wanted to join or not join; he was simply taken in when he came to the right ripeness, which was normally between the ages of eight and nine. There was, of course, some difference between the gangs of the proletariat and those of the more tender bourgeoisie. The former tried to preserve, at least to some extent, the grand tradition. They had quarters in empty houses or stable lofts, smoked clay pipes, rushed the can, carried lethal weapons, and devoted themselves largely to stoning cops and breaking into and looting the freight cars of the Baltimore & Ohio Railroad. The latter were a great deal milder and more elegant. They carried only clubs, and then only in times of danger; they never got any further along the road to debauchery than reading dime-novels and smoking cigarettes; and the only thing they ever stole (save, of course, ash-barrels and garbage-boxes on election night) was an occasional half-peck of apples, potatoes or turnips. These victuals were snatched on the run from the baskets that corner-grocers then set outside their stores, along with bundles of brooms, stacks of wooden kitchen-pails, and hog carcasses hanging from hooks.

I attained, by the age of eight, to a considerable proficiency in this larceny, and so did my brother Charlie. Our victim was usually Mr. Thiernau, a stout, bustling, sideburned man who operated a grocery-and-meat store at Gilmor and Baltimore streets, less than a block from our back gate. He wore invariably what was then the uniform of his calling—a long white apron stained with blood, a Cardigan jacket, and large cuffs made of some sort of straw. Around the little finger of his left hand ran a signet ring, and behind his right ear he carried his pencil. So far as I can remember, he never made any attempt to pursue the boys who looted him; in truth, I suspect that his baskets were set out as a kind of accommodation to them, with the aim of gaining their favor. Not infrequently they were delegated to buy supplies for their mothers, and on such occasions
* they always chose Mr. Thiernau's store, not that of the Knoops across the street. The Knoops, two brothers and a cousin, appear to have leaned toward Levirate ideas, for when the cousin died one of the brothers married his widow. They were Germans of large girth, gloomy aloofness and high commercial acumen, and they accumulated among them a considerable estate, but they never exposed anything that was edible on the sidewalk, and so the boys of the neighborhood were against

them. Even Mr. Thiernau, I believe, kept his best vegetables to be sold inside his store, not stolen in front of it.

One day, after my brother Charlie and I had made a fine haul of sweet potatoes, my father came home unexpectedly and caught us roasting them on a fire in the backyard. He demanded to know where we had got them from, and our guilty looks betrayed us. He thereupon made a great uproar, declaring that he would drown us, ship us to the Indian country or even hand us over to the child-stealers rather than see us grow up criminals. I put all the blame on Charlie, for he had actually made the snatch while I bossed the job and watched, and my father ordered him to return the potatoes to Mr. Thiernau at once, half burned as they were. Charlie set off boo-hooing, threw the potatoes into a garbage-box in the alley, and came home prepared to report that Mr. Thiernau had taken them back with polite thanks. But he delayed on the way to watch the Thiernau colored driver unload a cargo of dead hogs, and by the time he returned my father had apparently forgotten the matter, for we heard no more from him about it. We discovered the next day, however, that the hired girl had orders to supply us with potatoes whenever the roasting fever was on us, and for a week or so we patronized her. But her stock never seemed to have the right flavor, though it came from the same Thiernau's, and we eventually resumed our larcenies. They were terminated a year or so later by Mr. Thiernau's sudden death, which was a great shock to us, and naturally turned us to moral considerations and made us uneasily Hell-minded.

The Hollins street gang functioned as a unit only on occasions of public ceremonial—for instance, at election time. It began lifting boxes and barrels for the election night bonfire two or three weeks before the great day, usually under command of a large, roomy boy named Barrel Fairbanks, and they were commonly stored in the stable behind his house. If we managed to collar a paint barrel it was a feat that cheered us, for paint barrels burned with a fierce flame and made a great deal of smoke. The grocerymen and feed dealers of the neighborhood, knowing that we were on the prowl, tried to save their good boxes and barrels by setting out their decrepit ones, and we always accepted the suggested arrangement. It was only when there was a real famine in fuel that we resorted to taking back

gates off their hinges, and even then we confined ourselves to
gates that were ready to fall off of their own motion.

The first election night bonfire that I remember was built on
the evening of that day in November, 1888, which saw the
stuffings of Cleveland and Thurman knocked out of them by
Harrison and Morton. The returns were published from the
portico of a Democratic ward club at Lombard and Stricker
streets, across Union Square from our house, and the fire was
kindled at the crossing of Hollins and Stricker streets. As the
sad news dribbled along the Democrats fell into a low state of
mind, and some of them actually went home before the kegs
of beer that they had laid in were empty; but my father rejoiced, for as a high-tariff Republican he was bound in conscience to regard Cleveland as a fiend in human form. I recall
him coming down to the corner to see and applaud the fire,
which blazed higher than the houses along Hollins street. The
cops offered no objection to it, though in those days they were
all Democrats, for the flames did no damage to the solid Baltimore cobblestones that underlay them, and if they singed a
few trees it was only God's will. When the cobbles yielded to
asphalt, long after I was a grown man, election-night bonfires
were prohibited.

I recall one election night when the tough boys from the
region of the Baltimore & Ohio repair-shops, having had bad
luck in collecting material for their own fire, made an attempt
to raid ours. They arrived just as it was kindled. They were
armed with clubs, and made their attack from two sides, yelling
like Indians. We of Hollins street were ordinarily no match for
these ruffians, but that night there was an audience looking
on, so we fought fiercely, and finally managed to drive them
off. Some of them, retreating, carried off blazing boxes, but
not many. I got a clout across the arm that night, and nursed it
proudly for a week. I was in hopes that Dr. Wiley would order
the arm into a sling, but when he dropped in the next day he
could find nothing save a large blue bruise. When he began to
show signs of taking a routine look at my tongue, I slipped
away quickly, pleading an important engagement.

Every Baltimore boy, in those days, had to be a partisan of
some engine company, or, as the phrase ran, to go for it. The
Hollins street boys went for No. 14, whose house was in

Hollins street three blocks west of Union Square. Whenever an alarm came in a large bell on the roof of the engine-house broadcast it, and every boy within earshot reached into his hip-pocket for his directory of alarm-boxes. Such directories were given out as advertisements by druggists, horseshoers, saloonkeepers and so on, and every boy began to tote one as soon as he could read. If the fire was nearby, or seemed to be close to a livery-stable, a home for the aged, or any other establishment promising lively entertainment, all hands dropped whatever was afoot and set off for it at a gallop. It was usually out by the time we reached the scene, but sometimes we had better luck. Once we saw a blaze in a slaughter-house, with a drove of squealing hogs cremated in a pen, and another time we were entranced by a fire in the steeple of a Baptist church. Unhappily, this last ended as a dud, for the firemen quickly climbed up their high ladders and put it out.

The duties of a boy who went for an engine were not onerous. The main thing was simply to go for it. At an actual fire he could not distinguish between his own firemen and those of some other and altogether abhorrent company, for they all wore the same scoop-tailed helmets and the same black rubber coats. But he was expected nevertheless to go for them through thick and thin. If, venturing into a strange neighborhood, he was halted by the local pickets and asked to say what engine he went for, he always answered proudly and truthfully, even though the truth might cost him a black eye. I never heard of a boy failing to observe this obligation of honor. Even the scoundrels who went for No. 10, when we caught one of them in our territory, never tried to deceive us. The most they would do would be to retreat ten paces before letting off their clan cry. We would then proceed, as in duty bound, to hang them out, which is to say, to chase them off the soil of our Fatherland.

The frontiers of the various gangs in West Baltimore were known to all the boys denizened there, and it was not common for a boy to leave his own territory. If he did so, it was at the risk of being hung out, or maybe beaten. But fights between adjoining gangs were relatively rare, for the cops kept watch along the borders, and all hands avoided them diligently. Once the Hollins street gang, engaged in exploring Franklin Square, which was three blocks from Union Square, encountered a

gang that went for No. 8 engine, and a battle was joined. But
it had gone on for no more than a few minutes when a cop
came lumbering up Calhoun street, and both armies at once
fled northward, which is to say, into No. 8 territory. The No. 8
boys, though they were officially obliged to do us in at every
chance, concealed us in their alleys until the cop gave up the
chase, for in the presence of the common enemy gang differences sank to the level of the academic. Any boy in flight from
a cop was sure of sanctuary anywhere. In fact, a favorite way of
making a necessary journey through hostile lines was to do it
at a run, yelling "Cheese it! The cops!" Boys respected this
outcry even when they knew it was fraudulent.

There was in West Baltimore a neutral territory that all
gangs save the ruffians from the region of the B. & O. shops
respected—and they seldom invaded it, for they had better
hunting-grounds nearer their base. It was a series of open lots
beginning at Fulton avenue and Baltimore street, three blocks
from Union Square, and running westward until it was lost in
a wilderness of lime-kilns, slaughter-houses and cemeteries.
From east to west it must have been a mile long, and from
south to north half a mile wide. It is now covered with long
rows of the red brick, marble trimmed two-story houses that
are so typical of Baltimore, but in my nonage it was wild country, with room enough for half a dozen baseball diamonds, not
to mention huge thickets of Jimson weeds, nigger-lice, and
other such nefarious flora. The lower end, at Fulton avenue,
was much frequented by the colored men who made their livings beating carpets. They would erect poles, string them with
washlines, hang the carpets, and then flog them by the hour,
raising great clouds of dust. A little further to the westward
other colored men pursued the art and mystery of the sod-cutter.
They would load their rolled-up sods on wheelbarrows and
push them down into the city, to refresh and adorn the backyards of the resident bourgeoisie.

We Hollins street boys spent many a pleasant afternoon
roving and exploring this territory, which had the name of
Steuart's Hill. We liked to watch the operation of the lime-
kilns, all of them burning oyster shells, and the work of the
carpet-beaters and sod-cutters. But best of all we liked to visit
the slaughter-houses at the far western end. There was a whole

row of them, and their revolting slops drained down into a
deep gully that we called the Canyon. This Canyon was the
Wild West of West Baltimore, and the center of all its romance.
Whenever a boy came to the age when it became incumbent
on him to defy God, the laws of the land and his father by
smoking his first cigarette, he went out there for the operation.
It was commonly a considerable ceremony, with a ring of older
boys observing and advising. If the neophyte got sick he was
laid out on one of the lower shelves of the Canyon until he
recovered. If he began crying for his mother he was pelted
with nigger-lice and clods of lime.

The Canyon was also a favorite resort of boys who read
dime novels. This practice was regarded with horror by the
best moral opinion of the time, and a boy who indulged it
openly was given up as lost beyond hope. The best thing expected of him was that he would run away from home and go
west to fight the Indians; the worst was that he would end on
the gallows. In the more elderly years of my infancy I tried a
few dime novels, trembling like a virgin boarding an airship for
Hollywood, but I found them so dull that I could scarcely get
through them. There were other boys, however, who appeared
to be able to bear them, and even to like them, and these addicts often took them out to the Canyon to read in peace. No
cops ever showed themselves in that vicinity, which was probably, in fact, outside the city limits of Baltimore. It was an Alsatia without laws, and tolerated every sort of hellment. I have
seen a dozen boys stretched on the grass within a circumfer-
ence of fifty feet, all of them smoking cigarettes and reading
dime novels. It was a scene of inspiring debauchery, even to
the most craven spectator.

One afternoon, having been left behind when the Hollins
street gang made a trip to the Canyon, I set out alone to over-
take it. Just west of Fulton avenue, which is to say, in full sight
of householders and passers-by along Baltimore street, I was
held up with perfect technic by three boys of a strange gang.
One of them aimed a cap pistol at my head and ordered me to
stick up my hands, and the other two proceeded to frisk me.
They found a pocket-knife, a couple of sea-shells, three or four
nails, two cigarette pictures, a dozen chewing-tobacco tags, a
cork, a slate pencil, an almost fossil handkerchief, and three

cents in cash. I remember as clearly as if it were yesterday their
debate over the three cents. They were sorely tempted, for it
appeared that they were flat broke, and needed money badly.
But in the end they decided primly that taking it would be
stealing. The other things they took without qualm, for that
was only hooking.

When they turned me loose at last I ran all the way to the
Canyon, and sounded the alarm. The gentlemen of the Hollins
street gang were pleasantly engaged in throwing stones into a
pool of hog blood that had formed beneath the scuppers of
one of the slaughter-houses, but when they heard my story
they started for the scene of the outrage at once, scooping up
rocks on the way. They got there, of course, too late to capture
the bandits, but they patrolled the vicinity for the rest of the
afternoon, and revisited it every day for a couple of weeks,
hoping to make a collar, and get me back my handkerchief,
nails, slate pencil, and chewing-tobacco tags. I may say at once
that they were never recovered, nor did I ever see the robbers
again. They must have come from some remote part of West
Baltimore. Or perhaps they were prisoners escaped from the
House of Refuge.

This bastile was a mile westward, on the banks of Gwynn's
Falls. It was a harsh granite building surrounded by sepulchral
trees, and all the boys of West Baltimore feared it mightily. Its
population consisted of boys who had become so onery that
their own fathers resigned them to the cops. The general belief
was that a rascal who once entered its gates was as good as lost
to the world. If he ever got out at all, which was supposed to
be very unusual, the cops were waiting to grab him again, and
thereafter he made quick progress to the scaffold. I knew only
one boy who ever actually sat in its dungeons. He was a lout
of fourteen whose father kept an oyster-bay in Frederick avenue. The passion of love having seized him prematurely, he
got into a fight over a girl, and stabbed the other fellow with
an oyster-knife. I well recall the day the cops dragged him
through Union Square to the watch-house in Calhoun street,
and then hurried back to haul his victim to the University of
Maryland hospital in a grocery-wagon.

This affair caused a great sensation in Hollins street, for it
was the introduction of many of us to the hazards and terrors

of amour. We crowded around the watch-house a day or two later, waiting to hear the result of the cutthroat's trial, and slunk away in silence when a colored malefactor we knew came out and reported that he had been doomed to the House of Refuge, or, as we always called it, the Ref. We assumed as a matter of course that he had been sentenced for life. If he ever got out I didn't hear of it, and for all I can tell you he may be there yet, though the Ref was long ago transformed into a storehouse for the Baltimore sewer department. No member of the Hollins street gang ever entered its door. We had our faults, as I freely admit, but the immemorial timorousness of the bourgeoisie restrained us from downright felony. Two of the boys I chased cats with in 1888 drank themselves to death in their later years, two others went into politics, one became a champion bicycle racer, three became millionaires, and one actually died an English baronet, but none, to my knowledge, ＊ ever got to the death-house, or even to the stonepile.

In those days the nicknames of boys ran according to an almost invariable pattern, though all boys, of course, did not have them. The example of Barrel Fairbanks I have mentioned: he was too fat to be called simply Fats and not quite fat enough to be worthy the satirical designation of Skinny, so he took the middle label of Barrel. Any boy who happened to be lame was called Hop, anyone who had lost an eye was One-eye, and anyone who wore glasses (which was then very unusual) was Four-eyes. If a boy had a head of uncommon shape he was always called Eggy. The victims of such cruel nicknames never, so far as I can recall, objected to them; on the contrary, they appeared to be proud of their distinctions. Many nicknames were derived from the professions of their bearers' fathers. Thus the eldest son of a doctor was always Doc, and if a boy's father had the title of Captain—whether ship captain, fire captain, police captain, or military captain, it was all one—he was himself known as Cap. The eldest sons of all policemen above the grade of patrolmen took their fathers' titles as a matter of course. A block or two up Hollins street lived a sergeant whose son was called Sarge, and when the father was promoted to a lieutenancy the son became Loot. In case a boy's father had the military title of Major, which was not unusual in those days, for West Baltimore swarmed with householders who had been officers in the Civil War, he was called Major himself. I never knew a boy whose father was a colonel or general, but those to be found elsewhere in Baltimore undoubtedly followed the rule. The eldest sons of pedagogues were all called Professor, and if a boy's father was a professional gambler (there was such a boy in Hollins street) he was apt to be called either Colonel or Sport. Younger sons did not share in these hereditary honors, which went by primogeniture. The nicknames they bore, if they had any at all, were based upon their own peculiarities.

The latter-day custom of calling boys by their full given names was quite unknown. Every Charles was Charlie, every William was Willie, every Robert was Bob, every Richard was Dick and every Michael was Mike. I never heard a boy called Bill: the form was always Willie or Will. Bill was reserved for adults of the lower ranks, for example, ashcart drivers. My own stable-name, as I have noted, was Harry, and my immediate relatives so hail me to this day. My father's brother Henry, whose house was next door to ours in Hollins street, was Uncle Hen to us until the time of the World War, when the changing fashion converted him into the more decorous Uncle Henry. I had two uncles with the same given name of John: one was Uncle John to me and the other was Uncle Johnnie, though Uncle Johnnie was the elder. I had an uncle named William, but I still call him Uncle Will, though his son, more than forty years his junior, rates the formal William. My father was Gus to his wife and all his friends, though his sisters called him August, and his underlings called him Mr. August. My mother's given name was Anna, but my father always called her Annie, and she was Aunt Annie to the cousins next door. One of the rules of the time was that a boy named Albert was always called Buck, never Al. Only a boy with an unusual given name escaped these *Koseformen*. The name of Theodore, for example, which was seldom encountered in the pre-Roosevelt era, was never supplanted by Teddy or Ted, but always remained Theodore. There was a boy in Hollins street named Seymour, and he remained Seymour until he broke his leg, when he became Hop. But most boys were Eddie, Johnnie, Bob, Dick or Willie.

The humor of the young bourgeoisie males of Baltimore, in those days, was predominantly skatological, and there was no

sign of the revolting sexual obsession that Freudians talk of.
The favorite jocosities had to do with horse apples, O.E.A.
wagons and small boys who lost control of their sphincters at
parties or in Sunday-school; when we began to spend our
Summers in the country my brother and I also learned the
comic possibilities of cow flops. Even in the city a popular
ginger-and-cocoanut cake, round in contour and selling for a
cent, was called a cow flop, and little girls were supposed to
avoid it, at least in the presence of boys. Colored girls were fair
game for any prowling white boy, but there was never anything
carnal about hunting them; they were pursued simply because
it was believed that a nigger-louse burr, entangled in their hair
(we always kept stocks at hand in the season), could not be
removed without shaving their heads. Otherwise, the relations
between the races were very friendly, and it was not at all unusual for a colored boy from the alley behind Hollins street to
be invited to join a game of one-two-three, or a raid on Mr.
Thiernau's potatoes and turnips. Many of the cooks in our block
were colored women, though our own were always Caucasians
down to 1900 or thereabout. All surplus victuals and discarded
clothes were handed as a matter of course to the neighboring
blackamoors, and they were got in for all sorts of minor jobs.
There have been no race riots in Baltimore to this day, though
I am by no means easy about the future, for a great many anthropoid blacks from the South have come to town since the
city dole began to rise above what they could hope to earn at
home, and soon or late some effort may be made to chase
them back. But if that time ever comes the uprising will probably be led, not by native Baltimoreans, but by the Anglo-Saxon
baboons from the West Virginia mountains who have flocked
in for the same reason, and are now competing with the blacks
for the poorer sort of jobs.

The Baltimore Negroes of the eighties had not yet emerged
into the once-fine neighborhoods they now inhabit; they still
lived, in the main, in alleys, or in obscure side-streets. We boys
believed in all the traditional Southern lore about them—for
example, that the bite of one with blue gums was poisonous,
that those of very light skin were treacherous and dangerous, that
their passion for watermelon was at least as powerful as a cat's
for catnip, and that no conceivable blow on the head could

crack their skulls, whereas even a light tap on the shin would disable them. Mr. Thiernau once set me to tussling with a colored boy in his store, and I made desperate efforts to reach his shins with my heel, but he was too agile for me, and so he got the better of the bout. When I reached home my mother sniffed at me suspiciously, and then ordered me to take a bath and change my clothes from the skin out. The alley behind our house had some colored residents who had lived there for many years, but most of its inhabitants came and went rather frequently, with the rent-collector assisting them. He always appeared on Saturday evening, and if the rent was not ready he turned out his tenant at once, without bothering to resort to legal means. The furniture that he thus set out on the sidewalk was often in a fantastic state of dilapidation, but it always included some of the objects of art that poor blackamoors of that era esteemed—a blue glass cup with the handle off, a couple of hand-painted but excessively nicked dinner-plates, a china shepherdess without a head, and so on. These things had come out of trash-cans, but they were fondly cherished. Behind the alley in the rear of our house, cutting off the Negro cabins from the houses in Baltimore street, ran a blind and very narrow sub-alley, perhaps not more than three feet wide. It was considered a good joke to inveigle a strange boy into it, for it was full of fleas. There were many such blind alleys in West Baltimore. One of them, running off Gilmor street, a block or so from our house, was called Child-stealers' alley, and we avoided it whenever possible. It was supposed to be the den of a monster who stole little children and carried them off to unknown but undoubtedly dreadful dooms. Such criminals were never spoken of as kidnappers, but always as child-stealers. So far as I can recall, none of them ever actually stole a child; indeed, none was ever seen in the flesh. But they were feared nevertheless.

Like all other boys, my brother Charlie and I were always in a condition of extreme insolvency. My mother had read an article in an early issue of the *Ladies' Home Journal*[1] arguing that

---

[1]She had subscribed for it from its first issue, and continued to do so until her death in 1925. Once, when she somehow let her subscription lapse, she got a letter from Edward W. Bok, the editor, urging her not to desert him.

children should not be given money freely but required to earn it, and this became the rule of the house. My brother and I alternated in shining our father's Congress gaiters of a morning, and received five cents for each shine, then the standard price in Baltimore. For other chores we were paid on the same scale, and in good weeks our joint income reached sixty or seventy cents, and sometimes even a dollar. But it was never enough, so we supplemented it by various forms of graft and embezzlement. When my mother sent me to Hollins market with two or three dollars in hand and a list of supplies to be bought, I always knocked down at least a nickel. My brother and I also got a little revenue from Sunday-school collection money, for when we were given dimes we put in only nickels, and when we were given nickels we put in only pennies. All the male scholars save a few milksops followed the same system. The teachers must have been aware of it, but they never did anything about it. We picked up more money by walking to and from school—a round trip of at least three miles—and pocketing the three-cent fare each way. Sometimes, when a car was crowded we managed to elude the conductor, and so rode without paying. On some cars there was no conductor, and the driver had to see to the fares. Inasmuch as he couldn't leave his horses, there were channels running down the sides of the car to carry to him the coins inserted by passengers. When a dozen boys got on a car together, it was usually possible for at least half of them to dodge paying fare. The driver always made a pother, but every boy swore that it was his money that had rolled down. The ensuing debate could be easily protracted until we were at our destination.

When all such devices failed, and Charlie and I faced actual bankruptcy, we had to resort to more desperate measures. Here, unhappily, we were cribbed, cabined and confined by the notions of dignity that prevailed among the West Baltimore bourgeoisie. We somehow understood without being told that it would be unseemly for us to run errands for Mr. Thiernau, or to carry the marketing of strange ladies returning home from Hollins market, or to shovel snow off sidewalks in Winter, or to help hostlers with their horses, or carriage-washers at their work. But there was one labor that, for some reason or other, was considered more or less elegant, though it was strictly forbidden by all parents, and that was selling news-papers. In 1889 or thereabout my brother Charlie and I under-took it in the hope of accumulating quickly enough funds to buy a cat-and-rat rifle. We had an air-rifle, but wanted a cat-and-rat rifle, which used real cartridges, and our father's harsh and profane prohibition of it only made us want it the more. So we hoofed down to the alley behind the old *Evening World* office in Calvert street—a good mile and a half from Hollins street—and laid in six *World*s at half a cent apiece. Leaping on horse-cars and howling "Paper! Paper!" was a grand adven-ture, but we soon found that a great many tougher, louder and more experienced boys were ahead of us, and when we counted up our profits at the end of two or three hours of hard work, and found that we had made but six cents between us, we de-cided that selling papers was far from what it had been cracked up to be. Incidentally, we never got that cat-and-rat rifle.

School took in in those days early in September, and ran on until the end of June. There were very few holidays save the Saturdays and Sundays, and boys had to depend for their major escapes from learning upon the appearance of measles or chicken-pox in the house. But there was one day that was al-ways kept in Baltimore, and that was September 12, the anni-versary of the Battle of North Point. This historic action was fought at the junction of the Chesapeake Bay and the Patapsco river in 1814, and as a result of it Baltimore escaped being burned by the British, as Washington was. Moreover, it produced two imperishable heroes in the shape of a pair of Baltimore boys, Wells and McComas, who hid in a tree and assassinated the British commander, General Robert Ross. Yet more, Francis Scott Key, jugged on a British ship in Baltimore harbor, wrote "The Star-Spangled Banner" while the accom-panying bombardment of Fort McHenry was going on. Thus September 12 was always celebrated in Baltimore, and all the boys got a day off from school, which was to me a matter of special rejoicing, for the day was my birthday. The last dodder-ing veterans of the War of 1812 are dead now, and there is no longer a Defenders' Day parade, but September 12 remains a legal holiday in Maryland, and my birthday is still marked by blasts of patriotic rhetoric and artillery.

IX.
Cops and Their Ways

THE FIRST policeman I ever became acutely aware of on this earth was one Cookie, a short, panting fellow with the sagittal section of an archbishop. I was about six years old at the time, and along with my brother Charlie I was watching and admiring some older boys playing at par, which was the Baltimore name for leap-frog. This was on a hot Summer afternoon and at the corner of Hollins and Gilmor streets, not more than a hundred feet from our own front door. Suddenly one of the par-players stopped his play, turned pale, shook with a kind of palsy, pointed like a setter, and exclaimed "Cookie!" in a shrill, hysterical voice. The rest picked up the enemy at once. He was plodding along Gilmor street in the shadow of the high wall of the House of the Good Shepherd, stretching a * whole block down to Lombard street.

The next thing I recall is being dragged along at a speed of what seemed to be at least a mile a minute by the obese Barrel Fairbanks, with my brother tagging behind in tow of a boy named Socks Cromwell. Why we were in such haste I didn't gather at the minute, for I was yet unaware of the dreadful nefariousness of the police. Infants of six were still ignorant in such matters. They gaped at cops as innocently as they gaped at letter-carriers, garbage-men and organ-grinders' monkeys. But now my brother and I had been accepted as licensed followers, though still very far from members, of the Hollins street gang, and the facts quickly soaked into us when its lawful leaders ordered a halt in Booth alley behind our house, to catch breath and consider strategy.

Some were in favor of running on to Reveille's livery-stable, two blocks away, and hiding in the hay. Others proposed making a long detour around Reveille's and laying a course by forced draft out Fayette street to Steuart's Hill. There were objections to both plans. The Reveille brothers were hospitable to boys whose fathers stabled buggies in their establishment (which let in my brother and me), but for boys in general they had only a sour welcome, and none at all for boys in gangs. As for Steuart's Hill, it was at least six blocks away by the route suggested, and most of that route was uphill. Moreover, the Hill was likely to be swarming, on a Summer afternoon, with boys from strange gangs, and if they were in a mood of aggression they might break the truce usually prevailing there, and make short work of the Hollins street gang, burdened, as it was, by such raw and loutish troops as my brother and I.

All this may sound like a long council, but it actually took no more than half a minute. Finally, some smart fellow suggested that we send a spy to the end of the alley to find out if Cookie was still lumbering down on us. No one volunteered for that office, so the smart fellow had to undertake it himself. He sneaked up to Gilmor street along the back-fences, according to the approved technic for scouts in the Indian country, and peeped cautiously around the stable at the corner. Returning in a moment, his caution gone, he reported that Cookie had anchored in a cool spot along the convent wall, and was engaged in mopping his bald head and biting off a chew of tobacco. The hunt was thus over, for Cookie's ordinary jurisdiction did not extend to Booth alley, and he would follow boys there, it appeared, only in the heat of pursuit. No such heat was visible.

But the time and place seemed opportune for the older boys to instruct my brother and me in the tricks and deviltries of cops, and this they did at length. It was never safe, they explained, to let a cop come within reach. There was no telling what infamy he might be up to. For one thing, he might grab a more or less innocent boy, accuse him of breaking a window-pane in a house six blocks away, and proceed to do justice upon him on the spot, with the thin leather thong that flowed from the end of every cop's espantoon, enabling him to swing it ostentatiously as he patrolled his beat. For another thing, he might rush upon boys playing catty and break up the game in sheer ill-nature, with no excuse save the labored one that a flying catty had hit a baby carriage, and scared the infant half to death. For a third thing, he was an incurable tattle-tale, and delighted in writing down the names of boys detected in chasing cats, or throwing nigger-lice at colored girls, or blowing spitballs at the Salvation Army, and then blabbing on them to their fathers.

In brief, a cop was a congenitally iniquitous character, an enemy to society, a master of all the slimy devices of espionage and betrayal. He was against all the manly sports of boys of normal mind and high metabolism. If they started a ball-game in the street he would take his stand behind a tree a block away, watching for some violation of his arbitrary and incomprehensible regulations, and spoiling all the fun. He objected to the harmless pulling of girls' pigtails, to making bonfires in alleys, to setting dogs to fighting in Union Square, to catching goldfish in the pond there, to overturning and emptying ashboxes, to stealing rides on trucks or horse-cars, to hunting sparrows with air-rifles, to making game of cripples and idiots, to throwing horse-apples at aged or drunken men, to walking along the tops of backyard fences, to prodding mules with sticks, to pulling doorbells on Hallowe'en, to making sliding-places in the gutters in Winter, to scaring little girls with false-faces, to nailing up backyard gates, to putting on white pillow-slips after dark and terrorizing pious colored people, to yelling "Rats!" at * Chinese laundrymen, to upsetting the wooden Indians in front of cigar-stores.

Himself an habitual snitcher of peanuts and Johnny-bread from poor Italians, he prohibited lifting a few cheap turnips or carrots from the baskets outside the stores of rich grocerymen. When there was a funeral and boys collected on the sidewalk to see the pallbearers in their plug hats, he spoiled it by heaving into sight, and setting the whole gang to flight. When there was a fire, he made watching it hazardous, and no fun. No boy of any sense would approach voluntarily within half a block of a cop. If one came ambling down the street the sidewalk would clear as swiftly as if he had been Sitting Bull himself. A boy who had occasion to enter a livery-stable always peeped first, to make sure that no cop was there before him. A boy who turned a corner and came face-to-face with one took to flight at once, yelling "Cheese it!" to warn all other boys. Even girls felt uneasy when they saw a blue uniform, though cops never molested them. But from the moment a boy made the first faltering step toward manhood they had it in for him, and he had it in for them.

The one thing to be said in favor of these ruffianly kill-joys was that they were heavy on their feet, and hence easy to

out-run. There may have been lean and high-geared cops in
other communities, but I never heard of one in the West Baltimore I grew up in. They all wore extraordinarily thick and
uncomfortable-looking uniforms, in Summer as in Winter,
squeaky shoes with soles as solid as slabs of oak, and domed
helmets that always fell off when they attempted to run, scattering lead-pencils, peanuts, red bandana handkerchiefs and
chewing-tobacco, and maybe a few cigars, oranges or bananas.
A cop in pursuit of a boy had to hold on to his helmet with
one hand, and with the other clutch his revolver, lest it go off
in the holster flopping from his stern and shoot him in the leg.
Any boy in the full possession of his faculties could beat such a
mud-scow in a fair race. Even Barrel Fairbanks, fat as he was,
could do it. It was only the boy collared by stratagem—always
dirty—who was ever actually captured and switched.

So far as I can recall, this switching, when it was done, never
brought out any hullabaloo from the victim's parents. His father continued to speak to the cop amicably, and his mother
continued to threaten him with the cop when he failed to wash
behind his ears. Even the boys themselves did not object to the
switching *per se*; all they complained of was being switched by
the object of their common contempt and execration—an insult
rather than an injury. In those Mousterian days no one had yet
formulated the theory that a few licks across the backside would
convert a normal boy into a psychopathic personality, bursting
with Freudian complexes and a rage against society. It was still
universally considered that an occasional rataplan cleansed him
of false ideas and softened his native boorishness. School-teachers
whaled very freely, and with no more thought of tort than a
dentist pulling a tooth, and so did parents. On a window-sill
in the kitchen of our house in Hollins street lay a wooden
ruler that certainly gathered no cobwebs. Once, having tasted it
three times in a single morning, my brother Charlie sneaked it
away and buried it in the yard, but the next day there was another in its place, and no questions asked.

I remember well the first time a cop actually came into the
house: it must have been a year or so after our initiation into
the infamy of Cookie. The time was a Sunday morning, an
unusual one for callers, and when the doorbell rang Charlie
and I peeped out of a third-story window to see who was

there. When we saw the blue uniform we were almost paralyzed with fright—but not quite enough to keep us from piling into a cupboard in the rear room, pulling the door shut, and holding it tight. We stayed there until the bell rang for lunch, and even then we came down the stairs very gingerly, peeping over the banister to make sure that the monster had left. We gathered from my father's talk to my mother that he was one Lieutenant Smith, apparently a cop of great puissance. But we couldn't make out what he had come for, and we were too scared to ask. It was a great relief when we gathered that it was not for us.

Rather curiously, the most ferocious cop I ever knew was more tolerant of boys than the general, and enjoyed a kind of repute among them that was almost, though certainly not quite good. He was a huge Irishman of the name of Murphy, and he wore the heavy black mustache that went in those days with the allied sciences of copping and bartending. Murphy, I suspect, really wanted to be friends with the boys, but they never let him get near enough to them to show it. When we were playing ball in the street, he would come round the corner with a sort of ingratiating tread, much different from his standard plodding, and stand there rather wistfully as we yelled "Cheese it!" and galloped away.

Murphy reserved all his Berserker fury for the Aframericans who lived in Vincent alley, two blocks away. Our own dark neighbors in Booth alley were of a peaceful disposition, and the few ructions back there were almost always caused by visitors, but in Vincent alley the wars continued round the calendar, and were especially bloody on Saturday nights. I mean bloody in its literal sense. There were not many ladies of the Vincent alley set who had not been slashed more than once by the bucks they adored and supported, and I can recall no buck who had not had an ear bitten off, or a nostril slit, or a nose mashed. The alley began to buzz at 6 P.M. on Saturday, when such of its male inhabitants as worked at all came home with their pay, and by 8 o'clock Murphy was hard at it dragging the wounded out of its tenements and clubbing the felonious into insensibility.

There were in those days no patrol-wagons in Baltimore: a cop who made an arrest had to tool his prisoner to the nearest watch-house on foot, with such incidental help as he could get from friendly dray-drivers. Many's the time I have watched Murphy slide, shove and yank a frantic colored lady down the long path which ran obliquely (and still runs) through Union Square, with a huge gallery of white and black fans crowding after. The screams and contortions of such viragoes entertained us boys as neatly as a fire, and we learned a lot about anatomy and physiology from their remarks. Murphy never used his espantoon on females if he could help it, and when he couldn't he always bounced them gently—a tap just sufficient to cause a transient dizziness. He reserved his masterstrokes for males. One stupendous crack, and it was all over. If his customer revived before they got to the police-station it was so unusual as to amount to a marvel. When he applied himself seriously to a bad nigger there was one bad nigger less for a minimum of thirty days.

As I have said, this was before there were any patrol-wagons in Baltimore, or, at all events, in West Baltimore. When they came in at last, in the twilight of the eighties, Murphy seemed to lose form. It was only half a block from the hell-mouth of Vincent alley to the nearest box, and dragging his prisoners so short a distance, with help so quickly and easily obtainable, sapped his old pride of craftsmanship. More than once I observed him at the box looking baffled and foolish. When the wagon backed up he heaved his blackamoor aboard with a kind of resigned contempt, and barely spoke to the driver and footman. He belonged to the post-Civil War school of bare-hand cops, and was a fit match for Killer Williams of New York, though he never rose to any rank in his profession. In the end, if my recollection serves me, he was put on trial before the police commissioners on the charge of giving a bad nigger a clout of unnecessary violence. As I recall it, he was acquitted with honor, but the notion that anyone could imagine hitting a bad nigger too hard was beyond his comprehension, and he withdrew from the force. Baltimore, by 1890, was already fast degenerating, and so was civilization.

There were not only no patrol-wagons in service in Murphy's heyday, but also no ambulances. The cops had to get the sick and injured to hospital as best they could, and more often than not their best consisted only in commandeering a one-horse truck or ash-cart. In the case of patients emanating from Vincent alley that made no great difficulty, for no colored West Baltimorean of that era, so long as he retained his wits, would let the cops or anyone else take him to hospital. The word always meant to him the old University of Maryland Hospital at Lombard and Greene streets, and every Aframerican knew that it swarmed with medical students who never had enough cadavers to supply their hellish orgies, and were not above replenishing their stock by sticking a knife into a patient's back, or holding his nose and forcing a drink out of the black bottle down his throat.

The ordinary wounded of Vincent alley were patched up at a drug-store nearby, or by one of the sporty doctors who hung about the neighborhood livery-stables. If their injuries turned out to be beyond the science of these quacks, getting them to hospital was a laborious business—that is, in case they were conscious, and hence able to resist. Their struggles against being arrested were, in the main, only formal, and it took only a stroke or two of Murphy's wand to subdue them, but going to hospital was something else again. Not infrequently, in fact, it couldn't be managed without beating them into a coma, even with three or four cops and half a dozen civilian volunteers on the job. Once a patient was on his way, his neighbors gave him up as dead, and his lady friend began looking for a new admirer. There were, of course, aberrant cases of Aframericans, even in Vincent alley, who had been dragged to Lombard and Greene streets and yet returned, but they were very rare and carried a spookish and suspicious aura. Indeed, any blackamoor who had so survived was avoided by his fellows thereafter. He was one who had come unscathed from a charnel-house, and there were certainly reasonable grounds for surmising that he had escaped only by entering into some more or less diabolical pact with the doctors. No one wanted him about. He made everyone uncomfortable.

I must have been at least ten or eleven years old before my fear of cops began to abate. It was probably laid at last by two circumstances. The first was the fact that a young cop named Tom O'Donnell made a headline in the Baltimore *Sunpaper* one morning by excavating a burglar from the cellar of my father's warehouse in Paca street. Tom went in after the fellow alone, bare-handed and in complete darkness, and after he had emerged with his prisoner and dragged him to the nearest watch-house it was discovered that he had collared a desperate cop-hater with a long string of assaults and mayhems behind him. My father and his brother and the other business men of the vicinity thereupon waited on the police commissioners and demanded that Tom be promoted for his courage, and he was presently made a detective. He served in that office until only the other day, and I still see him on the streets occasionally, his eye continuing to oscillate for pickpockets, for an old cop never stops copping so long as he is on his legs. I got to know him very well in my days as a newspaper reporter, and spared no rhetoric when he made another dramatic collar, which was often. My father's high, astounding praise of him convinced my brother and me that there must be occasional cops who were not enemies of society, just as there were occasional Sunday-school teachers who were not idiots. It was disillusion and hence painful, but there was also some relief in it.

But what really shook us was the appearance in the next block of Hollins street of a boy who actually had a policeman for a father. It seemed wholly fantastic, but the evidence could not be gainsaid, for the boy admitted it himself, and we used to see his father coming home of an evening, exactly like any other father. He was a sergeant when he moved into Hollins street, but was presently promoted to a lieutenancy, and his son was thus known to us as Loot. We all liked him, and in his presence talk about the iniquity of cops had to be avoided. Gradually it fell off even when he wasn't present, and especially it fell off after he had invited us to his house to see his new steam-engine, and his father, in mufti, came down to the cellar and undertook to show us how to work it. He failed completely, as fathers always failed, and we began to realize that he was a human being almost like any other, at least when not in uniform. When the family moved away there was some recrudescence of cop-hating, but all the old steam was out of it.

Today the fear of cops seems to have departed teetotally from American boys, at least on the level of the bourgeoisie. I have seen innocents of eight or nine go up to one boldly, and speak to him as if he were anyone else. Some time ago the up-lifters in Baltimore actually organized a school for Boy Scouts with cops as teachers, and it did a big trade until the cops themselves revolted. What happened was that those told off to instruct the Scouts in the rules of traffic, first aid, the operation of fire-alarm boxes, etiquette toward the aged and blind, the elements of criminal law and other such branches got so much kidding from their fellows that they were covered with shame, and in the end the police commissioner let out the academy *sine die*, and restored its faculty to more he duties.

X.
Larval Stage of a Bookworm

* THE FIRST long story I ever read was "The Moose Hunters," a tale of the adventures of four half-grown boys in the woods of Maine, published in *Chatterbox* for 1887. *Chatterbox*, which now seems to be pretty well forgotten, was an English annual that had a large sale, in those days, in the American colonies, and "The Moose Hunters" seems to have been printed as a sort of sop or compliment to that trade, just as an English novelist of today lards his narrative with such cheery native bait as "waal, pardner," "you betcha" and "geminy-crickets." The rest of the 1887 issue was made up of intensely English stuff; indeed, it was so English that, reading it and looking at the woodcuts, I sucked in an immense mass of useless information about English history and the English scene, so that to this day I know more about Henry VIII and Lincoln Cathedral than I know about Millard Fillmore or the Mormon Temple at Salt Lake City.

"The Moose Hunters," which ran to the length of a full-length juvenile, was not printed in one gob, but spread through *Chatterbox* in instalments. This was an excellent device, for literary fans in the youngest brackets do their reading slowly and painfully, and like to come up frequently for air. But writing down to them is something else again, and that error the anonymous author of "The Moose Hunters" avoided diligently. Instead, he wrote in the best journalese of the era, and treated his sixteen-year-old heroes precisely as if they were grown men. So I liked his story very much, and stuck to it until, in a series of perhaps twenty sessions, I had got it down.

This was in the Summer of 1888 and during hot weather, for I remember sitting with the volume on the high marble front steps of our house in Hollins street, in the quiet of approaching dusk, and hearing my mother's warnings that reading by failing light would ruin my eyes. The neighborhood apprentices to gang life went howling up and down the sidewalk, trying to lure me into their games of follow-your-leader and run-sheep-run, but I was not to be lured, for I had discovered a new realm of being and a new and powerful enchantment. What was follow-your-leader to fighting savage Canucks on the Little Magalloway river, and what was chasing imaginary sheep to shooting real meese? I was near the end of the story, with the Canucks all beaten off and two carcasses of gigantic meese hanging to trees, before the author made it clear to me that the word *moose* had no plural, but remained unchanged *ad infinitum.*

Such discoveries give a boy a considerable thrill, and augment his sense of dignity. It is no light matter, at eight, to penetrate suddenly to the difference between *to, two* and *too,* or to that between *run* in baseball and *run* in topographical science, or *cats* and *Katz.* The effect is massive and profound, and at least comparable to that which flows, in later life, out of filling a royal flush or debauching the wife of a major-general of cavalry. I must have made some effort to read *Chatterbox* at the time my Grandmother Mencken gave it to me, which was at Christmas, 1887, but for a while it was no go. I could spell out the shorter pieces at the bottoms of columns, but the longer stories were only jumbles of strange and baffling words. But then, as if by miracle, I found suddenly that I could read them, so I tackled "The Moose Hunters" at once, and stuck to it to the end. There were still, of course, many hard words, but they were no longer insurmountable obstacles. If I staggered and stumbled somewhat, I nevertheless hung on, and by the Fourth of July, 1888, I had blooded my first book.

An interval of rough hunting followed in Hollins street and the adjacent alleys, with imaginary Indians, robbers and sheep and very real tomcats as the quarry. Also, I was introduced to chewing tobacco by the garbageman, who passed me his plug as I lay on the roof of the ash-shed at the end of the backyard, watching him at his public-spirited work. If he expected me to roll off the roof, clutching at my midriff, he was fooled, for I managed to hold on until he was out of sight, and I was only faintly dizzy even then. Again, I applied myself diligently to practising leap-frog with my brother Charlie, and to mastering the rules of top-spinning, catty and one-two-three. I recall well how it impressed me to learn that, by boys' law, every new top had to have a license burned into it with a red-hot nail, and that no strange boy on the prowl for loot, however black-hearted, would venture to grab a top so marked. That discovery gave me a sense of the majesty of the law which still sustains me, and I always take off my hat when I meet a judge—if, of course, it is in any place where a judge is not afraid to have his office known.

But pretty soon I was again feeling the powerful suction of beautiful letters—so strange, so thrilling, and so curiously suggestive of the later suction of amour—, and before Christmas I was sweating through the translation of Grimms' Fairy Tales that had been bestowed upon me, "for industry and good deportment," at the closing exercises of F. Knapp's Institute on June 28. This volume had been put into lame, almost pathological English by a lady translator, and my struggles with it awoke in me the first faint gutterings of the critical faculty. Just what was wrong with it I couldn't, of course, make out, for my gifts had not yet flowered, but I was acutely and unhappily conscious that it was much harder going than "The Moose Hunters," and after a month or so of unpleasantly wrestling with it I put it on the shelf. There it remained for more than fifty years. Indeed, it was not until the appearance of "Snow White" as a movie that I took it down and tried it again, and gagged at it again.

That second experiment convinced me that the fault, back in 1888, must have been that of either the brothers Grimm or their lady translator, but I should add that there was also some apparent resistant within my own psyche. I was born, in truth, without any natural taste for fairy tales, or, indeed, for any other writing of a fanciful and unearthly character. The fact explains, I suppose, my lifelong distrust of poetry, and may help to account for my inability to memorize even a few stanzas of it at school. It probably failed to stick in my mind simply because my mind rejected it as nonsense—sometimes, to be sure, very jingly and juicy nonsense, but still only nonsense. No doubt the same infirmity was responsible for the feebleness of my appetite for the hortatory and incredible juvenile fiction fashionable in my nonage—the endless works of Oliver Optic, Horatio Alger, Harry Castlemon and so on. I tried this fiction more than once, for some of the boys I knew admired it vastly, but I always ran aground in it. So far as I can recall, I never

read a single volume of it to the end, and most of it finished
me in a few pages.

What I disliked about it I couldn't have told you then, and I
can account for my aversion even now only on the theory that
I appear to have come into the world with a highly literal
mind, geared well enough to take in overt (and usually unpleasant) facts, but very ill adapted to engulfing the pearls of
the imagination. All such pearls tend to get entangled in my
mental *vibrissae*, and the effort to engulf them is as disagreeable to me as listening to a sermon or reading an editorial in a
second-rate (or even first-rate) newspaper. I was a grown man,
and far gone in sin, before I ever brought myself to tackle
"Alice in Wonderland," and even then I made some big skips,
and wondered sadly how and why such feeble jocosity had got
so high a reputation. I am willing to grant that it must be a
masterpiece, as my betters allege—but not to *my* taste, not for
me. To the present moment I can't tell you what is in any of
the other juvenile best-sellers of my youth, of moral and sociological hallucination all compact, just as I can't tell you what is
in the Bhagavad-Gita (which Will Levington Comfort urged
me to read in 1912 or thereabout), or in the works of Martin
Tupper, or in the report of Vassar Female College for 1865. I
tried dime-novels once, encouraged by a boy who aspired to
be a train-robber, but they only made me laugh. At a later
time, discovering the pseudo-scientific marvels of Jules Verne,
I read his whole canon, and I recall also sweating through a
serial in a boys' weekly called *Golden Days*, but this last dealt
likewise with *savants* and their prodigies, and was no more a
juvenile, as juveniles were then understood, than "Ten Thousand Leagues Under the Sea."

But before you set me down a prig, let me tell you the rest
of it. That rest of it is my discovery of "Huckleberry Finn,"
probably the most stupendous event of my whole life. The
time was the early part of 1889, and I wandered into Paradise
by a kind of accident. Itching to exercise my newly acquired
art of reading, and with "The Moose Hunters" exhausted and
Grimms' Fairy Tales playing me false, I began exploring the
house for print. The Baltimore *Sunpaper* and *Evening News*,
which came in daily, stumped me sadly, for they were full of
political diatribes in the fashion of the time, and I knew no

more about politics than a chimpanzee. My mother's long file
of *Godey's Lady's Book* and her new but growing file of the *Ladies' Home Journal* were worse, for they dealt gloomily with
cooking, etiquette, the policing of children, and the design
and construction of millinery, all of them sciences that still
baffle me. Nor was there any pabulum for me in the hired girl's
dog's-eared files of *Bow Bells* and the *Fireside Companion*, the
first with its ghastly woodcuts of English milkmaids in bustles
skedaddling from concupiscent baronets in frock-coats and
corkscrew mustaches. So I gradually oscillated, almost in despair, toward the old-fashioned secretary in the sitting-room,
the upper works of which were full of dismal volumes in the
black cloth and gilt stamping of the era. I had often eyed them
from afar, wondering how long it would be before I would be
ripe enough to explore them. Now I climbed up on a chair,
and began to take them down.

They had been assembled by my father, whose taste for literature in its purer states was of a generally low order of visibility.
Had he lived into the days of my practice as a literary critic, I
daresay he would have been affected almost as unpleasantly as
if I had turned out a clergyman, or a circus clown, or a labor
leader. He read every evening after dinner, but it was chiefly
newspapers that he read, for the era was one of red-hot politics,
and he was convinced that the country was going to Hell. Now
and then he took up a book, but I found out long afterward
that it was usually some pamphlet on the insoluble issues of
the hour, say "Looking Backward," or "If Christ Came to
Chicago," or "Life Among the Mormons." These works dis-
quieted him, and he naturally withheld them from his innocent first-born. Moreover, he was still unaware that I could
read—that is, fluently, glibly, as a pleasure rather than a chore,
in the manner of grown-ups.

Nevertheless, he had managed somehow to bring together a
far from contemptible collection of books, ranging from a set
of Chambers's Encyclopedia in five volumes, bound in leather
like the Revised Statutes, down to "Atlantis: the Antediluvian
World," by Ignatius Donnelly, and "Around the World in the
Yacht *Sunbeam.*" It included a two-volume folio of Shakespeare in embossed morocco, with fifty-odd steel plates, that
had been taken to the field in the Civil War by "William H.

Abercrombie, 1st Lieut. Company H, 6th Regiment, Md. Vol. Inftr.," and showed a corresponding dilapidation. Who this gallant officer was I don't know, or whether he survived the carnage, or how his cherished text of the Bard ever fell into my father's hands. Also, there were Dickens in three thick volumes, George Eliot in three more, and William Carleton's Irish novels in a third three. Again, there were "Our Living World," by the Rev. J. G. Wood; "A History of the War for the Union," by E. A. Duyckinck; "Our Country," by Benson J. Lossing, LL.D.; and "A Pictorial History of the World's Great Nations from the Earliest Dates to the Present Time," by Charlotte M. Yonge—all of them likewise in threes, folio, with lavish illustrations on steel, stone and wood, and smelling heavily of the book-agent. Finally, there were forty or fifty miscellaneous books, among them, as I recall, "Peculiarities of American Cities," by Captain Willard Glazier; "Our Native Land," by George T. Ferris; "A Compendium of Forms," by one Glaskell; "Adventures Among Cannibals" (with horrible pictures of missionaries being roasted, boiled and fried), "Uncle Remus," "Ben Hur," "Peck's Bad Boy," "The Adventures of Baron Münchhausen," "One Thousand Proofs That the Earth Is Not a Globe" (by a forgotten Baltimore advanced thinker named Carpenter), and a deadly-looking "History of Freemasonry in Maryland," by Brother Edward T. Schultz, 32°, in five coal-black volumes.

I leave the best to the last. All of the above, on my first exploration, repelled and alarmed me; indeed, I have never read some of them to this day. But among them, thumbing round, I found a series of eight or ten volumes cheek by jowl, and it appeared on investigation that the whole lot had been written by a man named Mark Twain. I had heard my father mention this gentleman once or twice in talking to my mother, but I had no idea who he was or what he had done: he might have been, for all I knew, a bartender, a baseball-player, or one of the boozy politicoes my father was always meeting in Washington. But here was evidence that he was a man who wrote books, and I noted at once that the pictures in those books were not of the usual funereal character, but light, loose and lively. So I proceeded with my inquiry, and in a little while I had taken down one of them, a green quarto, sneaked it to my bedroom, and stretched out on my bed to look into it. It was, as smarties will have guessed by now, "Huckleberry Finn."

If I undertook to tell you the effect it had upon me my talk would sound frantic, and even delirious. Its impact was genuinely terrific. I had not gone further than the first incomparable chapter before I realized, child though I was, that I had entered a domain of new and gorgeous wonders, and thereafter I pressed on steadily to the last word. My gait, of course, was still slow, but it became steadily faster as I proceeded. As the blurbs on the slip-covers of murder mysteries say, I simply couldn't put the book down. After dinner that evening, braving a possible uproar, I took it into the family sitting-room, and resumed it while my father searched the *Evening News* hopefully for reports of the arrest, clubbing and hanging of labor leaders. Anon, he noticed what I was at, and demanded to know the name of the book I was reading. When I held up the green volume his comment was "Well, I'll be durned!"

I sensed instantly that there was no reproof in this, but a kind of shy rejoicing. Then he told me that he had once been a great reader of Mark Twain himself—in his younger days. He had got hold of all the volumes as they came out—"The Innocents" in 1869, when he was still a boy himself; "Roughing It" in 1872, "The Gilded Age" in 1873, "Tom Sawyer" in 1876, "A Tramp Abroad" in 1880, the year of my birth, and so on down to date. (All these far from pristine firsts are still in the Biblioteca Menckeniana in Hollins street, minus a few that were lent to neighbor boys and never returned, and had to be replaced.) My father read them in the halcyon days before children, labor troubles and Grover Cleveland had begun to frazzle him, and he still got them down from the shelf on quiet evenings, after the first-named were packed off to bed. But a man of advancing years and cares had to consider also the sorrows of the world, and so he read in Mark less than aforetime.

As for me, I proceeded to take the whole canon at a gulp —and presently gagged distressfully. "Huckleberry Finn," of course, was as transparent to a boy of eight as to a man of eighty, and almost as pungent and exhilarating, but there were passages in "A Tramp Abroad" that baffled me, and many more in "The Innocents," and a whole swarm in "The Gilded Age." I well recall wrestling with the woodcut by W. F. Brown on page II3 of the "Tramp." It shows five little German girls swinging on a heavy chain stretched between two stone posts on a street in Heilbronn, and the legend under it is "Generations of Bare Feet." That legend is silly, for all the girls have shoes on, but what puzzled me about it was something quite different. It was a confusion between the word *generation* and the word *federation*, which latter was often in my father's speech in those days, for the American Federation of Labor had got under way only a few years before, and was just beginning in earnest to harass and alarm employers. Why I didn't consult the dictionary (or my mother, or my father himself) I simply can't tell you. At eight or nine, I suppose, intelligence is no more than a small spot of light on the floor of a large and murky room. So instead of seeking help I passed on, wondering idiotically what possible relation there could be between a gang of little girls in pigtails and the Haymarket anarchists, and it was six or seven years later before the "Tramp" became clear to me, and began to delight me.

It then had the curious effect of generating in me both a great interest in Germany and a vast contempt for the German language. I was already aware, of course, that the Mencken family was of German origin, for my Grandfather Mencken, in his care for me as *Stammhalter*, did not neglect to describe eloquently its past glories at the German universities, and to expound its connections to the most remote degrees. But my father, who was only half German, had no apparent interest in either the German land or its people, and when he spoke of the latter at all, which was not often, it was usually in sniffish terms. He never visited Germany, and never signified any desire to do so, though I recall my mother suggesting, more than once, that a trip there would be swell. It was "A Tramp Abroad" that made me German-conscious, and I still believe that it is the best guide-book to Germany ever written. Today, of course, it is archaic, but it was still reliable down to I908, when I made my own first trip. The uproarious essay on "The Awful German Language," which appears at the end of it as an appendix, worked the other way. That is to say, it confirmed my growing feeling, born of my struggles with the conjugations and declensions taught at F. Knapp's Institute, that German was an irrational and even insane tongue, and not worth the sufferings of a freeborn American. These diverse impressions have continued with me ever since. I am still convinced that Germany, in the intervals of peace, is the most pleasant country to travel in ever heard of, and I am still convinced that the German language is of a generally preposterous and malignant character.

"Huck," of course, was my favorite, and I read it over and over. In fact, I read it regularly not less than annually down to my forties, and only a few months ago I hauled it out and read it once more—and found it as magnificent as ever. Only one other book, down to the beginning of my teens, ever beset me with a force even remotely comparable to its smash, and that was a volume called "Boys' Useful Pastimes," by "Prof. Robert Griffith, A.M., principal of Newton High School." This was given to me by my Grandmother Mencken at Christmas, 1889, and it remained my constant companion for at least six years. The sub-title describes its contents: "Pleasant and profitable amusement for spare hours, comprising chapters on the use and care of tools, and detailed instructions by means of which boys can make with their own hands a large number of toys, household ornaments, scientific appliances, and many pretty, amusing and necessary articles for the playground, the house and out-of-doors." Manual training was still a novelty in those days, and I suspect that the professor was no master of it, for many of his plans and specifications were completely unintelligible to me, and also to all the neighborhood boys who dropped in to help and advise. I doubt, indeed, that any human being on earth, short of an astrophysicist, could have made anything of his directions for building boat models. But in other cases he was relatively explicit and understandable, and my brother Charlie and I, after long efforts, managed to make a steam-engine (or, more accurately, a steam-mill) according to his recipe. The boiler was a baking-powder tin, and the steam, issuing out of a small hole in the top, operated a sort of fan or mill-wheel. How we provided heat to make steam I forget, but I remember clearly that my mother considered the process dangerous, and ordered us to take the engine out of the cellar and keep it in the backyard.

*   I had no more mechanical skill than a cow, but I also managed to make various other things that the professor described, including a what-not for the parlor (my mother professed to admire it, but never put it into service), a rabbit-trap (set in the backyard, it never caught anything, not even a cat), and a fancy table ornamented with twigs from the pear tree arranged in more or less geometrical designs. "Boys' Useful Pastimes" was printed by A. L. Burt on stout paper, and remains extant to this day—a rather remarkable fact, for other boys often borrowed it, and sometimes they kept it on their work-benches for a long while, and thumbed it diligently. One of those boys was Johnnie Sponsler, whose father kept a store in the Frederick road, very near Hollins street. Johnnie was vastly interested in electricity, as indeed were most other boys of the time, for such things as electric lights, motors, telephones and door-bells were just coming in. He thus made hard use of Professor Griffith's Part VII, which was headed "Scientific Apparatus and Experiments," and included directions for making a static machine, and for electroplating door-keys. He later abandoned the sciences for the postal service, and is now, I believe, retired. "Boys' Useful Pastimes," and my apparent interest in it, may have been responsible for my father's decision to transfer me from F. Knapp's Institute to the Baltimore Polytechnic in 1892. If so, it did me an evil service in the end, for my native incapacity for mechanics made my studies at the Polytechnic a sheer waste of time, though I managed somehow to pass the examinations, even in such abysmal subjects as steam engineering.

The influence of "Huck Finn" was immensely more powerful and durable. It not only reinforced my native aversion to the common run of boys' books; it also set me upon a systematic exploration of all the volumes in the old secretary, and before I finished with them I had looked into every one of them, including even Brother Schultz's sombre history of Freemasonry in Maryland. How many were actually intelligible to a boy of eight, nine, ten? I should say about a fourth. I managed to get through most of Dickens, but only by dint of hard labor, and it was not until I discovered Thackeray, at fourteen, that the English novel really began to lift me. George Eliot floored me as effectively as a text in Hittite, and to the present day I have never read "Adam Bede" or "Daniel Deronda" or "The Mill on the Floss," or developed any desire to do so. So far as I am concerned, they will remain mere names to the end of the chapter, and as hollow and insignificant as the names of Gog and Magog.

But I plowed through Chambers's Encyclopedia relentlessly, beginning with the shortest articles and gradually working my way into the longer ones. The kitchen-midden of irrelevant and incredible information that still burdens me had its origins in those pages, and I almost wore them out acquiring it. I read, too, the whole of Lossing, nearly all of Charlotte M. Yonge, and even some of Duyckinck, perhaps the dullest historian ever catalogued by faunal naturalists on this or any other earth. My brother Charlie and I enjoyed "Our Living World" chiefly because of the colored pictures, but I also read long stretches of it, and astonished my father by calling off the names of nearly all the wild beasts when the circus visited Baltimore in 1889. Finally, I recall reading both "Life Among the Mormons" and "One Thousand Proofs That the Earth Is Not a Globe."

Thus launched upon the career of a bookworm, I presently began to reach out right and left for more fodder. When the * Enoch Pratt Free Library of Baltimore opened a branch in Hollins street, in March, 1886, I was still a shade too young to be excited, but I had a card before I was nine, and began an almost daily harrying of the virgins at the delivery desk. In 1888 * my father subscribed to *Once-a-Week*, the predecessor of *Collier's*, and a little while later there began to come with it a long series of cheap reprints of contemporary classics, running from Tennyson's poems to Justin M'Carthy's "History of Our Own Times"; and simultaneously there appeared from parts unknown a similar series of cheap reprints of scientific papers, including some of Herbert Spencer. I read them all, sometimes with shivers of puzzlement and sometimes with delight, but always calling for more. I began to inhabit a world that was two-thirds letterpress and only one-third trees, fields, streets and people. I acquired round shoulders, spindly shanks, and a despondent view of humanity. I read everything that I could find in English, taking in some of it but boggling most of it.

This madness ran on until I reached adolescence, and began to distinguish between one necktie and another, and to notice the curiously divergent shapes, dispositions and aromas of girls. Then, gradually, I began to let up.

But to this day I am still what might be called a reader, and have a high regard for authors.

XI.

First Steps in Divinity

IN THE days of my earliest memories my father had an acquaintance named Mr. Garrigues, a highly respectable man of French origin who operated a men's hat-store in West Baltimore, not far from our home in Hollins street. This hat-store of his, though it drove an excellent trade, occupied him only on week-days; on Sundays he threw himself, rather curiously for a man of his race, into superintending the Sunday-school of a little Methodist chapel in nearby Wilkens avenue. Early one Winter evening he dropped in while my brother Charlie and I were playing Indians up and down the front staircase, and proposed to my father that we be articled to his Sunday-school. I recall, of course, nothing of his argument, though my brother and I naturally eavesdropped; I remember only that it lasted but a few minutes, and that the very next Sunday afternoon Mr. Garrigues came to the house in a high silk hat, and conducted us to his seminary.

It was not until years afterward that I learned why my father had succumbed so quickly, or indeed at all. I understood by that time that he was what Christendom abhors as an infidel, and I took the liberty of expressing some wonder that he had been willing, in that character, to expose his two innocent sons to the snares of the Wesleyan divinity. He hemmed and hawed a little, but finally let go the truth. What moved him, he confessed, was simply his overmastering impulse to give over the Sunday afternoons of Winter to quiet snoozing. This had been feasible so long as my brother and I were puling infants and could be packed off for naps ourselves, but as we increased in years and malicious animal magnetism and began to prefer leaping and howling up and down stairs, it became impossible for him to get any sleep. So he was a set-up for Mr. Garrigues, and succumbed without firing a shot. "The risk," he went on to explain, "was much less than you seem to think. Garrigues and his Methodists had you less than two hours a week, and I

116

had you all the rest of the time. I'd have been a hell of a theologian to let them nail you."

I recall very little of his counter-revolutionary propaganda, and all that little took the form of a sort of satirical cross-examination, deliberately contrived to be idiotic. "Have they got you to Jonah yet? Have you heard about him swallowing the whale?" And so on. I recall even less of the teaching in the Sunday-school itself, though I apparently picked up from it some knowledge of the *dramatis personae* of the Old Testament. At all events, I can't remember the time when I did not know that Moses wrote the Ten Commandments with a chisel and wore a long beard; that Noah built an ark like the one we had in our Christmas garden, and filled it with animals which, to this day, I always think of as wooden, with a leg or two missing; that Lot's wife was turned into a pillar (I heard it as *cellar*) of table salt; that the Tower of Babel was twice as high as the Baltimore shot-tower; that Abraham greatly pleased Jahveh by the strange device of offering to butcher and roast his own son, and that Leviticus was the father of Deuteronomy. But all this learning must have been imparted by a process resembling osmosis, for I have no recollection of any formal teaching, nor even of any teacher.

The one thing I really remember about that Sunday-school is the agreeable heartiness of the singing. It is, of course, the thing that all children enjoy most in Sunday-schools, for there they are urged to whoop their loudest in praise of God, and that license is an immense relief from the shushing they are always hearing at home. Years later I lived for a while beside a Christian Science establishment in which the larval scientificoes were taught, presumably, that their occasional bellyaches were only mortal error, but all I ever heard of this teaching was their frequent antiphon of cheerful song, with each singer shrilling along in a different key. If the Bach Choir could work up so much pressure in its pipes, the Mass in B minor would become as popular as "Sweet Adeline." So far as I can make out, I attended Mr. Garrigues's hive of hymnody but two Winters, and yet I carried away from it a répertoire of Methodist shouts and glees that sticks to me to this day, and is turned loose every time I let three-bottle men take me for a ride.

My favorite then, as now, was "Are You Ready For the Judgment Day?"—a gay and even rollicking tune with a saving hint of brimstone in the words. I am told by Paul Patterson, who got his vocal training in the Abraham Lincoln Belt of Inner Illinois, that the No. 1 hymn there in the eighties was "Showers of Blessings," but in Baltimore, though we sang it, it was pretty far down the list. We grouped it, in fact, with such *dolce* but unexhilarating things as "In the Sweet By-and-By" and "God Be With You Till We Meet Again"—pretty stuff, to be sure, but sadly lacking in bite and zowie. The runner-up for "Are You Ready?" was "I Went Down the Rock to Hide My Face," another hymn with a very lively swing to it, and after "the Rock" came "Stand Up, Stand Up for Jesus," "Throw Out the Lifeline," "At the Cross," "Draw Me Nearer, Nearer, Nearer, Blessed Lord," "What a Friend We Have in Jesus," "Where Shall We Spend Eternity?" "The Sweet By-and-By," and "Hallelujah, Hallelujah, Revive Us Again," which last was cabbaged by the I.W.W. years later, and converted into proletarian ribaldry. We also learned the more somber classics—"Nearer, My God, To Thee," "Onward, Christian Soldiers," "Whiter Than Snow," "From Greenland's Icy Mountains," "Rock of Ages," "There is a Green Hill Far Away," and so on—but they were not sung often, and my brother and I had little fancy for them. It was not until I transferred to another Sunday-school that I came to know such lugubrious horrors as "There is a Fountain Filled With Blood." The Methodists avoided everything of that kind. They surely did not neglect Hell in their preaching, but when they lifted up their voices in song they liked to pretend that they were booked to escape it.

My early preference for "Are You Ready?" was no doubt supported by the fact that it was also a favorite among the Aframerican evangelists who practised in the alley behind Hollins street, alarming and shaking down the resident sinners. These evangelists did not confine themselves to Sundays, but worked seven days a week, and it seemed to me as a boy that there was always one of them in operation. They were both male and female. I recall clearly a female who wore a semi-ecclesiastical robe of violent purple, and had a voice so raucous that the white neighbors often begged the cops to chase her away. Whenever she was hustled out she kept on shouting warnings over her shoulder, always to the effect that the Day of Judgment was just round the corner. Her chief target was a low-down white man who lived in the alley with a colored woman, and had a large family of mulattoes. When he retreated into his house she howled at him through the window. So far as I know, she never made any impression on him, nor on his children, though his lady sometimes gave her a penny. This sinful white man, who never did any work, eventually disappeared, and the colored people reported that he had been killed in a brawl, and his body hustled to the University of Maryland dissecting-room. Of his children, one son was later reported to be hanged.

The evangelists always began their proceedings by lining out a hymn, and usually it was "Are You Ready?" It brought out all the colored people who happened to be at home, and in a few minutes white boys began to leap over the Hollins street back-fences to join the congregation. (In those days no self-respecting boy ever went through a gate. It was a point of honor to climb over the fence.) When the opening hymn reached its tenth and last stanza the evangelist would pray at length, mentioning salient sinners by name. Then there would be another hymn, and after that he would launch into his discourse. Its subject was always the same: the dreadful state of Aframerican morals in West Baltimore. It was delivered in a terrifying manner—indeed, it ran mainly to shrieks and howls—but it was seldom long, for the colored people preferred their theology in small and powerful doses. Then there would be another hymn, and the reverend would begin to show signs that a collection was impending. The moment those signs were detected nine-tenths of his audience vanished. Not infrequently, in fact, ten-tenths of it vanished, and all he could do, after mopping his brow and stuffing his handkerchief into his hat, was to shuffle on to some other alley.

We white boys always joined in the hymns, and listened to the sermons. From the latter we picked up a great deal of useful information about the geography, dimensions, temperature, social life and public works of Hell. To this day I probably know more about the matter than most ordained clergymen. The Hell we heard about was chiefly peopled, of course, by the colored damned; it was sometime later before I began to

understand clearly that there was also accommodation for Caucasians. We seldom attempted to rough-house these services,
though once in a while a boy whose people had family prayers
and who thus hated religion would heave a dead cat over the
fence or run down the alley yelling "Fire!" The colored communicants commonly gave ear with perfect gravity. Indeed,
the only one who ever ventured to dispute the theology on tap
was Old Wesley, the alley metaphysician, who reserved his caveats for the preaching of his brother, a divine who pastored a
tar-paper tabernacle down in Calvert county, and showed up
only to rowel and bedevil Wesley for living in adultery with
our next-door neighbor's colored cook.

It was the dream of every alley evangelist to be called to a
regular church, and sometimes that dream was realized. The
call consisted in renting a room in a tumble-down house, putting in a couple of rows of benches, and finding two or three
pious colored women to feed the pastor and pay the rent.
There was always a sign outside giving the name of the establishment, the name of the pastor (followed by D.D.), and the
order of services. These signs followed an invariable pattern,
with all the S's backward, and plenty of small *a*'s, *e*'s and *r*'s
scattered through the capitals. Such signs are still plentiful in
the poorer colored neighborhoods of Baltimore, and the old
church names survive—the Watch Your Step Baptist Temple,
the Sweet Violet Church of God, the Ananias Penecostal Tabernacle, and so on. One such basilica that I recall stood in the
middle of a lot down near the Baltimore & Ohio tracks, surrounded by Jimson weeds and piles of rusting tin-cans. The
sistren of the Ladies' Aid roved the vicinity, cadging contributions from white passers-by. Whenever my father and his
brother passed of a Sunday morning on their way to George
Zipprian's beer-garden across the tracks they gave up ten cents
apiece to the first collector who flagged them. They always
made her jab a hat-pin through her collection-card in their
presence, professing to fear that otherwise she might bilk the
pastor.

We were not permitted to enter any of these tabernacles, for
they were supposed to swarm with ticks, fleas, spiders, lice,
thousand-legs and other *Arthropoda*. But we were free to
attend the street-corner hullabaloos of the Salvation Army,

which was then a novelty in the United States, and almost as good as a circus. Here our training in Wesleyan hymnody stood us in good stead, for the hymns the Army howled were the same that we had howled ourselves in Mr. Garrigues's chapel. We let go with all brakes off, and greatly enjoyed the ensuing confessions of the saved. There was one old man who admitted such appalling crimes that we never got enough of him, and it was a sad day when he failed to appear, and one of the corner loafers intimated that he had been hauled off to a lunatic asylum. When the beautiful Amazons of God began circulating in the crowd with their tambourines we took to our heels, for we believed in conscience that salvation should be free.

Mr. Garrigues died suddenly in 1888, and my father thereupon shifted us to another and much larger Sunday-school, run by the English Lutherans in Lombard street. It met, unfortunately, on Sunday mornings, so he had to suffer some interruption of his afternoon nap, but as we grew older and more decorous that objection faded out. We liked it very much during the first few years, for the superintendent, Mr. Harman, was a Methodist at heart and often lined out the rousing hymns that we knew and esteemed. We also greatly enjoyed the cornet-playing of the treasurer, whose name I recall as Mr. Mentzer. He was an elegant fellow in a silky mustache, a white choker collar and an immaculate cutaway, and when he lifted his cornet to his lips it was with a very graceful flourish—at all events, it seemed so to us. As he let go *fortissimo* the whole Sunday-school seemed to heave, and the stained-glass rattled in the church upstairs. In the singing that went with his blasts of tone ordinary yelling was not enough; a boy of any spirit had to scream. More than once I came home hoarse, and was put to gargling with pain-killer.

The pastor of the church in those days was the Rev. Sylvanus Stall, D.D., a tall, gaunt Pennsylvanian with a sandy beard and melancholy voice. I find on investigation that he was precisely forty years old in 1887, but he seemed to my brother and me to be as ancient as Abraham. He looked at first glance like a standard-model Class B Protestant ecclesiastic, but there was much more to him than met the eye. One Sunday morning in 1889 or thereabout he showed up in Sunday-school with a strange contraption under his arm. Rapping for order, he announced that it was a newly invented machine that could talk like a human being, and not only talk but even sing. Then he instructed us to sing his favorite hymn, which was "God Be With You Till We Meet Again." We bawled it dutifully, and he explained that the machine would now bawl it back. "But not," he went on, "as loudly as you did. Listen carefully, and you will hear it clearly enough. The sound of the machine is very faint, but it is also very penetrating." So he turned it on, and we heard a phonograph for the first time. Ah, that it had been the last!

A little while later the good doctor quit pastoring to take the editorship of a church paper, with dashes into book-writing on the side. His first two or three books had such depressing titles as "Methods of Church Work," "Five-Minute Object Sermons" and "Bible Selections For Daily Devotion," and appear to have scored only successes of esteem. But in 1897, long after I had escaped his former Sunday-school and almost forgotten him, he brought out a little volume called "What a Young Boy Ought to Know," and thereafter he began rolling up money with such velocity that when he died in 1915 he was probably the richest Lutheran pastor, at least in the earned brackets, that the Republic has ever seen. For that little volume founded the great science of sex hygiene, which eventually developed into a major American industry, with thousands of practitioners and a technic become as complicated as that of bridge or chess.

He wrote all its official texts for male seekers—"What a Young Man Ought to Know," "What a Young Husband Ought to Know," "What a Man of Forty-five Ought to Know," and so on—and he inspired, copy-read and published all its texts for females, beginning with "What a Young Girl Ought to Know" and ending, I suppose, with "What a Decent Grandmother Ought to Forget." Indeed, he held the field unchallenged until the explosion of the Freud ammunition-dump of horrors, and by that time he was so well heeled that he could afford to laugh ha-ha. He left his money, I believe, to a college for training missionaries to the sexually misinformed and underprivileged, but where it is located I don't know and don't care.

Of the theology he radiated in his Baltimore days I retain precisely nothing. There was, in fact, little expounding of doctrine in his Sunday-school; the instruction, in so far as there was any at all, was predominantly ethical, and had as its chief apparent aim the discouragement of murder, robbery, counterfeiting, embezzlement and other such serious crimes, none of which occurred in the student body in my time. Those were the cradle days of religious pedagogy, and the teachers confined themselves mainly to expounding the week's International Sunday-school Lesson, and trying to induce their pupils to memorize the Golden Text. Inasmuch as I could never memorize anything, I failed regularly. But there was no penalty for failure, and it was hardly remarked, for virtually all the other boys in my class failed too.

Tiring of this puerile futility, I began to agitate for my release at the age of ten, and finally escaped when I went into long pants. My father, it turned out, had not underestimated * the potency of his evil influence: it left me an infidel as he was, and as his father had been before him. My grandfather died too soon to have much direct influence upon me, but I must have inherited something of his attitude of mind, which was one of large tolerance in theological matters. No male of the Mencken family, within the period that my memory covers, ever took religion seriously enough to be indignant about it. There were no converts from faith among us, and hence no bigots or fanatics. To this day I have a distrust of such fallen-aways, and when one of them writes in to say that some monograph of mine has aided him in throwing off the pox of Genesis my rejoicing over the news is very mild indeed.

XII.

The Ruin of an Artist

THE PIANO that introduced me to the tone-art was a Stieff square made in Baltimore, with a shiny black case, a music-rack that was a delirium of jig-saw whorls, and legs and ankles of the sort that survive today only on lady politicians. It came into the house in Hollins street on January 13, 1888, and there it groaned and suffered for twenty years, gradually taking on the unhealthy patina and tin-can tone of age. How many hours I gave over to banging it, first and last, I don't know, but certainly they must have been enough to set loose a couple of billion decibels. When, in 1906 or thereabout, I joined a music club, and we began to play occasionally in Hollins street, the infirmities of the old Stieff were remarked unpleasantly by the other members, and after a year or two of resistance I traded it in for an upright. Inasmuch as squares, by that time, had gone completely out of fashion, even on excursion boats and in houses of ill-fame, the dealer who acquired it could not find a buyer for it, and in the end he had to contribute it to a huge bonfire of unsalable instruments that the despairing piano men of the east staged at Atlantic City, to the accompaniment of considerable publicity. A few years later someone invented the trick of turning old squares into colonial desks, and there arose a sudden demand for them from antique manufacturers, with the prices soaring. The dealer spent his brief remaining days denouncing me for overreaching him, and his clamor in the saloons was largely responsible for the bad name that I still bear in Baltimore as a prince of pelf.

My first teacher was a gentleman I chiefly remember, not because of what he taught me, but because of the extraordinary luxuriance of his whiskers. Hair on the face, of course, was not unusual in the eighties; indeed, it was the rule, and I knew men with beards almost a yard long, and others who affected Burnsides, Dundrearys and even Galways. But foliage so wild and lawless as that of Mr. Maass—for such was his name—was nevertheless somewhat unusual. It was divided in the middle in such a way that it seemed to be blown apart by a gale of wind, and it swept so far to either side that it passed and concealed his narrow shoulders. He wore it, I learned, because he suffered from a weakness of the chest, and that same weakness had wrecked his career as a piano virtuoso. He was working at the time, in fact, as my father's bookkeeper, and he slipped away from his stool twice a week to fan my nascent talents and pick up an extra dollar. He was a patient and kindly man, and must have been a very fair teacher, for in hardly more than a year he got me through Ferdinand Beyer's Preliminary School for the Piano-Forte,[1] and even introduced me to some of the lesser horrors of Carl Czerny's School of Velocity.[2] But the weakness in the chest continued, and only too soon poor Mr. Maass had to give up both his teaching and his bookkeeping. A little while longer, and he was dead. I remember nothing of his funeral, and not much more of his pedagogy, but I recall very well his gentle spirit and his stupendous whiskers.

On his departure I fell into the hands of a series of lady   *
teachers, and they both wrecked my technic and debauched my taste. There were thousands of such damsels roving the American towns in the last century, radiating an influence for evil even worse than that of the contemporary white-slave traders, spiritualists and politicians. They charged a uniform price of twenty-five cents apiece for lessons, and derived their really living wages from the retailing of sheet music. Some of the music they taught me still exists in my library: "La Châtelaine," by A.

---

[1] I have the book yet, and lately paid a binder $7.50 to repair its dog's ears. In Grove's Dictionary of Music there is an article by the late Edward Dannreuther dismissing Beyer as "a fair pianist and tolerable musician whose reputation rests upon an enormous number of easy arrangements, transcriptions, potpourris, fantasias, divertissements, and the like, such as second-rate dilettanti and music-masters at ladies' schools are pleased to call amusing and instructive." Dannreuther's own compositions consisted, according to another writer in Grove, of "two sets of songs and one of duets." I pronounce a curse upon him in passing. He died in 1905, and is probably still in Purgatory. May he linger there for 10,000,000,000 more years!

[2] For Czerny I never developed any affection, and neither did any other male piano student of my generation. He was admired only by vinegary little girls who wore tight pigtails tied with pink ribbons, and played his infernal scales and arpeggios in a pretentious and offensive manner. So late as 1930, being in Vienna, I visited and desecrated his grave.

Leduc; "Danse Écossaise," by Fred T. Baker; the "Old Roman" march, by M. H. Rosenfeld (dedicated to "the Hon. Allen G. Thurman, the noblest Roman of them all"); "Monastery Bells," Leybach's Fifth Nocturne, the "Black Key" polka, the "Chopsticks" waltz, and other such rubbish. I achieved a considerable fluency in its performance, and at the age of ten was often put up to drive unwelcome guests out of the house.

This purpose, of course, was concealed from me, and I believed innocently that my proficiency was admired. The trick was played by my father. When some bore dropped in unexpectedly of an evening (which was no uncommon misadventure in those days, for there were no telephones) he would get out the jugs that were his tools of hospitality, yell upstairs for me to come down, set me at the Stieff square, and order me to play "something lively." I thereupon launched into a programme of marches and gallops, all of them executed with the loud pedal held down. If I let up long enough to attempt something soft and sneaking, he would stop me at once, and order me to turn on the juice again. This dreadful din went on until the guest withdrew. I remember trying to figure out why a rational man, entertaining his apparent friends, should want to deafen them, but the truth did not occur to me until long afterward. In fact, it did not occur to me even then; I derived it from one of my father's occasional confidences, which increased as I grew in years and discretion.

This unwitting service as bouncer made me a slave to the *forte* pedal, and I remain more or less under its spell to this day, as critics have often noted. My father was tone-deaf, and was thus not incommoded when, in reaching for the C below the bass clef, I hit B or D. He had been put to the fiddle in boyhood, but never got beyond the third position in Jacques-Féréol Mazas's Complete Violin Method: the rest of the book (which is still in the house) shows no pedagogical marks. He had two violins, but ventured to play them only when encouraged by libation. At such times he would tune up by performing "Yankee Doodle." If it sounded plausible he would proceed. Some years after his death I showed his violins to the late Albert Hildebrandt, of Baltimore, a friend of mine and a renowned violin expert. He dismissed one of them as trash, but told me that the other was an excellent German imitation of a sound Cremona model. He put it in order for me, and I was later offered $200 for it. Astounded, I called a family court of inquiry, and eventually excavated the fact that my father's stepmother had bought it for him on a visit to Leipzig in the sixties. She knew no more about violins than he did, but somehow she had managed to pick up a good one.

The lady music teachers, as I have said, undermined my virtuosity and vitiated my taste, but despite their hard efforts they did not destroy either altogether. I managed somehow to become a pretty good sight-reader, and I was soon proceeding by the way of the Strauss waltzes (which still delight me) to the whole salon répertoire of the time. There was some Mozart in it, and even some Beethoven, but it ran mainly to Moszkowski and his congeners. I well recall the sensation when Paderewski's minuet in G was added to it: people lined up for the music in the music-stores as they were soon afterward lining up for the Sousa marches. My command of waltzes, polkas, schottisches, mazurkas and so on, and later on of two-steps, kept me on the piano-stool at parties, and so I managed to get through * my nonage without learning to dance. I took a few belated lessons at the end of my teens, but turned out to be unteachable without recourse to complicated and costly apparatus, apparently because my center of gravity was not stable.

My real regret today, looking back over my career as a *Tonkünstler*, is that those preposterous lady Leschetizkys never gave me any instruction in elementary harmony. They avoided the subject, of course, simply because they knew nothing about it, and had, in fact, probably never heard of it. I don't recall any of them ever referring to a composition by naming its key; they always said it was "in three sharps," or "five flats," and never distinguished between major and minor. I was twelve years old before it dawned upon me that there must be ascertainable differences between chords, and it was a good while thereafter before I began to find out what those differences were. The creative frenzy of the mid-teen years prompted me to write a great many piano pieces, chiefly waltzes, but I had to harmonize them by the method of trial and error at the piano. If my inclination had run to songs this method might have made a George M. Cohan of me, or even an Irving Berlin. Perhaps fortunately, I was born with an intense distaste for vocal music, and to this day think of even the most gifted Wagnerian soprano as no more than a blimp fitted with a calliope. If a bass singer shows up at my funeral to sing "*Im tiefen Keller sitz' ich hier*" it will take the whole platoon of clergy and pallbearers to hold me down.

It was not until I was passing out of my teens that I ever opened a *Harmonielehre* and not until several years afterward that I began to associate familiarly with competent musicians. It was then too late for me to devote any serious attention to the subject, for I was in active practice as a reporter on a newspaper, and the job kept me jumping. That was long before it had occurred to anyone that reporters would be benefitted culturally by five-day weeks and time-and-a-half for overtime. I worked six days of twelve hours each, and often had to lend a hand on my day off. There was a year during which I accumulated no less than twenty full days of overtime. The city editor gave me what I thought was a handsome compensation by raising my pay $2 a week, letting me do copy-reading on the side for the experience, and adding five days to my annual vacation.

If I speak of my lack of sound musical instruction lightly, please do not be deceived. I was only dimly aware of it at the time, but it was really the great deprivation of my life. My early impulse to compose was no transient storm of puberty, explicable on purely endocrine grounds. It stuck to me through the years of maturity, and is still far from dead as I slide into the serenity of senility. When I think of anything properly describable as a beautiful idea, it is always in the form of music. Alcohol has the effect of filling my head with such ideas, and I daresay hashish would do even better. I have sketched out, in my day, at least ten sonatas for piano, and there was a time when I had accumulated fifty or sixty pounds of music-paper, all of it covered with pothooks. It ran, in the main, to waltzes, always my great delight, but it also included the score of a musical comedy put on by the boys at the Baltimore Polytechnic in 1895 or thereabout—most of it, of course, snitched from other composers. This musical comedy, despite a book that was frowned on as contumacious and even a bit salacious, made a great success, and I sat at the piano as its whole orchestra.

In those days I knew nothing about orchestra music, but when the music club I have mentioned began to function I

developed an interest in fiddles and flutes, and was soon writing for them. One of our first members, now long dead, was an Irishman named Joe Callahan, a charming fellow who loved   *
music to excess, but was of such limited skill as a violinist that he could be trusted only on the open strings. I wrote many parts for him in the safe keys of C and G major, and it gave him great delight to chime in, even though he could do it only occasionally. I also wrote violin and cello obbligatos for the songs of a lady singer who joined us for a while. Once I launched into the incredible project of arranging Dvořák's "New World" symphony for piano, violin and cello, and another time I actually made such an arrangement of Beethoven's No. 1. For years I collected orchestra scores, and what is more, studied them diligently, though I am almost as tone-deaf as my father, and could never get any more out of them than a ghostly reverberation, like the sound of a brass band heard from afar on a rainy night.

Meditating on this, my lifelong libido that has never come to anything, I become aware of the eternal tragedy of man. He is born to long for things that are beyond him, as flight through the air is beyond a poor goldfish in a globe, and stardom in Hollywood must remain forever outside the experience, though not outside the dreams, of all save a few hundred of the girls in the ten-cent stores. Not many men of my unhappily meagre equipment have ever had a better chance than I to fling their egos into the face of this world. I have, in fact, made a living for many years by thrusting myself upon the attention of strangers, most of them reluctant. I have written and printed probably 10,000,000 words of English, and continue to this day to pour out more and more. It has wrung from others, some of them my superiors, probably a million words of notice, part of it pro but most of it con. In brief, my booth has been set up on a favorable pitch, and I have never lacked hearers for my ballyhoo. But all the same I shall die an inarticulate man, for my best ideas have beset me in a language I know only vaguely and speak only like a child.

The loss to humanity, of course, is not serious enough to cause any general gloom. In truth, my real reason for failing to pursue music to a bitter finish was probably not, as I have intimated, that I was too busy with other things, nor even that I was too old when my first really good chance came. It was simply that I had no talent for it. This dreadful fact gradually forced itself into my consciousness as the years passed, helped along by the satirical efforts of musical friends, and today it is so firmly embedded that though I still itch I no longer scratch. But the underlying mystery remains. Why should a man so completely devoid of fitness for the tone-art yet have so powerful an impulse to practise it, and get so much pleasure out of it? I have no answer, but I suspect that my disease is more widespread than is generally assumed. Every concert audience probably swarms with baffled Beethovens and frustrated Wagners. I used to believe and argue that any person who had a genuine love of music would undertake some effort, soon or late, to make it, but even that I now doubt, for I know men who go to concerts almost as regularly as they eat, and sit at the phonograph or the radio by the hour, and yet have so little impulse to raise a din themselves, and so little curiosity about the ways and means of doing so, that they can't so much as pick out the scale of C major at the piano. As for me, I delight in the sound of horse-hair on catgut as honestly and as vastly as a cop delights in beer, and yet I am quite unable to tune a fiddle. The mystery is only one of a thousand that bedevil man in his swift and senseless flight through the world. The gods, in the main, are vicious, but now and then they show an unmistakable touch of humor.

My inclination toward the graphic arts began earlier and ended earlier than my devotion to music, and was much feebler. There are, in the family files, crude drawings dated 1886 and 1887, and a little while later, sitting under Mr. Paul at F. Knapp's Institute, I copied a whole series of the drawing-books then in fashion, and picked up some pale skill at draftsmanship as that science was then understood by German pedagogues. But my natural lack of manual dexterity hindered me here, and I never got beyond the elements. At Christmas, 1888, some one gave me a box of water-colors, and during the years following I made various attempts to use them. Having learned by reading that paintings were commonly done on canvas, I made a small wooden frame, stretched it with muslin borrowed from my mother's rag-bag, and was astonished and baffled to find that when water-colors were applied to it they all ran together. This unhappy *Jugendwerk* still survives. Also, there is a water-color on paper, signed "H. L. Mencken, July, 1892," which not only survives, but is framed in a gilt frame, and hangs on my office wall. It shows a scene along Jones falls, near our Summer home at Mt. Washington, and is anything but bad for a boy less than twelve years old. The rocks are painted in a thoroughly bold and modern manner, and the water falling over them actually looks like water. I have often thought of entering this composition in some free-for-all exhibition of Modernist Art—with the date and signature, of course, discreetly painted out.

XIII.

In the Footsteps of Gutenberg

O N NOVEMBER 26, 1887 my father sent his bookkeeper, Mr.
Maass, to the establishment of J. F. W. Dorman, at 217
East German street, Baltimore, and there and then, by the said
Maass's authorized agency, took title to a Baltimore No. 10 Self-
Inker Printing Press and a font of No. 214 type. The press cost
$7.50 and the font of type $1.10. These details, which I recover
from the receipted bill in my father's file, are of no conceivable
interest to anyone else on earth, but to me they are of a degree
of concern bordering upon the super-colossal, for that press determined the whole course of my future life. If it had been a
stethoscope or a copy of Dr. Ayer's Almanac I might have gone
in for medicine; if it had been a Greek New Testament or a set
of baptismal grappling-irons I might have pursued divinity. As it
was, I got the smell of printer's ink up my nose at the tender age
of seven, and it has been swirling through my sinuses ever since.

The press and type, of course, were laid in by my father against
Christmas, and were concealed for the nonce in a cupboard at
home, but my brother Charlie and I had a good look at them
before early candlelight of November 27. We decided that they
were pretty nifty, or, as the word was then, nobby. If Charlie,
comparing them to the velocipede that lay in wait for him, was
bemused by envy, he had only himself to blame, for he had delayed his coming into the world for twenty months after my
own arrival, and was still virtually illiterate. It was barely three
months, in fact, since he had begun to attend the sessions of F.
Knapp's Institute, and he yet had some difficulty in distinguish-
ing, without illustrative wood-cuts, between the words *cat* and
rat. Compared to him, I was so far advanced in *literae humaniores* as to be almost a savant. During the previous Summer
I had tackled and got down my first book, and was even then
engaged in exploring the house library for another. No doubt
this new and fevered interest in beautiful letters was marked in
the household, and set afloat the notion that a printing-press
would be to my taste. Indeed, I probably hinted as much myself.

If my mother approved, which she undoubtedly did, she must have developed a certain regret on Christmas Day, for my father undertook to show me how to work the press, and inasmuch as he knew no more about printing than Aristotle and had so little manual dexterity that he could not even lace a shoe, he made a ghastly mess of it. Before he gave it up as a bad job all the ink that came with the outfit had been smeared and slathered away, and at least half the type had been plugged with it or broken. I recall clearly that we ran out of white cards before noon, and had to resort to the backs of his business cards. By that time all the brass gauge-pins had been crushed, one of the steel guides that held cards against the platen was bent, and the mechanism operating the ink-roller was out of order. It was a sad caricature of a printing-press that went to the cellar at midday, when my mother ordered a halt and a clean-up.

Next morning, after my father shoved off for his office, I unearthed it and set to work to scrub the ink off it and make it go. Unfortunately, I had almost as little skill with my hands as my father, so it must have been New Year's Day, at the earliest, before I succeeded. My cash takings, that Christmas, had been excellent; in fact, I had amassed something on the order of $2. With this money I went down to Dorman's, bought a new can of ink and a large bottle of benzine, and also laid in a new font of type. With the press there had come a font of Black Letter and to it, apparently on the advice of Mr. Maass, who was an aesthete, my father had added one of Script. My own addition was a prosaic font of Roman, with caps only. I now had enough faces to begin printing on a commercial scale, and early in 1888 I was ready with the following announcement:

Up to this time I had always written my name Henry L., or
Harry, which last, as I have noted, has been my stable-name all
my life. My change to H. L. was not due to any feeling that the
form better became the dignity of a business man, but simply
to the fact that my father, in the course of his Christmas morning gaucheries, had smashed all my Black Letter lower-case *r*'s,
and I had to cut my coat to fit my cloth. During the ensuing
months I had some accidents of my own, and by the time I
began to print billheads I had wrecked the penultimate cap *M*
in my Roman font, and was forced to abbreviate Baltimore to
Balto. But I still had an undamaged *&* in Black Letter and also
a serviceable though somewhat mangey cap *C*, so I added "&
Co" to the style and designation of my house.

So far as I can remember, my father was my only customer.
His taste in typography, as in the other arts, was very far from
finicky, and his pride in the fact that I could print at all sufficed
to throttle such feeble qualms as he may have had. In February,
1888, he set off to one of the annual deliriums of the Knights
Templar, and I applied for, and got, the contract for printing
his fraternal *cartes de visite*. These cards were exchanged by brethren from North, East, South and West whenever two or more of
them happened to be thrown together in the saloons of the convention town. They followed a rigid model. Each showed the
name and home-town of the bearer, and a series of colored
symbols representing his Masonic dignities.

The symbols were naturally lacking in my composing-room,
and I had no idea where they were to be obtained. Moreover,
my Baltimore No. 10 Self-Inker was hardly fitted for work in
six or eight colors. But such impediments could not stump a
really up-and-coming business man. I simply put in the symbols by hand, and colored them with the water-colors that had
also been among my Christmas presents. My father professed
to be delighted with the cards, and on his return from the
convention told me that he had presented specimens of them
to Freemasons from points as far distant as Key West, Fla.,
Duluth, Minn., and Ogden, Utah, and that among the recipi-
ents were some of the most puissant and austere dignitaries of
the order, including two Governors and a dozen United States
Senators. This was my first attempt upon a national audience.
My bill for the job survives. It shows that I charged my father

8½ cents a dozen for the cards, including the hand-painting. Of the cards themselves, two or three also survive. They will go to the Bodleian after they have made the round of the American galleries.

In a little while I was branching out. On the one hand I issued a circular offering to print advertising at what, even in the primitive West Baltimore of that remote era, must have seemed to my competitors to be cut rates. And on the other hand, I launched into the publication of a newspaper in rivalry to the celebrated Baltimore *Sunpaper*, the news Bible at 1524 Hollins street as it has always been in every other respectable Baltimore household, then, now and forever. My circular offered to produce advertisements 2 by 2 inches in area, in any quantity below the astronomical, at the uniform rate of 4 cents a hundred. For an additional 2 cents a hundred I offered to blow them up to the magnitude of 3 inches by 3¼. This was as far as I could go, for it was the full size of the chase of my press. For business cards on plain white stock, "any size," I asked 5 cents a dozen, or 2 cents a quarter of a dozen. Why I assumed that anyone would want as few as a quarter of a dozen, or even a dozen, I don't recall: there must have been some reason, but it has slipped me. The "any size," of course, was only a euphemism: as I have said, my maximum size was 3 inches by 3¼. I never got any orders for these goods. I solicited my mother's trade, but she replied coldly that she was not in any commercial business, and had no use for cards or circulars. I also solicited my brother Charlie, but he was poor in those days, and believed that it was a kind of lunacy to lay out money on printed matter. He much preferred the black licorice nigger-babies sold by Old Man Kunker in Baltimore street, and commonly went about with his face mired by their exudations.

The newspaper I set up against the *Sunpaper* also came to nothing. It was doomed from the start, for it was afflicted by every malady that a public journal can suffer from—insufficiency of capital, incomplete news service, an incompetent staff, no advertising, and a press that couldn't print it. No copy of it survives, but I remember that it consisted of four pages, and was printed on scraps of wrapping-paper filched from the hired girl's hoard in the kitchen. I had to print each page separately, and to distribute the type between pages, for I hadn't enough to set up all four at once. Having no news service whatever, and not knowing where any was to be had, I compromised by lifting all of my dispatches out of my rival. In those days the Associated Press foreign report consisted largely of a series of brief bulletins, and the *Sunpaper* printed them on its first page every morning under the standing head of "Latest Foreign News." I chose the shortest, and when there were none short enough, chopped down the longer. Thus the most important item I ever printed was this:

Berlin, March 9—William I is dead aged 91.

This came out in my paper on March 15 or thereabout, a week after the *Sunpaper* had made it generally known in Baltimore, Washington, Virginia, West Virginia and the Carolinas. My domestic news came from the same source, and consisted wholly of telegraphed items, for they were usually short. I made no effort to cover local news, though there was then plenty of it in West Baltimore. Almost every day Murphy the cop made one of his hauls of ruffianly Aframericans in Vincent alley, and I could sit at my third-story office-and-bedroom window and see him drag them through Union Square to the watch-house at Calhoun and Pratt streets. It was common, also, for car-horses to fall dead in their tracks, for children to get lost, and for great gang-wars among the neighborhood dogs to tear up the Union Square lawns. But I never attempted to report any of these things. I remain a bad reporter, in fact, to this day. During my term of servitude as city editor of a Baltimore daily, long after my own paper blew up, I blushed inwardly every time I had to excoriate a member of the staff for failing to get the age, weight, color and address of a lady jugged for murdering her husband, or the names of the brave cops who had tracked her down.

Rather curiously, I can't recall the name of my paper, if, in fact, it had one. The chances are at least even that it didn't, for I was chronically short of what printers call sorts, and never wasted a single piece of type if I could help it. A little while later, probably during the ensuing Autumn, I discovered a perfect mine of supplies in the hell-box that stood outside the printing plant of Isaac Friedenwald & Son, in Paca street, across narrow Cider alley from my father's factory. It was Mr.

Maass who directed me to this Golconda, and I began to work it diligently. From it I recovered all sorts of mangey woodcuts, many empty ink-cans with a little ink remaining in them, a great deal of scrap paper and cardboard, and an occasional piece of condemned type, always badly battered. Unfortunately, this type was of small use to my newspaper, for the Friedenwalds were printers to the Johns Hopkins University, and laid claim to having the largest stock of foreign type-faces in the Western World, so when my eye lighted upon what looked to be a likely *E* it sometimes turned out to be a Greek *sigma* or a Hebrew *lamedh*. I could make nothing of these strange characters; in fact, I didn't know that they were characters at all, but took them to be the devices of unfamiliar branches of the Freemasons.

The Friedenwalds did not stop with such relatively intelligible alphabets, but boasted that they could print any language ever heard of on earth, and often surprised and enchanted the Johns Hopkins professors by making good. They had fonts of Arabic, Sanskrit, Russian, Coptic, Armenian and Chinese, not to mention Old Norse runes and Egyptian hieroglyphs. The specimens of these types that I recovered were always cruelly damaged, but nevertheless some of them were still legible, and if I had given them due study I might have become a linguist. But I usually traded them for marbles, chewing-tobacco tags or cigarette pictures with a neighbor who made lead soldiers of them in a mold he had somehow acquired, so I made no appreciable progress in the tongues.

Despite all these griefs and burdens, I stuck to my printing press through 1888, and it remained my favorite possession for several years afterward. Why my father, seeing my interest in it, did not buy me a larger and better one I do not know; probably it was because I wasn't aware that a larger and better one existed, and hence did not ask for it. I have found out since that Dorman had them with chases up to 6 by 8 inches, and that his catalogue listed two or three dozen different fonts of type, some of them with highly ornate faces in the rococo taste of the time. But though my press was a poor thing and my type gradually wore out to the point where all the letters printed like squashed *O*'s, my enthusiasm for printing did not die, and even when a rage for photography and then for chemistry

began to challenge it, in my early teens, it managed to continue
a sturdy undercover existence. When, on my father's death, as I
was eighteen, I was free at last to choose my trade in the world,
I chose newspaper work without any hesitation whatever, and,
save when the scent of a passing garbage-cart has revived my
chemical libido, I have never regretted my choice. More than
once I have slipped out of daily journalism to dally in its mere-
tricious suburbs, but I have always returned repentant and relieved, like a blackamoor coming back in Autumn to a warm
and sociable jail.

Aside from the direct and all-powerful influence of that
Baltimore No. 10 Self-Inker and the Friedenwald hell-box, I was
probably edged toward newspapers and their glorious miseries
by two circumstances, both of them trivial. The first was my
discovery of a real newspaper office in the little town of Ellicott
City, where we spent the Summers of 1889 and 1890. Ellicott City
was then a very picturesque and charming place, and indeed
still is, despite the fact that the heavy hand of progress is on it.
It is built along the two steep banks of a ravine that runs down
to the Patapsco, and many of the old stone houses, though
four stories high in front, scarcely clear their backyards in the
rear. It is the local legend that dogs, pigs, chickens and even
children have been known to fall out of these backyards into
and down the chimneys. The Baltimore & Ohio Railroad's old
main line to the West runs beside the river on a viaduct spanning the main street, and from this viaduct, in 1889, a long
balcony ran along the second story of a block of houses, with
an entrance from the railway station's platform. I naturally explored it, and was presently rewarded by discovering the
printing-office of the weekly Ellicott City *Times*.

The *Times*, even in those days, must have been an appreciably better paper than my own, but its superiority was certainly
not excessive. The chief article of equipment in its gloomy
second-story office was a Washington handpress that had
probably been hauled in on mule-back in the twenties or thirties, when the town was still Ellicott's Mills, and a famous
coaching-station on the road to the Ohio. I have seen many
Washington handpresses since, but never a hoarier one. Its
standards were oaken beams, and it looked to a marvelling boy
to be as massive as a locomotive. It was operated by a young

man and a boy, and I watched enchanted as the white paper was placed on the chase, the platen was brought down, and the printed sheets were lifted off. The circulation of the *Times* at that time was probably not more than 400, but it took the man and the boy all day to print an edition, for only one side could be printed at a time, and yanking the huge lever was a back-breaking job. I noted that the young man left most of the yanking to the boy, and encouraged him from time to time by loud incitements and expostulations. I found out that Thursday was press-day, and I managed to be on hand every time. If my mother had no commission for me in the village on a Thursday I always suggested one.

I was captivated not only by the miracle of printing, but also by the high might and consequence of the young man in charge of the press. He was genuinely Somebody in that remote and obscure village, and the fact radiated from him like heat from a stove. He never deigned to take any notice of me. He might give me a blank glance when he halted the press to take a chew of tobacco, but that was all. He became to me a living symbol of the power and dignity of the press—a walking proof of its romantic puissance. Years later I encountered him again, and got to know him very well, and to have a great affection for him. I was by then city editor of the Baltimore *Morning Herald*, now dead and forgotten, and he was the assistant foreman of its composing-room. No man in all my experience has ever met more perfectly the classical specifications for that office.

On a rush night he gave a performance that was magnificent. Arising in his pulpit, he would howl for missing takes in a voice of brass, always using the formula hallowed since Gutenberg's time: "What --- -- - ----- has got A 17?" His chief, Joe Bamberger, was also a foreman of notable talents, and knew how to holler in a way that made even the oldest printer gasp and blanche, but Josh Lynch—for such was his name—could outholler Joe a hundred to one, on the flat or over the jumps. He was a grand fellow, and he taught me a lot about the newspaper business that was not on tap in the *Herald* editorial-rooms. Above all, he taught me that a newspaper man, in the hierarchy of earthly fauna, ranked only below the assistant foreman of a composing-room, and that neither had any reason or excuse in law or equity to take any lip from any ——— in the whole —— world. He is dead now, but surely not forgotten. If I miss him in Hell it will be a disappointment.

The second experience that served to cake the ink upon me and doom me to journalism took the form of an overheard conversation. My father's Washington agent, Mr. Cross, paid a visit to us at Ellicott City one Sunday, and he and my father and my uncle Henry put in the afternoon drinking beer on the veranda of our house. They fell to talking of the illustrious personages they were constantly meeting in Washington—Senators who had not been sober for a generation, Congressmen who fought bartenders and kicked the windows out of night-hacks, Admirals in the Navy who were reputed to be four-, five- and even six-bottle men, Justices of the Supreme and other high courts who were said to live on whiskey and chewing tobacco alone. They naturally admired these prodigious men, and I crept up to hear them described and praised. But in the end Mr. Cross, who knew Washington far better than my father or my uncle, permitted himself a caveat of doubt. All such eminentissimos, he allowed, were mere passing shapes, as evanescent as the morning dew, here today and gone tomorrow. They had their effulgence, but then they perished, leaving no trace save a faint aroma, usually bad. The real princes of Washington, he said, were the newspaper correspondents. They outlasted Senators, Congressmen, judges and Presidents. In so far as the United States had any rational and permanent government, they were its liver and its lights. To this day, though reason may protest bitterly, I still revere the gentlemen of the Washington corps.

Other Christmas presents came and went, but there was never another that fetched and floored me like Dorman's Baltimore No. 10 Self-Inker Printing Press. The box of water-colors that set me to painting I have mentioned, and I have also al-
* luded to the camera that aroused in me a passion for photography, and then, by way of developers and toning solutions, for chemistry. But my career as a water-colorist was brief and not glorious, and the camera came after the period covered by this history. I recall a year when some one gave me a microscope, but it, too, held me only transiently, for one of the first things I inspected through it was a drop of vinegar, and the revolting

mass of worms that I saw kept me off vinegar for a year after-ward, and cured me of microscopy. Another year I received an electric battery, and for a while I had a swell time with it, but I began to neglect it when I discovered that it could not work a small arc-light that I had made of two charred matches. Yet another year I was favored with a box of carpenter's tools, but they must have been poor ones, for the saw would not saw, the plane would not plane, the hammer mashed my thumb, and the chisel cut my hand. Nor was I greatly interested in the steam-engine that appeared at Christmas 1889, or the steam railroad that followed the year after. The latter, indeed, was probably my brother Charlie's present, not mine, for he spent much more time playing with it than I did, and in later life he *
took to engineering, and laid many a mile of railroad line, and worked on many a bridge and tunnel.

It was the printing-press that left its marks, not only upon my hands, face and clothing, but also on my psyche. They are still there, though more than fifty years have come and gone.

XIV.

From the Records of an Athlete

I T ALWAYS astonishes people familiar with my present matronly figure to hear that I was a fast runner as a boy. It not
only astonishes them; it also makes them laugh. Nevertheless,
a fact remains a fact, no matter how much infidels may mock
it, and I like to recall this one whenever a steep stairway blows
me, or I begin to choke and gurgle in the act of lacing my
shoes.

Toward the end of the year 1890, when I was ten years old,
I made the 100 yards in 12⅖ seconds, wearing heavy Winter
underwear and timed by my father's Swiss repeater watch, then
the great glory of his jewel casket—that is, next to the massive
gold chain that anchored it to his person, the ruby-studded
Shriner's button that he wore in his coat-lapel, and the diamond solitaire that screwed into the façade of his boiled shirt.
To be sure, the distance for my dash was estimated by the eye, not
laid off by geometers, but all the same it must have been accurate to within 15 or 20 yards. I made it in less than 13 seconds,
not once but six or eight times in close succession, and would
have gone on running all afternoon if my mother had not in-
tervened on what I gathered to be hygienic grounds. I recall
clearly only her suggestion that my father must be going crazy.

He himself was surely no athlete. Once, seeking to edify my
brother Charlie and me, he essayed to jump over a bale of hay,
but only succeeded in landing on top of it belly-down, kicking
and hollering. When the mood to inspire us by boasting was
on him he liked to tell us that he had been a powerful swimmer
in his youth, but I never saw him in actual water save once, and
he then came out very promptly, shivering and upset. When a
natatorium was opened in Baltimore and I demanded to be
taken to it and taught the art, he kept on postponing the visit
until the place finally went bankrupt and closed. He also
claimed to be gifted as an oarsman, but on the only occasion
when I ever saw him enter a rowboat he upset it at the first

stroke, and got a good dousing, and was upbraided by my mother for resorting to the cup on a fine Summer afternoon, better fitted for nature study and other such sensible recreation.

As I have noted in a previous chapter, he was completely devoid of all the usual small skills. Never once, to my knowledge, did he ever undertake any of the repairs that are needed so incessantly in a dwelling-house, with children running wild in it. If a plank got loose in the backyard fence he had to send for a neighborhood handy-man to nail it tight, and if a spigot needed a washer it was a job for the plumber. If my brother and I, playing in the yard, tossed a ball into a rain-gutter, he sent us to the alley to find a colored boy to recover it. If the family dog choked on a bone he hustled it to Reveille's livery-stable two blocks away, to be succored by the Aframerican barber-surgeons there in practise. The grape vines in the backyard needed tying up now and then, what with blowing winds and climbing cats, but my father never undertook the job. My mother told me years later that he had tried it once, standing on a chair, but that the chair legs had sunk into the soft ground, and tumbled him head over heels.

He and his brother often sat in the Summer-house below the arbor on warm Sunday mornings, drinking beer and discussing the infamies of Terence V. Powderly, the Chicago anarchists, and other such scamps. The beer was usually Anheuser-Busch from St. Louis, and it came in flour-barrels holding 96 bottles, packed in straw. When a new barrel arrived my uncle would sometimes suggest waggishly that my father open it. Now and then he rose to the bait, but when he began work with a hatchet he made so much noise, broke so many bottles and so inevitably cut his hand that my uncle always had to finish the job. My uncle was more or less clumsy too, following the pattern of all the Menckenii since their escape from the Teutoburgerwald, but compared to my father he was almost a prestidigitator.

I have hitherto noted his prowess with firearms. All Winter long, throughout my nonage, the sideyard between our two houses was hung with the carcasses of wild ducks that had fallen to his aim. He would turn out before dawn, proceed to the Chesapeake marshes by train, and come rolling home in the late afternoon with dozens of them, mainly canvasbacks. They often hung in the yard for weeks, for his own family revolted against them by Christmas, and my mother had them on her blacklist, mainly because picking them was a painful chore and had the effect of filling hired girls with subversive ideas. Thus I grew up unaware that wild duck was a luxury open only to millionaires. Indeed, I was amazed years later to find it priced at $3 a portion on Delmonico's bill-of-fare. It was a quite common victual in the Baltimore of my youth—not so common, to be sure, as soft-crabs or shad-fish, but still very far from something to get excited about.

My uncle's hunting trips extended much further than the shores of the Chesapeake. Whenever he made a business journey, which was pretty often, he always took his guns along, and usually he would come back with many souvenirs and tall tales of the chase. He went all the way to Florida, which was then only a wilderness, to shoot alligators, and returned with the story that he had lured them out of the bayous by tying Negro babies to stakes along the bank. Whether or not this story was true I do not know, but my brother Charlie and I believed it firmly at the time.

On one of these Florida trips my uncle took along one of the drummers of Aug. Mencken & Bro., by name Christian
* Abner, a magnificently handsome Rhinelander who some years later returned home, married a wife with a substantial *dot*, and set up a carpet-sweeper factory. Abner sent his relatives in Cologne a glowing account of alligator-hunting in Florida, and urged them not to be upset by the use of Negro babies as bait. At first, he explained, he had shrunk from it himself as incompatible with Christian principles and German *Kultur*, but travel had a tendency to broaden the mind, and he had come to the view that it was bigotry to judge the *mores* of a new and progressive country by those of Europe, now so old and decadent. In later letters he confessed confidentially that he had proceeded experimentally to actual nigger-shooting in Georgia, but added in excuse and avoidance that he did not like it. To this day there is no taste for American ways among the bourgeoisie of Cologne, and no belief in American idealism.

Despite his brother's enthusiasm for the chase my father disliked it, and never owned a gun. The only lethal weapon I

could find in his effects after his death was his Knight Templar
sword, a sleazy blade that would have curled up if jabbed into
a tub of butter. It has now vanished, and I suspect that my
mother either had it buried in the backyard, or gave it to the
Salvation Army. A pair of dumb-bells survived in the cellar for
many years, but my father never touched them to my knowledge. They were of cast-iron, and weighed 15 or 18 pounds
apiece. My brother Charlie and I began to feel almost grown-up
when we could so much as lift them, but that is as far as we
ever got.

Our chief sports in those early days were running, climbing
backyard fences, and making long exploratory tramps to Steuart's
Hill or the other open country west of Hollins street. With the
boys of the neighborhood we played at least half a dozen different running games, and very often there were match races.
It was in these races that I developed the speed aforesaid. The
prime of my talent was reached before the age of twelve, but I
remained pretty fast until I had passed twenty and began to
put on blubber. Even to this day I could probably run down a
horse-car if there were any left in the world, and I still had my
old facility for sucking in air. All my muscles are in my legs. My
biceps are puny, and my fingers are so weak that a couple of
hours of playing the piano at high voltage makes them ache
and itch.

This relative feebleness above-decks prevented me from
shining as a boxer. Like every other boy in Hollins street I had
ambitions in that direction, for Jake Kilrain opened a saloon in ∗
nearby Baltimore street after John L. Sullivan finished him in
1889, and his familiar proximity inspired us all. We were free to
look at and venerate him as he stood in front of his place on
balmy days, his coat off and his shirt sleeves rolled up. His
forearms looked to us to be quite as massive as the hind legs of
elephants. But he was a very reserved and solemn fellow, and
never paid any attention to us. What little we learned of boxing
we learned by pummelling one another. But this was poor
sport, for there was one boy in the gang, Chauncey West by
name (the Chauncey was always pronounced *Chance-y*, not
Chawnce-y), who could lick any of the rest of us, or any two of
us, or indeed all of us put together.

One Summer day, while we were in the country, my father

came home with two pairs of boxing gloves, picked up at a bargain from an insolvent pugilist encountered in a saloon. They were much too big for my brother Charlie and me, but we finally managed to tie them on, and proceeded to bang each other all over the place. My mother was scandalized by these barbarities, and insisted on amending the house statutes by forbidding us (*a*) to clout each other above the neck, or (*b*) to fight at all unless my father or some other grown man was on hand to referee. Our first formal combat under these rules was our last. We staggered on for twenty rounds, with my father refereeing and keeping time, but I was in trouble after the tenth round, and in the twentieth Charlie floored me with a right hook to the neck, and I couldn't get up. After that I had no more stomach for boxing.

The one sport my father was really interested in was baseball, and for that he was a fanatic. This, of course, was before the days of the celebrated Baltimore Orioles, but nevertheless Baltimore had a very good team, and he attended its sessions at Oriole Park whenever he and it were in town together. When it was on the road, he would slip away from his office in the late afternoon to glim the score at Kelly's oyster house in Eutaw street. There were, in that era, no baseball extras of the newspapers, so the high-toned saloons of the town catered to the fans by putting in telegraph operators who wrote the scores on blackboards. Kelly's operator was supposed to be the fastest and most accurate in town. He sat in a little balcony half way up the wall of the barroom, and was so greatly respected that on a busy afternoon, with the Baltimores winning, he harvested treats running to twenty or thirty beers, and perhaps half as many cigars.

I often went with my father on his visits to Kelly's, for in those days I spent many of my free afternoons in his cigar factory in Paca street, watching and envying the stripper-boys, stealing cigar-bands, cigar-box nails and other such negotiable commodities, and excavating the wastebaskets in the office for postage stamps, worn-out pens and rubber bands. When he set out he would take me with him, and while he stood at the bar with one eye on the blackboard and a beer before him, I would be parked on the brass rail, with a glass of sarsaparilla in one hand and a pretzel in the other. I figure that before I was nine years old I had put down at least 5000 bottles of sarsaparilla and the same number of pretzels. In the end I got so used to sitting on brass bar rails that I could do so without holding on.

My father had a branch of his business in Washington, at the corner of Seventh and G streets, and connected with it there was a cigar-store. This cigar-store became the baseball head-quarters of Washington, and he got to know all the principal ball-players and managers of the time. Eventually, he bought an interest in the Washington club, and became its vice-president. In his papers I find a letter from its secretary, dated July 27, 1891, and running as follows:

Last time we went West rate was $30 each for 13 men. The R. R. Agents here have since formed a combination to squeeze us and now make the rate at $40.50 for each man. We understand this applies only to Washington. Won't you kindly see Barnie and see what rate he pays and see if you can't get same rate for our men from Baltimore? Route will be Balto to Cincinnati, to Columbus, to Louisville, to St. Louis, and then home.

Barnie was the manager of the Baltimore club. He and my father had frequent palavers in those days, not only about the extortions of the railroads, but also about the outrageous de-mands of the players, some of whom, though they were getting $1500 and even $1800 a year, had the impudence to ask for * more. These palavers were usually held in the Summer-house in Hollins street on Sunday mornings, and the Bolsheviks were summoned there, and put on the mat. Many a time I have seen six or eight head of stars assembled together, drinking beer and smoking ten-cent cigars in their uncomfortable Sunday clothes, and quailing under the moral indignation of Barnie and my father. The boys of the neighborhood flocked to the back-gate to get glimpses of them, and my brother Charlie and I would open it a few inches for particular friends, and so convert friends into slaves.

The most eminent of all the stars who suffered the correc-tion of their false thinking in the Summer-house was Matt Kilroy, a pitcher now somehow forgotten, though he was as vastly admired in his day as Amos Rusie afterward. He was an Irishman with eight brothers who were also ball-players, and my father toyed with the idea of organizing them into a nine and sending them on a tour of the country. Unfortunately, Kilroy belonged to Barnie, and Barnie hung on to him. My father sought surcease from this bafflement by naming a five-cent cigar after the great man, and employed his catcher, Sam Trott, to sell it. Sam was a novice to *Geschäft*, but he developed a considerable gift for it, and the Kilroy was thus a big success. When Kilroy himself blew up the five-center went with him, and Sam became Baltimore agent for a cigar factory in Philadelphia. He continued in the trade to the end of his life, and I often encountered him on the streets in his later years.

He was a handsome, four-square fellow with enormous shoulders, and every finger of his two hands was as gnarled as a cypress-tree. This was a souvenir of the days when catchers caught with their bare paws. He adopted a glove toward the end of his career, but it was too late either to save his hands or to change his technic. When a ball came zooming in from the outfield and an enemy player tried to steal home Sam always threw aside his glove and planted himself at the plate *au naturel*. He was an amiable man, and when my brother and I began to major in baseball he gave us a lot of useful advice. But he never managed to make a good player of either of us.

We could do little playing in the Winter, for the cops of West Baltimore objected to anything more serious than one-two-three in the street, and the nearest grounds were disputed by other boys, including, now and then, brigandish fellows from the vicinity of the Baltimore & Ohio railroad shops. When these ruffians were in a relatively mild mood they were content to chase us off the diamond, but when their glands were flowing freely they also cabbaged our bats, balls and gloves. In the Summers beyond the period I here embalm we had a better chance, for just behind our newly-acquired house at Mt. Washington there was a large hay-field, and the farmer who owned it was glad to rent us room enough for a diamond, once he had got in his hay. Along with the neighbor boys we paid him $15 a year for it, and had the place all to ourselves, morning, afternoon and evening, on Sundays as well as on week-days. Years ago our baseball field became part of the first golf course ever seen in Baltimore. That course is still in operation, but it now seems so far downtown that most of the

members of the Baltimore Country Club, which owns it, prefer the newer links ten miles out in the country.

The four Lürssen boys, who were our next-door neighbors,
were baseball fans of the first chop, and there were plenty of
other enthusiasts nearby, so we had games going on all the *
time. In the middle of Summer we often played until eight
o'clock in the evening, and when formal play had to be stopped
we put in another hour catching flies from the darkening sky.
Two miles nearer the city there was a little mill-town, Wood-
berry by name, that turned out an amazing number of first-rate
ball-players, for most of the jobs in the mills were for females,
which left the bucks all day to practise. One of the prodigies
thus given to humanity was Frank Foreman, a pitcher who
developed the widest and wickedest curves I have ever seen.
He got into the big leagues, and for all I know may be still
living in Baltimore, though very few Baltimoreans now recall
his once immortal name.

On Sundays he would sometimes bring his nine to our field,
and play a couple of games with scrub nines from Baltimore.
Inspired and inflamed by his incomparable virtuosity, I set up
for a pitcher, but nothing ever came of it, for I had little speed
and no control at all. When I ventured on an in-shoot it was apt
to be recovered, not by the catcher, but by the third baseman.
So the Lürssen boys, who were older than my brother and I,
retired me to the outfield, or, as it was then called, the farm, and
from there I slowly worked my way back as far as the position of
short-stop. One day a sizzler gave my left little finger a terrific
clout, and I was out of the game for weeks. The finger remains
slightly cauliflowered to this day—another reason, perhaps, why
I have never made much of a shine as a piano virtuoso.

My father seldom took any part in these games, though
some of the other men of the vicinity often did so. Once he
bought us an outfit of uniforms, but they didn't last long, for
we younger players quickly outgrew them, and the visitors
who were invited in from time to time had a habit of making
off with those issued to them. My own I'll never forget. It was
made of a woolen material as thick as a Scotsman's Winter underwear, and as I gradually increased in stature and bulk the
breeches pulled up until their bottoms were halfway between
my knees and my hips, and the shirt began to bind my chest

like a surgical bandage. My brother and I used to go to Mt. Washington on Sunday afternoons early in Spring, long before the family had moved out for the Summer, and there get in a lot of hard practice. I recall that we were always stiff in the legs and arms until the Wednesday following. But all this diligent work got me nowhere, and I began slowly to grasp the humiliating fact that I was not earmarked for a career of glory on the diamond. When the Baltimore Orioles started out to astound

* mankind with their new prodigies, in 1894, I withdrew in despair, though I remained a fan for a few years longer. Since 1900 I have seen but two professional baseball games.

XV.

The Capital of the Republic

M Y FATHER, in the days when I first knew him, visited his Washington office every Friday; after I went into pants he occasionally took me along. I recall standing between his knees as the train conductor came round, and hearing him protest that I was too young to pay any fare, even half-fare. Whether these protests were serious or not I don't know, but in all probability they were not, for the conductor was always in a very affable mood, and sometimes he let me work his ticket-punch on one of my father's business cards. The candy-butcher also showed me some attention, but that had plain self-interest in it, for he carried a basket containing oval boxes of figs, little red railroad lanterns full of candy pills, gumdrops in red, white and green, and other such favorite refreshments and souvenirs of the era, and my father was always good for a sale.

At that early period Washington was hardly more than a blur to me, and I divided my four or five hours there between admiring the meerschaum pipes and cigar-holders in the cigar-store connected with the branch office of Aug. Mencken & Bro., and accompanying my father on his subsequent rounds of his customers, many of whom kept either restaurants or saloons. He disappeared into his office the moment we got to Seventh and G streets, N.W., and spent the next hour or so auditing its books, with his agent standing by to answer questions. By that time I was half starved, so a great wave of hosannahs rolled through me when we started off for lunch. We usually ate, of course, in the restaurant of some customer, and no doubt we visited, first and last, a great many, but the one I remember best was kept by Mr. Burkhardt, who had once been my father's agent himself, but had now, by dint of diligence and thrift, acquired a business of his own. He always instructed his carver, a coal-black man called Snowball, to give me extra-large portions, and I always got them down. Indeed, I commonly ate so heartily that during the subsequent tour of saloons I had relatively little stomach for the pretzels that were handed down to me at my perch on the brass rail, and even gagged at drinking more than two or three bottles of sarsaparilla.

As I emerged from the fog of infancy Washington began to take on shape and substance, and pretty soon I was wallowing delightedly in its marvels. The greatest of them, in that era, was not the Capitol at the end of Pennsylvania avenue, nor even the Washington Monument, but the asphalt streets. Asphalt was then a novelty in the United States, and Washington was the only city that could show any considerable spread of it: in Baltimore it was still thought to be dangerous to horses. What I remember of it chiefly is the dreadful heat it threw up in Summer. The cobblestones of Baltimore, with their lush interstitial crops of grass, oats and Jimson weed, were cool in the warmest weather, but in Washington the white asphalt bounced the sun back into people's faces, and every stranger was told that in July and August the inhabitants abandoned their kitchen stoves altogether and cooked their meals on the street. This tale still pops up whenever there is an extraordinarily severe spell of heat, and it has probably gone out over the wires at least forty times. It was untrue when I first heard it as a small boy, and it remains untrue to this day, but for some reason or other people like to believe it, and so it hangs on.

Of my first trip to the top of the Washington Monument, which must have been made soon after it was opened in 1888, I recall only the fact that we descended by walking down the long, dark steps, and it seemed a journey without end. There was in those days a bitter debate as to whether a baseball thrown from the top of the monument could be caught by a catcher on the ground, and my father was much interested and full of mathematical proofs that it couldn't be done. Some time later it was tried, and turned out to be very easy. He also had a hand in a long and acrimonious discussion of curve pitching, one faction holding that the path of the ball was actually a curve and the other maintaining that the whole thing was only an optical illusion. Which side he took I don't recall, but I remember him coming home with the news that the reality of curves had been proved by setting up three stakes in a straight line at the Washington baseball grounds, and putting a pitcher to work on them. After knocking them down or missing them altogether for half an hour running he finally succeeded in pitching a ball clearly to leftward of the two end ones and as clearly to rightward of the middle one. This feat attracted a large crowd and was dealt with by the newspapers as if it had been some great public calamity or first-rate murder, but I was in school that day, and so had to miss seeing it. Later on my father undertook to show me how to curve a baseball, but inasmuch as he never could do it himself I made very little progress.

Most of my visits to Washington, at least from 1886 onward, must have been made after school let out in Spring, for I remember the town as always warm, and both my father and me as always thirsty. As he proceeded from one restaurant or saloon to another, usually with his agent, Mr. Cross, and palavered amiably with their proprietors, I sat on a long succession of brass rails, munching my pretzels and drinking my sarsaparilla. This life had its moments of boredom, especially when the visit to any given place was prolonged, but on the whole I enjoyed it, and to this day I retain a friendly feeling for saloons, though I seldom stand up at their bars, for I long ago associated myself with the Chinese doctrine that it is foolish to do anything standing up that can be done sitting down, or anything sitting down that can be done lying down. In the days before Prohibition, which were also the days before air-cooling, I doted on the cool, refreshing scent of a good saloon on a hot Summer day, with its delicate overtones of mint, cloves, hops, Angostura bitters, horse-radish, *Blutwurst* and *Kartoffelsalat*. It was always somewhat dark therein, and there was an icy and comforting sweat upon the glasses. The huge, hand-painted oil painting facing the bar, nearly always of Venus stripped for her weekly tub, was covered with netting to keep off the flies, and the mirror that framed the bartender was decorated with Winter landscapes drawn in soap. I have visited in my day the barrooms of all civilized countries, but none that I ever saw came within miles of a high-toned American saloon of the Golden Age. Today the influence of the cocktail lounge has brought in blue glass, chrome fixtures, and bars of pale and puny woods, but in the time I speak of saloon architects stuck to mirrors as God first made them, to honest brass, and to noble and imperishable mahogany.

My father sometimes took an afternoon off from his calls on

restauranteurs (for that is what they all liked to call themselves, including the unmistakable saloonkeepers) to show me the salient sights of the capital, or, perhaps more often, sent his office-boy with me while he struggled with accounts in his office. The majestic spectacle of the United States Senate was thus a commonplace to me before I was eight years old, and by the time I was ten I was a familiar of the Smithsonian and the National Museum. Both of the latter were even more meagre and measly then than they are now, but I was too young to know it, and hence enjoyed them immensely. There were two exhibits in the Smithsonian that fascinated me especially. The first, perhaps naturally, was the skeleton of a prehistoric monster, ten or twelve feet high at the shoulder. The second, rather curiously, was a primitive ox-cart with wheels made of solid slices of tree trunks. Why this last should have struck me so powerfully I do not know, but there is the fact. I wrote a description of it in my composition-book, and gained thereby the praise of Mr. Willie, son to the chancellor of F. Knapp's Institute. I also got his favorable notice by exhibiting a small bust of Abraham Lincoln, made of condemned and macerated paper money from the Treasury. Such busts are still obtainable in Washington, and honeymooners from the remoter villages of Virginia and Maryland often take them home. Their price runs in proportion to the face value of the deceased greenbacks in them. One containing the remains of mere $1 bills goes cheaply, but one made of $1000 bills costs a pretty penny. In my day the little hill on which the Washington Monument stands was still bestrewn with large chips of marble left by the builders. I recovered, first and last, at least a hundred pounds of them, and my brother Charlie and I hoarded them for a long while, for it was believed in Hollins street that soda-water could be made of them, though we never found out how. They disappeared eventually into a rockery that my mother made in the backyard.

At the Capitol and in the other public buildings of the town its magnificoes could be viewed only at a distance, but in the saloons they came down to earth, and laid themselves open to intimate inspection. Their principal resort was Shoomaker's old-time groggery in Pennsylvania avenue, but my father seldom visited it, so I had to get my eyeful of them at other

places, notably Mr. Burkhardt's. Mr. Burkhardt, I conclude on
reflection, must have specialized in the judiciary, for I recall a
great many customers who were addressed as Judge, or even
as Mr. Justice. These eminent men were quiet drinkers, but
assiduous. They apparently had short working-hours, for they
showed up at the bar early in the afternoon, and stuck around
until it was time for us to return to Baltimore. There was a very
old one, in a long-tailed black coat and white chin-whiskers,
who one day lifted me to speechless veneration by slipping me
a quarter. But the next time I encountered him he failed to
give me another, so I transferred my devotion to other gods.
There were also several Senators in the Burkhardt stock company, and a great many Congressmen. I noticed, boy as I was,
that Mr. Burkhardt kept his deference and solicitude for the
Senators and the judiciary, and had none left for Congressmen.
He addressed them familiarly as George, Jack and Bill, and
once I heard him invite one of them to get the hell out of the
place, and stay out. My father explained that this was because
Congressmen were too numerous in Washington to be of any
note; moreover, not a few of them were given to caterwauling
and wrestling in barrooms, a habit that he always deprecated.
They yet linger, I believe, in their lowly station, and are regarded by most Washingtonians as hardly worthy of common
politeness.

Of all the eminent men I had the honor of witnessing in
those days, the only one who ever showed me much personal
attention, and hence the only one I remember with any vivid-
ness, was Mr. McCarthy, a member of the higher joboisie of
the State Department. Mr. McCarthy was a hunchback, but
his infirmity did not damp his spirits, which were naturally very
gay. I can see him yet as he stood at the stately bar of Mr.
Burkhardt's restaurant, with his head scarcely reaching the
mahogany rail but his good right arm plenty long enough to
keep a firm hold on the glass of beer that the bartender had
just drawn for him. He could get down five or six in a row, and
yet retain both his courtly manners and his wide knowledge of
international affairs. My father relied upon him for confidential
information about the filthy schemes of the chancelleries of
Europe, and I relied upon him for a steady supply of foreign
postage stamps. He seemed to have something to do with

handling departmental mail, for his pockets were always full of
stamps from the farthest and most outlandish places, many of
which have long since disappeared from the stamp catalogues,
at least as current producers—for example, Korea, Montene-
gro, and Thurn und Taxis. He never failed to hand me a
handful, and I never failed, on returning home, to paste them
carefully in a blue-covered stamp-album that my mother had
given me. When, in the course of human events, I tired of
stamp-collecting, I turned over the album to my young sister,
Gertrude, and when she, in her turn, took to other concerns,
its contents passed to our niece Virginia, the daughter of my
brother Charlie, and she then handed it on to one of her cousins, and so on and so on. I suppose that Mr. McCarthy's
stamps are still cherished somewhere by some youngster or
other. As for Mr. McCarthy himself, he appears to have been
absorbed into the cosmos long years ago, but in my mind his
memory is still green.

Mr. Cross, who had succeeded Mr. Burkhardt as my father's
Washington nuncio, was another of my favorites, for he saved
up rubber-bands for me, let me inspect and handle the florid
meerschaum pipes in his showcase (one of them, I recall, was
priced $300), and was always good for a piece of cash money.
In those days the custom of tipping boys was as widespread in
the United States as it still is in England, and my brother Charlie and I derived a considerable revenue from it, especially in
Summer, when visitors often came to the country for all-day
visits. These visits sometimes strained my mother's housekeeping dangerously, and once or twice broke it down altogether,
but they were highly agreeable to Charlie and me, for that was
a scurvy fellow who did not fork up at least a quarter. One
Sunday when we were still at the Vineyard Mr. Cross staggered
us by slipping us a dollar each—a large sum for any boy to have
in his hands in the eighties, and perhaps roughly comparable
to a couple of shares of Eastman Kodak or Am. Tel. & Tel.
today. What is more, Mr. Cross kept to his mark thereafter, so
we were always rich during the week following one of his visits,
and regarded him at all times as a gentleman of surpassing elegance, which indeed he was. He was a handsome man with a
brisk coal-black mustache and prematurely white hair, and he
made a striking figure in the somewhat advanced tailoring that

he affected. One day he surprised us by bringing along a beautiful lady in a small bonnet and large bustle: in the course of time, I believe, they were married. But that must have been after he retired from the service of Aug. Mencken & Bro., and we saw him no more.

The old office at Seventh and G streets still stands, and when I last saw it it had changed little since 1889. There was the same areaway beside it, with the same pipe railing, and across the street the old building of the Patent Office looked exactly as I remember it as a boy. In the eighties the building next door was occupied by Mr. Voigt, a jeweler and one of my father's friends. On September 26, 1890, as I find by my father's bill-file, he bought a Swiss repeater watch from Mr. Voigt, paying $200 for it in cash—a strange transaction for him, for he commonly preferred barter, and settled most of his major bills in either cigars or leaf tobacco, or both. Even his tailor's bills were commonly paid that way—not directly to the tailor, but to a curious *entrepreneur* named Mr. Butke, who seems to have carried on a complicated series of similar transactions with half the business men of Baltimore. He would start out by finding someone who wanted the cigars or tobacco that he had got from my father, and end by finding someone who had something that the tailor wanted. The number of his intermediate trades varied from time to time, and often ran to many. He lived at Ellicott City, and was supposed to have mortgages on half the farms in the circumambient county. My father had some gifts as a trader himself, and so did his brother, but they were always a bit wary of Mr. Butke, for his talents began where theirs left off. They considered him, in fact, a public menace, but for many years they kept on dealing with him, hoping against hope that some day he would slip a cog and they would be able to throw him.

Mr. Voigt got cash for the Swiss repeater watch, I suspect, simply because Mr. Butke's diocese did not extend to Washington. The watch itself was my father's proudest possession until his death. It not only had a hand that made five jumps to the second; it was also fitted with a device which could be made to strike the hours, halves and quarters, thus telling the time in the dark. But my father never quite mastered the code of this device, so he could never really find out, in the dark,

just what time it was. Moreover, it was always much easier to
strike a match. In the days after his death, when I began to
wear the watch myself, this apparatus got out of order, and the
best watchmakers in Baltimore failed to cure it, though they
sent me very large bills. In the end the rest of the works also
went flooey, and I retired the piece to a safe-deposit box which
houses a series of family watches running back to the year
1700. At my own exitus they will be thrown into the market.
Meanwhile, I receive a bill from the bank every six months,
and they thus waste my substance and help to hold me in the
literary sweatshop.

I find by the bill-file that Mr. Voigt supplied many of the
articles of *virtu* that engauded our house in Hollins street in
my early days. There are bills for a cuckoo-clock, a music-box,
and other such things, beside a gold watch for my mother, and
* a chain and locket for it. Mr. Eckhardt, who was our neighbor
in Hollins street and operated an art works in downtown Baltimore street, was also active in this trade. His contributions
included the pier-glass that still stands in the old house; a photograph album bound in plush, with a music-box inside; a pair of
sombre steel engravings from paintings by Turner, showing
the English seaports of Hastings and Dover, each with a heavy
walnut frame; another steel engraving entitled "King Solomon
and the Iron Worker," apparently of Masonic significance; and
"1 pce. statuary" billed on October 19, 1885—unquestionably
the Rogers group, "Fooling Grandpa," that stood on a rococo
table in the parlor for many years, and is still cherished by my
sister. The music-box that came from Mr. Voigt's emporium in
1887, at the price of $125 cash in hand, was as large as (and
much resembled) a child's coffin,[1] and my father had to have a
special hollow-topped table made to accommodate it. It not
only played ten loud and swinging tunes—including Johann
Strauss's "Rosen aus dem Süden," and selections from "Boccaccio," "The Mascot" and "The Tales of Hoffmann"; it was
also outfitted with drums and bells, and when my brother

[1]It still exists, and after writing the above I measured it. It is two feet, seven
and a half inches long, fourteen inches wide, and ten inches high. It seemed
much larger as I recalled it from infancy. Indeed, I'd have guessed that it was
nearer four feet long.

Charlie and I set it going on a Sunday morning it shook the house. We employed it, boylike, to build up advantage in the neighborhood. Boys and girls who were polite to us were let in to listen to it perform, and a favored few of extraordinary amiability were permitted to wind it, and to turn the drums and bells off and on.

I always enjoyed the train ride to and from Washington, and in fact still prefer railroad travel to any other mode of conveyance by land. We used the B. & O. exclusively, not only because its ancient Baltimore station, Camden, was convenient to my father's office, but also as a matter of local pride and patriotism. The B. & O. made Baltimore, and Baltimoreans have never forgotten the fact. The company is tax exempt in Maryland to this day, and Baltimoreans going to New York would use its trains almost invariably if it had a tunnel through the North river. Its once famous flyer, the Royal Blue, did not go into service until 1890, but it had fast trains running between Baltimore and Washington so long ago as 1881, and by the middle eighties they were making the forty miles in fifty minutes, including the time wasted in getting in and out of the two cities. My father began to sell cigars to the B. & O. back in the seventies, when it added the first dining-cars to its star trains, and this business, along with the accompanying station-restaurant business, helped to put his firm on its feet. He died convinced that B. & O. trains were somehow superior to all others. If it were argued in his presence that they shipped a great deal of ballast dust and locomotive ash, then he would reply that those of both the Pennsylvania and the New York Central shipped even more, and that in any case no rational man could object to a nuisance that had its origin in immutable natural laws, and was thus in accord with the will of God. My father placed, in general, very little reliance upon heavenly legislation, but in this and a few other difficult situations he resorted to it to get rid of belly-achers and casuists.

XVI.
Recreations of a Reactionary

M Y FATHER and his brother and partner, like most reasonably successful American business men of the eighties,
always had plenty of time on their hands. The business they
were in had not yet been demoralized and devoured by the
large combinations of capital that were to come later on, and
there was room in their field, which was principally in the
Southeast, for all the firms in their line in Baltimore. They
* were thus on peaceful terms with their competitors, and regarded at least some of them with a kind of approval almost
akin to respect. They had a competent staff of drummers on
the road, their principal customers stuck to them pretty faithfully, and, though they gave a great deal of energy to excoriating labor agitators, they had very little labor trouble in their
own establishment.

My father's daily routine was no doubt quite typical of that
of hundreds of other Baltimore employers of the period. He
arose at what would be considered an early hour today, and
immediately after breakfast proceeded to his office. If we were
in the city he travelled by horse-car; if we were at Mt. Washington he drove his buggy, or, in impossible weather, went by
train. In either case he tackled his mail the moment he reached
his desk, which was a high one in the ancient mode, made for
use standing up. If the mail contained enough checks and orders to content him he was in good humor all morning, and
polite to the drummers who dropped in to sell him cigar-box
labels, cigar bands, advertising novelties, wrapping paper, and
other such minor supplies. But if the orders were light, or a
letter turned up news that another dead-beat in Georgia or
South Carolina had absconded, he would growl at these drummers in a most churlish way, and instruct the bookkeeper to
write letters to all his own drummers, accusing them formally
of wasting their time and his money on cards, dice, women
and the bottle. This routine was broken only by his weekly trip
to Washington.

On a normal morning all the cigars made in the factory the day before were waiting for his inspection in racks ranged in long rows. He would get to this job at about 10 A.M. and it took him probably half an hour. In theory, either he or his brother examined each and every cigar made in the place, but actually this was impossible; what they did was simply to draw out samples, feel of them critically, and set aside any plug or skipper that they discovered. A plug was a cigar so overstuffed with filler that sucking wind through it would probably be unfeasible, and a skipper was one so carelessly wrapped that the adjoining layers of wrapper did not overlap. There were plenty of days when my father found no case at all of either sort of pathology. When he encountered one he took the sick cigar upstairs, holding it at arm's length as if it had smallpox, and upbraided the offending cigarmaker. On his return he dropped it in a drawer which supplied complimentary smokes to truck-drivers, messenger boys who looked to be more than twenty-one years old, collectors for non-Masonic charities, bank runners, colored clergymen, and policemen below the rank of lieutenant.

The rest of the morning he devoted to a furious and largely useless figuring. He was immensely vain of his arithmetical capacities, and prepared elaborate cost-sheets long before they began to be whooped up at Harvard. They showed precisely what it stood the firm to produce 1000 of any one of the twenty or more brands of cigars on its list. Every time there was a ponderable change in the price of any kind of leaf tobacco, he recalculated those sheets. When the job was done he put them in one of the drawers of his desk, and that was the last anyone ever heard of them. His brother, who was not much interested in mathematics, gave them only a polite glance, and no one else in the place ever saw them at all, not even the bookkeeper.

A few minutes before one o'clock he suddenly clapped on his hat and dashed out for lunch. If the house in Hollins street was open he almost always lunched there; if not, he patronized one of the saloon-restaurants in the neighborhood, all of which advertised business men's lunches at the uniform price of twenty-five cents. When he went to Hollins street he made the round trip by horse-car and invariably took a nap after his meal. The scene or instrument of this nap was a frowsy old walnut and hair-cloth lounge in the dining-room, and the clearing off of dishes had to be deferred until a couple of Cheyne-Stokes snores notified the fact that he had passed out. After half an hour or so, he awoke with a start, looked about him wildly, reached for his hat, and started back to his office. To the casual eye he seemed to be in haste, but when he got to the office there was really next to nothing for him to do, and he usually spent the afternoon reading the *Tobacco Leaf* or the *Sporting Times* (this last for baseball news), searching out the ratings of prospective customers in the big Bradstreet book, or gossiping with his brother, the bookkeeper, or any caller who happened to drift in. At five-thirty he knocked off for the day.

I never knew him to visit his bank: all his routine business with it was transacted by the bookkeeper, and he never borrowed a nickel. Indeed, he regarded all borrowing as somehow shameful, and looked confidently for the bankruptcy and probable jailing of any business man who practised it regularly. His moral system, as I try to piece it together after so many years, seems to have been predominantly Chinese. All mankind, in his sight, was divided into two great races: those who paid their bills, and those who didn't. The former were virtuous, despite any evidence that could be adduced to the contrary; the latter were unanimously and incurably scoundrels.

He had a very tolerant view of all other torts and malfeasances. He believed that political corruption was inevitable under democracy, and even argued, out of his own experience, that it had its uses. One of his favorite anecdotes was about a huge swinging sign that used to hang outside his place of business in Paca street. When the building was built, in 1885, he simply hung out the sign, sent for the city councilman of the district, and gave him $20. This was in full settlement forevermore of all permit and privilege fees, easement taxes, and other such costs and imposts. The city councilman pocketed the money, and in return was supposed to stave off any cops, building inspectors or other functionaries who had any lawful interest in the matter, or tried to horn in for private profit. Being an honorable man according to his lights, he kept his bargain, and the sign flapped and squeaked in the breeze for ten years. But then, in 1895, Baltimore had a reform wave, the councilman was voted out of office, and the idealists in the City Hall sent word that a license to maintain the sign would cost $62.75 *a year.* It came down the next day.

This was proof to my father that reform was mainly only a conspiracy of prehensile charlatans to mulct taxpayers. I picked up this idea from him, and entertain it to the present day. I also picked up his doctrine that private conduct had better not be inquired into too closely—with the exception, of course, of any kind involving beating a creditor. In the Breckinridge-Pollard breach of promise case, a nation-shaking scandal in 1892, rating columns of verbatim testimony in the newspapers, he sympathized openly with Breckinridge, whom he had met in the Washington saloons, and denounced La Pollard as a scheming minx. In the matter of polygamy among the Mormons, which kept all the moral theologians of the country in a dither down to 1890, he was a champion of the Saints, and argued that it was nobody's damned business how many wives they had, so long as they paid their bills, which seemed to be the case.

He had little truck with the Germans who swarmed into Baltimore during the seventies and early eighties, and regarded most of them as idiots, but, like his father, he admired the so-called Pennsylvania Dutch, with whom he had constant business, for many of them were tobacco growers. In various salient respects, he would say, they were so loutish as to be hardly human, but nevertheless they abhorred debt, and that was enough. Contrariwise, he had a low opinion of the Virginians who had flocked to Baltimore after the Civil War, for though many of them were elegant and charming fellows, and a few were even the aristocrats they all claimed to be, they were usually very hard up, and anyone who gave them credit had a hard time getting his money.

As I have said, my father's work-day was usually pretty well over by the time he got back to his office from lunch, and he had the rest of the afternoon for recreation. If the Baltimore baseball club was playing in town he would go to the game; if it were on tour he would go to Kelly's oyster-house to learn the score. In Winter he waited for a customer to drop in, or one of his own drummers, and if his hopes were realized he would propose a drink in the saloon next door. Getting it down, and the others that always chased it, would occupy the time until five-thirty, when the cigarmakers came downstairs with their day's produce, the bookkeeper locked the safe, and the day was over. In that era all American business was carried on to the accompaniment of such libations. To let a customer go without offering him a drink was an almost unheard of insult. It was also considered unendurably boorish to refuse a drink when it was offered. There were bankers and brokers in South street, the Wall Street of Baltimore, who never got back from lunch at all. They ate in the luxurious bars of the neighborhood, and all their afternoon business, if they had any, was done in the same places.

My father preferred the saloon next to his office, not only because it was conveniently near, but also because it was kept by an old German named Ehoff, who pretended obligingly to be an extraordinarily innocent and credulous fellow. Many a time, as a small boy, I have sat on the brass rail, getting down my sarsaparilla and pretzel, and listened to my father complaining to Ehoff all over again, and perhaps for the fiftieth time, that his ice was stale, or telling him that the Brooklyn Bridge had fallen down, or that the Dutch were being driven out of Holland, or that Cardinal Gibbons had joined the A.P.A., or that Bismarck was moving to Baltimore and proposed to open a brewery. Ehoff, I suspected even then, knew better, but he always professed to be astounded. Thus he was a favorite among the business men of the vicinity, who all tried their fancy upon him. They avoided very diligently a saloon a bit up the street, kept by one William Ruth, for over its door hung a sign reading *Union Bar*. No one knew then that this Ruth, by the exercise of his generative powers a few years later, was to become the father of the imperishable Babe.

On afternoons when nothing better offered, my father and his brother lolled in their office concocting hoaxes and canards. Their masterpiece was the creation of a mythical brother named Fred, who went on living in gaseous form for many years; to this day a rheumy old Baltimorean sometimes stops me on the street to ask what has become of him. Fred was supposed to be a clergyman. Everyone knew that my grandfather was an infidel, so my father and his brother represented that Fred was a cruel burden and disgrace to him, and warned all comers to

avoid mentioning the clergy in his presence, lest his sorrow
suddenly overwhelm and unman him. The Fred legend gradually took on elaborate embroideries. Fred had been invited to
become chaplain of the United States Senate. He had converted 5,000 heathen in one week in Chicago. He had broken
into the old man's house, and tried to pray him up to grace.
He had bought Ehoff's saloon and Coblens's adjoining livery-
stable and was planning to build a church or a Bible factory
on the site. Finally, after my grandfather's death, they announced that Fred had been made a bishop, and there they let
him rest.

My father's solo flights, I must say as a more or less honest
historian, sometimes got perilously close to the line limiting
the best of taste. When he bought the Summer home at Mt.
Washington, one of the new neighbors asked him casually if he
had any plans for developing the place, which was somewhat
dilapidated. He replied solemnly that he proposed to give over
the long slope of lawn in front of the house to the breeding of
blooded hogs, a race of cattle too much neglected in Maryland. This news naturally staggered the neighbor, and he ran
about the vicinity spreading it. By the time the first delegation
of protest arrived my father was ready with large blue-prints of
the proposed piggery, prepared by a builder friend and showing the name "Pig Hill" on a banner hung between two immense flagpoles at the main entrance. The excitement began
to die down after we moved in and the long ranks of pens
continued *non est*, but there was a revival of it every time
workmen appeared to gravel a walk or repair a porch. Worse,
the name of "Pig Hill" stuck to the place, and was gradually
extended to the whole settlement. It survived, in fact, until the
city of Baltimore, proliferating northward, finally obliterated
both the settlement and the name.

There was something of the same barbarity, though it did
much less damage, in an operation against a German friend, a
gentleman who owned a wood-working factory. He was the
most inoffensive man imaginable, and his only known vice was
playing *Schafskopf* of an afternoon with a few friends. One day
he got into a row with a Maine lumber company about a
schooner load of lumber, and the company finally threatened
him with a lawsuit. This alarmed him greatly, so he dropped in

to consult my father. He was particularly concerned lest the noise and fumes of the dispute induce Bradstreet's, the commercial credit agency, to reduce his credit rating. My father offered at once to get a Bradstreet report on him to find out if anything of the sort had been done—and then spent the next two afternoons concocting a report that left nothing of him save a ruined name and his immortal soul.

This bogus report was typewritten on flimsy in exact imitation of a real one. It started off by saying that the old man was a once prosperous and respected *entrepreneur*, but that his gross neglect of his business had brought it down to the edge of bankruptcy. He left his office every day, it said, at 2 P.M., drove out to a notorious resort in the country (described so as to identify his own home), and there wasted what remained of his substance gambling with a gang of police characters. It added that he drank vast amounts of beer during this play, and was already showing signs of *mania à potu*. It ended by hinting that his family was considering having him put under restraint as *non compos mentis*, and that his creditors were forming a committee to join in the action.

The old man's response to all this nonsense was almost terrifying. He leaped in the air, began God-damning horribly in English and German, and talked wildly of shaking the dust of the United States from his feet and going back to his native Bremen. He laid the whole blame upon the lumber company, which was operated, so he said, by Yankee swindlers of a kind that, in any civilized country, would be looked to by the *Polizei*. He became so excited that my father grew alarmed, and began to confess in haste that the report was spurious. But by this time the victim was so wrought up that he wouldn't listen, and it was not until the bookkeeper was dispatched to Bradstreet's Baltimore office for a real one, and it turned out on inspection to be highly complimentary, that he recovered any calm. Even so, he kept on denouncing the lumber company, and it retained first place in his menagerie of monsters so long as he lived.

About this time the half-grown son of a neighbor at Mt. Washington became stage struck and began to prepare himself diligently for his chosen art. His preparations took the form of

dreadful howls and shrieks in the woods behind his home, designed to improve his breathing. This noise set all the dogs for
half a mile round to barking, and scared the horses, cats,
nurse-maids and small children of the settlement out of their
wits. My father's characteristic device for getting rid of the
nuisance was to complain to the police at the county seat that
a wild man was loose in the woods, devouring rabbits raw and
alive, and threatening cannibalism. The rural cops arrived on
horseback and at a gallop, surrounded the woods, discharged
their side-arms menacingly, and then rushed in and confronted
the astonished actor. It took my father a couple of days and
several boxes of Grade D cigars to convince them that some
miscreant had played a joke on them.

But such designs and inventions were, after all, only small
game. In his later years, reviewing his career as Münchhausen
and Joe Cook from the serene pinnacle of the forties, my father
dismissed them lightly as no more than inconsiderable im-
promptus. The true peak of his talent, he allowed, was reached
in his successful scheme to wreck the cigarmakers' union of
Baltimore, which called a strike along about 1889. In his own
shop the strike lasted only a few days, but the men stayed out
in some of the other shops of the town for weeks and months,
and as a result large numbers of them began to fall behind in
their rent and grocery-bills, and to hear unpleasantly from
their wives. The union had a war fund, but it wasn't large
enough to pay the strikers full benefits; the best it could offer,
at least toward the end, was free tickets to Philadelphia, which
then had so many shops that it was known as the Cigarmakers'
Heaven. The union sent hundreds of the strikers there, and
most of them got jobs, but other hundreds remained in Baltimore, and the war fund began to play out.

It was at this stage that my father formulated his scheme to
put the wounded enemy out of its misery. There were in the
cellar of every cigar-shop in town a great many supernumerary
cigarmakers' box-wood boards and cutting tools, left behind
by tramp workmen who had come in from nowhere, worked a
few weeks, got drunk and fired, and then vanished. The possession of such a board and set of tools was sufficient proof
that the bearer was a cigarmaker. The union was eager to clear

out all such casuals of the trade, for they were always half starved when they arrived, and it was thus easy for the bosses to induce them to work as strikebreakers.

When my father's spies reported that a dozen or more of them were being shipped to Philadelphia every day the inspiration for his museum piece seized him. If a board and a set of cutting tools made a cigarmaker, why not fashion a whole regiment of them out of the abandoned boards and tools in the cellar? To get the men was easy: there were hundreds and thousands of them in the flop-houses of Baltimore—sailors who had gone on drunks and missed their ships, farm-boys come to town to make their fortunes, old soaks not yet quite ready for the morgue, and a dozen other kinds of miserable and hopeless men. So an agent was sent down to the region of Pratt street wharf to round up a squad, and in a little while he returned with twenty-five. Each was given a cigarmaker's board, a set of cutting tools, a drink of horse-liniment, and fifty cents in cash, and instructed how to find the headquarters of the union, and what to say on reaching it. The agent then started them off, and in an hour they were all aboard a train for Philadelphia, each with a ticket in his hand that had cost the union $1.85, and a quarter for refreshments *en route*.

When the boards in the cellar of the Metropolitan Cigar Factory of Aug. Mencken & Bro. gave out those in the cellars of other factories were levied upon, and in the course of the next few weeks at least a thousand poor bums were run through the mill. They cost the union $2.10 apiece, and its remaining funds swiftly melted away. Finally, the spies brought news that it could go on for but one day more. My father always lingered over this part of the story. The union was now wrecked, but how could the fiends in human form in charge of it be made to understand clearly *how* it had been wrecked, and by whom? How could its defeat be converted into shame and vain repining? His solution, though it strained his powers to the utmost, was really very simple. He sent his agents down to Pratt street wharf to round up a dozen *one-armed* men, outfitted them with the usual boards and tools, and had them marched to union headquarters. The instant they got there the fiends tumbled to the trick that had been played on them. With low cries of dismay, they gathered up the few dollars remaining, rushed to the Baltimore & Ohio dépôt, and fled to Philadelphia themselves.

The union sneaked back into Baltimore afterward, but it was a long time afterward. While my father lived it troubled him no more. He died full of a pious faith that he had finished it.

XVII.
Brief Gust of Glory

I N MY boyhood in the Aurignacian Epoch of Baltimore the favorite bivouac and chapel-of-ease of all healthy males of tender years was the neighborhood livery-stable. I have since learned, by a reading in the social sciences, that the American livery-stables of that era were seminaries of iniquity, with a curriculum embracing cursing and swearing, gambling, cigarette-smoking, tobacco-chewing, the classical or Abraham Lincoln répertoire of lewd anecdotes, the design and execution of dirty pictures, and even the elements of seduction, burglary and delirium tremens. It may have been true, for all I know, in the pathological small towns that all social scientists appear to hail from, but certainly it was not true in West Baltimore. I was a regular student at Reveille's stable in Stricker street from the beginning of my seventh year to the end of my nonage, and as special student at Coblens's stable in Paca street, off and on, for most of the same period, but so far as I can recall I never heard a word uttered in either of them, or beheld any human act, transaction or phenomenon, that might not have been repeated before a bench of bishops.

On the contrary, they were both schools of decorum, operated by proud and even haughty men, and staffed by blackamoors of a generally high tone. No palpably dipsomaniacal or larcenous coon could survive more than a few days in any such establishment: there were too many valuable horses and rigs in hand to be trusted to the former, and too many valuable carriage-robes, buggy-whips, hassocks, etc., to be exposed to the latter. My father's No. 1 whip, hung up by the snapper in Mr. Reveille's office, had a gold band around the handle engraved with the insigne of the Ancient Arabic Order of Nobles of the Mystic Shrine, and in Mr. Coblens's office, where he commonly kept his No. 2 whip and his dayton-wagon, there was also a buffalo robe that he set great store by, although I should add that its hair had pretty well played out, and that after his death I gave it freely to the poor.

Mr. Coblens was a man of erect bearing, reserved manner, and great dignity. He wore none of the loud checks associated with his vocation, but was always clad in plain colors, and not infrequently appeared in a black cutaway. His only concession to the public expectation was a gray derby hat, very high in the crown. If you can imagine a Jewish colonel of a swagger cavalry regiment, then you have got him to the life. My father had a high regard for him, and often paused to discuss horses with him—a subject about which he knew everything and my father next to nothing. He seldom descended from his heights to speak to my brother or me. He knew us very well, and would indicate by a vague flicker of his eyes that he was aware of our presence, but it was not often that he said anything.

His cousin Felix was a far more cordial fellow. Felix was a bachelor in those days, and apparently a somewhat gay one, for more than once I saw him set out of an afternoon in a buggy shining like a $100 coffin, with sometimes a blonde lady beside him and sometimes a brunette. My brother and I, boylike, regarded his ease and success at gallantry with great respect. He was, indeed, one of our heroes, and also one of our friends. He was never too busy to explain to us, with the use of living models paraded by his blackamoors, the points of a harness horse, and he also had illuminating ideas about buggy architecture. When my father gave my brother Charlie and me the pony Frank, it was Mr. Felix who taught us how to handle him—no mean art, I assure you, for Shetland ponies not only kick like mules, but also bite like dogs, and no doubt would scratch like cats if they had claws. To this day I have a scar on my bosom, often passing for a war wound, that proves how effectively Frank could use his teeth.

In 1890 or thereabout my father traded two cases of Zimmer Spanish leaf tobacco for a gelding bearing the strange name (for a horse) of John. John was a trotter, and supposedly of some speed in harness, but my father could never get it out of him. The two did so badly together, indeed, that my father concluded that John must have rheumatism, and thereafter, for two or three months, the poor beast was the patient of a veterinarian who sent in large bottles of a fiery, suffocating liniment and even larger bills, but never did John any good. Mr. Felix, it appeared, had suspected all the while that the

trouble was predominantly in the driver rather than in the
horse, and eventually he volunteered to go out with my father
some afternoon, and make a scientific review of his driving. He
returned downcast. "Your pa," he said to me the next time I
dropped in, "is hopeless. It would take him two or three hundred years to learn to drive a cart-horse, let alone a trotter. He
holds the lines like a man dealing cards. If he ever got John to
really stepping he would fall out of the buggy and break his
neck."

A few days later, as if reminded by conscience that he may
have been hasty in dismissing his duty to the family, he amazed
and delighted me by offering to give *me* a few lessons. It was a
colossal opportunity to a boy of eleven, for Mr. Felix was an
eminent figure in the trotting world of Baltimore, and seldom
condescended to pedagogy. I had, as I recall it, only four or
five lessons, but when they were over Mr. Felix was so complimentary that I developed on the spot a complacency which
still survives after nearly fifty years, protecting me like an undershirt of concrete from the contumely of mankind. Indeed,
he said flatly, and I believe he meant it, that I had in me the
makings of a really smart harness driver. "By the time you
begin to shave," he concluded, "you'll be showing 'em."

By that time, alas, I had turned from equestrology to chemistry, and a little while later I abandoned chemistry for the kind
of beautiful letters on tap in newspaper offices. But for a couple
of years I drove John every day, and so gradually improved and
mellowed my technic. On Summer afternoons, when my father
and I were driving home to Mt. Washington, and the clomp-
clomp of a trotter's scissoring hooves began to sound behind
us on the Pimlico road speedway, he would silently hand me
the reins, and settle back to be torn between parental pride
and personal repining. I seemed to hear him groan now and
then, but he never said anything. When John, who was really
very fast, had left the other nag behind, and the brush was
over, he would quietly relight his cigar and resume the reins.
He never complimented me: it was too painful. Despite the
unction to my vanity that flowed out of these episodes, there
was also melancholy in them, and they implanted in me a lifelong conviction that children, taking one day with another,
must be damned pests.

But it was not the Coblens stable but the Reveille stable that was my chief haunt in boyhood. The Coblens stable was downtown in Paca street, a few yards from my father's place of business, but the Reveille stable was only two blocks from our home in Hollins street. My brother and I spent many happy hours there, watching the blackamoors currying, feeding and watering the horses, plaiting their tails, excavating and blacking their hooves, dosing them with Glauber's salts and condition powders, and treating their lampas (pronounced *lampers*) with red-hot pokers. This last was a horrifying spectacle, for lampas is an overgrowth of tissue behind the upper incisor teeth, and burning it out involved thrusting the poker into the poor horse's gaping mouth. But I learned before long that horses have very little sense of pain, if indeed any at all; and years afterward I saw one with a leg cut off in an accident munching the grass between the cobblestones as it lay on a Baltimore street, waiting for a cop to come out of a saloon to shoot it.

Mr. Reveille was a Frenchman who seemed venerable and even ancient to my brother and me, for he wore a long beard and always had on a black coat. He had two grown sons, both stout and hearty fellows, but, like their father, very dignified. There was a period when both the trotter John and the pony Frank (whose stable at the bottom of our backyard was transiently shut down) were quartered in the Reveille establishment, along with two buggies, a pony cart and several other rigs, so my brother and I had plenty of excuse for hanging about. The Reveilles always welcomed us gravely, and let us warm up, in Winter, in their tiny office, which was so filled with robes that there was scarcely room for the stove, always verging on white-hot. We admired especially the rack of whips, which included some virtuoso pieces by the Baltimore master-craftsmen of the time. A good whip might cost as much as $25, and we figured that the whole lot must be worth at least $1000.

The colored brethren who pontificated at Reveille's have all faded, with the flight of the years, into a brown smudge—all, that is, save Old Jim. Jim was the carriage-washer, and a fellow of vast size and unparalleled amiability. He was coal-black and built like a battleship, and when he got into his hip-high

rubber boots and put on his long rubber apron he looked like
an emperor in Hell. Jim's atelier was a skylighted space at the
rear of the carriage-house, paved with cobblestones and always
flowing with water. He got to work at six in the morning, and
was sometimes still going hard at nine at night. He had the
care of fifty or more buggies, and of perhaps as many other
vehicles, and he kept them clean and shining. His hardest time
came on Sunday morning, when he had to wash and polish all
the buggies in preparation for the pleasure jaunts of the afternoon. For this business he brought out his newest sponges and
cleanest chamois-skins. Also, he put on a black derby hat, never
worn on week-days.

In the intervals of his washing and polishing Jim took out
rigs to the homes of clients of the stable, and thereby sometimes acquired quiet brannigans, for it was the custom to reward him, not with money, but with drinks. My father kept a
special jug for the purpose. It was shared by the ice-man, but
Jim got most of it, for in view of his great bulk he was given a
much larger drink than the ice-man. He always downed it at a
gulp, and after it was down he would blink his eyes, rub his
belly, and say "Ah-h-h-h-h-!" This was a Baltimore custom of
the time, practised by most of the nobility and gentry and imitated by serving folk. Sometimes Jim also got a cigar. He
would light it at once, and stalk back to Reveille's smoking it
at an angle of forty-five degrees. When he reached the stable
he would choke it carefully and deposit it on a high ledge in
the brick wall, out of reach of his less Himalayan and reliable
colleagues.

My brother and I greatly admired Jim, and delighted in
watching him at work. He had a way of spinning buggy-wheels
that was really magnificent, and he worked with larger sponges
and broader chamois-skins than any other carriage-washer in
West Baltimore. The buggies of those days all had carpets, and
when there was nothing else to do he would get out a dozen
or so of them, and beat them. Sometimes he would find a
nickel or a dime under one of them. It always went into his
pocket, for it was the theory among the colored proletarians of
Baltimore in those days that whatever a white person lost or
mislaid he really didn't want. If he wanted it, he would ask for
it, and probably raise hell about it. Jim's income from this

source was not large, for he found a great many more pins than nickels. He always laid them aside carefully and then threw them into the manure-pit, for a pin in the frog of a horse's hoof might bring on calamity.

One day my brother and I were astonished to find Jim missing; it seemed almost as strange as finding Mr. Reveille missing, or the stable itself. His *locum tenens*, a short, spotty colored man named Browny, ordinarily a hostler, told us the sad news. Jim's youngest son, a youth of sixteen, had been blown up by an explosion in a one-horse soda-pop factory up a nearby alley, and Jim was off for the day, arranging for the interment of the few fragments that had been recovered. We had never heard of this son, but we were full of sympathy, and when Jim returned we tried to tell him so in the shy manner of boys. He replied that it was God's deliberate act and will, and that he did not mourn beyond reason. The son, he went on judicially, was not really bad, at least as sons went in an age of moral chaos, but nevertheless there was some worry in him, for now and then, like any other high-spirited colored boy, he got into trouble with the cops, and when that wasn't going on he wasted his substance on trashy yallah gals. Now he was far, far away, riding some cloud or rainbow, and hence safe from the hangman forever. He had even escaped, by the unusual manner of his death, the body-snatchers.

Two or three days later we saw a brisk-looking white man in a short yellow overcoat talking to Jim, and the day following Jim again disappeared. We heard from Browny that the brisk-looking man had been a lawyer, and that the talk had been of damages. Another talk, he said, was now proceeding downtown. Jim was gone a week, and then suddenly reappeared, but not to resume work. He showed up one morning in a stove-pipe hat and a long-tailed black coat, carrying an ebony cane with a bone head in the shape of a horse with widely distended nostrils tinted red, and green gems for eyes. His right-hand coat pocket was bulging with at least a quarter's worth of peanuts, and he invited all his old colleagues to thrust in their paws and help themselves. In his other coat pocket he had half a dozen apples for horses he especially liked, including the pony Frank but not the trotter John, and in the hand unburdened by the cane he carried a two-pound bag of lump-sugar.

In all four pockets of his white waistcoat were five-cent cigars, standing in rows like cartridges in a belt. He offered the cigars freely, and recommended them as the best in West Baltimore. He even offered one to Mr. Peter Reveille. His hip pockets were stuffed with chewing-tobacco.

Such was Jim in the full tide of his bereavement. Mr. Peter Reveille told us that the lawyer had offered him $250, but that Jim had stuck out for $300, and got it. He let it be known that he had demanded the money in $1 bills, but where he kept them we didn't know until later. Some of the hostlers were of the opinion that he had sneaked into the stable-loft by night and hidden them in the hay, and for a week or so a vain search for them went on. Browny insisted that they were in Jim's stove-pipe hat. He knew, as all of us knew, that policemen always kept their valuables in their helmets; *ergo*, why not Jim? But this theory blew up when Jim dropped in, a week or so later, without his hat, and complaining that two bad niggers from Vincent alley had knocked it off with clubs, and run away with it. The hat was gone, but Jim continued in funds for a long while afterward—indeed, for fully a month. He dropped into the stable almost daily, and never failed to distribute cigars, peanuts, and chewing tobacco, with sugar and apples for the horses. He appeared, at different times, in no less than five hats, and was often mildly in liquor. But he never brought any liquor on the premises, so the Reveilles, who had a large experience with the darker races, tolerated him patiently.

They knew that he would be back in his long boots and rubber apron soon or late, and he was. One morning early they found him at work, somewhat trembly and with a cut over his left eye, but otherwise as he had been in the days before wealth corrupted him. He had not been seen during the preceding week, and for a while his final adventures were unknown, for neither then nor thereafter did he ever mention them. But the other colored men gradually assembled and disgorged the story, and the cop on the beat helped out with a fact or two. It was really very simple. Jim, a decent widower, had been ganged and undone by the massed yallah gals of three alleys. They had all tackled him singly and failed, but when they tackled him in a body he succumbed.

The ensuing party raged for four days and four nights, with

continuous music by banjos, accordions, and bones. It began in a little saloon that was the G.H.Q. of one of the alleys, but gradually spread over the whole block, and ended at last in a loft over an empty stable. There was no hint whatever of carnality; the thing was purely alcoholic. After the first few hours each of the yallah gals sent for her regular fellow, and beginning with the second day all sorts of gate-crashers barged in. Thereafter there was a flow in and a flow out. Every hour or two some guest would collapse and roll home, and another would make the gate. Only Jim himself and a yallah gal named Mildred survived from beginning to end. Mildred, by that time, was in the first stages of *mania à potu*, and the cop on the beat, looking in, ordered her off the job, but Jim was still going strong.

Alas, he didn't go long, for a little while later the saloon-keeper's son Otto came in to say that time was called on the party. Otto and his brother Hermann had been hauling booze for it for four days and four nights, and both were badly used up. Hermann, in fact, had had to be put to bed. But it wasn't fatigue that made Otto call time; it was the fact that Jim's last dollar bill had been devoured. The father of Otto and Hermann was known to be a determined man, with the cops always on his side, so no one questioned the fiat. One by one, they simply faded away, leaving only Jim. He rolled himself in his long-tailed coat and lay down to a prodigal's dreams. He slept all the rest of that day, and all of the ensuing night to 5 A.M. Then he shuffled off to Reveille's stable, chased Browny away from his job, and resumed his station in life.

It was not until long afterward that my brother and I learned where Jim had kept his fortune while it oozed away. Mr. Reveille, worming the story out of the blackamoors, told my father, who told it to a neighbor, Mr. Scherer, whose boy Theodore, lurking about, overheard the telling, and brought it to us. The money had been in the care and custody of the saloonkeeper all the while. He doled it out to Jim dollar by dollar, marking the score on a blackboard behind his bar. He charged Jim a dollar a day "interest" for keeping it. When the final orgies began he charged a dollar for every day and a dollar for every night.

The Scherer boy reported that, in telling about this "interest," my father swore in a hair-raising manner. He had, in fact, a generally suspicious view of saloonkeepers. He would often say that while he knew and respected some upright men among them, only too many were disgraces to a humane and even noble profession.

XVIII.
The Career of a Philosopher

T HAT LEARNING and virtue do not always run together I learned early in life from the example of Old Wesley, a man of color living in the alley behind our house in Hollins * street. Wesley dwelt in illicit symbiosis with Lily, the stately *madura* cook of our next-door neighbors, and once a year his younger brother, who pastored an A.M.E. church down in Calvert county, dropped in on him to remonstrate against his evil ways. But Wesley always won the ensuing bout in moral theology, for he had packed away in his head a complete roster of all the eminent Biblical characters who had taken headers through No. 7, beginning with King David and running down to prophets of such outlandish names that, as I now suspect, many of them were probably invented on the spot. Moreover, Wesley could always floor his rev. brother with a final poser: How could he marry Lily so long as she had two other husbands, both of them united to her by impeccable Christian rites? Did the pastor propose the commission of trigamy? If so, then let him go down to the watchhouse in Calhoun street and ask the cops to show him chapter nine, verse twenty, in the big black lawbook behind the desk, a foot or two east of the water-cooler.

The pastor, I believe, never went. He had too healthy a respect for Wesley's scholarship in legal science, and indeed in all the other sciences, including especially those of an ethical or sacred nature. Thus the debate always petered out into futile logic-chopping, and the other residents of the alley, having crowded up to Wesley's open door for the show, got only headaches for their pains. Wesley would thereupon suggest that the pastor preach to them as a sort of solatium. Along with the other white boys of Hollins street, I heard more than one of those sermons, and I can testify that they were very powerful. Each had not only a subject, invariably the post-mortem dangers of sin, but also an object—one of the congregation assembled.

179

I remember well the day when it was Old Aunt Sophie's
turn. She was the widow of a black barber from Fauquier
county, Virginia, who had spent the years 1863 and 1864 caring
for the whiskers of General George H. Thomas, and since her
husband's death she had lived chastely on her pension, attending (on the sidewalk) all the funerals, white or black, in West
Baltimore, and lending a hand whenever special orgies were
staged in the colored churches. No more innocent person
lived on this earth. She had worn the same black veil for thirty
years, and it well indicated the sombre rectitude of her soul.
But the pastor lit into her as if she were a child-stealer or a pirate on the high seas, and after ten minutes of his discourse she
was flat on the cobblestones, suffocated by the fumes of brimstone and howling for deliverance.

*   Old Wesley himself listened to all these sermons politely,
though he was known to be an infidel, and had a long argument to prove that there was not enough coal and wood in
creation to stoke the fires of the Methodist Hell. He was, in
fact, very proud of his brother's homiletic talents, and when
the smaller colored boys on the edge of the crowd made
whoopee he would go among them with a lath and paddle
them far from gently. We white boys, knowing that the prevailing *mores* forbade him to paddle *us*, were bound in honor to
keep quiet, and this we always did. At the end of the sermon
we joined in the closing hymn—usually "Whiter Than Snow"
or "Are You Ready for the Judgment Day?" Then the pastor
would suggest an offering for his tarpaper tabernacle down in
Calvert county, and the assemblage would disperse in swift silence. But Wesley always put in a nickel, and sometimes a dime,
and I recall one day when his sinister eye halted so many fugitives that the total plate was nearly thirty-five cents. This would
be enough, said the grateful pastor, to replace a window-pane
in the tabernacle, broken by agents of Satan. For three and a
half years it had been sorely missed, for the butcher paper
pasted over the opening shut out the light.

The pastor's visitations always came in the Summer, and
usually in the afternoon. They quite upset Wesley's routine for
hot days. His Lily had to clear out at seven o'clock to get
breakfast for her white folks, but Wesley himself never arose
before eight. The first sign that he was astir would be the

appearance of their feather bed through the second-story front window of their four-room house. They apparently slept on it all the year round. On every fair morning, Wesley would shove it out of the window to air, and there it would remain until noon, unless storms came up in the meantime. He made his own breakfast, and then busied himself with undisclosed household tasks until eleven o'clock, when he took a walk around the block.

On his return, he had an armful of newspapers and other printed matter, dredged out of trash boxes on the way, and most of the afternoon he devoted to reading them. It was said that he could read any word, however hard. Colored schoolboys sometimes tackled him with appalling specimens, got from their teachers, but he was always ready to give them names, and to explain their significances. I myself, in the year 1889, sought to floor him with *phthisic*, then all the rage at my school. He called it off without a second's hesitation, and even offered to pronounce it backward. Its meaning? "It's one of them diseases," he said, "that you catch in the Fall of the year. It's something like what you call the heaves in a horse, and then again it ain't. There was a man up in Vincent alley died of it about the time the stockyards burned down. All the pallbearers took it, but none of them had it what you would call bad. Sometimes it don't amount to much."

In Summer, Wesley always did his reading across the alley from his house, in the shade of a white neighbor's backyard fence. He would bring out a kitchen chair shortly after noon, plant it carefully on the narrow and squidgy sidewalk, with its treacherous "she" bricks, and proceed solemnly to business. Years before, he had bought a pair of spectacles from a pack peddler, but he didn't need them, and seldom used them. He would read until three or four o'clock, and then he would be ready for easy and informative conversation until eight in the evening, when Lily returned from her place with a vast pan of victuals for their evening meal. Wesley, so far as I know, never ate lunch. Like most colored folk of the old school, he preferred to gorge at night, and to proceed direct from the table to bed. He was said once to have eaten a whole ham and a whole cabbage at a sitting, but I got that at third hand, and do not take responsibility for it.

I knew him best not as a gourmet but as a metaphysician. He had ready and overwhelming answers to all the questions that have baffled such professionals as Thomas Aquinas and Immanuel Kant, F. W. Nietzsche and William James. For example, What is truth? His answer, reduced to brevity, was as follows: "Truth is something that only damned fools deny." But how are you going to detect the damned fools? By the fact that they deny it. Is there a hole in this reasoning? Perhaps. But there are also holes, according to Kant, in the reasoning of Aquinas, and, according to Nietzsche and William James, in the reasoning of Kant, and so on to the end of the murky chapter.

Wesley had answers to all the other great riddles of the universe, and most of them were equally confident. He knew, for example, the causes of each and every one of the pestilences commonly afflicting Aframericans. Rheumatism, he explained, was due to bending over and lifting weights. The backbone, it appeared, crackled like a bent cornstalk. It could be restored to its natural shape and resilience only by adopting some sedentary avocation: this, in fact, was the reason Wesley himself lived at the cost and expense of Lily. His rheumatism, acquired during his former practice as a hod-carrier, still troubled him a bit, but sixteen years of ease had certainly improved it. He had got rid of the ague by carrying a horse chestnut in his pocket. Here the rationale was absurdly transparent. Horses and mules were notoriously immune to the ague; hence horse chestnuts would cure it. If there had been cow chestnuts or dog chestnuts, they would have cured it, too.

Wesley's pockets were full of many other such specifics. He carried a quince seed to hold in check the quinsy that beset him every Winter, some BB shot to prevent hiccoughs (the reasoning here I don't recall, or maybe never heard), and a small spring, apparently from a deceased firearm, to keep his wool in kink. This was before Aframerica began to patronize hair-straighteners. To Wesley, straight hair on a colored man was unearthly, and even alarming. The kinks, he taught, held the skull tight, and so kept the air out, and warded off headaches, blind staggers, and insanity. There had been a yellow fellow in Vincent alley with hair that was not only straight but also somewhat sandy. His fate was known to all. One windy night he went loony and cut his wife's throat, and a few months later, on a Friday that was the thirteenth of the month, he was hanged at the city jail.

Wesley seldom got farther than a block from his house in the alley behind Hollins street, but twice a year he went down into South Eutaw street near the railroad tracks to attend the meetings of a lodge that he belonged to. Its name I never discovered, or the character of its mysteries. Wesley always left home smoking a cigar, and, according to Lily, came back smelling of gin. The nearest route would have taken him past the University of Maryland Medical School at Lombard and Greene streets, but it was no secret that he always avoided the place by making a detour of six or eight blocks. This was not because he had any fear of the thousands of cadavers reported to be piled up like stove-wood in the university deadhouse. As I shall show, he regarded the departed as beneficent presences, or, at all events, as harmless. But he held it to be manifest that medical students were indistinguishable from demons. They lay in wait in dark Greene street with their dreadful hooks, saws, lassos, and knives, and when they had roped a poor colored man they dragged him into their den with hellish shrieks, sawed off his legs and arms, scalped him, and boiled down what remained of him to make medicine. There were, of course, no witnesses to prove these obscene rites, for there were no survivors, but the facts needed no testimony, for they were admitted *quod ab omnibus, quod ubique, quod semper.*

Wesley's attitude toward the dead was one of easy confidence. He believed that the overwhelming majority of them turned into angels, and that these angels were invariably white. "Who would be black if he could he'p it?" he would ask solemnly, not without a touch of pathos. And then, as usual, he would answer himself, "Angels *can* he'p it." The non-angelic dead were simply probationers, roving the vicinity of their coffins (and hence extremely numerous in graveyards) until their cases could be adjudicated. Wesley rejected the idea of Hell, not only for the reason I have stated a while back, but also on legalistic grounds. There would be a profound irrationality, he argued, in punishing evildoers in one world for what they had done in another. Was a chicken thief in Calvert county jailed in Baltimore? Obviously not. The very cops would laugh at the idea. He had other reasons, too, but what they were I forget.

It was in the year 1891 that Wesley had a chance to test his faith in the beneficence of the departed. One day Lily came home from her place complaining of a terrible misery in the head. Wesley put her to bed at once, and sat up all night tearing towels and sheets into strips, soaking them in Dr. Jackson's Reliable Vinegar Liniment for Man and Beast, and binding them tightly to her head. But the air must have got in nevertheless, for by dawn Lily was out of her wits, and carrying on so loudly that the neighbors were all aroused, and came flocking in to assist at the bedside, and to tell one another when they had seen Lily last, and what she had said to them. Presently someone got word to Dr. Benson, the young white medico who had just opened an office in Hollins street, and he came rushing out of his back gate with his nightshirt stuffed into his trousers, and his shiny new black bag bulging reassuringly. But the science of young Dr. Benson, though it was extraordinarily fresh, and indeed came down almost to that precise moment, was insufficient to save poor Lily, and as the whistle down at the Mount Clare carshops blew for seven o'clock she gave up the ghost.

Wesley took his calamity like the philosopher that he was. Nor did he blanch when word came that the burial society to which Lily had belonged for eighteen years, dutifully paying in fifteen cents every week, was insolvent, and could not meet its liability of forty dollars. He borrowed two dollars from young Dr. Benson, produced eleven dollars and some odd cents from a mysterious cigar box, and talked the undertaker, Brother James Gadsden, into giving him credit for what was needed to make up twenty-five. Thus Lily, though she missed the gaudy Class A Nazarene funeral that she had looked forward to for so many years, was at least assured of dignified interment, and in an hour or two Brother Gadsden and his son Joe arrived with a neat black box, and she was duly laid out in the little parlor. A plate rested on her chest, and as the neighbors and the public generally filed past there was an occasional tinkle. Wesley raked in the money from time to time, not wanting to expose kindly friends to temptations beyond human endurance. By evening he had nearly a dollar and a half, and this he gave to

Brother Gadsden to affix a copious but somewhat rusty crêpe to the spot on the front-door frame where a bell would have been if there had been one. A postal card was sent to the clerical brother down in Calvert county, inviting him to conduct the obsequies if his ecclesiastical and private engagements permitted. Wesley didn't expect him to show up, and he didn't. His professional view of Lily's morals was very low.

No less than two brave spirits, one of them the alley half-wit and the other a dubious-looking mulatto from the region behind Hollins Market, offered to sit up with Lily, but Wesley waved them away. There would be no death watch, he announced, and no wake. Along about nine o'clock in the evening he adjourned proceedings for the day, jammed a chair against the front door to keep it shut, made a solitary supper of cold meats, and went to bed in the little room above the chamber of death. The neighbors marveled at this fortitude. What if Lily should take to walking? What if her ghost began to moan? What if the Devil dropped in to look her over?

They listened cautiously for a while, but if they heard anything it was only Wesley's snores. His nursing duties the night before and all the excitement of the day had worn him out, and he was quickly asleep. There was no room in his philosophy for fear of the dead. If they became angels, they were, of course, harmless, and if they were put on probation, they naturally carried themselves very discreetly, in the hope of early release. It was only when those fiends, the medical students, disturbed them in their graves, dragging them out of the earth to rend and cook them, and leaving screwdrivers, broken knives, cigarette butts, and whiskey bottles in their empty coffins —it was only then that they went on in a riotous and alarming manner, and even so their worst screams were simply calls for help. Treat them with reasonable politeness, and they were no more evil than policemen, who responded in the same way to the same dose. Wesley had confidence in Lily. Living, she had paid his rent for many years, and provided him with nourishing board. Dead, she would certainly not afflict him.

But that, alas, is precisely what she did. The details are not all clear, but Wesley seems to have shown a brave and tolerant spirit. It was not until the grisly hour before dawn that he appeared at the door of his neighbors, the Perkinses, and rapped

softly. Three of the seven Perkins children slept on pallets in
the front room, and they let him in and called their father.
Wesley was almost apologetic—not for himself but for Lily.
"She don't seem to be restin'," he explained, "as well as she
ought. Otherwise, I don't know *what* to call it. No sooner was
I asleep than she pulled off my covers. Then I went to sleep
again, and she pulled 'em off again. That went on six or seven
times. Then she commenced to blow in my face. And then she
buzzed like a mosquito. And then she meeowed like a cat. And
then—well, I thought I'd better clear out, and maybe she
could get some rest. I don't know *what's* troublin' her."

The Perkins children were scared half to death. It had been
bad enough to sleep with only a thin wall between them and
Lily; now that she was aprowl, the thing became appalling. But
their parents, who told the whole neighborhood about it later,
were not alarmed, or even surprised. They suggested that Lily,
on her deathbed, had probably forgotten to tell Wesley something, and that it was still lying on her mind and driving her
thoughts from celestial matters. Wesley himself had to admit the
plausibility of the hypothesis. The next day he told Brother
Gadsden, the undertaker, that she was most likely trying to tell
him where he would find the cigar box and its hoard of nickels
and pennies. In life, it appeared, she had never suspected that
he knew about it all the while and had even burgled it modestly once or twice. But Brother Gadsden, though naturally a
stupid fellow, came back with a series of disconcerting questions. "If she didn't know it when she was alive," he demanded,
"is that any sign she didn't know it soon as she was dead? Can't
a ghost *see*? And wasn't the box standing right there on the
mantelpiece, plumb empty?"

So far as I know, Wesley never resolved the riddle. It seemed to
bother him a great deal during the weeks following, and may
have had something to do with his early demise. He was always
bringing it up, and laboring it futilely. He even talked to himself about it. When the neighbors ceased to think of him as a
lone and lorn widower, and so ceased to feed him, he turned
anti-social, and was presently in the hands of the cops. Jailed
for stealing two hams and a sack of flour from a grocer's delivery wagon, he came down with pneumonia in his damp dun-

geon. With the unhappy alacrity of his race, he was dead in five days, and a week later the medical students had him. I have never known a more gifted metaphysician, or one who came to a sadder end.

XIX.
Innocence in a Wicked World

Bombazine is often spoken of by authors, usually in a sneering way, but the only person I ever knew to wear it was Aunt Sophie, the ancient colored woman mentioned in the last chapter. As I recall it, it was a somewhat stiff and shiny fabric, apparently black at the start, but converted by the oxygen of the air into a sinister, malarious polychrome like that of the waters of a stagnant frog pond. Aunt Sophie wore it on all public occasions, along with a long crêpe veil of the same unappetizing color. As the widow of a military barber, she was in receipt of a modest pension from the United States Treasury, and on it she lived at ease in her little four-room house, and even in a kind of opulence.

Her days were very busy. Whenever there was a funeral in West Baltimore, whether in a white street or a colored, she arrived in good time and planted herself on the sidewalk. She carried a white cambric handkerchief that, under the ravages of time, had taken on the texture of a lace curtain, and as the pallbearers emerged with the departed she always applied it politely to her eyes. If the cortege went to any church within walking distance, she hustled along beside it, and since the hack horses of those days were encouraged to move slowly, she usually beat them to the sacred edifice by at least a length, and grabbed a decorous seat near the door. There she mourned quietly in the character of an old friend, or even of a relative, if the departed happened to be colored, and in that of a family retainer if he or she were white. She was, in fact, more or less related to fully half the black folk in our neighborhood, for most of them had come from either Fauquier county, Virginia, where her husband was born, or Calvert county, Maryland, where she was born herself. And all the white folks knew and esteemed her.

This funeral-going occupied a large part of her time, and it was seldom that she got through two days running without putting on her uniform of woe. Among her own people her

absence from the forefront of mortuary orgies was always remarked, and often it had a moral significance. For she was a
woman of strict Christian principles, and permitted herself no
compromise with sin. Thus she took her station at least five or
six doors away from the house of sorrow when Lily, the con-
sort of Wesley the metaphysician, was laid to rest, for their
long association had been unblessed by any sacrament. And
when the yellow fellow in Vincent alley ran amuck one night
and slit his wife's weasand, and was duly hanged for it at the
city jail, she refused primly to patronize the ensuing ceremoni-
als in any way, shape or form, though they attracted all the
other colored people for a mile around, and also all the white
boys who could escape their mothers' vigilance. My brother
and I both sneaked into the tiny parlor to see the corpse, and
were haunted for many nights afterward by the marks of the
rope on its gaunt, felonious neck.

Old Sophie was made welcome at funerals, for she was very
well regarded throughout West Baltimore. The only time she
was ever turned away, to my knowledge, was when Joe Gans,
the colored pugilist, was buried. Joe was so eminent a character among his own people that his funeral had to be divided
into three cantos and held successively in three different
churches to accommodate the immense concourse. Even so,
many more appeared than could get in to hear and see, and his
heirs and assigns, at the last moment, made a rule that only
those who arrived in carriages should be admitted. This barred
out Aunt Sophie, for she had no carriage and was too thrifty a
woman to blow in four dollars—the extortionate price for the
day—on a public hack. Worse, the baffled crowds outside the
three churches were so large and turbulent, despite the bellowing and scuffling of the police, that she never got within
half a block of poor Joe's bones. Thus she appeared, unwittingly, to be operating her familiar moral boycott on him, but
as a matter of fact she admired him vastly, and had proofs, as
she said, that he had died in the bosom of the A.M.E. Church
and confident of a glorious resurrection.

The one curse of Aunt Sophie's otherwise peaceful and happy
life was her fear of the murderous villains she called body-snatchers.
These body-snatchers were not grave-robbers, but criminals who
engaged in the far worse business of manufacturing cadavers for

the trade. Sophie's fear of them actually had some ground in logic, for in the early eighties one Emily Brown, another respectable old Baltimore colored woman, had been murdered by two thugs, and her remains sold to the janitor of the University of Maryland Medical School for fifteen dollars. The pursuit and trial of the assassins gave Baltimore, white and black, a show that was remembered for years afterward. They had represented to the janitor that they were undertakers trying to get rid of an insolvent client, so he was cleared of all guilt, but they themselves were hanged. The janitor was very careful after that, but most colored people believed that he still had murderers in his employ, and only the bravest or craziest ever ventured to pass the Medical School after dark.

Aunt Sophie held the view that his agents were on the prowl, not only in the immediate vicinity of his grisly den but also all over West Baltimore. Thus, when she had to be abroad by night she kept to well-lighted streets, and whenever it was possible induced someone else to go along. When she was alone her eye was alert for policemen, and after she had passed one she always looked back over her shoulder two or three times, to make sure that he was still there, and ready to protect her if necessary. Most of the cops knew her, and now and then one of them would have some fun by letting off a fearful whoop after she had gone by. In such cases it was hard for her to make up her mind whether she should rush back to him or gallop on.

One dismal Autumn night, on her way down Hollins street to her A.M.E. tabernacle in Stockton street, she was suddenly alarmed by the sound of stealthy footsteps behind her. She quickened her pace, but the steps continued close; in fact, they gradually came closer. Finally she broke into what, in spite of her rheumatism, must be described as a kind of run, but there was no speed in it, and the sinister steps still followed her. She was convinced that her last hour had come, and was preparing to die howling and scratching when suddenly she saw a policeman on the other side of the dark street. At once she swung round, and confronted her pursuer, who turned out to be a young white man.

"I know what you is!" she screamed. "You's a body-snatcher! Begone, you wicked rapscallion! Don't you lay none o' your dirty hands on *me*!"

But the young white man only laughed, and when the cop ambled across the street to see what the uproar was about, he laughed too. It was a disconcerting dénouement, certainly, and as Aunt Sophie thought it over during the days following, she began to read very unpleasant significances into it. In the end she went about the neighborhood warning all persons of color that the police had entered into a corrupt compact with the body-snatchers, and that the streets were more unsafe by night than ever before. She became, like all other persons with grievances against the government, somewhat extravagant in her denunciations, and playful cops liked to set her off when a crowd of loafers was at hand. Before her scare wore off, she went to the length of threatening to arm herself with her late husband's sword, and to run it through anyone who approached her after nightfall, whether cop or layman. It was news to most people that colored barbers in the Union Army had been armed with swords, but so far as I can recall, no one ever raised the point. Nor did anyone ever see the sword.

The little parlor in Aunt Sophie's house remained substantially as her husband Jeems had left it. He had practised his profession intermittently, charging five cents flat for shaving either a face or a scalp, but his pension put him above worldly cares, and most of his time had been given to the art of painting in oils. There were several examples of his genius on the walls of the room—one a picture of a full-rigged ship laboring in a pea-green ocean. Jeems had to pick up his paints and brushes where he could find them, usually in trash cans, so his color schemes were sometimes very unusual. He once did a portrait of Old Wesley, using coal-black paint for the face. This greatly offended Wesley, who was of a rich chestnut color and liked to believe that he had Indian blood.

Sophie left Jeems's mirror on the wall after his death, along with the wooden shelf beneath it bearing his razor, comb, and brush. His operating chair presented no problem, for it was an ordinary cane-seat chair of the period, with the lost canes replaced by strips of wood from a soapbox. A large wooden spittoon filled with sawdust still stood under the mirror; for Jeems had chewed tobacco in the Army to relieve his frequent toothaches, and never gave up the practice afterward. Against the farther wall stood a scuffed Victorian side table with a cracked marble top, and on it were the *objets d'art* that Sophie had collected in her tours of the kitchens and backyards of the adjacent white folks.

The most striking of these ornaments was a large Dresden cupid with both wings missing and a crack across the face which gave it the appearance of a prizefighter staggering up for the twentieth round. There was also a glass bell covering a stuffed canary that had lost its tail and one of its eyes. Propped against the bell were several pieces of curved colored glass, all relics of deceased goblets or bottles. Some souvenirs of the Philadelphia Centennial of 1876 were also in the collection—one of them an oyster shell embellished with a sketch of Independence Hall in full color. Sophie had not visited the exposition herself; in fact, she had never been farther north in this world than Harlem Square in Baltimore. But as its white frequenters gradually discarded their souvenirs of it, she acquired them and, having acquired them, cherished them.

She used to make regular rounds of all the white folks' kitchens in the neighborhood—that is, of all wherein she was reasonably sure of a welcome. The cooks of her own race were glad to see her, for she knew all the gossip, both white and colored, and was full of wise advice to those having trouble with their husbands, their children, their madames, or the police. She usually appeared at mealtimes and always refused the first ten or twenty invitations to have a bite. But in the end she would sit down, and if she happened to be in good form she devoured enough to feed a longshoreman, though she couldn't have weighed much more than a hundred pounds. If anything was left over, she wrapped it in a newspaper and took it home. No one ever saw her buy anything, whether food or clothing. She ate, so to speak, on the country, and her wardrobe had been fixed and complete for years. Her pension went (*a*) for her rent, which was $1.25 a week, (*b*) to the funds of the A.M.E. Church in Stockton street, (*c*) to funeral collections, and (*d*) into a dime savings bank down in Baltimore street. When she died at last, and a young white lawyer in the neighborhood volunteered, as *amicus curiae*, to investigate her affairs, he found that she had amassed the substantial sum of $67.10.

Her visits to our kitchen were always made at about four o'clock in the afternoon, for she knew that my mother had tea at that time, and that she was sure of four or five cups of it, and a slab of whatever cake happened to be current. Her favorite was raisin bread, which she liked with plenty of powdered sugar. A whole dynasty of our hired girls, white and black, thus fed her. Sometimes, in the course of her formal refusals to have any refreshment, she would rush out of the kitchen door, but she always returned before the teapot was cold. In Summer, however, her refusal of iced tea was real, for she regarded ice as a poison almost as deadly as cucumbers. She liked her drinks very hot, and one of our hired girls once told me that she could eat a red pepper straight out of the tarragon-vinegar cruet without batting an eye.

Aunt Sophie lived to a great age, and in her last years was somewhat shaky. One day, in my hearing, my mother asked her how old she was, precisely. She thought sombrely for a minute or two, and then answered that she must be well along toward thirty. This was in 1897 or thereabout, and she had been married to her Jeems some time before the Civil War. Another day my mother asked her why she didn't move back to Calvert county, where she had nephews to look after her, including two preachers, and her pension would make her a grand lady. Again she gave herself to meditation, and then answered simply, "They ain't never no parades in the country."

XX.

Strange Scenes and Far Places

To my brother Charlie and me our father seemed to be a tremendous traveler—indeed, almost a Marco Polo. His trips to buy tobacco ranged from New York State and Connecticut in the North to Cuba in the South, and from the wilds of the Pennsylvania Dutch in the East to Wisconsin in the West, and he also made at least one journey a year to some national potlatch of the Freemasons. In this last mysterious order he never attained to any eminent degree or held any office, but he was enrolled in both of its more sportive and expensive sub-divisions, the Knights Templar and the Shriners. At the orgies of the Knights Templar he appears to have arrayed himself in a uniform resembling that of a rear-admiral, for in the wardrobe that he took with him there were a long-tailed blue coat with brass buttons, a velvet chapeau with a black feather, a silk baldric, and a sword. With them he carried the red fez that marked him a member of the Ancient Arabic Order of the Nobles of the Mystic Shrine. Whether or not the Shriners and the Knights met jointly I don't know, but every time he returned from a muster of either the one or the other or both he brought back souvenirs of the convention and the convention town, and these entertained Charlie and me in a very agreeable way, and gave us considerable credit, when they were exhibited, among the boys of the neighborhood. Other such objects of art and instruction flowed in from his tobacco-buying trips, so that the house was always well supplied. I recall especially some ornate fans from Havana, some jars of guava jelly from the same place, a large book illustrating the objects of interest in St. Louis, a photograph of the bar of the Palmer House in Chicago, showing (not very clearly) its floor of silver dollars, and a book of views along the French Broad river in North Carolina, apparently a souvenir of a visit to Asheville. My father's traveler's tales were full of thrills to Charlie and me, especially those that had to do with bullfighting in Cuba. My mother always protested against them as horrifying and

brutalizing, but we never got enough of them. Or of his accounts of strange victuals devoured and enjoyed in far places. I
well remember his return from Kansas City, probably in 1889
or thereabout, with the first news that had ever reached Hollins street of a dessert called floating-island, then apparently a
novelty in the world. We made him describe it over and over
again, and in the end some effort was made to concoct it in the
family kitchen, but that effort came to naught.

Our own travels, down to the end of the eighties, had been
very meagre. I had been to Washington often, and Charlie
rather less often, but neither of us had ever been far enough
from home to have to stay overnight, and neither of us had
ever eaten in a dining-car or slept in a sleeper. It was thus a
gaudy piece of news when, in the first days of 1891, my grandfather Abhau let it be known that he had some long-neglected
relatives in faraway Ohio, and was of a mind to pay them a
visit, and take me along. These relatives were new to me, and
even my mother had only the vaguest idea of them. They were
the descendants, it appeared, of my grandfather's elder sister,
who had been so much his senior that she might have been his
aunt. On arriving in the United States at some undetermined
time in the past, they had bought a lottery ticket on the dock,
won a substantial prize (my grandfather's estimate of it ranged
up to $20,000), and used the money to buy a couple of fine
farms on the borders of the Western Reserve in Ohio, not far
from Toledo. My grandfather now proposed to wait upon
them, and to stop on the way to see some friends in Cleveland.
Himself of no experience as a land traveler (though he had
made some sea voyages as a youth), he wanted companionship
for the journey, and as his oldest grandchild I got the nomination. It was to me as exciting a surprise as being appointed
hostler to Maud S. or president of the Foos candy factory
down the alley behind Hollins street.

The preparations for the journey took a couple of weeks, at
least. There was, first of all, the matter of my trousseau. What
was the climate of Northern Ohio in Winter? No one seemed
to know, so my mother proceeded on the assumption that it
must be pretty terrible. I thus drew a new and well-padded
overcoat from Oehm's Acme Hall, and a new Winter cap with
ear-flaps from Mr. Garrigues, the Bible-searching hatter in

Baltimore street. Simultaneously, my mother began assembling
a large stock of extra-heavy stockings and underclothes, and a
great battery of mufflers, mittens and pulse-warmers, and to it
was added a pair of massive goloshes. All these things had to
be tried on, and some of them were broken in by being worn
on my daily journeys to F. Knapp's Institute, for the weather in
Baltimore had conveniently turned very cold. But I had no
appetite in days so electric for the proceedings at F. Knapp's
Institute, and for the first and last time in my school life I came
home at the end of January with bad marks. Of the many sciences taught there that month, the only one that I really paid
any attention to was geography, and in geography my studies
were confined to the State of Ohio. I learned to my satisfaction
that Toledo was very near its western frontier, and hence
within handy reach of the spot where Sitting Bull had just
been killed; that the village we were bound for was only a few
miles from Lake Erie, which was twice as large as Chesapeake
Bay and probably jammed to the brim with oysters, crabs and
shad-fish; and that Cleveland was celebrated all over the world
for the magnificence of its Euclid avenue, lined with the *pa-
lazzi* of Christian millionaires.

My father entered the picture in the closing days of our
preparations. He came home one day with the tickets, including the Pullman tickets, and proceeded to instruct me in the
technic of getting to bed at night and up again the next morning on a sleeper. He said that he would see us off at Camden
Station, Baltimore, and, if there was time enough, make sure
that we were properly stowed, but on the chance that the train
would not halt more than a few minutes, he would also request
his Washington agent, Mr. Cross, to take a look at us when we
reached Washington. We were to travel, of course, by Baltimore & Ohio, and the route ran through Washington and
Pittsburgh. I recall nothing of our actual departure, nor of Mr.
Cross's inspection in Washington, but I remember very well my
father's last-minute fears that I might not have enough money
for possible expenses. My grandfather was the treasurer of the
expedition, but inasmuch as he was an ancient of sixty-four
there was always the chance that he might stray off and get
lost, or fall into the hands of bunco-steerers, or succumb to
amnesia, or lose his faculties otherwise, so it was necessary for

me to be financed on my own. Every time my father thought of another of these contingencies he gave me another dollar bill, and urged me to store it safely. By the time we finally shoved off I had them secreted all over my person, and on our return two weeks later I managed to omit a couple from my settlement of accounts. With these, after a discreet interval, my brother Charlie and I bought a new air-rifle. The marks of its darts are still in the door of a cupboard on the third floor of Hollins street.

My grandfather and I changed trains at Pittsburgh in the morning, and I had my first glimpse of a quick-lunch counter. The appearance of a white waiter behind it was a piquant novelty to me, for all the restaurants I knew in Baltimore and Washington were served by blackamoors. I remember that the white coat of this Caucasian appeared to show a certain lack of freshness, but I forgot the fact when he shoved a huge stack of wheat cakes before me, with a large pitcher of syrup beside it, and then politely turned his back. At home the syrup pitcher was rigorously policed, and emptying it over a pancake brought a reprimand, if not a box of the ears, but in Pittsburgh there seemed to be no rules, so I fell to in a large and freehand way. Once or twice I noticed my grandfather looking at me uneasily, and making as if to speak, but he actually said nothing, and by the time we had to rush for our train the wheat cakes were all gone, and so was most of the syrup. There was also a plate of bread on the table, but I never touched it. As we left I saw the waiter return the slices to a pile on a shelf behind the counter. This gave me a considerable shock, and set me to wondering if the wheat cakes had also passed over some other plate before they reached mine. But I was too full of them to worry much, and after what seemed a very brief ride through country covered with snow, we reached Cleveland and were met by my grandfather's friend, Mr. Landgrebe.

Mr. Landgrebe turned out to be a very pleasant man, and * when we got to his house he produced a young son, Karl, slightly older than I, who was agreeable too. How long we stayed in Cleveland I don't know, but it must have been no more than two days. But though the time was short, Mr. Landgrebe showed us all the marvels of the town, including not only the millionaires' elegantly hand-tooled castles along

Euclid avenue, with every lawn peopled by a whole herd of cast-iron deers, dogs, cupids and Civil War soldiers, but also the infernal valley wherein the oil of these millionaires was processed and barreled, and a lunatic asylum in which, presumably, the victims of their free competition were confined. My grandfather, a man of tender heart, was much upset by the carryings-on of the Napoleons, George Washingtons and Pontius Pilates in the wards, and shushed me with some asperity whenever I ventured to giggle. It was my first visit to a lunatic asylum, and I enjoyed it in the innocent and thankful manner of any normal boy of ten. There was one poor maniac who entertained me particularly, for his aberration took the form of rolling up thin cylinders of paper and sticking them in his nose and ears. When I got home and told my brother Charlie about the wonderful things I had seen on my travels, he pronounced this lunatic the most wonderful of all. My own first choice, after mature reflection, was the trolley-car that ran past the Landgrebe house in Cleveland. There had been one in Baltimore for six months, but its route lay far from Hollins street, so I knew nothing about it. What struck me especially about the Cleveland car was the loud, whistling buzz that its trolley made as it came down the street. This buzz could be heard *before* the noise of the car itself was detectable—a marvelous indicator, to me, of the unearthly powers of electricity. But Charlie, who was less than nine years old, stuck to the lunatic.

When we finally got to the farms of my grandfather's kinfolk the snow had melted and the whole countryside was an ocean of mud, but by the next morning I had forgotten it, for by that time I was on easy terms with the boys and girls of the two houses, and thereafter they showed me what, in those days, was called an elegant time. I had already spent two Summers at the Vineyard, and was thus more or less familiar with rural scenes, but the Vineyard, after all, was only ten miles as the bird flies from Baltimore, and we were only Summer sojourners. Here were real farms inhabited by real farming people, and in their daily life there was something every minute that was new to me, and full of fascination. I got to know cows and hogs familiarly, and learned to esteem them. I helped the younger Almroths (it was at their house that we stayed) to crack walnuts in the barn, to fetch up apples from the cellar, and to haul wood for the great egg-stoves that kept us warm. The enormous country dinners and suppers, with their pyramids of fried chicken and their huge platters of white home-cured hog-meat, swimming in grease, stoked and enchanted my vast appetite, and I rolled and wallowed at night in the huge feather-beds. It was pleasant to go out of a morning with Mr. Almroth, and watch him (from a safe distance) blow out stumps with sticks of dynamite. It was even more pleasant to go into the woods with his two older sons, and help stack the firewood that they cut. One day I labored so diligently at this task that I got into a lather and picked up a sore throat, and the next day Mrs. Almroth cured it with a mixture of honey and horse-radish —a prescription that went far beyond anything Dr. Wiley ever ordered. The days ran by as fast as the Cleveland trolley-car, and the evenings around the egg-stove in the parlor were trips to a new and romantic world. The youngsters and I stuffed doughnuts, tortured the house dogs and swapped riddles out of Dr. Ayer's Almanac while my grandfather and the elders searched the remotest reaches of their genealogy, and the village schoolma'm (who boarded out during the term, and was the Almroths' guest that Winter) sat by the lamp on the table reading a book that seemed to me to be the thickest on earth. Before we left I sneaked a look at its title, and when we got back to Baltimore I borrowed it from the branch of the Pratt Library in Hollins street, but I never managed to get beyond its first chapter. It was "St. Elmo," by Mrs. Augusta Jane Evans Wilson.

The Almroths, it appeared, were professing Christians, and on the Sunday following our arrival they took my grandfather and me to their church, which stood in the midst of a slough in the village, and was, as I recall, of some branch or other of the Lutheran communion. We got in late and my grandfather diffidently declined to go forward to the Almroth pew, but slipped into a seat near the door and dragged me with him. But if he thought to escape the glare of notoriety by that device he was badly fooled, for at the close of the proceedings an officer arose near the pulpit and read a report on the attendance for the day. When he came to "Number of visitors present: two" the whole congregation arose as one Christian and rubber-necked East, West, North and South until we had been located. There was indeed such a hubbub that my grand-father was induced to arise and make a bow. As we were passing out afterward he was introduced to the pastor and all the notables of the congregation, including many who welcomed him in German, for the whole Lake Erie littoral was full of Germans. The pastor eyed me speculatively and seemed about to try me out on the Catechism, but just then a female customer began to whoop up his sermon in high, astounding terms, and I escaped under cover of his grateful thanks.

But of all the incidents of that memorable journey to the Wild West the one that sticks in my recollection most firmly was the last, for it was aided in gaining lodgment by an uneasy conscience. My grandfather and I, on our return, were hardened travelers, and dealt with train conductors, Pullman porters and such-like functionaries in a casual and confident manner. We arrived at Washington very early in the morning, and my father's plenipotentiary, Mr. Cross, was there to meet us. His face, when we sighted him on the platform, was very grave, and he approached us in the manner of a man charged with an unhappy duty. It took the form of handing us a telegram. My grandfather blanched when he saw it, and passed it to me without reading it, for telegrams always alarmed him. I opened it at his nod, and then proceeded to read it to him in a chastened whisper, as follows:

Frank Cross,   Baltimore, February 26, 1891
    Aug. Mencken & Bro.,
        Seventh and G streets, N.W.,
            Washington, D.C.

            Mr. B. L. Mencken is dead.

                                        Habighurst.

Mr. Habighurst was my father's bookkeeper, and Mr. B. L. Mencken was my other grandfather, the progenitor, chief justice and captain general of all the American Menckenii. My grandfather Abhau was silent on the short trip back to Baltimore, and remained silent as we boarded a horse-car at Camden Station and rode out to Hollins street, our bags piled beside the driver. We got off at Stricker and Lombard streets, and made for the house across Union Square. As we came to the fishpond in the center of the square I saw that there was a black crêpe on the handle of the doorbell, in token of filial respect to the dead patriarch. The sight made me feel creepy, for that was the first crêpe I had ever seen on a Mencken doorbell. But I was only ten years old, and the emotions of boys of that age are not those of philosophers. For a brief instant, I suppose, I mourned my grandfather, but before we had crossed the cobblestones of Hollins street a vagrom and wicked thought ran through my head. I recognized its enormity instantly, but simply could not throttle it. The day was a Thursday—and they'd certainly not bury the old man until Sunday. No school * tomorrow!

NEWSPAPER DAYS
1899–1906

MAY 20, 1904

Preface

THE RECOLLECTIONS here embalmed, I should say at once, have nothing in common with the high, astounding tales of journalistic derring-do that had a considerable run several years ago, after the devourers of best-sellers had begun to tire of medical memoirs. In the second half of the period here covered I became a city editor, which is to say, a fellow of high mightiness in a newspaper office, and at the very end I was lifted by one of fate's ironies into even higher dignities, but the narrative has principally to do with my days as a reporter, when I was young, goatish and full of an innocent delight in the world. My adventures in that character, save maybe in one or two details, were hardly extraordinary; on the contrary they seem to me now, looking back upon them nostalgically, to have been marked by an excess of normalcy. Nevertheless, they had their moments—in fact, they were made up, subjectively, of one continuous, unrelenting, almost delirious moment—and when I revive them now it is mainly to remind myself and inform historians that a newspaper reporter, in those remote days, had a grand and gaudy time of it, and no call to envy any man.

In the long, busy years following I had experiences of a more profound and even alarming nature, and if the mood were on me I could fill a book with inside stuff almost fit to match the high, astounding tales aforesaid. I roamed, in the practise of my trade, from the river Jordan in the East to Hollywood in the West, and from the Orkney Islands in the North to Morocco and the Spanish Main in the South, and, like every other journalist, I met, listened to and smelled all sorts of magnificoes, including Presidents and Vice-Presidents, generals and admirals, bishops and archbishops, murderers and murderesses, geniuses both scientific and literary, movie and stage stars, heavyweight champions of the world, Class A and Class B royalties, judges and hangmen, millionaires and labor goons, and vast hordes of other notables, including most of the recognized Cæsars and Shakespeares of journalism. I edited both newspapers and magazines, some of them successes and some

of them not, and got a close, confidential view of the manner
in which opinion is formulated and merchanted on this earth.
My own contributions to the mess ran to millions of words,
and I came to know intimately many of its most revered con-
fectioners. More than once I have staggered out of editorial
conferences dripping cold sweat, and wondering dizzily how
God got along for so many years without the *New Republic*
and the Manchester *Guardian*. And at other times I have
marvelled that the human race did not revolt against the imposture, dig up the carcass of Johann Gutenberg, and heave it
to the buzzards and hyenas in some convenient zoo.

A newspaper man in active practise finds it hard to remain a
mere newspaper man: he is constantly beset by temptations to
try other activities, and if he manages to resist them it takes a
kind of fortitude that less protean men, badgered only by their
hormones and their creditors, never have need of. I was born,
happily, with no more public spirit than a cat, and have thus
found it relatively easy to throw off all the commoner lures,
but there have been times when the sirens fetched me clearly
below the belt, and I did some wobbling. In 1912, though no
one will ever believe it, I was groomed surreptitiously as a dark
horse for the Democratic Vice-Presidential nomination, and if
one eminent American statesman, *X*, had not got tight at the
last minute, and another, *Y*, kept unaccountably sober, I might
have become immortal. Two years later I was offered $30,000
cash, deposited in bank to my order, to write anti-Prohibition
speeches for the illiterates in the two Houses of Congress. A
little further on an Episcopal bishop asked me to tackle and try
to throw a nascent convert, female and rich, who had thrice
slipped out of his hands at the very brink of the font. Another
time the prophet of a new religion, then very prosperous in
the Middle West, offered to consecrate me as a bishop myself,
with power to bind and loose; and almost simultaneously I was
arrested on Boston Common on a charge of vending obscene
literature to the young gentlemen of Harvard. I have seen
something of the horrors of war, and much too much of the
worse horrors of peace. On five separate occasions I have been
offered the learned degree of *legum doctor*, though few men
are less learned in the law than I am, or have less respect for it;
and at other times I have been invited to come in and be

lynched by the citizens of three of the great Christian states of the Union.

Such prodigies and monstrosities I could pile up for hours, along with a lot of instructive blabbing about what this or that immortal once told me off the record, for I have had the honor of encountering three Presidents of the United States in their cups, not to mention sitting Governors of all the states save six. But I bear in mind Sir Thomas Overbury's sneer at the fellow who "chooseth rather to be counted a spy than not a politician, and maintains his reputation by naming great men familiarly," and so hold my peace: let some larval Ph.D. dig the dirt out of my papers marked "Strictly Private: Destroy Unread" after I shove off for bliss eternal. In the present book my only purpose is to try to recreate for myself, and for any one who may care to follow me, the gaudy life that young newspaper reporters led in the major American cities at the turn of the century. I believed then, and still believe today, that it was the maddest, gladdest, damndest existence ever enjoyed by mortal youth. At a time when the respectable bourgeois youngsters of my generation were college freshmen, oppressed by simian sophomores and affronted with balderdash daily and hourly by chalky pedagogues, I was at large in a wicked seaport of half a million people, with a front seat at every public show, as free of the night as of the day, and getting earfuls and eyefuls of instruction in a hundred giddy arcana, none of them taught in schools. On my twenty-first birthday, by all orthodox cultural standards, I probably reached my all-time low, for the heavy reading of my teens had been abandoned in favor of life itself, and I did not return seriously to the lamp until a time near the end of this record. But it would be an exaggeration to say that I was ignorant, for if I neglected the humanities I was meanwhile laying in all the worldly wisdom of a police lieutenant, a bartender, a shyster lawyer, or a midwife. And it would certainly be idiotic to say that I was not happy. The illusion that swathes and bedizens journalism, bringing in its endless squads of recruits, was still full upon me, and I had yet to taste the sharp teeth of responsibility. Life was arduous, but it was gay and carefree. The days chased one another like kittens chasing their tails.

Whether or not the young journalists of today live so

spaciously is a question that I am not competent to answer, for
my contacts with them, of late years, have been rather scanty.
They undoubtedly get a great deal more money than we did in
1900, but their freedom is much less than ours was, and they
somehow give me the impression, seen at a distance, of complacency rather than intrepidity. In my day a reporter who
took an assignment was wholly on his own until he got back to
the office, and even then he was little molested until his copy
was turned in at the desk; today he tends to become only a
homunculus at the end of a telephone wire, and the reduction
of his observations to prose is commonly farmed out to literary
castrati who never leave the office, and hence never feel the
wind of the world in their faces or see anything with their own
eyes. I well recall my horror when I heard, for the first time, of
a journalist who had laid in a pair of what were then called bicycle pants and taken to golf: it was as if I had encountered a
stud-horse with his hair done up in frizzes, and pink bowknots
peeking out of them. It seemed, in some vague way, ignominious, and even a bit indelicate. I was shocked almost as much
when I first heard of reporters joining labor unions, and describing themselves as wage slaves. The underlying ideology
here, of course, was anything but new, for I doubt that there
has ever been a competent reporter in history who did not regard the proprietors of his paper as sordid rascals, all dollars
and no sense. But it is one thing (a) to curl the lip over such
wretches, and quite another thing (b) to bellow and beat the
breast under their atrocities, just as it is one thing (a^2) to sass a
cruel city editor with, so to speak, the naked hands, and another thing (b^2) to confront him from behind a phalanx of
government agents and labor bravoes. The a operations are
easy to reconcile with the old-time journalist's concept of
himself as a free spirit and darling of the gods, licensed by his
high merits to ride and deride the visible universe; the b's must
suggest inevitably a certain unhappy self-distrust, perhaps not
without ground.

Like its companion volume, "Happy Days" (1940), this
book is mainly true, but with occasional stretchers. I have
checked my recollections whenever possible, and found them
reasonably accurate. For the rest, I must throw myself upon
the bosom of that "friendly and judicious reader" to whom

Charles Lamb dedicated the Essays of Elia—that understanding fellow, male or female, who refuses to take "everything perversely in the absolute and literal sense," but gives it "a fair construction, as to an after-dinner conversation."

BALTIMORE, 1941.   H. L. M.

Table of Contents

I.
Allegro Con Brio

M Y FATHER died on Friday, January 13, 1899, and was bur- *
ied on the ensuing Sunday. On the Monday evening
immediately following, having shaved with care and put on my
best suit of clothes, I presented myself in the city-room of the
old Baltimore *Morning Herald*, and applied to Max Ways, the
city editor, for a job on his staff. I was eighteen years, four
months and four days old, wore my hair longish and parted in
the middle, had on a high stiff collar and an Ascot cravat, and
weighed something on the minus side of 120 pounds. I was
thus hardly a spectacle to exhilarate a city editor, but Max was
an amiable fellow and that night he was in an extra-amiable
mood, for (as he told me afterward) there was a good dinner
under his belt, with a couple of globes of malt to wash it down,
and all of his reporters, so far as he was aware, were transiently
sober. So he received me very politely, and even cordially. Had
I any newspaper experience? The reply, alas, had to be no.
What was my education? I was a graduate of the Baltimore
Polytechnic. What considerations had turned my fancy toward
the newspaper business? All that I could say was that it seemed
to be a sort of celestial call: I was busting with literary ardors
and had been writing furiously for what, at eighteen, was almost an age—maybe four, or even five years. Writing what—
prose or verse? Both. Anything published? I had to play dead
here, for my bibliography, to date, was confined to a couple of
anonymous poems in the Baltimore *American*—a rival paper,
and hence probably not admired.

   Max looked me over ruminatively—I had been standing all
the while—and made the reply that city editors had been
making to young aspirants since the days of the first Washington hand-press. There was, unhappily, no vacancy on the staff.
He would take my name, and send for me in case some catastrophe unforeseen—and, as I gathered, almost unimaginable
—made one. I must have drooped visibly, for the kindly Max
at once thought of something better. Did I have a job? Yes, I

was working for my Uncle Henry, now the sole heir and assign of my father's old tobacco firm of Aug. Mencken & Bro. Well, I had better keep that job, but maybe it might be an idea for me to drop in now and then of an evening, say between seven thirty and seven forty-five. Nothing, of course, could be promised; in fact, the odds against anything turning up were appalling. But if I would present myself at appropriate intervals there might be a chance, if it were God's will, to try me out, soon or late, on something commensurate with my undemonstrated talents. Such trial flights, it was unnecessary to mention, carried no emolument. They added a lot to a city editor's already heavy cargo of cares and anxieties, and out of the many that were called only a few were ever chosen.

I retired nursing a mixture of disappointment and elation, but with the elation quickly besting the disappointment—and the next night, precisely at seven thirty-one, I was back. Max waved me away without parley: he was busy jawing an office-boy. The third night he simply shook his head, and so on the fourth, fifth, sixth and seventh. On the eighth—or maybe it was the ninth or tenth—he motioned me to wait while he finished thumbing through a pile of copy, and then asked suddenly: "Do you ever read the *Herald*?" When I answered yes, he followed with "What do you think of it?" This one had all the appearance of a trap, and my heart missed a couple of beats, but the holy saints were with me. "I think," I said, "that it is much better written than the *Sunpaper*." I was to learn later that Max smelled something artful here, but, as always, he held himself well, and all I could observe was the faint flutter of a smile across his face. At length he spoke. "Come back," he said, "tomorrow night."

I came back, you may be sure—and found him missing, for he had forgotten that it was his night off. The next night I was there again—and found him too busy to notice me. And so the night following, and the next, and the next. To make an end, this went on for four weeks, night in and night out, Mondays, Tuesdays, Wednesdays, Thursdays, Fridays, Saturdays and Sundays. A tremendous blizzard came down upon Baltimore, and for a couple of days the trolley-cars were stalled, but I hoofed it ever hopefully to the *Herald* office, and then hoofed it sadly home. There arrived eventually, after what seemed a geological epoch by my calendar, the evening of Thursday, February 23, 1899. I found Max reading copy, and for a few minutes he did not see me. Then his eyes lifted, and he said casually: "Go out to Govanstown, and see if anything is happening there. We are supposed to have a Govanstown correspondent, but he hasn't been heard from for six days."

The percussion must have been tremendous, for I remember nothing about getting to Govanstown. It is now a part of Baltimore, but in 1899 it was only a country village, with its own life and tribulations. No cop was in sight when I arrived, but I found the volunteer firemen playing pinochle in their engine-house. The blizzard had blockaded their front door with a drift fifteen feet high, but they had dug themselves out, and were now lathering for a fire, though all the water-plugs in the place were still frozen. They had no news save their hopes. Across the glacier of a street I saw two lights—a bright one in a drugstore and a dim one in a funeral parlor. The undertaker, like nearly all the rest of Govanstown, was preparing to go to bed, and when I routed him out and he came downstairs in his pants and undershirt it was only to say that he had no professional business in hand. The druggist, hugging a red-hot egg-stove behind his colored bottles, was more productive. The town cop, he said, had just left in a two-horse buggy to assist in a horse-stealing case at Kingsville, a long drive out the Belair pike, and the Improved Order of Red Men had postponed their oyster-supper until March 6. When I got back to the *Herald* office, along toward eleven o'clock, Max instructed me to forget the Red Men and write the horse-stealing. There was a vacant desk in a far corner, and at it, for ten minutes, I wrote and tore up, wrote and tore up. Finally there emerged the following:

A horse, a buggy and several sets of harness, valued in all at about $250, were stolen last night from the stable of Howard Quinlan, near Kingsville. The county police are at work on the case, but so far no trace of either thieves or booty has been found.

Max gave only a grunt to my copy, but as I was leaving the office, exhausted but exultant, he called me back, and handed me a letter to the editor demanding full and friendly publicity, on penalty of a boycott, for an exhibition of what was then called a kinetoscope or cineograph. "A couple of lines," he said, "will be enough. Nearly everybody has seen a cineograph by now." I wrote:

At Otterbein Memorial U.B. Church, Roland and Fifth avenues, Hampden, Charles H. Stanley and J. Albert Loose entertained a large audience last night with an exhibition of war scenes by the cineograph.

I was up with the milkman the next morning to search the paper, and when I found both of my pieces, exactly as written, there ran such thrills through my system as a barrel of brandy and 100,000 volts of electricity could not have matched. Somehow or other I must have done my duty by Aug. Mencken & Bro., for my uncle apparently noticed nothing, but certainly my higher cerebral centers were not focussed on them. That night I got to the *Herald* office so early that Max had not come back from dinner. When he appeared he looked me over thoughtfully, and suggested that it might be a good plan to try my talents on a village adjacent to Govanstown, Waverly by name. It was, he observed, a poor place, full of Methodists and Baptists who seldom cut up, but now and then a horse ran away or a pastor got fired. Reaching it after a long search in the snow, and raking it from end to end, I turned up two items— one an Epworth League entertainment, and the other a lecture for nearby farmers, by title (I have the clipping before me), "Considering the Present Low Price of Hay, Would It Not Be Advisable to Lessen the Acreage of Hay for Market?" Max showed no enthusiasm for either, but after I had finished writing them he handed me an amateur press-agent's handout about a new Quaker school and directed me to rewrite it. It made twenty-eight lines in the paper next morning, and lifted me beyond the moon to Orion. On the night following Max introduced me to two or three reporters, and told them that I was a youngster trying for a job. My name, he said, was Macon. They greeted me with considerable reserve.

Of the weeks following I recall definitely but one thing—that I never seemed to get enough sleep. I was expected to report at the cigar factory of Aug. Mencken & Bro. at eight o'clock every morning, which meant that I had to turn out at seven. My day there ran officially to five thirty, but not infrequently my uncle detained me to talk about family affairs, for my father had died intestate and his estate was in process of administration, with two sets of lawyers discovering mare's nests from time to time. Thus it was often six o'clock before I escaped, and in the course of the next hour or so I had to get home, change my clothes, bolt my dinner, and return downtown to the *Herald* office. For a couple of weeks Max kept me at my harrying of the remoter suburbs—a job, as I afterward learned, as distasteful to ripe reporters as covering a fashionable church-wedding or a convention of the W.C.T.U. I ranged from Catonsville in the far west to Back River in the east, and from Tuxedo Park in the north to Mt. Winans in the south. Hour after hour I rode the suburban trolleys, and one night, as I recall uncomfortably over all these years, my fares at a nickel a throw came to sixty cents, which was more than half my day's pay from Aug. Mencken & Bro. Max had said nothing about an expense account, and I was afraid to ask. Once, returning from a dismal village called Gardenville, a mile or two northeast of the last electric light, I ventured to ask him how far my diocese ran in that direction. "You are supposed to keep on out the road," he said, "until you meet the Philadelphia reporters coming in." This was an ancient Baltimore newspaper wheeze, but it was new to me, and I was to enjoy it a great deal better when I heard it worked off on my successors.

But my exploration of the fringes of Baltimore, though it came near being exhaustive, was really not long drawn out, for in a little while Max began to hand me city assignments of the kind that no one else wanted—installations of new evangelical pastors, meetings of wheelmen, interviews with bores just back from Europe, the Klondike or Oklahoma, orgies of one sort or another at the Y.M.C.A., minor political rallies, concerts, funerals, and so on. Most of my early clippings perished in the great Baltimore fire of 1904, but a few survived, and I find from them that I covered a number of stories that would seem as antediluvian today as a fight between two brontosauri—for example, the showing of a picture-play by Alexander Black (a series of lantern-slides with a thin thread of banal recitative), and a chalk-talk by Frank Beard. When it appeared that I knew something of music, I was assigned to a long series of organ recitals in obscure churches, vocal and instrumental recitals in even more obscure halls, and miscellaneous disturbances of the peace in lodge-rooms and among the German singing societies. Within the space of two weeks I heard one violinist, then very popular in Baltimore, play Raff's Cavatina no less than eight times. The *Herald*'s music critic in those days, an Englishman named W. G. Owst, was a very indolent fellow, and when he discovered that I could cover such uproars without making any noticeable bulls, he saw to it that I got more and more of them. Finally, I was entrusted with an assault upon Mendelssohn's "Elijah" by the Baltimore Oratorio Society—and suffered a spasm of stage fright that was cured by dropping into the Pratt Library before the performance, and doing a little precautionary reading.

Thus the Winter ran into Spring, and I began to think of myself as almost a journalist. So far, to be sure, I had been entrusted with no spot news, and Max had never sent me out to help a regular member of the staff, but he was generous with his own advice, and I quickly picked up the jargon and ways of thought of the city-room. In this acclimatization I was aided by the device that had helped me to fathom Mendelssohn's "Elijah" and has always been my recourse in time of difficulty: what I couldn't learn otherwise I tried to learn by reading. Unhappily, the almost innumerable texts on journalism that now serve aspirants were then still unwritten, and I could find, in fact, only one formal treatise on the subject at the Pratt Library. It was "Steps Into Journalism," by E. L. Shuman of the Chicago *Tribune*, and though it was a primitive in its class it was very clearly and sensibly written, and I got a great deal of useful information out of it. Also, I read all of the newspaper fiction then on paper—for example, Richard Harding Davis's "Gallegher and Other Stories," Jesse Lynch Williams's "The Stolen Story and Other Stories," and Elizabeth G. Jordan's "Tales of the City-Room," the last two of which had but lately come out.[1]

How I found time for this reading I can't tell you, for I was kept jumping by my two jobs, but find it I did. One night,

[1]It must have been a little later that I read "With Kitchener to Khartoum," "From Capetown to Ladysmith" and the other books of George W. Steevens, of the London *Mail*. They made a powerful impression on me, and I still believe that Steevens was the greatest newspaper reporter who ever lived.

sitting in the city-room waiting for an assignment, I fell asleep, and the thoughtful Max suggested that I take one night off a week, and mentioned Sunday. The next Sunday I stayed in bed until noon, and returned to it at 8 P.M., and thereafter I was ready for anything. As the Spring drifted on my assignments grew better and better, and when the time came for high-school commencements I covered all of them. There were five in those days, beginning with that of the City College and ending with that of the Colored High-school, and I heard the Mayor of Baltimore unload precisely the same speech at each. Max, who knew the man, complimented me on making his observations sound different every time, and even more or less intelligent, and I gathered the happy impression that my days as an unpaid volunteer were nearing their end. But a city editor of that costive era, at least in Baltimore, could take on a new man only by getting rid of an old one, and for a month or so longer I had to wait. Finally, some old-timer or other dropped out, and my time had come. Max made a little ceremony of my annunciation, though no one else was present. My salary, he said, would be $7 a week, with the hope of an early lift to $8 if I made good. I would have the use of a book of passes on the trolley-cars, and might turn in expense-accounts to cover any actual outlays. There was, at the moment, no typewriter available for me, but he had hopes of extracting one from Nachman, the business manager, in the near future. This was followed by some good advice. *Imprimis*, never trust a cop: whenever possible, verify his report. *Item*, always try to get in early copy: the first story to reach the city-desk has a much better chance of being printed in full than the last. *Item*, be careful about dates, names, ages, addresses, figures of every sort. *Item*, keep in mind at all times the dangers of libel. Finally, don't be surprised if you go to a house for information, and are invited to lift it from the *Sun* of the next morning. "The *Sun* is the Bible of Baltimore, and has almost a monopoly on many kinds of news. But don't let that fact discourage you. You can get it too if you dig hard enough, and always remember this: any *Herald* reporter who is worth a damn can write rings around a *Sun* reporter."

This last was very far from literally true, as I was to discover when I came to cover stories in competition with such *Sun*

reporters as Dorsey Guy and Harry West, but there was nevertheless a certain plausibility in it, for the *Sun* laid immense
stress upon accuracy, and thus fostered a sober, matter-of-fact
style in its men. The best of them burst through those tram-
mels, but the rank and file tended to write like bookkeepers. As
for Max, he greatly favored a more imaginative and colorful
manner. He had been a very good reporter himself, with not
only a hand for humor but also a trick of pathos, and he tried
to inspire his slaves to the same. Not many of them were equal
to the business, but all of them save a few poor old automata
tried, and as a result the *Herald* was rather briskly written, and
its general direction was toward the New York *Sun*, then still
scintillating under the impulse of Charles A. Dana, rather than
toward the Baltimore *Sun* and the *Congressional Record*. It was
my good fortune, during my first week on the staff, to turn up
the sort of story that Max liked especially—the sudden death
of a colored street preacher on the street, in the midst of a
hymn. I was not present at the ringside, and had to rely on the
cops for the facts, but I must have got a touch of drama into
my report, for Max was much pleased, and gave me, as a reward, a pass to a performance of Rose Sydell's London Blondes.

I had gathered from the newspaper fiction mentioned a few
pages back that the typical American city editor was a sort of
cross between an ice-wagon driver and a fire-alarm, "full of
strange oaths" and imprecations, and given to firing whole files
of men at the drop of a hat. But if that monster actually existed
in the Republic, it was surely not in the Baltimore *Herald* office. Max, of course, was decently equipped for his art and
mystery: he could swear loudly enough on occasion and had a
pretty hand for shattering invective, but most of the time, even
when he was sorely tried, he kept to good humor and was polite to one and all. Whenever I made a mess of a story, which
was certainly often enough, he summoned me to his desk and
pointed out my blunders. When I came in with a difficult story,
confused and puzzled, he gave me quick and clear directions,
and they always straightened me out. Observing his operations
with the sharp eyes of youth, I began to understand the curious equipment required of a city editor. He had to be an incredible amalgam of army officer and literary critic, diplomat
and jail warden, psychologist and fortune-teller. If he could

not see around corners and through four or five feet of brick he was virtually blind, and if he could not hear overtones audible normally only to dogs and children he was almost deaf. His knowledge of his town, as he gathered experience, combined that of a police captain, an all-night hackman, and a priest in a rowdy parish. He was supposed to know the truth about everyone and everything, even though he seldom printed it, and one of his most useful knowledges—in fact, he used it every day—was his knowledge of the most probable whereabouts of every person affected with a public interest, day or night.

Max had these skills, and many more. How he would have made out on the larger papers of a later period, with their incessant editions, I do not attempt to guess, but in his time and place he was a very competent man, and had the respect as well as the affection of his staff. In person he was of middle height, with light hair that was beginning to fall out, and an equator that had already begun to bulge. What remained of his hair he wore longish, in what was then called the football style. He affected rolling collars, and sometimes wore a Windsor tie. His colored shirts, in the manner of the day, were ironed to shine like glass, and his clothes were of somewhat advanced cut. We younger reporters modelled ourselves upon him in dress as in mien. The legends that played about him were mainly not of a professional nature, but romantic. He was a bachelor, and was supposed to be living in sin with a beautiful creature who occasionally took a drop too much, and exposed him to the embarrassment of her caterwauling. Whether or not that creature had any actual existence I can't tell you: all I can say is that I never saw her, and that the only time I ever visited Max in his quarters (he was laid up with pink-eye) I found him living *a cappella* upstairs of a French restaurant, and waited on by the proprietor's well-seasoned and far from aphrodisiac wife.[2]

---

[2]When he quit the *Herald* Max went into politics, and lived to be one of the Democratic bosses of Baltimore. But the first time he ran for elective office he was beaten, mainly, so it was reported, because many voters assumed from his name that he was a Jew, and others suspected that he might even be a Chinaman. He was actually of Scotch-Irish, Welsh, English and Pennsylvania German stock. He later married the charming secretary of the Governor of Maryland, and became the father of a son and a daughter who followed him into the newspaper business. He died in 1923.

It was a pleasant office that I found myself entering. Many of the reporters, to be sure, were rummy old-timers who were of small ability and no diligence, but they were all at least amiable fellows, and working beside them were some youngsters of superior quality. The *Herald* Building was new, and its fifth-floor city-room was one of the most comfortable and convenient that I have ever seen, even to this day. But in many respects it would seem primitive now: it had, for example, but two telephones—one belonging to each of the two companies that then fought for subscribers in Baltimore. Both were Paleozoic instruments attached to the wall, and no one ever used them if it could be avoided. There was no telephone on the city editor's desk until my own time in that office, beginning in 1903. The office library, save for a dog's-eared encyclopedia with several volumes missing, was made up wholly of government reports, and the only man who ever used it was an old fellow who had the job of compiling cattle and provision prices. He finished work every day at about 5 P.M. and spent an hour reading in the encyclopedia. There was no index of the paper, and no office morgue. The city editor kept a clipping file of his own, and when it failed him he had to depend upon the shaky memories of the older reporters.

The city staff, save for such early birds as the court reporter, came to work at half an hour after noon, and every man was responsible for his bailiwick until 11 at night. The city editor himself began work an hour earlier and worked an hour or so later. There were no bulldogs or other early editions. The first mail edition did not close until after midnight. In consequence, there was no hurry about getting stories on paper, except very late ones. Rewrite men were unheard of. Every reporter, no matter how remote the scene of his story, came back to the office and wrote it himself. If he lagged, his copy was taken from him page by page, and he was urged on by the grunting and growling of the city editor, who was his own chief copyreader, and usually wrote the head on the leading local story of the night. A great deal of copy was still written by hand, for there were not enough typewriters in the office to go round, and every time Nachman, the business manager, was asked to buy another he went on like a man stabbed with poniards. But every reporter had a desk, and every desk was equipped with a spittoon. This was a great convenience to me, for I had acquired the sinful habit of tobacco-chewing in my father's cigar factory, and am, in fact, still more or less in its loathsome toils.

The office was kept pretty clean by Bill Christian, a barber who had got the job of building superintendent because Colonel Cunningham, the managing editor, liked his tonsorial touch. Bill was allergic to work himself, but he rode herd diligently on his staff of colored scavengers, and the whole editorial floor was strangely spick and span for that time. Even the colonel's own den was excavated at least twice a month, and its accumulation of discarded newspapers hauled out. Bill failed, however, to make any progress against the army of giant cockroaches that had moved in when the building was opened, three or four years before. On dull nights the copy-readers would detail office-boys to corral half a dozen of these monsters, and then race them across the city-room floor, guiding them with walking-sticks. The sport required some skill, for if a jockey pressed his nag too hard he was apt to knock off its hind legs.

II.
Drill for a Rookie

M Y FIRST regular assignment as a reporter was South Baltimore, or, to speak technically, the Southern police district. It was, as I shall remark again in Chapter XVIII, a big
territory, and there was always something doing in it, but
though my memories of it are copious and melodramatic, I
must have spent only a few weeks in it, for by the end of the
Spring, as I find by a promenade through the *Herald*'s files, I
was covering Aframerican razor-parties in the Northwestern,
which was almost as black as Mississippi, and making occasional dips into the Western, which embraced the largest and
busiest of Baltimore's five Tenderloins.

In those days a reporter who had durable legs and was reasonably sober tended to see a varied service, for it was not unusual for one of his elders to succumb to the jug and do a
vanishing act. More than once during my first weeks, after
turning in my own budget of assaults, fires, drownings and
other such events from the Southern, I was sent out at eleven
o'clock at night to find a lost colleague of the Eastern or
Northeastern, and pump his news out of him, if he had any. It
* was by the same route, in July, that I found myself promoted
to the Central, which was the premier Baltimore district, jour-
nalistically speaking, for it included the busiest of the police
courts, a downtown hospital, police headquarters, the city jail,
and the morgue. The regular man there had turned up at the
office one noon so far gone in rum that Max relieved him of
duty, and I was gazetted to his place as a means of shaming
him, for I was still the youngest reporter in the office. When he
continued in his cups the day following I was retained as his
locum tenens, and when he went on to a third day he was reduced to the Northern police district, the Siberia of Baltimore,
and I found myself his heir.

This man, though we eventually became good friends, resented his demotion so bitterly that for weeks he refused to
speak to me, but I was too busy in my new bailiwick to pay any

attention to him. Its police court was the liveliest in town, and had the smartest and most colorful magistrate, Gene Grannan by name. He was always willing to help the press by developing the dramatic content of the cases before him, and during my first week he thus watered and manured for me a couple of stories that delighted Max, and boosted my own stock. Such stories were almost a *Herald* monopoly, for *Sun* reporters were hobbled by their paper's craze for mathematical accuracy, and most *American* reporters were too stupid to recognize good stuff when they saw it. Max helped by inventing likely minor assignments for me, and one of them I still remember. It was a wedding in a shabby street given over to second-hand shops run by Polish Jews and patronized by sailors. The bride had written in demanding publicity, and I was sent to see her— partly as a means of gently hazing a freshman, but also on the chance that there might be a picturesque story in her. In the filthy shop downstairs her father directed me to the second floor, and when I climbed the stairs I found her in process of being dressed by her mother. She was standing in the middle of the floor with nothing on save a diaphanous vest and a flouncy pair of drawers. Never having seen a bride so close to the altogether before, I was somewhat upset, but she and her mother were quite calm, and loaded me with all the details of the impending ceremony. I wrote the story at length, but Max stuck it on his "If" hook, and there it died.

But such romantic interludes were not frequent. My days, like those of any other police reporter, were given over mainly to harsher matters—murders, assaults and batteries, street accidents, robberies, suicides, and so on. I well recall my first suicide, for the victim was a lovely young gal who had trusted a preacher's son too far, and then swallowed poison: she looked almost angelic lying on her parlor floor, with a couple of cops badgering her distracted mother. I remember, too, my first autopsy at the morgue—a most trying recreation for a hot Summer day—, and my first palaver with a burglar, and my first ride with the cops in a patrol-wagon, but for some reason or other my first murder has got itself forgotten. The young doctors at the City Hospital (now the Mercy Hospital) were always productive, for they did a heavy trade in street and factory accidents, and a very fair one in attempted suicides. In those days carbolic acid was the favorite drug among persons who yearned for the grave, just as bichloride of mercury was to be the favorite of a decade later, and I saw many of its customers brought in—their lips swollen horribly, and their eyes full of astonishment that they were still alive. Also, I saw people with their legs cut off, their arms torn off, their throats cut, their eyes gouged out. It was shocking for a little while, but then no more. Attached to the City Hospital was the first Pasteur Institute ever set up in America, and to it came patients from all over the South. It was in charge of an old doctor named Keirle, and usually he managed to save them, but now and then one of them reached him too late, and died of rabies in frightful agony. He let me in on several of these death scenes, with the poor patient strapped to the bed and the nurses stepping warily. When the horror became unendurable the old doctor would take over with his hypodermic. He was a humane and admirable man, one of the few actual altruists that I have ever known, and I marvel that the Baltimore which has monuments to the founder of the Odd Fellows and to the president of a third-rate railroad has never thought to honor itself by erecting one to his memory.

On July 28, 1899, when I was precisely eighteen years, ten
* months and sixteen days old, I saw my first hanging; more, it was a hanging of the very first chop, for no less than four poor blackamoors were stretched at once. When I was assigned to it as legman for one of the older reporters I naturally suffered certain unpleasant forebodings, but the performance itself did not shake me, though one of the condemned lost his black cap in going through the trap, and the contortions of his face made a dreadful spectacle. The affair was staged in the yard of the city jail, and there was a large gathering of journalists, some of them from other cities, for quadruple hangings, then as now, were fancy goods. I went through the big iron gate at 5 A.M., and found that at least a dozen colleagues had been on watch all night. Some of them had sustained themselves with drafts from a bottle, and were already wobbling. When, after hours of howling by relays of colored evangelists, the four candidates were taken out and hanged, two of these bibbers and six or eight other spectators fell in swoons, and had to be
* evacuated by the cops. The sheriff of Baltimore was required

by law to spring the trap, and he had prepared himself for that office by resorting to a bottle of his own. When it was performed he was assisted out of the jail yard by his deputies, and departed at once for Atlantic City, where he dug in for a week of nightmare.

I saw a good many hangings after that, some in Baltimore and the rest in the counties of Maryland. The county sheriffs always took aboard so much liquor for the occasion that they were virtually helpless: they could, with some help, pull the trap, but they were quite unable to tie the knot, bind the candidate, or carry off the other offices of the occasion. These were commonly delegated to Joe Heine, a gloomy German who had been chief deputy sheriff in Baltimore for many years, and was such a master of all the technics of his post that no political upheaval could touch him. So far as I know, Joe never actually put a man to death in his life, for that was the duty of the sheriff, but he traveled the counties tying knots and making the condemned ready, and there was never a slip when he officiated. I missed the great day of his career, which fell in 1904 or thereabout, for I was becoming bored with hangings by that time, and when a nearby county sheriff invited me to one as his private guest and well-wisher, I gave my ticket to my brother Charlie. This was Charlie's first experience and he saw a swell show indeed, for the candidate, a colored giant, fought Joe and the sheriff on the scaffold, knocked out the county cops who came to their aid, leaped down into the bellowing crowd, broke out of the jail yard, and took to an adjacent forest. It was an hour or more before he was run down and brought back. By that time all the fight had oozed out of him, and Joe and the sheriff turned him off with quiet elegance.

But a reporter chiefly remembers, not such routine themes of his art as hangings, fires and murders, which come along with dispiriting monotony, but the unprecedented novelties that occasionally inspire him, some of them gorgeous and others only odd. Perhaps the most interesting story I covered in my first six months had to do with the purloining of a cadaver from a medical college. The burglar was the head *Diener* of the dissecting-room, and he packed the body in a barrel and shipped it to a colleague in the upper Middle West, where there was a shortage of such provisions at the time. Hot weather coming on *en route*, it was discovered, and for a week we had a gaudy murder mystery. When the *Diener* shut off the uproar by confessing, it turned out that the maximum punishment he could be given, under the existing Maryland law, passed in 1730, was sixty days in the House of Correction. On his return to duty the medical students welcomed him with a beer party that lasted forty-eight hours, and he boasted that he had been stealing and shipping bodies for years. But the cops, discouraged, did nothing about it.

At a somewhat later time, after I had forsaken police reporting, the moral inadequacy of the ancient Maryland statutes was revealed again. This time the culprit was a Methodist clergyman who operated one of the vice crusades that then afflicted all the big cities of the East. The cops, of course, were violently against him, for they could see nothing wrong about honest women making honest livings according to their talents. When the pastor charged that they pooh-poohed him because they were taking bribes from the girls they determined to get him, and to that end sneaked a spy into the Y.M.C.A. One night soon afterward the pastor visited the place with a Christian young man, and the spy, concealed in a cupboard, caught the two in levantine deviltries. The former was collared at once, and the State's attorney sent for. Unhappily, he had to advise the poor cops that the acts they laid to their prisoner were not forbidden by Maryland law, which was singularly tolerant in sexual matters. The maximum penalty it then provided for adultery, however brutal and deliberate, was $10 fine, with no alternative of imprisonment, and there was no punishment at all for fornication, or for any of its non-Euclidian variations. The cops were thus stumped, but they quickly resolved their dilemma by concealing it from the scared pastor, and giving him two hours to get out of town. He departed leaving a wife and five children behind him, and has never been heard from since. The Legislature being in session, the cops then went to Annapolis and begged it to sharpen the laws. It responded by forbidding, under heavy penalties, a list of offenses so long and so bizarre that some of them are not even recorded in Krafft-Ebing.

I myself, while still assigned to the Central district, covered a case that well illustrated the humanity of the old Maryland

statute. The accused was a man who had run away from Pittsburgh with another man's wife, and they had come to Baltimore in the drawing-room of a sleeper. The lady's husband,
having got wind of their flight, wired ahead, asking the cops to
arrest the pair on their arrival. The cops refused to collar an
apparently respectable female on any such charge, but they
brought in the man, and he was arraigned before Gene Grannan. As a matter of law, his guilt had to be presumed, for the
Court of Appeals of Maryland had decided only a little while
before that when a man and a woman went into a room together and locked the door it would be insane to give them
the benefit of the doubt. Moreover, the prisoner, advised by a
learned police-station lawyer, admitted the charge freely, and
confined his defense to swearing that the crime had not been
committed until after the train crossed the Maryland line. If he
were sent back to Pennsylvania for trial he would be in serious
difficulties, for the penalty for adultery there was almost as
drastic as that for arson or piracy, but in Maryland, as I have
said, it was a mere misdemeanor, comparable to breaking a
window or spitting on the sidewalk. Grannan doubted the
truth of the defense, but decided that a humane judge would
have to accept it, so he fined the culprit $2, and the pair re-
sumed their honeymoon with loud hosannas. When a Pennsylvania cop showed up the next day with extradition papers he
was baffled, for the man had been tried and punished, and
could not be put in jeopardy again.

Grannan held a session of his court every afternoon, and I
always attended it. It was seldom, indeed, that he did not turn
up something that made good copy. He had been, before his
judicial days, chief of the Baltimore & Ohio's railroad police, *
and thus had a wide acquaintance among professional criminals, especially yeggmen, and held the professional respect of
the cops. In that remote era there was no file of finger-prints at
Washington, and even the Bertillon system was just coming
into use. The cops, in consequence, sometimes picked up an
eminent felon without knowing who he was. But if he came
before Grannan he was identified at once, and started through
a mill that commonly landed him in the Maryland Penitentiary.
That institution, which occupied a fine new building near the
city jail, then had as its warden a reformed politician named

* John Weyler. He had been a tough baby in his day, and was even suspected of a hand in a homicide, but when I knew him he had said goodbye to all that, and was an excellent officer. I dropped in on him two or three times a week, and usually picked up something worth printing. He had a strange peculiarity: he never came outside the prison walls save when it was raining. Then he would wander around for hours, and get himself soaked to the skin, for he never used an umbrella. Once a month his board of visitors met at the Penitentiary, and he entertained the members at dinner. These dinners gradually took on lavishness and gaiety, and during one of them a member of the board, searching for a place marked "Gents," fell down the main staircase of the place and had to be sent to hospital. After that Weyler limited the drinks to ten or twelve a head.

Another good source of the kind of news that Max Ways liked was old fellow named Hackman, the superintendent of the morgue. The morgue was housed in an ancient building at the end of one of the city docks, and Hackman seldom left it. There was a sort of derrick overhanging the water, and on it the harbor cops would pull up the floaters that they found, and let them dry. Some of them were covered with crabs and barnacles when they were brought in, and Hackman had a long pole for knocking such ornaments off. How greatly he loved his vocation was shown when a new health commissioner fired him, and he refused to give up his keys. The health commissioner thereupon called for a squad of cops, and went down to the morgue to take possession by force, followed by a trail of reporters. But Hackman was defiant, and when firemen were sent for to aid the cops, he barricaded himself among his clients, and declared that he would never be taken alive.

The ensuing battle went on all afternoon, and was full of thrills. The cops refused to resort to firearms and the firemen refused to knock down the door with their hose, so Hackman seemed destined to hold out forever. Every now and then he would open the door for a few inches, and howl fresh defiance at the health commissioner. Finally, one of the reporters, Frank R. Kent, of the *Sun*, sneaked up along the wall, and thrust in his foot the next time the door was opened. Before Hackman could hack Kent's foot off the cops rushed him, and the

morgue was taken. The poor old fellow burst into tears as he
was being led away. The morgue, he wailed, was his only solace, almost his only life; he had devoted years to its upkeep
and improvement, and was proud of its high standing among
the morgues of Christendom. Moreover, many of the sponges,
cloths and other furnishings within, including the pole he used
to delouse floaters, were his personal property, and he was
being robbed of them. The health commissioner promised to
restore them, and so Hackman faded from the scene, a victim
to a Philistine society that could not fathom his peculiar ideals.

There were press-agents in those days as in these, and
though they had not reached the dizzy virtuosity now on tap
they nevertheless showed a considerable ingenuity and daring.
One of the best I encountered in my first years remains unhappily nameless in my memory, though I well recall some of his
feats. He slaved for Frank Bostock, a big, blond, tweedy, John
Bullish Englishman who had leased an old cyclorama in Baltimore and put in a wild animal show. Even before the doors
were open the agent bombarded the local newspapers with
bulletins worthy of the best tradition of Tody Hamilton, press-
agent for P. T. Barnum—battles between tigers and boa con-
strictors, the birth of infant giraffes and kangaroos, the sayings
of a baboon who could speak Swahili, and so on. When, after
the opening, business turned out to be bad, he spit on his
hands, and turned off some masterpieces. The one I remember
best was the hanging of a rogue elephant, for I was assigned to
cover it. This elephant, we were informed, had become so or-
nery that he could be endured no longer, and it was necessary
to put him to death. Ordinarily, he would be shot, but Bostock, as a patriotic and law-abiding Englishman, preferred
hanging, and would serve as executioner himself.

The butchery of the poor beast—he looked very mangey
and feeble—was carried out one morning in the Bolton street
railroad yards. First his legs were tied together, and then a
thick hawser was passed around his neck and pulled tight, and
the two ends were fastened to the hook of a railroad crane.
When Bostock gave the signal the crane began to grind, and in
a few minutes the elephant was in the air. He took it very quietly, and was pronounced dead in half an hour. A large crowd
saw the ceremony, and after that business at the Bostock zoo

picked up. The press-agent got rid of the S.P.C.A. by announcing that the elephant had been given six ounces of morphine to dull his sensations. His remains were presented to the Johns Hopkins Medical School for scientific study, but no one there was interested in proboscidean anatomy, so they finally reached a glue factory.

Six months later the Bostock zoo gave the Baltimore newspapers a good story without any effort by its press-agent. On a cold Winter night, with six inches of sleet in the streets, it took fire, and in a few minutes all its major inmates were burned to death and the small fry were at large. The pursuit of the latter went on all night and all the next day, and the cops turned up an occasional frost-bitten monkey as much as a week later. No really dangerous animal got loose, but the town was in a state of terror for weeks, and many suburban dogs, mistaken for lions or tigers, were done to death by vigilantes. I recall picking up a powerful cold by wallowing around the night of the fire in the icy slush.

But the best of all the Baltimore press-agents of that age was a volunteer who worked for the sheer love of the science. His name was Frank Thomas, and he was the son of a contractor engaged in building a new courthouse. There were to be ten or twelve huge marble pillars in the façade of the building, and they had to be brought in from a quarry at Cockeysville, fourteen miles away. The hauling was done on trucks drawn by twenty horses. One day a truck lost a wheel and the pillar aboard was broken across the middle. Frank announced at once that a fossil dog had been found in the fracture, and supported the tale by having a crude dog painted on it and the whole photographed. That photograph made both the *Herald* and the *American*, though the suspicious *Sunpaper* sniffed at it. It took the geologists at the Johns Hopkins a week to convince the town that there could be no canine fossils in sedimentary rocks. A bit later Frank made it known that the new courthouse would be fitted with a contraption that would suck up all sounds coming in from the streets, and funnel them out through the sewers. In his handout he described eloquently the comfort of judges and juries protected against the noises of traffic and trade, and the dreadful roar of the accumulated sounds as they emerged from the sewers along the waterfront.

Frank indulged himself in many other inventions, and I handled most of them for the *Herald*, for the courthouse was in
my parish. When the building was finished at last he published
an illustrated souvenir book on it, and I wrote the 8000 words
of its text. My honorarium was $25.

His days, alas, were not all beer and skittles, for putting up a
large building in the heart of a busy city is a job shot through
with cephalalgia. While it was under way a high board fence
surrounded it, and on that fence were all the usual advertising
signs, most of them hideous. The *Herald* started a violent
crusade against them, arguing that they disgraced the courthouse and affronted all decent people. I was assigned by Max
Ways to write some of the indignant stories we printed, and
thus I met Frank in the dual rôle of friend of his fancy and
enemy of his fence. So far as I could make out, the *Herald*'s
crusade had no support whatsoever in public sentiment—in
fact, it became more and more difficult to find anyone to en-
dorse it—but it roared on for months. The fence came down
at last at least three or four weeks later than it would have
come down if there had been no hullabaloo, for Frank had
iron in him as well as imagination, and held out defiantly as
long as he could.

It was a crusading time, with uplifters of a hundred schools
harrying every major American city, and every newspaper of
any pretensions took a hand in the dismal game. I recall crusades against sweat-shops, against the shanghaiing of men for
the Chesapeake oyster fleet, and against dance-halls that paid
their female interns commissions on the drinks sold. I had a
hand in all of them, and if they filled me with doubts they also
gave me some exhilarating experiences. With the cops I toured
the bastiles of the waterfront crimps, and examined the jails
that they maintained for storing their poor bums, and with
health department inspectors I saw all the worst sweat-shops of
the town, including one in which a huge flock of hens was kept
hard at work laying eggs in a filthy cellar. In the war upon
bawdy dance-halls I became a witness, unwillingly, against the
cops, for I was put on the stand to testify that I had seen two
detectives in one of them, and that the detectives must have
been aware of what was going on. The poor flatfeet were unquestionably guilty, for I had discussed the matter with them

in the place, but I managed to sophisticate my testimony with so many ifs and buts that it went for nothing, and they were acquitted by the police board. That was my first and last experience as an active agent of moral endeavor. I made up my mind at once that my true and natural allegiance was to the Devil's party, and it has been my firm belief ever since that all persons who devote themselves to forcing virtue on their fellow men deserve nothing better than kicks in the pants. Years later I put that belief into a proposition which I ventured to call Mencken's Law, to wit:

Whenever *A* annoys or injures *B* on the pretense of saving or improving *X, A* is a scoundrel.

The moral theologians, unhappily, have paid no heed to this contribution to their science, and so Mencken's Law must wait for recognition until the dawn of a more enlightened age.

III.

Sergeant's Stripes

W HEN I project my mind back into space and time it gathers in more pictures from my days as a police reporter than from any other period, and they have more color in them, and a keener sense of delight. But they were actually not long, for before I had been on the *Herald* staff a year I was promoted out of the world of common or dirt felony and assigned to cover the more subtle skullduggeries of the City Hall. This promotion was surely not to be sniffed at, for the City Hall assignment was then regarded by all reporters as something choice and important, and is so regarded, in fact, to this day. Moreover, it gave me more chance to shine than I had had in police work, and so got me frequent offers from the other Baltimore papers, and jacked up my salary on the *Herald*. I find by an old account-book that my first raise from $7 to $8 a week was not lifted to $10 until the beginning of 1900, but during the ensuing Summer I was promoted to $14, in December to $16, and in February, 1901, to $18. But during my first weeks in the City Hall I was homesick for Gene Grannan and the cops, the jail and the morgue. I was still very green—indeed, much greener than I was aware of in my youthful vanity—and it took me some time to fathom the art of handling politicians. Even the ordinary routine of City Hall reporting was full of snares, and I fell into some of them.

One fetched me on my very first day in the new service. There had been a municipal election during the previous Spring, and though its results were long known and its victors in office, the official returns had not yet been published by the Board of Election Supervisors. They were now, it appeared, to be given to a waiting world. Unhappily, I was slowed down in my tour of the City Hall by my unfamiliarity with its very geography, and when I got to the office of the supervisors at last it was closed for the day. I can still remember every twinge of my terror. What if I fell down on the story? The least penalty I could imagine would be return to a police assignment—and maybe not even a good one. So I hopped a trolley-car and tracked down the secretary to the board—an amiable politico whose name was Deane. He was sitting down to supper, but I conveyed to him enough of my alarm to induce him to come down to his office at once, open his safe, and give me a copy of the returns. When I got to the *Herald* office late, and Max Ways froze me with a growl, I thought it best to tell him the truth. He received it with a tolerant smile. "If you were older," he said, "you'd have known better. Such official documents are not worth so much trouble. If you had come in without it I could have got a proof of it from Jim Doyle [city editor of the *American*] or Hallett [city editor of the *Sun*]. But don't think that I blame you. We live and learn."

My relief was stupendous, and I chalked up one more article in my long bill of debts to Max. Soon afterward he quit the *Herald* and newspaper work, and was succeeded by a new city editor who had been, only lately, a City Hall reporter himself, so I had to hustle, and hustle I did. My job was gradually made pleasant, though surely not lightened, by the fact that the Mayor then in office—he had come in but a short time before—was an extremely eccentric and rambunctious fellow, so full of surprises that he had already acquired the nickname of Thomas the Sudden. His name was Hayes, and he was at one and the same time a very shrewd lawyer, an unconstructed Confederate veteran, a pious Methodist, and a somewhat bawdy bachelor. He was a wiry little fellow with a high forehead and a gigantic black moustache, and was the precise image of the Nietzsche depicted in Hans Olde's familiar drawing. There never lived on this earth a more quarrelsome man. He never had less than six feuds going at once, and some of them reached unparalleled altitudes of raucousness. When he could not fetch his enemies by any other method he sued them in the courts, and during all of his four-year term the appellate judges of Maryland were kept humping by his litigations. There was in Baltimore at the time another litigant of ferocious assiduity, to wit, Charles J. Bonaparte, who was a grand-nephew of Napoleon I and was later to become Secretary of the Navy and then Attorney General in the Cabinet of Roosevelt I. But Bonaparte usually lost his cases, and in fact frittered away on them the better part of an inherited fortune of $1,000,000, whereas Hayes invariably won.

His method of celebrating victory was to go on a grand drunk. One evening, in the course of such a drunk, he arrived home in a state of incoördination, and fell down a stairway in his house, breaking a leg. After that, for a couple of months, the City Hall reporters of Baltimore had to see him in bed, and loud and long were the snorts and screams of moral indignation that issued from it. He lived with his sister, an old maid schoolma'm, and she tried her best to police him, but with very little success. Propped up in a frayed and filthy nightshirt, he chewed tobacco all his waking hours, and spit the juice into space without stopping to aim. On a table beside his bed was a box of five-cent cigars, but I never saw him smoke one, and he never offered one to a visitor. It was his theory that his enemies in and out of the City Hall were taking advantage of his disablement to ruin his administration, reduce Baltimore to bankruptcy, and undermine civilization, and in support of that theory he was always ready with great masses of evidence, some of it more or less plausible, but most of it plainly bogus. We reporters had to sift the little that could be printed from the mass that was poisonously libellous, and sometimes the job was anything but easy. But we liked the old boy nevertheless, for good stories radiated from him like quills from the fretful portentine, and if we had to scrap two-thirds of his fulminations there was always enough left to keep us rich in copy.

He was one of the most brazen boasters I have ever encountered, but I soon learned from him the immoral but useful lesson that boasters are not necessarily liars. He was, in fact, a really first-rate public official, and he pretty well cleaned out the corruption that had burdened Baltimore for generations, and set up so rational and efficient a municipal administration that its momentum is still visible, though he has been dead many years. His chief enemy, rather curiously, was another Confederate veteran whose honesty and competence were as notable as his own. This was Major Richard M. Venable, a member of the City Council and one of the stars of the Maryland bar. Though the two were on the same side at bottom, and both served Baltimore magnificently, they always differed in detail, and inasmuch as neither could ever imagine the slightest decency in an opponent, they carried on their wars *à outrance* and kept the town in a dither. Once they landed before the Court of Appeals at Annapolis on nine separate points of law, and though Venable was the more learned lawyer, and by far, Hayes won on every point. His celebration went on for weeks, and in the course of it he issued statements sneering at Venable as a putrid pettifogger, questioning the election returns that put him in the Council, and even hinting that there was something phony about his war record. None of them were ever printed.

Venable was also a bachelor, and a personage quite as picturesque as Hayes himself. He was of great stature, had a belly so vast that his waistcoat looked like a segment of balloon, and wore a huge and bristling beard. He kept house in a sort of one-man monastery in a decayed downtown street, and was beautifully served by a staff of colored servants. One dull Sunday evening, seeking only to set him to talking, I asked him how he managed to run his establishment so well. He replied that there were two reasons. The first was that no white women were allowed in the house, and the second was that he had a standing offer to his servants to pay them half again as much as anyone else was willing to pay them. He had two great hates, one against women and the other against Christianity. His large library was principally made up of works on theology, and he read them constantly, and damned them violently. He was, in fact, the premier town atheist of his generation, and after his death it was reported that he had left orders that his ashes were to be disposed of by throwing them into any convenient ashcan. If he actually left such orders they were disregarded; instead, his ashes were scattered in Druid Hill Park, for in his last days he had been a member of the Park Board. His loathing of women embraced the whole sex, but its worst poisons were concentrated on a lady eminent in good works. It was a common joke in Baltimore city-rooms to send a new reporter to him for verification of a presumed report that he was about to marry her. His roars usually scared the reporter out of a month's growth.

The major easily dominated both houses of the City Council, and it usually served him docilely in his gory wars on Mayor

Hayes. It consisted, then as always, of a scattering of intelligent raisins in a big loaf of dunderheads. One of its members was a brewery collector, another was a writer of dime novels, and two others were operators of O.E.A. (*i.e.*, odorless excavating apparatus) companies, which is to say, they were engaged professionally in cleaning the privies that survived in thousands of Baltimore backyards until 1915 or thereabout, when the sewerage system was completed. The rest sloped down to saloonkeepers, small trucking contractors, and miscellaneous ward-heelers. The major rode these poor idiots in a bold and berserk fashion, and whenever one of them ventured to vote against him, which was not often, he gave a magnificent exhibition of moral indignation. They trembled under his bellowing, but like inferior men at all times and everywhere, ended by admiring him vastly, and even, in their dull way, loving him. Sometimes he would gather them together in one of the council chambers after a meeting had adjourned, and delight them with Rabelaisian anecdotes in the manner of Abraham Lincoln. He had a large répertoire, and his delivery was aided considerably by his commanding mien and florid beard.

It was part of my job, of course, to cover the sessions of the Council, and I always enjoyed them greatly. Inasmuch as there were two houses I was given an assistant for the duration, but I usually managed to look in at both chambers, and never missed the upper one when Major Venable was on his legs. The hour of meeting was 5 P.M. and the sessions often lasted until 8. We reporters were allowed 50 cents a head by our papers for supper money, and usually victualled before returning to our offices, for in those primitive days the maniacal demand for early copy that now palsies journalism was unheard of. Across the street from the City Hall there was a saloon in which a dinner consisting of a coriaceous T-bone steak, a dab of fried potatoes, a slice of rye bread and a cup of coffee could be had for a quarter, and most of the reporters patronized it, and so made a profit of the other quarter. But there was one among them of more voluptuous inclinations, and he soon convinced me that it was better to eat a more elegant dinner. He was Frank Kent, of the *Sun*. He had discovered that such a meal was on tap in a hotel in Calvert street, and thereafter he and I ate it every Council night. Sometimes we had to add ten cents to the fifty to cover our checks, but we were reckless fellows, and did not begrudge any kindness to our pyloruses.

This epicureanism rather set us apart from the other City Hall reporters, and our singularity was even more unpleasantly marked when we gave Major Venable aid and applause in his war upon what had been known for years and years as "the meritorious measure." This was an ordinance put through whenever the Council adjourned for its Summer recess, giving every reporter who had covered its proceedings a gratuity of $150. It had been passed yearly since the Civil War, and maybe since the Revolution, but the major announced that he was implacably agin it, and, what is more, that he would attack it in a taxpayer's suit if it were passed. Frank and I, having convinced ourselves virtuously that any such gratuity was an insult to journalism, let it be known that we'd refuse the money if the major came to grief, and this got us some unpopularity among our colleagues, but when he won hands down the matter was quickly forgotten, and we were again on good terms with all hands. There were so many sources of news in the City Hall that it was impossible for one reporter to cover all of them, so we had perforce to pool our daily accumulations. How that arrangement once broke down, and how human ingenuity restored it, will be told in Chapter XVIII.

The examples of Hayes and Venable were proofs enough that honest and competent men could sometimes get on the public payroll, and I soon found many more on lower levels. Hayes's secretary, a courtly Irishman named William A. Ryan, was one, and another was a man named Julius Freeman, who was deputy city register: both knew their jobs and gave the city hard and faithful service. A third was a curious character named McCuen, a bachelor like Hayes and Venable, and like Venable again, the master of a fierce set of whiskers. McCuen's were almost as red as blood, and he wore them parted in the middle, and drawn out into two horns. He came from South Baltimore, and his past was that of any other neighborhood politico, but when Hayes made him superintendent of lamps and lighting he took his duties with great gravity, and was soon discharging them in a highly efficient and even stylish manner. All day he slaved in his office, and half the night he roved the streets, spotting lights that were not working, and picking out places to set up new ones. For the first time in its history Baltimore was decently lighted. Moreover, McCuen replaced thousands of the old rickety lamp-posts with new ones of excellent design, and in general showed an aesthetic sense that was astounding in a politician. But now and then he reverted unaccountably to more primitive canons of taste, and once he spent a lot of money putting colored lights into a fountain in one of the city reservoirs. The effect was that of an explosion of stick-candy, but more Baltimoreans admired it than laughed at it, and the lights remain in place to this day, forty years afterward.

At about the same time a Civil War veteran who was superintendent of the City Hall decided that the large bronze lamps which flanked its main entrance were too dirty to be endured, and had his men give them a coat of bright green paint. This improvement set loose an uproar, for the patina on them had been accumulating for thirty years, and was much prized by the town cognoscenti. I well recall the distress of the poor old man when he finally took in the notion that his honest effort to imitate the arty McCuen had resulted in a *faux pas*. I really felt sorry for him, but my responsibility to my own art had to be considered first, so I helped to heap ribaldry upon him. The Baltimore cartoonists had a grand time while his agony lasted. McKee Barclay of the *Evening News* did a plate showing all the principal local monuments bedizened in the new manner, including the Washington column striped like a barber's pole. It took the City Hall scavengers two weeks to scrape the paint off the lamps, and in doing so they removed the patina too.

The City Hall seemed dullish after the Central police district, but even so it had its moments. There was a battle in the war between Hayes and Venable every few weeks, and in the intervals the members of the various city boards locked horns, and gave us good shows. During the Winter smallpox broke out in Baltimore, and patients dragged out of the alleys by the cops were stored every afternoon in the City Hall annex, an old school building occupied by the Health Department, a block or so away from the Hall itself. Whenever a wagonload accumulated it was started for the pest-house down the harbor. Visiting the Health Department every day, we reporters had to pass within a few feet of these candidates for the potter's field. To protect us the doctors vaccinated us once a week. The vaccinations produced less effect on me than so many gnat bites, for my arm had been scraped back in 1882 by our family physician, Dr. Z. K. Wiley, and when he did a job of that kind he left behind him a scar like a shell crater, good for a generation.

Hayes distrusted all his official advisers, and especially his legal staff, but he had a kitchen cabinet that had his confidence, composed mainly of third-rate politicians. One Sunday I printed in the *Herald* what purported to be a report of its latest star-chamber proceedings, and the buffoonery was so well received that I went on with it thereafter from week to week. In a little while one of the members offered to give me more or less accurate minutes of its actual sessions if I would agree to treat him politely. I agreed readily, and after that my stories were accepted in the City Hall as authentic. Hayes himself tried to worm out of me the source of my information, but the pieces were unsigned, and I refused to admit that I was writing them. His suspicions were finally fixed on a quite innocent member, and this unfortunate was expelled from the cabinet, and threatened with the loss of his city job. It is a remarkable fact that the member who really leaked was never detected, and indeed never even suspected. I kept on writing this somewhat obvious stuff until my term of servitude in the City Hall ended. Even today I occasionally meet an old-time politician who remembers it uneasily, and tries to induce me to tell him who blabbed. More than once my report of the cabinet's debates, touched up artistically, ruined some design of Hayes and his torpedoes, and covered Major Venable with soothing unguents. But the major never admitted that he read such trivia. He was essentially a serious man.

Hayes himself came to a bad end. After his four-years' term as Mayor he dropped out of politics, and resumed his law practise, which was mainly devoted to criminal business. He knew how to holler in court and was thus successful before juries, but in Maryland most criminal trials go on without juries, even in capital cases, and he made much less impression on judges. A Methodist by early training, he gradually gave over the jug and devoted himself more and more to Christian endeavor. He became the superintendent of a Methodist Sunday-school, and inveigled the *Sunday Sun* into printing his weekly observations on the International Sunday-school Lessons. These observations were of a high degree of fatuity, and when I became Sunday editor of the *Sun* myself, in 1906, I killed them. In his last years, which were lonely and unhappy, for his schoolma'm sister had died, his income was diminishing and his services to Baltimore were beginning to be forgotten, he wasted at least half his time on his theological debauchery, greatly to the distress of his former secretary, Ryan, who was a very intelligent man, and moreover, a Catholic. Ryan himself had made progress in politics, and was by now collector of customs. I dropped in on him often, and we moaned over poor Hayes's deterioration, but there was nothing that we could do about it. When he died at last his funeral orgies were on a scale fit for a bishop, or even an archangel, and the Methodists of Baltimore still remember him as a prophet comparable to Nehemiah, Habakkuk or Deuteronomy. But to all the less sanctified Baltimoreans he has grown vague, and there is no public memorial to him in the town.

He was the last of the Civil War veterans to reach high public office there, and even during his term as Mayor the old city was changing. The great fire of 1904 was to hasten its transmogrification, and today it bears little resemblance to the Baltimore of my first memories. But in my reportorial days there were still whole sections, especially along the waterfront, that still looked and smelled exactly as they must have looked and smelled in 1861. The Back Basin, which made up into the town so far that its head was only four blocks from the main crossroads, received the effluence of such sewers as existed, and emitted a stench as cadaverous and unearthly as that of the canals of Venice. In Summer it took on extra voltage, and became almost unendurable, but the old-time Baltimoreans pretended that they didn't notice it, and even professed to believe that it was good for their sinuses and a prophylactic against the ague. During the crusading era the local newspapers often set up demands that something be done about it, but it continued to afflict the town until the new sewerage system was completed, and the Back Basin was reduced to the humble status of a receptacle for rain water. Once a *Herald* editorial writer proposed in print, and quite seriously, that a dam be built across the mouth of the Basin, to the end that the water backed up at high tide might be released suddenly when the tide was low. His theory was that the resultant flood would carry off all the dead dogs, decayed bunches of bananas and multitudinous worse filth that floated on the Basin's surface. When an Old Subscriber wrote in asking what would happen to the shipping in the lower harbor when this flood roared down the Patapsco, the editorial writer was indignant, and accused various reporters of writing the letter.

My days in the City Hall, like my days as a police reporter, were not long, but by the time they were over I had begun to think of myself as a journeyman journalist, and was so accepted by the elder brethren of the craft. It was not unusual for me to be taken off the job for a day or two, or even for a week or two, and assigned to some other work. After the middle of 1900 I had a hand in nearly all the big stories that engaged the Baltimore newspapers. Even in 1899 I had been told off to do the election-day lead, and given three columns for it. It was a story of some importance, for up to that time Baltimore had never seen an election day without at least one murder. But the tide was now flowing toward peace and decorum, and though I roved the town all day, looking for dead and wounded, I had to base my lead on the surprising fact that no one had been killed, and only a few poor bums hurt. The next year I was put to writing a pre-election series of instructions to voters, for the election laws had been lately changed by taking all party emblems off the ballots, which thus became Chinese puzzles to the plain people, who had been voting for either Abraham Lincoln's beard or the Democratic rooster for years. At the time I performed this educational service I had just passed my twentieth birthday, and could not vote myself until nearly a year later.

I was used to newspaper hours by now, and liked them. On Summer nights it was always beginning to grow cool when I got home—sometimes as early as one o'clock, but usually nearer three. I got in some reading in the quiet of the house, and slept like a top. Arising at ten or thereabouts, I had a couple of hours for my literary enterprises before going to work. I lost a good many days off, but those that I got were very pleasant, for they gave me some extra time for writing, and in the evening I went to the theatre. As older men dropped out I inherited Saturday as my day off—the choice one of the whole week, for there were matinées on it, and some sort of newspaper party was always staged after work on Saturday night. I began to reflect upon my trade, and to discern some of its principal virtues and defects. Of the latter, the worst was the fact that it worked me too hard, but though I was aware of it I did not resent it, for I was still full of the eagerness of youth, and hot to see the whole show. Of the former, the greatest was that a newspaper man always saw that show from a reserved seat in the first row. The rest of humanity had to wait in line and struggle for places, but not a reporter. He was always expected, and usually welcomed. He got into places by a side door. To this day it always irritates me absurdly to have to stand in line, even for a few minutes—say at a ticket-window or on a customs pier. It seems to me to be an intolerable affront, not only to my private pomp and circumstance, but also to the honor of the Fourth Estate.

IV.
Approach to Lovely Letters

WHEN I told Max Ways, on applying for a job on the *Herald*, that I had been busting with literary ardors for four or five years I was stating a simple fact. It must have been before 1895 that I made my first formal attempt to do something for publication: it was an article on a chemical invention of my own—a platinum toning bath for silver photographic prints. All the photographic magazines of the time rejected it, and it never got into print until 1925, when the late Isaac Goldberg published it in a book called "The Man Mencken." I was in those days vacillating between chemistry and journalism, and two teachers at the Baltimore Polytechnic, from which I was graduated in 1896 as the youngest member of my class, had something to do with my final choice. I had got interested in chemistry through photography, and in photography through the gift of a camera at Christmas, 1892, just as I had got interested in journalism through the gift of a printing-press at Christmas, 1888.

By 1894 I had a laboratory in Hollins street, and was engaged in eager but usually inconclusive experiments. All the orthodox accidents happened to me, including four or five explosions and an inhalation of bromide gas that nearly strangled me, and no doubt had something to do with the sore throat that pestered me for years afterward. If I had encountered a competent teacher of chemistry at the Polytechnic I'd have gone on in that science, and today I'd be up to my ears in the vitamines, for it was synthetic chemistry that always interested me most. But the gogue told off to nurture me succeeded only in disheartening me, so I gradually edged over to letters, helped by another gogue who really knew his stuff, and, what is more, loved it. He was a young *Cand. jur.* named Edward S. Kines, who had but recently graduated from the Baltimore City College, and was pursuing his legal studies of an evening at the University of Maryland Law School. He taught English literature at the Polytechnic, and judged by any plausible standard must have been set down a bad teacher, but somehow or other he managed to impart to me, and to a few other boys, his honest enthusiasm for what then passed in schools for good books. My reading, up to the time he began to operate on me, had been scattered and futile, but he gave it direction, and I was soon leaping and prancing through the whole classical répertoire, and enjoying it. I even tackled such revolting doses as Butler's "Hudibras," Herbert's "The Temple," the contributions to the *Spectator* by Eustace Budgell, and Colley Cibber's Apology.

Kines, so far as I know, had no literary ambitions of his own: he was content to spout his favorite passages, and in his later years he devoted himself assiduously to his trade as a trial lawyer. Nor was there much scratching for the *cacoethes scribendi* among his pupils. Indeed, I can recall but one who ever spoke of writing. He was Arthur W. Hawks, who had a brother on the *Herald* staff, and was to join it himself a little while before I did. It may be that the example of the two Hawkses led me to the *Herald* instead of to the *Sun*, but on that point my memory is cloudy, and I am sure that they knew little about my actual attempts at writing, at any rate before 1898. I recall going out to the Baltimore baseball grounds in 1895, and doing a play-by-play report of a game between the famous Baltimore Orioles and some visiting nine, but though I was delighted the next morning to find that it coincided with the stories in the newspapers I never showed it to anyone. Nor did I solicit opinion on any of the verse that I began to do about the same time. Indeed, I have always been shy about showing my writings to other people, though it would certainly be an exaggeration to call me, generally speaking, a violet; and to this day I have never asked anyone to read a manuscript of mine, or even a printed book. My first production was a satirical poem on a baseball theme, and I sent it to the Baltimore *American* unsigned, and was amazed to see it in print. After that I favored the *American* with almost daily contributions, but only one more was ever printed. At the Polytechnic my yearning to make the staff of the school paper was thwarted by the class politicians, and when the time came to concoct a class play I was not invited to help write it, but put to banging the piano for the performance.

To a youngster of my inclinations the literary movement of the nineties was naturally a cosmic event, and I followed it as best I could, with no one to guide me, once I had departed from Kines. I remember haunting a newsdealer's shop in West Baltimore, hot to grab every new magazine as it came out, and first and last I must have waded through scores of them. The majority were idiotically eccentric: there was one, for example, in which the illustrations, printed separately, were pasted in, and another that sold pretentiously for a cent. But my critical faculties were still embryonic, and I devoured the bad with the good. The *Chap-Book* and the *Lark* went through my mill, but so did many an arty monstrosity that lasted but one number. I recall, however, enjoying *M'lle New York* better than most, for there was in it a writer named James G. Huneker whose illuminating sophistication and colorful, rapid style gave me a special thrill. Years later I was to know him well and see much of him, but in 1895 he was as far out of my world as Betelgeuse.

When I began to find my way about the *Herald* office I discovered to my delight that I was on the actual frontiers of lovely letters, for all those members of the staff who showed a mental age above thirteen were consumed by either one or the other of two then prevalent ambitions: to write the book of a comic opera, or to set up a weekly journal of literary, theatrical, musical and political opinion. The elder Hawks, Wells, was actually engaged upon the former, and though, as a young reporter, I was not admitted to his confidences, his brother Arthur sneaked some of its lyrics to show me, and we agreed that they were masterpieces. No weekly ever precipitated itself from the current dreams, but a monthly called *Dixie* was really in existence, and if the contributions of the local literati made no noise, the magazine was at least getting notice for some of its illustrations. They were done by a pen-and-ink artist named G. Alden Peirson. Turning away from the uptown prides and glories of Baltimore, he went down to the waterfront for his subjects, and there produced some very charming drawings.[1] The newspaper artists of the town were naturally miles behind

---

[1]*Dixie* lasted from January, 1899, to April, 1900. The rest of its illustrations scarcely got above the candy-box-top level. Its literary contents were even worse.

him, but they, too, had their quest for an earthly Grail. It took them to a dark office in an old building under the elevated in North street, where there lurked a syndicate man who was always ready to buy a comic drawing of the sort then in fashion. Unhappily, there had to be a he-and-she joke to go with it, and inventing these jokes usually stumped the artists. When they could not find a literary reporter able to supply one, they went to the Pratt Library and dug it out of the back files of *Puck*, *Judge* or *Texas Siftings*. The market price for joke and drawing was $1.

There were some high-toned literati living in Baltimore in those days—for example, Edward Abram Uffington Valentine, who printed a book of poems in 1902 that got very good reviews—but I never met any of them, and there was little to lift me, after I got used to it, in the endless gabble that went on in the *Herald* office about the weekly that never came to birth. My own aspirations were gradually turning from poetry to prose. I had a drawer full of verse, but I was making fewer and fewer additions to it. A large part of it consisted of dreadful imitations of Kipling, who was then my god, and the rest was made up of triolets, rondeaux and other experiments in the old French forms that Austin Dobson and Andrew Lang had brought in. In the Autumn of 1900, when I was given a weekly column on the editorial page, and invited to do my damnedest, I unearthed a lot of these *Jugendwerke*, and so saved the labor of writing new stuff. They were all pretty bad, but they seemed to be well received in the office, and in December I received the singular honor of being invited by the new managing editor, Carter, to do a poem for the first page. It was not, to be sure, quite original, for it was based upon a French piece lately published by Edmond Rostand, roundly denouncing the Boer   * leader, Oom Paul Kruger. Carter put Rostand's French into English prose, and I turned it into burning tetrameter, with poor old Oom reduced to a greasepot at the end. It was blowsy stuff, God knows, but Carter professed to like it, and, good or bad, there it glowed and glittered in long primer italic on page one—a glory that no other American poet, however gifted, has ever achieved, at least to my knowledge. My column ran on until my reserves of prosody began to be depleted. I then diluted it with more and more prose, and finally it became prose altogether. Beginning in June, 1901, it took the form of a weekly tale of ancient Rome, in which all the characters were American politicians, thinly disguised. Every tale ended with the hanging of the principal personage. I don't recall how many such pieces I did, but it was well beyond thirty, and toward the end of the series I was hard put to invent something new every week, and yet keep within the formula.

My poetical contributions to the editorial page in 1900 and 1901 made up most of the contents of my first book, "Ventures Into Verse," though it did not come out until 1903. It was a typical product of the aesthetic movement of the time, then gradually subsiding. Its projectors were two young fellows named Marshall and Beek, who had formed a firm to do fine printing and taken into partnership an artist named Gordon. The three came to me asking that I suggest a likely source of copy for a small volume that would show off their advanced typography, and I naturally nominated myself. Marshall set the book by hand, and there were decorations by Gordon, and by another artist named John Siegel. The press-run was 100 copies, of which I got half and the firm got half. Some were bound à la Roycroft, in rough binders' boards with red labels, but most were issued in plain brown paper. I sent ten of my copies to the principal critical organs of the time, and presented the rest to libraries or to friends. As incredible as it may seem, the book got good notices, but only three orders for it ever reached Marshall, Beek and Gordon. My presentation copies seem to have been preserved in odd corners, for when American firsts began to bring fantastic prices, in 1925, a good many appeared in the market, and at one time a clean specimen brought as much as $225. All those that had gone to public libraries were stolen. Some ass spread the story that I was buying up the copies offered by dealers, and burning them. It was, of course, not true. I can recall buying but one copy, and that one I gave to a friend. It cost me $130.

Meanwhile, I was devoting all my meagre leisure to writing. I still did an occasional poem, and some of them were published in magazines. The first to make high literary society, so far as I can recall, was a rhymed address to my hero Kipling, urging him to forget politics and go back to Mandalay. It was written in the Autumn of 1899, while I was in the midst of my apprenticeship as a police reporter, and I sent it to the *Book-man*, then edited by Harry Thurston Peck. It went in anonymously and with no return address on the manuscript, and I was both surprised and enchanted when it came out in the December issue. I wrote to Peck at once, admitting its paternity with suitable blushes, and was surprised again when one of his assistants replied politely, and enclosed a check for $10. I quote from the letter:

> As we are paying you more than we usually do for poems, you may judge from that fact that the poem appealed to us. We may add, also, that the poem has been quoted quite a little in the newspapers.

I recall a curious detail of the day the December *Bookman* appeared on the newsstands in Baltimore. When I discovered my verses in it I was so addled that I was quite unfit for work, and decided to seek peace and recuperation in the old Odeon Theatre in Frederick street, to which I had the entrée. The Odeon was a burlesque house, and while I sat in a stage box, reading my burning lines over and over again, two comedians broke slapsticks over each other's fundaments, and the ladies of the ensemble engaged in what were then called muscle dances. But the manager of the house, James Madison, was himself a writer,[2] and when he dropped in on me and I showed him the magazine he joined in my rejoicings. On returning to the *Herald* office, I told Max Ways my purple secret, and he spread it in the office. That night Colonel Cunningham, who was presently to retire as managing editor, paused on his way through the city-room to compliment me officially.

I sold verse during the following Winter to *Life*, to *Leslie's Weekly*, to the *National Magazine* and to the *New England Magazine*, but in the main I wrote short stories, and most of them landed eventually in magazines. In an old account-book I find a record of my operations: it is interesting chiefly because it shows that the magazines I attempted are nearly all long gone and forgotten, for example, the *Criterion*, the *Broadway*,

---

[2]He wrote vaudeville sketches and dialogues for Dutch, Irish and Jewish comedians, and had a large following. Later on he abandoned that art for the book business, and is at present (1941) the publisher of an excellent monthly for bibliophiles.

Judge, *Puck*, the *Black Cat*, *Munsey's*, *Success*, *Ainslee's*, *Leslie's*
(the monthly, not the weekly), *Lippincott's*, the *Youth's Companion*, *McClure's*, *Everybody's*, *Pearson's*, *Golden Days*, the
Critic, the *World's Work*, the *Century*, *Hearst's*, *Town Topics*,
the *Metropolitan*, the *Argosy*, *Harper's Weekly*. Eheu! it is a roll
of the noble dead. The *Bookman* under Peck was the best literary monthly the United States has ever seen; *Munsey's*, *Mc-
Clure's* and *Everybody's* had immense circulations; the *Youth's
Companion* was read by every American boy; the *Black Cat*
was "the story-telling hit of the century"; and a barber-shop
without *Puck* and *Judge* would have seemed as nude as one
without the *Police Gazette*. But now they are all in the shades,
and only a few doddering oldsters recall even their names.

The *Criterion*, then edited by Emory Pottle, husband of
Juliet Wilbor Tompkins, was the only solvent survivor of the
literary movement of the nineties. I banged away at Pottle for
a good while without shaking him, but finally he bought a
short story called "The Heathen Rage," born of my trip to Jamaica (Chapter V), and after that I sold him others. For one of
them, I find by my records, he paid me $51 and for another
$34.35. It was a day of close prices. My steadiest customer in
the long run, however, was not Pottle, but Ellery Sedgwick,
then editor of *Frank Leslie's Popular Monthly* and later to be
editor of the *Atlantic Monthly*. Sometime in 1901 he bought
two of my short stories, and thereafter he bought others.
Moreover, he sent me criticisms of those he rejected, and then,
as later on, I learned a lot from him. He also put me to work
writing articles under the *nom de plume* of John F. Brownell.
Leslie's was illustrated, and Sedgwick would first pick up a good
series of photographs, and then have me write a text to fit
them. One such series, as I remember, had to do with the
Hagenbeck Zoo at Hamburg. I had never been to Hamburg
(and, in fact, never got there until 1938), but I was by now a
journeyman reporter, so I did an article that apparently pleased
the readers of *Leslie's*, and Sedgwick offered me a job on his
home-office staff. The salary he named was more than I was
getting on the *Herald*, and he proposed to add a round-trip
railroad pass to Baltimore once a month, but I declined at
once, for I had already made up my mind that I didn't want to
live in New York. Many other offers to move there came later,

and beginning with 1914 I actually had an office in the town
for twenty years on end, but I stuck to living in Baltimore,
which suited me, and still suits me, precisely. While I was an
editor of the *Smart Set* and then of the *American Mercury* I
commuted to New York as often as weekly, but I stayed at the
Algonquin, and never had any permanent quarters.

I was reasonably successful as a writer of short stories, and
sold virtually every one I wrote, though not always at the first
attempt. One of my good markets was *Short Stories*, and I also
had a welcome from Karl Edwin Harriman, then editor of the
Red Book. Toward the end of 1901 I sold two stories to the
Youth's Companion that somehow got pigeon-holed in the office, and were not exhumed and published until more than
thirty years later. At that time the editor sent me proofs of
them, and invited me to make any changes that a generation of
experience might suggest, but I passed them without changing
a word. They were on the bad side as stories, but they were no
worse than the general. Until I joined the staff of the *Smart Set*
as its book reviewer, in 1908, I had sold it but one piece of
copy—a poor little triolet—and even that never got into the
magazine, for I discovered at once that I had already used it in
my *Herald* column, and had to recall it. Between 1899 and
1902 I must have bombarded the *Smart Set* with at least forty
other pieces of verse, always in vain.

How I managed to find time for all this writing, considering
the heavy work I was doing for the *Herald*, I simply can't tell
you. My output during my first years on the staff, in and out of
the office, was really enormous, for in addition to my short
stories and doggerels, I wrote a great many articles for other
papers, and began work on a novel. The novel, happily, never
got very far. Its scene was Elizabethan England, and Shakespeare was to have been one of the characters. It blew up when
I discovered that I knew no more about Elizabethan England
than about the M. M. III age of Crete. I was constantly turning up news and feature stories in Baltimore that were of interest in other cities, and selling them there. The first paper I thus
broke into was the Philadelphia *Inquirer*, and it was soon followed by the New York *Morning Telegraph*, and then, after a
while, by the New York *Sun*. My contributions to the *Sun*
were mainly interviews with an imaginary Civil War colonel

from the Eastern Shore of Maryland, who was supposed to be the world's greatest authority on the mint julep. Unless my memory plays me false they started that controversy about the proper compounding of the julep which still rages.

Nor did I confine myself, in my reachings out for fresh fields and lusher pastures, to this great Republic. There was in New York in those days a Rhinelander named Henry W. Fischer who made a living translating news items from the chief European papers, and selling them in the United States. The cable service of the time was much leaner than it is today, so there was room for him. It occurred to me that I might set up a similar service from the Far East, and to that end I approached various newspapers in that region, offering to send them occasional American letters in return for the right to mine their news columns. A number bit, and in a little while I was the American correspondent of the Hongkong *Press*, the Kobe *Chronicle*, the Nagasaki *Press*, and the *Ceylon Observer* of Colombo, and had letter-heads printed to prove it. Unfortunately, I soon learned that very few American newspapers were interested in Far Eastern news, and my cash takings remained scanty. Finally, I decided to go to New York to consult Fischer, with a view to an amalgamation. I found him in carpet-slippers at his home in Bensonhurst, and remember clearly his brief comment when I recited to him the list of my papers. It consisted of the single word "Jesus!" But we quickly came to terms, and the amalgamation was effected on the spot. That is to say, I gave him my business, such as it was, and he returned to Manhattan with me and took me to Lüchow's in Fourteenth street, where he bought me an excellent lunch and half a dozen horns of Würzburger.

I have said that I never met any of the recognized literati of Baltimore, but I should mention one exception. He was Jean Havez, who had been a reporter on the *Evening News* only a short time before, and was now eminent as the author of "Goodbye, Booze!," "Everybody Works But Father," and "He Cert'n'y Was Good to Me," all of them great popular successes. Havez was of French parentage, and a fellow of huge bulk, powerful thirst, and notable amiability. Whenever he returned to Baltimore from Broadway for a visit to the home folks there was a party that lasted for days. While one of them was going on, toward the end of 1900, Lew Dockstader came to town with his minstrel company, and tried to induce Jean to write some local stanzas for his songs. But Jean was too busy to fool with such chicken feed, and for some reason that I forget turned the job over to me. I wrote the stanzas in a few hours, and went to Ford's Opera House that night to hear Lew sing them, full of agreeable anticipations. But he had got an overdose of Jean's party during the afternoon, and when he came upon the stage it was apparent to the judicious that he was not altogether himself. In consequence, he made a horrible mess of my poor jocosities, but the customers roared none the less, for a theatre audience will always laugh at the mention of a familiar name by a comedian, no matter how idiotic the joke he makes on it. Later in the week Lew pulled himself together and did better, and after the Saturday matinée he handed me $10 for my labor. A month later I collared another ten-spot by doing parodies for a Democratic mass-meeting.

But though all these extra-mural activities brought in money, and I was soon earning more outside the office than in it, I began to be conscious of a lack of direction, and tried a number of times to decide formally what I really wanted to do, and to get on with the doing of it. Such advice as I sought usually turned out to be bad, and in consequence I did a great deal of wobbling. I tried all sorts of things, including even advertising writing, but they satisfied me as little as the concoction of verse, which had begun to pall dismally. My short stories, as I have said, were doing pretty well, and I got some comfort and solace in the writing of them from another youngster in the office, Leo Crane by name and secretary to the managing editor by trade. Crane was writing short stories too, and making *Harper's* with them, which was even better than I was doing. But it gradually dawned on me that fiction was not my *forte*, and I did none after 1902. The Boston lemon-squeezer, Richard G. Badger, tried to inveigle me, in that year, into letting him bring out a volume of my stories, but when, after a considerable correspondence, I discovered that he expected me to pay for it, I fled from his blandishments. He gave me to understand that he thought me one of the coming masters of the short story in America, but I was already in grave doubt about that. For two years I let the matter lie there. Then, through the theatre, I became interested in George Bernard Shaw, and through Shaw I found my vocation at last. My first real book, begun in 1904, was a volume on his plays and the notions in them, critical in its approach. It was the first book about him ever published, and it led me to begin a larger volume on Nietzsche in 1907, and to undertake a book on Socialism two years later, in the form of a debate with a Socialist named La Monte, now recusant and forgotten. After that I was a critic of ideas, and I have remained one ever since.

In all probability, my various false starts did me no harm, though I was undoubtedly delayed in coming to fruit by trying to do too many things at once. My work for the *Herald* was enough in itself to keep one man busy, and I recall many times when I finished a day so nearly worn out that I could barely keep my eyes open. More than once I produced 5000 words of news copy between noon and midnight—not in a single continuous story, which might have been easy enough, but in a miscellany of perhaps twelve or fifteen, every one of them requiring some legging. The newspaper padrones of that era, like the steel magnates, had not yet discovered that over-long hours greatly diminish the amount of good work done. A little while ago I spent an uncomfortable afternoon going through the files of the *Herald*, reading my contributions to it in 1900 and 1901. I discovered that I had done a great deal of shabby writing, full of clichés and banalities. But it was well regarded in the office at the time, and was at its worst appreciably better than the work of many of my colleagues. Not until a somewhat
* later date did anything properly describable as good writing become the rule on the *Herald*. At least half the members of the staff had literary ambitions of some sort or another, but not one of them ever got anywhere as a writer in the years following. Several took to executive work and became city editors and managing editors, but more became press-agents, and still more left journalism altogether. That is its continuing tragedy: it opens all sorts of outside opportunities to its slaves, and so loses them. I have known newspaper men who have become bank presidents, judges, United States Senators, Governors, generals in the Army, and even bishops. One of the

worst who ever lived, Warren Gamaliel Harding, actually became President of the United States. And in Baltimore, during
the thirteen years of horror, the best bootician in service was a
former newspaper artist.

V.

Fruits of Diligence

THE ASSIDUITIES described in the preceding chapters had rewards both subjective and objective, for I not only enjoyed every minute of every day, but also got a good many friendly grunts from Max Ways, and, though I didn't know it, substantial promotion was just around the corner. Unhappily, my hustling bore rather heavily upon a constitution that had some holes in it, and so early as the Spring of 1900 I began to lose weight, and to show other symptoms of exhaustion. From my childhood I had been badgered by disorders of the upper respiratory tract. Every Autumn, on returning to school, I suffered for several weeks from a bleariness that seems, in retrospect, to have been the beginnings of hay-fever, and during my chemical days I picked up a sore throat that stuck to me more or less steadily for ten years.

In most ways, to be sure, I was a perfectly healthy animal, for I could eat and digest anything colorably organic, I recovered quickly from all minor wounds and infections, and to this day I have never had a headache. But there was always something unpleasant going on in my nose or throat, and it took the faculty a long while, not to mention a considerable shedding of blood, to repair the blunders of Yahweh there, and launch me on the robustness that marked my thirties and forties. How many times I went on the table I don't recall precisely, but it must have been half a dozen at least. My tonsils were removed no less than twice—a complete impossibility, as I well know, but nevertheless I was present both times. Even after all that butchery hay-fever remained, and it was not until I was fifty years old that it ever showed any sign of yielding—whether to the vaccines that I was taking by the pint or to the belated mercies of higher powers I do not know.

When, in June of 1900, the fatigues of a hard Winter began to blossom into downright debility, I waited on our old family physician, Dr. Z. K. Wiley,[1] and he talked so mysteriously and so dolefully about tuberculosis that I got alarmed, and rushed off at once to a specialist downtown. This specialist was a competent journeyman of the transition stage between sweet spirits of nitre and the barbituric acid compounds: he was enough of a modernist to wear the first white coat I had ever seen on a doctor in private practise, but he stuck to a carpet on the floor of his surgery, and there was a huge (and rusty) static electricity machine in a corner. He listened to my chest sounds for half an hour or so, pulled down a couple of books, meditated profoundly, and then said that if I wanted to keep out of trouble I had better take a sea voyage, preferably in a sailing ship. His precise diagnosis, whatever it was, he did not mention, and I never learned it afterward, though I assumed that he had heard something upsetting in my bronchial tubes, or maybe even my lungs. There were craft sailing out of Baltimore, he went on, that offered what I needed in a very cheap and convenient form. They were the small schooners that went to the Bahamas every Spring to bring back pineapples. They were not licensed to carry passengers, but he reckoned that my newspaper connections would enable me to get rid of that difficulty.

When I brought this advice to Max Ways he was full of sympathy, and proceeded immediately to practical aid. I had two weeks' vacation coming to me, and to them, he said, he would add another week to make up for the days off that I had lost. (I had actually lost at least fifteen, but let it go.) Furthermore, if I wanted to add a fourth week I might take it without salary: beyond that he could not go without risking a row with the business office. This seemed fair to me, and Max added to my gratitude by ordering our shipping reporter to go down to the wharves at once, book passage for me on the next pineapple schooner to sail, and arrange the matter of the passenger license with his friend Bill Stone, the collector of customs. The shipping reporter came back presently with the news that the last schooner of the season had cleared that very morning, but he added consolingly that there was a banana boat sailing for

[1]He is dealt with at length in Chapter VII of *Happy Days*.

the West Indies in two days, and that Old Man Buckman, the Baltimore banana king of the time, was willing to let me sign on it as supercargo. My duties and wages would be nothing, and if I paid $2.50 a day for my transportation and subsistence it would be enough.

I went down to Bowley's Wharf the next morning to have a look at the banana boat. It was a small British tramp of the kind that used to be rolled out along the Clyde as Fords were later to be littered along the River Rouge. Such paint as it showed was in patches of different colors, all of them hideous, and the only members of the crew in sight were a couple of Chinamen. It was the *Ely* of Cardiff, Captain Corning, and only the other day I went through a dusty old book at the Baltimore Customshouse to learn its official specifications. Its registered tonnage, I found, was 541 tons,[2] and it carried a crew of nineteen men. But as it lay there at Bowley's Wharf on that far-off June morning, gradually disgorging its cargo of green bananas, it loomed high above the express wagons on the quay, and seemed almost oceanic beside the bumboats that clustered about it. The heady smell of the tropics gushed from it, and as I gaped at it a strange-looking yellow-faced man in white duck clothes and a Panama hat came out of Old Man Buckman's office and went aboard. Only a few months before I had read Lafcadio Hearn's "Two Years in the French West Indies," and now the glamor of it rose up to enchant me all over. I had never been to sea, and here I was making ready to sail not only the great Atlantic but also the romantic Caribbean. In ten days or less I'd be loitering beneath the palm trees, and plucking bananas, cocoanuts, pineapples, oranges, lemons, limes, coffee, chocolate, nutmegs, cinnamon and allspice from the vine.

I recall nothing of our departure: my first recollection is of the sneaking, poisonous roll of the Atlantic outside the Chesa-

[2] I take this from the clearance papers, but should add that Captain Corning told me the tonnage was 800. There are, in fact, four sorts of tonnage—the net, which is lowest; the gross, the deadweight, and the displacement, which is highest. Inasmuch as port charges are commonly based on tonnage, the masters of tramp steamers pretend to the lowest that the customs authorities will tolerate. The tonnage of large passenger liners, of course, is reckoned as liberally as possible, to fetch customers.

peake capes. We cleared the capes during the night, and when I came on deck next morning we were already out of sight of land. To Captain Corning the day was fair and the sea calm, but not to me. In brief, I was seasick, and after I had refused breakfast and made a couple of melancholy trips to the *leeward* rail (I had read enough maritime literature to know *that*) the good captain unearthed a dilapidated deck-chair, had it taken up to the starboard wing of the bridge, and invited me to use it. The air up there, he said, was fresher than below, and I'd thus recover the quicker. I lolled in the chair all day and all the following night, with my mouth open and my eyes rolling, and was still full of misery the next morning, but toward midday I began to recover, and by the second night I was on my legs again, and very hungry. What I needed now, said the captain, was some physic, so he got out his medicine-chest and handed me a pill—the largest and blackest, I believe, ever seen on earth. Its effects were almost those of siege artillery, but it did me no harm, and I was presently sitting on the after-deck eating a plate of clam chowder with the captain.

It was his theory that clam chowder was the queen of all human victuals, and he ate it in large bowls every day. He said he bought it in cans, which was reassuring, for I had taken a look into the galley, and the Chinese cook, naked to the waist and barefooted, was certainly not appetizing. While we thus ate our first meal together (there was nothing beyond the chowder save crackers and bananas) a strange shape suddenly appeared from the depths of the ship. It was that of a skinny old man wearing greasy dungarees and carpet slippers, and showing four or five days' growth of gray beard. His right arm was extended and from his hand hung a strip of what appeared to be bacon—held as gingerly as one might hold a dead rat by the tail. It turned out that he was the Scotch chief engineer, and that he had a complaint. "Is this the sort of meat," he croaked, "to feed a British crew?" "What's the matter with it?" demanded the captain. "There's worms in it," said the chief engineer. "How do you know?" said the captain. "I bit into one," said the chief engineer. "Well, then," said the captain, "spit it out and go to Hell. Back to your engine-room!"

The captain appeared to be glad of my company, for the commander of a British ship is a lonely man, and we ate

together for the remainder of the voyage. It lasted eight days
altogether—six days to Port Antonio on the north coast of
Jamaica, and two days up the coast and back. The total distance covered was something under 1800 miles, but the *Ely*
had been built, not for speed but for economy, and it took a
brisk tail wind to lift her to nine knots. On the fourth day we
passed the little island of San Salvador, where Columbus first
sighted America, and the captain made a course close inshore,
so that I could see the cairn on the beach that marks the most
fateful landfall in all history. We were among the islands after
that, with great masses of yellow seaweed floating by on the
ever bluer water, and flying-fish leaping among them, and
strange birds coming out to have a look. On a day so bright
that it was blinding I caught glimpses of both Cape Maysi,
Cuba, and the western mountains of Haiti, but it was not until
the next morning, just before daylight, that we made Port
Antonio. The east began to show streaks of pink as we entered
the little harbor, and so I got my first sight of the tropics in the
vast splendors of dawn.

It was a spectacle so superb that I stood on deck silent and
almost abashed. As the sun cleared the horizon and its first rays
broke through the palms of Upper Titchfield they picked up a
thousand gaudy hues, and in a few minutes the whole scene
was shimmering like the image in a kaleidoscope. I had always
thought of the tropics as luxuriant, but somehow, despite the
word-painting of Hearn, I had overlooked their magnificent
color. Now I got all that color with the light exactly right, and
behind it, gradually fading into blue and gray, stretched the
immense escarpment of the Blue Mountains, just short of a
mile and a half high. And down from the heights, borne by the
land-breeze of the dawn, came the indescribable tropical smell
—half sweet and half sour, laden with strange and lovely scents,
but also with whiffs of decay. I was brought back to the rusty
and decrepit *Ely* by the clatter of oar-locks: a small boat was
making out from the shadows of the shore. When it came close
I saw a very impressive man standing in its stern—coal black as
to complexion, but clad in immaculate white ducks and a sun
helmet. He was some sort of port functionary, and he entered
upon an official parley with the captain. "How many?" I heard

him bellow, and the captain bawled back "Nineteen officers and hands and one passenger." Passenger? Wasn't I on the ship's papers as supercargo? The captain recalled the fact instantly and corrected his report. "I meant to say," he howled, "*twenty* officers and hands, and *no* passengers." The functionary made no reply, and I was soon preparing to go ashore.

But at the last minute the captain proposed that I stay aboard while he ran up the coast to load bananas, and in an hour we were off. How far we went I have forgotten, but I recall going ashore at a little place called Port Maria, and wandering through a village that looked precisely like an African kraal, even to the high-pitched thatched roofs and the stilts under the wicker houses. The captain went along and we palavered with the females of the settlement, and watched their naked children at play, while the bucks hauled bananas out to the *Ely* in surf-boats. When it was time for us to return to the ship there was a warning blast of its siren, and all the children dived under the houses. We got back to Port Antonio on the second morning following, again at dawn, and I saw the show of light and color all over again. The *Ely* did not enter the harbor, but only slowed down outside, and I went ashore in a surf-boat, along with four or five banana-checkers of the white race, and a dozen black roustabouts. One of the checkers was a ventriloquist, and he entertained the rest of us by evoking sepulchral shrieks of "Help!" and "Murder!" from the depths of the Caribbean, and turning the livers of the poor Afro-Jamaicans to water.

When we parted the captain and I agreed to meet again in Baltimore on my return, and we did so a couple of months later. I took him to lunch and he asked for clam chowder: he was still eating it every day. He was a Blue Nose from Nova Scotia, and not very communicative, but on this occasion he confided to me an aspiration that, so I learned afterward, was shared by all the merchant masters in the West Indies trade. It was to get a towing line, some happy day, aboard a disabled steamship of large tonnage, and so strike a blow for humanity and collar the captain's share in a juicy pot of salvage. Whether or not this chance for Service ever came to him I never heard, but years afterward, crossing the Atlantic in a luxurious

Doppelschraubenschnellpostdampfer, I met another captain of
* the Spanish Main to whom it had. He was a Dane from
Schleswig, and his share of the honorarium, so he told me, ran
to $30,000. He invested it in certain mysterious speculations
in the Oriente province of Cuba, and when I encountered him
he had on a Panama hat that had cost him $125 wholesale, and
was passing out Upmann cigars at least eight inches long.

I put in a couple of weeks roving and seeing Jamaica, and
was delighted enormously by its varied but always gorgeous
scenery. I crossed the island on a train that ducked through
twenty-four tunnels in forty miles, and between them ran
along gorges thick with bamboo and brilliant with crocuses of
a hundred colors and a thousand patterns. On another train I
traveled westward over the high country, and spent a night at
the very English hill-station of Mandeville, where I dined on a
cut from a pale, bluish joint of island beef, with two vegetables
that tasted like stewed hay. I put up at the old Myrtle Bank
Hotel in Kingston (soon to be destroyed in the great earthquake of 1907), and there became acquainted with planters'
punch, a drink that I have esteemed highly ever since, and also
with an exiled native king from the Mosquito Coast, who lived
in gloomy splendor on an official solatium of £1 a day and
spent all his time trying to grasp the game of billiards. And I
went up to Spanish Town, the old capital of the island, and
there searched the records for vestiges of my father's mother's
people, the McClellans, who had lived in Jamaica nearly a
century before.

These records were in charge of a colored intellectual who
wore the thick spectacles with Oxford frames that still mark a
learned blackamoor in the British West Indies. He brought
out a dozen elephant folios from his catacombs, and deputed a
lowly clark, a mulatto with sandy hair, to help me explore
them. All the clark and I could find was the will of my great-
great-uncle, Jeremiah, who had died in Kingston back in the
early forties. He had left, it appeared, a small legacy to my
grandmother, then still a child, but whether she ever got it I
do not know: I suppose that I must assume that she did, for his
executor was a clergyman. This Jeremiah never married, but
there was in him none the less a strong strain of philoprogeni-
tiveness, and I discovered that his descendants were numerous

all over the southern parishes of the island, and that some of the latest generation had reverted to an almost burnt cork complexion. On my return to Baltimore I spread the news, and acquired thereby a standing in the inner Confederate circles of the town that was very useful to me in my later newspaper work.

Kingston itself was an ancient and romantic town, and I spent some agreeable mornings wandering along its sea-front or rambling through its market, which swarmed with native farmers from back in the brush. They offered all sorts of comestibles that were new to me—for example, cacao beans, plantains, mangoes, and cashew nuts, all of them still unknown in the United States. They had heaps of pimento berries, from which allspice is made, spread out on newspapers, and here and there was a country butcher with rounds and chops of goat meat. I learned to smoke and like the dark, spicy Jamaican cigars, and I had a colored tailor sitting at his booth by the market place make me a suit of white ducks. They were ready in two hours and cost £1, then the standard price for a Class A suit in Kingston. The tailor told me that he had other and cheaper models, some as low as eight shillings, but that he never recommended them to distinguished visitors. I also made acquaintance with a Jamaican soft-drink called cola—the progenitor, I suspect, of Coca-Cola, which was yet concealed in the womb of time. And, as a fanatical Kiplingite, I was enchanted to observe Mulvaney, Learoyd and Ortheris, direct from "Soldiers Three," strutting along the streets of the town with their swagger sticks, tomcatting the more likely black gals, and taking their ease in the less refined bars.

All these studies and recreations were very pleasant, but my time was running short, so I shoved back to Port Antonio to find a ship for home. I learned at once that a Norwegian tramp of about the size and speed of the *Ely* would be clearing in a few days, and I booked passage at once. The next day was a Sunday, and I resolved to spend it sitting on the veranda of the old Titchfield Hotel, listening to the gabble of the supercargoes, plantation overseers and English remittance men who then constituted the society of the place. They started off after breakfast with a series of magnificent tales of love, trading and carnage, for it was not often that they encountered a new listener who was really eager to listen. But suddenly, in the midst

of a hair-raising anecdote about cannibalism in Haiti, two of
them rose quietly and faded away, and then two more followed,
and then three, and in half a minute I was alone with the ra-
conteur, an Irishman who claimed to be the son of a Spanish
duke. Finally, even *he* made off at a quick sneak, and I looked
behind me anxiously, almost expecting to see a crocodile bearing down, or even a shark. But all I could find was an old man
with a long white beard, buttoned up in a black frock coat of
the vintage of 1880. He looked harmless enough, certainly, but
I was soon to learn that he was the most dangerous carnivore
on the island, for what he packed was a messianic delusion.

In brief, he was tortured by a libido to save the souls of
carnal wayfarers, and in order to feed and furnish it he maintained at his own expense a Methodist chapel down in the
town. The cost was no burden to him, for he had come to Jamaica back in the first days of the banana business, and picked
up plenty of easy money. Now his whole time was given over
to his missionarying, and every Sunday morning he swooped
down on the Titchfield veranda and tried to round up the
damned assembled there. As I learned afterward, only strangers somewhat gone in liquor ever succumbed to him, and
when they got back from his services they always reported a
terrible experience. Being sober at the time, I resisted, and inasmuch as I was already something of an amateur theologian,
and hence familiar with all the classical grips and grapples, I
resisted to some effect. But I am glad to testify today, after
so many years, that never in this life have I gone to the mat
with a tougher evangelist. He beat any Christian Scientist ever
heard of, or any Presbyterian, however ferocious, or any foot-
wash Baptist. I have been tackled in my day by virtuosi ranging
from mitred abbots to the kitchen police of the Salvation
Army, but never have I had to fight harder to preserve my
doctrinal chastity. Over and over again the old boy got to my
chin or midriff with scriptural texts that had the impact of a
mule's hoof, and when he turned from upbraiding to cajolery,
and began to argue that my sufferings in Hell would be upon
his head, I almost threw up the sponge. Indeed, if it had not
been for the audience lying in wait (I could hear it panting
behind the jalousies), I'd have gone down to his gospel mill
with him, if only to get rid of him, but as it was I was in honor

bound to resist, and in the end he gave up in despair, and shuffled off down the path to the town. The loafers, when they sneaked back, stood me a communal drink, and I surely needed it. Some years later, on returning to Port Antonio, I was told that the old man had got himself into a wilder and wilder lather as his years advanced, and that he finally prayed himself to death.

The Norwegian tramp that brought me home, though it was as slow as the *Ely* and little if any larger, turned out to be a great deal cleaner and more shipshape. The young captain, who told me that he owned a 3/70ths interest in it, his father an 18/70ths, and his rich Uncle Olaf a 32/70ths, had his wife with him—a handsome and charming blonde from Bergen, with enlightened ideas about eating and drinking, and a flair for interior decoration in the provincial Scandinavian mode. Every chair in the cabin had a knitted tidy on it, and there were window-boxes at all the portholes, with geraniums growing in them. We dined at 1 P.M., which is to say, we *began* to dine at 1 P.M. The meal itself, prepared by an excellent Danish cook, lasted until 3, and then the steward came in with a large Gjedser cheese, a plate of crackers, a pot of coffee and a bottle of Madeira, and we lingered over them until 4 or even 5. The captain and his wife were eager propagandists for the Norwegian *Kultur*, and they told me so much about Ibsen, then still a dubious character in America, that I became, a few years later, Baltimore's recognized authority on the subject, and even went to the length of reading all the plays, including "The Warriors at Helgeland," perhaps the worst play ever written. I blush to say that I can't remember the name of this amiable and excellent pair, though I seem to recall that it was something on the order of Olsen, Jensen, Hansen, Knutson, Halvorsen or Magnussen. They were intelligent and kindly people, and the captain was a brisk and competent mariner.

But even the briskest mariner collides now and then with what the marine insurance policies call an act of God, and this happened to my friend somewhere or other off the Middle Atlantic coast. It was a misty morning, and in consequence he could not leave the bridge, so I climbed up to keep him company. Suddenly there was a thinning of the mist, and a lightship loomed up off the *starboard* bow. In other words, we were *inside* the light-ship—and maybe only a few yards from the beach. The captain had yanked the wheel out of the quartermaster's hands in a split second, and the ship heeled over alarmingly as we made a quarter turn on the nautical equivalent of a ten-cent piece. We continued due East for two hours at least, and the next morning, though the sky was as clear as crystal, the captain approached the Delaware capes as cautiously as a sheep approaching a coyote, and, in fact, did not venture to enter at all until another ship came along and showed the way.

That my trip to Jamaica had done me any good did not appear immediately. I was still underweight, and as Summer faded into Autumn I developed a cough. The specialist, however, professed to believe that his prescription had worked, and I was presently so busy that I forgot my malaises. I wrote three pieces for the *Sunday Herald* on my adventures, illustrated by halftones from photographs that I had bought on the island. I was ready and willing to write three more, or a dozen more, but Colonel Cunningham got rid of me by saying that a stringent economy order had just come up from the business office, and that he'd catch hell if he authorized any more halftones. I continued skinny until 1904, as the frontispiece to this work shows, but after that I gradually picked up weight, and by the time I was thirty I was so rotund that another specialist put me on one of the first of the reducing diets.

VI.

The Gospel of Service

IT WAS in the month of May, 1901, that I got my first really juicy out-of-town assignment—and began to develop in a large way my theory that Service is mainly only blah. The scene was the town of Jacksonville, Fla., and I had been sent there to cover the great fire of May 3, the largest blaze in American history between the burning of Chicago in 1871 and the burning of Baltimore in 1904. It destroyed, as I learn from an encyclopedia, no less than 2361 buildings, stretching over 196 city blocks and 450 acres: all I can add to these statistics is that when I arrived by train, all set to load the wires with graphic prose, there seemed to be nothing left save a fringe of houses around the municipal periphery, like the hair on a friar's head. Only one hotel was left standing, and, so far as I could discover, not a single other public convenience of any sort, whether church, hospital, theatre, livery-stable, jail, bank, saloon, barbershop, pants-pressing parlor, or sporting-house.

But what so powerfully reinforced my growing suspicion of Service was not this scene of desolation, but the imbecility of the public effort to aid its ostensible victims. In every American community of Christian pretensions, North, East, South and West, busy-bodies began to collect money and goods for their succor the moment the first bulletins came in, and by the time I reached what was left of the Jacksonville railroad station the first relief shipments were on their way. The *Herald* started a communal subscription at the drop of the hat, and had cabbaged half a carload of eleemosynary supplies before I left for the South. The city editor (not Max Ways, but one of his successors) favored me from hour to hour with dispatches recording the progress of this philanthropy. The first one, I recall, announced that the boys at the Pimlico race-track had contributed 100 second-hand horse-blankets, and on its heels came one reporting that the saloonkeepers of Baltimore had matched them with 100 cases of Maryland rye.

When I took these dispatches to the Mayor of Jacksonville I

expected (at least officially) that he would burst into tears and bid me thank the good people of Baltimore for their generosity, but what he actually did was to laugh. I must confess that, at thought of the horse-blankets, I had to smile myself, for the temperature in Jacksonville was rising 80 degrees, and most of the dispossessed householders, white and black, were camping out gaily in their erstwhile backyards, and refreshing themselves with swims in the St. Johns river. The Mayor was amused, but not surprised, for he had telegrams on his desk showing that many other Northern cities were even more idiotic than Baltimore. St. Paul, it appeared, was sending a couple of bales of old fur coats, and Boston was loading a car with oil-stoves. Even some of the nearby towns, though they should have known better, had contributed supplies almost as insane. Thus, a large box of woolen mittens had already come in from Montgomery, Ala., and Winston-Salem, N. C., had sent a supply of the heavy, sanitary red underwear for which it was then famous.

But it was the Maryland whiskey, not the Pimlico horse-blankets, that really flabbergasted the Mayor. He was far from a Prohibitionist, but the fire had given him plenty of worries, and he did not welcome the new one provided by those hundred cases of rye. What would he do with them when they arrived—supposing they escaped the hobos and railroad men on the way? If he distributed them as medical supplies every white man in Jacksonville would be in a state of liquor within an hour, and probably half of the blackamoors. If he put his town cops to guarding them he would lose his police force, which was sorely needed. And if he asked for a detail from the Florida militia, which was flocking into town from the swamps to the southward, there would be a military drunk of a virulence unparalleled since Sherman's march to the sea, with a good deal of promiscuous shooting.

I had no suggestion to offer His Honor, and left him. I wrote a column and a half on the scene of desolation, and then went to inquire of the railroad men when the first car from Baltimore could be expected. They knew nothing about it, and had never even heard of it. Indeed, it was not until hours later that I got a bulletin from Baltimore saying that it had just started, and in the same bulletin came news that it was now

two cars instead of one. The second, it appeared, was loaded
mainly with medical and chirurgical *matériel*, including a bale
of splints, five gallons of sulphuric ether, half a ton of bandages,
a crate of wooden legs, and twenty Potter's Field coffins in
shooks. Inasmuch as no one had suffered anything worse than
a few singes in the fire, and all the other survivors were in ro-
bust health and excellent spirits, this shipment seemed somehow irrational, but figuring out what to do with it was the
Mayor's grief, not mine, and I confined myself to trying to
learn when it would arrive.

The Mayor, when I saw him again that evening, was not as
put out about the medical supplies as I expected, for he said
that the militiamen from the Everglades would undoubtedly
begin shooting one another anon, and it would be handy to
have the splints and coffins, if not the wooden legs. But when
I told him (as I had just been advised by a latter bulletin) that
the freight of the medical car included a dozen cases of champagne, he immediately took a graver view of the situation, and,
in fact, showed a considerable perturbation. This seemed unreasonable to me, for I believed the cops and militiamen, all of
them unschooled in the ways of the northern Babylons, would
probably take to their heels in alarm the moment the first
champagne cork popped, but when I said so to the Mayor he
replied that a moral question was involved—in brief, that
champagne was still regarded by the decent people of Florida
as a lecherous drink, and that having it on his hands might
embarrass him politically almost as much as having a trunk full
of tights. I could see this point of view and even sympathize
with it, though I was young at the time, so I proposed to His
Honor that he commandeer the champagne the instant it arrived, wrap it in the horse-blankets from Pimlico, and lock it
up in the catacombs under City Hall, for such future reference
as human ingenuity and the course of events might suggest.
Whether or not this was actually done I do not know to the
present day, as the narrative following will show.

It was now late at night, and I began to think about a place
to sleep. As I have said, there was only one hotel left standing,
and when I got to it I found that it was swamped by guests—
some of them newspaper reporters like myself, but most of
them insurance adjusters, brick and lumber salesmen, and

agents for sprinkling systems and fire extinguishers. They were sleeping five and six in a room, and all the upstairs corridors were full of cots. Every one of the arm-chairs in the lobby had been grabbed by a sleeper, and others were snoring on the dining-room tables. The night-clerk, a very affable fellow, received my importunities politely, but shook his head. Finally, he had a bright idea. Between the lobby and the dining-room there was a small ladies' parlor, and in it was a grand piano, with a heavily embroidered spread covering it. Why not remove the spread, roll it up for a pillow, and then turn in *under* the piano? I'd thus have the whole space beneath the instrument to myself, a larger area than anyone else had, and I'd be protected from the hooves of guests stumbling through the parlor in the dark. The idea seemed magnificent, and in five minutes I was berthed behind the pedals and sound asleep.

Unhappily, I was not booked for an easy night, for before I got halfway through my first dream a squad of moron soldiery took up post on the veranda outside the parlor window, to guard a burned bank across the street, and their simian gabble and guffawing made me toss and moan, dead tired though I was. But the worst was reserved for 3 A.M. or thereabouts. The goofs had brought a primeval machine-gun with them, and one of them, thinking he saw ghouls in the ruins of the bank, suddenly turned it on. With the sounding-board of the piano directly over my head I got the full force of the reverberation —indeed, I got a great magnification of it. It took on the proportions of the explosion of a battleship, and when I fetched up with a start my head banged the hull of the piano, and I got a bump that stuck to me until I was back in Baltimore. The night-clerk patched me up with vinegar and butcher-paper from the kitchen, but I slept no more that night.

All the next day I devoted to badgering the railroad men about the two relief-cars, and all of the day following, with occasional pauses to file instalments of my thriller on the ruins. No report of them had come in. No one had any notion where they were. Meanwhile, my city editor bombarded me with demands that I get and send a statement from the Mayor, setting forth Jacksonville's gratitude. Rather curiously for so philosophical a man, he raised scruples about giving it to me. What if the cars never arrived at all? What if they were wrecked along the way, and the whole world learned that they had not got in? Inspired and goaded by my city editor, I labored with His Honor, and in the end he compromised with his conscience by requiring me to swear that if he gave me a statement I would not send it until the cars were safe in port. I was ready, by that time, to agree to anything, and after a conference with his advisers he produced the document. It turned out, after all that backing and filling, to be only a carbon of one that had been dispatched to Savannah, Atlanta, New Orleans, and various other nearby cities, with the name of Baltimore inserted in a blank left for the purpose. It began by saying that the people of Jacksonville were completely overcome by the astounding generosity and loving-kindness of the (Baltimore) humanitarians, and would never forget it so long as the pleasant and mutually profitable business relations between Jacksonville and (Baltimore) continued. It went on in this vein for 500 or 600 words, and then closed with some sly remarks about the salubriousness of the Florida climate, and the incomparable flavor of the citrus fruits. This was before the great Florida land boom, so there was no mention of real estate opportunities, but the general tenor of it was certainly very complacent, and I heard when I got home that some of the horse-lovers of Pimlico, on reading it, said they wished they had kept their blankets.

Armed with the carbon, I spent the evening in the railroad yards searching for the two cars of relief supplies, and not finding them. Along about ten o'clock the fireman of a switching engine told me that he had seen a couple of suspicious-looking cars on a siding about a mile out of town, and I hoofed there to have a look. I got to the place all right, and even found the cars, only to learn that they were two old wrecks loaded with razor-back hog hides from Waycross, Ga. I turned sadly away, and started down the long, long trail back to stricken but contented Jacksonville. I had gone hardly a third of the distance when a yahoo militiaman jumped from behind a gondola, and jammed his bayonet into my front. He was taking his stance to shove it through me when I managed to yell. This set him to yelling too, and in a moment two more privates, a corporal, a sergeant, and finally a lieutenant rushed up. It appeared that the yahoo charged me with looting, though there was nothing within half a mile that any sensible man would loot. I demanded trial on the spot, and it was presently in progress, with the lieutenant serving as both president and judge-advocate. He was an ill-favored fellow, and if he lived to 1934 he probably got a part in "Tobacco Road," but he knew something about the rules of evidence, and so acquitted me with honor, and even offered me a chew from his plug as a solatium.

There ensued three days and three nights of fevered hunting for those cars, gladdened on the afternoon of the third day by a telegram from the Seaboard's division superintendent at Savannah saying that they had been found on a siding near a water-tank called Jones. I tried to wire to Jones, but was told that there was no operator there, nor indeed anything save the tank itself and an old man who spent his time plugging its leaks with rosin. I laid off the third night, and had a fair sleep, and then spent the next morning writing a long piece describing the grateful gloats and sobs of the starving and shivering Jacksonville populace as the cars rolled in, and the supplies were distributed. I figured on filing this palpitating stuff the instant they really arrived, or were reported anywhere below the Georgia frontier, but when they failed to turn up at 6 P.M. I filed it anyhow, and was encouraged two hours later by a complimentary telegram from the home office.

Bucked up by this appreciation, I decided to put in another night in the yards, looking for the cars. When I got there no one had seen them, or heard anything about them, but while I stood talking with the yardmaster, wondering whether I had better give up, they suddenly appeared from nowhere, directly before our eyes. They were running next to the caboose of a way-freight, and how they got there I never learned. The door of one hung by a single hinge, but when it came to a halt I could find no sign that it had been burgled, and the railroad men showed no predatory interest in its contents. On both sides of each car were muslin banners (or what was left of them) reading:

BALTIMORE MORNING HERALD
RELIEF TRAIN FOR
JACKSONVILLE FIRE SUFFERERS

The railroad men snickered quietly at the words "train" and "sufferers," and began pulling the signs down—as I gathered from their talk, to make shirts for their children. I filed the Mayor's long-delayed statement before turning in, and slept late the next morning, for my mission of mercy was over. At noon or thereabout I dropped into His Honor's office, and he promised to do something about the cars as soon as he could come round to it—that is, if the anthropoid militiamen did not seize them meanwhile, and spirit them away to the Everglades. He even suggested politely that if I would stick about a day or two longer a couple of the bottles of Maryland rye would be mine for the asking. But I needed sleep more than stimulants, and, what is more, I was lathering for a square meal, for the catering arrangements at Jacksonville, even disregarding the fire, were much less elaborate in those days than they are today, and I was tired of tough hog-meat and greasy corn-pone. That night I boarded a train for Baltimore, and the next day, at a meal-stop called Norlina, near the border between North Carolina and Virginia, I tackled a platter of country victuals that still sticks in my mind after forty years. It was, in quality, superb, for it consisted principally of chicken fried to perfection, with hominy cakes and cream gravy. In quantity, it was colossal, and the half hour allowed for devouring it was enough to dispose of only about a third of it. The rest, according to the custom of travelers in that age, I stuffed into my pockets, and I was still at work on it when we crossed the James river.

A year later I was sent back to Jacksonville to find out how the town was making out. I found, as I expected, that the fire had been the luckiest act of God in all its history. The marsh that used to lie between it and the channel of the St. Johns river, generating mosquitoes and malaria, was now filled with the debris, and dozens of new warehouses were going up. A little while later Congress ordered the 19-foot channel dredged to 24 feet, and then to 30. During the next decade the population of Jacksonville more than doubled, and today it is a metropolis comparable to Nineveh or Gomorrah in their prime, with the hottest night-clubs between Norfolk and Miami, and so many indigenous salvage-crews of humanitarians that Florida can't contain them, and they are constantly reaching out for more distant clients. When, in 1904, Baltimore itself had a

big fire, they proposed to send up enough oranges (some of
them almost fresh) to supply 500,000 people for 100 days, but
the Baltimore authorities declined them.

My exertions on my mission seem to have been well received
in the *Herald* office, for during the following year I was given
a number of other interesting out-of-town assignments. I recall, for example, being sent to the battlefield of Antietam, in
Western Maryland, to cover the dedication of a soldiers' monument by the immortal McKinley. He was to become an angel
only a couple of months later, but he did not know it at the
time, and so made a roaring speech from an open-air stand on
a very hot day. There were scores of reporters present, including a large squad of Washington correspondents wearing cutaway coats and carrying doggy walking-sticks. This was the
first time that I had ever come into contact with such eminent
journalists, and you may be sure that I gaped at them with every
show of respect. Inasmuch as McKinley's secretary, George B.
Cortelyou, had brought along copies of the presidential
speech, it was not necessary to risk sunstroke by listening to it,
so I spent the hour of its delivery roving about the grounds. A
large marquee had been erected for the accommodation of
distinguished guests, and in it I found a dozen or more United
States Senators loading up on fried chicken and champagne.
Late in the afternoon the whole party returned to Washington
on a special train provided by the Baltimore & Ohio Railroad,
and I heard the same Senators go through a long programme
of American folk-song, including "The Old Black Bull." There
were no ladies present, for in those days the female politician
had not yet begun to spoil junkets.

Various assignments took me to Washington, and there
came eventually the glorious day when I sat in the Senate
press-gallery for the first time. Like all the really massive experiences of life, it turned out to be more or less disappointing. I
also made a number of trips to Annapolis, to help my betters
cover the Maryland Legislature, and there I sniffed for the first
time the peculiar smell that radiates from all such bodies—that
sickening mixture of stale beer and free lunch, contributed by
the city members, and cow and sweat, contributed by the yokels. In the years since I have smelled it in six or eight other
state capitals, and have never been able to detect a difference of

more than two per cent. between one and the next. But the best of all the assignments that came to me in those happy days, and indeed the best of my whole career on newspapers, I had to miss. It was the Martinique volcano story of 1902. The first blow-off of Mont Pelée, of course, happened too suddenly to be covered, but when the Navy started a couple of rescue ships for the island there was room on them for a few reporters, and Carter got a place for the *Herald*, and assigned me to it. The boys on those rescue ships saw the most stupendous spectacle ever staged on earth, for when they heaved in sight of the island the volcano went off again, and with ten times the violence of the first time. The ships were rocked by the blast and covered with ashes, but no one was hurt. All the reporters vomited purple copy, and for a week afterward it filled the American newspapers. Alas, none of it was mine, for on the day before the ships sailed I was served with a summons in a lawsuit relating to my father's estate, and my lawyer warned me that if I disregarded it I might land in jail on my return, and my mother might lose a piece of property. No one else was sent.

VII.

Scent of the Theatre

THE REPORTER covering the theatres for the *Herald*, during
my first year on the staff, was Theodore M. Leary, a
charming young Irishman who was a graduate of the Johns
Hopkins and whose father, a general in the Army, was com-
mandant at Fort McHenry, the Baltimore military post. The
job, in those days, was not a full-time one, and Leary was often
given other assignments. In June, 1900, he was sent to Philadelphia to help Al Goodman, the political reporter of the paper,
cover the Republican National Convention. The importance
of the job impressed him vastly, and when his train reached
Wilmington he put off a telegram to Max Ways, announcing
the fact. Half an hour later, having got to Philadelphia, he sent
another, reading:

> Have arrived safely. Delegates pouring in. Prepare for at least a
> column and a half tonight.

The waggish Max passed these telegrams around the office,
and when Leary returned he was given a heavy dose of kidding.
But he threw it off by doing excellent work, and was soon
ranked among the four or five best reporters on the paper.
Such a youngster, when assigned to the theatres, was always
marked, in those days, by the theatrical managers of New York,
and in a little while he began to receive offers from this one or
that one to go on the road as press-agent of a traveling company. At the beginning of the season of 1901–2 he finally succumbed, and at his suggestion I was given his place. Thus I
escaped the City Hall at last, and in the intervals of covering
the theatres took general assignments. In October I was made
Sunday editor, but continued to do the theatres and also to
write for the editorial page.

Baltimore then had two first-class playhouses, Ford's Opera
House and the Academy of Music, a third that played dollar
shows, a fourth that offered vaudeville, a fifth that had a stock
company, a sixth that played only melodrama, and a couple of

burlesque houses. There was a change of bill in each of them every week, and every change of bill had to be noticed. The theatre reporter (or, as he was called, the dramatic editor) commonly did the principal attraction of the week, but when Robert I. Carter became managing editor of the *Herald* at the end of 1900 he took over the leading notice himself, for he had formerly been a dramatic critic, was still greatly interested in the theatre, and knew more about plays than any other man I had encountered up to that time. Thus, when I succeeded Leary, it was only the second choice that fell to me, but I was very well content, for two times out of three Carter would pick the more serious plays, which left me the comedies and musical pieces. I recall, for example, that I did "Florodora" when it first came to Baltimore, and liked it so well that I dropped in at every subsequent performance of the week, usually just as the famous sextette was coming on. In the first theatre page that I got out as Sunday editor, the piano score of the sextette was reproduced as a background for a photograph of the six elegant bucks and six gorgeous wenches who danced and sang it.

On Monday evenings, after Carter had dictated his own notice and I had written mine, he would invite me to his office, and instruct me in the technic of reviewing. He believed, and taught me, that a dull notice, however profound, was not worth printing. "The first job of a reviewer," he would say, "is to write a good story—to produce something that people will enjoy reading. If he has nothing to say he simply can't do it. If he has, then it doesn't make much difference whether what he says is fundamentally sound or not. Exact and scientific criticism is not worth trying for, especially on a provincial paper. Don't hesitate to use the actors roughly: they are mainly idiots. And don't take a dramatist's pretensions too seriously: he is usually only a showman." Carter warned me against associating with theatrical people, but added that he meant performers, not authors or managers. In search of material for my daily column of theatrical gossip I tackled all members of the latter two classes who visited Baltimore, and thereby got to know many notables of the time, for example, Daniel Frohman, Victor Herbert, Clyde Fitch, Paul Armstrong, Augustus Thomas, Charles Klein and A. M. Palmer. Charles Frohman I never met. When he came to town he secreted himself mysteriously, and getting to see him was an elaborate business, almost as difficult as seeing the Pope. When, in the end, I was solemnly invited to the felicity of waiting on him, I refused, for I had seen a good many of his plays by that time, and come to the conclusion that he was a fraud.

But I naturally met all of the salient press-agents of the era, for they came to my office as soon as they got to town. Most of them were former newspaper reporters, and all that I can remember were very pleasant fellows. One of the liveliest was a Dane with the strange name of A. Toxen Worm, who stood at the head of the craft but is now forgotten. Another who was good company was a tall, slim, handsome blond young man named Herbert Bayard Swope, who interrupted a successful newspaper career to whoop up the English actor, Martin Harvey. Harvey seemed to me to be a ham, but Swope I came to terms with quickly, and we have been on a footing of mutual esteem and suspicion ever since. In 1912 he was married in Baltimore, and I was best man at his wedding. In 1906 I was drafted for the same delicate office by Channing Pollock, who then combined press-agenting and play-writing, but I had to function *in absentia*, for at the last moment he and Anna Marble decided to be married in Canada. Many other press-agents of that era were interesting and able men, among them, Paul Wilstach, who whooped up Richard Mansfield and actually believed that he was the greatest actor on earth; James Forbes, who labored for many bad stars, including Robert Edeson; Eugene Walter, who did the same, again including Edeson; Bayard Veiller, who represented, among other first-chop performers, his own excellent wife, Margaret Wycherly; and Frank J. Wilstach, who was Paul's elder brother, and served, at different times, De Wolf Hopper, E. H. Sothern, Julia Marlowe, Viola Allen, William Faversham and Mrs. Leslie Carter. These were all clever fellows, and every one of them made his mark in the years following. Paul Wilstach wrote a number of successful plays, accumulated a competence, and retired in bachelor splendor to a romantic old estate on the Potomac. Forbes, in 1906, wrote "The Chorus Lady," which broke records on Broadway; Walter, in 1908, alarmed and delighted it with "The Easiest Way"; and Veiller had two big successes in 1918 and 1928—"Within the Law" and "The Trial of Mary Dugan."

Frank Wilstach wrote no plays, but devoted all his leisure to a dictionary of similes that had a cordial reception when it came out at last, and remains the standard work in its field. He collected its contents as he toured the country ahead of his various troupes, and always carried a large ledger for recording them. I supplied him with scores, including many that I invented on the spot, with modest credit to such authors as Aristotle, Confucius and John Calvin. Frank died in 1933 and Forbes five years later, but the rest still flourish.

In 1902, coming to Baltimore ahead of Robert Edeson, Forbes confided to me that he had planted an illustrated article on his star's achievements at field sports, and asked for my help in making the photographs. Edeson, as a matter of fact, knew no more about field sports than a mother superior, but we soon borrowed an outfit of guns, fishing tackle, shooting jackets, hip boots and so on, and went out to Druid Hill Park with a photographer. The time was mid-morning, and the park was deserted. For the fishing pictures a small pond served as stream, and then Edeson changed to the shooting jacket and began to draw beads on imaginary birds. Suddenly a mounted cop came galloping over a hill, and put the whole party under arrest. He had heard, he said, several shots. Didn't we know that it was a serious offense to shoot birds in a public park? We protested that no shot had been fired, and handed over the gun to prove it. We also offered to let the cop search us for cartridges. But he insisted that he had heard at least three shots from the other side of the hill. Why, else, should he have charged us at a gallop? The mystery was never solved. We finally talked the cop out of calling the wagon, but he went away muttering. To this day his imbecile, puzzled face returns to me in my dreams, and wakes me in a sweat. Druid Hill Park, as every Afro-Baltimorean knows, is infested by witches, but who ever heard of a witch using firearms?

Paul Armstrong I met for the first time when he came to Baltimore to put on his first play, "St. Ann." He had been working for Hearst as a sports reporter specializing in pugilism, and had saved enough money to buy scenery and hire a company. All the regular managers of the time had refused the play, and Armstrong was already full of a loathing for them that continued to his death. It turned out to be a dreadful *réchauffé* of Sardou, Pinero and Augustus Thomas, and the opening performance was a nightmare to both audience and dramatist. One of the principal actors showed up drunk and had to be fired, and then another actor, though sober, undertook to beat up Armstrong for an imaginary insult to the leading woman. Armstrong, who was a tough fellow, knocked out this poor fish, so there were two vacancies in the cast, and when a girl who had a small part began to be saucy she was fired too, and there were three. The first act wobbled, the second was worse, the third became downright maniacal, and the fourth was never finished. These proceedings, and especially the bout between Armstrong and the actor, made excellent newspaper fodder, and it was my sworn duty to describe them in the *Herald*. Armstrong, as a newspaper man, understood my position and did not resent my story. Instead, he seemed grateful that I had tamed it down as much as possible, and we straightway became warm friends. A few years later he was the king of Broadway, with three big successes running at once. Having thus fallen into funds, he decided to become a landed proprietor in Maryland, where, as he used to say, there were more shades of green in Spring than anywhere else on earth. He bought an ancient and dilapidated estate below Annapolis, and moved there with his wife and three little girls, and after that I used to see a lot of him, for I spent many weekends with him and he seldom passed through Baltimore without looking me up.

One day in the Spring of 1915 I received a letter from him, dated Atlantic City, saying that he was laid up there by a heart attack, and asking me to arrange for his treatment at the Johns Hopkins Hospital. I did so at once, and in a few days he was at the hospital under the care of Dr. Lewellys F. Barker, the successor of Osler as its chief physician. Dr. Barker found that his heart was very badly impaired, and warned him that he'd have to avoid excitement if he expected to live. Armstrong promised solemnly to go on a Mark Twain regimen—doing all his writing in bed, and leaving every sort of business to his confidential agent, Ben Piazzi. But he had hardly got back to New York before he became involved in a lawsuit, and before long he was engaged in his usual fights with actors. By the end of the Summer he was dead. He was a curious man, and had some talent.

His plays, to be sure, were mainly trash, but nevertheless they were very adroitly constructed, and he made success after success, some of them record-breaking. Despite his truculent ways and fearsome makeup—he wore a Buffalo Bill goatee and a two-gallon hat, and liked striking clothes and flashy jewelry —he was a simple-minded fellow at bottom, and more than once, listening to him expound the plot of a new play at his dinner-table, I have seen tears roll down his cheeks. He probably earned more money than any other dramatist up to his time, whether here or in Europe. His revenues from a single one-acter, played by two companies in vaudeville, ran, to my personal knowledge, beyond $2000 a week for two years on end. He was preparing, in his last days, to invade the movies in the grand manner, and if he had lived ten years more he'd have died a multi-millionaire, for he was already master of all the eye-popping, heart-breaking and liver-scratching devices that the movie Shakespeares were to develop only long afterward. At least five years before D. W. Griffith exacerbated the soul of humanity with "The Birth of a Nation" Armstrong was entertaining me with projects for historical films on twice its scale, with such excursions and alarms in them that they would have paled it. He died at forty-six, leaving three widows. Both of the two that I knew were beautiful and charming women.

I met a great many other dramatic authors in those days, and also most of the current composers of operettas and musical comedies. Reginald De Koven I remember mainly for the fact that he was in liquor every time I had him under my eye, and Victor Herbert because of his marked German accent. Herbert had been brought up in Stuttgart, where his mother had married for the second time, and he looked, talked and carried himself far more like a Württemberger than like the Irishman that he was. He spent a couple of Summers in Baltimore as the director of pop concerts. A man of large bulk, with a neck that required a No. 20 collar, he suffered much from the heat. I used to drop in on him between numbers, and usually found him sitting in his dressing-room in his undershirt, drinking Rhine wine and damning the thermometer. During one especially hot spell he wrecked four or five shirts of an evening, and had to put on a fresh collar after every number. Once, to make conversation, I asked him how he had got the idea for the lovely gipsy love-song in "The Fortune Teller." He replied that he didn't know. "I was aware," he said, "that Eugene Cowles would sing it, and when I sat down to write it I had his voice in mind. After that, I just wrote it." Another popular composer of the time, Willard Spenser, told me that he fetched up melodies by improvising at a church organ. This Spenser was a tall, cadaverous fellow with wispy side-whiskers, and looked more like a Presbyterian deacon than a composer for the theatre. He was, in fact, very prim and pious, and never visited back-stage if he could help it. His two operettas, "The Little Tycoon" and "The Princess Bonnie," were enormous successes, but today they are as teetotally forgotten as "Erminie" or "Fra Diavolo."

It was usual, when a new play had its first performance in Baltimore, for colleagues from New York, Philadelphia and Washington to come to town for the event, and I thus became acquainted with a number of them. One was Acton Davies, of the New York *Evening Sun*, a short, squatty fellow with a high piping voice and a somewhat effeminate manner. One night he appeared for the opening of a new Clyde Fitch play, and after the first act became engaged in a debate in the lobby of Ford's Opera House with the author, whose voice was even higher than his own, and whose manner was even more girlish. Pres-
* ently they were joined by a Baltimorean who surpassed both of them in both respects. In a few minutes the three were surrounded by an appreciative gallery, and when it began to applaud and wise-crack Charlie Ford had to shut off a possible riot by shooing them into the house. The older dramatic critics, in those days, wore opera cloaks and plug hats, and looked a good deal like melodrama villains. They were mainly ignoramuses, though some of them could write. The dean of the corps was William Winter, of the New York *Tribune*, who would sometimes take three of the wide columns that his paper then affected to review a Shakespearean performance. Four-fifths of his critique, of course, was written in advance, and consisted of a pedantic discourse on the play. He was a violent opponent of all novelty in the theatre, and spent his last years denouncing Ibsen, Hauptmann and Shaw. He died in 1917, aged eighty-one. If he had lived into the Eugene O'Neill era

he'd have suffered so powerfully that his death would have been a kind of capital punishment.

Winter, like most of the other dramatic critics of the time, tried to write plays himself, but never with any success. There were, however, a few of the brethren who kept resolutely on their own side of the footlights. To be precise, there were two that I knew of—Stuffy Davis of the New York *Globe* and my- *
self. In 1903 we organized a national association called the Society of Dramatic Critics Who Have Never Written Plays, and began to hold quarterly conventions in Brown's Chophouse, in New York, then the chief boozing-ken of theatrical business men. We got friendly notice in the stage weeklies, and several other colleagues applied for membership, but it always turned out, on investigation, that they had plays under way in secret, and were thus frauds. Stuffy kept the oath of the organization until his lamented death, but soon afterward I succumbed so far as to write a couple of one-acters. I consoled my conscience, which was still functioning more or less in those days, by maintaining that they were unplayable. When they were actually played I began to wobble, and in 1919 I had wobbled so far that I wrote a full-length play in collaboration with George Jean Nathan. But though Nathan thus sinned with me, he professed to support the principles of the Davis-Mencken society, and the two of us cleared our skirts by refusing to let the play be done on Broadway. One manager offered us $10,000 cash for the refusal of it, but we had gone too far by then to turn back, and had to say no. To this day it has never been played.

One of the most competent young dramatic editors of the early century was Will A. Page, of the Washington *Post*. In the Autumn of 1901, soon after I had taken over the job in Baltimore, he moved there to be press-agent for a new stock company organized by George Fawcett. Fawcett was an educated *
and intelligent man, and his company soon made a big success. His beautiful wife, Percy Haswell, was the competent leading woman, and the leading man was Frank Gillmore, a handsome young Englishman who was later to become the head of Actors' Equity. The stage manager of the company was Percy Winter, old William's son, and its youngest member was a

youth named Frank Craven, afterward to be well known as both actor and dramatist. The Fawcett company opened in "The Liars" and then proceeded to a series of other plays of the same amusing and civilized sort. Almost every night I dropped in at the theatre for a palaver with Page, and he was soon reinforcing Carter's attempt to make me take the drama seriously. It was from him that I first heard of George Bernard Shaw, and he fanned my interest in Ibsen, first set going by the episode described at the end of Chapter V. One day at the beginning of the season of 1902–3 he asked me if I thought that the Baltimore public would stand for a production of Ibsen's "Ghosts," which had been recently suppressed in London and was poison to all the current William Winters. I was naturally
* hot for it, and on November 12 the play was put on, with Mary Shaw as Mrs. Alving, Frederick Lewis as Oswald, Maurice Wilkinson as Pastor Manders, Charles A. Gay as Engstrand, and Virginia Kline as Regina.

The first night was somewhat exciting, for the house manager, misunderstanding the action, jumped to the conclusion that Mrs. Alving was trying to seduce Oswald, and rushed out of the house exclaiming "We'll all go to jail!" The next day the critic of the *Sun* deplored "the revolting theme" and "the ghastly story," and the *American* and *News* lamented that such immoral and pathological stuff should be shown in a Christian city, but, with Carter's eager approval, I beat the drum for it in the *Herald*, and Baltimore received it without any further sign of moral trauma. It had, in fact, a good week, and after that the cast presenting it was detached from the Fawcett company and took it on the road. First and last, it was shown for three years. Other plays of pathological and subversive flavor were added to the little troupe's répertoire, but "Ghosts" remained its stand-by. Miss Shaw not only played it in scores of remote towns, some of them deep in the Bible Belt; she also lectured on it at many bucolic colleges, and always escaped without encountering anything worse than a few bewildered belches. From time to time fresh actors were thrown into the male parts, but Virginia Kline stuck to the end.

The "Ghosts" week was the high point of the Fawcett company. Page tried to get the American rights to the early Shaw plays, and had a brisk correspondence with Shaw on the subject, but they could not come to terms. In 1903 he left the company, and when business turned bad Fawcett resorted to such obvious boob-squeezers as "The Three Musketeers," "Monte Cristo" and "Blue Jeans." When he quit at last he was succeeded by a manager of such small experience in the theatre that he was constantly appealing to newspaper men for advice. I was promoted to city editor at about the same time, and was followed as dramatic editor by a smart young reporter named Eugene Bertram Heath, who quickly became this manager's * chief confidant and fatal curse. When Heath first came to work on the *Herald* a careless city editor, remembering only that his given name was somewhat romantic, entered him on the pay-roll as Percy, and Percy he remained to the end of his days. He lived to do the American book of "Sari," a great musical suc-cess, and to become a considerable figure in Hollywood. His counsel to Fawcett's unhappy heir and assign was chiefly wag-gish. Noting that the leading woman of the company was a blonde of large curves, he suggested that she be cast as Hamlet, *à la* Sarah Bernhardt. The manager fell for it—and to every-one's astonishment the week showed good takings. Percy then proposed satirically that her talents be turned loose upon "The Two Orphans," and when it, too, showed a profit, he advised that it be followed by a different version of the same play. The result was a gay and delirious week, for the actors trying to play the second version could not forget the first, and wal-lowed in confusion from curtain to curtain. Percy will appear again in Chapter XV. He was a man of parts. Unhappily, he had taken on family responsibilities, and when a good offer to go on the road as a press-agent came to him he accepted it, and Baltimore knew him no more.

I naturally received such offers myself, but I always refused them, for I was determined to stay in Baltimore. One of those offers was from E. H. Sothern. It was harder to resist certain more subtle approaches. Once I got word that David Belasco, then at the height of his celebrity, desired my opinion on a play, and it was hinted that he would expect to pay a substantial honorarium for it. I declined without thanks, for I regarded Belasco as a mountebank, and knew that what he wanted was not my judgment on a play but my support for all his trashy enterprises. The attempts of local managers to fetch me

* sometimes almost succeeded. When Charlie Ford would call
me up at home, and tell me with trembling voice that a traveling press-agent was too drunk to function, and ask me in
God's name to take over his work for a couple of days, I was
unpleasantly tempted, but my natural cynicism always came to
my aid, and I ducked. There were also blandishments from
actors, but here it was easier going, for I knew very few of
them, and never had anything to do with them. Once, after I
had written a somewhat tart notice of Richard Mansfield's
performance in Schiller's "Don Carlos," he invited me to dine
with him on his private car and favor him with my notions in
more detail, but I replied that I was too busy to come. He
thereupon sent me a large photograph of himself, elegantly
inscribed.

My general view of the theatre, in truth, was always somewhat skeptical. I continued to do an occasional review even
after I became city editor, and when the *Herald* blew up at last
and I transferred to the *Sun* I became its principal reviewer,
though not its dramatic editor. Not many plays of any real interest came out in those days. The favorite dramatists were
such cheap jacks as Clyde Fitch and Charles Klein, and the
dominant managers were such charlatans as Charles Frohman,
Belasco, and Klaw and Erlanger. During the Winter of 1905–6,
working for the *Sun*, I wrote twenty-three unfavorable notices
in a row. Charlie Ford thereupon complained bitterly that I
was ruining his business, and protested that he was not to
blame, for he had to take whatever plays the Theatrical Trust
sent him. On reflection, I found myself sympathizing with
him, and thereupon asked to be relieved. I have never written
a line of dramatic criticism since.

VIII.
Command

W̲HEN C̲ARTER appointed me Sunday editor toward the
end of 1901 I was as green as grass, and made heavy
weather of it for the first few weeks. It may seem strange, but I
can't recall the name of the man I succeeded. Whoever he was,
he must have left the office as well as the job, for I got no instruction from him, and had to find my own way. In those
days, as in these, reporters were taught nothing about printing, nor even about make-up, and it was rare for one of them
to so much as peep into the composing-room, the engraving
department, the stereotype foundry, or the press-room. Thus
when I made my appearance in the first-named I was almost
helpless. But Joe Bamburger, the foreman, was a sympathetic
fellow, and so was his assistant, Josh Lynch, and in a little while
they had broken me in. I naturally developed a grateful affection for them, and I think they liked me too, for we remained
on friendly terms until both were dead. In a little while we fell
into the habit of victualling together every Saturday evening
between the time the last page of the Sunday supplement
closed and the time the first page of the news section was
ready. We always stopped first at a saloon in Fayette street, and
there laid in a couple of beers. Then we proceeded to an eating-
house in Baltimore street, where the principal dish was a beef
stew so nourishing and so cheap that Joe called it the Workingmen's Friend. We ate it every Saturday, to the accompaniment
of butter-cakes and coffee, and then returned to the *Herald*
office to search the supplement, which was just coming up
from the cellar, for bulls. We always found them, and always
blamed one another. Joe was a tall, slim, solemn-looking fellow with a black beard, but when the spirit moved him he could
swear magnificently. He was a pious Catholic, denounced the
new heresy of birth control as mortal sin, and had eleven or
twelve children. Josh was short and stout, with a gift for profanity that was more explosive than Joe's, but perhaps fell below
it in reach and endurance. Joe would often say: "Josh is an

inhuman bluff." Both were first-rate printers, trained in the days before the linotype had reduced printing to the level of typewriting, and I learned more about the newspaper trade from them than I ever learned from anyone in the editorial department with the one exception of Max Ways.[1]

Save on a few metropolitan papers, the Sunday editor of today is not much concerned about his pages of colored comics, for they are supplied by syndicates, and most of them are printed by outside contractors, far from the office. But in 1901 there were no syndicates, and every paper had to prepare and print its own. This work, untrained as I was, gave me endless torment, for I quickly found that comic artists were a temperamental and nefarious class of men, that engraving departments were never on time, that pressmen had an unearthly talent for printing colors out of register, so that a blue spot intended to represent an eye usually appeared clear outside the cheek, and that plates plainly marked red were often printed as yellow, and *vice versa*. The first page of the color sheet, in those days, was seldom given over to comics, which were still regarded as somewhat *infra dig.*; its more usual adornment was a large picture of a damsel in an hour-glass corset and trailing skirts, labeled "The Summer Girl," "The Spirit of Thanksgiving," or something of the sort. The artists who drew these sugar-teats were even worse characters than the concocters of comics, and needed more policing. If one of them delivered a drawing on schedule he was sure to be *non est* when the time came to block out the color plates, and if he did the color plates promptly it always turned out that he had done them wrong. There were weeks when I spent at least two-thirds of my working hours wrestling with these criminals. They were, taking one with another, very affable fellows, and they used to try to mollify me by presenting me with large colored drawings of beautiful gals without any clothes on, but my professional relations with them were usually strained, and it never gave me any pain when I heard that one of them had broken a leg or got soaked for heavy alimony by his wife. Toward the end of 1902, happily for my sanity, syndicated comics began to appear,

[1]There is more about them in Chapter XIX following, and yet more on pp. 139 and 140 of my book, Happy Days.

and I need not say that I subscribed to them with cheers. The very names of the first ones are now forgotten—Simon Simple, Billy Bounce, the Teasers, the Spiegelburgers. Finally came Foxy Grandpa, and we were on our way. Even so, it was necessary to keep a comic artist or two on call, for now and then the business office sold a quarter-page ad on a comic page, and something had to be cooked up to go 'round it. I not only had to supervise the preparation of this home-made stuff, but also to supply the ideas for it. The only ideas that the comic artists of that age ever produced on their own were either too banal to be used, or too lascivious.

Some time ago I put in a gloomy afternoon in the Pratt Library in Baltimore, going through the files of the *Sunday Herald* for the period of my editorship. There was little in them to lift me. A whole page was given over every week to the dismal humors of M. Quad—Mr. Bowser, the Limekiln Club, the *Arizona Kicker*, Major Crowfoot, and so on. Quad was an old-time printer whose actual name was Charles B. Lewis. He was the last of the long line of American newspaper humorists which began with Seba Smith (Major Jack Downing), and ran through H. W. Shaw (Josh Billings), D. R. Locke (Petroleum V. Nasby) and C. F. Browne (Artemus Ward) to Bill Nye and Bob Burdette. George Ade and Finley Peter Dunne were already blazing new paths in Chicago, but as yet they were not syndicated, and I had to do without them. I paid Quad $5 a week for his page, which included the matrices for four or five illustrations. He was already an old man, and from his home in Brooklyn he farmed out his work to various bright young reporters in New York. All of his features followed precise patterns, and it was child's play to write them.

Another stand-by of the *Sunday Herald*—and of scores of other Sunday papers—was the weekly travel article of Frank G. Carpenter. He was the Marco Polo of his generation, and had been roving the world since 1881. The stuff that he sent back from such places as Tierra del Fuego, Lapland and Cochin-China was excessively dull, and the photographs that came with it made engravers weep, but there was a superstition on the *Herald* that the customers liked travel articles, and so I had to print him. One day a young man walked into the office with the news that he was barging into the trade in competition

with Carpenter. He had with him, and exhibited, some specimens of his art: they had to do, as I recall, with South America. They were so much better than Carpenter's that I took
on this newcomer at once. His name was Frederic J. Haskin,
and he came from Quincy, Ill. He demanded $10 a week,
whereas Carpenter had got but $5, but I was so glad to get
rid of Carpenter that I strained my budget to pay it. Haskin
continued to do his own traveling and writing for some years
thereafter, but then he began to give over most of his time to
selling his stuff, and hired assistants to fetch it in. He was a
superb salesman, and at his peak was probably the most successful syndicate man in America, with a weekly foreign letter,
a daily article from Washington, and a questions-and-answers
service that still exists. He began to publish books for the
one-book-a-year trade in 1911, with such titles as "The American Government," "The Panama Canal" and "10,000 Answers to Questions," and ran up such sales that the regular
publishers of the country were staggered. I got to know him
very well, and every time he dropped off in Baltimore we
gave over the evening to drinking Pilsner and laughing at the
human race. His journalistic bee-hive in Washington turned
out some notable graduates, for example, Louis Brownlow,
the expert on municipal government, and Harvey Fergusson,
the novelist.

My own writing for the *Sunday Herald* was pretty well
confined to the theatre pages: I had too many troubles to do
much else. Those pages, as such things ran in that era, were
not bad. I devoted them to plays rather than to actors, and
made a point of giving some account of every new drama of
any importance that reached the stage, whether in this country
or Europe. Not many that were worth describing came along,
and I was often reduced to wasting space on trash, but now
and then a Shaw or a Hauptmann stepped up to the bat for
me, and I was happy. The frenzied encomiums on actors that
poured in from press-agents I cut down to brief paragraphs
and printed literally, with a heading reading "What the Press-
Agents Say." There was a weekly letter about stage doings in
New York by Charles Henry Meltzer, who had been dramatic
critic for the New York *Herald* and *World* and one of the

associates of James Huneker on *M'lle New York*. My main effort, outside the theatre pages, was devoted to reforming the archaic typography of the Sunday paper, and trying to get rid of its ancient features. As I have said, I succeeded with Carpenter but failed with M. Quad. One of its worst relics of a more innocent day was a full page of fraternal order news—supplied free by the secretaries of the various lodges, but so badly written that copy-reading it was a heavy chore. The theory in the office was that this balderdash made circulation—that all the joiners of the town searched it every Sunday morning for their own names. This seemed to me to be bad reasoning, for any given joiner was bound to be disappointed nine Sundays out of ten. One Sunday I quietly dropped the page—and not a single protest came in.

Carter quit as managing editor at the end of 1902 and was succeeded by Lynn R. Meekins, of whom a great deal will be heard in Chapters XIX and XX. Meekins, after spending a couple of weeks surveying the office, decided that the city-room, since Max Ways's time, had been going downhill. This was something that was palpable to the meanest understanding, and no one knew it better than I, who had emerged from the place only a little while before. A good many of the more competent men of Ways's days had disappeared, and their places had been taken by third-, fourth- and fifth-raters. That they wrote bad stuff was not unnatural, but that it got into the paper was really shocking. I well recall my writhing discomfort over some of it. When, in the Autumn of 1901, the immortal McKinley was done to death by one of Hitler's agents, and his remains were dragged through Baltimore on their way to Washington, the following paragraph was actually printed in a *news* story:

In the silent masonry of men's souls all over this fair land of ours you hold a place today with Washington and Lincoln—a place no power can plead away—a place God-given by right of honor and justice, peace and equity, faith and hope. Vale McKinley!

This drivel, it appears, was highly esteemed by the city editor of the time. Carter should have killed it, but Carter was but little interested in the news department, and seldom read the proofs that reached his desk every night. Meekins was much more attentive, and during his first month he got rid of several of the worst word-painters. But a lot of muck remained, and he decided finally to put in a new city editor. When he offered the job to me I was really astonished, and, what is more, considerably alarmed. It was, to be sure, a step up that must have flattered any youngster of twenty-three, but I knew that reorganizing the staff would be a difficult job, and I was in fear that I'd have special difficulties with some of the older men, several of whom, at one time or another, had been my superiors. But Meekins was optimistic, and my fear turned out to be without ground. With one or two exceptions, all the old-timers gave me hearty support, and at Meekins's suggestion I got rid of the worst of the rag-tag and bob-tail by firing a whole platoon of them on my first day at the city-desk.

This was wise surgery, but it left the staff much depleted, and my job for a while was less that of a city editor than that of a rewrite man. In fact, I usually put in all my time from 9 P.M. onward rewriting leads, leaving my assistant, Joe Callahan, to run the desk. Meekins was pleased with the improvement in the paper, and especially with the disappearance of fustian and hooey, but when he discovered what I was doing he prohibited it, and ordered me to stick to my proper duties. My model and idol, in those days, was the New York *Sun*, and I made desperate efforts to bring the *Herald* up to its standard of good writing. This, of course, was impossible, for there were no such reporters in Baltimore as those who adorned the *Sun*, but nevertheless some progress was made, and after the staff had been strengthened with a few good men the *Herald* began to shine. To this day, in fact, no American provincial paper that I can recall has ever been so briskly written. We were often beaten on news by the Baltimore *Sunpaper*, but our bright young men wrote rings around it every day.

I soon found, as every young city editor must find, that Sunday night brings the zero hour of the week. There is, ordinarily, very little news stirring, and that little tends to be a great deal less than exhilarating. Everything really interesting and instructive falls off on Sunday, from murders to dog-fights. The courts, the City Hall, and a dozen other principal sources of news are closed, and the public orgies of the day are of a predominantly chaste and diuretic character.[2] That was a red-letter Sunday, in 1903, when news came in that a colored lodge of Odd Fellows, excursioning on the Chesapeake in a barge towed by a tug, had been run down by a banana boat, and another when a wild man was reported loose in the woods over Baltimore's northern city-line, with every dog barking for miles around, and all women and children locked up. I got special delight out of the wild man, for I had invented him myself, and no one else knew that he was imaginary save Tom Dempsey, an old-time police lieutenant, who had kindly helped me with the job. The other cops took him quite seriously, and hunted him with loud shouts and the frequent discharge of their pistols. Before the day was over they had roped and brought in at least a dozen poor bums, and put them through very stiff workouts in the back room. When Monday dawned, and Baltimore resumed its usual carnalities, the wild man was forgotten, but Dempsey and I revived him the next Sunday, and so every week for a month following. The story was spoiled at last when an alarmed magistrate, believing the bogus evidence offered by the cops against a half-wit stranger that they had collared, sentenced him to six months in the House of Correction.

I discovered one day that what would now be called an Open Forum was in operation on Sunday afternoons in a hall over a West Baltimore livery-stable, and assigned a reporter without too much conscience to have a look. He came back with a swell story about a riotous debate between a Single Taxer and a Socialist, with the Socialist pulling a butcher-knife and the Single Taxer leaping out of a window. The two came in the next day to protest that the matter had been exaggerated, but I nevertheless continued the same reporter on the job, and in a little while he had peopled the Open Forum with a whole stock company of fantastic characters, some of them still remembered in Baltimore. His imagination was of high

[2]In these days, of course, there is always a heavy grist of fatal automobile accidents, but it is seldom that anyone of any importance is killed. Politicians have learned to reserve their radio crooning and other prophesying for Sunday nights, but their blather commonly comes by wire, and thus does not help city editors.

octane content, but his literary style ran to long and tortured sentences. I took over the burden of reading copy on him, and usually managed to translate him into reasonably clear English. Unhappily, I eventually lost him, for his writing was so bad that it got him a job as editorial writer on another paper. His efforts, while he lasted, reduced the whole Open Forum movement in Baltimore to the level of barroom humor, and to this day no one there cares what is said or advocated by the orators who rant and roar in such quarters. They can argue for Communism all they please, or even for cannibalism, adultery or kidnaping. The very cops listen placidly.

For a while this sort of thing entertained me pleasantly, but in the end it began to bore me. I was, I suspect, a bad city editor. My interest in what is called spot news had begun to wither after I was graduated from police reporting myself, and I was now chiefly intent on making the *Herald* better written. Any reporter who could write reasonably well seemed a good one to me, and any one who couldn't a mutt. This judgment could be defended like any other, but there was also a good deal to be said against it. I took a number of long chances with stories chiefly fanciful, but curiously enough, picked up no libel suits save with those that were substantially true. The worst of these litigations (which always alarm a newspaper office, however easy their defense may look) was launched by a lady who, according to the cops, was a common prostitute. She was the widow of an Italian who had also left another widow, and this other one had later married a Chinaman. One night Widow No. 1 was jugged for street-walking, and the cops mistook her for Widow No. 2. When the *Herald* reported the next morning, relying on their dope, that she was the Chinaman's wife she instructed her solicitor to enter suit. We thought we had her, for dozens of cops volunteered to testify that she was free of both the white and black races, and hence had no reputation to lose, but the judge ruled out all this testimony on the ground that it had nothing to do with our false and foul allegation that she had married a Chinaman. Even a street-walker, he said, might object to that, at least in the eye of the law. We seemed to be lost, but at the last minute the lady's solicitor, not content to let well enough alone, rose up to address the jury. Within two minutes his eloquent description of her mental anguish had the twelve jurymen snickering, and in five minutes they were howling, along with the learned judge. Our own lawyer kept silent, and the jury gave us a verdict without leaving the box.

Not infrequently the long hours and endless vexations of my job worked me down so far that I was in a state bordering on paranoia. The *Herald* office, by this time, had a complete outfit of telephones, and mine rang an average of once a minute. I had to keep track of the comings and goings of thirty men, some of them with a high talent for disappearing. It was a for-midable business, when a big fire broke out or a nice murder was announced, to round up enough of them to cover it, and once they got out of sight it was quite as harassing to recover them. Very often, at the end of a long afternoon, I'd sneak out of the office for a little peace, and let it sweat and fester on its own. Sometimes I would go to a French restaurant a few blocks away, where a slow but sound meal was to be had for sixty cents, and the proprietor (who was also the chef) turned up a new wife (who was also the cashier) every month. That refuge was spoiled one night when two of these wives had it out with crockery just as I was about to sit down to a plate of onion soup. I then took to making quiet round trips to Wash-ington, and dining on the train. In those days every city editor had a pocketful of annual passes: I had them myself, in fact, on every railroad east of St. Louis or north of Atlanta, and also on all the coastwise steam-packets. The dining-car dinners I thus engulfed were seldom very appetizing, but it was refreshing to escape from the city-room for a while and rest my eyes on the frowsy wilderness that runs between Baltimore and Washing-ton. When I saw a yap at a cross-roads, waiting on his mule for the train to pass, I forgot the hookworms and other parasites at work upon his liver and lights, and almost envied him.

But despite all these woes I still had a reasonably pleasant time, and my leisure, though scanty, was at least more than I had enjoyed as a reporter. One of its fruits was a sharp revival of my interest in music. Carter had given me a start in that direction, and now I was helped on by the learned conversa-tion of our music critic, Owst, who was an abyss of thorough-bass, and set me to studying a textbook of that science; by daily contact with Lew Schaefer, one of the reporters, who * devoted his own leisure to writing piano pieces for children; and, above all, by the untutored but very real enthusiasm of my assistant, Joe Callahan. Joe was perhaps the worst violinist who ever lived; in fact, his technic went but little beyond the open strings; but he knew a great many musicians, and brought me into contact with them. It was through him that I met Fred Gottlieb, a rich brewer who was also an amateur flautist, and Al Hildebrandt, a violin-dealer by trade who played the cello for the fun of it, and remained one of my warmest friends to the end of his days. There were also Isidor Goodman, the night editor, who had once played the flute in a circus band, and Emanuel Daniel, assistant sporting editor, who passed in the office under the nickname of Schmool, and was a violinist. Under Joe's conniving, Schmool, Al and I took to playing trios, and in a little while other amateurs joined us, and then a few professionals, and by 1904 we had a club meeting regularly. It exists to the present day, and I never miss one of its Saturday night sessions when I am in Baltimore. I am now the only survivor of its original members. Goodman never belonged to it, but he and I often played together, for he had a girl who was a singer, and he liked to play flute obbligatos to her singing, while I did the piano accompaniment. For these refined soirées we commonly borrowed a small studio in a piano-dealer's establishment, a block from the *Herald* office. There was never any audience, for Goodman believed that his technic had degenerated since his circus days, and was shy of criticism. As for me, I banged away innocently, and often drowned out both the poor girl's voice and her admirer's tootling.

*   Goodman had an elder brother named Al who was the *Herald*'s political reporter. He had a bald head and a Van Dyke beard and was old enough to be my father, but we got on very well, and he taught me a great deal about the science of politics as he had observed it. It was his theory that all reformers were either frauds or idiots, and that some of them were both. He believed that practical politicians, taking one with another, made the safest and most competent public officials, if only because they were intelligent. He granted somewhat grudgingly that there were occasional thieves among them, but he argued that their worst corruptions were cheaper to the taxpayer than the insane wastes of the uplift. It was from him that I first heard all the familiar maxims of American statecraft, for example, "In politics a man must learn to rise *above* principle," and "When the water reaches the upper deck follow the rats." Al took me to my first pair of national conventions—those of 1904. In theory I was his superior officer, but I was glad to go as his legman, for he knew all the politicians, high and low, and was full of illuminating confidences about them. I recall his telling me in St. Louis that William Jennings Bryan, though a teetotaler, was a glutton, and predicting that he would eat himself to death. This prophecy was a long time coming true, but after twenty-two years it came true at last.

Al always wrote a long political disquisition for the Sunday *Herald*, and usually composed it in the city-room on Saturday afternoon, when there was comparative quiet there. He looked upon the typewriter as a new-fangled absurdity, and always wrote by hand. Ever and anon he would pause in his work, slap his bald head, clear his throat, and deliver himself of a soliloquy of his own composition. It began as follows:

Yes, my belovéd bullpups: it was not always thus. So his arse hit the ceiling with great éclat, and the little birds sang hallelujah.

This went on for a minute or two, and then rounded up with a quotation from "Barbara Frietchie": *

> "Strike, if you must, this old gray head,
> But spare your country's flag," she said.

Once a female reporter, overhearing this ritual, complained to me that it was painful to her pruderies. I invited her to do her work thereafter in the press-room, for I admired Al, and greatly enjoyed his observations, however vulgar. He and his brother Isidor had nicknames for all the office boys, usually borrowed from the Yiddish nomenclature, and often indecent. They also had nicknames for most of the reporters and editors. I daresay they had one for me, too, and maybe a blistering one, but if so I never heard it. City editors, in those days, were addressed familiarly by their given names by all save the youngest reporters, but even in those days city editors were treated a bit tenderly.

The supreme climax and boiling point of my service in that office I reserve for Chapter XIX.

IX.
Three Managing Editors

I N THE days of which I write the chief editorial dignitary on every American daily paper was called the managing editor, and his jurisdiction extended, not only over all the news departments, but also over the editorial page. He was himself, in fact, the chief editorial writer, and on most papers his only help in that line came from two or three ancient hulks who were unfit for any better duty—copy-readers promoted from the city-room to get rid of them, alcoholic writers of local histories and forgotten novels, former managing editors who had come to grief on other papers, and a miscellany of decayed lawyers, college professors and clergymen with whispered pasts. Some of these botches of God were pleasant enough fellows, and a few even showed a certain grasp of elemental English, but taking one with another they were held in disdain by the reporters, and it was almost unheard of for one of them to be promoted to a better job. Everyone believed as an axiom that they lifted four-fifths of their editorials from other papers, and most authorities held that they bitched them in the lifting. If anyone in the city-room had ever spoken of an editorial in his own paper as cogent and illuminating he would have been set down as a jackass for admiring it and as a kind of traitor to honest journalism for reading it at all. No editorial writer was ever applied to for a loan, or invited to an office booze-party.

But the managing editor, though he also wrote editorials, escaped the infamy of the caste, no doubt because he was mainly concerned with news, and usually emanated from the news department himself. He was, indeed, the chief hero of all the younger reporters, even when they denounced him for overworking and underpaying them, and they tried to model their mien and metaphysic on his—that is, provided he were not, by an office calamity, a teetotaler or an opponent of smoking. Myths about him were always in circulation, some of them based upon actual feats of professional or other derring-do, but most of them purely imaginary. Colonel A. B.

Cunningham, managing editor of the *Herald* when I joined its
staff in 1899, was generally depicted, by office gossip, as a very
truculent and even bloodthirsty man, with a long record of
carnage behind him. His career in the Confederate Army was
assimilated to those of Jeb Stuart, J. S. Mosby and Joe Wheeler,
and it was believed that he had refused to come in after Appomattox, but chosen rather to flee to Egypt, where he gradually
cooled himself off by slaughtering dervishes. He had worked
as a reporter on the St. Louis *Post-Dispatch* under the celebrated John Albert Cockerill, and out of the fact developed a
legend that he had once fought a duel with Cockerill, with
bowie knives as weapons.

The colonel's aspect gave a certain amount of support to his
reputation, for he was tall, well-built and of military bearing,
had flashing black eyes under heavy brows, and wore his wavy,
coal-black hair brushed back from his forehead. His head, in
fact, was a fine one, and his smooth-shaven face was not un-
handsome. But he was actually a much milder man than his
lieges believed, and it was only when he was in his cups that he
made any noise in the office. The facts about him came out in
1906, when he reached the dignity of inclusion in "Who's
Who in America." He was a native, it appeared, of Minden, a
small town in northwestern Louisiana, just under the Arkansas
line, and he was less than fifteen years old when the Civil War
began. But despite his tender years he enlisted in the Eighteenth Louisiana Infantry, and after that, in succession, in the
Fifth Texas Cavalry and McNelly's Scouts, and fought doggedly until the end of the war. After Appomattox he put in a
few years at flag-stop colleges in Louisiana, and then, in 1874,
he was offered a commission in the Egyptian Army, which was
being reorganized on a grandiose scale by the spendthrift Is-
mail. Many other ex-Confederates received similar offers, and
some actually went to Egypt, but Cunningham apparently
never made the trip, though he kept his title of colonel (*bey*)
for the rest of his life. It was, in its way, a kind of gilding of the
lily, for all Southern editors in that era were colonels by brevet,
and many of them, especially in the smaller towns, are so to
this day. When I became managing editor of the *Herald* myself, in 1905, I was usually so addressed in communications
from confrères below the Potomac.

The colonel seldom showed himself in the city-room, save to stalk through it, but he knew all the reporters by name, and sometimes joined in their extramural activities. At the time of the first election I ever helped to cover there was a dollar pool in the office on the majority of the winning candidate, and the colonel won it. It amounted to $50 or $60, and he blew in the money royally on a midnight supper to the staff. Toward the end of the party, which was large and loud, someone remembered that the annual ball of the Nonpareil Social Club was going on in a shabby hall near the waterfront, and it was resolved to look in. The Nonpareil was one of two rival organizations of Baltimore harlots, or, perhaps more accurately, of their male parasites and protectors, and its functions were always attended by large delegations of whiskey drummers, brewery collectors, professional bondsmen, minor court officials, and cops in mufti. By the time we got to the hall it was pretty late, and the festivities on the floor were abating, but the colonel revived them by taking a seat in the front row of the gallery, and heaving handfuls of small silver overboard. No less than three times he had $10 bills changed into dimes, and every time he went into action all the waiters on the floor dropped their trays and began to scramble for the money. The third time a committee consisting of two distinguished madames and a deputy sheriff came up to the gallery to protest. They said the honor of his presence was appreciated, but that his largess was incommoding the service of drinks and wrecking the ball. He professed to be offended, and threatened to denounce the affair in a *Herald* editorial as snobbish and anti-social, but he was only having his joke, and in a little while he gave the signal for us to withdraw. On the street outside, stimulated by the dawn, he lined us up along the curbstone, and gave the signal for one of those combats in uresis which festive males of *Homo sapiens* have been carrying on since the days of Abraham. It was won easily by a young reporter with powerful reflexes, whose name sounded something like Macon.

When the rival organization, the Rogers Pleasure Social, gave a ball a few weeks later, it sent a special committee to the *Herald* office to invite the colonel and his suite, but he said he had had enough of sexual society for a while, and refused to come. The rest of us, however, went in strength, and had the pleasure of witnessing a battle with beer bottles between two madames. Both were blooded, and the cops made a great pother of dragging them apart and carting them to hospital. Many of the more nefarious political clubs of the town gave somewhat similar parties, and we were usually invited. I remember one especially, for it was arranged in layers, with the wives and daughters of the ward heelers entertained on the second floor and the fancy women on the third. The former danced to a five-piece orchestra and the latter to a hand-organ. When we reporters arrived at the street door and made ourselves known we were ushered at once to the third floor.

The colonel had only contempt for the public attentions that pursue newspaper editors. He never went to a banquet if he could help it, and never signed manifestoes or sat on committees. The only public office he ever accepted was membership on the Baltimore School Board, which was unpaid. This was in 1901 or thereabout, and an effort was being made at the time to rid the Baltimore schools of the dirt pedagogy that had prevailed in them since colonial times, and to substitute the new wizardries from Teachers College, Columbia. The president of the board was a local corporation lawyer of the highest elegance, and one of the members was Dr. Daniel Coit Gilman, president of the Johns Hopkins University. I was assigned to cover the meetings for the *Herald* and commonly returned from them with the colonel, riding on the rear platform of a trolley-car. He never made any suggestions about the way the story was to be written, but in the confidence of a smoke together he often thought aloud about his fellow-members, most of whom he put in the debased class of uplifters. One evening he asked me if I had taken notice of one who spoke habitually in despairing tones, wore a long-tailed coat, and looked the perfect Christian philanthropist. "That poor eunuch," he said, "claims to be the father of five or six children. Turn your mind to the physiology of mammalian reproduction, and see if you can imagine it." I had to confess that I couldn't.

When it came to salaries the colonel was excessively hardboiled, for the *Herald*, in those days, was poor compared to the *Sun* and *News*: even his own pay, as I learned on becoming managing editor myself and snooping through the books, was never more than $90 a week. But he stuck to his men when they got into trouble, and it was on such occasions that his Southern fire was oftenest manifested. I well recall a case in point, for I was a figure in it. It came in the first years of the century, when not only the public schools, but also all the other municipal departments of Baltimore, including even the police force, were in the clutches of primeval New Dealers. Presently the poor cops had a new and terrifying master—a retired Army captain with a walrus moustache who had been sitting for years in the window of the Athenaeum Club in Charles street, glaring at the passers-by. His name was Hamilton, and he was the perfect model of the *Rittmeister* of tradition—stiff, vain, boorish and stupid. He set the cops to saluting on all occasions, ordered the old ones to train off their bay-windows, and put the whole unhappy outfit to drilling in the hot sun.

These reforms made for news, but getting it was something else again. When I was assigned to headquarters, and made my first call at the new chief's office, he let me stand for at least ten minutes while he busied himself with the papers on his desk. The second day I stood for fifteen minutes, and the third day for twenty minutes, and when the old boy looked up at last he would bark as if I had been an insurance agent or a collector for the orphans. After that I kept out of his office, and my information about his doings was derived from cops who were as friendly to newspaper reporters as they were hostile to their new commander. The inevitable result was that the *Herald* printed some stories that annoyed him, and in a little while he wrote a letter to the colonel, complaining that I never came near his office and that my reports of his doings were faked. This was a serious charge and the colonel ordered me up for trial the next morning. My defense was brief: I simply told the truth. The colonel was not long in reaching his verdict. "Go back to that goddam son-of-a-bitch," he roared, "and tell him * with my compliments that a *Herald* reporter kisses *no* man's arse." I relayed this communiqué to Hamilton through one of his stooges, and he was polite enough thereafter. Before long he had got the cops into such a mess that he had to be kicked out, and they returned joyously to Bach.

When the *Herald* was sold to Wesley M. Oler, a rich Balti- * morean who had made his money in the ice business and eventually rose to be president of the American Ice Company, the colonel's position became very uncomfortable, for Oler was a Republican and wanted to use the paper to promote his political aspirations, which were wide and deep. The colonel, of course, was a Democrat. After a series of squabbles he quit his job and started an afternoon paper of his own, but it blew up quickly, and he became the Baltimore agent of the Associated Press.[1] His successor was Robert I. Carter, who had been recommended to Oler by the Tafts of Cincinnati, where he had worked on the *Times-Star* and assisted in launching William Howard of that ilk as a statesman. On all imaginable counts he was at the opposite pole from the colonel. A native of Massachusetts and a graduate of Harvard, with a game leg, a conservative paunch and a red Van Dyke beard, he looked the college professor far more than the newspaper editor, and in all his tastes, methods of work, theories of journalism and habits of mind he differed abysmally from his predecessor. At the start the boys in the *Herald* office hardly knew what to make of him, for it was quickly bruited about that he could speak seven (soon lifted to seventeen) languages, and he alarmed everybody on his second night by showing up in a dinner coat. But it soon became apparent that he was anything but a dilettante, and when he fired several old-timers, ordered some raises in salaries, and put a rambunctious female reporter in her place, office opinion began to swing toward him, and the usual legends about him were hatched. One was to the effect that he had killed a man in Cincinnati, and another accounted for his game leg by a fall off a fire-escape leading down from the boudoir of a rich brewer's beautiful fourth wife. He was reputed to be wealthy himself, and there were two theories about the origin of his hoard: one being that he was an heir of the Carter's Ink fortune and the other that he was an heir of the Carter's Little Liver Pills fortune.

My own relations with him have been described more or less in Chapter VII. He was a highly civilized and very charming man, and his influence upon me at a time when I was in some

---

[1]He died in Baltimore in 1915. Born in 1846, he was 54 years old in 1900, but to us young reporters he seemed a patriarch.

danger of yielding to the Philistinism which then dominated
Baltimore journalism was powerful and all to the good. He
made it plain to me, and to others, that it was quite possible to
be a good newspaper man, and still cherish some pretense to
decent tastes. His own eager interest in the fine arts, and especially in music and the drama, was contagious, but he was as far
from being priggish as the old colonel himself. On the contrary, he was a very amiable and expansive fellow, fond of good
eating and drinking, and tolerant of the so-called Bohemianism
of the city-room, though he kept aloof from it himself. He
fired the old-timers, not primarily because they were boozers,
but because they were booze-grafters, and hence disgraceful to
the paper.

The job he had taken on was not an easy one, for the departure of Cunningham, followed soon by that of Max Ways,
and then by that of Nachman, the business manager, had left
the *Herald* organization crippled and demoralized. Carter
tried out several new city editors in succession, but they fell
very far short of Ways. He was burdened with editorial writers even worse than usual, and was reduced at one time to
inviting members of the city staff to contribute volunteer
editorials. But his most severe headaches came from above,
not below. Oler was a poor substitute for William Howard
Taft, though he had the same itch to shine in statecraft. He
was a tall, thin, dour Methodist with a funereal black beard,
and never got to first base in politics, though he once collared
a great deal of notice (at least in his own paper) by inducing
Theodore Roosevelt, then President, to ride over from Washington to visit him in his suburban mansion. Roosevelt, who
made the trip on horseback, followed by a squad of sweating
Army officers, let it be known that Oler was a man of astounding abilities and would make a superb United States
Senator, but no one else ever believed it. To replace the smart
and competent Nachman as business manager he brought in
a Canadian named Peard—a majestic and singularly handsome fellow with no more capacity for the job than a police
sergeant. So the *Herald* gradually got into difficulties, and
Carter's hard work went for nothing. He modernized the typography of the paper, reformed some of its archaic Southern

practises, and brought in a few good men, but in the end he had to confess failure. After two years and two months of it he resigned in January, 1903, and was succeeded by Lynn R. Meekins.[2]

Of the three managing editors that I sat under on the *Herald* Meekins was the most competent, and by long odds, but he came into the office carrying several handicaps, and it took him some time to get rid of them; indeed, it was not until the great Baltimore fire of 1904 brought out his quick resourcefulness and high capacity for command that he was generally accepted in the office. His first handicap was that he had got most of his training on the Baltimore *American*, a rival that was not even given the flattery of fear, but simply held in contempt. His second was that he had spent most of his seventeen years there writing editorials—a trade, as I have said, that no reporter respected. His third, and heaviest, was that he was reported to be a Methodist, and what is worse, a Methodist of the so-called Methodist Protestant sub-sect, which, even in 1903, was already whooping up Prohibition. When his membership in this infamous outfit was confirmed there was something close to moral indignation in the office, and one of the artists actually announced that, provided he could find a better job elsewhere, he would resign in protest.

Nor did Meekins's first tour of inspection reassure the brethren, for he turned out to be a slight, clerical-looking fellow wearing a small gray moustache and scholarly spectacles, with a voice that never arose to the barks and snarls proper to a managing editor. But though the legend of his anti-social heresies persisted for a year, it was soon apparent to the more judicious that he was anything but a milksop. On the contrary, he turned out to be bold and even pugnacious, and in a little while he was carrying on a revolt against Peard's

[2]Carter joined the New York *Herald* after leaving Baltimore, and became editor of its Paris edition and one of the confidential men of James Gordon Bennett. He had traveled very widely as a young man and now traveled even more. I encountered him occasionally in New York after he left Baltimore, but eventually lost sight of him. He disappeared from Who's Who in America after the 1912–13 edition. He was 32 years old when he came to the *Herald* in Baltimore.

ineptitudes downstairs, and getting rid of a lot of dead wood in the editorial rooms. My own inclination was to see something in him, for he had two novels behind him and was a frequent contributor to *Harper's Magazine*; and that inclination was converted into an active prejudice pro when he called me into his office one day and told me that my salary as Sunday editor was to be increased $5 a week. This was the first time since I had joined the *Herald* that I had ever got a raise without first being offered a better job elsewhere, and the miracle naturally filled me with amiable sentiments. Nor was my delight diminished when he told me that I needed better help in my job, and ordered me to find a couple of likely young aides, male or female. What he had to say about the Sunday edition, some of it favorable but most of it critical, was searching and sensible, and I soon discovered that he knew more about such things than anyone else in the office. This, I must confess, seemed incredible in an editorial writer— until presently I learned that, in the interval between writing editorials for the *American* and coming to the *Herald*, he had been the first managing editor of the *Saturday Evening Post*, then just started on its opulent career of fostering the national letters.

But the fact remained that Meekins, compared to Cunningham or even to Carter, was a subdued and highly respectable fellow, and that life in the *Herald* office began to lose something of its old wild glitter. He was not, it soon appeared, an actual Prohibitionist, but he had a low opinion of the more alcoholic journalists of the era, and began to ease them out one by one. The *Herald* office thus became much more efficient than it had ever been before, but it ceased to be as merry as it once was, and if the men got more money they enjoyed less recreation, as recreation was then understood. We had another Methodist in the office, a reporter named Stockbridge, but he was so pleasant a fellow that no one held it against him, though we showed our dissent from his superstitions by giving him the satirical title of Bishop. When, in July, 1903, Pope Leo ∗ XIII died, and the cardinals began hustling to Rome to elect his successor, an office wag put the following notice on the city-room bulletin-board:

FOR POPE:
The Right Rev. Jason Stockbridge, D.D.,
Bishop of Sodom and Gomorrah *in partibus infidelium*
Subject to the Democratic primaries

This jocosity, though it lay snugly within the traditional
Herald pattern of office humor, outraged Meekins, and he not
only ordered it removed at once but went through the forms
of an investigation that lasted for two weeks. While his inquiries were going on I trembled lest he accuse some innocent
member of the staff, and so force me to step up and confess the
truth, which was that I had done the deed myself. But the investigation frittered out without an indictment, and it was
years later, after the *Herald* had been long buried, and forgotten by all save its alumni, that Meekins told me he had recognized my literary style at once. His failure to accuse me was
* revelatory of his peculiar character: he was fundamentally a
somewhat prissy fellow, but he always refrained from wreaking
his prissiness on others. Until his professional exploits at the
time of the fire of 1904 won him unanimous acceptance at last,
he remained a suspicious person to most of the reporters, for it
was still a cardinal article of office doctrine that a Methodist
(despite the glaring contrary example of Bishop Stockbridge)
was necessarily and *ipso facto* a devious, inimical and mean fellow, bent only on afflicting and injuring the human race. But
Meekins was constantly doing things that made that easy formula untenable, and the ground was thus gradually preparing
for his elevation to respect and esteem in 1904. If there had
never been any fire it might have been delayed, and without
question it would have stopped short of canonization, but
certainly it would have come.

Meekins had been born in a small village on the Eastern
Shore of Maryland, where Yahweh remains a threatening character to this day, and if he kept some of the theological naïveté
of his native wildwood, he also showed a good deal of country
humor. He took the horrible alarms and vicissitudes of newspaper life without too much seriousness, and was full of sharp
judgments of men and events. He viewed editorial writers
much as reporters viewed them, though he had been one for
so many years himself, and at a later period, when he resumed

the shroud of the craft in the service of Hearst, he cackled over its futilities every time we met. It was his theory that no editorial that showed genuine sense was fit to print, or, indeed, could be printed without danger. He could write very good ones on occasion, for he had a clear mind and a first-rate English style, but he got more fun, I am sure, out of writing the bad ones—for example, arguments in favor of new parks and a reformed police force, and obituary encomiums of dead local worthies, nine-tenths of whom he knew personally to be either idiots or scoundrels. The Hearst paper he worked for was the heir of both his first love, the Baltimore *American*, and the Baltimore *News*. Its leading editorials were mainly canned goods from the New York headquarters of the chain; his job was simply to keep the home fires burning. A conservative by instinct, he was amused rather than outraged by the exuberance of the Hearst typography, and used to defend it wryly on the ground that it at least enabled him to fill a lot of space at small expense of labor.

As an author himself he took a great deal of interest in my own literary strivings. His advice in that department was always sound, and he was ever ready with it. He knew most of the American literati of the Howells generation, and was full of illuminating anecdotes about them. His own writings were in their manner, but he was very hospitable to the newcomers who finally unhorsed them, and he did a great deal of miscellaneous reading, even in his busiest days as managing editor of the uremic *Herald*, and, later, as its publisher. Unlike Carter, he had no appetite for music and very little for the theatre, but his knowledge of books was enormous, and he set me to reading many a tome that I might have missed otherwise. I suspect that it was largely his influence that caused me to resolve, when the *Herald* finally went down, to subordinate executive work, during the rest of my days, to writing. In all probability he lived to regret that he had not done so himself.[3]

[3]Meekins died in 1933 in London, where his only son was commercial attaché of the American embassy.

X.

Slaves of Beauty

IT WAS not until I became Sunday editor that I had any offi-cial relations with the fantastic Crocodilidæ known as news-paper artists, but I had naturally encountered a number of them in my days as a reporter. The first one I ever saw in the flesh, so far as I can recall, was an Irishman wearing a seedy checked suit, a purple Windsor tie, a malacca stick, and a *bou-tonnière* consisting of two pink rosebuds fastened together with tinfoil. This was in a saloon near the *Herald* office in the year 1899, and I remember saying to myself that he certainly looked the part. It appeared at once that he also acted it, for when the bartender hinted that the price of beer was still five cents a glass, cash on delivery, the artist first snuffled up what remained of the foam in his schooner, and then replied calmly that it was to be charged to his account. I was still, in those days, a cub reporter, and full of an innocent delight in the wonders of the world. The decaying veteran at my side had invited me out, as he put it, to introduce me to society, and while he did the introducing I bought the beer. He now nudged me, and whispered romantically that the artist had spent his last ten cents for the *boutonnière*: it had been bought, it appeared, of a street vendor in front of police headquarters —a one-armed man who was reputed to get his stock by raid-ing colored graveyards by night. This vendor trusted no one below the rank of a police lieutenant, so the rosebuds had to be paid for, but bartenders showed more confidence in hu-manity. After the artist had filled his pockets with pretzels and stalked out grandly, flirting his malacca stick in the manner of James A. McNeill Whistler, the old-timer explained that he was honorable above the common, and always paid his reckon-ings in the long run. "Whenever," I was informed, "some woman with money gets stuck on him, or he sells a couple of comics to a syndicate, he goes around town settling up. Once I saw him lay out $17 in one night. He had to beat it from England in a cattle-boat. There was a rich Jewish duke packing a gun for him."

I never saw this marvel again, for a few days later he was shanghaied on the Baltimore waterfront, and when, after a couple of months of bitter Winter weather down Chesapeake Bay, he escaped from the oyster fleet by legging it over the ice, he made tracks for Canada and the protection of the Union Jack, leaving more than one bartender to mourn him. But in the course of the next half dozen years, first as Sunday editor, then as city editor, and finally in the austere misery of managing editor, I made acquaintance with many other artists, and acquired a lot of unpleasant information about their habits and customs. They ranged from presumably respectable married men with families (sometimes, indeed, with two families) down to wastrels who floated in from points South or West, remained only long enough to lift an overcoat and two or three bottles of Higgins's drawing ink, and then vanished as mysteriously as they had come. A few of them even neglected to draw their pay—always to the indignation of the office cashier, who had to carry a small and incredible overage on his books until he got up nerve enough to buy the city editor a couple of drinks, and so discharge his debt for theatre passes. But whatever the differences marking off these jitney Dürers into phyla and species, they all had certain traits in common, mostly productive of indignation in editors. Each and every one of them looked down his nose at the literati of journalism, and laughed at them as Philistines almost comparable to bartenders or policemen. One and all had an almost supernatural talent for getting out of the way when fire broke out in a medical college or orphan asylum, and there were loud yells for illustrative art. And so far as I can recall, there was never one who failed, soon or late, to sneak something scandalous into a picture at the last moment, to the delight the next morning of every soul in town save what we then called the Moral Element.

I write, of course, of an era long past and by most persons forgotten, and I have no doubt that artists are now much changed, whether on newspapers or off. Some time ago a man in charge of the art department of a great metropolitan daily told me that fully a third of his men read the *Nation*, and that

many of the rest had joined the C.I.O. and were actually paying their dues. He even alleged that there were two teetotalers
among them, not to mention a theosophist. In my time nothing of the sort was heard of. The artists of that day were all
careless and carnal fellows, with no interest in their souls and
no sense of social responsibility. Their *beau idéal* was still the
Rodolfo of "La Bohème," and if not Rodolfo, then some salient whiskey drummer, burlesque manager or other Elk; for
the contemporaneous Roosevelts, Willkies, Hulls, Ma Perkinses,
Bishop Mannings and John L. Lewises they had only razzberries. Long before naked women were the commonplaces of
every rotogravure supplement—indeed, long before rotogravure supplements were invented—large drawings of ladies in
the altogether, usually in the then fashionable sepia chalk,
decorated every newspaper art department in America. It was
believed by young reporters that artists spent all their leisure in
the company of such salacious creatures, and had their confidence. Even the most innocent young reporter, of course, was
aware that they used no living models in their work, for everyone had noted how they systematically swiped from one another, so that a new aspect of the human frame, or of a dog's,
or cat's, or elephant's frame, once it had appeared in a single
newspaper in the United States, quickly reappeared in all the
rest. But the artists fostered the impression that they did hand-
painted oil-paintings on their days off, direct from nature un-
adorned. They let it be known that they were free spirits and
much above the general, and in that character they sniffed at
righteousness, whether on the high level of political and economic theory or the low one of ordinary police regulations.

*   I well recall the snobbish rage of a primeval comic-strip artist
whom I once rebuked for using the office photographic equipment to make counterfeit five-dollar bills. It was on a Sunday
morning, and I had dropped into the office for some reason
forgotten. Hearing me shuffling around, he bounced out of
the darkroom with a magnificent photograph of a fiver, cut
precisely to scale, and invited me to admire it. I knew it would
be useless to argue with him, but I was hardly prepared for his
screams of choler when I grabbed the phoney, tore it up, and
made off to the darkroom to smash the plate. He apparently
regarded my action, not only as a personal insult, but also as an

attentat against human enlightenment. If the word *bourgeois* had been in circulation at the time he would have flung it at me. As it was, he confined himself to likening my antipathy to counterfeit money to Lynn Meekins's Methodist aversion to drunkards, and laughed derisively at all the laws on the statute-books, from those against adultery to those prohibiting setting fire to zoos. I fired him on the spot, but took him back the next day, for good comic-strip artists were even more rare in that age than they are today.

Another that I fired—for what reason I forget—refused to come back when I sent for him, and I found on inquiry that he had got a job making side-show fronts for a one-ring circus. He produced such alarming bearded ladies, two-headed boys and wild men of Borneo that the circus went through the Valley of Virginia like wildfire, and in a little while he had orders from four or five of its rivals. By the end of a year he was the principal producer of side-show fronts south of the Mason & Dixon Line, and had three or four other artists working for him. Also, he had a new girl, and she appeared in public in clothes of very advanced cut, and presently took to drink. Undaunted, he put in another, and when she ran away with a minstrel-show press-agent, followed with a third, a fourth, and so on. Finally, one of them opened on him with a revolver, and he departed for Scranton, Pa. When he edged back to Baltimore a month or two later, glancing over his shoulder at every step, his business had been seized by his assistants, and the last I heard of him he was working for a third-rate instalment house, making improbable line drawings of parlor lamps, over-stuffed sofas, washing-machines, and so on. Many other artists of that time went the same sad route. Starting out in life as painters of voluptuous nudes in the manner of Bouguereau, they finished as cogs in the mass production of line-cuts of ladies' hosiery.

In the heyday of this fellow I had a visit one day from a sac-erdotal acquaintance—a Baptist clergyman who pastored a church   * down in the tidewater Carolinas. His customers, he told me, had lately made a great deal of money growing peanuts, and a new brick church was approaching completion in his parish. In this church was a large concrete baptismal tank—the largest south of Cape Hatteras—and it was fitted with all the latest gadgets, including a boiler downstairs to warm the water in cold weather. What it still lacked, said the pastor, was a suitable fancy background, and he had come to see me for advice and help on that point. Would it be possible to have a scene painted showing some of the principal events of sacred history? If so, who would be a good man to paint it? I thought at once of my side-show-front friend, and in a little while I found him in a barrel-house, and persuaded him to see the pastor.

The result was probably the most splendiferous work of ecclesiastical art since the days of Michelangelo. On a canvas fifteen feet high and nearly forty feet long the artist shot the whole works, from the Creation as described in Genesis I to the revolting events set forth in Revelation XIII. Noah was there with his ark, and so was Solomon in all his glory. No less than ten New Testament miracles were depicted in detail, with the one at Cana given the natural place of honor, and there were at least a dozen battles of one sort or another, including two between David and Goliath. The Tower of Babel was made so high that it bled out of the top of the painting, and there were three separate views of Jerusalem. The sky showed a dozen rainbows, and as many flashes of lightning, and from a very red Red Sea in the foreground was thrust the maw of Jonah's whale, with Jonah himself shinning out of it to join Moses and the children of Israel on the beach. This masterpiece was completed in ten days, and brought $200 cash—the price of ten side-show fronts. When it was hung in the new Baptist church, it wrecked all the other evangelical filling-stations of the lower Atlantic littoral, and people came from as far away as Cleveland, Tenn., and Gainesville, Va., to wash out their sins in the tank, and admire the art. The artist himself was invited to submit to the process, but replied stiffly that he was forbidden in conscience, for he professed to be an infidel.

The cops of those days, in so far as they were aware of artists at all, accepted them at their own valuation, and thus regarded them with suspicion. If they were not actually on the level of water-front crimps, dope-pedlars and piano-players in houses of shame, they at least belonged somewhere south of sporty doctors, professional bondsmen and handbooks. This attitude once cost an artist of my acquaintance his liberty for three weeks, though he was innocent of any misdemeanor. On a cold Winter night he and his girl lifted four or five ash-boxes, made a roaring wood-fire in the fireplace of his fourth-floor studio, and settled down to listen to a phonograph, then a novelty in the world. The glare of the blaze, shining red through the cobwebbed windows, led a rookie cop to assume that the house was afire, and he turned in an alarm. When the firemen came roaring up, only to discover that the fire was in a fireplace, the poor cop sought to cover his chagrin by collaring the artist, and charging him with contributing to the delinquency of a minor. There was, of course, no truth in this, for the lady was nearly forty years old and had served at least two terms in a reformatory for soliciting on the street, but the lieutenant at the station-house, on learning that the culprit was an artist, ordered him locked up for investigation, and he had been in the cooler three weeks before his girl managed to round up a committee of social-minded saloonkeepers to demand his release. The cops finally let him go with a warning, and for the rest of that Winter no artist in Baltimore dared to make a fire.

But it was not only artists themselves who suffered from the harsh uncharitableness of the world; they also conveyed something of their Poësque ill fortune to all their more intimate associates. I never knew an artist's girl, however beautiful, to marry anyone above a jail warden or a third-string jockey, and most of the early photo-engravers came to bad ends, often by suicide. The engravers used various violent poisons in their work, including cyanide of potassium. It was their belief that a dose of cyanide killed instantly and was thus painless, but every time one of them rounded out a big drunk by trying it he passed away in a tumultuous fit, and made a great deal of noise. The survivors, however, no more learned by experience than any other class of men, and cyanide remained their remedy of choice for the sorrows of this world. They had in their craft a sub-craft of so-called routers, whose job it was to deepen the spaces between the lines in line-cuts. This was done with a power-driven drill that bounced like a jumping-jack and was excessively inaccurate. If the cut was a portrait the router nearly always succeeded in routing out the eyes. Failing that, he commonly fetched one of his own fingers. Many's the time I have seen a routing machine clogged to a standstill by a

mixture of zinc eyes and human tissue, with the router jumping around it with his hand under his arm, yelling for a doctor
or a priest.

In those days halftones were not much used in newspapers,
for it was only a few years since Stephen H. Horgan, of the
New York *Tribune*, had discovered that they could be stereo-
typed. Most provincial stereotypers still made a mess of the job,
so line-cuts were preferred, and relatively more artists were
employed than today. Nevertheless, photographs were needed,
if only to be copied in line, and every paper of any pretensions
had at least one photographer. The first I recall on the *Herald*
was a high-toned German of the name of Julius Seelander,
who had served his apprenticeship in his native land. He wore
a beard trimmed to display the large stickpin that glowed from
his Ascot necktie: it was, in fact, *two* pins, with a filigree silver
chain connecting them. Julius was an excellent technician, but
had a habit of aesthetic abstraction in emergencies. Once, in
bitter Winter weather, I took him along when I was assigned
to go down the Chesapeake on an ice-boat, to cover the succoring of a fishing village that had been frozen in for weeks.
We got to the place after a bumpy struggle through the ice,
and Julius took a dozen swell pictures of the provisions going
ashore and the starving oystermen fighting for them on the
wharf. But when we got back to the office, and I was in the
midst of my story, he came slinking out of his darkroom to
confess that he had made all of the photographs on one plate.
He said he was throwing up his job, and asked me to break the
news to Max Ways: he was afraid that if he did so himself Max
would stab him with a copy hook or throw him out of the
window. But when I told Max he was very little perturbed, for
he believed that all photographers, like all artists, were as grossly
unreliable and deceptive as so many loaded dice, and it always
surprised him when one of them carried out an assignment as
ordered. The next day Julius was back in his darkroom, and so
far as I know, nothing more was ever said about the matter.

But the most unfortunate camp-follower of art that I ever
knew was not a photographer, nor even a photo-engraver, but
a saloonkeeper named Kuno Something-or-other, who had a
great many artists among his customers. When, in 1900, he

opened a new saloon, they waited on him in a body, and offered to decorate its bare walls without a cent of cost to him, save only, of course, for their meals while they were at work, and a few drinks to stoke their aesthetic fires. Kuno, who loved everything artistic, jumped at the chance, and in a few days the first two of what was to be a long series of predacious frauds moved in on him. The pair daubed away for four or five hours a day, and it seemed to him, in the beginning, to be an excellent trade, for they not only got nothing for their services, but attracted a number of connoisseurs who watched them while they worked, and were good for an occasional flutter at the bar. But at the end of a couple of weeks, casting up accounts with his bartender, Kuno found that he was really breaking less than even, for while the credit side showed eight or ten square feet of wall embellished with beautiful girls in transparent underwear, the debit side ran to nearly 100 meals and more than 500 beers, all consumed by the artists.

Worse, the members of the succeeding teams were even hungrier and thirstier than the first pair, and by the time a fourth of one wall of the saloon was finished Kuno was in the red for more than 500 meals and nearly 7000 beers, not to mention innumerable whiskeys, absinthes and shots of bitters, and a couple of barrels of paint. The easy way out would have been to throw the artists into the street, but he respected the fine arts too much for that. Instead, he spent his days watching the Work in Progress and his nights trying to figure out how much he would be set back by the time it was finished. In the end these exercises unbalanced his mind, and he prepared to destroy himself, leaving his saloon half done, like a woman with one cheek made up and the other washed.

His exitus set an all-time high for technic, for he came from Frankfurt-an-der-Oder, and was a Prussian for thoroughness. Going down to the Long Bridge which spanned the Patapsco below Baltimore, he climbed on the rail, fastened a long rope to it, looped the other end around his neck, swallowed a dose of arsenic, shot himself through the head, and then leaped or fell into the river. The old-time cops of Baltimore still astound rookies with his saga. He remains the most protean performer they have ever had the pleasure of handling post-mortem.

XI.

The Days of the Giants

NOT INFREQUENTLY I am asked by young college folk, sometimes male and sometimes female, whether there has been any significant change, in my time, in the bacchanalian virtuosity of the American people. They always expect me, of course, to say that boozing is now at an all-time high, for they are a proud generation, and have been brought up to believe that Prohibition brought in refinements unparalleled on earth since the fall of Babylon. But when I speak for that thesis it is only to please them, for I know very well that the facts run the other way. My actual belief is that Americans reached the peak of their alcoholic puissance in the closing years of the last century. Along about 1903 there was a sudden and marked letting up—partly due, I suppose, to the accelerating pace and hazard of life in a civilization growing more and more mechanized, but also partly to be blamed on the lugubrious warnings of the medical men, who were then first learning how to reinforce their hocus-pocus with the alarms of the uplift.

In my early days as a reporter they had no more sense of civic responsibility than so many stock-brokers or policemen. A doctor of any standing not only had nothing to say against the use of stimulants; he was himself, nine times out of ten, a steady patron of them, and argued openly that they sustained him in his arduous and irregular life. Dr. Z. K. Wiley, our family practitioner, always took a snifter with my father when he dropped in to dose my brother Charlie and me with castor oil, and whenever, by some unusual accident of his heavy practise, he had any free time afterward, he and my father gave it over to quiet wrestling with the decanters. His favorite prescription for a cold was rock-and-rye, and he believed and taught that a shot of Maryland whiskey was the best preventive of pneumonia in the R months. If you object here that Dr. Wiley was a Southerner, then I answer at once that Dr. Oliver Wendell Holmes was a Yankee of the Yankees, and yet held exactly the same views. Every schoolboy, I suppose, has heard by this time of Dr. Holmes's famous address before the Massachusetts Medical Society on May 30, 1860, in which he argued that "if the whole materia medica, as now used, could be sunk to the bottom of the sea, it would be all the better for mankind —and all the worse for the fishes"; but what the pedagogues always fail to tell their poor dupes is that he made a categorical exception of wine, which he ranked with opium, quinine, anesthetics and mercury among the sovereign and invaluable boons to humanity.

I was thus greatly surprised when I first heard a medical man talk to the contrary. This was in the Winter of 1899–1900, and the place was a saloon near a messy downtown fire. I was helping my betters to cover the fire, and followed them into the saloon for a prophylactic drink. The doctor, who was a fire department surgeon, thereupon made a speech arguing that alcohol was not a stimulant but a depressant, and advising us to keep off it until the fire was out and we were relaxing in preparation for bed. "You think it warms you," he said, sipping a hot milk, "but it really cools you, and you are seventeen point eight per cent. more likely to catch pneumonia at the present minute than you were when you came into this doggery." This heresy naturally outraged the older reporters, and they became so prejudiced against the doctor that they induced the Fire Board, shortly afterward, to can him—as I recall it, by reporting that he was always drunk on duty. But his words made a deep impression on my innocence, and continue to lurk in my mind to this day. In consequence, I am what may be called a somewhat cagey drinker. That is to say, I never touch the stuff by daylight if I can help it, and I employ it of an evening, not to hooch up my faculties, but to let them down after work. Not in years have I ever written anything with so much as a glass of beer in my system. My compositions, I gather, sometimes seem boozy to the nobility and gentry, but they are actually done as soberly as those of William Dean Howells.

But this craven policy is not general among the literati, nor was it to be noted among the journalists of my apprentice days. Between 1899 and 1904 there was only one reporter south of the Mason & Dixon Line who did not drink at all, and he was considered insane. In New York, so far as I could

make out, there was not even one. On my first Christmas Eve
on the *Herald* but two sober persons were to be found in the
office—one of them a Seventh Day Adventist office-boy in
the editorial rooms, and the other a superannuated stereotyper
* who sold lunches to the printers in the composing-room.
There was a printer on the payroll who was reputed to be a
teetotaler—indeed his singularity gave him the nickname of
the Moral Element—, but Christmas Eve happened to be his
night off. All the rest were full of what they called hand-set
whiskey. This powerful drug was sold in a saloon next door to
the *Herald* office, and was reputed to be made in the cellar by
the proprietor in person—of wood alcohol, snuff, tabasco sauce,
and coffin varnish. The printers liked it, and got down a great
many shots of it. On the Christmas Eve I speak of its effects
were such that more than half the linotype machines in the
composing-room broke down, and one of the apprentices ran
his shirt-tail through the proof-press. Down in the press-room
four or five pressmen got hurt, and the city edition was nearly
an hour late.

Nobody cared, for the head of the whole establishment, the
revered managing editor, Colonel Cunningham, was locked
up in his office with a case of Bourbon. At irregular intervals
he would throw a wad of copy-paper over the partition which
separated him from the editorial writers, and when this wad
was smoothed out it always turned out to be part of an interminable editorial against General Felix Agnus, editor of the
American. The General was a hero of the Civil War, with so
much lead in his system that he was said to rattle as he walked,
but Colonel Cunningham always hooted at his war record, and
was fond of alleging—without any ground whatsoever—that
he had come to America from his native France in the pussy-
like character of a barber. The editorial that he was writing that
Christmas Eve was headed, in fact, "The Barber of Seville." It
never got into the paper, for it was running beyond three
columns by press-time, and the night editor, Isidor Goodman, killed it for fear that its point was still to come. When
the Colonel inquired about it two or three days afterward he
was told that a truck had upset in the composing-room, and
pied it.

The hero of the *Herald* composing-room in those days was

a fat printer named Bill, who was reputed to be the champion beer-drinker of the Western Hemisphere. Bill was a first-rate linotype operator, and never resorted to his avocation in working-hours, but the instant his time was up he would hustle on his coat and go to a beer-house in the neighborhood, and there give what he called a setting. He made no charge for admission, but the spectators, of course, were supposed to pay for the beer. One night in 1902 I saw him get down thirty-two bottles in a row. Perhaps, in your wanderings, you have seen the same—but have you ever heard of a champion who could do it *without once retiring from his place at the bar*? Well, that is what Bill did, and on another occasion, when I was not present, he reached forty. Physiologists tell me that these prodigies must have been optical delusions, for there is not room enough in the coils and recesses of man for so much liquid, but I can only reply *Pfui* to that, for a record is a record. Bill avoided the door marked "Gents" as diligently as if he had been a débutante of the era, or the sign on it had been "For Ladies Only." He would have been humiliated beyond endurance if anyone had ever seen him slink through it.

In the year 1904, when the *Herald* office was destroyed in the great Baltimore fire, and we had to print the paper, for five weeks, in Philadelphia, I was told off to find accommodation for the printers. I found it in one of those old-fashioned $1-a-day hotels that were all bar on the first floor. The proprietor, a German with goat whiskers, was somewhat reluctant to come to terms, for he had heard that printers were wild fellows who might be expected to break up his furniture and work their wicked will upon his chambermaids, but when I told him that a beer-champion was among them he showed a more friendly interest, and when I began to brag about Bill's extraordinary talents his doubts disappeared and he proposed amiably that some Philadelphia foam-jumpers be invited in to make it a race. The first heat was run the very next night, and Bill won hands down. In fact, he won so easily that he offered grandly to go until he had drunk *twice* as much as the next best entry. We restrained him and got him to bed, for there had been some ominous whispering among the other starters, and it was plain that they were planning to call in help. The next night it appeared in the shape of a tall, knotty man from Allentown,

Pa., who was introduced as the champion of the Lehigh Valley. He claimed to be not only a beer-drinker of high gifts, but also a member of the Bach Choir at Bethlehem; and when he got down his first dozen mugs—the boys were drinking from the wood—he cut loose with an exultant yodel that he said was one of Bach's forgotten minor works. But he might very well have saved his wind, for Bill soon had him, and at the end of the setting he was four or five mugs behind, and in a state resembling suffocation. The next afternoon I saw his disconsolate fans taking him home, a sadder and much less melodious man.

On the first two nights there had been only slim galleries, but on the third the bar was jammed, and anyone could see that something desperate was afoot. It turned out to be the introduction of two super-champions, the one a short, saturnine Welshman from Wilkes-Barré, and the other a hearty blond young fellow from one of the Philadelphia suburbs, who said that he was half German and half Irish. The Welshman was introduced as the man who had twice drunk Otto the Brewery Horse under the table, and we were supposed to know who Otto was, though we didn't. The mongrel had a committee with him, and the chairman thereof offered to lay $25 on him at even money. The printers in Bill's corner made up the money at once, and their stake had grown to $50 in forty minutes by the clock, for the hybrid took only that long to blow up. The Welshman lasted much better, and there were some uneasy moments when he seemed destined to make history again by adding Bill to Otto, but in the end he succumbed so suddenly that it seemed like a bang, and his friends laid him out on the floor and began fanning him with bar-towels.

Bill was very cocky after that, and talked grandiosely of taking on two champions at a time, in marathon series. There were no takers for several nights, but after that they began to filter in from the remoter wilds of the Pennsylvania Dutch country, and the whole *Herald* staff was kept busy guarding Bill by day, to make sure that he did not waste any of his libido for malt liquor in the afternoons. He knocked off twenty or thirty challengers during the ensuing weeks, including two more Welshmen from the hard-coal country, a Scotsman with an ear missing, and a bearded Dunkard from Lancaster county.

They were mainly pushovers, but now and then there was a tough one. Bill did not let this heavy going interfere with the practise of his profession. He set type every night from 6 P.M. to midnight in the office of the *Evening Telegraph*, where we were printing the *Herald*, and never began his combats until 12.30. By two o'clock he was commonly in bed, with another wreath of laurels hanging on the gas-jet.

To ease your suspense I'll tell you at once that he was never beaten. Germans, Irishmen, Welshmen and Scotsmen went down before him like so many Sunday-school superintendents, and he bowled over everyday Americans with such facility that only two of them ever lasted more than half an hour. But I should add in candor that he was out of service during the last week of our stay in Philadelphia. What fetched him is still a subject of debate among the pathologists at the Johns Hopkins Medical School, to whom the facts were presented officially on our return to Baltimore. The only visible symptom was a complete loss of speech. Bill showed up one night talking hoarsely, the next night he could manage only whispers, and the third night he was as mute as a shad-fish. There was absolutely no other sign of distress. He was all for going on with his derisive harrying of the Pennsylvania lushers, but a young doctor who hung about the saloon and served as surgeon at the bouts forbade it on unstated medical grounds. The Johns Hopkins experts in morbid anatomy have never been able to agree about the case. Some argue that Bill's potations must have dissolved the gummy coating of his pharyngeal plexus, and thus paralyzed his vocal cords; the rest laugh at this as nonsense savoring of quackery, and lay the whole thing to an intercurrent laryngitis, induced by insufficient bedclothes on very cold nights. I suppose that no one will ever know the truth. Bill recovered his voice in a couple of months, and soon afterward left Baltimore. Of the prodigies, if any, that marked his later career I can't tell you.

He was but one of a notable series of giants who flourished in Baltimore at the turn of the century, bringing the city a friendly publicity and causing the theory to get about that life there must be delightful. They appeared in all the ranks of society. The Maryland Club had its champions, and the cops had theirs. Some were drinkers pure and simple; others specialized

* in eating. One of the latter was an old man of easy means who lived at the Rennert Hotel, then the undisputed capital of gastronomy in the terrapin and oyster country. But for some reason that I can't tell you he never did his eating there; instead, he always took dinner at Tommy McPherson's eating-house, six or eight blocks away. He would leave the hotel every evening at seven o'clock, elegantly arrayed in a long-tailed black coat and a white waistcoat, and carrying a gold-headed cane, and would walk the whole way. Tommy's place was arranged in two layers, with tables for men only alongside the bar downstairs, and a series of small rooms upstairs to which ladies might be invited. The cops, goaded by vice crusaders, had forced him to take the doors off these rooms, but he had substituted heavy portières, and his colored waiters were instructed to make a noise as they shuffled down the hall, and to enter every room backward. The old fellow I speak of, though there were tales about his wild youth, had by now got beyond thought of sin, and all his eating was done downstairs. It consisted of the same dishes precisely every night of the week, year in and year out. First he would throw in three straight whiskeys, and then he would sit down to *two* double porterhouse steaks, with *two* large plates of peas, *two* of French fried potatoes, *two* of cole-slaw, and a mountain of rye-bread. This vast meal he would eat to the last speck, and not infrequently he called for more potatoes or bread. He washed it down with two quarts of Burgundy, and at its end threw in three more straight whiskeys. Then he would light a cigar, and amble back to the Rennert, to spend the rest of the evening conversing with the politicoes who made their headquarters in its lobby.

One day a report reached the *Herald* office that he was beginning to break up, and Max Ways sent me to take a look. He had, by then, been on his diet for no less than twelve years. When I opened the subject delicately he hooted at the notion that he was not up to par. He was, he told me, in magnificent health, and expected to live at least twenty years longer. His excellent condition, he went on to say, was due wholly to his lifelong abstemiousness. He ate only a sparing breakfast, and no lunch at all, and he had not been drunk for fifteen years—that is, in the sense of losing all control of himself. He told me that people who ate pork dug their graves with their teeth, and praised the Jews for avoiding it. He also said that he regarded all sea-food as poisonous, on the ground that it contained too much phosphorus, and that fowl was almost as bad. There was, in his view, only one perfectly safe and wholesome victual, and that was beef. It had everything. It was nourishing, palatable and salubrious. The last bite tasted as good as the first. Even the bones had a pleasant flavor. He ate peas and potatoes with it, he said, mainly to give it some company: if he were ever cast on a desert island he could do without them. The cole-slaw went along as a sort of gesture of politeness to the grass that had produced the beef, and he ate rye-bread instead of wheat because rye was the bone and sinew of Maryland whiskey, the most healthful appetizer yet discovered by man. He would not affront me by presuming to discuss the virtues of Burgundy: they were mentioned in the Bible, and all humanity knew them.

The old boy never made his twenty years, but neither did he ever change his regimen. As the uplift gradually penetrated medicine various doctors of his acquaintance began to warn him that he was headed for a bad end, but he laughed at them in his quiet way, and went on going to Tommy's place every night, and devouring his two double porterhouses. What took him off at last was not his eating, but a trifling accident. He was knocked down by a bicycle in front of the Rennert, developed pneumonia, and was dead in three days. The resurrection men at both the Johns Hopkins and the University of Maryland tried to get his body for autopsy, and were all set to dig out of it a whole series of pathological monstrosities of a moral tendency, but his lawyer forbade any knifeplay until his only heir, a niece, could be consulted, and when she roared in from Eufaula, Ala., it turned out that she was a Christian Scientist, with a hate against anatomy. So he was buried without yielding any lessons for science. If he had any real rival, in those declining years of Baltimore gastronomy, it must have been John Wilson, a cop: I have always regretted that they were never brought together in a match. Once, at a cop party, I saw John eat thirty fried hard crabs at a sitting—no mean feat, I assure you, for though the claws are pulled off a crab before it is fried, all the body-meat remains. More, he not only ate the crabs, but sucked the shells. On another occasion, on a bet, he ate a ham and a cabbage in half an hour by the clock, but I was not present at that performance. When, a little later, he dropped dead in the old Central station-house, the police surgeons laid it to a pulmonary embolus, then a recent novelty in pathology.

XII.

The Judicial Arm

M Y RECOLLECTION of judges and my veneration for them go back a long way before my newspaper days, for I was a boy not more than eight or nine years old when my father began taking me on his tours of the more high-toned Washington saloons, and pointing out for my edification the eminent men who infested them. Not a few of those dignitaries were ornaments of the Federal judiciary, and among them were some whose names were almost household words in the Republic. But it was not their public fame that most impressed me; it was the lordly and elegant way in which they did their boozing. Before I really knew what a Congressman was I was aware that Congressmen were bad actors in barrooms, and often had to be thrown out, and years before I had heard that the United States Senate sat in trials of impeachment and formerly had a say in international treaties I had seen a Senator stricken by the first acrobatic symptoms of delirium tremens. But though I search my memory diligently, and it is especially tenacious in sociological matters, I can't recall a single judge who ever showed any sign of yielding to the influence. They all drank freely, and with a majestic spaciousness of style, but they carried their liquor like gentlemen.

Boy-like, I must have assumed that this gift for the bottle ran with their high station, and was, in fact, a part of their professional equipment, for I remember being greatly astonished years later, when I first encountered, as a young reporter, a judge definitely in his cups. There was nothing to the story save the bald fact that the poor old man, facing a hard calendar in equity on a morning when he was nursing a hangover from a Bar Association banquet, had thrown in one too many quick ones, and so got himself plastered. When he fell sound asleep in his pulpit, with his feet on the bench, there was a considerable pother, and by the time I wandered upon the scene his bailiffs had evacuated him to his chambers and doused him with ice-water, and he was rapidly resuming rationality, as his loud swearing indicated. Being still innocent, I reported the facts truthfully to Max Ways, and was somewhat puzzled when he ordered me to write a brief piece saying that His Honor had been floored at the post of duty by stomach ulcers, but was happily out of danger. Later on, as my journalistic experience widened, I saw many judges in a more or less rocky state, though I should add at once that I never saw another in that condition on the actual bench or within its purlieus, and that most of those I encountered were very far from their own courts. Indeed, I gradually picked up the impression that judges, like police captains, never really let themselves go until they were away from home. In those days all the police captains of the Eastern seaboard, whenever they felt that they couldn't stand the horrors of their office another minute, went to Atlantic City, and there soused and bellowed incognito, without either public scandal or danger to their jobs. Sometimes as many as a dozen gathered in one saloon—two or three from New York, a couple each from Philadelphia, Baltimore and Washington, and maybe the rest from points as far west as Pittsburgh. In the same way judges commonly sought a hide-away when the impulse to cut loose was on them; in their own archdioceses they kept their thirsts in hand, and so avoided the prying eyes of the vulgar.

At the time I began to find my way about as a reporter there
* was a rich old fellow in Baltimore who gave a big stag dinner every year at the Maryland Club. He was himself of no prominence, and his dinner had no public significance: it was simply that he loved good eating and enlightened boozing himself, and delighted in getting a group of men of the same mind about him. He had begun long before with a relatively small party, but every year the grateful patients suggested that it would be nice to include this or that recruit, and in the era I speak of the feast had grown to be very large and surpassingly elaborate, with seventy or eighty head of guests at the long table, as many colored waiters toting in the oysters, wild duck and terrapin, a large staff of sommeliers at the wine-buckets, and a battery of bartenders out in the hall. One year a judge was among the delegation of stock-brokers, bank presidents, wine-agents, Tammany leaders and other dignitaries who came down from New York, and the next year he brought another,

and the year following there were three, and then six, and so on. They greatly enjoyed the entertainment, and no wonder, for it was in the best Maryland Club manner; and the host, on his side, appreciated having so many men of mark at his board. But in the course of time it began to be hard on the families of some of the judges, and almost as hard on the cops and newspaper reporters of Baltimore.

For every time there was a dinner it launched a drunk in the grand manner, and every time there was such a drunk the job of rounding up the judiciary took two or three days, and was full of embarrassments and alarms. Many of the other guests, of course, also succumbed to the grape, but no one ever seemed to care what had become of them. A Tammany leader could disappear for two days, and cause no remark; even a bank president would not be posted at Lloyd's until the third day. But judges, it appeared, were missed very quickly, if not by their catchpolls then certainly by their wives and daughters, and by the late afternoon of the day after the dinner inquiries about this or that one would begin to come in from the North. Not infrequently the inquiry would be lodged in person by a frantic daughter, and when she was put off by the cops with weasel words she would tour the newspaper offices, declaring hysterically that her pa must have been murdered, and demanding the immediate production of his carcass.

The cops were indifferent for a plain reason: they always knew where the missing judges were. So, in fact, did everybody know, but it was not etiquette to say so. For aside from a few very ancient men who had gone direct from the dinner to the nervous diseases ward of the Johns Hopkins Hospital, and were there undergoing the ammonia cure, all the recreant Pontius Pilates were safely housed in the stews of Baltimore, which were then surpassed in luxury and polish only by the stews of St. Louis. Every such establishment had appropriate accommodations for just such clients. They would be lodged in comfortable rooms, watched over by trustworthy bouncers, entertained with music, dancing and easy female conversation, and supplied with booze until they seemed about to give out, whereupon they would be put on strict rations of milk and soda-water and so prepared for restoration to the world. All the chatelaines of the Baltimore houses of sin were familiar with that kind of trade, and knew precisely how to handle it, for they got a great deal of it, year in and year out, from Washington. Having handled maniacal Senators and Ambassadors, not to mention even higher dignitaries, they were not daunted by a sudden rush of harmless judges.

Unhappily, it was hard to convince the daughters of the missing jurists that they were comfortable and happy, and under no hazards to either their lives or their morals. Every such inquirer refused violently to be placated with generalizations: she demanded to be taken to her father instantly, and allowed to convoy him home. Inasmuch as no one dared to tell her where he was, it became the custom to say that he had gone down to a ducking club on the Eastern Shore of Maryland, and was there engaged in shooting mallards and canvasbacks. But there were always daughters who declared that their fathers were not marksmen, and in fact had a fear of guns, and sometimes it took a good deal of blarney to convince them that duck-shooting could be learned in half an hour, and was done with air-rifles or sling-shots. Even those who swallowed the lie often made trouble, for they usually proposed to proceed to the duck country at once, and I recall one who spent two days and nights roving the Eastern Shore, seeking some trace of a tall old man wearing a heavy white moustache, weighing 220 pounds, and dressed in a broadcloth cutaway and striped pants. It would have done no good to tell this poor lady that her father was still wearing the evening clothes that he had put on for the dinner. All the visitors, in fact, continued in their tails until the time came to wash them up and start them home. The champion in my day went on thus for four days and nights, and when the whistle was blown on him at last his judicial collar, white lawn tie and boiled shirt were in a truly scandalous state. Within the month following his return to duty, so I was told afterward, he sentenced five men to death.

How the old boys accounted for their disappearance to their daughters, once they had got back to their hotels and changed clothes for the journey home, I do not know, and never inquired. I suppose that a daughter is bound in law to believe anything her father tells her, especially if he be a judge, and I assume that judges, having been lawyers, have good imaginations and ready tongues. All I can tell you is that this annual man-hunt was a headache to the city editors of Baltimore, and to their faithful reporters. We had to keep watch on the whole gang for two or three days and nights, ever full of a pardonable hope that this one or that one would fall out of a window, brain a piano-player, drop dead of *mania à potu*, or otherwise qualify for our professional attentions. It would never do to be beaten on such a story—if such a story ever bobbed up. But it never did. The judges all got home safely, and whenever it turned out that one of them had left his watch behind, or his wallet, or his plug hat, the cops always recovered it promptly, and turned it over to the host, who saw that it was restored to its owner.

There was in those days a standard Maryland dinner for all festive occasions, and it was eaten five hundred times a year in the more polished hotels and clubs of Baltimore. It had the strange peculiarity of being wholly devoid of vegetables: every item on the bill save the salad was protein, and even the salad had slices of ham in it. It began with Chesapeake Bay oysters, proceeded to Chesapeake Bay terrapin, went on to Chesapeake Bay wild ducks, and then petered out in lettuce salad with Smithfield ham, and harlequin ice-cream. Sometimes a thin soup was served between the oysters and the terrapin, but often not. The oysters were not the rachitic dwarfs now seen on dinner tables, but fat, yellow, eunuchoid monsters at least six inches long; indeed, they were frequently nearer ten than six. A stranger to the Maryland cuisine, confronting such an oyster for the first time, usually got into a panic, but his host always bucked him up to trying it on his esophagus, and when he did so it commonly went down without choking him, for an oyster is a very pliant and yielding animal, and is also well lubricated. To cut up one would be regarded, in Maryland, as an indecency to be matched only by frying soft crabs in batter or putting cream into terrapin stew. The last two crimes against humanity obtain in New York, Philadelphia and Washington, but not in Baltimore. Soft crabs are always fried (or broiled) there in the altogether, with maybe a small jock-strap of bacon added, and nothing goes with terrapin save butter, seasoning and a jigger or two of sherry. Today a Marylander will give humble thanks to God for any kind of wild duck he can shoot, trap, beg, bootleg or steal, but in the Golden Age he offered his guests only the breasts of canvasbacks. Along with the orthodox dinner that I have outlined went an equally rigid programme of drinks. If cocktails were served before going to the table they had to be Manhattans, for no Baltimorean of condition ever drank gin: it was for blackamoors only, with a humane reservation in favor of white ladies suffering from female weakness. With the terrapin came sherry, or maybe Madeira, and with the duck, champagne, or maybe Burgundy. The rest of the dinner was washed down with champagne only, and the more of it the better.

This bill-of-fare, with all the drinks save the cocktails included, cost $10 a plate in any good Baltimore hotel. In that age of low living costs it was a high price, and the persons who paid it tried to get the worth of their money by guzzling all the champagne they could hold. As a young reporter I covered many such dinners, and saw some drinking bouts of very high amperage. The annual banquet of the Merchants and Manufacturers Association, then the chief organization of the local Babbitti, always ended in one of them. The chief speaker was usually either the Governor of some Southern state or a United States Senator, but it was seldom that his remarks were heard by anyone save the reporters and a few old Presbyterian misers, for all the rest of the guests were far gone by the time he got up, and not infrequently he was pretty well smeared himself. As I have noted, it was nothing to me to see a Senator in his cups, but it always shocked the Presbyterians, and after every dinner they proposed that the next one be dry. This proposal, when it got into the newspapers, set off a debate that went on for weeks and invariably ended in one way, with Colonel Cunningham and General Agnus joined in brotherly amity on the triumphant wet side. No M. & M. party was ever even ostensibly dry until the Prohibition murrain came down upon the country. The classical Maryland dinner was one of that great curse's first victims, and has never been revived, for when Prohibition went out at last new game laws came in, and it would be impossible today to assemble enough canvasback ducks to feed 500 men, or even fifty. In the midst of the thirteen doleful years the M. & M. itself gave up the ghost, and was absorbed by a new organization which devotes itself mainly to shipping and manufacturing statistics, and is not interested in the good living which once made Baltimore the envy of every other American city save New Orleans.

XIII.

Recollections of Notable Cops

SOME TIME ago I read in a New York paper that fifty or sixty college graduates had been appointed to the metropolitan police force, and were being well spoken of by their superiors. The news astonished me, for in my reportorial days there was simply no such thing in America as a book-learned cop, though I knew a good many who were very smart. The force was then recruited, not from the groves of Academe, but from the ranks of workingmen. The best police captain I ever knew in Baltimore was a meat-cutter by trade, and had lost one of his thumbs by a slip of his cleaver, and the next best was a former bartender. All the mounted cops were ex-hostlers passing as ex-cavalrymen, and all the harbor police had come up through the tugboat and garbage-scow branches of the merchant marine. It took a young reporter a little while to learn how to read and interpret the reports that cops turned in, for they were couched in a special kind of English, with a spelling peculiar to itself. If a member of what was then called "the finest" had spelled *larceny* in any way save *larsensy*, or *arson* in any way save *arsony*, or *fracture* in any way save *fraxr*, there would have been a considerable lifting of eyebrows. I well recall the horror of the Baltimore cops when the first board to examine applicants for places on the force was set up. It was a harmless body headed by a political dentist, and the hardest question in its first examination paper was "What is the plural of *ox*?," but all the cops in town predicted that it would quickly contaminate their craft with a great horde of what they called "professors," and reduce it to the level of letter-carrying or school-teaching.

But, as I have noted, their innocence of *literae humaniores* was not necessarily a sign of stupidity, and from some of them, in fact, I learned the valuable lesson that sharp wits can lurk in unpolished skulls. I knew cops who were matches for the most learned and unscrupulous lawyers at the Baltimore bar, and others who had made monkeys of the oldest and crabbedest judges on the bench, and were generally respected for it. Moreover, I knew cops who were really first-rate policemen, and loved their trade as tenderly as so many art artists or movie actors. They were badly paid, but they carried on their dismal work with unflagging diligence, and loved a long, hard chase almost as much as they loved a quick, brisk clubbing. Their one salient failing, taking them as a class, was their belief that any person who had been arrested, even on mere suspicion, was unquestionably and *ipso facto* guilty. But that theory, though it occasionally colored their testimony in a garish manner, was grounded, after all, on nothing worse than professional pride and *esprit de corps*, and I am certainly not one to hoot at it, for my own belief in the mission of journalism has no better support than the same partiality, and all the logic I am aware of stands against it.

In those days that pestilence of Service which torments the American people today was just getting under way, and many of the multifarious duties now carried out by social workers, statisticians, truant officers, visiting nurses, psychologists, and the vast rabble of inspectors, smellers, spies and bogus experts of a hundred different faculties either fell to the police or were not discharged at all. An ordinary flatfoot in a quiet residential section had his hands full. In a single day he might have to put out a couple of kitchen fires, arrange for the removal of a dead mule, guard a poor epileptic having a fit on the sidewalk, catch a runaway horse, settle a combat with table knives between husband and wife, shoot a cat for killing pigeons, rescue a dog or a baby from a sewer, bawl out a white-wings for spilling garbage, keep order on the sidewalk at two or three funerals, and flog half a dozen bad boys for throwing horse-apples at a blind man. The cops downtown, especially along the wharves and in the red-light districts, had even more curious and complicated jobs, and some of them attained to a high degree of virtuosity.

As my memory gropes backward I think, for example, of a strange office that an old-time roundsman named Charlie had * to undertake every Spring. It was to pick up enough skilled workmen to effect the annual re-decoration and refurbishing of the Baltimore City Jail. Along about May 1 the warden would telephone to police headquarters that he needed, say, ten head of painters, five plumbers, two blacksmiths, a tile-setter, a

roofer, a bricklayer, a carpenter and a locksmith, and it was
Charlie's duty to go out and find them. So far as I can recall, he
never failed, and usually he produced two or three times as
many craftsmen of each category as were needed, so that the
warden had some chance to pick out good ones. His plan was
simply to make a tour of the saloons and stews in the Marsh
Market section of Baltimore, and look over the drunks in congress assembled. He had a trained eye, and could detect a plumber
or a painter through two weeks' accumulation of beard and
dirt. As he gathered in his candidates, he searched them on the
spot, rejecting those who had no union cards, for he was a firm
believer in organized labor. Those who passed were put into
storage at a police-station, and there kept (less the unfortunates who developed delirium tremens and had to be handed
over to the resurrection-men) until the whole convoy was
ready. The next morning Gene Grannan, the police magistrate,
gave them two weeks each for vagrancy, loitering, trespass, committing a nuisance, or some other plausible misdemeanor, the
warden had his staff of master-workmen, and the jail presently
bloomed out in all its vernal finery.

Some of these toilers returned year after year, and in the end
Charlie recognized so many that he could accumulate the
better part of his convoy in half an hour. Once, I remember, he
was stumped by a call for two electricians. In those remote
days there were fewer men of that craft in practise than today,
and only one could be found. When the warden put on the
heat Charlie sent him a trolley-car motorman who had run
away from his wife and was trying to be shanghaied for the
Chesapeake oyster-fleet. This poor man, being grateful for his
security in jail, made such eager use of his meagre electrical
knowledge that the warden decided to keep him, and even requested that his sentence be extended. Unhappily, Gene Grannan was a pretty good amateur lawyer, and knew that such an
extension would be illegal. When the warden of the House of
Correction, which was on a farm twenty miles from Baltimore,
heard how well this system was working, he put in a requisition
for six experienced milkers and a choir-leader, for he had a
herd of cows and his colored prisoners loved to sing spirituals.
Charlie found the choir-leader in no time, but he bucked at
hunting for milkers, and got rid of the nuisance by sending the

warden a squad of sailors who almost pulled the poor cows to pieces.

Gene had been made a magistrate as one of the first fruits of the rising reform movement in Baltimore, and was a man of the chastest integrity, but he knew too much about reformers to admire them, and lost no chance to afflict them. When, in 1900, or thereabout, a gang of snoopers began to tour the red-light districts, seeking to harass and alarm the poor work-ing women there denizened, he instructed the gals to empty slops on them, and acquitted all who were brought in for doing it, usually on the ground that the complaining witnesses were disreputable persons, and could not be believed on oath. One day, sitting in his frowsy courtroom, I saw him gloat in a positively indecent manner when a Methodist clergyman was led out from the cells by Mike Hogan, the turnkey. This holy man, believing that the Jews, unless they consented to be baptized, would all go to Hell, had opened a mission in what was then still called the Ghetto, and sought to save them. The adults, of course, refused to have anything to do with him, but he managed, after a while, to lure a number of *kosher* small boys into his den, chiefly by showing them magic-lantern pic-tures of the Buffalo Bill country and the Holy Land. When their fathers heard of this there was naturally an uproar, for it was a mortal sin in those days for an orthodox Jew to enter a *Goy Schul*. The ritual for delousing offenders was an arduous one, and cost both time and money. So the Jews came clamor-ing to Grannan, and he spent a couple of hours trying to figure out some charge to lay against the evangelist. Finally, he ordered him brought in, and entered him on the books for "annoying persons passing by and along a public highway, disorderly con-duct, making loud and unseemly noises, and disturbing religious worship." He had to be acquitted, of course, but Gene scared him so badly with talk of the penitentiary that he shut down his mission forthwith, and left the Jews to their post-mortem sufferings.

As I have noted in Chapter II, Gene was a high favorite among us young reporters, for he was always good for copy, and did not hesitate to modify the course of justice in order to feed and edify us. One day an ancient German, obviously a highly respectable man, was brought in on the incredible charge of beating his wife. The testimony showed that they had been placidly married for more than 45 years, and seldom exchanged so much as a bitter word. But the night before, when the old man came home from the saloon where he played *Skat* every evening, the old woman accused him of having drunk more than his usual ration of eight beers, and in the course of the ensuing debate he gave her a gentle slap. Astounded, she let off an hysterical squawk, an officious neighbor rushed in, the cops came on his heels, and so the old man stood before the bar of justice, weeping copiously and with his wife weeping even more copiously beside him. Gene pondered the evidence with a frown on his face, and then announced his judgment. "The crime you are accused of committing," he said, "is a foul and desperate one, and the laws of all civilized countries prohibit it under heavy penalties. I could send you to prison for life, I could order you to the whipping-post [it still exists in Maryland, and for wife-beaters only], or I could sentence you to be hanged. [Here both parties screamed.] But inasmuch as this is your first offense I will be lenient. You will be taken hence to the House of Correction, and there confined for twenty years. In addition, you are fined $10,000." The old couple missed the fine, for at mention of the House of Correction both fainted. When the cops revived them, Gene told the prisoner that, on reflection, he had decided to strike out the sentence, and bade him go and sin no more. Husband and wife rushed out of the courtroom hand in hand, followed by a cop with the umbrella and market-basket that the old woman had forgotten. A week or two later news came in that she was ordering the old man about in a highly cavalier manner, and had cut down his evenings of *Skat* to four a week.

The cops liked and admired Gene, and when he was in good form he commonly had a gallery of them in his courtroom, guffawing at his whimsies. But despite his popularity among them he did not pal with them, for he was basically a very dignified, and even somewhat stiff fellow, and knew how to call them down sharply when their testimony before him went too far beyond the bounds of the probable. In those days, as in these, policemen led a social life almost as inbred as that of the justices of the Supreme Court of the United States, and outsiders were seldom admitted to their parties. But reporters were exceptions, and I attended a number of cop soirées of great elegance, with the tables piled mountain-high with all the delicacies of the season, and a keg of beer every few feet. The graft of these worthy men, at least in my time, was a great deal less than reformers alleged and the envious common people believed. Most of them, in my judgment, were very honest fellows, at least within the bounds of reason. Those who patrolled the fish-markets naturally had plenty of fish to eat, and those who manned the police-boats in the harbor took a certain toll from the pungy captains who brought up Baltimore's ✳ supplies of watermelons, cantaloupes, vegetables, crabs and oysters from the Eastern Shore of Maryland: indeed, this last impost amounted to a kind of *octroi*, and at one time the harbor force accumulated so much provender that they had to seize an empty warehouse on the waterfront to store it. But the pungy captains gave up uncomplainingly, for the pelagic cops protected them against the thieves and highjackers who swarmed in the harbor, and also against the land police. I never heard of cops getting anything that the donor was not quite willing and even eager to give. Every Italian who ran a peanut stand knew that making them free of it was good institutional promotion and the girls in the red-light districts liked to crochet neckties, socks and pulse-warmers for them. It was not unheard of for a cop to get mashed on such a girl, rescue her from her life of shame, and set her up as a more or less honest woman. I knew of several cases in which holy matrimony followed. But the more ambitious girls, of course, looked higher, and some of them, in my time, made very good marriages. One actually married a banker, and another died only a few ✳ years ago as the faithful and much respected wife of a prominent physician. The cops always laughed when reformers alleged that the wages of sin were death—specifically, that women who sold their persons always ended in the gutter, full of dope and despair. They knew that the overwhelming majority ended at the altar of God, and that nearly all of them married better men than they could have had any chance of meeting and roping if they had kept their virtue.

One dismal New Year's day I saw a sergeant lose an excellent chance to pocket $138.66 in cash money: I remember it brilliantly because I lost the same chance at the same moment.

There had been the usual epidemic of suicides in the waterfront flop-houses, for the dawn of a new year turns the thoughts of homeless men to peace beyond the dissecting-room, and I ac- companied the sergeant and a coroner on a tour of the fatal scenes. One of the dead men was lying on the fifth floor of a decaying warehouse that had been turned into ten-cent sleeping quarters, and we climbed up the long stairs to inspect him. All the other bums had cleared out, and the hophead clerk did not offer to go with us. We found the deceased stretched out in a peaceful attitude, with the rope with which he had hanged himself still around his neck. He had been cut down, but then abandoned.

The sergeant loosed the rope, and began a search of the dead man's pockets, looking for means to identify him. He found nothing whatever of that sort, but from a pants pocket he drew out a fat wad of bills, and a hasty count showed that it contained $416. A situation worthy of Scribe, or even Victor Hugo! Evidently the poor fellow was one of the Russell Sages that are occasionally found among bums. His money, I suppose, had been diminishing, and he had bumped himself off in fear that it would soon be all gone. The sergeant looked at the coroner, the coroner looked at me, and I looked at the sergeant. Then the sergeant wrapped up the money in a piece of newspaper lying nearby, and handed it to the coroner. "It goes," he said sadly, "to the State of Maryland. The son-of-a-bitch died intestate, and with no heirs."

The next day I met the coroner, and found him in a low frame of mind. "It was a sin and a shame," he said, "to turn that money over to the State Treasury. What I could have done with $138.67! (I noticed he made a fair split, but collared one of the two odd cents.) Well, it's gone now—damn the luck! I never *did* trust that flat-foot."

XIV.

A Genial Restauranteur

I AM well aware that the word *restauranteur*, as it appears in the title of this chapter, contains an *n* that the French eschew; my plea in confession and avoidance must be that I am not writing French but American, and, specifically, the American in vogue on the newspapers of my native Baltimore in my salad days as a journalist. No reporter of that era ever thought of referring to a respectable saloonkeeper as a saloonkeeper: the term was reserved, at least in print, for such dubious characters as Bob Fosbender, whose place at Pine and Raborg streets was the very Capitol of the Western red-light district— and when I say Capitol I mean exactly that, for the representative assembly of the adjacent landladies, always called simply the Senate, met in his back room once a week. All saloonkeepers above Bob's social and moral level, with one exception, were restauranteurs, with the *n*, and all that were personally known to newspaper men, and held in reasonable esteem, rated the *genial* in front of *restauranteur*.

This large company included even Frank Junker, probably one of the least genial men, in actuality, that ever suffered from varicose veins, the occupational malady of all the old-timers of his profession. He was a stout, short, silent, suspicious German who was a Scotsman in all save the husk or rind, and he owned a modest but very profitable saloon opposite the Baltimore City Hall. Having learned by experience that municipal job-holders, as a class, were grasping and cantankerous men, he did not cater to them, but directed his lures (*a*) to the musicians, stagehands and ham actors of the old Holliday Street Theatre, which was half a block away, and (*b*) to journalists. Neither of these groups had any great amount of money, but they could be trusted to spend all they had, and, moreover, they spread their boozing over both day and night. Like any other downtown saloonkeeper Frank had plenty of business in daylight hours, but at night most of the streets near the City Hall were as dead as Herculaneum, and many of the genial restauranteurs in them actually closed at 9 P.M. But not this one, for he had learned that that was the hour when musicians and actors began to duck out for really earnest drinking, and he knew, too, that journalists hardly got under way until an hour or two later. Thus his place was crowded every night, and I have seen it so jammed at midnight that Frank and his bartender, Emil, had to call off all mixed drinks, and serve only straight whiskey and beer.

I have spoken of the actors as hams, and that, unhappily, was what they were, for the Holliday Street was one of the oldest theatres in America, and had long since descended to Theodore Kremer and Charles E. Blaney melodramas. It had a matinée every day (heavily patronized by night-shift street-car conductors and motormen, and their doxies), and before every performance, no matter what the weather, the orchestra, playing as a brass band, performed on the portico over the entrance. This was tough work in Winter, and the work indoors, Winter or no Winter, was almost as onerous, for there was continuous music while a melodrama was going on, and the musicians had to look sharply or miss their cues. The hottest
* spot was that of Hank Schofield, the bull-fiddler, for on his vigilance depended the success of every scene of lust, vengeance or despair. Whenever the villain was on the stage, which was nearly always, Hank had to accompany his lubricious rascalities *pizzicato*, and when the comic man split his pants the sound had to be caught and augmented *col arco*. Even the love scenes gave Hank no rest, for it was the convention in those days to signalize every kiss with a jocose *glissando*, and that *glissando* always started in the bull-fiddle.

Thus Hank was pretty dry by the time the evening performance was over, and nearly every night he sat at one of Frank's greasy tables with several other *Tonkünstler* and discussed the decay of their chosen art. By the time we journalists began to drop in some of these artists were more or less lit, and so the evening's ceremonies started off in a very friendly manner. On our side there was a fixed ritual. We were organized into a professional society known as the Stevedores' Club (the name, of course, was a subtle reference to the unloading of schooners), and as soon as a *minyan* was present Frank was elected an honorary member. He always received this distinction with modest deprecation and embarrassment, and apparently lived and died without ever figuring out why he got it so often. But he knew the rule that a new member was expected to set up the drinks, and in consequence we always got a round free. Once the experiment was tried of electing him *twice* in a night, but he failed to hear the second election, and the scheme was abandoned. But at about the same time we invented and established a rule that *guests* could treat the house, though members were forbidden to do so. The Holliday Street Theatre boys kept this rule alive by steering in a steady stream of ham actors, all of whom were welcomed with flattering speeches. The musicians were not members of the Stevedores' Club, but when they had a ham in tow they were free to sit in.

How long the club went on I don't know, for it was in existence years before my time, and there were vestiges of it visible so late as 1915, long after I had become a managing editor and was no longer eligible. At its peak, say in 1900, it had about a dozen regular members, and a dozen more who dropped in off and on. Not only was its direct patronage valuable to Frank; it also helped him to wealth by enabling him to stay open beyond the Baltimore closing hour, which in those days was midnight. The news of this immunity getting about, he was soon catering to a large body of miscellaneous night-hawks, including printers, post-office clerks, bank watchmen, and even street cleaners. We objected to the last-named on the ground of their smell, and they were finally excluded, but the rest kept coming, and Frank wore out a cash-register a year ringing up their money. In 1904, when his place was burned in the great Baltimore fire, the insurance he received, added to his accumulations, gave him the impressive cash capital of $175,000, and with it he built a stag hotel and was quickly rolling in an income even larger than his old one. Unhappily, his dignity as host of his hotel required him to wear his Sunday suit every day, and he soon began to pine away, and was presently no more.

As I have said, it was the presence of the Stevedores' Club that enabled him to keep open after hours, for we journalists naturally had some drag with the cops, and when we represented to Ned Schleigh, their captain in that precinct, that it was inhuman to ask us to clear out at midnight, perhaps in the midst of a belated meal, he allowed that the point was well

taken, and instructed his flatfeet to act accordingly. But the
reform wave that began to afflict Baltimore at the turn of the
century was especially hard on cops, and in 1901 or thereabout
a new chief of police took to sending squads of plain-clothes
men from remote precincts into the downtown areas of sin,
seeking to catch the regular watch in derelictions. One night
such a gang of shoo-flies, as they were called, bust into Frank's,
and though the members of the Stevedores' Club set up a
dreadful bellow, and threatened to break and jail the sergeant
in command, Frank got a summons, and we were put to the
trouble of having it torn up next morning.

This episode greatly incensed Ned Schleigh, the captain, not
only because it revealed to the people of Baltimore a crass violation of the liquor laws in his bailiwick, but also and more
especially because it flouted his lawful command and authority.
He responded by stationing one of his own cops, in full uniform, at the back door we used for getting in and out of the
place, and that cop stood on guard there every night for something on the order of six months, for it took that long for the
reform movement to subside. His instructions were to inform
any raiders who showed up that the place was already in the
custody of Schleigh himself, who had raided it only half an
hour before. No more appeared, but the six months included a
hard February, and the poor cop on duty at the back door,
whose name was Joe, suffered painful frostbites until his native
intelligence suggested that he come in now and again, and
thaw out behind Frank's stove. Every time he came in he got a
shot of Class C rye, so the arrangement was satisfactory to all
hands. When the reformers were thrown off at last, and Christian peace and order were restored in Baltimore, we persuaded
the Police Board to promote Joe to a sergeancy.

Frank, as I have remarked, was a man without social graces,
and it was rare for him to say more than *Wie geht's* to a customer, whether journalistic or other. But he was highly skilled
at his social-minded craft, and thus enjoyed a kind of esteem
that, in a more responsive man, would have passed for popularity. He understood very well the principle that a glass of
beer running to less than sixteen ounces or costing more than
five cents is an economic atrocity. He also had the acumen to
charge only ten cents for deviled crabs, with an inside rate of

five cents to members of the press. Thus his customers ate well and drank freely, and in his nightly election to honorary membership in the Stevedores' Club there was really almost as much good will as self-interest. When he opened his stag hotel the club followed him, but the place was rather too elegant for the literary trade, and most of the members presently deserted it for the establishment of a compatriot with goat whiskers, known to everyone as Weber and Fields. Weber and Fields was only one man, but no one could make out which of the two comedians he resembled most, so he was named for both. His place was in a dark alley behind the Baltimore *Sun* office, and his small bar was packed every night. He was himself a beer-drinker of great gifts, and was reputed to get down fifty shells a day. The shell he used had a false bottom, but even so his daily ration sounded impressive, and he enjoyed a high degree of public respect.

Those members of the Stevedores' Club who stuck to the splendors of Frank's stag hotel had a somewhat quiet time of it, for the roomers at the place went to bed early, and there was little outside trade in the bar. The bartender, in fact, knocked off every night at midnight, and Frank himself withdrew soon afterward, worn out by the abrasions of his boiled shirt and Sunday suit. This left the main deck in charge of a night-clerk nearly eighty years old, with a young fellow named Rudolph as his only aide. Rudolph served as bell-hop, house dick, and night bartender and oyster-shucker. The night-clerk's faculties were so far clouded by age that he could be disregarded, which reduced the problem before the club to this: how to get rid of Rudolph long enough to pillage the bar and oyster-bar? It was solved night after night by tipping him off that some member not present had just sneaked in with a female, and disappeared up the stairway behind the elevator. This set him to searching the house, and while he was so engaged a leisurely burglary was effected. After the fraud had been worked on him forty or fifty times he began to show signs of tumbling, so the club withdrew. The stag hotel, in fact, was never very popular with the brethren.

But Frank's old place opposite the City Hall had been their favorite for years, and so long as it survived it was the home port of all Baltimore journalists of the malt-liquor moiety.

They used, of course, other saloons—or, as the cops of the era preferred to call them, kaifs—, but Frank always got them in the end. When his bartender, Emil, set up business on his own the boys attended the opening, and some of them dropped in occasionally afterward, but inasmuch as the new establishment was in a remote suburb, half a mile beyond the rail-head of the nearest trolley line, getting to it was a fatiguing business. Once, when Emil threw a party to celebrate the fifth anniversary of the death of Bismarck, the full strength of the club waited on him, taking along the band of the Holliday Street Theatre. But when the band marched up the road from the trolley, playing brisk Sousa marches, the whole suburb turned out of bed to hoot and holler, for it was after midnight, and in those pre-radio days decent people in such neighborhoods were in the hay by 9:30. The cops who were summoned joined the party and became such life as it had, but it never had much, and it was not repeated.

There were other restauranteurs in the Baltimore of that time who will get friendly notice if the true history of the town is ever written, which is, alas, improbable. I remember, for example, John Roth, who kept a swell place in Fayette street, next door to the *Herald* office, with a pool parlor up-stairs. He was the *beau idéal* of an old-time saloonkeeper, with a walrus moustache, a large paunch, and the manners of an ambassador. He never went behind his own bar, but always stood in front of it, near the entrance, so that he could greet incoming clients. On the wall opposite was the largest hand-painted oil-painting of Venus rising from her bath in all the Baltimores. His free lunch was very well spoken of, and he offered a business men's lunch at midday that was worth twice its *prix fixe* of twenty-five cents. But the best free lunch of the era was to be had at the Diamond in Howard street, kept by Muggsy McGraw and Wilbert Robinson, two heroes of the old Baltimore Orioles. Muggsy was too contentious a man to make a good saloonkeeper, and in a little while he vanished from the place, but the fat and amiable Robinson continued on duty for several years, always standing in front of the bar like John Roth. The free lunch at the Diamond was based on an immense chafing-dish of hot dogs, always bubbling, but it also included roast beef, *Schwartenmagen*, and a superior brand of rat-trap cheese. There was a high-toned colored man behind the counter, and any customer of reasonably neat appearance was free to eat all he could hold. The only persons who were barred out as a class, so far as I can recall, were newspaper artists. Robbie had a very low opinion of them, and when one of them wandered in and had to be bounced, he always did it personally.

The most austere restauranteur in Baltimore, and perhaps in the United States, was one Kepler, who kept a place in North street near the City Hall. He was a grave, even sombre man who smiled only once or twice a week. I seldom entered his door, but one snowy night in the Winter of 1900–01 I came near having the honor of being assassinated in front of his bar. The assassin was a minor labor leader who had developed a   *
hate for me because I had written a story revealing him as the caitiff of a fight in a bawdy-house, and he came into the place looking for me, apparently on the mistaken theory that I frequented it. Pulling out two pistols he laid them on the bar, and announced his purpose, naming me by name. Kepler was for trying moral suasion on him, but one of my *Herald* colleagues, who happened to be drinking in the place, preferred more direct action. Seizing a quart bottle of Maryland rye that was on the bar, he brought it down on the labor leader's head, knocking him out at one crack. He then dragged the poor fellow's carcass out into the street, and shoved it into a snow drift. There it lay until the cops came along and sent it to hospital. When, a little while later, I ran into its owner on the street, he seemed to be completely restored, but had no more murder in his heart. The whole thing, he assured me, was a mistake. He was only trying to scare Kepler.

The most hated saloonkeeper in Baltimore in those days— that is, among journalists—was Mike Ganzhorn, who kept a small stag hotel in Baltimore street, with an ornate bar and eating-room downstairs. He was the only member of the whole fraternity who was never, under any circumstances, mentioned in print as a genial restauranteur. Indeed, he never got any mention at all, save only when there was a fight in his bar, or a guest committed suicide upstairs. Mike's crime was that he had once told someone who had told someone who had told someone that he could buy any newspaper man in Baltimore for a drink. This libel rankled for years. It rankled mainly be-cause there was so much truth in it. Mike had taken in slightly too much territory, but there was certainly enough sound ground in the middle to sustain him.

XV.
A Girl from Red Lion, P.A.

SOMEWHERE IN his lush, magenta prose Oscar Wilde speaks of the tendency of nature to imitate art—a phenomenon often observed by persons who keep their eyes open. I first became aware of it, not through the pages of Wilde, but at the hands of an old-time hack-driver named Peebles, who flourished in Baltimore in the days of this history. Peebles was a Scotsman of a generally unfriendly and retiring character, but nevertheless he was something of a public figure in the town. Perhaps that was partly due to the fact that he had served twelve years in the Maryland Penitentiary for killing his wife, but I think he owed much more of his eminence to his adamantine rectitude in money matters, so rare in his profession. The very cops, indeed, regarded him as an honest man, and said so freely. They knew about his blanket refusal to take more than three or four times the legal fare from drunks, they knew how many lost watches, wallets, stick-pins and walking-sticks he turned in every year, and they admired as Christians, though deploring as cops, his absolute refusal to work for them in the capacity of stool-pigeon.

Moreover, he was industrious as well as honest, and it was the common belief that he had money in five banks. He appeared on the hack-stand in front of the old Eutaw House every evening at nine o'clock, and put in the next five or six hours shuttling merrymakers and sociologists to and from the red-light districts. When this trade began to languish he drove to Union Station, and there kept watch until his two old horses fell asleep. Most of the strangers who got off the early morning trains wanted to go to the nearest hotel, which was only two blocks away, so there was not a great deal of money in their patronage, but unlike the other hackers Peebles never resorted to the device of driving them swiftly in the wrong direction and then working back by a circuitous route.

A little after dawn one morning in the early Autumn of 1903, just as his off horse began to snore gently, a milk-train got in from lower Pennsylvania, and out of it issued a rosy-cheeked young woman carrying a pasteboard suitcase and a pink parasol. Squired up from the train-level by a car-greaser with an eye for country beauty, she emerged into the sunlight shyly and ran her eye down the line of hacks. The other drivers seemed to scare her, and no wonder, for they were all grasping men whose evil propensities glowed from them like heat from a stove. But when she saw Peebles her feminine intuition must have told her that he could be trusted, for she shook off the car-greaser without further ado, and came up to the Peebles hack with a pretty show of confidence.

"Say, mister," she said, "how much will you charge to take me to a house of ill fame?"

In telling of it afterward Peebles probably exaggerated his astonishment a bit, but certainly he must have suffered something rationally describable as a shock. He laid great stress upon her air of blooming innocence, almost like that of a ca-vorting lamb. He said her two cheeks glowed like apples, and that she smelled like a load of hay. By his own account he stared at her for a full minute without answering her question, with a wild stream of confused surmises racing through his mind. What imaginable business could a creature so obviously guileless have in the sort of establishment she had mentioned? Could it be that her tongue had slipped—that she actually meant an employment office, the Y.W.C.A., or what not? Pee-bles, as he later elaborated the story, insisted that he had cross-examined her at length, and that she had not only reiter-ated her question in precise terms, but explained that she was fully determined to abandon herself to sin and looked forward confidently to dying in the gutter. But in his first version he reported simply that he had stared at her dumbly until his amazement began to wear off, and then motioned to her to climb into his hack. After all, he was a common carrier, and obliged by law to haul all comers, regardless of their private projects and intentions. If he yielded anything to his Caledo-nian moral sense it took the form of choosing her destination with some prudence. He might have dumped her into one of the third-rate bagnios that crowded a street not three blocks from Union Station, and then gone on about his business. In-stead, he drove half way across town to the high-toned studio

of Miss Nellie d'Alembert, at that time one of the leaders of *
her profession in Baltimore, and a woman who, though she
lacked the polish of Vassar, had sound sense, a pawky humor,
and progressive ideas.

I had become, only a little while before, city editor of the
Herald, and in that capacity received frequent confidential
communications from her. She was, in fact, the source of a
great many useful news tips. She knew everything about everyone that no one was supposed to know, and had accurate advance information, in particular, about Page 1 divorces, for
nearly all the big law firms of the town used her facilities for
the manufacture of evidence. There were no Walter Winchells
in that era, and the city editors of the land had to depend on
volunteers for inside stuff. Such volunteers were moved (*a*) by
a sense of public duty gracefully performed, and (*b*) by an enlightened desire to keep on the good side of newspapers. Not
infrequently they cashed in on this last. I well remember the
night when two visiting Congressmen from Washington got
into a debate in Miss Nellie's music-room, and one of them
dented the skull of the other with a spittoon. At my suggestion
the other city editors of Baltimore joined me in straining journalistic ethics far enough to remove the accident to Mt. Vernon
place, the most respectable neighborhood in town, and to lay
the fracture to a fall on the ice.

My chance leadership in this public work made Miss Nellie
my partisan, and now and then she gave me a nice tip and
forgot to include the other city editors. Thus I was alert when
she called up during the early afternoon of Peebles' strange
adventure, and told me that something swell was on ice. She
explained that it was not really what you could call important
news, but simply a sort of human-interest story, so I asked
Percy Heath to go to see her, for though he was now my successor as Sunday editor, he still did an occasional news story,
and I knew what kind he enjoyed especially. He called up in
half an hour, and asked me to join him. "If you don't hear it
yourself," he said, "you will say I am pulling a fake."

When I got to Miss Nellie's house I found her sitting with
Percy in a basement room that she used as a sort of office, and
at once she plunged into the story.

"I'll tell you first," she began, "before you see the poor

thing herself. When Peebles yanked the bell this morning I was sound asleep, and so was all the girls, and Sadie the coon had gone home. I stuck my head out of the window, and there was Peebles on the front steps. I said: 'Get the hell away from here! What do you mean by bringing in a drunk at this time of the morning? Don't you know us poor working people gotta get some rest?' But he hollered back that he didn't have no drunk in his hack, but something he didn't know what to make of, and needed my help on, so I slipped on my kimono and went down to the door, and by that time he had the girl out of the hack, and before I could say 'scat' he had shoved her in the parlor, and she was unloading what she had to say.

"Well, to make a long story short, she said she come from somewheres near a burg they call Red Lion, P.A., and lived on a farm. She said her father was one of them old rubes with whiskers they call Dunkards, and very strict. She said she had a beau in York, P.A., of the name of Elmer, and whenever he could get away he would come out to the farm and set in the parlor with her, and they would do a little hugging and kissing. She said Elmer was educated and a great reader, and he would bring her books that he got from his brother, who was a train butcher on the Northern Central, and him and her would read them. She said the books was all about love, and that most of them was sad. Her and Elmer would talk about them while they set in the parlor, and the more they talked about them the sadder they would get, and sometimes she would have to cry.

"Well, to make a long story short, this went on once a week or so, and night before last Elmer come down from York with some more books, and they set in the parlor, and talked about love. Her old man usually stuck his nose in the door now and then, to see that there wasn't no foolishness, but night before last he had a bilious attack and went to bed early, so her and Elmer had it all to theirself in the parlor. So they quit talking about the books, and Elmer began to love her up, and in a little while they was hugging and kissing to beat the band. Well, to make a long story short, Elmer went too far, and when she come to herself and kicked him out she realized she had lost her honest name.

"She laid awake all night thinking about it, and the more she thought about it the more scared she got. In every one of the books her and Elmer read there was something on the subject, and all of the books said the same thing. When a girl lost her honest name there was nothing for her to do excepting to run away from home and lead a life of shame. No girl that she ever read about ever done anything else. They all rushed off to the nearest city, started this life of shame, and then took to booze and dope and died in the gutter. Their family never knew what had became of them. Maybe they landed finally in a medical college, or maybe the Salvation Army buried them, but their people never heard no more of them, and their name was rubbed out of the family Bible. Sometimes their beau tried to find them, but he never could do it, and in the end he usually married the judge's homely daughter, and moved into the big house when the judge died.

"Well, to make a long story short, this poor girl lay awake all night thinking of such sad things, and when she got up at four thirty A.M. and went out to milk the cows her eyes was so full of tears that she could hardly find their spigots. Her father, who was still bilious, give her hell, and told her she was getting her just punishment for setting up until ten and eleven o'clock at night, when all decent people ought to be in bed. So she began to suspect that he may have snuck down during the evening, and caught her, and was getting ready to turn her out of the house and wash his hands of her, and maybe even curse her. So she decided to have it over and done with as soon as possible, and last night, the minute he hit the hay again, she hoofed in to York, P.A., and caught the milk-train for Baltimore, and that is how Peebles found her at Union Station and brought her here. When I asked her what in hell she wanted all she had to say was 'Ain't this a house of ill fame?,' and it took me an hour or two to pump her story out of her. So now I have got her upstairs under lock and key, and as soon as I can get word to Peebles I'll tell him to take her back to Union Station, and start her back for Red Lion, P.A. Can you beat it?"

Percy and I, of course, demanded to see the girl, and presently Miss Nellie fetched her in. She was by no means the bucolic Lillian Russell that Peebles's tall tales afterward made her out, but she was certainly far from unappetizing. Despite her loss of sleep, the dreadful gnawings of her conscience and the menace of an appalling retribution, her cheeks were still rosy, and there remained a considerable sparkle in her troubled blue eyes. I never heard her name, but it was plain that she was of four-square Pennsylvania Dutch stock, and as sturdy as the cows she serviced. She had on her Sunday clothes, and appeared to be somewhat uncomfortable in them, but Miss Nellie set her at ease, and soon she was retelling her story to two strange and, in her sight, probably highly dubious men. We listened without interrupting her, and when she finished Percy was the first to speak.

"My dear young lady," he said, "you have been grossly misinformed. I don't know what these works of fiction are that you and Elmer read, but they are as far out of date as Joe Miller's Jest-Book. The stuff that seems to be in them would make even a newspaper editorial writer cough and scratch himself. It may be true that, in the remote era when they appear to have been written, the penalty of a slight and venial slip was as drastic as you say, but I assure you that it is no longer the case. The world is much more humane than it used to be, and much more rational. Just as it no longer burns men for heresy or women for witchcraft, so it has ceased to condemn girls to lives of shame and death in the gutter for the trivial dereliction you acknowledge. If there were time I'd get you some of the more recent books, and point out passages showing how moral principles have changed. The only thing that is frowned on now seems to be getting caught. Otherwise, justice is virtually silent on the subject.

"Inasmuch as your story indicates that no one knows of your crime save your beau, who, if he has learned of your disappearance, is probably scared half to death, I advise you to go home, make some plausible excuse to your pa for lighting out, and resume your care of his cows. At the proper opportunity take your beau to the pastor, and join him in indissoluble love. It is the safe, respectable and hygienic course. Everyone agrees that it is moral, even moralists. Meanwhile, don't forget to thank Miss Nellie. She might have helped you down the primrose way; instead, she has restored you to virtue and happiness, no worse for an interesting experience."

The girl, of course, took in only a small part of this, for Percy's voluptuous style and vocabulary were beyond the grasp of a simple milkmaid. But Miss Nellie, who understood English much better than she spoke it, translated freely, and in a little while the troubled look departed from those blue eyes, and large tears of joy welled from them. Miss Nellie shed a couple herself, and so did all the ladies of the resident faculty, for they had drifted downstairs during the interview, sleepy but curious. The practical Miss Nellie inevitably thought of money, and it turned out that the trip down by milk-train and Peebles' lawful freight of $1 had about exhausted the poor girl's savings, and she had only some odd change left. Percy threw in a dollar and I threw in a dollar, and Miss Nellie not only threw in a third, but ordered one of the ladies to go to the kitchen and prepare a box-lunch for the return to Red Lion.

Sadie the coon had not yet come to work, but Peebles presently bobbed up without being sent for, and toward the end of the afternoon he started off for Union Station with his most amazing passenger, now as full of innocent jubilation as a martyr saved at the stake. As I have said, he embellished the story considerably during the days following, especially in the direction of touching up the girl's pulchritude. The cops, because of their general confidence in him, swallowed his exaggerations, and I heard more than one of them lament that they had missed the chance to handle the case professionally. Percy, in his later years, made two or three attempts to put it into a movie scenario, but the Hays office always vetoed it.

How the girl managed to account to her father for her mysterious flight and quick return I don't know, for she was never heard from afterward. She promised to send Miss Nellie a picture postcard of Red Lion, showing the new hall of the Knights of Pythias, but if it was ever actually mailed it must have been misaddressed, for it never arrived.

XVI.

Scions of the Bogus Nobility

O F LATE years, as I have noted in my Preface, American newspaper reporters have come to think of themselves as proletarians, and reach out for communion with coal-miners, truck-drivers, pipe-fitters, bricklayers, and other such wage slaves. It was certainly not so in my early days in the craft. We young journalists, to be sure, were far from snobbish, and in the saloons we frequented we had very amicable relations with various classes of workingmen, notably printers, policemen, musicians and hackmen; nevertheless, we always kept a little distance, and our eyes, when they rolled at all, rolled in the other direction. The hero of our dreams was not Sam Gompers or Gene Debs, but Richard Harding Davis, who was reputed to own twenty suits of clothes, or James Creelman, who had interviewed the Pope. And we were always susceptible to the glamor of less eminent colleagues who had any claim, however false, to high connections, however mysterious. That was a shabby newspaper staff, at least in the big cities, which could not show at least one son of a Civil War general, or nephew of an archbishop, or French count.

In the *Herald* office we had two of the last named, though I should add that neither called himself an actual count. Both were content to let it be known that they were cadets of French families running back to Charlemagne, and would be eating very high on the hog if they could only get their rights. One, * when in his cups, spoke of himself as Jean-Baptiste du Plessis de Savines, and the other allowed that he was Jacques de Corbigny. Naturally enough, du Plessis de Savines could not hope to rate his full style and appellation in the turmoil of a newspaper office, so he did not object seriously when Max Ways renamed him Jones. It was a plebeian name—but so, he believed, were all British names. As for Jacques de Corbigny, he was Jake to everyone from Colonel Cunningham down to the office boys, and also to all the functionaries in the Baltimore sties of justice, where he served the *Herald* as court reporter.

Jones oscillated through various jobs in my day, but all of them were of the desk variety, and usually he was telegraph editor. The night report of the Associated Press was then very meagre and in consequence he had a good deal of time on his hands, especially after midnight. In such hours of relaxation he liked to gather a group of young reporters about him, and astonish them with tales of his high doings in a dozen fields of enterprise. He had fought the ten duels that all French counts of his generation had to ring up, and one of them, as the custom provided, was with M. de Blowitz, Paris correspondent of the London *Times*. In addition, he had served his orthodox six years in the Foreign Legion, had escaped in nothing save his pants and hat from an intrigue with a Spanish infanta, had stolen two girls from the Prince of Wales (afterward Edward VII), had climbed the Matterhorn, and had blacked the eyes of both Jake Kilrain and James Gordon Bennett. So far he only ran true to type. But in addition he claimed to be the most adept church organist since Johann Sebastian Bach, and it was in that unusual character that he appeared in some of his most edifying anecdotes.

I well recall one that had to do with his appearance as guest organist at Trinity Church in New York. The news that he was to perform, so he said, brought in such a mob of fans from all over the East that the church was packed. Unhappily, it was discovered at the last minute, just as he was taking off his shoes to fall to, that something was wrong with the organ, and the sexton who usually looked after it not only could not remedy the trouble but even failed to find out what it was. Jones said that his own extraordinarily acute ear solved the mystery at once, though he let the sexton sweat a while in malice: there was something ailing the huge pedal pipe that sounded eighteen octaves below middle C. This pipe was at least two feet in diameter, and its length was such that it ran half way up the steeple. There should have been a man-hole in it at the bottom, but Jones could not find one, so while the expectant audience buzzed, scratched itself and blew spitballs, he climbed up to the steeple to look down the open top, as a laryngologist looks down the trachea of a radio crooner.

I shall not detain you with the details: suffice it to say that he lost his balance and plunged headlong down the tube.

Fortunately, he was a close fit, so the air was compressed as he went along, and when he landed at last in the conical war-nose of the pipe the jar was no greater than that of a fall on the ice. Nor was there any danger of suffocation, for the organ-pump was still working, and it was easy to turn a stiff breeze into the pipe. But how to get out? Jones confessed that, for a while, he was baffled. He could hear what was going on outside, and he soon picked up the news that the sexton proposed to attempt his rescue with an ax. The rector, it appeared, objected to this, and so did Jones, for he knew the crude technic of sextons, and feared that the ax which liberated him might also decapitate him. In the end he hit on a better scheme, and shouted a command that it be executed. It consisted in sending for riggers, hoisting the pipe out of the steeple, turning it upside down, and then bouncing out Jones on a leap-tick of pew-cushions heaped up on the sidewalk.

There were sassy young reporters who refused to believe this story, and some of them asked searching and embarrassing questions, with diagrams designed to show its impossibility, but Jones always stuck to it, and many who doubted when they first heard it came to believe afterward. It was only one chapter in a long saga of his adventures as a performer of sacred music. One of his favorite tricks, he said, was to search out a pipe whose sound made the stained-glass windows of the church vibrate in unison, and then pop them off in the midst of a solemn anthem, to the alarm of the clergy, choir and congregation. He said he had learned how to do this trick with an ordinary parlor, or reed-organ, and once utilized his skill to liberate a baby in arms from a bank vault. The baby's mother, it appeared, had put it in the vault without notifying the bank personnel, and as a result it had been imprisoned when the time-lock clamped down. When Jones was sent for he borrowed an organ from a nearby Sailors' Bethel, found a note in it that would vibrate steel, and so shook the time-lock to pieces. Why the mother had chosen a bank vault for storing her baby, and how she managed to stow it away without being noticed, he did not say.

Toward the end of his life Jones forgot his noble French ancestry, and began shopping around the world for forefathers, and even for fathers. Whenever a bulletin would come in announcing the death of some eminent man he would stagger out into the city room with the Associated Press flimsy, apply his handkerchief to his eyes, and sob piteously. The city editor was then expected to engage him in the following dialogue:

City Editor—What are you blubbering about?
Jones—So-and-so is dead.
City Editor—Well, what of it? What do you care for that ————?
Jones (in a sepulchral whisper)—He—was—my—father.

Everyone would then offer him formal condolences, and he would return to his desk much comforted. Sometimes he would have to be comforted two or three times a week. These raids upon the Christian sympathies of the city editor became so frequent that they irked him, and he terminated them with a bang on the night of November 7, 1901, when news came in of the death of Li Hung Chang. He was aided by a gang of ruffianly copy-readers, organized for the purpose. When Jones appeared with his flimsy and his tears they let fly with ink- and paste-pots, copy-hooks and spittoons. One of them even let go an old typewriter. Jones quit a little while later, and everyone was amazed when word drifted in that he was actually working as organist in a Presbyterian church in a poor suburb—and claiming to be a son of both John Calvin and John Knox.

Jake was a man of more modest pretensions: the most he ever alleged was that his father had been, at one and the same time, a Confederate general, a French nobleman, and a graduate of both Oxford and Cambridge. Unlike Jones, who was very abstemious, Jake was a lusher; indeed, there was a period, say from 1899 to 1902, when he was probably the ranking lusher of the whole region between the Mason & Dixon Line and the James river. He was magnificently ombibulous, drinking anything that contained ethyl alcohol, whatever its flavor or provenance. By day he would sustain himself as court reporter mainly by resorting to the hand-set whiskey that the printers guzzled at night, and in the evening he would always drop in at Frank Junker's saloon for the session of the Stevedores' Club, with its diligent unloading of schooners of beer. But whenever anything else offered, he got it down, giving thanks to God. Once I saw him drink a quart of apricot brandy at a sitting, and at other times I watched him as he dispatched Angostura, Fernet Branca and Boonekamp bitters by the goblet, all without chasers.

Jake was a tall, sturdy and even herculean fellow, with the wide, confident mouth of a carp or orator, but there came eventually a time when his heroic physique went back on him, and the young doctors at the City Hospital took him on as an out-patient and laboratory animal. So far as I could make out they could never agree on a diagnosis. One held that there was nothing wrong with him save a gastritis so acute that the lining of his stomach had turned to a kind of asphalt, and another that he was in the last stages of cirrhosis of the liver. There were others who voted for Bright's disease, cholelithiasis and scurvy, and a larval psychiatrist held out for paresis, for in those days that malady was still ascribed to drink. Jake himself also favored paresis, for he had noted in his court work that it frequently afflicted distinguished members of the bar. One night he was reciting his symptoms in Junker's when Joe, the cop on the beat, dropped in for his hourly shot of rye, and stood listening in uncomfortable fascination. Finally Joe gave a shiver, and burst out with "Goddam if I don't believe I got the same goddam thing." Jake glared at him for half a minute with singeing scorn, and then replied:

"So you have got paresis, too, have you? A *cop* with paresis? Well, of all the infernal impertinence ever heard of on earth! What ails you, Joe, is *jim-jams*. In order to have paresis you have to have *brains*."

Whatever it was that afflicted Jake, it presently threw him, and he had to be sent to St. Agnes' Hospital, which then specialized in treating the wounded garrison-troops of the Baltimore barrooms. The lower floor of the institution, called Hogan's Alley, was always full of them, and Jake found many old friends there, including a rich theatre manager who came down with *mania à potu* twice a year, and always celebrated his cure by giving the good sisters who ran the place some elegant present—one year a *porte cochère*, the next year a new boiler for their heating plant, the third a stained-glass window for their chapel, and so on. There were iron bars on the windows of Hogan's Alley and the inmates lived under rigid discipline, which included complete abstention from alcohol, but they were allowed visitors, were fed upon hearty victuals, and in general led a very easy life.

Jake had a girl known to the boys as the Battleship—a vast,

rangy creature built on his own scale, with the broad shoulders and billowing bosoms of a Wagnerian contralto. She came to see him one evening as in duty bound—and an hour later the gentlemen of Hogan's Alley were all full of liquor and cutting wild capers. The sisters, after quieting them, made a search for the source of their supply, but could not find it. Two days later the Battleship made another call—and Hogan's Alley had another too-cheerful night. When it happened a third time the sisters put two and two together, the Battleship was barred from the place, and Jake himself was requested to find some other asylum. They never learned the technic of the smuggling, but Jake himself later revealed it. The Battleship, on each visit, had stowed two quarts of rye between the huge hemispheres of her bosom, and then slipped them quietly to the idol of her dreams, who disposed of them at a dollar a big drink.

Jake's expulsion turned out to be a great stroke of luck for him. The institution he transferred to was a suburban drink-cure run by an enlightened medico who, after curing him, put him to work as a capper in the downtown saloons. All Jake had to do was to keep a sharp lookout for gentlemen showing the first signs of delirium tremens, and report their names to the medico, who thereupon alarmed their families, and usually got them as patients. Jake had comfortable quarters over the dead-house of the drink-cure, and a liberal expense-account. For two or three years he led the life of Riley, and was much envied by all the other boozers of Baltimore. Then, one morning, he dropped dead in a barroom, and was given a neat Odd Fellows funeral by the medico. Some time later a *Herald* reporter digging up a story at the Health Department happened upon Jake's death certificate. It showed that he was born in Philadelphia, that his father's name was something on the order of Schultz, Schmidt or Kraus, and that he had been baptized Emil.

XVII.
Aliens, but Not Yet Enemies

T HE CURRENT American concept of the German as an excessively sly, bellicose and sinister fellow, apt at any moment to panic the radio audience with false news or blow up a
gas-works, was undreamed of in my early days in journalism.
We thought of him then as predominantly benignant and not
too smart, and that view was fostered by the German reporters
who swarmed in all the big cities of the East and Middle West.
In every such city there was at least one German daily, with a
staff like any other newspaper and not infrequently of considerable importance in local politics. In Baltimore there were
two, not to mention four or five weeklies, and on these sheets
were some of the most eminent and popular reporters of the
town. They covered spot news, to be sure, only sketchily, for a
four-alarm fire was nothing to them unless the owner of the
burned premises happened to be a German, or, at worst, an
Austrian or a Swiss; but ever and anon they had a complicated
and hair-raising German suicide to trade for a colored murder,
or a riot at a *Gesangverein* rehearsal for a City Hall story, and
at all times they were salient figures in what may be called the
social life of the Fourth Estate.

If there was any member of our Stevedores' Club who stood
out head and shoulders above all the rest of the members, as
Ward McAllister rose above the sea-level of the New York 400,
then it was certainly John Gfeller of the *Deutsche Correspondent*,
a Züricher with a flowing yellow moustache, and a full-dress
outfit of frock coat, plug hat and ivory-headed walking-stick
that set him off magnificently. Save when he had to cover the
wedding of a brewer's daughter or some other such overshad-
owing and interminable shambles, he showed up at Junker's
saloon every night at midnight, and there he led all the other
Stevedores in their unloading of schooners. He was the first
man of whom I ever heard it said that his legs were hollow, and
the last of whom I ever believed it. Malt liquor seemed to have
no more effect upon him than so much sarsaparilla, and in all

my acquaintance with him I saw him flustered but once, and that was after he had been induced to drink eight or ten mint juleps on a hot July afternoon.

A drinking club always develops a ritual, and the Stevedores' followed the pattern. The basic design of its evening program was simply to shake poor Junker down for free beers, but there was also singing, and in this John naturally led, for he not only had the highest tenor voice in the club, but also a large repertory of robustious songs, most of them relics of his student days in Switzerland. With one or two exceptions the other members knew no more German than so many Irish cops; nevertheless, they learned many of John's songs by rote, as the Welsh and Slovak miners in the Bach Choir at Bethlehem, Pa., learn the Bach cantatas. And even when they were vaguest about the rest of the words they could at least chime in on the choruses, and this they did in voices of brass, always to Junker's alarm, for he lived in fear that, in spite of the immunity the presence of newspaper men was supposed to give him, the cops would clamp down on him for keeping open after hours.

One of the favorites of the club was a song by the celebrated Viktor von Scheffel, whooping up the victory of the primeval Nazis over the Romans under P. Q. Varus in the year 9 A.D.—a victory that threw the Romans over the Rhine for keeps, and made its scene, the Teutoburger Forest, sacred ground in German history. It is now nearly forty years since I last joined in singing this composition, but I remember its opening as clearly as if John were still uprisen before me, beating time with a foam-scraper:

> Als die Römer frech geworden,
>   Zum, ze rum zum, zum, zum, zum;
> Zogen sie nach Deutschlands Norden,
>   Zum, ze, rum zum, zum, zum, zum.

All the students' *Liederbücher* indicate that every *zum* should have been a *sim*, but in our ignorance we followed John without question, and when we came to the imitation of trumpets in the next strophe we converted them into calliopes, Junker or no Junker, *Polizeistunden* or no *Polizeistunden*. John knew all the seven stanzas, and would sing them with voluptuous gusto, especially the one telling how Varus, in departing swiftly through a swamp, left both of his boots and one of his socks behind, but the rest of us confined ourselves to the choruses, and did not stop to question this somewhat strange account of Roman military costume.

The German reporters led lives that were the admiration of many of their American colleagues, for, as I have said, their papers were not much interested in ordinary news, and there was no court-martial if one of them missed a bank robbery or even a murder, provided, of course, no German were involved. Their main business was to cover the purely German doings of the town—weddings, funerals, concerts, picnics, birthday parties, and so on. This kept them jumping pleasantly, for there were then 30,000 of their compatriots in Baltimore, and most of the 30,000 seemed to be getting on in the world, and were full of social enterprise. It was not sufficient for a German reporter to report their weddings as news: he also had to dance with the bride, drink with her father, and carry off a piece of the wedding cake, presumably for his wife. At a funeral of any consequence—say, that of a saloonkeeper, a pastor, or the head basso of a singing society—his duties were almost as onerous as those of a *Totsäufer* for a brewery,[1] and if he quit before the last clod hit the coffin it was an indecorum. When there were speeches, which was usually, he had to make one, whether at a birthday party, a banquet of the German Freemasons, Knights of Pythias or Odd Fellows, or the opening of a new picnic-grounds, saloon, or Lutheran church. Whenever refreshments were offered, which was always, he had to eat and drink in a hearty and demonstrative manner, and he was remiss in his duties if he failed to sneak in a nice notice for the lady who had prepared the *Sauerbraten* or the *Häringsalat*. In his reports all malt liquor had to be superultra, and all potato salad the best yet seen on earth.

The fattest regular story of the German brethren in my time was the monthly arrival of the North German Lloyd immigrant ship at Locust Point. All leaves were canceled on that day, and the instant the ship tied up at the Baltimore & Ohio pier its decks swarmed with journalists. Even at the turn of the cen-

---

[1] A *Totsäufer* is a brewery's customers' man. One of his jobs is to weep and beat his breast at the funeral of a saloonkeeper.

tury, of course, most of the actual immigrants aboard were Slavs or Jews, but there were still some Germans, and among them there were bound to be a number of characters worth embalming in print—say, a barber who had once shaved Bismarck, or a man with nineteen children, or a Prussian lieutenant whose foot had slipped in one way or other, forcing him, as the Germans say, to go 'round the corner. The captain of the ship always spread a buffet luncheon for the reporters, and they always got down a couple of barrels of Munich beer. During his stay in port the captain would be entertained extensively by the German societies, for the commander of a North German Lloyd liner was a notable in all respectable German circles, and even a young third officer was a social lion and a swell catch. The German reporters attended all such functions officially, and stayed until the band went home.

But the story that came nearest to straining their powers in the days when I knew them best was the opening of the Anheuser-Busch Brewery's Baltimore branch in 1900. To cover that historic event the *Deutsche Correspondent* threw in its whole local staff, and with them came the chief editor, an editorial writer, and the circulation manager. How much space the affair got the next morning I forget, but it must have been many, many columns, despite the fact that several of the older reporters blew up in the course of the evening, and had to be laid out in the cold-storage room to recover. The rival *Journal* not only sent its whole staff but also a photographer. The photographer went down for a count of two or three hundred before he had so much as unlimbered his camera, and was fired on the spot, but when he recovered he rejoined the festivities, and did prodigies with his second wind. A great many reporters from the American papers of Baltimore were also present, and to this day the old-time journalists of the town recall the Anheuser-Busch party as indubitably tops in its class. No other brewery ever came within miles of it.

The lordly life of the German colleagues spread the rest of us with the sickly green of envy, but the gods seem to have become envious also, for the great Baltimore fire of 1904 dealt heavy licks to their papers, and World War I finished them. One of the two German dailies succumbed to the first of these calamities, and the other to the second, and all save one of the weeklies went down the chute with the latter. As a result, a great many merry fellows were out of jobs. A few were slipped upon the public payroll by friendly politicians, and a few more managed to make the grade on English newspapers, but the rest had a hard time of it, for their labors, though delightful, had not been lucrative. Indeed, I can recall but one German reporter who ever accumulated any considerable capital, and that one was such a marvel that he was generally regarded as almost inhuman. He was a tall, sallow Oldenburger of the name of Delmenhorst, and in the course of four years' service, at a salary of $15 a week, he saved the neat sum of $16,500. With this he returned to Germany, bought a brickyard in a county town of Brandenburg, and survived into quite modern times—opulent, comfortable, and universally respected.

His wealth, of course, did not flow from his salary: a schoolboy could figure *that*, or even a schoolma'm. He gathered it in simply by turning all the other usufructs of his calling into quick assets. When he went to a German birthday party, and there was on the table a round of *Rinderbrust mit Meerrettig* that met his notions, he not only gobbled down 10,000 or 20,000 calories of it, but lamented loudly that his wife was not present to enjoy it. The hostess, flattered by the encomium of an expert, thereupon always insisted that he take a couple of thick slabs home with him, and in the course of packing them she usually added a bowl of *Bohnensalat*, a chocolate *Torte*, and maybe a bottle of Liebfraumilch or a dozen bottles of beer. Similarly, if paprika chicken was the main dish, he departed with a whole fowl, and if there was roast goose with red cabbage he got enough of each to feed his wife for two or three days.

At the start, so I was told by his fellow-Germans, he confined himself to her actual victualling, but in a little while he began to arrive home with so much provender that she could not get it all down, or even the half of it, so it occurred to him that it might be a good idea for her to take a boarder. The first boarder, a bookkeeper in a sauerkraut factory, put on weight so fast that everyone remarked it, and soon there were eager applications for the second spot. Within a month there were six highly appreciative paying guests at the table, and soon afterward the Delmenhorsts moved to a larger house, put in a colored maid, and increased their clientèle to ten, and then finally to twelve. Simultaneously, they began weeding out such poor fellows as bookkeepers, and substituting bachelors and widowers who could pay better, for example, assistant brewmasters, secretaries of building associations, and interpreters for the North German Lloyd.

Delmenhorst had to sweat hard to round up enough chow for a dozen men. Sometimes he covered eight or ten weddings, birthday parties and other such orgies in an evening, and had a dreadful time promoting a sufficiency of handouts without eating himself to death. But he gradually developed a technic that saved his life, and after a while he hired a colored boy to accompany him from feast to feast with a toy wagon, to haul the loot home. Whenever, by some unhappy accident, there were not enough parties of a night to load the wagon Mrs. Delmenhorst put her boarders on bologna, rat-trap cheese and rye-bread, but that happened very seldom, for the Germans of Baltimore, as I have said, were very social in those days, and loved to stuff their friends. Such wines and beers as he accumulated Delmenhorst sold to the boarders at a discount of twenty per cent., and when his stock began to go beyond their capacity he disposed of the beer to private friends at the same rate, and the wine to the proprietor of a wine-room in East Baltimore.

Nor was it only food and drink that he accumulated. Once a rich baker, celebrating not too quietly the bankruptcy of a rival, gave him a hand-painted oil-painting of the castle at Heidelberg, and he sold it within a week for $17, and another time he wangled a barrel of chinaware from a china-dealer in Gay street. That he ever collected cash was not established to public knowledge, for the matter was naturally kept confidential, but after his return to Germany his old colleagues used to declare that he did, and even professed to know his prices. For an ordinary wedding story, they said, he expected (and usually got) $5, but if it was in moneyed circles, and the bride was so homely that it took some straining of conscience to call her ravishing, he raised the ante to $10, $15, or $25. A pious Lutheran, he never charged anything for funerals, but he would take $5 for a christening, and when he dealt with a silver or golden wedding in the upper brackets the sky was the limit. All saloonkeepers had to pay double, and all brewers quadruple. Thus, for four years, Delmenhorst held up the banner of the foreign-language press in Baltimore, and then, his wife having taken on such weight that her health broke down, he and she departed for fresh fields in Brandenburg. They sailed from Baltimore by the North German Lloyd, traveling on passes. There was a gaudy farewell party on the ship—paid for by the line. For the first time in the four years Delmenhorst took nothing home from the table.

XVIII.
The Synthesis of News

ONE OF the first enemy reporters I came to terms with in the days of my beginnings was an amiable, ribald fellow with a pot belly and a pointed beard, by name Leander J. de Bekker. He hailed from Kentucky by way of Cincinnati and Chicago, and was proud of the fact that he was of Dutch descent. The Dutch, he told me at our first meeting, were the champion beer-drinkers of Christendom, and had invented not only free lunch but also the growler, which got its name, so he said, from the Dutch word *grauw*, signifying the great masses of the plain people. This de Bekker and I made many long and laborious treks together, for he was doing South Baltimore for the *American* when Max Ways sent me there to break in for the *Herald*, and South Baltimore was a vast area of indefinite boundaries and poor communications, with five or six miles of waterfront. At its upper end were the wharves used by the Chesapeake Bay packets, and at its lower end the great peninsula of Locust Point, given over mainly to railroad-yards and grain elevators, but adorned at its nose by Fort McHenry, the bombardment of which in 1814, allegedly by a B——h fleet, inspired Francis Scott Key to write "The Star-Spangled Banner."

There was always something doing in that expansive territory, especially for a young reporter to whom all the major catastrophes and imbecilities of mankind were still more or less novel, and hence delightful. If there was not a powder explosion at Fort McHenry, which was armed with smooth-bore muzzle-loaders dating from 1794, there was sure to be a collision between two Bay packets, and if the cops had nothing in the way of a homicide it was safe to reckon on a three-alarm fire. The blackamoors of South Baltimore were above the common in virulence, and the main streets of their ghetto— York street, Hughsie street and Elbow lane—always ran blood on Saturday nights. It was in Hughsie street, one lovely Summer evening in 1899, that I saw my first murderee—a nearly decapitated colored lady who had been caught by her beau in treason to her vows. And it was in the jungle of warehouses and railroad tracks on Locust Point that I covered my first fire.

De Bekker and I and the reporter for the *Sunpaper* (I forget his name) attended all these public events together, and since de Bekker was the eldest of the trio, and had a beard to prove it, he set the tone and tempo of our endeavors. If, on an expedition to the iron wilds of Locust Point, he decided suddenly that it was time for a hiatus and a beer, we downed tools at once and made for the nearest saloon, which was never more than a block away. Unhappily, the beers of those days, especially along the waterfront, ran only a dozen or so to the keg, and it was thus sometimes difficult for us youngsters, after two or three of them, to throw ourselves into gear again. At such times de Bekker's professional virtuosity and gift for leadership were demonstrated most beautifully.

"Why in hell," he would say, "should we walk our legs off trying to find out the name of a Polack stevedore kicked overboard by a mule? The cops are too busy dragging for the body to ask it, and when they turn it in at last, maybe tomorrow or the day after, it will be so improbable that no union printer in Baltimore will be able to set it up. Even so, they will only guess at it, as they guess at three-fourths of all the names on their books. Moreover, who gives a damn *what* it was? The fact that another poor man has given his life to engorge the Interests is not news: it happens every ten minutes. The important thing here, the one thing that brings us vultures of the press down into this god-forsaken wilderness is that the manner of his death was unusual—that men are not kicked overboard by mules every day. I move you, my esteemed contemporaries, that the name of the deceased be Ignaz Karpinski, that the name of his widow be Marie, that his age was thirty-six, that he lived at 1777 Fort avenue, and that he leaves eleven minor children."

It seemed so reasonable to the *Sun* reporter and me that we could think of no objection, and so the sad facts were reported in all three Baltimore morning papers the next day, along with various lively details that occurred to de Bekker after he had got down another beer. This labor-saving device was in use the whole time I covered South Baltimore for the *Herald*, and I never heard any complaint against it. Every one of the three city editors, comparing his paper to the other two, was surprised and pleased to discover that his reporter always got names and addresses right, and all three of us were sometimes commended for our unusual accuracy. De Bekker, I should add, was a fellow of conscience, and never stooped to what he called faking. That is to say, he never manufactured a story out of the whole cloth. If, under his inspiration, we reported that a mad dog had run amok down the Point and bitten twenty children, there was always an actual dog somewhere in the background, and our count of the victims was at least as authentic as any the cops would make. And if, when an immigrant ship tied up at the North German Lloyd pier, we made it known that fifteen sets of twins had been born during the voyage from Bremen, there were always some genuine twins aboard to support us.

Thus, in my tenderest years, I became familiar with the great art of synthesizing news, and gradually took in the massive fact that journalism is not an exact science. Later, as I advanced up the ladder of the press, I encountered synthesists less conscientious than de Bekker,[1] and indeed became one myself. It was well for me that I showed some talent, else my career might have come to disaster a year or so later, when I was promoted to the City Hall. There I found myself set against two enemy reporters of polished technic and great industry—Frank Kent of the *Sunpaper* and Walter Alexander of the *American*. Kent was a youngster only a little older than I was, but he was a smart fellow, and Alec was already covering his third or fourth city administration, and knew every rat-hole in the City Hall. He remained there for years afterward, and became, in the end, a bottomless abyss of municipal case and precedent. Mayors, comptrollers, health commissioners, city councilmen and other such transient jobholders consulted him as diligently as they consulted the daily racing dope. Even in 1900 he knew more than any of them, and was thus a formidable competitor.

---

[1] He left Baltimore in 1901 to join the staff of the Brooklyn *Standard-Union*, and afterward worked for the New York *Tribune* and *Evening Post*. In 1908 he published a dictionary of music, and in 1921 a work on words and phrases in collaboration with Dr. Frank H. Vizetelly, editor of the Standard Dictionary. He died in 1931.

Once I had got my legs, Kent and I tried to rope him into a
camorra such as de Bekker operated in South Baltimore, but
he knew very well that he would contribute a great deal more
to its assets than we would, so he played coy, and there was
seldom a day that he didn't beat us. One week he let us have it
daily with both barrels, and we got into trouble with our city
editors. There was, of course, only one remedy, and we were
forced into it in haste. Thereafter, we met every afternoon in
Reilly's ale-house opposite the City Hall, and concocted a fake
to bounce him. That fake appeared the next morning in both
the *Sun* and the *Herald*, with refinements of detail that coincided perfectly, so all the city editors of the town, including
Alec's, accepted it as gospel. For a week or two Alec tried to
blitz and baffle us with real news beats, but when we proceeded
from one fake a day to two, and then to three, four, and even
more, he came in asking for terms, and thereafter the three of
us lived in brotherly concord, with Alec turning up most of the
news and Kent and I embellishing it. Our flames of fancy having been fanned, we couldn't shut them off at once, but whenever we thought of a prime fake we let Alec have it also. If it
was so improbable that his somewhat literal mind gagged at it
we refrained from printing it ourselves, but in such cases we
always saved it from going to waste by giving it to the City
Hall man of the *Deutsche Correspondent*, a Mannheimer who
was ready to believe anything, provided only it was incredible.
Once we planted on him an outbreak of yellow fever in the
City Jail, but inasmuch as his account of it was printed in German, and buried in columns of gaudy stuff about German
weddings, funerals, bowling contests, and other such orgies,
our city editors never discovered it.

Kent and I remained in the City Hall about a year, and until
the end of that time our relations with Alec were kindly and
even loving; in fact, we continued on good terms with him
until his lamented death many years afterward. Unhappily, our
successors never got next to him as we had, and in consequence
he beat them almost every day, and often in a dramatic and
paralyzing manner. In the end it was impossible for any rival
reporter to stand up to him, and the rich *Sun* had to shanghai
him from the poor *American* to avoid disgrace and ruin. More
than once Baltimoreans of public spirit, even in the City Hall,

proposed that he be elected Mayor himself, and in perpetuity, but like nearly every other good newspaper man, he looked on political office as ignominious, and preferred to remain a reporter. When he died at last the City Hall flag was at half-mast for a week.

The failure of the post-Kent-Mencken flight of City Hall reporters to bring him to a stand as the Old Masters had done was probably due not only to the natural recession of talent among them, but also to a curious episode that had made a dreadful pother on the *Herald* and was still remembered uneasily by all the journalists of Baltimore. The central figure of that episode was a reporter whose name I shall suppress, for he was unhappily an addict to the hand-set whiskey of the Baltimore printers, and spent a large part of his time sleeping it off in police-stations. Let there be a murder, a fire or even an earthquake, and he would snore through it in one of the roomy barroom chairs that were then provided for the use of professional witnesses, straw bondsmen, and cops on reserve. Max Ways was a man of enlarged views, and had no objection to alcoholism as such, but a narcolept was of little more use to him than a dead man, and one rainy Sunday in the early Winter of 1898–99, being somewhat exacerbated by drink himself, he had the culprit before him, and gave him such a bawling out that even the office boys were aghast.

Moreover, that bawling out was reinforced by an ultimatum. If, by 6 P.M. of that same day, the culprit did not appear in the office with a story worth at least two sticks[2] he was to consider himself fired for the nth and last time, with no hope of appeal, pardon, commutation or reprieve, whether in this world or the next. The poor fish, alarmed, shuffled off to police headquarters and begged the cops to help him, but they reported that the bleak, filthy weather had adjourned all human endeavor in the town, and that they had nothing in hand save two lost colored children and a runaway horse. He then proceeded to such other public offices as were open, but always he met with the same response. Somewhere or other he picked up the death of a saloonkeeper, but the saloonkeeper was obscure, and thus worth, at most, only a few lines. It began to look

[2]A stick is about two inches of type.

hopeless, and he slogged on despairingly, soaked by the rain and scarcely knowing where he was going.

This woeful tramp took him at last to the shopping district, and he started to plod it just as dusk was coming down. Simultaneously, the arc-lights which, in that era, hung outside every store of any pretensions began to splutter on, and in his gloomy contemplation of them he was suddenly seized with an idea— the first, in all likelihood, that had occurred to him for long months, and maybe even years. Those arc-lights were above the range of pedestrians on the sidewalks, but it would be easy to reach any of them with an umbrella. Suppose a passer-by carrying a steel-rodded umbrella should lift it high enough to clear another passer-by's umbrella, and its ferrule should touch the steel socket that held the lower carbon of one of the lights, and suppose there should be some leakage of electricity, and it should shoot down the umbrella rod, and into the umbrella's owner's arm, and then, facilitated by his wet clothes, down his legs and into the sidewalk—what would be the effect upon the man? The speculation was an interesting one, and the poor fish paused awhile to revolve it in his deteriorated mind.

The next morning the *Herald* printed a story saying that a man named William T. Benson, aged forty-one, a visitor from Washington, had made the experiment accidentally in West Baltimore street, and had been knocked, figuratively speaking, into a cocked hat. There was a neat description of the way the current had thrown him half way across the street, and a statement from him detailing his sensations *en route*. He had not, he said, lost consciousness, but gigantic pinwheels in all the colors of the rainbow whirled before his eyes, and in the palm of his right hand was a scarlet burn such as one might pick up by grasping a red-hot poker. Moreover, his celluloid collar had been set to smoking, and might have burst into flames and burned his neck if a stranger had not rushed up and quenched it with his handkerchief. The young doctors at the University Hospital, so it appeared, regarded Mr. Benson's escape alive as almost miraculous, and laid it to the fact that he had rubber heels on his shoes. Fortunately, their science was equal to the emergency, and they predicted that their patient would be as good as new, save for his burned hand, by morning. But they trembled to think of the possible fate of the next victim.

This story, which ran well beyond two sticks and rated a display head, saved the narcolept's job—but only temporarily. By ten o'clock the next morning more than 200 Baltimore merchants had called up the electric company and ordered the lights in front of their stores taken away at once. By noon the number was close to a thousand, and by 3 P.M. the lawyers of the electric company were closeted with Nachman, the business manager of the *Herald*, and his veins were running ice-water at their notice of a libel suit for $500,000. They were ready to prove in court, they said, that it was as impossible to get a shock from one of their lights as from a child's rattle. The whole apparatus was fool, drunk, boy, idiot, suicide, and even giraffe proof. It had been tested by every expert in the nation, and pronounced perfect.

What became of the poor fish no one ever learned, for he got wind of the uproar before coming to the office the next day, and in fact never came at all, but vanished into space. The check-up that went on, with half the staff thrown into it, produced only misery of a very high voltage. The cops knew nothing of any such accident, the doctors at the University Hospital had no record of it, and the only William T. Benson who could be found in Washington had not been in Baltimore for nine years. Nor was there any lifting of the gloom when the *Herald*'s own lawyer was consulted. This gentleman (he afterward reached the eminence of a Federal circuit judge) was one of those old-fashioned attorneys who saw every case as lost, and liked to wring their clients' hearts. If the *Herald* went into court, he said, he would have to stand mute, for there was no conceivable defense, and if it offered a compromise the electric company would be insane to take anything less than $499,999.99. The most that could be hoped for was that a couple of implacable utilities-haters would sneak past the company's fixers and get on the jury, and there scale down the damages to something less brutal—say $250,000 or $300,000.

During the month following the *Herald* printed twenty or thirty news stories acknowledging and denouncing the fake, and at least a dozen editorials apologizing for it, but many of the merchants had become immovably convinced that what could be imagined might some day actually happen, so the revenues of the electric company continued depleted, and the bellowing of its lawyers broke all records. When the case was finally set down for an early trial every *Herald* man felt relieved, for it was clearly best to get the agony over, go through a receivership, and start anew. On the day before the day of fate there was really a kind of gaiety in the office. Once more it was raining dismally, but everyone was almost cheerful. That afternoon a man carrying a steel-rodded umbrella lifted it to clear another pedestrian's umbrella in West Baltimore street, and the ferrule touched the lower carbon-socket of one of the few surviving arc-lights. When the cops got him to hospital he was dead.

I tell the tale as it was told to me: it all happened before I joined the staff. My own talent for faking fell into abeyance after I left the City Hall, and especially after I became city editor. In that office, in fact, I spent a large part of my energy trying to stamp it out in other men. But after I was promoted to managing editor, it enjoyed a curious recrudescence, and my masterpiece of all time, with the sole exception of my bogus history of the bathtub, printed in the New York *Evening Mail* on December 28, 1917, was a synthetic war dispatch printed in the *Herald* on May 30, 1905. The war that it had to do with was the gory bout between Japan and Russia, and its special theme was the Battle of Tsushimi or Korea Straits, fought on May 27 and 28. Every managing editor on earth knew for weeks in advance that a great naval battle was impending, and nearly all of them had a pretty accurate notion of where it would be fought. Moreover, they all began to get bulletins, on May 27, indicating that it was on, and these bulletins were followed by others on the day following. They came from Shanghai, Hongkong, Foochow and all the other ports of the China coast. They were set in large type and printed under what were then called stud-horse heads, but they really offered nothing better than rumors of rumors. Everyone knew that a battle was being fought, and everyone assumed that the Japanese would win, but no one had anything further to say on the subject. The Japs kept mum, and so did the Russians.

Like any other managing editor of normal appetites I was thrown into a sweat by this uncertainty. With the able aid of George Worsham, who was then news editor of the *Herald*, I

had assembled a great array of cuts and follow stuff to adorn
the story when it came, and though the *Herald* had changed
to an evening paper by that time, he and I remained at our
posts until late in the evenings of May 27 and 28, hoping
against hope that the story would begin to flow at any minute,
and give us a chance to bring out a hot extra. But nothing
came in, and neither did anything come in on May 29—that is,
nothing save more of the brief and tantalizing bulletins from
the China coast. On the evening of this third day of waiting
and lathering I retired to my cubby-hole of an office—and
wrote the story in detail. The date-line I put on it was the
plausible one of Seoul, and this is how it began:

> From Chinese boatmen landing upon the Korean coast comes the
> first connected story of the great naval battle in the Straits of Korea
> on Saturday and Sunday.

After that I laid it on, as they used to say in those days, with
a shovel. Worsham read copy on me, and contributed many illuminating details. Both of us, by hard poring over maps, had
accumulated a knowledge of the terrain that was almost fit to
be put beside that of a China coast pilot, and both of us had by
heart the names of all the craft in both fleets, along with the
names of their commanders. Worsham and I worked on the
story until midnight, and the next morning we had it set in
time for our noon edition. It began on Page 1 under a head
like a fire-alarm, jumped double-leaded to Page 2, and there
filled two and three-quarters columns. It described in throbbing phrases the arrival of the Russians, the onslaught of the
Japs, the smoke and roar of the encounter, and then the gradual rolling up of the Jap victory. No one really knew, as yet,
which side had won, but we took that chance. And to give
verisimilitude to our otherwise bald and unconvincing narrative, we mentioned every ship by name, and described its fate,
sending most of the Russians to the bottom and leaving the
field to Admiral Count Heihachiro Togo. With it we printed
our largest, latest and most fierce portrait of the admiral, a
smaller one of his unhappy antagonist, Admiral Zinivy Petro-
vitch Rozhdestvensky, and a whole series of pictures of the
contending ships, with all the Russian marked either "damaged" or "sunk."

Thus the *Evening Herald* scored a beat on the world, and, what is more, a beat that lasted for nearly two weeks, for it took that long for any authentic details of the battle to reach civilization. By that time, alas, our feat was forgotten—but not by its perpetrators. Worsham and I searched the cables from Tokyo, when they began to come in at last, with sharp eyes, for we lived in fear that we might have pulled some very sour ones. But there were no such sour ones. We had guessed precisely right in every particular of the slightest importance, and on many fine points we had even beaten the Japs themselves. Years later, reading an astonishing vivid first-hand account of the battle by an actual participant, Aleksei Silych Novikov,[3] I was gratified to note that we were still right.

[3]Translated as Tsushima; New York, 1937.

XIX.

Fire Alarm

A̲T MIDNIGHT or thereabout on Saturday, February 6, 1904, I did my share as city editor to put the *Sunday Herald* to bed, and then proceeded to Junker's saloon to join in the exercises of the Stevedores' Club. Its members, having already got down a good many schooners, were in a frolicsome mood, and I was so pleasantly edified that I stayed until 3:30. Then I caught a night-hawk trolley-car, and by four o'clock was snoring on my celibate couch in Hollins street, with every hope and prospect of continuing there until noon of the next day. But at 11 A.M. there was a telephone call from the *Herald* office, saying that a big fire had broken out in Hopkins Place, the heart of downtown Baltimore, and fifteen minutes later a reporter dashed up to the house behind a sweating hack horse, and rushed in with the news that the fire looked to be a humdinger, and promised swell pickings for a dull Winter Sunday. So I hoisted my still malty bones from my couch and got into my clothes, and ten minutes later I was on my way to the office with the reporter. That was at about 11:30 A.M. of Sunday, February 7. It was not until 4 A.M. of Wednesday, February 10, that my pants and shoes, or even my collar, came off again. And it was not until 11:30 A.M. of Sunday, February 14—precisely a week to the hour since I set off—that I got home for a bath and a change of linen.

For what I had walked into was the great Baltimore fire of 1904, which burned a square mile out of the heart of the town and went howling and spluttering on for ten days. I give the exact schedule of my movements simply because it delights me, in my autumnal years, to dwell upon it, for it reminds me how full of steam and malicious animal magnetism I was when I was young. During the week following the outbreak of the fire the *Herald* was printed in three different cities, and I was present at all its accouchements, herding dispersed and bewildered reporters at long distance and cavorting gloriously in strange composing-rooms. My opening burst of work without a stop ran to sixty-four and a half hours, and then I got only six hours of nightmare sleep, and resumed on a working schedule of from twelve to fourteen hours a day, with no days off and no time for meals until work was over. It was brain-fagging and back-breaking, but it was grand beyond compare—an adventure of the first chop, a razzle-dazzle superb and elegant, a circus in forty rings. When I came out of it at last I was a settled and indeed almost a middle-aged man, spavined by responsibility and aching in every sinew, but I went into it a boy, and it was the hot gas of youth that kept me going. The uproar over, and the *Herald* on an even keel again, I picked up one day a volume of stories by a new writer named Joseph Conrad, and therein found a tale of a young sailor that struck home to me as the history of Judas must strike home to many a bloated bishop, though the sailor naturally made his odyssey in a ship, not on a newspaper, and its scene was not a provincial town in America, but the South Seas. Today, so long afterward, I too "remember my youth and the feeling that will never come back any more—the feeling that I could last forever, outlast the sea, the earth, and all men . . . Youth! All youth! The silly, charming, beautiful youth!"

Herald reporters, like all other reporters of the last generation, were usually late in coming to work on Sundays, but *that* Sunday they had begun to drift in even before I got to the office, and by one o'clock we were in full blast. The fire was then raging through a whole block, and from our fifth-floor city-room windows it made a gaudy show, full of catnip for a young city editor. But the Baltimore firemen had a hundred streams on it, and their chief, an old man named Horton, reported that they would knock it off presently. They might have done so, in fact, if the wind had not changed suddenly at three o'clock, and begun to roar from the West. In ten minutes the fire had routed Horton and his men and leaped to a second block, and in half an hour to a third and a fourth, and by dark the whole of downtown Baltimore was under a hail of sparks and flying brands, and a dozen outlying fires had started to
* eastward. We had a story, I am here to tell you! There have been bigger ones, of course, and plenty of them, but when and where, between the Chicago fire of 1871 and the San Francisco earthquake of 1906, was there ever one that was fatter,

juicier, more exhilarating to the journalists on the actual ground? Every newspaper in Baltimore save one was burned out, and every considerable hotel save three, and every office building without exception. The fire raged for a full week, helped by that bitter Winter wind, and when it fizzled out at last the burned area looked like Pompeii, and up from its ashes rose the pathetic skeletons of no less than twenty overtaken and cremated fire-engines—some of them from Washington, Philadelphia, Pittsburgh and New York. Old Horton, the Baltimore fire chief, was in hospital, and so were several hundred of his men.

My labors as city editor during that electric week were onerous and various, but for once they did not include urging lethargic reporters to step into it. The whole staff went to work with the enthusiasm of crusaders shinning up the walls of Antioch, and all sorts of volunteers swarmed in, including three or four forgotten veterans who had been fired years before, and were thought to have long since reached the dissecting-room. Also, there were as many young aspirants from the waiting-list, each hoping for his chance at last, and one of these, John Lee Blecker by name, I remember brilliantly, for when I told him to his delight that he had a job and invited him to prove it he leaped out with exultant gloats—and did not show up again for five days. But getting lost in so vast a story did not wreck his career, for he lived to become, in fact, an excellent reporter, and not a few old-timers were lost, too. One of the best of them, sometime that afternoon, was caught in a blast when the firemen began dynamiting buildings, and got so coagulated that it was three days before he was fit for anything save writing editorials. The rest not only attacked the fire in a fine frenzy, but also returned promptly and safely, and by four o'clock thirty typewriters were going in the city-room, and my desk was beginning to pile high with red-hot copy.

Lynn Meekins, the managing editor, decided against wasting time and energy on extras: we got out two, but the story was too big for such banalities: it seemed like a toy balloon in a hurricane. "Let us close the first city edition," he said, "at nine o'clock. Make it as complete as you can. If you need twenty pages, take them. If you need fifty, take them." So we began heaving copy to the composing-room, and by seven o'clock there were columns and columns of type on the stones, and picture after picture was coming up from the engraving department. Alas, not much of that quivering stuff ever got into the *Herald*, for a little before nine o'clock, just as the front page was being made up, a couple of excited cops rushed in, howling that the buildings across the street were to be blown up in ten minutes, and ordering us to clear out at once. By this time there was a fire on the roof of the *Herald* Building itself, and another was starting in the press-room, which had plate-glass windows reaching above the street level, all of them long ago smashed by flying brands. We tried to parley with the cops, but they were too eager to be on their way to listen to us, and when a terrific blast went off up the street Meekins ordered that the building be abandoned.

There was a hotel three or four blocks away, out of the apparent path of the fire, and there we went in a dismal procession —editors, reporters, printers and pressmen. Our lovely first edition was adjourned for the moment, but every man-jack in the outfit believed that we'd be back anon, once the proposed dynamiting had been done—every man-jack, that is, save two. One was Joe Bamberger, the foreman of the composing-room, and the other was Joe Callahan, my assistant as city editor. The first Joe was carrying page-proofs of all the pages already made up, and galley-proofs of all the remaining type-matter, and all the copy not yet set. In his left overcoat pocket was the front-page logotype of the paper, and in his left pocket were ten or twelve halftones. The other Joe had on him what copy had remained in the city-room, a wad of Associated Press flimsy about the Russian-Japanese war, a copy-hook, a pot of paste, two boxes of copy-readers' pencils—and the assignment-book!

But Meekins and I refused to believe that we were ship-wrecked, and in a little while he sent me back to the *Herald* Building to have a look, leaving Joe No. 2 to round up such reporters as were missing. I got there safely enough, but did not stay long. The proposed dynamiting, for some reason unknown, had apparently been abandoned, but the fire on our roof was blazing violently, and the press-room was vomiting smoke. As I stood gaping at this dispiriting spectacle a couple of large plate-glass windows cracked in the composing-room under the roof, and a flying brand—some of them seemed to be six feet long!—fetched a window on the editorial floor just below it. Nearly opposite, in Fayette street, a sixteen-story office building had caught fire, and I paused a moment more to watch it. The flames leaped through it as if it had been made of matchwood and drenched with gasoline, and in half a minute they were roaring in the air at least 500 feet. It was, I suppose, the most melodramatic detail of the whole fire, but I was too busy to enjoy it, and as I made off hastily I fully expected the whole structure to come crashing down behind me. But when I returned a week later I found that the steel frame and brick skin had both held out, though all the interior was gone, and during the following Summer the burned parts were replaced, and the building remains in service to this day, as solid as the Himalayas.

At the hotel Meekins was trying to telephone to Washington, but long-distance calls still took time in 1904, and it was fifteen minutes before he raised Scott C. Bone, managing editor of the Washington *Post*. Bone was having a busy and crowded night himself, for the story was worth pages to the *Post*, but he promised to do what he could for us, and presently we were hoofing for Camden Station, a good mile away—Meekins and I, Joe Bamberger with his salvage, a copy-reader with the salvage of the other Joe, half a dozen other desk men, fifteen or twenty printers, and small squads of pressmen and circulation men. We were off to Washington to print the paper there—that is, if the gods were kind. They frowned at the start, for the only Baltimore & Ohio train for an hour was an accommodation, but we poured into it, and by midnight we were in the *Post* office, and the hospitable Bone and his men were clearing a place for us in their frenzied composing-room, and ordering the press-room to be ready for us.[1]

Just how we managed to get out the *Herald* that night I can't tell you, for I remember only trifling details. One was that I was the principal financier of the expedition, for when we pooled our money at Camden Station it turned out that I

[1] Bone was an Indianan, and had a long and honorable career in journalism, stretching from 1881 to 1918. In 1919 he became publicity chief of the Republican National Committee, and in 1921 he was appointed Governor of Alaska. He died in 1936.

* had $40 in my pocket, whereas Meekins had only $5, and the
rest of the editorial boys not more than $20 among them.
Another is that the moon broke out of the Winter sky just as
we reached the old B. & O. Station in Washington, and shined
down sentimentally on the dome of the Capitol. The Capitol
was nothing new to Baltimore journalists, but we had with us
a new copy-reader who had lately come in from Pittsburgh,
and as he saw the matronly dome for the first time, bathed in
spooky moonlight, he was so overcome by patriotic and aesthetic sentiments that he took off his hat and exclaimed "My
God, how beautiful!" And a third is that we all paused a second
to look at the red glow over Baltimore, thirty-five miles away
as the crow flies. The fire had really got going by now, and for
four nights afterward the people of Washington could see its
glare from their streets.

Bone was a highly competent managing editor, and contrived somehow to squeeze us into the tumultous *Post* office.
All of his linotypes were already working to capacity, so our
operators were useless, but they lent a hand with the make-up,
and our pressmen went to the cellar to reinforce their *Post*
colleagues. It was a sheer impossibility to set up all the copy we
had with us, or even the half of it, or a third of it, but we nevertheless got eight or ten columns into type, and the *Post* lent
us enough of its own matter to piece out a four-page paper.
In return we lent the hospitable *Post* our halftones, and they
adorned its first city edition next morning. Unhappily, the
night was half gone before Bone could spare us any press time,
but when we got it at last the presses did prodigies, and at
precisely 6.30 the next morning we reached Camden Station,
Baltimore, on a milk-train, with 30,000 four-page *Herald*s in
the baggage-car. By 8 o'clock they were all sold. Our circulation hustlers had no difficulty in getting rid of them. We had
scarcely arrived before the news of our coming began to circu-
late around the periphery of the fire, and in a few minutes
newsboys swarmed in, some of them regulars but the majority
volunteers. Very few boys in Baltimore had been to bed that
night: the show was altogether too gaudy. And now there was
a chance to make some easy money out of it.

Some time ago I unearthed one of these orphan *Herald*s

from the catacombs of the Pratt Library in Baltimore, and gave it a looking-over. It turned out to be far from bad, all things considered. The story of the fire was certainly not complete, but it was at least coherent, and three of our halftones adorned Page 1. The eight-column streamer-head that ran across its top was as follows:

HEART OF BALTIMORE WRECKED BY
                GREATEST FIRE IN CITY'S HISTORY

Well, brethren, what was wrong about that? I submit that many worse heads have been written by pampered copy-readers sitting at luxurious desks, with vassals and serfs at their side. It was simple; it was direct; there was no fustian in it; and yet it told the story perfectly. I wrote it on a make-up table in the *Post* composing-room, with Meekins standing beside me writing a box for the lower right-hand corner of the first page, thanking the *Post* for its "proverbial courtesy to its contemporaries" and promising formally that the *Herald* would be "published daily by the best means it can command under the circumstances."

Those means turned out, that next day, to be a great deal short of ideal. Leaving Joe Callahan, who had kept the staff going all night, to move to another and safer hotel, for the one where we had found refuge was now in the path of the fire, Meekins and I returned to Washington during the morning to make arrangements for bringing out a larger paper. We were not ashamed of our four pages, for even the *Sunpaper*, printed by the Washington *Evening Star*, had done no better, but what were four pages in the face of so vast a story? The boys had produced enough copy to fill at least ten on the first day of the fire, and today they might turn out enough to fill twenty. It would wring our gizzards intolerably to see so much good stuff going to waste. Moreover, there was art to consider, for our two photographers had piled up dozens of gorgeous pictures, and if there was no engraving plant left in Baltimore there were certainly plenty in Washington.

But Bone, when we routed him out, could not promise us any more accommodation than he had so kindly given us the first night. There was, it appeared, a long-standing agreement between the *Post* and the Baltimore *Evening News*, whereby each engaged to take care of the other in times of calamity, and the *News* staff was already in Washington cashing in on it, and would keep the *Post* equipment busy whenever it was not needed by the *Post* itself. Newspapers in those days had no such plants as they now boast: if I remember rightly, the *Post* had not more than a dozen linotypes, and none of them could chew up copy like the modern monsters. The prospect seemed depressing, indeed, but Bone himself gave us a shot of hope by mentioning casually that the Baltimore *World* appeared to have escaped the fire. The *World*? It was a small, ill-fed sheet of the kind then still flourishing in most big American cities, and its own daily editions seldom ran beyond four pages, but it was an *afternoon* paper, and we might hire its equipment for the night. What if it had only four linotypes? We might help them out with hand-set matter. And what if its Goss press could print but 5,000 six- or eight-page papers an hour? We might run it steadily from 6 P.M. to the middle of the next morning, bringing out edition after edition.

We got back to Baltimore as fast as the B. & O. could carry us, and found the *World* really unscathed, and, what is more, its management willing to help us, and as soon as its own last edition was off that afternoon Callahan and the gentlemen of the *Herald* staff came swarming down on its little office in Calvert street. The ensuing night gave me the grand migraine of my life, with throbs like the blows of an ax and continuous pinwheels. Every conceivable accident rained down on us. One of the linotypes got out of order at once, and when, after maddening delays, Joe Bamberger rounded up a machinist, it took him two hours to repair it, and even then he refused to promise that it would work. Meekins thereupon turned to his desperate plan to go back to Gutenberg and set matter by hand—only to find that the *World* had insufficient type in its cases to fill more than a few columns. Worse, most of this type appeared to be in the wrong boxes, and such of it as was stand-ing on the stones had been picked for sorts by careless printers, and was pretty well pied.[2]

---

[2]Perhaps I should explain some printers' terms here. The stones are flat ta-bles (once of actual stone, but now usually of steel) on which printers do much of their work. Type is kept in wooden cases divided into boxes, one for

Meekins sent me out to find more, but all the larger printers of Baltimore had been burned out, and the only supply of any size that I could discover was in the office of the *Catholic Mirror*, a weekly. Arrangements with it were made quickly, and Joe Bamberger and his gallant lads of the union rushed the place and proceeded to do or die, but setting type by hand turned out to be a slow and vexatious business, especially to linotype operators who had almost forgotten the case. Nor did it soothe us to discover that the *Mirror*'s stock of type (most of it old and worn) was in three or four different faces, with each face in two or three sizes, and that there was not enough of any given face and size to set more than a few columns. But it was now too late to balk, so Joe's goons went to work, and by dark we had ten or twelve columns of copy in type, some of it in eight-point, some in ten-point and some in twelve-point. That night I rode with Joe's chief of staff, Josh Lynch, on a commandeered express-wagon as these galleys of motley were hauled from the *Mirror* office to the *World* office. I recall of the journey only that it led down a steep hill, and that the hill was covered with ice. Josh howled whenever the horse slipped, but somehow or other we got all the galleys to the *World* office without disaster, and the next morning, after six or eight breakdowns in the pressroom, we came out with a paper that at least had some news in it, though it looked as if it had been printed by country printers locked up in a distillery.

When the first copy came off the *World*'s rickety Goss press Meekins professed to be delighted with it. In the face of almost hopeless difficulties, he said, we had shown the resourcefulness

---

a character. As it is set up by the compositor it is placed in galleys, which are brass frames, and then the galleys are taken to the stone and there made up. Sometimes, after the printing has been done, the type is returned to a stone, and left there until a convenient time to return it to the cases. To pick sorts is to go to such standing type and pick out characters that are exhausted in the cases. Pied type is type in such confusion that it cannot be returned to the cases by the usual method of following the words, but must be identified letter by letter. To forget the case, mentioned below, is to lose the art of picking up types from the boxes without looking at them. The boxes are not arranged alphabetically, and a printer learns the case as one learns the typewriter key-board. A face of type is a series of sizes of one design. The face in which this line is set is called Scotch Modern and the size is eight point. The text above is in eleven and one-half point Scotch Modern.

of Robinson Crusoe, and for ages to come this piebald issue of
the *Herald* would be preserved in museums under glass, and
shown to young printers and reporters with appropriate remarks. The more, however, he looked at it the less his enthusiasm soared, and toward the middle of the morning he decided
suddenly that another one like it would disgrace us forever,
and announced at once that we'd return to Washington. But
we knew before we started that the generous Bone could do
no more for us than he had already done, and, with the *Star*
monopolized by the Baltimore *Sun*, there was not much chance
of finding other accommodation in Washington that would be
better than the *World*'s in Baltimore. The pressure for space
was now doubled, for not only was hot editorial copy piling up
endlessly, but also advertising copy. Hundreds of Baltimore
business firms were either burned out already or standing in
the direct path of the fire, and all of them were opening temporary offices uptown, and trying to notify their customers
where they could be found. Even in the ghastly parody printed
in the *World* office we had made room for nearly three columns
of such notices, and before ten o'clock Tuesday morning we
had copy for ten more.

But where to turn? Wilmington in Delaware? It was nearly
seventy miles away, and had only small papers. We wanted accommodation for printing ten, twelve, sixteen, twenty pages,
for the *Herald* had suffered a crippling loss, and needed that
volunteer advertising desperately. Philadelphia? It seemed fantastic, for Philadelphia was nearly a *hundred* miles away. To be
sure, it had plenty of big newspaper plants, but could we bring
our papers back to Baltimore in time to distribute them? The
circulation men, consulted, were optimistic. "Give us 50,000
papers at 5 A.M.," they said, "and we'll sell them." So Meekins,
at noon or thereabout, set off for Philadelphia, and before dark
he was heard from. He had made an arrangement with Barclay
H. Warburton, owner of the Philadelphia *Evening Telegraph*.
The *Telegraph* plant would be ours from 6 P.M., beginning
tomorrow, and it was big enough to print any conceivable
paper. Meekins was asking the Associated Press to transfer our
report from Baltimore to Philadelphia, and the International
Typographical Union to let our printers work there. I was to
get out one more edition in Washington, and then come to

Philadelphia, leaving Callahan in charge of our temporary office in Baltimore. But first I was to see Oscar G. Murray, president of the B. & O. Railroad, and induce him to give us a special train from Philadelphia to Baltimore, to run every night until further notice.

The B. & O.'s headquarters building in Baltimore had been burned out like the *Herald* office, but I soon found Murray at Camden Station, functioning grandly at a table in a storage warehouse. A bachelor of luxurious and even levantine tastes, he was in those days one of the salient characters of Baltimore, and his lavender-and-white striped automobile was later to become a major sight of the town. When he gave a party for his lady friends at the Stafford Hotel, where he lived and had his being, it had to be covered as cautiously as the judicial orgies described in Chapter XII. He looked, that dreadful afternoon, as if he had just come from his barber, tailor and haberdasher. He was shaved so closely that his round face glowed like a rose, and an actual rose was in the buttonhole of his elegant but not too gaudy checked coat. In three minutes I had stated my problem and come to terms with him. At two o'clock, precisely, every morning a train consisting of a locomotive, a baggage-car and a coach would be waiting at Chestnut Street Station in Philadelphia, with orders to shove off for Baltimore the instant our *Herald*s were loaded. It would come through to Camden Station, Baltimore, without stop, and we could have our circulation hustlers waiting for it there.

That was all. When I asked what this train would cost, the magnificent Murray waved me away. "Let us discuss that," he * said, "when we are all back home." We did discuss it two months later—and the bill turned out to be nothing at all. "We had some fun together," Murray said, "and we don't want to spoil it now by talking about money." That fun consisted, at least in part, of some very exuberant railroading. If we happened to start from Philadelphia a bit late, which was not infrequent as we accumulated circulation, the special train made the trip to Baltimore at hair-raising speed, with the piles of *Herald*s in the baggage-car thrown helter-skelter on the curves, and the passengers in the coach scared half to death. All known records between Philadelphia and Baltimore were broken during the ensuing five weeks. Finally the racing went so far beyond the seemly that the proper authorities gave one of the engineers ten days lay-off without pay for wild and dangerous malpractice. He spent most of his vacation as the guest of our printers in Philadelphia, and they entertained him handsomely.

But there was still a paper to get out in Washington, and I went there late in the afternoon to tackle the dismal job. The best Bone could do for us, with the Baltimore *News* cluttering the *Post* office all day and the *Post* itself printing endless columns about the fire still raging, was four pages, and of their thirty-two columns nearly thirteen were occupied by the advertisements I have mentioned. I got the business over as soon as possible, and returned to Baltimore eager for a few winks of sleep, for I had not closed my eyes since Sunday morning, and it was now Wednesday. In the *Herald*'s temporary office I found Isidor Goodman, the night editor. He reported that every bed in downtown Baltimore was occupied two or three deep, and that if we sought to go home there were no trolley-cars or night-hacks to haul us. In the office itself there was a table used as a desk, but Joe Callahan was snoring on it. A dozen other men were on the floor.

Finally, Isidor allowed that he was acquainted with a lady who kept a surreptitious house of assignation in nearby Paca street, and suggested that business was probably bad with her in view of the competing excitement of the fire, and that she might be able in consequence to give us a bed. But when we plodded to her establishment, which was in a very quiet neighborhood, Isidor, who was as nearly dead as I was, pulled the wrong door-bell, and a bass voice coming out of a nightshirt at a second-story window threatened us with the police if we didn't make off. We were too tired to resist this outrage, but shuffled down the street, silent and despairing. Presently we came to the Rennert Hotel, and went in hoping to find a couple of vacant spots, however hard, on a billiard-table, or the bar, or in chairs in the lobby. Inside, it seemed hopeless, for every chair in sight was occupied, and a dozen men were asleep on the floor. But there was a night-clerk on duty whom we knew, and after some mysterious hocus-pocus he whispered to us to follow him, and we trailed along up the stairs to the fourth floor. There he unlocked a door and pointed dramatically to a vacant bed, looking beautifully white, wide and deep.

We did not wait to learn how it had come to be so miraculously vacant, but peeled off our coats and collars, kicked off our shoes, stepped out of our pants, and leaped in. Before the night-clerk left us we were as dead to this world and its sorrows as Gog and Magog. It was 4 A.M. and we slept until ten. When we got back to the *Herald*'s quarters we let it be known that we had passed the night in the house of Isidor's friend in Paca street, along with two rich society women from Perth Amboy, N.J.

That night we got out our first paper in Philadelphia—a gorgeous thing of fourteen pages, with twenty columns of advertising. It would knock the eyes out of the *Sun* and *Evening News*, and we rejoiced and flapped our wings accordingly. In particular, we were delighted with the *Evening Telegraph*'s neat and graceful head-type, and when we got back to Baltimore we imitated it. Barclay Warburton, the owner of the *Telegraph*, came down to the office to see us through—elegantly invested in a tail coat and a white tie. Despite this unprofessional garb, he turned out to be a smart fellow in the pressroom, and it was largely due to his aid that we made good time. I returned to Baltimore early in the morning on the first of Oscar Murray's special trains, and got a dreadful bumping on the curves and crossings. The circulation boys fell on our paper with exultant gurgles, and the next night we lifted the press-run by 10,000 copies.

We stayed in Philadelphia for five weeks, and gradually came to feel almost at home there—that is, if anybody not born in the town can ever feel at home in Philadelphia. The attitude of the local colleagues at first puzzled us, and then made us snicker in a superior way. Save for Warburton himself, not one of them ever offered us the slightest assistance, or, indeed, even spoke to us. We were printing a daily newspaper 100 miles from base —a feat that remains unparalleled in American journalism, so far as I know, to this day—and it seemed only natural that some of the Philadelphia brethren should drop in on us, if only out of curiosity. But the only one who ever appeared was the managing editor of one of the morning papers, and he came to propose graciously that we save him a few dollars by lending him our halftones of the fire. Inasmuch as we were paying his paper a substantial sum every day for setting ads for us—the *Evening Telegraph* composing-room could not handle all that crowded in—we replied with a chilly nix, and he retired in a huff.

There was a press club in Philadelphia in those days, and its quarters downtown offered a convenient roosting-place for the hour or two after the night's work was done. In any other American city we'd have been offered cards on it instantly and automatically, but not in Philadelphia. At the end of a week a telegraph operator working for us got cards for us in some unknown manner, and a few of us began using the place. During the time we did so only one member ever so much as spoke to us, and he was a drunken Englishman whose conversation consisted entirely of encomiums of Barclay Warburton. Whenever he saw us he would approach amiably and begin chanting "Good ol' Bahclay! Good ol' Bahclay! Bahclay's a good *sawt*," with *sawt* rhyming with *caught*, and apparently meaning *sort*. We agreed heartily, but suffered under the iteration, and presently we forsook the place for the saloon patronized by the *Herald* printers, where there was the refined entertainment described in Chapter XI.

Meekins's arrangements for getting out the *Herald* so far from home were made with skill and worked perfectly. Callahan remained in Baltimore in charge of our field quarters outside the burned area, and on every train bound for Philadelphia during the afternoon he had an office-boy with such copy as had accumulated. At six o'clock, when the *Evening Telegraph* men cleared out of their office, we opened a couple of private wires, and they kept us supplied with later matter. Even after the fire burned out at last Baltimore was in an appalling state, and there were plenty of old Baltimoreans who wagged their heads despairingly and predicted that it would never be rebuilt.
* One such pessimist was the Mayor of the town: a little while later, yielding to his vapors, he committed suicide. But there were optimists enough to offset these glooms, and before we left Philadelphia the debris was being cleared away, many ancient and narrow streets were being widened, and scores of new buildings were started. All these debates and doings made for juicy news, and the men of the local staff, ably bossed by Callahan, poured it out daily. Meekins would come to Philadelphia two or three times a week to look over his faculty in exile, and I would drop down to Baltimore about as often to

aid and encourage Joe. We had our own printers in Philadelphia and our own pressmen. Our circulation department performed marvels, and the advertising department gobbled up all the advertising in sight, which, as I have said, was plenty. The *Herald* had been on short commons for some time before the fire, but during the two or three months afterward it rolled in money.

Once I had caught up on lost sleep I prepared to do a narrative of the fire as I had seen it, with whatever help I could get from the other *Herald* men, but the project got itself postponed so often that I finally abandoned it, and to this day no connected story has ever been printed. The truth is that, while I was soon getting sleep enough, at least for a youngster of twenty-four, I had been depleted by the first cruel week more than I thought, and it was months before I returned to anything properly describable as normalcy. So with the rest of the staff, young and old. Surveying them when the hubbub was over, I found confirmation for my distrust, mentioned in Chapter XI, of alcohol as a fuel for literary endeavor. They divided themselves sharply into three classes. Those who had kept off the stuff until work was done and it was time to relax—there were, of course, no all-out teetotalers in the outfit —needed only brief holidays to be substantially as good as new. Those who had drunk during working hours, though in moderation, showed a considerable fraying, and some of them had spells of sickness. Those who had boozed in the classical manner were useless before the end of the second week, and three of them were floored by serious illnesses, one of which ended, months later, in complete physical and mental collapse. I pass on this record for what it is worth.

XX.

Sold Down the River

AFTER FIVE weeks in Philadelphia we moved back to Baltimore. The steel skeleton of the *Herald* Building was still
standing, and it might have been furnished with a new skin
and viscera as the other burned office-buildings of Baltimore
were furnished, but the city had seized it to widen a street, and
the place where it stood soon became the Courthouse Plaza,
which is today given over to parked automobiles. I had visited
its ruins a number of times during the month after the fire, and
once shinned up its shell to the fifth floor, and investigated the
mortal remains of the editorial rooms. It was easy to find the
place where my desk had stood, though the desk itself was
only a heap of white dust, for its hardware survived and so did
the frame of the goose-neck light that had stood upon it. I also
found my old copy-hook, twisted as if it had died in agony,
and I have it yet. But all the clippings and other records that
had stuffed the drawers of the desk were gone, and I thus lost
many souvenirs of my earliest days, including a collection of
pieces of hangmen's ropes. In that era the sheriff pontificating
at a Maryland hanging always cut up the rope afterwards to
give to his fans, and the reporters on hand were included. If
my collection had survived I suppose I'd have presented it,
soon or late, to the Smithsonian, but it is no more, and I do
not repine.

The indefatigable Meekins, with such help as he could
squeeze out of Peard, the general manager, had leased an old
car-barn in South Charles street, just outside the area of the
fire, and there he set up fifteen or twenty linotypes, and a second-
hand Hoe press that he had found in New York. I have seen
much worse newspaper offices in my time. At the start the editorial rooms were in a little three-story building across an alley
from the barn, but that turned out to be an inconvenient arrangement, and we soon moved into the barn itself, which was
wide and deep. This put the whole operation of the paper,
from the writing and editing of copy to the printing and deliv-

ery, on one floor—a scheme that has been adopted deliberately, in recent years, by a number of mid-Western dailies that happened to have room enough for it. We got out a pretty good paper, and circulation showed some gains, but the post-fire burst of advertising did not last, and by the beginning of Summer the *Herald* was in difficulties. The advertising trend, even in those days, was away from morning papers, and it was especially marked in Baltimore, where the *Evening News*, published by Charles H. Grasty, was making inroads on the morning *Sun*. In the morning field we had not only the *Sun* to face, but also the *American*; in the evening field there was nothing beside the *News* save the *World*, which had hardly any advertising at all.

So Peard decided to switch from morning to evening—and then, at the last moment, had an attack of caution, and ordered Meekins to keep the morning going until we could make out how the evening was doing. It was characteristic of that well-meaning but highly unjournalistic man that he never stopped to figure out how one staff could produce two papers. Not a single extra man was hired. Meekins was managing editor of both, and I was city editor of both. This preposterous arrangement went on for a single week, and then we all blew up. During that week I never got home at all, but slept, when I slept at all, on a couch in the office—usually from 2 A.M. to 6 or 7. It was the end of August, 1904, in sticky Summer weather, and the car-barn was only a block from the waterfront, in the hottest part of Baltimore. Changes of clothes were sent to me from home, but the only baths I got were from a fire-hose in the press-room.

Launched under such disadvantages, the *Evening Herald* was naturally something of a scarecrow, and its reception by the gentry and commonalty of Baltimore was far from enthusiastic. Grasty's *Evening News* was then, as always, a bad newspaper, but it was not quite as bad as the *Evening Herald*, and the advertisers of the town showed no sign of deserting him to fatten us. Peard and his men in the business office tried to put all the blame on the editorial department, but we bit and scratched back, and after an insane week of his noble experiment the morning *Herald* was abandoned, and we began to get out an evening edition that looked more or less like a newspaper.

But the Sunday morning paper was continued, and so my work-day on Saturday ran from 7 A.M. to 1 or 2 A.M. Sometimes I was able to snatch a nap in the afternoon, but more often I was not, and the thing I principally remember about the time is that I always slept so late on Sunday morning that I was unable to sleep Sunday night, and that it commonly took me until Wednesday to oscillate back to my normal hours. We all sweated and schemed, but it gradually became plain that without fresh money and new and wonder-working management the *Herald* was doomed. Natural forces were also in operation against us, for the great reduction in the number of American daily papers that marked the 20's and 30's was already beginning. Baltimore had five in 1904, and in 1903 it had had six, but today it has but three.

In the midst of these dismal struggles, at some time or other in 1905, Meekins's title was changed to that of editor-in-chief, and I was made managing editor in his place, with Joe Callahan succeeding me as city editor. It was a step that must have caressed inevitably the gills of any youngster of twenty-five, for though I was well aware of the *Herald*'s gloomy prospects, it was nevertheless a daily newspaper, and in a city of more than 500,000 people. Most of my fellow-freshmen of 1899 were still reporters, and some were out of jobs, but here was I, by the sheer power of a singular virtue, rising to great and puissant dignities, and ready to become (as I suspected) the Ajax of a new crop of legends as astonishing as those which swathed Cunningham, Carter and Meekins himself. It was a great day when I overheard an office-boy speak of me, to a colleague, as the Old Man, and another when the office stationery came back from the printers with Meekins's name blacked out and mine printed above it. But as the duties of my new office took me deeper and deeper into the affairs of the paper I became better and better aware of its parlous state. Meekins told me daily of his palavers with Peard and with Oler, the iceman who owned the paper, and what he had to report was predominantly depressing. On those rare days when news came down from the business office uptown that a new 300-line ad had been snared he and I would go to Joyce's Hotel opposite Camden Station and blow ourselves to a swell dinner.

It would be an error, however, to say that I was ever despondent, or anything remotely resembling it. I was still only twenty-five—and at twenty-five the hot ichor of youth is still roaring in the veins. I argued, even against the wise Meekins, that the paper could still be saved, and both of us certainly shirked no blood and sweat to that end. Having no responsibility for the editorial page, I leaped from crag to crag in the news department, and kept a constant eye on composing-room and press-room. If a desk man was out of service I took over his duties for the day; if there was a rush of business in the city-room I sat in as an extra copy-reader; once, for a month running, I got out the woman's page; and whenever Meekins was off the job I lent a hand with the editorial page. It was a busy and exhilarating life, despite all the lugubrious bulletins from the front office, and I enjoyed it immensely. But all the while, I am sure, I was accumulating a conviction that executive posts were not for Henry, and formulating plans, if only unconsciously, to avoid them in the still dim future. Meekins himself, as I have said in Chapter IX, probably contributed more to that determination than either he or I realized at the time.

I recall, in point, the day when the proofs of my first real book, "George Bernard Shaw: His Plays," came in. It was a small volume, else I could not have found the time to write it at all, but it was nevertheless a book, set up and to be published by a real publisher, and I was so enchanted that I could not resist taking the proofs to the office and showing them to Meekins—on the pretense, as I recall, of consulting him about a doubtful passage. He seemed almost as happy about it as I was. "If you live to be two hundred years old," he said, "you will never forget this day. It is one of the great days of your life, and maybe the greatest. You will write other books, but none of them will ever give you half the thrill of this one. Go to your office, lock the door, and sit down to read your proofs. Nothing going on in the office can be as important. Take the whole day off, and enjoy yourself." I naturally protested, saying that this or that had to be looked to. "Nonsense!" replied Meekins. "Let all those things take care of themselves. I *order* you to do nothing whatsoever until you have finished with the proofs. If anything pops up I'll have it sent to *me*." So I locked myself in as he commanded, and had a shining day indeed, and I can still remember its unparalleled glow after all these years.

On January 20, 1906, there was a mysterious confab in the business office uptown, and the next day the *Herald* announced that "at a meeting of the board of directors of the *Herald* Publishing Company the resignation of Mr. Frank F. Peard as president and general manager was received with regret." On the same day Meekins appeared on the flagstaff of the paper as president and publisher, and under his name was this:

Henry L. Mencken, *Secretary and Editor*

The details of Peard's exitus I never heard, and in fact I never inquired about them. He was always extremely polite to me, but my communion with him had early convinced me that his talents, however distinguished, did not lie in the newspaper field. He had many other irons in the fire, and at one time made a weekly trip to New York to function as secretary of a typewriter company. The only part of the paper that he showed any genuine interest in was the financial page. To embellish it he saddled us with a stock tipster who used the *nom de plume* of G. de Baldevinus—an amiable old fellow who was well liked in the office, but guessed wrong almost as often as our racing tipster. Baldevinus did all his work in the composing-room, where he used one of the stones as a desk, and in the course of an average afternoon he would receive six or eight telephone calls from Peard, who played the stock market steadily, and lost nine times out of ten.

Both Peard and Oler were naturally fertile in editorial ideas, all of them bad. Whenever Oler sent in a request that something be printed about himself or one of his friends the resultant copy was marked "Ice," which was our ground-rules equivalent of the usual newspaper "Must." I can recall forlorn days when the city-room copy-hook was almost choked with "Ice" stuff. Peard's orders were quite as numerous, and even more demoralizing. Once, at Christmas time, he let the advertising manager of a Baltimore department-store sell him the notion that it would be fine propaganda for the *Herald* if we could induce every trolley passenger to add a penny to his nickel fare, as a Christmas offering to the conductors. A smart reporter was assigned to work up the idea, and he did it in a series of stories full of sly satire that Peard swallowed without suspicion. Some of the conductors threw the pennies in the passengers' faces, for that was before effective fare-registers had been invented, and any conductor with his wits about him was a man of means, for he could easily knock down five times his wages. Others got into rows with their motormen, who tried to muscle in on the swag—which never, I believe, amounted to anything. We received hundreds of letters denouncing us as rogues and imbeciles, mainly on the ground that giving money to the conductors would only incite the trolley monopoly to cut their wages.

Peard was always an easy mark for press-agents, and especially for those representing what he regarded as prospective advertisers. It would be unjust to blame him here, for we were desperately in need of more lineage, but his seductions were often very embarrassing to the editorial department. More than once a good reporter, assigned to write some extravagant piece of balderdash, bucked violently and threatened to resign. Inasmuch as I always sympathized with him heartily, I was debarred from putting any pressure on him, and had to resort to cajolery. Even non-advertisers found Peard willing and eager—for example, the Christian Scientists. That was in the days before the late Charles Scribner had given them a salutary trouncing in the matter of the E. F. Dakin book on Ma Eddy, which they tried in vain to suppress. In every American city they had a committee on publication which roved the newspaper offices, confidently demanding space for the lectures of their traveling exegetes. When they first appeared in the *Herald* office I threw them out, but they soon came back with a chit from Peard, and for a couple of years we had to make room for their nonsense. The copy-desk struck back by converting it into even worse nonsense, and by writing idiotic heads on it, so I had to watch it carefully.

But now Peard had faded out at last,[1] and Meekins was in full charge of the paper, with only Oler over him. I was secretary of the company, but so far as I can recall there was never any meeting of the board; in fact, I never heard the names of the members thereof, if any. Meekins's principal job was to

[1] In his later years he made a considerable success in the insurance business in California, and died there in 1925.

blackjack money out of the reluctant and now terrified Oler. He was successful for a few months, but after that Oler began to dry up, for he had become convinced at last that his political career was under the curse of God. In the early Spring of 1906 a number of the larger advertisers of Baltimore, concluding that it might be good *Geschäft* to keep the *Evening Herald* alive, if only for use as a club against Grasty and his *Evening News*, appeared with an offer to chip in enough to meet our weekly deficits. Meekins and I added a bottle of claret to our dinner at Joyce's that night, but when the advertisers began to mention actual money it appeared that the best they were willing to do was far short of our needs, and after some vain gabble they took to the woods. From that time onward it was only a matter of standing the death-watch. Finally, on June 17, we printed the following on the editorial page:

NOTICE

Tomorrow the property of the *Herald* Publishing Company will pass into new hands, and there will be no further publication of the *Sunday Herald*, the *Evening Herald*, or the *Weekly Herald*.

"New hands" was something of a euphemism. We had virtually nothing to sell, for all our mechanical equipment was mortgaged, and our morning Associated Press membership, save for the Sunday edition, had been forfeited by our switch to the evening field. Nevertheless, the other Baltimore papers seem to have put up a nominal sum to get rid of the wreck, for I discovered years later, on searching the corporation records of the Baltimore *Sun*, that its share had been $3,125. The staff, during the last year, had gradually reduced itself, for everyone suspected what was coming, and at the time of the final crack no one was much perturbed, at any event in the editorial department. Nearly all the boys found new jobs without difficulty, some in Baltimore and the rest in other cities, and those who didn't went into other trades. Joe Callahan, the city editor, started a weekly paper for builders and contractors that still survives and is still prosperous, though Joe himself is long dead.

As for me, I was, like Meekins, in apparent difficulties, for it is a newspaper maxim that when a paper blows up the chances of its hirelings landing new jobs run in inverse proportion to their rank. The office-boys are at work again the next day, and good reporters are snapped up quickly, but managing editors are out on a limb, for vacancies in their gloomy trade come rarely and are usually filled by promotion, and if they look for lesser posts they encounter the same prejudice that afflicts ex-managers in the theatre. But I was lucky, for all three of the larger dailies of Baltimore offered me jobs, and I took the first offer that reached me. It came from Grasty of the *Evening News*: he wanted me to be his news editor. But after a couple of weeks in the job I decided finally that executive work was not to my taste, and in a little while I transferred to the *Sunpaper* as Sunday editor, a more leisurely and literary job. Soon I was set to writing editorials, and after that my contributions to the various *Sunpapers*—morning, evening and Sunday— were destined to go on with only an occasional break until the early days of 1941. Since 1910, save for a brief and unhappy interlude in 1938, I have never had a newspaper job which involved the control of other men's work, or any responsibility * for it.

HEATHEN DAYS
1890–1936

*   MARCH 30, 1942

Preface

WHEN I finished "Happy Days" in August, 1939, anchored to an Underwood Noiseless Portable in the lovely Summer home of Dr. and Mrs. Frederic M. Hanes, high up in the North Carolina mountains, it would have astonished me unfeignedly if one of the native necromancers had dropped in from a neighboring Alp and told me that two similar volumes would follow it. I had had a grand time doing the book, but it seemed to me that one dose of my *curriculum vitae* was enough for posterity, and with the troubles of the teens peeping round the *corner in my memory, I was rather glad to be shet of the subject. It soon appeared, however, that I was in the hands of higher powers, some of them supernatural but most of them merely human. The latter were customers who began writing in suggesting that I do a companion volume on my early newspaper adventures, and in a little while I had so far succumbed to their blarney that a couple of chapters thereof were sketched out. This was in 1940. The project occupied me off and on during the year, but in the main I worked on my "New Dictionary of Quotations," and when 1941 dawned "Newspaper Days" was still only a fragment. I thereupon decided, heroically but idiotically, to jam through both books together, and the result was that I landed in hospital in April, with the dictionary finished but "Newspaper Days" yet very far short of it. After I got out of their animal-house the resurrection men ordered me to take a holiday, and I went to Cuba by sea—probably my last ocean trip on this earth. I spent a couple of lazy weeks in Havana and its environs, hearing some excellent music, watching (and getting converted to) the cavortings of a Russian ballet company, and putting away large quantities of the nourishing Cuban victuals. When I got back to Baltimore I had so far recovered that I had a sudden burst of energy, and was soon knocking off what remained of "Newspaper Days" at the rate of 3,000 words a day—my all-time high for sustained writing. The MS. was in the hands of the Knopfs by June 18, and on June 24 I was writing to Blanche: "I note your acceptance of 'Newspaper Days.' It is naturally gratifying to a young author."

The present volume is a kind of by-product of the burst of
energy just mentioned. When I came to the end of the period
marked off for "Newspaper Days," I simply could not stop, but
kept on going until I had accumulated four or five redundant
chapters. When wind of these reached Harold W. Ross, the
alert editor of the *New Yorker*, he collared them for his instructive weekly, and urged me to go on to more. When "Newspaper Days" came out in the Autumn of 1941 there was further
heat from customers, and even a few whiffs from reviewers, so
the present volume gradually and inevitably took form. It
covers a wider range of time than either of its predecessors, for
in it I have included a couple of chapters that belong to my
Erinnerungen aus dem fröhlichen Bubenleben but somehow
failed to fit into "Happy Days," and on the other end I bring it
down to 1936. But there is no continuity in it, and none was
attempted. It is simply a series of random reminiscences, not
always photographically precise, of a life that, on the whole,
has been very busy and excessively pleasant. Like any other
man I have had my disasters and my miseries, and like any
other author I have suffered from recurrent depressions and
despairs, but taking one year with another I have had a fine
time of it in this vale of sorrow, and no call to envy any man.
Indeed, I seem to have been born without any capacity for
envy, and to the fact, no doubt, is due a large part of my habitual tranquility, not to say complacency. But in part that con-
tentment of spirit is due also to a kind of caginess that has
dissuaded me, at all stages of my life, from attempting enterprises clearly beyond my power. Sticking always to what I
could do with reasonable comfort, I have escaped the pains
of complete bafflement, and thus have no motive, whether
Freudian or other, for begrudging the other fellow his competence. Indeed, I simply can't imagine competence as anything
save admirable, for it is very rare in this world, and especially in
this great Republic, and those who have it in some measure, in
any art or craft from adultery to zoölogy, are the only human
beings I can think of who will be worth the oil it will take to
fry them in Hell.

Despite my two previous miscalculations, this third volume
of my more or less accurate memories will probably be my last,
for I begin to be impressed, at sixty-two, with the cogency of

the Chinese warning that "it is later than you think"; and if I actually do any more dredging out of the past it will undoubtedly be in a more chastened and scientific mood. The hereditary pedant in me has made me a diligent conservator of records, and in the files in my cellar are enough of them to entertain a whole herd of nascent Ph.D.'s—records of forty-three years on newspapers, of forty as a writer of books, of twenty-five as a reviewer, of twenty as a magazine editor. These vocations have overlapped, but they have also intermingled, and some of my chronicles are thus rather complicated. When I was engaged a little while back in trying to get some order into them, I was struck by the thought that every man given over professionally to hearing and seeing things ought to be allowed two lives— one to hear and see and the other to set down what he has heard and seen. But inasmuch as no such thought seems to have occurred to the Creator of the species, I am doomed to an inevitable but sorry compromise. Having now done three volumes of my recollections, I shall turn away from the past for a while and devote myself to hearing and seeing some more. I can only say of the present volume, as I said of its two predecessors, that it is not sober history but yarning, and is thus devoid of any purpose save to entertain. If it fails there it is a flop indeed. The title, alas, comes a good deal short of satisfying me. In its provisional or studio form I thought of the book as "Miscellaneous Days," for it covers a long period and shows me at ages ranging from the agonies of nonage to the beginnings of senility. But there were objections to "Miscellaneous Days" that need not be gone into here, so I began concocting various other titles, all of them bad—"Busy Days," "Gaudy Days," "Red-Letter Days," "Assiduous Days," and so on. Finally, I hit on "Heathen Days," which is probably worse than any of them. The precisely right title would be "Happy Days III," just as the precisely right title for "Newspaper Days" was "Happy Days II," but it is now too late to undo the mistake I made in 1941.

In my efforts to keep down my errors in names, dates and other facts to a reasonable minimum I have thrown myself on the kindness of several friends with better memories than my own—especially, George Jean Nathan, my former associate in many a gay enterprise; A. H. McDannald, my companion in one that is herein described at some length; Dr. Paul de Kruif, a partner in another; and Richard J. Beamish, now a member of the Public Utility Commission of Pennsylvania, but formerly a reporter as I was, and a much better one. Most of all I owe thanks to another old colleague and friend—Edgar Ellis, librarian of the Baltimore *Sunpapers*. Mr. Ellis has not only built up a newspaper morgue of the first class; he has also learned how to find his way about in it, so that its veriest scrap of information is immediately at his hand. I called on him for help at least two dozen times while the pages following were in progress, and not once did he fail me. Without his aid, always generously given, my record would show a great many more stretchers than now adorn it.

BALTIMORE, 1942.   H. L. M.

Table of Contents

I.
Downfall of a Revolutionary
[1890]

O F ALL the eminent characters who flourished in the West
Baltimore of my infancy, the one most venerated by the
boys of my generation was Hoggie Unglebower, an uncouth
youth whose empire and influence, radiating out from an
humble stable in the alley which ran behind our house in Hollins street, covered altogether an area of at least half a square
mile. No storekeeper of that time and place was better known,
whether for good or for evil, nor any cop, however heinous,
nor any ma'am in the public school up Hollins street hill, nor
bad nigger in Vincent alley, nor blind man in practice at Hollins market. Between the longitude of the market and the wilderness of Steuart's Hill, all through a chunk of territory four
or five blocks thick, he was a hero to every boy above the age
of seven.

The reader of today, soaked in the Freudian sewage for so
many years, will assume at once, I suppose, that Hoggie must
have been a Lothario, and his headquarters a seraglio. Nothing
could have been further from the truth. He was actually almost
a Trappist in his glandular life, and his hormones never gave
him any visible trouble until much later on, as I shall show in
due course. In the days of his greatest glory his view of all
human females was predominantly disdainful, but it never led
him to use them wickedly, or even impolitely. When a hired
girl issued into the alley to flag a rag-and-bone man or hunt
for a lost garbage box he would whistle at her satirically and
shout "Ah, there!" but at the same time he always took off his
hat. To women of greater age and station he was courteous to
an extreme degree, and when he visited a neighboring dwelling with his terriers to purge it of rats he always wiped his feet
at the back door, and never failed to address the lady of the
house as Ma'am.

No, Hoggie was not carnal in the Catechism sense, and I
incline to think that that was one of the reasons all the boys so

greatly respected him. The male infantry of today, debauched
by Progressive Education and the sex hygiene quackery, are
said to be adepts at the arts of love before they are more than
half house-broken, but that was certainly not true in my time.
The boys of that Mousterian generation, until adolescence came
down upon them, regarded girls with frank aversion, and had
as little truck with them as with cats or cops. It is, of course, a
fact that the probable delights of amour were occasionally discussed, but it was always vaguely and with a considerable uneasiness, for any move to put a concrete project into effect
would have involved a close approach to females, and that was
never done if it could be helped. What made Hoggie a personage was nothing in that line; it was mainly, and perhaps even
only, his successful and notorious resistance to the doctrine
that cleanliness is next to godliness.

In his father's stable he led the life dreamed of as ideal by all
normal boys, then, now, and forever. No one, it appeared, had
any authority (at all events any authority that he recognized)
to make him comb his hair, or brush his clothes, or shine his
shoes, or wash behind the ears. He wallowed there day in and
day out, including especially Sundays, in such slops as every
normal boy longs to own, but is seldom permitted to have.
Preferring the society of horses and dogs to that of men, he
lived among them freely and unashamedly, sleeping with them,
eating with them, and sharing his confidences with them. He
got his hair cut when he damned well pleased, and it wasn't
often. Hating neckties, he never wore them. When he thirsted,
he drank from the end of the stable hose, and if anyone stopped
to gape at him he squeezed the hose (which was old, soft and
full of holes) and sent a fine stream into the gaper's eye.

In brief, a magnificent specimen of Natural Man, somehow
surviving unscathed every corruption of an effete and pusillan-
imous civilization. He came of a bourgeois family and had
been to school, but had fought off successfully every effort to
denaturize him. His days were busy, and full of enterprises
that, to us boys, were important, difficult and romantic. He
was the architect, builder and navigator of the largest and fastest
double-decker sleds known in West Baltimore, and probably
the best repairer of boys' wagons ever seen in Christendom.
He knew how to knock a barrel to pieces without splitting any

of the staves, and how to put it together again. He could teach tricks to horses, and had so far mastered their vocabulary of whinnies and pawings that he carried on long conversations with them, often laughing at their pawky humor. He was a dog doctor of great gifts, and kept a large stock of medicines for his patients on a shelf in the stable. To cops, despite all their clubs, handcuffs and sidearms, he presented a calm and unflickering eye, and they had a high respect for him, for when he went to the aid of one who was overwhelmed by a passel of bad niggers, the bad niggers lost consciousness almost instantly, and awoke in the watch-house with huge bumps on their heads. Hoggie, disdaining firearms, did his fighting with clubs, and had an arsenal of them ready to hand—little ones for light jobs, and thick, warty shillalahs for really earnest work. When he came down upon a skull something gave way, and it was never Hoggie or his weapon.

He was the best dog-trainer for miles around, and could transfer even the sorriest mutt into a competent ratter. For this purpose he liked to have them young; indeed, he preferred to begin on them as soon as their eyes were open. At that age, of course, they were no match for actual rats, and even the more active sort of mice had the edge on them. To equalize the odds, Hoggie would catch infant rats in a trap, pull their teeth with a pair of pliers, and then throw them into a barrel with a couple of his pupils. As the latter gained in strength and technique, he would test them with rats of gradually larger growth, retaining at first one tooth each, and then two, and then four or five, and finally a whole set, upper and lower. Now and then a freshman was badly mauled in these exercises, but Hoggie did not despair, for he knew that any sort of educational process was bound to be painful, and he preferred the hard way for dogs as for men. His graduates were all recognized virtuosi. One day he let me go along as he took one to a hay-and-feed warehouse for a final examination. The candidate was only a spindly black-and-tan, but within three minutes by the watch he had unearthed, run down and killed a whole bucket of rats, some of them of the fearsome sewer variety, with fangs two inches long.

Hoggie admired dogs, and was admired by them in turn, though his medicating of them ran to heroic measures. His usual prescription for the common run of canine malaises was the better part of half a pound of Glauber's salts. The colored quacks who practised a Dahomeyan farriery in Reveille's livery stable down the street hesitated to give so large a dose to anything short of a cart horse, but Hoggie believed that it was foolish to temporize with disease, and proved it by curing most of his patients. He was also adept at surgery, and could point to at least a dozen dogs that he had treated successfully for broken bones. He sutured the lacerations that followed dogfights with the thick, black thread used by shoemakers, and always waxed it carefully before setting to work. He was, I believe, the first canine dentist ever in practice in Baltimore; to this day, in fact, they are rare. He pulled the damaged teeth of his patients with the same pair of pliers that he employed to prepare rats for his academy, and sometimes he had to pull very hard. I heard him say once that most dogs, like most human beings, were born with too many teeth, and that getting rid of half a dozen or so toned up their systems and improved their dispositions.

No one that I ever heard of approached him in the delicate art of trimming puppies' tails. His technique was of the whirlwind variety: the tail was off before the puppy had a chance to be alarmed. In my earliest days he had a formidable rival in old Julius, an Aframerican *mohel* with headquarters in Reveille's stable, but as the years passed he gobbled all of Julius's practice, and in the end his mastery was admitted by everyone. In that era the different breeds of dogs in vogue nearly all wore their tails clipped, so Hoggie was kept busy. I have seen him knock off six or eight of an afternoon, with the whole Hollinsstreet gang for a gallery. Our own dogs, from the early eighties onward to the middle nineties, all passed through his hands, and every one of them was friendly to him afterward, and wagged its stump whenever it encountered him. He also treated dogs when they took to nibbling grass in the yard or showed other signs of indisposition—always with that massive dose of Glauber's salts as a starter. He had plenty of other medicines, and used them freely on occasion, but he depended mainly on the Glauber's salts, just as Dr. Wiley, our family doctor, depended on castor oil.

Hoggie's incurable boyishness was shown by the fact that,

for all his fondness for horses and dogs, he hated cats with a
blind and implacable hatred, and spent a great deal of his time
tracking them down and executing them. There was a time,
indeed, when his chronic war upon them aroused some ill-will
in the neighborhood—but not, of course, among the boys.
What was done about it I forget, but for a while he locked
himself in his stable, and refused to have any truck with human
society. Even the cops were given to understand that their
room was preferred to their company. But then a stray cat
scratched a baby down the block, and under cover of the ensuing uproar Hoggie emerged from his solitude, and resumed
his crusade. I well recall the day when, as a gesture of triumph,
he threw eight dead cats into the alley in one lot, and got into
a row with the street cleaner who had to haul them away. The
street cleaner, it appeared, held that a person engaged in such
wholesale slaughters should dispose of his own dead, and not
dump them on public officials. He cited the example of the hotels which carted off their own garbage, and that of the candy
factory down the alley which kept a wagon to handle its own
boiler ashes, but Hoggie refused to allow any weight to the
argument. So far as he was concerned, he said, the cats could
lie in the alley until the Judgment Day, along with the rats that
he heaved out almost daily—the melancholy refuse of his college for puppies. The street cleaner muttered a while longer
and threatened several times to submit the whole matter to
Murphy the cop, but in the end he loaded the cats upon his
cart, and during the weeks that followed he loaded many others. Until a fresh generation of kittens worked its way in from
Hollins market, the Union Square neighborhood was almost
as bare of *Felidae* as Greenland. A few, of course, survived in
houses, but they were kept as closely penned as canary birds.

The boys of the Hollins-street gang believed, like well-
educated American boys everywhere else, that cats had nine
lives, but Hoggie dissented. He admitted freely that no cat within
his experience ever had so little as one life, but he insisted that
his researches indicated that five was the limit. Indeed, it was
only battle-scarred old Toms who went even that far: the average free-lance cat, depleted by its wandering, precarious life,
was disposed of finally after being killed three or four times.
One day the alley metaphysician, Old Wesley, undertook to

point out a possible statistical fallacy in this doctrine. What evidence was there, he demanded, that the Toms which Hoggie killed five times had not been killed four times before by other executioners, thus making up the classical nine? This argument, rather to the astonishment of his listening admirers, floored Hoggie completely. The louder he howled against it, the more he became confused and out of temper, and in the end he was reduced to the sorry expedient of denouncing Wesley as a sassy nigger, and threatening to set the medical students on him. His failure in the debate, and above all his resort to what amounted to forensic blackmail, lowered his stock with the boys of Hollins street, but not for long. In a little while he recovered face gloriously by staging, in the privacy of his stable, a dog-fight that went down into history as the most gory ever seen in West Baltimore.

Despite his unhappy encounter with Old Wesley, he was commonly on good terms with the colored people who lived in the alley, and exercised a general jurisdiction over them, milder and more understanding than that of the cops. They had a high respect for him, and went to him in their troubles, though in his practice as dog-doctor and cat-and-rat exterminator he was uncomfortably close to a medical student. He did not hold himself out as skilled at human medicine, but the bottles he kept for dosing dogs were at the disposal of any blackamoor who wanted to try them, and many professed to be benefited. In particular, the liniment he used on dogs run over by carts was said to be very efficacious against rheumatoid afflictions in *Anthropoidea*. Once he scared off all his Aframerican patients by stuffing a dead cat with oats, and using black shoe-buttons for its eyes. This gruesome object, while it remained on exhibition, kept all the colored people out of his stable, though we white boys thought it was very nobby. It didn't last long, for the huge, ferocious rats of Hollins market quickly heard of it, and one night they rushed the stable and devoured it, eyes and all. All that remained of it the next morning was a carriage-bolt that Hoggie had employed to counteract the flaccidity of the oats.

His downfall I can place with reasonable accuracy in the year 1890, when I was ten years old and he must have been about twenty-two or -three. One afternoon in Summer, on my way to Reveille's livery stable to visit my father's horse, John, who was laid up with epizootic, I encountered Hoggie at the corner of Baltimore street in such vestments that I stopped dead in my tracks, and gaped at him as if he had been a cop in motley or a two-headed boy. He had on a brand-new suit of store clothes, golden brown in color, and wore a pair of the immense yellow shoes then in fashion—as wide, almost, as a street-car at the ball of the foot, but stretched out to a long point at the toe. On his head was a cart-wheel straw hat with a brim at least six inches deep, and a gorgeous red-and-white ribbon. His collar, which was of fresh celluloid, rose above a boiled shirt that gleamed like snow on the Alps, and around it he wore a bright green four-in-hand tie, with the ends tucked over to expose a stud that glittered like a diamond, but was no doubt something else. He was shaved so closely that his neck and chin were criss-crossed with red gashes, and the rest of his face was a brilliant vermilion. Finally, and most amazing of all, his hair—at least such of it as I could see below his hat—was cropped to its roots according to the best technique of Barber Lehnert. As I passed him, I caught a gust of Jockey Club scent, familiar to me as the special favorite of our current hired girl. I was so astounded that I passed him without greeting him, staring foolishly. He paid no attention to me, but stalked along painfully, like a man in a barrel. I spread the news over the neighborhood, and Hoggie's secret quickly leaked out.

He had succumbed at last, after all his years of outlawry, to one of the most conventional of human weaknesses: he had fallen in love. The ancient psychosis that had floored and made a mock of Marc Antony, Dante and Goethe—but *not* Shakespeare, Napoleon Bonaparte or George Washington—had now fetched him too. Some inconsiderable and probably pie-faced slip of a girl, name unknown, had collared him, tamed him, and made of him the dreadful popinjay that I had seen. The rest of the pathetic story follows classical lines, and is soon told. Hoggie disappeared from his stable, and was reported to be occupying a bedroom in the Unglebower family home, and actually eating at table. In a little while he vanished altogether, and reports came in that he was married to the lady, living in far Northwest Baltimore, and at work as a horse-car driver. That was the last I ever heard of him.

II.

Memoirs of the Stable

[1891]

Horses, taking one with another, are supposed to be the stupidest creatures (forgetting, of course, horse-lovers) within the confines of our Christian civilization, but there are naturally some exceptions, and they probably include the whole race of Shetland ponies. During the interminable epoch stretching from my eleventh year to my fourteenth I was on confidential terms with such a pony, and came to have a very high opinion of his sagacity. As the phrase ran in those days, he was as sharp as a trap, and also excessively immoral. The last word, I should say at once, I do not use in the Puritan or Freudian sense, for Frank was a gelding; what I seek to convey is simply the idea that he was also a cheat, a rogue and a scoundrel. Nearly all his waking hours were given over to deceiving and afflicting my brother Charlie and me. He bit us, he kicked us, he stepped on our toes, he crowded us against the walls of his stall, and he sneezed in our faces, and in the intervals he tried to alarm us by running away, or by playing sick or dead. Nevertheless, we loved him, and mixed with our affection there was a great deal of sincere admiration.

Where he was bred we never heard, and, boy-like, did not inquire. One day in the Autumn of 1891 a couple of carpenters appeared in Hollins street and began to throw up a miniature stable at the end of the long backyard, and by the time they got the roof on Frank was in it, along with a yellow go-cart, a tabloid buggy with fringe around its top, a couple of sets of harness, and a saddle. It soon turned out that there was not room enough in the stable for both the go-cart and the buggy, so the buggy was moved to Reveille's livery-stable two blocks away, where my father's horse John was in residence. Simultaneously, a colored intern was brought in from the same place to instruct Charlie and me in the principles of his art, for we were told that we were to have the honor of caring for Frank. Inasmuch as we had been hanging about stables since infancy,

watching the blackamoors at their work, this hint that we needed tutelage rather affronted us, but we were so delighted by the privilege of becoming hostlers—the dream of every American boy in that horsy age—that we let it pass, and only too soon we learned that there was a great deal more to servic- *
ing a Shetland pony than could be picked up by watching blackamoors service full-grown horses.

Charlie, I believe, got the first kick, but I got the first bite. It was delivered with sly suddenness on the second morning after the intern from Reveille's had graduated me *cum laude* and gone back to his regular job. He had cautioned me that, in currying any sort of horse it was necessary to pay particular heed to the belly, for it tended to pick up contamination from the stall litter, and he had added the warning that the belly was a sensitive area, and must be tackled gently. I was gentle enough, goodness knows, but Frank, as I was soon to learn, objected to any sort of currying whatsoever, top or bottom, and so, when I stooped down to reach under his hull—he was only nine hands high at the withers—he fetched me a good nip in the seat of my pants. My reaction was that of a coiled spring of high tension, and it was thus hardly more than a split second before I was out in the yard, rubbing my backside with both hands. When I tell you that Frank laughed you will, of course, set me down a nature-faker; all the same, I tell you that Frank laughed. I could see him through the window above his feed-trough, and there were all the indubitable signs—the head thrown back, the mouth open, the lips retracted, the teeth shining, the tears running down both cheeks. I could even hear a sound like a chuckle. Thereafter I never consciously exposed my ca-boose to him, but time and again he caught me unawares, and once he gave me a nip so severe that the scar remains to this day. Whenever I get to hospital—which is only too often in these later years—the sportive young doctors enter it upon their chart as a war wound.

Frank quickly developed a really marvelous technic of es-cape. He had a box-stall that, considering his size, was roomy, and Charlie and I kept it so clean that the hostlers from all the other stables in the alley would drop in to admire it. There was a frame of soft red clay to ease his forefeet, and a large piece of rock-salt to entertain him on lazy afternoons. He got hearty meals of substantial horse-victuals three times a day, and in cold weather the water used to mix his mill-feed was always warm. Through the window above his trough he could look out into the yard, and a section of it about twenty feet square was fenced off to give him a paddock. In this paddock he was free to disport a couple of hours every day, save only when there was snow on the ground. But when he was in it he devoted most of his time to hanging his head over the paling-fence, lusting for the regions beyond. Just out of his reach was a peach tree, and beyond it a pear tree, both still young and tender. One fine Spring day, with both trees burgeoning, he somehow cracked the puzzle of the catch on the paddock gate, and by the time he was discovered he had eaten all the bark off the peach tree, from the ground to a height of four feet. Charlie and I found it hard to blame him, for we liked the peach gum ourselves and often chewed it, flies and all, but my mother wept when the tree died, and the paddock gate was outfitted with an iron bar and two chains.

Frank never got through it again—that is, by his own effort. But one day, when a feeble-minded hired girl left it open, he was in the yard instantly and made a killing that still lives in the family tradition. Rather curiously, he did not molest the pear tree, but by the time he was chased back to his own ground he had devoured a bed of petunias, all my mother's best dahlias, the better part of a grape vine, and the whole of my father's mint patch. I have been told by eminent horse-lovers that horses never touch mint, but I am here dealing, not with a horse, but with a Shetland pony. Frank gradually acquired many other strange appetites—for example, for ice cream. Every time it was on tap in the house he would smell it and begin to stamp and whinny, and in the end it became the custom to give him whatever happened to be left. Once, when the hired girl got salt into it and the whole batch was spoiled, he devoured all of it—probably a gallon and a half—and then drank two buckets of water. He also ate oranges (skin and all), bananas (spitting out the skin), grapes, asparagus and sauerkraut. One day Charlie tried him with a slab of rat-trap cheese, but he refused it. Another day Charlie gave him a piece of plug tobacco wrapped in a cabbage leaf, but again without success. This last trick, in fact, offended him and he sought revenge at once. When he bit through the cabbage into the tobacco he gave a sudden and violent cough, and the plug hit Charlie in the eye.

When we were in the country in Summer Frank had my father's horse John for a stable-mate, and they got on together well enough, though it was plain to see that Frank regarded John as an idiot. This was a reasonable judgment, for John, who was a trotter, was actually very backward mentally, and could be easily scared. Whenever the two were in pasture together Frank would alarm John by bearing down upon him at a gallop, as if about to leap over him. This would set John to running away, and Frank would pursue him all over the pasture, whinnying and laughing. John himself could no more laugh than he could read and write. He was a tall, slim sorrel with a long, narrow head, and was so stupid that he even showed no pride in his speed, which was considerable. Life to him was a gloomy business, and he was often in the hands of horse-doctors. If there was a stone on the road he always picked it up, and when we were in the country and Charlie and I had charge of him we never bedded him down for the night without investigating his frogs. In the course of an average Summer we recovered at least twenty nails from them, not to mention burrs and splinters. Like most valetudinarians he lived to a great age. After my father's death we sold him to an animal show that had Winter quarters in Baltimore, and he spent his last years as a sort of companion to a herd of trained zebras. The zebras, I heard, had a lot of fun with him.

One night, an hour or so after midnight, there was a dreadful kicking and grunting in our stable in the country, and my father and Charlie and I turned out to inquire into it. We found John standing in the middle of his box-stall in a pitiable state of mind, his coat ruffled and his eyes staring. Frank, next door, was apparently sleeping soundly. We examined John from head to foot, but could find nothing wrong, so we contented ourselves with giving him a couple of random doses from his enormous armamentarium of medicine bottles, and talking to him in soothing tones. He seemed quite all right in the morning, and my father drove him to and from town, but that night there was another hullabaloo in the stable, and we had to turn out again. On the day following John was put to

grass and Charlie and I went for a colored horse-doctor in
Cross Keys, a nearby village. He advised us to throw away all
of John's medicines, and prescribed instead a mild course of
condition powders, with a handful of flaxseed once a day. This
was begun instantly, but that night the same dreadful noises
came from the stable, and again the night following, and again
the night after that, and so on for a week. Two or three other
horse-doctors were called in during that time, but they were all
baffled, and John took to looking seedy and even mangy. Meanwhile, my father began to suffer seriously from the interruptions to his sleep, and talked wildly of having the poor horse
shot and his carcass sent to a glue-factory. Also, he began to
discover unpleasant weaknesses in his old friend Herman Ellis,
from whom John had been bought. Ellis, hitherto, had been
held up to Charlie and me as a model, but now it appeared
that he drank too much, kept two sets of books, was a Methodist, and ought to be expelled from the Freemasons.

Charlie and I, talking the business over at length, came to
the conclusion eventually that there must be more to it than
met the eye, and so decided to keep watch at the stable.
There was already floating through our minds, I think, some
suspicion of Frank, for we were at pains to prevent him learning what we were up to. At our bedtime we sneaked into the
carriage-house on tiptoe, and there made ourselves bunks in
the family dayton-wagon. We were soon sound asleep, but at
the usual time we were aroused by a great clomping and
banging in the stalls adjoining, and turned out to take a
stealthy look. It was a moonlight night, and enough of the
gentle glare was filtering into the stable to give us an excellent view. What we saw scarcely surprised us. All the uproar,
we discovered, was being made by Frank, not by John. Frank
was having a whale of a time flinging his heels against the sides
of his stall. The noise plainly delighted him, and he was laughing gaily. Presently poor John, waking in alarm, leaped to his
feet and began to tremble. At this Frank gave a couple of final
clouts, and then lay down calmly and went to sleep—or, at all
events, appeared to. But John, trying with his limp mind to
make out what was afoot, kept on trembling, and was, in fact,
still half scared to death when we announced our presence and
tried to comfort him.

My father had arrived by this time, his slippers flapping, his suspenders hanging loose and blood in his eye, and we soon made him understand what had happened. His only comment was "Well, I'll be durned!" repeated twenty or thirty times. We soon had a bridle on Frank, with a strap rigged from it to his left hind leg, and if he tried any more kicking that night he knocked himself down, which was certainly no more than he deserved. But we heard no more noise, nor was there any the next night, or the next, or the next. After a week we removed the strap, and then sat up again to see what would happen. But nothing happened, for Frank had learned his lesson. At some time or other while the strap was on, I suppose, he had tried a kick— and gone head over heels in his stall. He was, as I have said, a smart fellow, and there was never any need to teach him the same thing twice. Thereafter, until the end of the Summer, he let poor John sleep in peace. My father fired all the horse-doctors, white and black, and threw out all their remedies. John recovered quickly, and a little while later did a mile on the Pimlico road in 2.17½—not a bad record, for he was pulling a steel-tired buggy with my father and me in it, and the road was far from level.

In that same stable, the next Summer, Frank indulged himself in a jape which came near costing him his life. To recount it I must describe briefly the lay-out of the place. He inhabited a box-stall with a low wall, and in that wall was a door fastened by a movable wooden cleat. He was in the habit of hanging his head over the door, and drooling lubriciously, while Charlie and I were preparing his feed. This feed came down from the hayloft through a chute that emptied into a large wooden trough, and he often saw us start the feed by pulling out a paddle in the chute. One night either Charlie or I neglected to fasten the door of his stall, and he was presently at large. To his bright mind, of course, the paddle was easy. Out it came, and down poured an avalanche of oats—a bushel, two bushels, and so on to eight or ten. It filled the trough and spilled over to the floor, but Frank was still young and full of ambition, and he buckled down to eat it all.

When Charlie and I found him in the morning he was swelled to the diameter of a wash-tub, his eyes were leaden, and his tongue was hanging out dismally, peppered with oats that he had failed to get down. "The staggers!" exclaimed Charlie, who had become, by that time, an eager but bad amateur horse-doctor. "He is about to bust! There is only one cure. We must run him until it works off." So we squeezed poor Frank between the shafts of the go-cart, leaped in, gave him the whip, and were off. Twice, getting down our hilly road to the pike, he sank to his fore-knees, but both times we got him up, and thereafter, for three hours, we flogged him on. It was a laborious and painful business, and for once in his life Frank failed to laugh at his own joke. Instead, he heaved and panted as if every next breath were to be his last. We could hear his liver and lights rumbling as we forced him on. We were so full of sympathy for him that we quite forgot his burglary, but Charlie insisted that we had to be relentless, and so we were. It was nearing noon when we got back to the stable, and decided to call it a day. Frank drank a bucket of water, stumbled into his stall, and fell headlong in the straw. We let him lie there all afternoon, and all of the night following, and for three days thereafter we kept him on a strict diet of condition powders and Glauber's salt.

The bloating that disfigured him, when it began to go down at last, did not stop at normalcy, but continued until he was as thin as a dying mule, and that thinness persisted for weeks. There came with it, perhaps not unnaturally, a marked distaste for oats. His old voluptuous delight in them was simply gone. He would eat them if nothing else offered, but he never really enjoyed them again. For a year, at least, we might have made him free of a feed-trough full of them without tempting him. What John thought of the episode we could never find out. My guess is that he was too dumb to make anything of it.

III.

Adventures of a Y.M.C.A. Lad
[1894]

W HEN I reach the shades at last it will no doubt astonish
Satan to discover, on thumbing my *dossier*, that I was
once a member of the Y.M.C.A. Yet a fact is a fact. What is
more remarkable, I was not recruited by a missionary to the
heathen, but joined at the suggestion of my father, who enjoyed and deserved the name of an infidel. I was then a little
beyond fourteen years old, and a new neighborhood branch of
the Y, housed in a nobby pressed-brick building, had just been
opened in West Baltimore, only a few blocks from our home in
Hollins street. The whole upper floor was given over to a gymnasium, and it was this bait, I gathered, that fetched my father,
for I was already a bookworm and beginning to be a bit
round-shouldered, and he often exhorted me to throw back
my shoulders and stick out my chest.

Apparently he was convinced that exercise on the wooden
horse and flying rings would cure my scholarly stoop, and
make a kind of grenadier of me. If so, he was in error, for I
remain more or less Bible-backed to this day, and am often
mistaken for a Talmudist. All that the Y.M.C.A.'s horse and
rings really accomplished was to fill me with an ineradicable
distaste, not only for Christian endeavor in all its forms, but
also for every variety of callisthenics, so that I still begrudge
the trifling exertion needed to climb in and out of a bathtub,
and hate all sports as rabidly as a person who likes sports hates
common sense. If I had my way no man guilty of golf would
be eligible to any office of trust or profit under the United
States, and all female athletes would be shipped to the white-
slave corrals of the Argentine.

Indeed, I disliked that gymnasium so earnestly that I never
got beyond its baby-class, which was devoted to teaching
freshmen how to hang their clothes in the lockers, get into
their work-suits, and run round the track. I was in those days
a fast runner and could do the 100 yards, with a fair wind, in

something better than fourteen seconds, but how anyone could run on a quadrangular track with sides no more than fifty feet long was quite beyond me. The first time I tried it I slipped and slid at all four corners, and the second time I came down with a thump that somehow contrived to skin both my shins. The man in charge of the establishment—the boys all called him Professor—thereupon put me to the punching-bag, but at my fourth or fifth wallop it struck back, and I was floored again. After that I tried all the other insane apparatus in the place, including the horizontal bars, but I always got into trouble very quickly, and never made enough progress to hurt myself seriously, which might have been some comfort, at least on the psychological side. There were other boys who fell from the highest trapezes, and had to be sent home in hacks, and yet others who broke their arms or legs and were heroic figures about the building for months afterward, but the best I ever managed was a bloody nose, and that was caused, not by my own enterprise, but by another boy falling on me from somewhere near the roof. If he had landed six inches farther inshore he might have fractured my skull or broken my neck, but all he achieved was to scrape my nose. It hurt a-plenty, I can tell you, and it hurt still worse when the Professor doused it with arnica, and splashed a couple of drops into each of my eyes.

Looking back over the years, I see that that ghastly gymnasium, if I had continued to frequent it, might have given me an inferiority complex, and bred me up a foe of privilege. I was saved, fortunately, by a congenital complacency that has been a godsend to me, more than once, in other and graver situations. Within a few weeks I was classifying all the boys in the place in the inverse order of their diligence and prowess, and that classification, as I have intimated, I adhere to at the present moment. The youngsters who could leap from bar to bar without slipping and were facile on the trapeze I equated with simians of the genus *Hylobates*, and convinced myself that I was surprised when they showed a capacity for articulate speech. As for the weight-lifters, chinners, somersaulters, leapers and other such virtuosi of striated muscle, I dismissed them as *Anthropoidea* far inferior, in all situations calling for taste or judgment, to school-teachers or mules.

I should add that my low view of these prizemen was unaccompanied by personal venom; on the contrary, I got on with them very well, and even had a kind of liking for some of them—that is, in their private capacities. Very few, I discovered, were professing Christians, though the Y.M.C.A., in those days even more than now, was a furnace of Protestant divinity. They swore when they stubbed their toes, and the older of them entertained us youngsters in the locker-room with their adventures in amour. The chief free-and-easy trysting-place in West Baltimore, at the time, was a Baptist church specializing in what was called "young people's work." It put on gaudy entertainments, predominantly secular in character, on Sunday nights, and scores of the poor working girls of the section dropped in to help with the singing and lasso beaux. I gathered from the locker-room talk that some of those beaux demanded dreadful prices for their consent to the lassoing. Whether this boasting was true or not I did not know, for I never attended the Sabbath evening orgies myself, but at all events it showed that those who did so were of an antinomian tendency, and far from ideal Y.M.C.A. fodder. When the secretaries came to the gymnasium to drum up customers for prayer-meetings downstairs the Lotharios always sounded razzberries and cleared out.

On one point all hands were agreed, and that was on the point that the Professor was what, in those days, was called a pain in the neck. When he mounted a bench and yelled "Fellows!" my own blood always ran cold, and his subsequent remarks gave me a touch of homicidal mania. Not until many years afterward, when a certain eminent politician in Washington took to radio crooning, did I ever hear a more offensive voice. There were tones in it like the sound of molasses dripping from a barrel. It was not at all effeminate, but simply saccharine. Had I been older in worldly wisdom it would have suggested to me a suburban curate gargling over the carcass of a usurer who had just left the parish its richest and stupidest widow. As I was, an innocent boy, I could only compare it to the official chirping of a Sunday-school superintendent. What the Professor had to say was usually sensible enough, and I don't recall him ever mentioning either Heaven or Hell; it was simply his tone and manner that offended me. He is now dead,

I take it, for many years, and I only hope that he has had good luck *post mortem*, but while he lived his harangues to his students gave me a great deal of unnecessary pain, and definitely slanted my mind against the Y.M.C.A. Even when, many years later, I discovered as a newspaper correspondent that the Berlin outpost thereof, under the name of the *christliche Verein junger Männer*, was so enlightened that it served beer in its lamissary, I declined to change my attitude.

But I was driven out of the Y.M.C.A. at last, not by the Professor nor even by his pupils in the odoriferous gymnasium —what a foul smell, indeed, a gymnasium has! how it suggests a mixture of Salvation Army, elephant house, and county jail!—but by a young member who, so far as I observed, never entered the Professor's domain at all. He was a pimply, officious fellow of seventeen or eighteen, and to me, of course, he seemed virtually a grown man. The scene of his operations was the reading-room, whither I often resorted in self-defense when the Professor let go with "Fellows!" and began one of his hortations. It was quiet there, and though most of the literature on tap was pietistic I enjoyed going through it, for my long interest in the sacred sciences had already begun. One evening, while engaged upon a pamphlet detailing devices for catching boys and girls who knocked down part of their Sunday-school money, I became aware of the pimply one, and presently saw him go to a bookcase and select a book. Dropping into a chair, he turned its pages feverishly, and presently he found what he seemed to be looking for, and cleared his throat to attract attention. The four or five of us at the long table all looked up.

"See here, fellows," he began—again that ghastly "fellows!" —"let me have your ears for just a moment. Here is a book"— holding it up—"that is worth all the other books ever written by mortal man. There is nothing like it on earth except the One Book that our Heavenly Father Himself gave us. It is pure gold, pure meat. There is not a wasted word in it. Every syllable is a perfect gem. For example, listen to this—"

What it was he read I don't recall precisely, but I remember that it was some thumping and appalling platitude or other— something on the order of "Honesty is the best policy," "A guilty conscience needs no accuser," or "It is never too late to mend." I guessed at first that he was trying to be ironical, but it quickly appeared that he was quite serious, and before his audience managed to escape he had read forty or fifty such specimens of otiose rubbish, and following nearly every one of them he indulged himself in a little homily, pointing up its loveliness and rubbing in its lesson. The poor ass, it appeared, was actually enchanted, and wanted to spread his joy. It was easy to recognize in him the anti-social animus of a born evangelist, but there was also something else—a kind of voluptuous delight in the shabby and preposterous, a perverted aestheticism like that of a latter-day movie or radio fan, a wild will to roll in and snuffle balderdash as a cat rolls in and snuffles catnip. I was, as I have said, less than fifteen years old, but I had already got an overdose of such blah in the McGuffey Readers and penmanship copybooks of the time, so I withdrew as quickly as possible, unhappily aware that even the Professor was easier to take than this jitney Dwight L. Moody. I got home all tuckered out, and told my father (who was sitting up reading for the tenth or twentieth time a newspaper account of the hanging of two labor leaders) that the Y.M.C.A. fell a good deal short of what it was cracked up to be.

He bade me go back the next evening and try again, and I did so in filial duty. Indeed, I did so a dozen or more nights running, omitting Sundays, when the place was given over to spiritual exercises exclusively. But each and every night that imbecile was in the reading-room, and each and every night he read from that revolting book to all within ear-shot. I gathered gradually that it was having a great run in devotional circles, and was, in fact, a sort of moral best-seller. The author, it appeared, was a Methodist bishop, and a great hand at inculcating righteousness. He not only knew by heart all the immemorial platitudes, stretching back to the days of Gog and Magog; he had also invented many more or less new ones, and it was these novelties that especially aroused the enthusiasm of his disciple. I wish I could recall some of them, but my memory has always had a humane faculty for obliterating the intolerable, and so I can't. But you may take my word for it that nothing in the subsequent writings of Dr. Orison Swett Marden or Dr. Frank Crane was worse.

In a little while my deliverance was at hand, for though my

father had shown only irritation when I described to him the
pulpit manner of the Professor, he was immediately sympathetic when I told him about the bishop's book, and the papu-
liferous exegete's laboring of it. "You had better quit," he said,
"before you hit him with a spittoon, or go crazy. There ought
to be a law against such roosters." *Rooster* was then his counter-
word, and might signify anything from the most high-toned
and elegant Shriner, bank cashier or bartender to the most
scurvy and abandoned Socialist. This time he used it in its
most opprobrious sense, and so my career in the Y.M.C.A.
came to an end. I carried away from it, not only an indelible
distrust of every sort of athlete, but also a loathing of Methodist bishops, and it was many years afterward before I could
bring myself to admit any such right rev. father in God to my
friendship. I have since learned that some of them are very
pleasant and amusing fellows, despite their professional enmity
to the human race, but the one who wrote that book was certainly nothing of the sort. If, at his decease, he escaped Hell,
* then moral theology is as full of false alarms as secular law.

IV.
The Educational Process
[1896]

W HY MY father sent me to the Baltimore Polytechnic I
have never been able to make out, though from time to
time I have fetched up various more or less colorable theories
—and seen them go to pot when confronted with the known
facts. I had, as a boy, the usual boyish interest in making things,
but I soon discovered that I had no talent for it, and so my
interest gradually died down. My mother was full of stories of
my striking incapacity for the constructive chores of the household; indeed, she depicted me as only a little less incompetent
than my father, who could not mount a ladder without falling
off or drive a nail without mashing his thumb. One Summer,
when we were at our country place, she gave me the job of
making a table for a storeroom and I fell to work reluctantly
but violently, using a pile of old joists and flooring as materials.
When the thing was done it was so massive and clumsy that I
could not move it into the corner where it was to stand, and
the hired girl had to be called in to help. It stood in that corner until the house was sold after my father's death, and I
heard later from the buyer that he had a dreadful time getting
rid of it. Since it would not go through either of the doors of
the room, it had to be knocked to pieces on the spot, and this
turned out to be a laborious job, for I had put it together
with fifty-penny iron nails running fourteen to the pound,
and had not been stingy with them. These nails had rusted,
and the only way to get them out was to split the wood, which
was anything but easy, for the joists were of yellow pine of
irregular grain and very knotty. By the time the buyer poured
this tale into my ear I had passed through the Polytechnic and
held its diploma, but if I had been put to making another such
table I'd have made it just as badly, for I don't recall learning
anything of a mechanical nature while I was a student. I enjoyed
some of the shop work, especially the wood-turning and blacksmithing, but that was mainly because it was a rather hazardous

kind of play; it left no more sediment of profit in my mind
than the prayers the president of the school used to let go in
the assembly-room every morning.

My actual interests, in those days, lay far from tools and
machinery. I was fascinated, on the one hand, by the art of
writing and on the other by the science of chemistry, and both
obsessions had been set going by Christmas presents—the first
by that of a printing-press and the second by that of a camera.
The two fought it out in my psyche all the while I was in the
Polytechnic, and it was only in my last year that the writing
insanity won. My first effort to write for publication was a sort
of compromise between them, for it took the form of a report
on a platinum solution that I had devised for toning silver
prints. This was during the Summer of 1894, when I was still
less than fourteen years old. Writing won in the end largely if
not principally because the brethren who expounded *literae
humaniores* at the Polytechnic were both enthusiasts, whereas
the brother who taught chemistry knew very little about it and
* appeared to have only mild interest in it. Of the former, there
were two, and both of them, by the ordinary academic standards of the time, were bad teachers. Moreover, they failed as
moral exemplars, for one chewed tobacco incessantly and the
other often showed up in class of a morning with bleary eyes
and a breath like a sailor home from the sea. But they had in
common an ardent and almost pious delight in good writing,
and in their catch-as-catch-can way they managed somehow to
convey it to such of the boys as were susceptible to such infections. Neither taught composition *qua* composition, but they
knew where the best models of it were to be found, and I recall
brilliantly over all these years what delights shot through me
when one of them set me to reading the *Spectator* and the other
introduced me to Thackeray. No other gogues in the place
matched them in fanning my private fires, so I got more out of
them than from all the rest, and what I got was better lasting.
Between them they converted me into one of the most assiduous customers that the Enoch Pratt Free Library in Baltimore
has had in its whole history. There were Winters when I visited
it almost every week-day, and before I began to be fetched by
the literary movement of the nineties I had read at least half of
the classical English répertoire.

But I don't want to say that the other gogues at the Polytechnic were all hams, for some of them were clearly not, especially two teachers of mathematics, a subject in which I had little interest. To one of these obscure Bernoullis I owe a massive debt, and it is a pleasant privilege to acknowledge it gratefully after fifty years. He was a man named Uhrbrock, an eccentric bachelor of unknown provenance and training, and his learning in his chosen art probably went but little beyond the algebra that he taught. But he had the great merit of believing in all seriousness that algebra was a discipline of stupendous importance to civilization, and in consequence he imparted it with a degree of zeal amounting almost to frenzy. When I proceeded to the Polytechnic from F. Knapp's Institute in 1892, I was quite innocent of it, for old Professor Knapp had different ideas, and the idiot gogues who sorted out incoming boys thus put me in the lowest class. In all other respects I was ready to enter the next higher class, but the idiots stuck to the letter of their rules. In some way or other Uhrbrock heard of this, and at once offered to tutor me privately—that is, if I were willing to stay an hour after school every day until he judged that I knew enough to be promoted. I was willing, and he fell on me in his most furious manner. For a few days my head swam, but after that I began to take in algebra by the eye, the ear and the pores of my skin, and by the middle of the second week I knew everything that the boys were supposed to learn that first year. Uhrbrock thereupon took me before the committee of idiots, demanded that I be examined, stood by menacingly while they questioned me, and terrorized them into passing me with a mark of 100. The next day I was promoted, and ever since that time, down to the present glorious day, I have been a year ahead of schedule on my progress through life. I say this because, on age alone, I really belonged in the lowest class. But Professor Knapp and his goons had done such a good job of teaching me all the branches save algebra that I had almost accumulated the extra year, and it needed only Uhrbrock's philanthropy to give it to me.

I call it philanthropy advisedly, though in general philanthropy seems to me to be a purely imaginary quantity, like demi-virginity or one glass of beer. Even here, I suppose, I am forgetting the lust to teach—a passion apparently analogous to concupiscence or dipsomania, and, in the more extreme varieties of pedagogues, maybe quite as strong. I daresay that Uhrbrock was full of it, but I must point out in fairness that his yielding to it went a good deal further than has ever been usual in his order. If he merely lusted to teach he might have worked out his libido within the ordinary patterns of the place; as it was, he stepped outside them, and put himself to purely gratuitous trouble. If I had to stay after school every day, in hot September weather, then so did he. Moreover, his willingness to do this for a perfect stranger certainly had some sort of altruism in it, at least to the extent that you will find altruism in the operations of the F.B.I. or the Boy Scouts. He had never seen or heard of me before, and in fact had to ask my name ten or twenty times before he remembered it. Nor was I the bright and shining sort of youngster who may be expected to attract adult notice and favor; on the contrary, I was more unprepossessing than otherwise, with a bulging cranium, round shoulders, bow legs, and very little show of the prancing masculine gorgeousness that developed later. Thus I was very grateful to Uhrbrock for what he did for me, and shall go on thinking of it as philanthropy. In the years following, I should add in candor, he made some efforts to cash in on it. I was by that time the city editor of a newspaper in Baltimore, and he was involved in a row with his superiors—a row that went on for a long, long while. Whenever it rose to special venom he would visit me at my office and try to induce me to print his diatribes against his opponents. Inasmuch as those diatribes had but slight support in any facts known to me and many of them were packed with libel *per se*, I had to put him off, but I was always very polite to him, and whenever the chance offered to give him a little sneaking aid I seized it. In the end his enemies got him and he was drummed out of the public school system, and soon afterward he died.

He was a competent teacher, and rammed the mysteries of algebra into his boys with great success. Some of them actually became so proficient that they could solve the problems he set to them without any sort of cheating. His colleagues of the mathematical faculty were generally less proficient, and it was therefore the custom of the school to use cribs against them.

One of these colleagues, an old fellow who had been a pedagogue for many years, and showed all the traditional stigmata
of the craft—a pasty complexion, chalky fingers, and a preference for white neckties and black alpaca coats—eventually gave
great delight to his pupils by going crazy. His infirmity crept *
upon him slowly, and in its earlier stages all that was noticed
was that he was more crabbed than usual. When a boy went to
the blackboard to solve a problem in geometry or trigonome-
try he would fall upon the poor fellow like a cat playing a
mouse, and try to rattle him with frequent cries of "Nonsense!",
always pronounced with the two syllables equally stressed. Nine
times out of ten the boy had a copy of the solution in his hand,
lifted from the textbook, and had simply transferred it to the
board, but the old man nevertheless found plenty to object to.
In the end he began to question and deride the book itself, and
it dawned upon the boys that he had gone *mashuggah*. Proof
positive followed almost instantly, for he took to felicitating
and whooping up the occasional boys who were too stupid to
use the book solutions, or maybe even too honest. In a little
while some smartie tried him out with a solution so fantasti-
cally imbecile that the dullest boys laughed at it. When he
praised it as a masterpiece everyone knew for sure that his
mind had happily given way, and thereafter all of his students
were magnificently at ease in his classroom. My own class,
which visited him twice a week, had a rollicking time. The
more fatuous the solution offered, the better he liked it, so we
gave him what he wanted, and got high marks day after day.
Now and then, to test the progress of his malady, we put up
controls armed with cribs from the textbook. Each and every
time he drove them from the blackboard with yells of "Nonsense!" and we thus established the fact that he was not recovering. The boys of all his classes naturally kept his lunacy to
themselves, and it was weeks before any of the other gogues
noticed it. The poor old fellow was then relieved of his duties,
and his successor gave us a really savage working out. At the
end of that year more than half the boys in my class were
plucked in mathematics, but the administration let them go on
the ground that we had all suffered through no fault of our
own. No boy, of course, was conscious of any actual suffering.

This unhappy gogue was a pretty good teacher in his days of

normalcy, though not as good as Uhrbrock. Most of the other
members of the faculty, with the shining exception of the two
who professed English literature, ranged downward from indifferent to unspeakable. The great sciences of anatomy and
physiology, naturally extremely interesting to adolescent boys,
were in charge of a superannuated homeopath armed with a
textbook in which all the abdomen south of the umbilicus was
represented by a smooth and quite uneventful surface, exactly
like the figleaf section of a female acrobat's pink tights. The
homeopath, who must have gone through some sort of medical college in his time, was apparently convinced that he could
never arouse any interest in his subject with such reticent materials, for he made no effort whatsoever to teach it. Instead,
he devoted his lecture periods to rambling harangues on all
sorts of non-anatomical subjects, and every boy knew that all
who listened with any show of attention would get high passing marks at the end of the year. His principal business was
really not teaching at all, but the coopering of boys injured in
the shops. This happened very frequently, and he seldom got
through one of his harangues without having to stop to sew
up a cut or pull out a splinter. His assembled students always
watched these manipulations with fascination, and some of
them, called on for occasional help, became skillful operating-
room orderlies. It was not often that a boy was hurt seriously,
but once it happened in my presence. The victim was a handsome young fellow who was so well liked that he had been made
president of my class. Like all the rest of us, he had been warned
against the extreme dangers of using a power plane to dress
thin pieces of wood, but one day he chose to disregard them,
his piece of wood gave way, the fingers of his right hand were
sucked into the revolving blades, and he lost every finger save
the thumb. I was standing not six feet away from him, and the
bloody spectacle shocked me even more than it did the victim,
who bore it very bravely. We did not take him to the homeopath, but rushed him to the City Hospital, which was separated
from the Polytechnic only by an alley. There the surgical interns stopped the hemorrhage and sewed up the stumps, but
his fingers were gone forever—a cruel calamity to an ambitious
youngster. One of the boys retrieved them from the pile of
shavings under the plane, and brought them to the hospital,

hoping that they could be sewed on, but the interns said that in the then state of surgery it could not be done.

There was a medical school attached to the hospital, and its students loafed and skylarked in the alley separating them from the Polytechnic. We were on friendly terms with them, and they entertained us by showing off their horrors. Also, they were of assistance to us in our wars with unpopular teachers. After we had bombarded one such unfortunate with all the classical weapons, including live rats and hydrogen sulphide, the medical students gave us an ear from an Aframerican cadaver, and we stuffed it into his inkwell. But this *attentat*, despite its boldness and ingenuity, was a failure, for the gogue, a very stupid fellow, fished the ear out of his ink and dropped it into his wastebasket without a word, and we spent the next week trying to figure out whether he had really recognized it for what it was. There was a faction that proposed to give him another and surer shock by getting a whole Aframerican head from the medical students and propping it up on his desk, but the students refused to supply it. The disappearance of an ear, they said, would pass unnoticed, but if they made off with a head there would be an inquiry and maybe a good deal of unpleasantness. Some years after this it was discovered that the *Diener* in the dissecting-room of the college had been carrying * on for years a brisk trade in entire cadavers. He filched them from the morgue in the basement, crammed them into barrels, and shipped them to fly-by-night medical colleges in the West. By the time he was taken I was already out of the Polytechnic and working as a newspaper reporter, and it fell to me to cover the story of his arrest, trial and jugging.

The shop-work at the Polytechnic, as I have said, interested me very little, save for that in the wood-turning and blacksmith shops. For some reason or other I got pleasure out of making the puerile gimcracks that were the chief product of the former, and there was always the stimulating possibility that one of the pointed tools we used would dig into the wood—we called it catching a crab—and make a kind of explosion. Such accidents always brought the gogue in charge of the shop at a run, and he would stop all work and deliver himself of a long monitory lecture. He was an old fellow in a skullcap that made him look like a rabbi and his lectures were heavy going. We took his warnings lightly, but once I saw a block of maple, caught in a crab, fly from the lathe with such force that when it hit the guilty boy in the forehead he went out like a pug caught in the jaw. By the time he revived and we took him to the homeopath he had a bump on his forehead as big as an egg. Another time, in the same shop, a power-operated band-saw broke, and the boy using it was wound up in the blade. His injuries, however, consisted only of a few minor cuts, and the homeopath soon had him patched up and on his way home. I liked the blacksmith shop because it was full of sparks and noise, and also, I suppose, because it was dirty. In it, after four or five months of hard struggle, I made a small iron hook that I still use as a paperweight. In it I also received the only injury I suffered in four years at the Polytechnic. It was, naturally enough, a burn, and I got it by picking up a piece of iron that looked cold to the eye but was actually still very hot. Having got hold of it, I couldn't let go, and in consequence my hand was burned badly enough to give me three or four days' holiday. I often worked in the chemical laboratory after school hours, but was never hurt there, though I had several narrow escapes. One day a boy working next to me filled a test-tube with nitric acid, plugged it with a cork, and proceeded in all innocence to heat it over a Bunsen burner. When it went off I managed to duck the murderous spatter, but the boy responsible got a big splash down one of his bare arms, and before I could douse him with an alkali a sizable groove was burned into his flesh.

It was the custom at the school for the boys of the senior class to make an ambitious piece of machinery, and my class undertook a 100-horsepower triple-expansion marine engine. The plans came from the Naval Academy at Annapolis and the castings were made outside, but we did all the machining. I say we, but my own share was confined to finishing the crosshead brasses, for my talents were too modest for me to be entrusted with anything more vital. I worked on those brasses all year, and ruined two or three sets of castings before I produced a finished set that fit. The best machinist in my class, a really competent fellow, got the lordly job of boring the cylinders, and was a hero in consequence. He and the instructor, who knew his subject as few other teachers in the place knew theirs, spent a lot of time counselling and helping me, but my con-genital incapacity for mechanical operations kept me in the baby class. My diligence, however, got its reward, for at the end of the year, though I must have been a headache to him, the instructor gave me a good mark.

The president of the Polytechnic, in those remote days, was a retired naval lieutenant—a tall, slim, elegant fellow wearing the mustache and goatee of Admiral Winfield Scott Schley, then a common make-up among naval officers. He was sup-posed to teach us the higher arcana of steam engineering, but he was so bad a teacher that we had to get whatever we actually learned of the subject from the instructor in the machine-shop. I well recall my difficulties in trying to puzzle out the mysteries of an indicator diagram—a sort of chart showing the perfor-mance of a steam-engine. After listening to the lieutenant for a month or two I gave it up as hopeless, but a little while later the machine-shop instructor made it plain to me in ten minutes. I forgot it, of course, within twenty-four hours after the Polytechnic's diploma was in my hands, as I forgot virtually everything else that I had, at least in theory, learned there. At the present moment I am probably as far from a mechanical genius as it is possible for the free white Ameri-can to get, and still maintain any degree of public veneration. A gasoline engine is as completely mysterious to me as the way of a serpent upon a rock, and when a fuse blows out in my house and I have to replace it the job takes me the better part of an hour.

The naval lieutenant had the easy ways of a sailor and was very popular with the boys. When they started an insurrection in the room of some numskull gogue he would let them roar on for five or ten minutes before coming in to put it down. Such events were commonly followed by mass trials, with himself as judge, but he seldom found anyone guilty and when he did so his punishments were so trivial as to be almost re-wards. He had, like any other man of service on the high seas, an eye for female pulchritude, and was known to receive visits from the fair in his office after school hours. Inasmuch as the boys who observed this always reported that his visitors were beauties on the order of the loveliest actresses portrayed on the cigarette-cards of the time, the news only increased his popularity. But not with the gogues who were his subordinates. They were, in the main, creatures so unattractive to either sex that it would be impossible to imagine even Lydia Pinkham calling on them, so they viewed his gallantries with bilious eyes, and in the end one of them laid charges against him with the school board. Those charges, as reported in the newspapers, were rather vague, but it was easy to gather that they accused the old boy of levantine carnalities. By the time they came out I had left the Polytechnic, but I was interested enough to inquire how the surviving boys had taken the business, and got an answer that pleased me greatly. The day after the outcry, as the lieutenant entered the assembly-room to lead in morning prayers, the whole student body rose as one boy and launched into such a riot of cheers that the cop on the beat came rushing in. A little later, apparently fearing that the names of definite ladies might be brought into the case, he resigned without standing trial, and on his departure got another deafening round of huzzahs. He was succeeded by another naval lieutenant, and this one, after a while, was also beset by the school wowsers. They charged him with resorting to the jug during school hours, and he demanded and received a public trial. Acquitted triumphantly, he got a reception from the boys almost but not quite equalling the deafening approbation of his predecessor. The latter remains to this day the greatest hero the Baltimore Polytechnic has ever produced. The boys, I am told, still cheer him at football games, though they were not born at the time of his troubles, and many of them are the sons of men who were not then born.

If I had encountered a good teacher of chemistry at the Polytechnic, it is very probable that I'd be a chemist at this moment, with a swell job on the staff of the du Ponts and maybe a couple of new synthetic rubbers or super-cellophanes to my credit. My chief interest was always in organic chemistry, but the best that was offered by the gogue aforesaid was a childish high-school course in inorganic analysis, so I began, in a kind of despair, to work off my steam in literary endeavor. My early compositions, of course, were mainly in verse, for poetry is much easier to write than prose. During my last year in school I turned out many a fair set of dithyrambs, most of them in imitation of Rudyard Kipling, who had become my

adoration, and the rest in the old French forms that were favored by the literary movement of the nineties. I recall that at
one time, probably during my last year at the Polytechnic, I
resolved solemnly to write at least one poem a day, and that I
kept it up for several weeks. But it was more than a year after
my graduation before anything of mine ever got into print.
During my school days I nursed a flaming ambition to be admitted to the staff of the school paper, but I kept it to myself,
and was never asked to join by the politicoes who bossed such
things. As a sort of final blast at the gogues the boys of my
class concocted a satirical musical comedy, but though I wrote
a couple of lyrics for it I had no hand in the prose scurrilities
which made it a great success, and at the one performance I
was told off to play the piano. Some of the more tender gogues
were so outraged by the sneers at them that they talked boldly
of holding up several diplomas, but the old lieutenant with the
stable of lovely sweeties was still president, and he put down
his heavy quarter-deck foot upon the project.

I made a pretty good scholastic record during my four years
at the Polytechnic, despite my lack of interest in most of the
subjects it presumed to teach. In the literary branches I really
shined, and I found mathematics easy, though I disliked it. At
the end of my term of servitude there was a general examination for the purpose of awarding a gold medal offered by the
Alumni Association to the master scholar of the whole herd.
This award was made on the basis of the examination alone,
and classroom marks were not taken into account. The first
day was devoted to English, and I was passed at the head of my
class. The next day there was an examination in something else
that happened to be easy for me, and I passed first again. When
I got home with this news my father went into a state of mys-
tical exaltation, and then stepped out of it with an offer to give
me $100 in cash if I remained in first place at the end of the
examinations. This seemed a hard order, for there were subjects ahead—for example, electricity—of which I knew precisely nothing, but a hundred dollars, in those days, was a
fabulous fortune to a boy, and I resolved to make the attempt.
My experience with Uhrbrock, four years before, had taught
me something, to wit, that with hard application a subject that
engaged a class a whole year could be wolfed in a few days.

Favored by the fact that there was a free day between adjoining examinations, I gave it over to relentless boning up on the subject just ahead, and the result was, to make a long and painful story short, that I passed all the examinations and came out at the head of my class; indeed, I came out with a general average that has not been surpassed at the Polytechnic, so far as I know, to this day. Fortune, of course, gave me a good deal of assistance, for I was born lucky. When I came, for example, to the examination in electricity I discovered to my enchantment that the twelve questions on the paper all covered ground that I had traversed the night before, my nose in the book and the midnight oil burning. In consequence, my answers were perfect, and the amazed and disgusted gogue in charge of the examination had to give me a mark of 100. In addition to the alumni medal there was a special medal for the ranking scholar in electricity—and I had won it!

But giving it to me was something else again. The poor gogue, justifiably horrified, came out the next day with an announcement that monthly marks would be taken into account in awarding the medal, which would hand it over to a boy who really knew something about the subject. This seemed to me to be reasonable and fair, and I was glad to see him get it, but my father professed to be outraged and talked wildly of going into court for an injunction against the school board. It took me some time to argue him out of this, but in the end he calmed down, and when I brought him the news that I was to be allowed to make a speech at the commencement he forgot the matter. That speech must have been a dreadful thing, indeed, for I was still very young in those days, and had not yet acquired my present facility for rabble-rousing. But my father listened to it very politely, and he and his agents applauded it loudly when it was over. I was myself too elevated to be conscious of its badness, for his check for $100 was in the inside pocket of my tailcoat. It was not until I was approaching twenty-five that I ever earned $100 in one lump again.

V.
Finale to the Rogue's March
[1900]

WHEN I was disgorged by the Polytechnic I went to work
in my father's cigar factory, theoretically to learn the tobacco business, but *Geschäft* was not to my taste, and when my
father died in 1899 I quit at once and got myself a job as a cub
reporter on the old Baltimore *Morning Herald*, now extinct
and almost forgotten. At the start, of course, I was not entrusted with news stories of any importance, but simply served
as a leg man for my elders and betters. One of the first big
stories I thus helped to cover was the hanging of four blackamoors at the Baltimore City Jail. It was worth, by the standards of the time, two or three columns of space, so the
reporter assigned to it was a fellow of some esteem in the office, despite an unhappy weakness for drink. As for me, I had
no responsibility beyond getting the correct spelling of the attending ecclesiastics' names, taking down the last words (if
any) of the condemned, and inquiring into the undertaking
arrangements. But that programme was quickly blown up by
the fact of my senior's addiction to the so-called hand-set whiskey of the Baltimore printers, which kept him sound asleep in
the warden's office all the while the hanging was going on, got
him fired when we returned to our own office, and set me to
writing the story. The taste of the period, in all such branches
of composition, was for prose so colorful as to be virtually
purple, and I must have laid on my pigments with a shovel,
for the city editor gave me a very kind look when the proofs
came down, and I had first call on every similar assignment
afterward.

I found the work light and instructive, and there was plenty
of it to do, for a movement was afoot in my native Maryland at
the time to "hang out," as the phrase went, the whole criminal
population of the state, at all events in the higher brackets. The
notion that murderers, rapists and other such fiends in human
form were simply unfortunates suffering from mental croups

and catarrhs, and that the sensible way to deal with them was to send them to luxurious sanatoria, and there ply them with nourishing victuals, moral suasion and personality tests—that notion was still hidden in the womb of the future. The prevailing therapy was a great deal harsher: in fact, it came down from the rough-and-ready days of Leviticus and Deuteronomy, and its only recent improvements had been developed during the California gold rush. It consisted, in brief, in pursuing the erring with cops, posses and bloodhounds, putting them on trial before hanging judges, and then dispatching them as promptly as possible. As a young reporter I observed and recorded all branches of this *régimen*, and enjoyed them all. But I enjoyed especially the terminal part, for my lifelong interest in theology was already well developed, and it gave me a great kick to hobnob and palaver with the divines who comforted the doomed.

These divines, of course, were mainly Aframericans, for the great majority of culprits hanged below the Mason and Dixon Line were of that great race, but though it is usually thought of down there as somewhat backward I never saw any sign of professional incompetence in its pastors. On the contrary, they were almost invariably smart and snappy fellows, well grounded in the Sacred Scriptures and the masters of an adroit and effective homiletic technic. The job they had on their hands, in the normal case, was certainly no easy one. What they had to do was to convince a blackamoor taken red-handed in some brutal and deliberate atrocity, usually freely admitted, that he would nevertheless get a free pardon for it post-mortem, and in fact become an angel in Heaven, white in color and of the highest repute, within ten minutes of his exitus from this earth. There were, to be sure, parts of this that needed no arguing, for they were not disputed. Every colored brother in the death-house, like every colored person of his class outside, believed in Heaven and Hell, looked forward to a drum-head trial for his sins after death, and had an unshakable faith that, in case of acquittal, he would be turned into a Caucasian angel. But that was only the half of it, and what remained must have been a great deal harder to inculcate, for it collided with everything that the candidate had been taught by other clergymen his whole life long. One and all they had concentrated on the pains and penalties of Hell, and had warned him *appassionata* and *con amore* that he would be inevitably fried in its fires if he did not curb his evil propensities. But now, having yielded the last measure of devotion to those propensities, he was asked to believe that he would escape Hell altogether, and even meet with what amounted to special handling in Heaven.

It seemed irrational, surely, and not a few of the colored boys wrestled with it dismally for weeks and months. If things would actually be so facile and comfortable beyond the grave, then why all the horrible talk about the boiling sulphur and steaming geysers of Hell? And if Hell was a myth, then why ever be good at all, even in intent? Such were the questions the death-house divines had to answer, and how they answered them I can't tell you with any definiteness, though I often listened to their explanations for hours. They must have been experts at suggestion and virtuosi at untangling complexes, though both suggestion and complexes were unheard of at the time. All I can say is that, when the job was done at last, the client still retained his full faith in Hell, along with the utmost confidence in its system of justice, and yet was completely convinced that he would escape its fires. In his terminal days, in fact, he usually gloated openly over his approaching apotheosis, and not infrequently showed a certain smugness. Let the sheriff do his damndest: he might hang a poor coon, but out of that coon, like a butterfly from a caterpillar, would emerge a celestial creature with large, snowy wings and a complexion to match that of any white lady in the land, however rich and beautiful.

Such ideas naturally take away the sting of death, and it was not uncommon for the postulants to go to the gallows as jauntily as if they were going to a barber shop. I saw some who actually pranced—that is, to the extent that it was possible in their long black gowns, and with their arms tied behind them. When they had anything to say in their last minutes, which was usually, it was always of an extremely optimistic nature, and whenever they mentioned individuals by name—say the sheriff, the warden, the pastor, or a guard of the death-watch—it was in terms of praise. I recall one—it was on the Eastern Shore of Maryland—who devoted most of his farewell remarks to whooping up the jail cook, for the whole time since his trial

had been eased by fried chicken and hominy cakes three times
a day. Another even had a kind word for the Governor who
had refused to reprieve him, and expressed regret that his approaching translation would make it impossible for him to
vote at the coming election, in which the Governor would be
running for a second term. But mostly, of course, they talked
of themselves, for the glories that awaited them naturally en-
grossed them. I have never heard more eloquent descriptions
of the geography, social life and public improvements of Heaven
than some of those that were thus loosed by uneducated but
not untutored Aframericans upon audiences of newspaper reporters, professional jurymen, country constables and courthouse loafers.

There was, however, one exception to the general rule I have
set forth, and him I encountered in the city jail of Baltimore—
an ancient granite structure in the feudal style of architecture,
with crenellated battlements along the tops of its walls, and
accommodation in its death-house, in those days, for a dozen
head of condemned. It was a gloomy place, God knows, and
not all the colored theologians of Baltimore, working in eight-
hour shifts for weeks on end, could lift its darkness for the
unhappy blackamoor I speak of. For he had been, in his time,
a preacher himself, and though he had later turned apostate
and was now awaiting hanging for murdering a whole family,
he still retained his old talent for the sacred sciences, and especially for theological disputation. Thus he sassed back when
the death-house clergy began to operate on him, and in a little
while he had them completely flabbergasted. Unhappily, his
success against them was his undoing, for he retained, like any
other sane colored man, his full belief in Hell, and the more he
proved that their talk of his becoming an angel was hooey, the
more he convinced himself (and them) that he was headed for
the brimstone. This naturally upset him considerably, and as
the day of his departure approached he became more and more
alarmed. On the morning thereof he was in a really appalling
state. All he had to do, if he wanted to see a swarm of devils
with their pitchforks, was to shut his eyes. Even his appetite
left him, and he actually refused the magnificent breakfast that
was brought to him. He was to be hanged, if the sheriff was
not diverted by some other duty, at 10 A.M., and by 9.45 he

was making such heavy weather of it that the jail doctor, a very humane man, decided to give him a shot of morphine.

I was present when this shot went into his arm, and noted the dose—three grains. Inasmuch as a quarter of a grain is ordinarily enough to quiet a patient, and two grains enough to quiet him forever, it was apparent that the doctor was taking no chances. He watched with satisfaction, and I watched with him, the rapidly gathering effects of the drug. First the candidate ceased to moan and bellow, then his speech became thick, then his eyes began to roll, then he sat down on his bed, and then he looked at us blankly, apparently not recognizing us. The minutes, meanwhile, were ticking on, and the doctor himself grew uneasy. In fifteen more of them his patient would be blotto, and hanging him might present serious technical difficulties. Where was the sheriff? Why the delay? Just then a deputy came galloping from the warden's office with the news that the sheriff was on the telephone—an arduous business in those days—, trying to track down a rumor that the Governor had decided to grant the condemned a five-days' reprieve.

The doctor lost no time. He was in the warden's office in ten seconds, and back with the sheriff in half a minute. "Either you hang this coon at once," he roared, "or he'll die in your face! He has got enough morphine aboard to knock off an archbishop. Look at him! He doesn't know whether he is here or in Indianapolis, Indiana. In an hour he'll be dead. Get a hump on! Get a hump on! You were supposed to hang him at ten o'clock, and it's now ten six. Do you want to go to jail for contempt of court? Get a hump on! Get a hump on!"

The sheriff, in a panic, got it on instanter, and in two minutes the condemned was being half led and half carried down the corridor, his eyes rolling more and more and his head beginning to roll too. There was some difficulty about getting him up the steps of the scaffold, but a dozen jail guards leaped forward to help, and at ten o'clock, sixteen minutes and twenty seconds A.M. he went through the trap. His eyes were closed in his last moments and his knees were buckling, but not from fear. He had forgotten all about the Christian Heaven and Hell, and was neck-deep in the poppy Paradise of the Chinese.

After a colored undertaker had made off with the remains the sheriff finally got the Governor's office by telephone, and learned that the report of a reprieve had been a canard. The next day, encountering the jail doctor in a saloon, I asked him what he would have done if it had turned out to be true.

"I'd have made out a death-certificate," he replied calmly, blowing the foam off a schooner, "saying that he died of fright."

"But," I persisted, "you couldn't have signed it. You know the law: it provides that there must be a coroner's inquest after every death in jail, and that the coroner must sign the death-certificate."

"As for that," he replied, still calm, "the coroner and I have an understanding. We always coöperate professionally."

VI.

Notes on Palaeozoic Publicists
[1902]

IT IS the fashion today, in newspaper circles, to sniff at press-agents, and even to spit at them: in the *Editor and Publisher*, the trade journal of the daily press, they are treated as if they were lepers, or even infidels. That was certainly not my own feeling about them in the days when I had most to do with them, *circa* 1902. I had by then become what was called the dramatic editor of the *Morning Herald* in Baltimore, and one of my jobs was to receive the press-agents who traveled ahead of itinerant theatrical troupes, whooping up the genius of their stars. Nine-tenths of these brethren seemed to me to be very pleasant fellows, and some of them were so smart that they afterward made considerable splashes in the world, whether inside the bounds of the theatre or out—for example, Eugene Walter, Channing Pollock, the Wilstach brothers, Charles Emerson Cook, Bayard Veiller and Herbert Bayard Swope. Nearly all had been newspaper men in their time, and good ones. I cannot say that I was very generous about giving them space; on the contrary, I held them down to short commons, and often spoiled the little matter I printed by adding clownish glosses to it; nevertheless, I got on with them very well, and made some friendships among them that endure to this day.

In that remote era some of the primeval press-agents of the post-Civil War period still survived, and still wore the long-tailed coats, loud waistcoats and plug hats that had then gone with their art and mystery. The first agent who ever called on me, in fact, was of that already archaic company. He was at least sixty years old, and looked to me to be a hundred. His talk was all about Lotta, Maggie Mitchell, Charlotte Cushman, Mary Anderson and other such old-timers, though he was actually working for a young female star who, according to his story, had but lately escaped from a convent in Mauch Chunk, Pa. All his purple prose about her was done with a lead-pencil on large sheets of ruled yellow paper, for he regarded the typewriter as effeminate. Another elderly visitor who made a great impression on me was a splendid creature of the name of Marcus B. Mayer. He had been an opera manager in his day, and had carried over into press-agentry the uniform of that calling—a fur overcoat, a white waistcoat elegantly embroidered, and a gold-headed walking stick. What star he represented I forget, but I remember that he offered me no handout at all, but unloaded his encomiums of him (or her) *viva voce*, and left me to write my own advance notice. In it I limited the star to a few lines, and devoted the rest of my space to Marcus himself. The local theatre manager protested against this, but Marcus was rather pleased, and sent me a signed photograph of himself in token of the fact.

Of a different type was Punch Wheeler, who had come into the theatre from the circus, and affected the make-up of a Mississippi river gambler of 1875 or thereabout—a loud checked suit, a yellow waistcoat embroidered with roses, and a red satin cravat run through a diamond ring. A little while before this time Punch had been a manager on his own account, operating a fly-by-night opera company in what is now called the Drought Bowl. The star thereof was a Baltimorean named Jerome Sykes, who was later to become a favorite on Broadway. (His best rôle there was that of Foxy Quiller in the musical comedy of the same name: I can still hear his sonorous reading of its tag-line: "'Aha,' said Foxy Quiller, with a crafty leer!") When the company started out from New York for the Western steppes there was not enough money in the till to hire a chorus, so Punch had a dozen sightly kickers painted on the back-drop. Anon and anon he would duck ahead of the troupe to arrange its bookings, and in every town he would let the local Frohman name the opera to be played. If the Frohman said "Carmen" or "Il Trovatore" or "The Chimes of Normandy" he would bill the town accordingly, for he had picked up a stock of miscellaneous lithographs in Cincinnati, and was his own billsticker as well as his own advance agent. But no matter what opera was billed, Jerome and his four or five associates, when they got to the town, would sing "The Mascot," for that was the only opera all of them knew.

The audiences out in the sticks seldom protested, for most

of them were hearing their first opera, and the brisk, voluptuous tunes of "The Mascot" were very ingratiating. Nor did they object to the fact that the chorus was painted on the scenery, for they assumed that such was the custom in opera. Jerome had a loud voice, and made enough noise to give solid support to the female singers, who shrieked their damndest. The company thus did very well in the cow country, and Punch accumulated so much money that on one or two occasions he actually paid salaries. But when, having got to El Paso, he decided to dip over the Rio Grande into Mexico, he and his poor troupers came suddenly and dramatically to grief, for there was a law in Mexico in those days, passed to fetch phony one-ring circuses, making it a criminal offense to advertise an attraction and then not give it. Punch found out about it when Jerome and the company began to warble "The Mascot," for the Frohman at Juárez had asked for "Carmen," and that is what Punch had billed. In the middle of the first act the Mexican cops closed in, the audience (which knew every note of "Carmen") demanded its money back, and Punch, Jerome and the others were locked up in an adobe jug full of scorpions. Jerome, who knew "Carmen," got out the next day by singing the whole score, including the overture, the choruses, and even the soprano and contralto solos, to the chief of police, and a little while later the chief also turned loose the other singers, as innocent victims of the wicked Punch, but it took Punch himself a week or more to beat the rap, and cost him not only all his cash in hand, but also the costumes and scenery of the company, including the back-drop with the chorus painted on it.

I enjoyed his visit to Baltimore immensely, and gave him a good deal more space than his attraction—an "Uncle Tom" company working its way back to New York from the Deep South—was worth. There was nothing intellectual about him, but he was a very amusing fellow, with an endless saga of adventures in the cause of art. When I asked him, on getting acquainted with him, why he continued to wear his fire-alarm make-up, he said that he had got so used to it that he felt almost naked in ordinary clothes. Sometimes, when he hit a town where he wasn't known, the cops would take him for a three-card monte operator, and set a watch on him. Whenever

he noticed a couple of dicks trailing him, he would lead them
to the main street of the town, pull out a Bible, and begin
preaching salvation to the passersby. He was not, of course, in
earnest, but he told me that this satirical whooping of the
gospel often made converts, and that he figured he had saved
at least two hundred head of rubes from Hell. Once he actually
converted one of the dicks tailing him. Another time, somewhere in Tennessee, a committee waited on him to offer him
the pastorate of a new Baptist church. He got out of it by saying that he was under a vow to wear his checked coat and embroidered vest all the rest of his life, which wouldn't do, of
course, for an ecclesiastic, even in Tennessee.

　　The undisputed king of theatrical press-agents, in my time,
* was A. Toxen Worm, a Dane of circular cross-section, immense
appetite, and low humor. He usually dined alone, mainly because it was impossible to find anyone who could keep up with
his eating, or even watch it without swooning. One Sunday
evening, happening to be in Philadelphia, I encountered him
in the main dining-room of the Bellevue-Stratford just as he
was finishing dinner. In those days a dinner-check running
beyond $2 was almost unheard of in America, but I noticed
that Toxen's was for $6.70. Moreover, it included no charges
for drinks, for, as he told me, his kidneys were acting badly,
and he was transiently on the wagon. His last course, as I could
see by the debris, was a gigantic ice-cream sculpture covered
with spun sugar, of the kind served at wedding breakfasts.
Three waiters hung about him, panting. It was one of his quiet
Sunday evenings.

　　But if eating was his principal business in life, practical joking
was his recreation, and in his time he pulled off some masterpieces. In his own view, so he once told me, he reached his
all-time high in a joke at the expense of an English theatrical
manager named Hubert Something-or-other. Hubert was a
pleasant fellow, but not too bright: in appearance and manner
he came close to realizing what was then the average American's notion of a London clubman. He wore cutaway coats,
high Piccadilly collars and pants with bold stripes, and from his
neck hung a monocle on a wide black ribbon. His mind leaned
toward the literal side, and its operations tended to be deliberate. He was married for a time to a well-known American

actress, and accompanied her on the road as her company manager. One night, while she was playing at the Academy of Music in Baltimore, I met him in the lobby, and he began telling me an interminable anecdote about some friend of his—a man he described as one of nature's noblemen. But despite his admiration for the fellow, and their intimacy, he could not recall his name. Finally, he appealed to me for help. "You *must* have met him," he said. "Everybody knows him. He was Miss ——'s second husband, the one just before me."

One day Toxen met him in St. Louis, and found him in a low state of mind. He was homesick, it appeared, for London, and especially for its tranquil society. He tired of the wild boozing of America, and longed for the quiet stimulation of afternoon tea. "Don't worry any more," said Toxen. "I can fix it. How would you like to have tea tomorrow afternoon with a lovely lady and her five beautiful daughters—just the two of us—no mob?" Hubert thought it would be perfect, and the next day he arrayed himself in his best cutaway, bought a gardenia for his buttonhole, and, with Toxen steering, took a hack for the house. It turned out to be a fine old mansion in a quiet side street—somewhat decayed outwardly, to be sure, but very ornate inside. The parlor furniture was massive gilt, and there was a thick red carpet on the floor. Hubert liked his hostess instantly, and was delighted by her five daughters, all of whom seemed, rather curiously, to be of an age. Soon tea was served, and Hubert stood up to drink it, his cup and saucer in hand. The prettiest of the five daughters was in front of him, and he turned upon her his best tea-party chit-chat. She professed to be charmed, and moved closer and closer to him. Finally, she was so close that he took an involuntary step backward—and collided with the stern of her Mamma. "See here, you goddam son-of-a-bitch," roared Mamma, "what in hell do you think this is—a whore house?"

In telling the story, Toxen used to say that Hubert dropped cup and saucer, leaped into the hall, grabbed his hat and stick, and ran all the way back to the hotel. Toxen said that he had had to give the madame and the girls $20 for their entertainment, but declared that it would have been cheap at twice the price. Hubert, of course, said nothing, and after a while skeptics began to allege that Toxen had invented the whole story—that

nothing of the sort had ever happened. In order to lay this
doubt he reenacted the show in Philadelphia, with a couple of
witnesses invited. The witnesses swore that Hubert actually fell
for it all over, and in a large way. This time the madame not
only bawled him out, but also cracked a saucer over his head,
and the girls ganged on him with loud screams, and gave him
the bum's rush.

Toxen indulged himself in many other such jocosities as he
traveled the country ahead of theatrical troupes, and as time
passed, and his technic improved, they tended to become more
and more cruel. Once, in Louisville, he tipped the cops that a
fellow agent named Charlie Connolly was an absconding bank
cashier from Seattle, and Charlie spent a couple of days in a
very uncomfortable jail. Another time he hired a loose girl in
Buffalo to swear out a warrant against the most respectable
agent on the road, alleging seduction under promise of marriage, though everyone knew that the accused was completely
innocent. He did a heavy trade in bogus telegrams, most of
them of an alarming character. The Frohman brothers, Charles
and Daniel, had a brother named Gus who often went on the
road for them, and Toxen sent them frequent messages announcing that Gus was locked up for jumping a board bill, or
had married a chorus girl, or broken his leg, or committed
suicide. His schemes often showed a macabre flavor. He would
call up the cops, and tell them that there had been a murder in
some theatre, or he would recruit pallbearers for a man who
was still alive, or he would spread the story that a fellow agent
had been rushed to hospital with smallpox or delirium tremens.

All this went on for years, and there was naturally a considerable accumulation of soreness. In the end the boys combined
against Toxen, and resolved to give him a massive dose out of
his own bottle. The scene was Denver, and he fell quite easily,
for one of his weaknesses was vanity. Thus, when the manager of
a local theatre told him in confidence that a rich widow of the
town, observing him in the lobby, had got mashed on him he
saw nothing impossible in it, and when a note arrived the next
day, inviting him to call on her, he not only accepted, but began
to throw out hints about a conquest. It was quickly arranged
that he should wait upon her at her swell apartment on the top
floor of Denver's newest and most elegant apartment-house,

and he presented himself at the time fixed wearing his best party clothes, elegantly shaved and perfumed, and carrying a bouquet of orchids. When he rang the bell it was opened by a swarthy maid of gigantic size, and he was invited to enter. The instant he did so one of the boys, previously concealed in the hallway, rushed up and locked the door on him.

Toxen remained in that apartment for three days and three nights. It consisted of one small room, a bath and a kitchenette. The maid was an Indian of a mental age of six or seven years and knew only that she was to keep him from escaping, and dole out to him an occasional ham sandwich. There was no fire-escape, and the telephone wires had been cut. During the long watches of the night Toxen slept on the floor, and the maid snored in the kitchen. By day he spent his time trying to devise some means of escape, but he never managed it, for he was afraid to yell for help and the maid grabbed him and threw him every time he tried to pick the lock of the door. As a practical joke it was almost as successful as his own masterpieces, but as a lesson to him it was a complete failure. Two days after the boys liberated him he was busy once more with his bogus telegrams and his phony tips to the cops.

VII.

The Tone Art
[1903]

* WHEN IT was discovered by the music critic of the *Morning Herald*, a little while after I went to work as a cub reporter, that I could play the piano from the printed music and knew how many sharps were in the key of C major, he began borrowing me from the city editor to cover his third-, fourth- and fifth-string concerts, for he was not only a lazy dog but also had a sensitive ear, and it pained him to have to listen to the false notes so often struck at such affairs. As for me, I did not mind them, for my own playing, like Beethoven's, was pretty inaccurate, and my general taste in music was still somewhat low. I got no extra pay for this service, and indeed no allowance of time: all my regular work had to be done before I could go to a concert, and as a result I often arrived late, and heard only the terminal or Cheyne-Stokes tumults of the performers. But when a Summer opera company was in town, or Sousa's band, or anything else of that loud and hearty order, I usually managed to get, as the phrase then went, a larger load of it, even at the expense of missing two-thirds of a colored murder, or the whole of a Democratic ward meeting. During my first Summer I thus heard the whole répertoire of bad opera from "Cavalleria Rusticana" to "The Chimes of Normandy," not once but three or four times, and in the intervals of this caterwauling I dropped in now and again on half a dozen Italian bands.

These bands were then at the height of their popularity in the United States, and every trolley park had one. They all put on substantially the same programme every night, beginning with one of the more deafening Rossini overtures and ending invariably with "The Star-Spangled Banner," played a couple of tones above the usual key of B flat to show off the trumpets, for the Spanish-American War was only a few years in the past, and patriotism was still bubbling in the national heart. There were two great set pieces that were never missed: indeed, the audiences of the day would have set down an Italian band leader as a fraud if he failed to play them. One was the sextette from "Lucia di Lammermoor," done with all the trumpets and trombones lined up on the apron of the platform, and the other was the anvil chorus from "Il Trovatore," with a row of real anvils in the same place, and a series of electric wires so arranged that big blue sparks were struck off as the gentlemen of the percussion section clouted the anvils with real hammers. For this last effect, of course, the lights were always turned out. It had been invented years before, so I learned long afterward, by the celebrated Patrick Sarsfield Gilmore, the greatest of all American bandmasters, but by the turn of the century he was dead and forgotten, and the wops who worked his masterpiece all claimed credit for it.

They were, in fact, assiduous copy-cats, and whenever one of them hit on anything really new the rest imitated it at once. As a result it was hard to tell one Italian band from another. They not only played the same programme every night; they also wore the same florid uniforms, and their leaders all exhibited the same frantic gestures and the same barbaric haircuts. Any leader who, on coming to the coda of a Rossini overture, with its forty or fifty measures of tonic and dominant chords, did not throw his arms about like a maniac and contrive to make his back hair (it was always long and coal black) flap up and down like a loose hatch in a storm, would have seemed extremely strange. As a matter of record, no such leader was known to musical zoölogists—that is, not until I invented one myself.

This was in 1903 or thereabout, after I had been promoted to the office of dramatic editor. In that rôle, as I have said, I was in charge of all advance notices of musical and theatrical shows, and spent a part of every day receiving press-agents. One day a member of the corps dropped in to introduce, according to the custom then prevailing, a band leader who had just come to town, and the leader informed me, as usual, that he had written a Baltimore *Morning Herald* march and proposed to dedicate it to me as a tribute to my national and even international celebrity as a friend of sound music. This, of course, was an old gag, and it made no impression on me. Every Italian leader had a portfolio of dog's-eared marches that he renamed

after the principal papers of whatever city he happened to be
playing in, and dedicated to such members of the staffs thereof
as handled advance notices. I was thus not interested, for at
least six other *Morning Herald* marches had been dedicated to
me during my first few months in office. But there was something unusually attractive about this last imitator of imitators
of imitators, and after the formal ritual was over I invited him
to sit down, and asked him how the world was using him.

He was very young, and, as I could quickly see, not too sure
of himself. He had come to the United States, he said, in the
hope of getting a desk as a clarinetist in a first-rate symphony
orchestra, but he found that it was the prevailing theory among
the Germans who then conducted all American orchestras that
the only good clarinetists were either Frenchmen or Belgians,
and so he had been refused even an audition. He had thereupon joined an Italian band at $14.50 a week, and after a little
while the *padrone* who owned it, and a dozen others exactly
like it, had offered him the baton of one of them, at an advance, I gathered, to not more than $25. It was with this outfit
that he had come to Baltimore, and as we got on easy terms he
confessed to me that he greatly feared the competition of the
six or eight other bands then playing in town, for his own was
made up mainly of riffraff.

One of his tuba players, he said, could play only by ear, and
was in fact not a musician at all but a barber, and that very
morning at rehearsal it had been necessary to fire the second
snare-drummer, a Black Hander from Palermo, for trying to
disembowel a piccolo player with one of his drum-sticks. This
snare-drummer was now threatening to throw a bomb at the
opening concert. The only oboist in the band, who had to
double in the English horn, was naturally insane, for mental
aberration is almost normal among oboists, but he was worse
than the common run, for his lunacy took the form of trying
to blow the oboe and the English horn at once—a preposterous feat, of no practical use or sense. As for the six trumpet
players—the very sinew and substance of a brass band—, three
were red-ink drunkards, two were grappo addicts, and the
sixth had to wear a false moustache to throw off the police,
who suspected him of a trunk murder in Akron, O., and
wanted to sweat him.

The woes of this earnest young Italian aroused my sympathy, for I was young myself in those days and had many tribulations of my own. Unhappily, I could think of no way to help him against that crew of scalawags, for my experience of musicians had already gone far enough to convince me that there was no cure for their eccentricities. Every band leader in America had the same troubles, and also every orchestra conductor, even the most eminent. There was boozing in the Boston Symphony, and gang-wars were not unheard of at the rehearsals of the New York Philharmonic. He would have to take his band as he found it, and content himself with doing his level damndest: the Good Book itself said that angels could do no more. But there was still some chance of giving him help in the field of public relations, and I let my mind play upon the subject while he talked. Eventually I fished up an idea.

Why, I asked him, go on leading an *Italian* band? There were hundreds, and maybe even thousands of them, in the country, and they were all precisely alike, at least in the eyes of their public. Why not start out from the reasonable assumption that that public was more or less fed up with them, and proceed to give it something different? The professor pricked up his ears, and so did the press-agent, and my fancy began to flow freely. Why not have at the fortissimo fans with a *Spanish* band? Why not, indeed? The Spaniards, who had been fiends in human form only a few years ago, were now fast gathering popularity in the United States—a phenomenon that follows all American wars. Nothing had been too evil to say of them while they were butchering Cubans and Filipinos, but the moment Uncle Sam had to take over the job himself they began, in retrospect, to seem innocent and even humane. Spanish singers were returning to the Metropolitan Opera House, and American women were again wearing red and yellow, the Spanish colors.

The leader and his press-agent concurred after only brief hesitation, and soon we were engaged in preparing an announcement. The name of the band, it appeared, was to be the Royal Palace Band and Drum Corps of Madrid. Its leader was Lieut. José de la Vega of the Spanish Army, a son to the commander of the battleship *Vizcaya*, sunk by Schley at Santiago. The lieutenant himself had been present at that engagement as

chief bugler of the battleship *Infanta Maria Teresa*, and had
been blown overboard by one of Schley's shells, and then rescued by Schley's gallant jackies, and brought to Tampa and
nursed back to normalcy by a beautiful American nurse named
Miss Mary Smith, and had fallen in love with her and was
about to marry her. The press-agent, a competent craftsman,
thought of many interesting details, and even the leader, as he
heated up, made some useful contributions. When the question of language was adverted to he relieved the press-agent
and me by saying that he knew a few words of Spanish—*Cuanto?*
De quien es esta sombrero? Siento! La cerveza no es buena, and
so on—enough to fool Americans. So far as I was aware, there
was only one actual Spaniard in Baltimore, and he was a man
of eighty, floored by rheumatism. There were, of course, plenty
of Cubans and Porto Ricans, but none of them would speak to
a Spanish officer.

The scheme was launched the next week, and to the tune of
considerable friendly réclame in the local press. No one, to my
knowledge, detected the imposture, not even the critic of the
Baltimore *Sunpapers*, who was not let in on the secret. The
leader and his men wore the same uniforms that they had been
wearing all the while, and played the orthodox programme,
with the addition of the *habanera* from "Carmen" and "La
Paloma." The only real concession to verisimilitude was offered
by the press-agent, who had a large Spanish flag made and
hung it behind the band. At the end of the first half of the first
concert the large audience leaped to its feet and cheered, and
when the last note of the evening was played there was so vociferous a demand for encores that Lieut. de la Vega did "La
Paloma" twice more, the second time *pianissimo* with the
lights dimmed. During the intermission I encountered one of
the professors at the Peabody Conservatory of Music, and he
told me that he was greatly enjoying the evening. Italian bands,
he said, drove him wild, but the Spaniards at least knew how to
get decent sounds out of the woodwind. "If this fellow," he
said, "would sneak in four or five Italian trumpet players he
would have a really good band."

Unhappily, the innovation, though an artistic success, was
killed in its infancy by the Italian *padrone* who owned the
band. When he heard that it had gone Spanish he raised a

considerable pother, mainly on prudential grounds. If the
news ever got to Italy, he said, he would be disgraced forever,
and the Black Hand would probably murder his old mother.
Moreover, he was presently reinforced by the members of the
band, and especially by the gorilla moiety thereof. They demanded an immediate raise of $2 a week as compensation for
the infamy of being turned into Spaniards, and when it was
refused they took to sabotage. On the opening night of the
second week, when the time came to launch the first dose of
"La Paloma," the whole band began to play "Funiculi-Funicula"
instead, greatly to Lieut. de la Vega's astonishment and chagrin. There was, of course, nothing for him to do save go along,
but during the intermission he gave the performers a piece of
his mind, and they responded by threatening to plant a bomb
under his podium. Before the end of that second week the
band was demanding a raise of $4, and the *padrone* came to
Baltimore to make peace. The upshot was that in return for a
solemn promise to let his old mother in Naples live he burned
the Spanish flag, fired the press-agent, and ordered Lieut. de la
Vega to resume the style and appellation of Antonio Bracciolini,
which he had been before. A little while later the band gave
place to another from the same stable, and in the course of
time, I suppose, it succumbed to the holocaust which engulfed
all the Italian bands in America. I never heard from Lieut. de
la Vega-Bracciolini again. But now and then I got news of the
press-agent. He was going about the country telling newspaper colleagues that I was a smartie who deserved a kick in
the pants.

I got to know a good many other musicians in those days,
and found many of them pleasant fellows, though their ways of
life were strange. I well recall a talented lady pianist who came
to Baltimore for six seasons running, and each time brought a
new husband, always of a new nationality. The last that I saw
was a Turk, and afterward, so I have heard, she proceeded to a
Venezuelan, a South African Dutchman and a native of Monte
Carlo, but on that point I can't speak from personal knowledge. I also remember a French tenor who traveled with no
less than three wives, but that was before the passage of the
Mann Act. Two of them sang in the chorus of his company,
and while they were on the stage the third took care of their

and her own infants in the baggage-room. This company had
come up from South America, and carried on its affairs according to provincial Italian principles. Everything was sung in the
fashion of the sextette in "Lucia"—that is, with the singers in a
long row at the footlights. This was done even in the final agonies of "Traviata," with *Violette* dying of tuberculosis. As the
curtain fell the lady playing the rôle—she weighed at least 200
pounds—was lined up with *Alfred, Annina, Germont* and *Dr.
Grenvil,* howling *Gran Dio! morir si giovane!* (Great God! to
die so young!) in a voice of brass. One warm evening, approaching the opera-house somewhat late, I could hear the
screams of the polygamous tenor two blocks away. He was
throwing a lot of violent and supernumerary high C's, many of
them *sforzando,* into *Deserto sulla terra.*

I soon found that, among the instrumental players, the register of the instrument apparently had some effect upon the
temperament of the artist. The bull-fiddle players were solid
men who played the notes set before them, however difficult,
in a dogged and uncomplaining manner, and seldom gave a
conductor any trouble, whether by alcoholism or Bolshevism.
The cellists were also pretty reliable fellows, but in the viola
section one began to encounter boozers, communists and
even spiritualists, and when one came to the fiddlers it was
reasonable to expect anything, including even a lust to maim
and kill. So, also, in the brass and woodwind. No one ever
heard of a bassoon or tuba player saying or doing anything
subversive, but the trumpeters were vain and quarrelsome, the
flautists and clarinetists were often heavy drinkers, and the oboists, as I have noted, were predominantly *meshuggah.* Learning
these instructive facts, I began to have some sympathy with
orchestra conductors, a class of men I had hitherto dismissed
as mere athletes, comparable to high-jumpers, circus acrobats
and belly-dancers. I now realized that their lives were full of
misery, and when, a few years later, I became well acquainted
with a number of them, it seemed only natural to learn that
they were steady readers of Schopenhauer and Nietzsche and
heavy consumers of aspirin, mineral oil and bicarbonate of soda.

Indeed, my gradually growing familiarity with musicians
taught me many interesting things about them, and also helped

my comprehension of the general mystery of man. It did not surprise me to discover that a great many of them, in their professional capacity, hated music, for I was already aware that most bartenders of any sense were teetotalers and that some of the most eminent medical men at the Johns Hopkins Hospital took patent medicines when they were ill, but it *did* surprise me to find that this animosity to the tone art as a trade was often accompanied by a deep love of it as a recreation. I well recall my delight when I was invited by a Baltimore brewer to * a party at his brewery in honor of a dozen members of the Boston Symphony Orchestra, and saw them strip off their coats and fall upon a stack of chamber music that kept them going until 4 A.M. These men, all of whom were first-rate performers, had put in the early part of the evening playing a heavy concert, with a new tone-poem by Richard Strauss, bristling with technical snares, as its principal ingredient. They agreed unanimously that Strauss was a scoundrel, that his music was an outrage upon humanity, and that anyone who paid good money to hear it was insane. Yet these same men, after nearly two hours of professional suffering, now spent four more hours playing for the pleasure of it, and one of the things they played with the greatest gusto was Strauss's serenade in E flat for wind instruments, opus 7. All they got for their labor, save for a keg of beer to each man and the applause of the brewer and of the customers he had invited to meet them, was a hot inner glow, obviously extremely grateful. As I sat listening to them I could not help pondering upon the occult satisfaction that arises from the free and perfect performance of a function, as when a cow gives milk or a dog chases a cat. If the stars were sentient they would no doubt get the same kick out of their enormous revolutions, otherwise so pointless. These reflections, in some way or other, induced me to resume music myself, abandoned since my boyhood, and I was presently playing trios and quartettes with an outfit that devoted four hours of every week to the job—that is, two hours to actual playing and the other two to the twin and inseparable art of beer-drinking.

The members of this little club were all very much better performers than I was, and it puzzled me at the start to find them so tolerant of my inferiority. I discovered the secret when, after a little while, they took in a recruit even worse, for I was a good deal less pained by the dreadful sounds he made than cheered by his pious enthusiasm. In brief, he really loved music, and that was enough to excuse a great many false entrances and sour notes. I could stand him, at least up to a point, just as the rest could stand me, again up to a point. That club goes on to the present day, though I am the only survivor of the era of my own admission. It has included through the years some first-rate professionals and it has also included some amateurs hardly worth shooting, but they have got on together very amicably, and though they are now mainly elderly men, with kidneys like sieves, they still meet once a week, Winter or Summer, in war-time or peace-time, rain or shine. From end to end of World War I an Englishman sat between two Germans at every meeting, and in World War II a Czech has his place, and two Jews flank the Germans. What this signifies I refrain, on the advice of counsel, from venturing to suggest: in all probability it is downright unlawful. But there it is.

The club, in its day, has had some men of more or less note among its members, and there were times during its earlier stages when the question of honorifics presented a certain difficulty. Should a distinguished university, governmental or ecclesiastical dignitary be addressed by his simple surname or given his title? In the case of those who sat regularly the problem was soon solved in the Rotarian fashion by calling him Julius or Charlie, but when he came only occasionally it was got round by giving him a satirical lift. Thus a plain Mister became Doctor, a Doctor became Professor, and a Professor became *Geheimrat.* If there had ever been a colonel in the club we'd have made him a general, and if there had ever been an archbishop we'd have addressed him as Your Eminence or perhaps even Your Holiness. Once, when a baron sat in for a few sessions, we called him Count, and another time we promoted a judge to Mr. Chief Justice. The club has always had a few non-performing members, but they have been suffered only on condition that they never make any suggestions about programmes or offer any criticism of performances. The same rule has applied to occasional guests: they are welcome if they keep their mouths shut and do not sweat visibly when the flute is half a tone higher than the first violin, but not otherwise.

The club has never gone on the air or had its disturbances recorded on wax, but nevertheless it has done more than one
humble service to the tone art, and in the dark forward and
abysm of the future those services may be acknowledged and
even rewarded. For one thing, it has produced, from its composers' section, at least one peerless patriotic hymn, to wit, "I
Am a 100% American," by William W. Woollcott. This magnif- *
icent composition has everything. It is both chaste and voluptuous. It radiates woof and it reeks with brrrrrrr. I am frankly
tender toward it, for when the inspiration for it seized the
composer I had the honor of taking it down at the piano: he
was, at the moment, suffering from a sprained arm, and moreover, he plays no instrument save the triangle, and that only in
a dilettante fashion. A print of it exists and may be found in
libraries, but so far it has not got its deserts from the public.
Perhaps it will take a third World War or even a fourth to bring
it out. National hymns, as everyone knows, sometimes linger a
long while in the dog-house before they win universal acceptance and acclaim. Even "The Star-Spangled Banner" was formally adopted by Congress only a few years ago; indeed, it
outran "God Bless America" by hardly more than a neck.

But the greatest of all of Willie Woollcott's inspirations was
his plan to play the first eight Beethoven symphonies seriatim,
with only brief halts for refreshments between them. He omitted the Ninth only because the club's singing section, at that
time, lacked castrati, and in fact consisted of but two men,
both of them low, growling basses. We had excellent arrangements of the first eight symphonies, and after debating the
project for two or three years resolved at last to give Willie's
bold project a whirl. This must have been in 1922 or thereabout, when the club had the largest membership in its history,
including a great many bold and reckless men, some of them
aviators or ex-marines. Willie not only supplied the idea; he
also proposed to supply the scene—his house in a dense woods
near Baltimore, with no neighbors within earshot—and the
refreshments. It seemed a reasonable arrangement, and so we
fell to—at 4 o'clock of a Summer afternoon.

The First Symphony was child's play to us, and we turned it
off in record time, with a pause of only ten minutes afterward.
By six o'clock we had also finished the Second, and then we

stopped for cocktails and dinner. After dinner there was some relaxation, and we dallied a bit with some excellent malt liquor, so that it was eight o'clock before we tackled the Eroica. It began so badly that we played the first movement twice, but after that it picked up momentum, and by 9.30 we had finished it. Then we paused again, this time for sandwiches, a walk in the woods—it was a lovely moonlit night—and another resort to the malt, but at 11.30 or maybe a little later we were back in the trenches, and the Fourth was begun. For some reason or other it went even worse than the Eroica, though it actually makes much less demand on technic, and the clock must have been near to 1 A.M. when we decided finally that it had been done well enough. Our struggles with it had naturally tired us, so we decided to knock off for an hour and find out what the malt had to offer in the way of encouragement.

This hiatus, unhappily, was a fatal one, for when the time came to resume the hullabaloo it was discovered that two of the members had sneaked off for home, and that two more were so sound asleep that we could not arouse them without risk of hurting them. Thus the C minor was begun under unfavorable circumstances, and by the time it was over the band was reduced to what amounted to a mere fragment, and the four-hand piano was making so much noise that the other surviving instruments were barely audible. The Pastoral followed at once, but how it was done I can't say, for I fell asleep myself somewhere in the *scherzo*, and by the time Willie got me back on the piano bench the end had been reached and there was a debate going on about No. 7. It was now nearly 5 A.M., and the east was rosy with the dawn. One faction, it appeared, was in favor of giving up and going home; another insisted that a round of ham and eggs and a few beers would revive us enough to take us to the end. As to what actually happened there are two legends. The official story, inscribed by Willie upon the scrolls of the club, is that we tackled the Seventh, banged through it in circus time, and then dispatched the Eighth. A rump account says that we blew up in the middle of the Seventh, leaped to the Eighth, blew up again, and were chased out by our host, assisted by his hunting dogs. According to this rump account, but three performers were left at the end—the *primo* pianist, one fiddler and a man trying to play a basset-horn.

My own feeling is that in such bizarre matters precise facts are only intrusions. If we actually played the eight symphonies, then no other group of *Tonkünstler* has ever done it, on this or any other earth. And if we only tried, then no one else has ever tried.

VIII.

A Master of Gladiators
[*1907*]

IT ALWAYS amazes me how easily men of the highest talents and eminence can be forgotten in this careless world—for example, the late Abraham Lincoln Herford, manager of the incomparable Joe Gans, lightweight champion of the world. Even Joe himself, though he was probably the greatest boxer who ever lived and unquestionably one of the gamest, is mentioned only rarely by the sporting writers, and in his native Baltimore there is no memorial to him save a modest stone in an Aframerican graveyard, far off the usual lines of tourist travel. It may be that pilgrims occasionally visit it, but if so they have to use large-scale maps, showing every culvert and hot-dog stand. Joe's funeral was a stupendous event, with services running seriatim in three different churches, ten or twelve choirs moaning sad music, and no colored Baltimorean absent who could get the afternoon off and squeeze in, but since then the dead gladiator's fellow blackamoors have let his memory fade, and gone flocking after newer and lesser heroes. There is no Gans boulevard, avenue, street or even alley in the Harlem of Baltimore, and no Gans park. Some years ago I heard talk of raising a monument to Joe in Perkins Square, hard by his humble birthplace, with a marble effigy of him in ring costume on top of it, but the scheme faded out as all plans and projects among the colored people have a way of doing. If it is ever revived I hope to be invited to participate, for my admiration for Joe was high while he lived and has not abated since his decease. Specifically, I offer herewith to contribute $100 in cash money whenever a sufficiently reliable committee opens subscription books. By reliable, of course, I do not mean one certified by the S.E.C. or by a gang of colored pastors or gamblers, but one certified by the Baltimore cops.

* But if Joe was great, then Al Herford must have been great also, for he grasped Joe's genius when it was still occult to other men, and nursed it to flower with both skill and tenderness. Of Al's origins I know nothing, for I did not become acquainted with him until he was already well up in the world, and president *and* treasurer of the Eureka Athletic and Social Club. Under the laws prevailing in Maryland in those days, it was forbidden to give boxing exhibitions for hire, but any group of fans was free to form a club to stage them in private, and that is what the Eureka brethren did, with Al acting as their agent and adviser. Their meetings were held every Friday evening at the old Germania Maennerchor hall in Lombard street, and ran about three hours, with a fifteen-round bout at the end, usually between heavyweights. According to the by-laws of the club each member paid his weekly dues as he came in, and the rate for those who wanted seats near the ring was considerably higher than for those who were content to sit in the gallery. Al always opened the proceedings by reading the minutes of the last meeting. They described briefly the bouts that had entertained the members, and then went on to a technical commentary upon them, frequently of great acuteness. If there had been any distinguished new members present, say a party of Congressmen from Washington, Al recited their names, and bade them welcome to the club. At the end of the minutes he called for motions from the floor, and some member always moved that the club make up a purse and buy the president *and* treasurer a diamond ring or stick-pin. Al handed over the gavel, at this point, to Ernie Gephart, who was secretary and time-keeper of the club, but after the motion had been put and carried (as it was invariably, and unanimously) he returned long enough to announce that subscriptions might be paid to the doorkeeper on the way out.

Al never bored the members with financial statements, though he always stressed the *and* in "president *and* treasurer," for the by-laws made them virtually supererogatory. According to Article II all the money collected in dues went into a pot in the custody of the president *and* treasurer, and out of it he paid all the necessary expenses of the meetings—for example, for hall rent, announcements in the newspapers, stationery and postage, the fees of the sporty young doctor who served as the club's surgeon, and the honoraria of the pugs invited to exhibit their art. If anything was left over, which was usually the case, it was given to the president *and* treasurer, as a small return for

his services. This simple system worked beautifully, and had
the approval of the Baltimore cops. They came to the meetings
in large numbers, and were so well appreciated by the other
members that the doorkeeper, by a tacit but general understanding, always forgot to collect their dues. Sometimes, when
a couple of extra-fat captains were present at the ringside, Al
would have a little fun with them by announcing that they
would go on for six rounds at the next meeting. He also had a
line of spoofing for visitors from Washington, and did not hesitate to refer to the most puissant Senators, and even judges, by
their Christian names. The other members were delighted to
belong to a club which included so many illustrious men.
More than once I have sat at the ringside with a Senator or
Governor to either side of me, and two or three stars of the
Federal judiciary just behind.

Al was not only president *and* treasurer of the club, but also
its announcer, and his introductions always showed an exuberant fancy. When two colored flyweights were brought on for a
preliminary he presented them as Young Terry McGovern of
San Francisco and Young Joe Gans of Australia. Nearly everyone knew, of course, that they were actually water-boys from
the Pimlico racetrack, but the members liked Al's style, and
always professed to believe him. His humor was protean, and
never flagged. When two boys sailed into each other with unusual vehemence and the members began to howl, he would
signal Ernie Gephart to let the rounds run on, and whenever,
on the contrary, a bout was tame, he would cut them short. Once
I saw a set-to between two ferocious colored youths, Young
Corbett, of Yarmouth, England, and the Zulu Whirlwind, of
Cape Town, South Africa, in which the average length of the
five rounds, by actual timing, was twelve and a half minutes,
and another time I saw Ernie put through a flabby six-round
bout in ten minutes flat, with the pauses for wind, massage and
hemostasis included.

Al was very inventive, and many of his innovations stuck. He
was, I believe, the first announcer in Europe or America to call
the penultimate bout of an evening the semi-windup. I recall
that some of the more literate members of the Eureka Club
snickered at the neologism, and that I was brought up by it
myself. But in a little while it had swept the boxing world, and

it is now used without any thought of vulgarity by such purists as John F. Kieran and Grantland Rice. Al, a little later, began to call the second from the last bout the semi-semi-windup, and the third from the last the semi-semi-semi-windup, but these innovations never took, and he proceeded no further. He did not invent the battle-royal, but I believe it is only just to say that he greatly developed it. One of his contributions was the scheme of dividing the four boys into three very small ones and one very tall one: this favored a brisk entertainment, for the dwarfs always ganged on the giant and knocked him out, usually by blows behind the ear. Another of Al's improvements was the device of dressing the colored boys who fought in battles-royal, not in ordinary trunks, but in the billowy white drawers that women then wore. The blacker the boy, the more striking the effect. In all such massacres, of course, the scheme of holding back time on a good round was carried out. So long as the members kept on guffawing and hollering Al let the boys clout away.

Al, in his private life, was a very generous fellow, but in his character of president *and* treasurer of the club he kept a sharp eye on its funds. The standard fee for preliminary boys of no experience was $4, win or lose, but he seldom paid it without a struggle, which meant that he seldom paid it at all. Once, after a long evening marked by extraordinary carnage, I sat with him in his bureau under the stage while the boys came in to collect their money. I recall a pair of young featherweights who could barely stand up—Young Jeffries, of Honolulu, and Young Fitzsimmons, of Yale University. Both of Jeffries' eyes were blacked, his nose was only a squash, and he claimed that he had broken all five fingers of his right hand. The Yale boy had been used even worse, and when I entered the bureau the club surgeon was giving him a ticket to the free surgical clinic at the University of Maryland Hospital. They had fought six really terrific rounds, and the club referee, Jim O'Hara, had let them go on after the fourth only because he could not make out which was getting the worse beating. But Al conceived it to be his duty as treasurer of the club to challenge them, and challenge them he did. "What!" he roared. "Have you bastards the nerve to come down here and talk of money after doing a *brother* act? Do you think this place is a dancing-school? Back

to the Y.M.C.A., and fight with feather-pillows! I could sue
you in the courts. I could sick the cops on you. Never let me
see you again. Here [to Jeffries] is two dollars, and here [to
Fitzsimmons de Yale] is a dollar and a half. Now scram before
I get mad and kick you to hell out of here."

On this occasion, unhappily, Al went a shade too far, for the
next day he was waited on by Lawyer Melville W. Fuller Fineblatt, secretary of the Central Police Court Bar Association,
and forced to disgorge. Lawyer Fineblatt not only collected
the balance of the four dollars that was due to each boy under
the rules, but also three dollars a head for medical expenses,
and a fee of twenty dollars for himself. The alternative to cough-
ing up, he said firmly, would be a prosecution for violating the
laws against giving public boxing exhibitions, allowing smoking in a theatre, maintaining a nuisance, embezzling trust
funds, and contributing to the delinquency of minors. Al entered a long and indignant account of the episode in the minutes, and read it at the next meeting of the club, but when he
came to the statement that the boys had put on a fake some of
the members began to laugh, and he pursued the matter no
further. But he continued to labor it *in petto*, and nine or ten
years later, after public boxing exhibitions had become lawful
in Maryland and the Eureka Athletic and Social Club had with-
ered away, he was still talking darkly of having Lawyer Fineblatt
disbarred.

How much he made out of Joe Gans, first and last, I can't
tell you, for he kept his books in his hat, but I knew the man,
and am morally certain that he never collared more than fifty
percent, or maybe sixty percent, of Joe's earnings. If this seems
a large cut, then don't forget that many of the other pug managers of the time took seventy percent, and even eighty; indeed, there were some who took all, less enough, of course, to
victual their boys, and keep them housed and clothed. Joe's
own share was surely considerable, for when he retired from
the ring for the first of his fifteen times he had saved enough to
open a gaudy night-club in Baltimore—the first black-and-tan
resort the town had ever seen. To be sure, it blew up quickly,
* and Joe died in a low state, financially speaking, but nevertheless the money he lost had passed through his hands.

Al taught him a lot, not only about the business of boxing,

but also about the carriage and conduct of a professional man, and Joe became widely known as the most gentlemanly pugilist then on earth. His manners were those of a lieutenant of the guards in old Vienna, and many managers sent their white boys to him to observe and learn. When he was shoveled away at last, Al undertook the tutelage of a colored boxer named Young Peter Jackson, a heavyweight. Peter was an apt pupil, and soon became famous for his elegance. Unhappily, he lacked Joe's natural grace, and was in fact a squat, clumsy fellow with a coal-black hide and a shaven head. Once he made a tour of England under the eye of an English manager named Jolly Jumbo, and the sports were so delighted by his suave ways that, on his return to America, they chipped in money for a farewell present. Jolly Jumbo was deputed to select it. Forgetting Peter's depilated poll, he chose a set of gold-mounted military brushes.

Another of Al's protégés (in his announcements and harangues to the club he always pronounced the word pro-teege) was a heavyweight who shined for a brief season, but then took to heavy eating and lost his wind, and eventually got so dreadful a beating from Philadelphia Jack O'Brien that he retired from the ring and opened a saloon. I was present at his Waterloo, sitting with my knees touching the ropes, and remember it because of the poor fellow's extraordinary loss of blood, chiefly from his nose. Directly beside me sat Judge John H. Anderson, sporting editor of the *Morning Herald* and the first Harvard Phi Beta Kappa man ever to occupy such a position. The judge, who had got his title, not on the bench but at the race-track, wore a round beard *à la* James A. Garfield, and was extremely dignified and even formal in appearance and manner. I well recall his profane protests when the unhappy heavyweight's gore began to sprinkle his beard. He did not object to the rosin dust that overspread it at every meeting of the club, nor even to an occasional drop of blood, but when great gouts began to hit his foliage he set up a hell of an uproar, and if the heavyweight had not gone to the mat a little while later I have no doubt that he would have forced Al to stop the bout. When the Prohibition infamy hit the country in 1920 the heavyweight converted his saloon into a speakeasy, and was soon raided by Federal agents. The first jury acquitted him, for it was made up largely of members of Al's old club, and so did the second, third, fourth, fifth, sixth, seventh and eighth. But on his ninth appearance the district attorney took precautions, and he was duly found guilty and sentenced to three months in jail. While he was cooped there he was allowed to have his meals sent in from outside, and in a couple of weeks his gluttony had reduced him to such a state that he needed medical advice. He thereupon asked and was given permission to send for one of the visiting physicians of the Johns Hopkins Hospital—a very skillful and high-toned consultant. Simultaneously, he read in the Baltimore *Sunpaper* that his favorite niece, a pretty girl then in the foolish stage of her life, had been nabbed as a witness to a roughhouse in a rowdy suburban night-club. This smudge upon the honor of his house affected him deeply, and when the doctor waited upon him at the jail he was actually in tears. "My God, doctor," he moaned, "just think of it, just think of it! I been so ashamed to look anybody in the eye that for two days I ain't been out of my cell."

IX.

A Dip into Statecraft

[1912]

S OME TIME ago, in writing a book for the edification of the young, I let fall the remark that, in the now forgotten year of 1912, I was a candidate for the Democratic nomination for Vice-President of the United States. It is almost incredible that an author of my experience should have made such a slip. I must have been very well aware, even in the cachexia of composition, that the only effect of my statement would be to provoke a storm of snorts, and get me classed among the damndest liars on earth. That, indeed, is exactly what happened, and during the month after the book came out (it had a very fair sale) I received 30,000 or 40,000 letters full of hoots and sneers. Nevertheless, my statement was true in the most precise and literal sense, and I hereby reiterate it with my hand upon the Holy Scriptures. I was actually a candidate as I said, but I should add at once, before historians begin to rush up with their proofs, that I did not get the nomination.

Perhaps the best way to tell the story, which is mercifully brief, will be to start out with a cast of characters. Here it is:

The Hon. J. Harry Preston, mayor of Baltimore, and a man of aggressive and relentless bellicosity.

Charles H. Grasty, editor of the Baltimore *Sunpapers*, an enemy to Preston, and a sly and contriving fellow.

H. L. Mencken, a young journalist in the employ of Grasty as columnist and trigger-man.

Scene: Baltimore.

Time: The weeks preceding the Democratic National Convention of 1912.

That was the year when the late Woodrow Wilson was nominated and so began his dizzy rise to immortality. Grasty was for him, but Preston was against him and in favor of Champ Clark of Missouri. This difference was only one of hundreds that lay between them. They quarreled all the time, and over

477

any proposition that could be dissected into alternatives. If Preston, as mayor, proposed to enlarge the town dog-pound, Grasty denounced it in both morning and evening *Sunpapers* as an assault upon the solvency of Baltimore, the comity of nations, and the Ten Commandments, and if Grasty argued in the *Sunpapers* that the town alleys ought to be cleaned oftener Preston went about the ward clubs warning his heelers that the proposal was only the opening wedge for anarchy, atheism and cannibalism. It was impossible to unearth anything against Preston's private character, though every *Sun* reporter, under Grasty's urging, made desperate efforts to do so, for he was a respectable family man, a vestryman in an Episcopal church with a watchful rector, and a lawyer of high standing at the bar. But in his rôle of politician, of course, he was an easier target, and so his doings in the City Hall were gradually assimilated (at least in the *Sunpapers*) to those of Tweed in New York, the *ancien régime* in France, and the carpet-baggers in the South.

Grasty, on his side, was vulnerable in the reverse order. That is to say, he could not be accused of political corruption, for it was notorious that he had no political ambitions, but in his private life there was more encouraging material, for several times, in the past, he had forgotten himself. The dirt thus dredged up was gradually amalgamated into the master charge that he had been run out of Kansas City (where he formerly lived) for a series of adulteries of a grossly levantine and brutal nature. This charge Preston not only labored at great length in his harangues to the ward clubs; he also included it in his commencement addresses to the graduates of the Baltimore high-schools and his speeches of welcome to visiting Elks, Shriners, Christian Endeavorers and plumbers' supply dealers; moreover, he reduced it to writing, signed his name to it with a bold flourish, and printed it as paid advertising in the *Sunpapers* themselves.

The revenues from this advertising were gratefully received by Grasty, for the *Sunpapers*, in those days, were using up almost as much red ink in the business office as printer's ink in the press-room. But against that pleasant flow of the wages of sin there had to be set off the loss from the municipal advertising, which Preston, though a Democrat, diverted to a Republican paper. It took him a long while to clear it out of the

Sunpapers, but clear it out he did at last. Any City Hall functionary who, by force of old habit, sent in an announcement of a tax sale or a notice of an application to open a hat-cleaning parlor was fired forthwith and to the tune of loud screams of indignation. To meet this devastating attack the whole staff of the two *Sunpapers* spent half its time in concocting reprisals. No story against Preston was too incredible to be printed, and no criticism too trivial or irresponsible. If the blackamoors in the death-house at the Baltimore City Jail had signed a round robin accusing him of sending them poison in cornpone or snuff, it would have gone into type at once.

My own share in this campaign of defamation was large and assiduous. In my daily column on the editorial page of the *Evening Sun* I accused Preston of each and every article in my private catalogue of infamies. Once I even alleged that he was a Sunday-school superintendent—and was amazed to discover that it was true. I had nothing against him personally; on the contrary, I was fond of him, thought he was doing well as mayor, and often met him amicably at beer-parties. But in his character of enemy of Grasty, and hence of the *Sunpapers*, I was bound by the journalistic code of the time to deal him a lick whenever I could, and this I did every day. On some days, in fact, my whole column was devoted to reviling him. Why he never hit back by accusing me of adultery, or, at all events, of fornication, I do not know, but no doubt it was because he was too busy amassing and embellishing his case against Grasty.

The plain people of Baltimore naturally took his side against the *Sunpapers*. They are always, in fact, against newspapers, and they are always in favor of what reformers call political corruption. They believe that it keeps money in circulation, and makes for a spacious and stimulating communal life. Thus they cheered Preston every time he appeared in public, and especially did they cheer him every time the *Sunpapers* published fresh allegations that he and his goons, having made off with everything movable in the City Hall, were beginning on the slate roof and the doorknobs. This popularity had a powerful effect on the man himself, for he was not without the vanity that afflicts the rest of us. He began to see himself as a great tribune of the people, ordained by God to rescue them from the entrapments of a dissolute journalism, by libel out of crim.

con. More, he began to wonder if the job of mayor of Baltimore was really large enough for his talents. Wasn't there something grander and juicier ahead? Didn't the Bible itself guarantee
that a good and faithful servant should have a reward? What
if the people of Maryland should decide to draft the man who
had saved the people of Baltimore, and make him their Governor and Captain-General? What if the people of the whole
United—

But this last wayward thought had to wait until, early in
1912, the Democrats of the nation decided that Baltimore should
be their convention city. Preston, as mayor, had a large hand in
bringing the party national committee to that decision. He not
only made eloquent representations about the traditional delights of the town, especially in the way of eating and drinking;
he also agreed to raise a fund of $100,000 to pay the costs of
the show, and made a big contribution to it himself, for he was
a man of means. During the Spring the wild fancies and surmises that were devouring him began to emerge. One day the
Republican paper getting the city advertising suggested that he
would make a magnificent candidate for the Vice-Presidency,
the next day he received hundreds of spontaneous letters and
telephone calls from his job-holders, urging him to accept the
plain call of his country, and the third day his campaign was
in the open, and throwing out dense clouds of sparks and
smoke. It soon appeared that he had an understanding with
Champ Clark. Clark had already rounded up a majority of
the delegates to the coming convention, but he needed more,
for the two-thirds rule still prevailed. Why couldn't the Baltimore gallery, packed and fomented by Preston, panic enough
waverers to give Clark the nomination? It seemed an enlightened trade, and it was made. If Preston delivered the goods
and Clark became the standard-bearer, Preston would have
second place.

It was at this point that Grasty conceived his hellish plot,
and the rest of the story is soon told. Under the presidential
primary law then on the books in Maryland every candidate
for the Presidency who itched for the votes of the state's delegates had to file his name "before the first Monday in May"
preceding the convention, and with it deposit $270 in cash
money. Under the same law candidates for the Vice-Presidency

lay under the same mulct. If no candidate submitted to it, the
state convention was free to instruct the delegates to the national convention to vote for anyone it fancied, but if there
were two who had paid up it had to make its choice between
them, and if there was but one it had to instruct the delegates
to vote for him. The agents of Wilson, Clark and all the other
contenders for first place on the ticket had entered their ap-
pearances and paid their fees, but no candidate for the Vice-
Presidency had been heard from. Preston, of course, knew the
law, but he was a thrifty fellow and saw no reason why he
should waste $270, for he figured with perfect plausibility that
he would be the only aspirant for second place before the state
convention.

Grasty's sinister mind grasped this point a day or two before
I was sailing for Europe on a holiday. Summoned to his office,
I sat enchanted while he unfolded his plan. It was to wait until
the very last minute for filing names of Vice-Presidential candidates, and then rush an agent to Annapolis, properly equipped
with $270 in cash, to file *mine*. "Go back to your office," he
instructed me, "and write a letter of acceptance. Say in it that
you are sacrificing yourself to save the country from the menace of Preston. Lay it on with a shovel, and take all the space
you want. To be sure, you'll be in the middle of the Atlantic
when the time comes, but I'll send you a wireless, so you'll
know what to say when the New York *Herald* reporter meets
you at Cherbourg. The joke will wreck Preston, and the shock
may even kill him. If he actually shoots himself I'll tone down
your statement a bit, but write it as if he were still alive and
howling. Imagine the scene when the state convention is forced
to instruct the delegates to the national convention to vote for
you! Here is the law: read it and laugh. It is really too rich,
especially this point: the delegates to the national convention
will have to vote for you *as a unit* until 'in their conscientious
judgment' you are out of the running. That may not come until
days and even weeks after the convention starts. All the Wilson
men will throw you votes to annoy Clark. Now get busy with
your letter of acceptance before I laugh myself to death."

On the fatal evening I was aboard ship in lat. 50 N, long. 15 W,
gulping down beer with my traveling companion, A. H. McDannald, another *Sunpaper* man, and keeping a sharp lookout for a

page-boy with a radio envelope. McDannald was in on the plot, and helped me to itch and pant. We got through beer after beer—one, two, three, six, ten, *n*. We wolfed plate after plate of sandwiches. We returned to beer. We ordered more sandwiches. The hours moved on leaden feet; the minutes seemed to be gummy and half dead. Finally, we were the only passengers left in the smokeroom, and the bartender and waiters began to shuffle about pointedly and to douse the lights. Just as darkness closed in on us the page-boy came at last. He had two messages for McDannald and three for me. Both of McDannald's read "Sorry to have missed you; bon voyage," and so did two of mine. The third read: "Everything is off. Say nothing to anyone."

It was not until I got home, four weeks later, that I found out what had happened. Grasty, it appeared, had been so taken by the ingenuity and villainy of his scheme that when he went to the Maryland Club the next afternoon for his daily ration of Manhattan cocktails he couldn't resist revealing it—in strict confidence, of course—to one of the bibuli there assembled. I should say that the bibulus was normally a very reliable man, and carried in his breast a great many anecdotes of Grasty that
* Preston would have given gold and frankincense to hear, but this time he was so overcome by the gorgeousness of the secret that he took a drop too much, and so blabbed. This blabbing was done in the sanctity of the club, but Preston had his spies even there. Thus, when Grasty's agent appeared at the office of the Secretary of State at Annapolis, at the very last minute for filing names, with $270 in greenbacks held tightly in his fist, it was only to find that Preston's agent had got there two minutes before him, and was engaged with snickers and grimaces in counting out the same sum.

I thereby missed my purple moment, and maybe even immortality. Now that the facts are before a candid world, let the publicists of the *Nation*, the *New Masses* and the *New Republic* speculate upon the probable effects upon history—nay, upon the very security and salvation of humanity—if Grasty's scheme had worked. I offer them the job without prejudice, for no matter how powerfully their minds play upon it their verdict will be only moot. It was not until years later that I discovered that the Constitution of the United States, Article II, Section

1, provides that no person shall be eligible for the Presidency, and *pari passu* for the Vice-Presidency, "who shall not have attained to the age of thirty-five years." On that July day of 1912 when the Hon. Thomas R. Marshall of Indiana got my job I was precisely thirty-one years, ten months and twenty-three days old—and the Constitution was still in force.

X.

Court of Honor
[*1913*]

ONE OF the oldest of legal wheezes is to the effect that no man should sit as judge in his own case. You will find it in the "Sententiae" of Publilius Syrus, written in the First Century B.C., and it must have been ancient when Publilius lifted it—as he lifted everything else—from some forgotten Greek. In all the years since his time no one, so far as I can discover, has ever ventured to dispute it. It is one of the few propositions that Leftists and Rightists agree on, and even judges on the bench—or, at all events, those among them who give their dismal trade any thought at all—speak well of it. But is it really true? Sometimes I find myself in doubt, just as I sometimes find myself in doubt that two and two are four, or that Jonah actually swallowed the whale. Especially do these wayward misgivings beset me when my memory plays with a case of extra-legal adultery that I became privy to in New York City in the year 1912. In that case one and the same man was not only both judge and complainant, but also prosecuting attorney, yet the verdict that he handed down was fair, equitable and just, and the sentence that he pronounced was notably humane.

Needless to say, he was not a common or dirt judge, deteriorated and debauched by years of listening to lying witnesses and nefarious lawyers. He was not even, in fact, a man of any learning in the law: he was simply a theatrical manager, and even more ignorant than most of them are. He kept an office in the heart of the theatrical district, but most of his revenues came from what was then called the sticks. If he had a success on Broadway he thought of it only as a means of extracting money from the people beyond the two rivers. Any run of more than forty nights was enough to start him off. He would flood the provinces with propaganda whooping up the play as the greatest hit since "The Two Orphans," and in a few weeks he would follow that propaganda with a series of road companies, all of them outfitted with frantic press-agents and inflam-

484

matory billing. The press-agents he selected with care, mainly from among men who had had circus or bicycle-race experience, and the billing he wrote and designed himself, but to the casting of his companies he gave only casual attention, for it was his firm conviction that the provinces could not distinguish between geniuses and hams, and indeed were more apt to be pleased by hams than by geniuses. Whenever he was preparing a fresh assault upon them he would send in an order to a theatrical agency for so many head of bucks and so many head of wenches (this is how he always spoke of his hirelings) and in a little while rehearsals would be under way. But now and then, of course, he picked up a performer in some other manner—say through a letter of introduction from a theatre manager in Anniston, Ala., or Xenia, O., or a rare crash of his office trenches and pill-boxes.

This last happened in the case of the lady who was the culprit in the trial I am about to describe. She hailed from Nebraska, and had got her early training in a company playing "The Fatal Wedding" under canvas. When the rough travel and bad eating in the Western wilderness began to tell on her, she threw up her job and headed for New York. She had $375 in her stocking—the savings of two years of hard work—, and with this to sustain her she took a modest room in the forties and began a siege of the Broadway agents and managers. My friend's office was on her daily route, but it was a long while before he ever saw her, or even heard of her, for his office boy chased her out every time she showed up. This happened in all the other offices also, and she began to be uneasy, for her money was fast disappearing. One morning, after my friend's office boy—a gigantic lout who, in these days, would be called a gorilla—had been especially unkind to her, she burst into tears and dropped into a chair by the door to have her cry out. My friend, happening to come in at that moment, was struck by something or other in her appearance, and, being in a benignant mood, invited her into his private office to talk it over. The net result was not only a job, but also a love affair. In brief, my friend got mashed on her, and within a week she had moved from her meagre lodgings in the forties to a comfortable apartment in the fifties, and had a large outfit of new clothes, with a fur coat to top it off.

But though she was properly grateful, and told everyone she met (including me) that my friend was a prince and had a heart of gold, she still itched for the stimulation of the footlights, and in a little while she began agitating for a part in one of the road companies. My friend was not averse to giving her a chance, for he believed that she was probably bad enough, professionally, to please the provinces, but his feelings toward her were still very tender, and he was loath to be separated from her, maybe for four or five months. Presently he solved the problem by organizing a company to play one of his recent forty-night sensations in towns close to New York. The farthest it would get, according to the route laid out, would be Scranton, Pa., and during a large part of its tour, so he hoped, it would be playing at a dollar-top neighborhood theatre in Brooklyn. The girl was accordingly given the job of leading woman, and after two weeks in Pennsylvania and New Jersey, was safely anchored in Brooklyn for the run. This arrangement, for a while, was satisfactory to all parties at interest. The girl spent her days, save when there were matinées, on Manhattan Island, kept her clothes at the apartment in the fifties, and usually, though not always, returned there after the evening's performance in Brooklyn.

My friend, after the opening, never looked in on the company, for he was a very busy man, but he had a spy who visited it at intervals and reported on anything amiss—say, too much boozing by the company manager or some unusual butchery of the lines by the actors. One day, during the fourth or fifth week of the Brooklyn run, this spy came in with very unpleasant news. It was to the effect that the leading lady was carrying on injudiciously, not to say feloniously, with the leading man. They visited each other's dressing-rooms far more than they had any need for, and several times they had been detected in prolonged strangle-holds behind the back-drop. On the evenings following matinée days, when the girl, on the score of fatigue, remained in Brooklyn overnight, they disappeared together and were never seen by the other members of the company. The spy, as in duty bound, shadowed them on such an evening, and found them ducking into the leading man's quarters at a third-rate hotel. My friend was naturally upset by this report, but he had some suspicion of his spy, and so borrowed another one from a brother manager, and sent him to Brooklyn to check up. This second spy made the same report precisely. The girl was thereupon ordered to report in New York at 11 o'clock the next morning to stand her trial.

I was not, of course, present at this proceeding, but my friend described it to me at great length the next time I was in New York, and I am sure that he gave me a reasonably accurate account of it, for he was a truthful fellow, despite his business, and he had a special confidence in and kindness for me, for I was the only dramatic reviewer in America, save only Stuffy Davis of the New York *Globe*, who had never tried to sell him a play. He said that the girl appeared at his office promptly, and declined his offer to let her have counsel. Instead, she made a complete confession, instantly and without urging, and in it went much further than either of the spies had alleged. It was quite true, she said, that she and the leading man were carrying on as alleged. It had begun, in fact, before the end of the first week in Brooklyn, and it was still in progress. Moreover, she refused flatly to make any promise of an abatement, either then or thereafter, though she admitted freely that her conduct was clearly immoral.

My friend told me that this confession not only shocked him, but also greatly astonished him. He had, of course, heard "Rigoletto" and hence knew that women were mobile, but here, it seemed to him, mobility had quite run amuck. The insult to his vanity he could bear, for he was a philosopher, but the puzzle that went with it really racked him. Why on earth should a girl apparently sane engage in any such degrading and irrational malpractises with an obscure and ignominious actor, a cheap clown in a No. 5 road company, a mere ham? Why should she turn from a salient and even (in her world) distinguished man and take up with so grotesque a nonentity? My friend, who had no false modesty, told me that he put the question to her plainly. On the one side, he reminded her, was himself—a fellow of large means and generous impulses, a figure of consequence on Broadway, her tried friend and benefactor, and last but not least, a man who wore expensive and well-cut clothes and was commonly conceded to be of imposing presence. On the other was that wretched ham—a poor fish who would never get beyond the lowest rounds of his

profession and was doomed to penury all his life long; moreover, a grotesque figure in his cheap and flashy garments, with
a hair-cut that no he-man would tolerate, a ring on his finger
set with a bogus diamond, a preposterous walking-stick, and a
complexion that inevitably suggested (when his make-up was
washed off) both inebriety and malnutrition. What had become of the boasted sagacity of the female sex? How could any
woman abandon and betray so upstanding and admirable a
man as my friend and make off with that hideous caricature?

She had, it appeared, an answer ready. She had pleaded
guilty, but nevertheless she was not without a defense. She did
not deny the tremendous disparity between my friend and the
actor. On the contrary, she admitted it freely, and even added
that it was greater than had been represented. "I am here to
tell you honestly," she said to my friend, "that you are the most
elegant man I have ever met. No one could be more attractive
to a sensible woman. You are rich, generous, smart, celebrated
and handsome. I love to hear you talk, and I even like to see
you eat. You have treated me better than a queen. When I put
you beside that ham it really makes me laugh: compared to you
he is a rat beside a hippopotamus. But"—and she paused a bit,
as an actress would, to drive the point home—"but you are
here in New York, rolling in your glory—and I am out there in
the wilds of Brooklyn, alone and forlorn, trying to get that
terrible play over to great gangs of smelly idiots.

"Have you ever tried to figure out what that means to a refined woman? Can you imagine yourself making up in a damp,
drafty dressing-room night after night, and then going out on
that creaky stage and speaking the same lines over and over
again to those blockheads? No; I thought not. But that is what
I have to do, and, believe me, it is no easy job. Sometimes I
make such a mess of my performance that I burst into tears at
every exit. Well, every time I do that there is that ham standing
in the wings. He comes up to me, puts his arms around me,
and says 'You are wonderful tonight, darling! I watched you
fascinated. You really moved me.' Do I swallow it? Naturally
not. I know that I have been lousy,[1] but there he is waiting for

[1]This term was still a novelty in 1912, even on Broadway. It came in toward
the end of 1911.

me, to tell me that I haven't. Let me say to you that such words are music to the ear of a woman. They fetch us every time. Maybe, if it had been anywhere else but Brooklyn I might have pulled myself together and given that ham a clout over the ear, but the first time he tried me it was pouring down rain outside and the audience smelled like a cat-show, and so I fell for it. After that he had me. I knew it was crazy, but I simply couldn't resist. He never had anything to say about himself: it was always *me, me, me*. He had me acting rings around Nazimova. He got me so that when I looked in my dressing-room mirror I saw Lillian Russell. So that is my story, and you can take it or leave it."

My friend told me that it took him no more than a minute to reach his decision; he had formulated it, in fact, before the girl finished her speech. As friend, as philanthropist, as man, he was injured, outraged—but as psychologist he was hooked and landed. What answer, indeed, could he make to the girl's argument? He could think of none whatsoever. His verdict simply had to be self-defense, and his sentence was so mild that it amounted to a parole: he bade her return to Brooklyn and try to avoid the ham as much as possible. He even let her keep the apartment in the fifties, though in view of the circumstances he had his own belongings moved out by his spy the next morning.

XI.

A Roman Holiday
[*1914*]

MOST OF my traveling, whether by land or by sea, has been done on business, and in consequence there has usually been a good deal more hard labor in it than *dolce far niente*. For twenty years on end I had jobs as a magazine editor in New York but kept my home in Baltimore, which meant that I had to make the round trip every couple of weeks, and sometimes oftener. These journeys, if I had been able to look out of the train windows, would have made me minutely familiar with all the scenery along the two hundred miles, but as it was I always had to keep my nose buried in manuscripts, and seldom saw anything save an occasional sash-weight factory or cow, glimpsed vaguely out of the corner of my eye. When this servitude ended, at the beginning of 1934, I employed a statistician to figure out how many words I had read during the twenty years, but when his report came in it was so full of plus and minus signs and unintelligible gabble about skew distributions and coefficients of correlation that I threw it away in disgust, and fell back on my own bare-hand guess, which was 50,000,000 words. My longer journeys, before, during and after the same time, were made principally for newspapers, and save when I contrived to get myself lost were even worse, for they were punctuated day and night by telegrams from managing editors reading "Where is your second follow lead?", "Please call in between 11.30 P.M. and 11.40 Eastern Standard Daylight Time," or "Your story differs from the A.P. in the following particulars. . . . Please confirm or correct." All the reporters that I traveled with got the same telegrams, and not infrequently, when I received an especially outrageous one, I would change the address on it and pass it to one of my colleagues. Unhappily, the other boys and gals resorted to the same trick, with the effect that on a bad night I was bombarded with remonstrances from managing editors stretching from San Diego to Boston. No one, of course, save a greenhorn or a lunatic ever answered such messages, but nevertheless they were irritating, and after reading them for a couple of weeks I was almost in a mood for the plunge into delirium tremens that they had been accusing me of, usually only covertly but sometimes in plain English, all the while.

But there were a number of times when I threw off such chains, and traveled for the pure deviltry of it, and it is such trips that I always remember most vividly when I am laid up with rheumatism and try to forget it in memories of my dead life. Of all those unofficial or illicit journeys, the one that I recall with the most pleasure is a jaunt in reverse along the route of the classical Grand Tour of Europe, made in the Spring of 1914 in the company of two Baltimore friends, W. Edwin Moffett and A. H. McDannald, the latter my companion on a previous pilgrimage, already mentioned in Chapter IX. Moffett is now a bull-fiddle virtuoso of such wizardry that I have actually seen and heard a symphony concert audience rise up and cheer him, and McDannald has gone so far in learning that he is the editor-in-chief of an encyclopedia, but in 1914 they were both simple fellows out for a gaudy time, as I was myself, and we unquestionably had it in Italy, Switzerland, Germany and France, not to mention the Atlantic Ocean and the Mediterranean Sea. We made the eastward ocean trip in a second-string Cunarder called the *Laconia*, one of the first of the so-called tour-ships. It was slow but very comfortable, and when we left New York we looked forward to nine lazy days to Gibraltar. We planned to spend them in the smokeroom, for all three of us believed that the glare of the sun on deck was deleterious, and had tried to put away temptation by making a pact to hire no deck-chairs. This, of course, got the deck-stewards down on us, but the bar-stewards were very polite and assiduous, and it was generally understood before we reached Nantucket light that one of the best corners in the smokeroom was ours. But our dream of crossing the ocean in peace and comfort did not last much longer, for on the first day out the usual pests got together to form the usual committees, and there\after we were beset day and night by women selling tickets to concerts, chances on raffles, or knitted neckties made by inmates of the Sailors' Orphans' Home at Liverpool, or worse still, trying to wheedle us into going to mask balls, joining in folk-song

festivals, or making speeches. Moffett put off these harpies for
a few days by pointing to his right ear and bellowing "Deef!
Deef!" and Mac pretended that I was a homicidal maniac and
he my keeper, but the gals quickly got on to these subterfuges,
and settled down in brutal earnest to fetch us.

We were, however, tough guys in those days, and as incredible as it may seem we actually came into sight of the coast of
Portugal without going to a single dance, concert, raffle, spelling-
bee, debate, sing-song or mass-meeting, and without contributing a single nickel to any home for decrepit sailors, or their
(probably illegitimate) offspring, or their deserted wives, or
their sorrowing old fathers and mothers, from the Orkney islands to Capetown. Every time the smokeroom stewards saw
us throw off another solicitor they set up the drinks on the
house, for, as they told us, it was unprecedented for a male
passenger in the Cunard to escape his inevitable doom for such
a stretch of time. Many, of course, held out for a day or two,
and a few extraordinarily recalcitrant curmudgeons stood it for
three days, or even four, but never since the *Britannia* sailed
from Liverpool on July 4, 1840 had anyone ever survived so
long as a week. This happy state of affairs prevailed until the
night before we made Gibraltar, and we attained to such eminence aboard that not a few other passengers, escaping momentarily from whatever horror was afoot, came to the
smokeroom door to gape at us and admire us. But after dinner
that evening the massed committees of the ship's company
combined to assault and rout us, and after an all-too-brief and
far from glorious struggle we were had.

I need not add, I hope, that it was not argument that took
us, nor anything properly describable as an appeal to our better
nature: it was simply the use of female pulchritude, and in the
rawest and most unsportsmanlike fashion. Hitherto all the ladies who had tackled us had been mature and even more or
less overripe damsels of the sort who naturally take to good
works, whether on land or sea. The worst of them came close to
looking like members of the W.C.T.U., and even the best, when
they were not plainly retired opera singers or cashiered stock-
company actresses, carried about them a faint, sickening suggestion of Christian Endeavor. But now all that orthodox but
puerile technic was out of the window, and the master-minds of

the committees, laying their heads together, were trying us with a new and far sharper excalibur. In brief, they rounded up the three rosiest, sweetest, triggest, archest, sauciest and all-round charmingest cuties in the ship, and set them on us as a pot-hunter might turn a pack of bloodhounds upon a poor fieldmouse. We had never seen these cuties before, for they had spent all their time dancing in the social hall, and our own station, as I have said, had been in the smokeroom, but now, as they bore down upon us with pretty giggles, we got a massive eyeful, and in ten seconds we were undone. Nor did we recover when they began unloading the selling-talk that the committeemen had prepared for them. What they wanted us to do, they explained ever so alluringly, was to squire them to a mock wedding that was presently to be staged in the dining-room, which had been cleared for the occasion. They were to appear at this mock wedding in the character of bridesmaids, and we were to be ushers. No rehearsal, they assured us, would be necessary. So far as our own participation was concerned, it would be a wedding like any other, and if occasional prompting turned out to be necessary they would supply it, at the same time hanging on to our arms. All the speaking parts were in other hands. *Allons*, comrades, the audience waits! Moffett, with a faint blush for the smokeroom stewards who glared reproachfully from behind their bar, offered his arm to a blonde who looked like Lillian Russell at the age of seventeen, Mac grabbed a little brunette who seemed to be of mixed Russian, French, Spanish, Algonquin and angel blood, and I was left with a red-haired girl so lovely that when I looked at her I saw only an explosion of rubies and amethysts.

Thus we were bagged, and thus we marched ignominiously to the dining-room, each hanging on to his Delilah. A large company of poor fish was already assembled, and the chief bore of the ship, a loud, officious, Rotarian-sort of fellow, was planted under an arch of British flags in the low comedy rôle of the officiating clergyman. Presently the ship's bugler blew five or six measures of the "Lohengrin" wedding march, the bride and groom marched in from the pantry, the best man and chief bridesmaid fell in behind them, and Moffett, Mac and I, with our trio of palpitating pretties, took up the rear. Of the bride I can only recall that she was a fair specimen of run-of-the-mine goods, and of the bridegroom only that he looked considerably alarmed. Later on I heard that the bride actually had her eye on him, and that they became engaged while visiting the grave of Percy Bysshe Shelley at Rome. But on that point I have only rumor, and moreover, it is irrelevant. What I remember most clearly, and indeed with a sort of dizzy dazzle, is the marriage service that the Rotarian began to read. It opened as follows:

Dearly beloved, we are gathered here together in the face of this company to join together this man and woman in asceptic matrimony, which is commended by Mendel, Ehrlich, Metchnikoff and others to be honorable among men, and therefore is not to be entered into inadvisedly or carelessly, or without due surgical precautions, but reverently, cleanly, sterilely, soberly, scientifically, and with the nearest practicable approach to chemical purity.

And so on, and so on. The audience, at first, was astonished into silence, but in a little while a few women began to titter, and soon there were snorts all over the room. The three cuties took it very merrily, and mine gave me more than one dig in the ribs with her incomparable elbow. Meanwhile, the Rotarian boomed on in roaring tones, calling upon the bridegroom to say so plainly if he were suffering from any "lesion, infection, malaise, congenital defect, hereditary taint or other impediment," and finally commanding him to produce medical certificates or forever hold his peace. At this, the bridegroom took a long envelope from his inside pocket and handed it to the Rotarian, who broke its seal in a very ceremonious manner, withdrew a paper fluttering a red ribbon, and proceeded to read from it as follows:

We, and each of us, having subjected the bearer to a rigid clinical and laboratory examination, do hereby certify that, to the best of our knowledge and belief, he is free from all disease, taint, defect, deformity or hereditary blemish. Temperature *per ora*: 98.6. Pulse: 76, strong. Respiration: 28.5. Wassermann: minus two. Phthalein: first hour, 46 per cent; second hour, 21 per cent. White blood corpuscle count: 8,925. Free gastric hydrochloric acid: 11.5 per cent. No stasis. No lactic acid.

By this time the dining-room was in an uproar, and the three cuties seemed to be on the point of busting with laughter. I was somewhat amused myself, and, in secret, delighted, but I was even more astounded, for *I had written that wedding service myself.* Yea, I had not only written it, but printed it, to wit, in the *Smart Set* for October 1913, pp. 63 *ff.*[1] Thus I listened to the Rotarian's somewhat sketchy and ruffianly version of it with all the fascination that enthralls any dramatic author when he sees his own play on the stage, and while the thing was going on I gave scarcely a thought to the throbbing virgin at my side. Nor did Mac pay any attention to his delectable brunette, for he had read the piece in the magazine and knew that I had written it. When the show was over, to great salvos of huzzahs at the end, the three cuties deserted us for their regular platoons of beaux, and we resumed our pews in the smokeroom. It may be that the Rotarian, in one of his innumerable bulletins and speeches to his suffering fellow-passengers, had given proper credit to the author, but if so we heard nothing of it, and Mac, who was a *legum baccalaureus* of the University of Virginia and full of lingering Confederate warlust, was all for suing him in the courts for infringement of copyright. This seemed a bad idea to me, for the copyright had been taken out, not in my name, but in that of the *Smart Set,* and anything we recovered from the Rotarian would go to John Adams Thayer, then the proprietor of the magazine. Inasmuch as Thayer was already very well heeled, I could see no sense in engorging him further, but Mac insisted that important principles were at stake, and also conjured up a number of interesting questions of law. Could we sue the Rotarian in Gibraltar, where we were due to land the next morning, or would we have to wait until we got back to New York? Furthermore, wasn't the Cunard Steamship Company responsible, as *particeps criminis,* and if so couldn't we proceed against it in admiralty, libel the *Laconia,* hang up the tour, and expose the ship to hundreds of claims for damages to the other passengers? Mac had no law-books with him, and in fact had not looked

---

[1] It was entitled A Eugenic Wedding and was signed Owen Hatteras, a *nom de plume* I used in those days whenever my monthly contributions to the *Smart Set* were so numerous that they could not all be published under my own name. With the title changed to Asepsis: A Deduction in *Scherzo* Form, it was reprinted in my Book of Burlesques; New York, 1916.

into one since he took his degree in 1898, but he kept on laboring the matter until the smokeroom stewards turned out
the lights on us at 3 A.M. and we had to go to bed. The next
morning, after we had landed on the Rock and were getting
down *Humpen* of bicarbonate of soda in its only drug-store,
he resumed the subject, but as the bicarbonate began to open
the pores of his mind he forgot it, and after that I heard no
more from him about it. Whether or not the Rotarian really
lifted my play without credit I do not know to this day. If he
did, then I forgive him belatedly and wish him good luck in his
chosen career, whatever it may be.

A few days later the *Laconia* reached Naples and we went
ashore through the barrage of bumboats, broken-down steam-
launches and other such crazy craft that once made a riot of
that lovely port. The depth of water at the docks was then insufficient to float an ocean steamer, and passengers had to be
ferried in row-boats. These row-boats were operated by members of the Black Hand, and they hated one another almost as
much as they hated humanity in general. Thus getting to land
was a more or less hazardous business, for the instant a passenger appeared at the gangway all the Black Handers for a block
around began to fight for his business. Nor was the battle over
when one of them got him, for the rest proceeded to ram the
victorious boat, and to prod both its operator and its passenger
with their oars. It was very uncommon for a passenger to get
ashore without being doused, and not infrequently he lost his
baggage. On the quay he went through another similar maul-
ing, for the customs-house red-caps, all of them gorillas brought
in from the penitentiaries of Sicily, fought for him just as the
boatmen had fought for him. It is a literal fact that it took Ed,
Mac and me two hours to get through the customs, though
we had nothing to declare and the actual officials were very
polite. All the delay was caused by our porters, who had to
fight for us from the moment they collared us until they finally
landed us on the street. This fighting, of course, was not done
in silence. The screaming and howling, in fact, were even worse
than the jostling, and by the time the three of us got to our
hotel in the Via Caracciolo we were pretty well worn out.

This, of course, was before the days of Mussolini, and Italy was still innocent of efficiency engineering. Exactly twenty years later, in 1934, I returned to Naples, again by sea. I was aboard a German liner of at least twice the tonnage of the *Laconia*, but it tied up at a dock with the greatest ease and even elegance. Looking ashore, I could see nothing of the frantic Black Handers of 1914. At the far end of the dock a long row of taxicabs was lined up, and between them and the ship stood four or five men in uniform. Whenever a passenger went ashore one of these functionaries approached him politely, asked him if he required a taxi, whistled for one if he said yes, and then put him aboard it with a deep bow. There was no more uproar than you will hear in the middle of the Mojave Desert, and not the slightest sign of excitement. Going ashore for a little walk, I seemed to be in a city that had died and been embalmed. Where were the sellers of dirty postcards that had swarmed over Ed, Mac and me in 1914? Where were the loud and urgent guides to Pompeii, to the art galleries, to the bawdy-houses? Where were the hawkers plastered with lottery-tickets? Where was all the old-time hullabaloo? Alas, it had gone with the wind, and a Fascist calm prevailed. After walking for a while I came to a little square, and there, across the grass, I saw an evil-looking youth who took me back twenty years. He saw me too, and began to approach me in a stealthy, furtive way, pausing anon to glance back over his shoulder. If any human being ever had seller of dirty postcards written on his face it was that unappetizing young wop, and I halted to give him a chance to make his sales approach. I was not, of course, in the market for his wares, but I yearned to hear him for old time's sake. But when he was not more than fifteen feet from me he stopped suddenly, stared over my shoulder like a pointer become aware of a quail, turned white with an unearthly greenish cast, and then made off to starboard with long, nervous, skulking strides, and vanished into the shadows of an alley. As he disappeared I about-faced to find out what had alarmed him. Half a block away I saw a perfect simulacrum of Benito Himself—an obvious plain-clothes man in the Fascist béret, his legs planted firmly, his arms folded in authoritative challenge, an imitation of the Mussolini frown upon his face. Such were the hazards of an innocent and industrious dirty-postcard vendor under the New Order in Italy.

Such was life in sterilized and dephlogisticated Naples, once so gay with iniquities and stinks. Such, I reflected sadly, was human progress.

But in 1914 Naples was still as free and natural as it had been in the days when its bristling walls scared off Hannibal. Its main streets had not been swept since the Sixteenth Century, and in many of its alleys there was an accumulation of garbage going back to Roman times. Ed, Mac and I had a grand time exploring its marvels and devouring its garlicky and excellent victuals. One day we went out to Capri and got lost among its vineyards, and another day we hoofed the ruins of Pompeii and were introduced by a friendly guide to an antique factory adjacent, where we saw the workmen turning out Roman bronzes by the gross, all plainly marked 200 B.C., to reassure tourists. At night we would resort to the Galleria Umberto and listen to the singing contests going on there all the time. We had two large rooms at our hotel, with a magnificent bathroom adjoining, including a shower. On the morning after our arrival I arose before the others, and went to this bathroom to take a bath. First I soaped myself from head to foot and then I got under the shower and turned the handle. But no water came out. Seeing a small stool in a corner, I mounted it to investigate, but I could not solve the mystery, and soon the soap got into my eyes and blinded me, and I had to call for help. Mac responded by beating on all the pipes with the heel of one of his shoes, but the more practical Ed went to the telephone and called up the office. The clerk below, it appeared, could not understand English, and Ed's Italian was far from perfect. While I tried to mop off the soap with a towel ten feet long I could hear him roaring into the 'phone: "Da wat' no come in da pipe! Da dam machina no worka! Senda da chief engineer dam quicka!"

In a few minutes there was a rap at the door, and Mac admitted a chambermaid. She was armed with a broom, a bucket, a mop and various other apparatus, and turned out, fortunately, to have a few words of German, so I soon explained to her, clad in that mainsail of a towel, what was wrong. She was an efficient woman, as efficiency ran in Italy in those days, and instantly fell to work. First, she turned on the water full tilt— but it still refused to flow. Then she put the stool into the tub,

mounted it, withdrew a large hairpin from her hair, and proceeded to investigate the sprinkler. The first hole she tackled
turned out to be solid with rust, but she managed by hard
gouging to coax a drop of water out of it. Encouraged, she
turned to a hole in the center of the sprinkler, and gave it a
sudden and powerful jab. There was a large scab of rust inside,
apparently covering half a dozen holes. When this scab gave
way it gave way all over, and as a result she got a rush of water
squarely in the eye, and went over backward, yelling blue murder. The scene followed the most austere lines of classical farce;
in fact, it was worthy of Billy Watson's Beef Trust. Ed, Mac
and I whooped and roared in our vulgar mirth, but when the
lady became bellicose we threw her out, and I resumed my
bath. When we shoved off for Rome the hotel's bill showed an
item of two lire for repairing the shower, but Mac threatened
suit and we got away without paying it.

We arrived in Rome late at night, and after taking a walk and
a couple of drinks rolled into the hay. The next morning we
were up bright and early, and on our way to St. Peter's. There
we put in two or three hours admiring its wonders, especially
the immense *pissoir* on the roof—the largest in Europe—, and
by noon we found ourselves in the alley between the cathedral
and the Vatican, thumbing through postcards at a stand there
set up. While we were so engaged an American we had met on
the ship strolled up, and the four of us decided to lunch together. But before we could set off for an eating-house we
noticed a group of people gathered about a priest a little farther up the alley, with the priest haranguing them violently. It
seemed worth looking into, so we approached the group and I
noted that the priest was talking German. From his remarks it
quickly appeared that his customers were pious pilgrims from
Vienna, that they had been forty-eight hours in day-coaches
on the way—I could well believe it by their smell—, that they
had an appointment to be received by the Pope, that the time
set was only a few minutes hence, and that their pastor was
giving them a last-minute refresher course in Vatican etiquette.
Over and over again he explained to them the stage management of a papal audience, and cautioned them to behave in a
seemly and Christian manner. They would be lined up on their
knees, he said, and His Holiness would walk down the line,

blessing them as he went and offering them his ring to kiss. Under no circumstances were they to attempt to kiss his hand, but only the ring. "Nicht die Hand!" he kept on repeating. "Küsst den Ring!" Nor did he stop with this brief, almost military order: he also went into the considerations lying behind it. What a scandal it would be, he said, if the illustrious Pope of Rome, the spiritual father of the whole universe, were exposed in his own almost sacred person to the lewd osculation of the vulgar! What an insult to His Holiness, and what a source of obscene joy to the vast hordes of infidels! His ring was provided as a means of warding off any such calamity. It, and not his hand, was to be kissed. "Nicht die Hand, Kinder! Küsst den Ring!"

So saying, he signaled the pilgrims to follow him. As they moved over toward a door making into the Vatican I looked at Mac, Mac looked at Ed, Ed looked at the stranger from the *Laconia*, and the stranger looked at me. Why not, indeed? The group was large enough for us to be lost in it, and the pilgrims seemed to be of very low mental visibility. As for the priest, he was marching ahead of them, with his back to them and us. We therefore ducked among them, and in a minute we were marching down one of the long corridors of the Vatican, headed for the audience chamber. I expected to see a large hall elegantly turned out, with maybe a couple of pictures by Raphael or Leonardo on its walls, but the priest actually led us into a series of modest rooms that looked like parlors in a bourgeois home. They were arranged *en suite*, and the Pope, I gathered, would traverse them one after another. The priest was in the room nearest His Holiness's entrance, but when he issued a command that we fall on our knees it was relayed down the line, and we all obeyed. Mac kneeled to my left and Ed to my right and beyond Ed was the stranger. We waited patiently, but in some uneasiness. What if we were detected? Would the Swiss guards who stood at every door simply throw us out, or would it be a matter for the police? We had not long to suffer, for in a minute there was a murmur in the room beyond us and in an-
* other minute the Pope was passing before us, holding out his ring to be kissed.

He was Pius X, born Sarto, already an ancient man and beginning to break up. From the floor where we kneeled he looked tall, but I doubt that he was so in fact. His skin was of a startling whiteness, and he stooped from the effects of a large swelling at the back of his neck—not, of course, a goitre, but of the same general dimensions and aspect. As he came into our room, preceded by a chamberlain and followed by two guards, an ormolu clock on the marble mantelpiece struck twelve. He moved slowly and with effort, and appeared to be almost unaware of his visitors, though he held out his hand for the kissing of his ring, and smiled wanly. Save for the whispered words of his blessing he said nothing, and neither did any of the pilgrims. He had been Pope, by now, for eleven years, and was close to eighty years old. A man of deep piety and simple tastes, he had resisted, back in 1880, an effort to make him Bishop of Treviso, but a few years later he had been caught by the cogs of the Roman escalator and by 1893 he was the Cardinal Patriarch of Venice and ten years later he was Pope. His reign, alas, had not been any too peaceful: there had been struggles with France, turmoils among the Italian bishops, and all sorts of vexatious disputes—about the powers and jurisdictions of the Papal courts, the text of canon law, the nomination of bishops, the reform of the breviary and of church music, and so on without ceasing. He looked immensely old as he passed so slowly before us, and pretty well worn out. But he walked without help, and in less than two minutes he was gone. This was in May, 1914. Two months later a shot was fired at Sarajevo in faraway Bosnia, and on August 2 World War I began. His Holiness survived that blasting of all his hopes of peace on earth by less than three weeks. On August 20 he was dead.

Once he vanished, Mac, Ed, the stranger and I made tracks out of the room, for we feared that the priest might come back and discover us. Without anyone to guide us, we got lost at once, and were presently astonished to find ourselves in the Sistine Chapel. It was quite empty, and we hid there for ten minutes—long enough to throw off the scent. Then we tried the first long corridor that offered, and at its end found a door * which took us out into the glare of noontime Rome. A horse-hack was waiting nearby, and in it we rode grandly to our hotel. There was a large assemblage of *Laconia* passengers in the dining-room, and some of them asked us where we had been. When we replied that we had been undergoing the

honor of an audience with the Pope there were sniffs of incredulity, and mingled with that incredulity there was not a little
hostility. Some of those other passengers were pious Catholics
come to Rome for the express purpose of paying their respects
to His Holiness, but when they had gone to the American
College that morning to apply for an audience they had been
told that it would involve a great many onerous formalities and
probably a long wait. So many applications were piled up, in
fact, that the best the clergy at the college could promise, even
to a ninth-degree Knight of Columbus and his lady, was a
possible look-in some time in July. Actual bishops, it appeared,
were hanging about for weeks before their numbers turned
up. Moreover, all the lay applicants were warned that their
appointments, if, when and as obtained at all, would be for
designated weeks, not for specific days, and that they might
have to stand by from end to end of those weeks, the men in
boiled shirts and tail coats and the ladies in black gowns with
long sleeves. If, at the moment of their summons, they were
not so arrayed, they would miss their turns, and maybe have to
wait three months before they were called again.

All of this, naturally enough, had filled the pilgrims with
unpleasant sentiments, and they were in no mood to listen
with any appreciation to the tale of our own exploit. It was already very hot in Rome, and they could well imagine what it
would be like in July or August to sit in unventilated hotel
rooms for a week on end, clad in boiled shirts and long sleeves.
At the start, they eased their minds by denouncing us as liars of
unparalleled effrontery, but as we added various details in
support of our narrative, they had to admit that we were probably telling something more or less resembling the truth, and
thereupon they took refuge in the theory that our uninvited
visit was not only an insult to the Pope, but also a carnal and
blasphemous attack upon Holy Church itself, and upon the
True Faith that it inculcated. The Knights of Columbus present were all too old and bulky to hope to beat us up, but they
talked darkly of employing Black Handers for the purpose, and
even hinted that they knew a Jesuit who could supply the Black
Handers. We replied primly that there was a lawyer in our
outfit, and that if any such threats were carried out he would
know how to launch the secular law upon all persons responsi-

ble. This seemed to daunt the knights, who had a high reverence for the police of all nations, and they gradually subsided into mutterings about the impertinence of Protestants, and, even worse, of infidels, and the need of laws barring them from the capital of Christendom. All we could reply to that was that Teddy Roosevelt and William Jennings Bryan were both Protestants, and that Thomas Jefferson had been an infidel. It was a somewhat feeble argument, and we did not press it. In consequence, the debate gradually petered out, and when we left at last the knights and their ladies had gone back to discussing the discomforts of boiled shirts and long sleeves in hot weather.

Having now seen both St. Peter's and the Vatican and enjoyed the distinction—whether honorable or infamous—of having been received by the Pope in private audience, we decided that we had given enough time to Rome and its environs, and the next day we set out for Munich by the Brenner Express. We had an instructive and somewhat noisy time in that beautiful city, but for the purposes of the present narrative what we saw, heard and did during our visit is neither here nor there.

XII.

Winter Voyage
[1916]

IN THE closing days of 1916, having been hired by a news-paper to investigate the war raging in Europe, I sailed from New York in a Danish ship, and seventeen days later found myself in Copenhagen. It was a slow trip, even for war time, but my recollections of it do not have to do with its duration, but with two relatively minor details: (*a*) the excessively mixed and belligerent nature of the ship's company, and (*b*) the stupendous eating and drinking that went on aboard. Nearly every nationality that I had heard of up to that time was represented among the passengers, and each *bloc* hated and reviled all the others. It did not surprise me, of course, to find the Germans and French on somewhat distant terms, or the Poles and Austrians, but I was certainly amazed when it turned out that the Danes, Norwegians, Swedes and Finns were bitter enemies, each to the other three, that the only Scotsman refused to speak to the Englishmen, and that the French actually joined the Germans in contemning and excoriating the Italians.

* At meals I sat at the doctor's table, with a Russian general in the place of honor at the other end. This general, who wore stupendous Hindenburg mustaches, glared at his trough-fellows through breakfast, lunch and dinner, and refused either to speak to them or to answer them when they spoke to him. The theory arose that he probably knew no language save Russian, so a Czech who spoke it was brought up from the second cabin to tackle him. The general, for perhaps five minutes, took no notice whatever, but the Czech was a persistent fellow, and finally dredged a single sentence out of those fearful mustaches. He reported that it was a profane declaration, *in Russian*, that the general could not speak Russian. How he talked to his adjutant, who sat beside him, I do not know, for they exchanged only grunts at meals, and between meals they disappeared.

All during those intervals, I suppose, the general slept in his cabin, for it is hard to imagine anyone keeping awake after the gargantuan feeds he got down. Certainly they never ran to less than 45,000 calories apiece, not counting bread, butter and the sugar in the coffee. Well do I recall his breakfast on the first day out, for it was a rough morning, and most of the other passengers at our table confined themselves to toast and tea. But not the general. He began with three oranges *au naturel*, followed them with a large plate of oatmeal swimming in cream, topped it with a double order of ham and eggs, and then proceeded to run through all the Danish delicacies on the table—six or eight kinds of smoked fish, as many of sausage, a bowl of pickled pigs' ears, another of spiced lambs' tongues, a large slab of Gjedser cheese, and five or six slices of toasted rye-bread spread with red caviare. To wash down this mammoth *frokost* he drank four cups of coffee and two of tea. When he finished at last a couple of waiters rushed up to help him to his feet, but he shook them off, arose with the dignity of Neptune emerging from the sea, and stalked away in his best parade-ground manner. His adjutant, following at a respectful six paces, wobbled precariously, for the ship was doing a forty-degree roll, but the general was still as perpendicular as a meridian of longitude when he disappeared down the corridor to his quarters.

By lunchtime the weather had moderated considerably, and all hands at the table were ready for earnest eating, but the general was in full form by now and managed to grab so much of everything that there was little left for the rest of us. He was aided in this enterprise by the fact that the rules of the Danish merchant marine in those days—and, for all I know, the constitution of Denmark—ordained that everything after the soup should be brought to the table on large platters and passed round. This passing round, of course, should have started with the ship's doctor at the head of the table—an old man in a long beard, and himself, as it soon appeared, no contemptible glutton—but the waiters had to come in through a door that was just behind the general's chair, and he thus got first whack at them—no doubt illegally, but none the less effectively, for he grabbed their arms if they tried to pass him. The pièce de résistance at that first lunch was a pair of gigantic cabbages stuffed with sausage meat and decorated with potato balls, beets and turnips cut into fancy designs, and hard-boiled eggs. The general nabbed the larger of the two cabbages, and had got half of it down before the other one could be carved by the doctor and served to the remaining fourteen men at the table. The doctor, incensed, instructed the waiters to make a detour around the general thereafter, but he turned out to have a reach like a gorilla, and when one of them presently staggered in with a huge plate of spare ribs and sauerkraut he had nailed two-thirds of the spare ribs and nearly all the sauer-kraut before you could say Jack Robinson. And so with every other dish that followed—maybe six or eight in all, for the Danes fed their customers as if fattening them for slaughter. But it was not until the end of lunch that the general let go the last link of his virtuosity. By that time, though we had got only his meagre leavings, we were all pretty well filled, and hence hardly fit to do justice to the gigantic board of Danish pastry that ended the meal. But not the general. There were twelve separate and distinct kinds of pastry on it—and he grabbed two of each. When, having got them down, he began work on six cups of coffee, his mustaches glittered like a Christmas tree with the accumulated marmalade, powdered sugar and whipped cream.

The ship's doctor, during the two or three days following, tried various schemes to curb and baffle the old boy, but they all failed, and the only remedy remaining was to order double rations for the table. This was done, and an extra waiter was added to help rassle them, but the general improved as the service improved, and at the end of the first week the double rations had to be lifted to treble. Rather curiously, we never saw him take a drink of anything alcoholic. For a couple of days after this abstemiousness was remarked a theory floated about that he was off the stuff in compliment to King George V of England, who had gone on the water-wagon at the begin-ning of the war, but in the end most of the other men at the table chose to believe rather that he knocked off a quart or so of vodka before every meal, in the quiet of his quarters. We discussed him constantly despite his presence, for it was as-sumed as a matter of course that he knew no English, which was the common language of the table. Because of his mus-taches the boys gave him the name of the Walrus. He never took any notice of these debates about him, nor did he show any resentment when all hands downed tools to watch him snare a whole leg of veal, or wolf another double dozen of Danish pastries. These pastries changed at every meal: it was the boast of the line that the same one was never served twice. The Walrus ate two of each variety at lunch and three at dinner. At the end of the long voyage, as we were all shivering in the customs shed at Copenhagen, he addressed a fellow passenger for the first time—and in excellent English. "I knew," he said, "that you called me the Walrus, but I didn't give a damn." Then he made off in the car of the Russian minister to Denmark, and was seen no more.

His avoidance of alcohol would have made him a marked man on that ship, even if he had confined himself to ordinary eating, for he was the only teetotaler, whether actual or apparent, among the passengers. The rest guzzled day and night, full of a resigned belief that a German submarine might fetch them all at any minute. We were at sea on New Year's Eve, somewhere off the coast of Greenland. It was too cold to go on deck, so the whole ship's company gathered in the smoke-room in the early afternoon, and gradually worked up a party of the very highest amperage. It appeared that it was the custom of the line for the ship's band, on such gala occasions, to play the national airs of all the countries represented among the passengers, but this time the captain forbade it, for he feared riots. Along toward midnight one of the Americans aboard * played a joke on the band (and the captain) by digging up a *potpourri* of harmless German folk-songs (it began with "O Tannenbaum") and asking the leader to put it on. The leader, who was also the bull fiddler, was so far gone in liquor by now that he could hardly stand up to his instrument, so he agreed amiably and at once plunged into the music. He either did not know, or had forgotten in his cups, that it ended with "Die Wacht am Rhein." Before he could pull up he was down to "Lieb' Vaterland, magst ruhig sein," and a Class A rough-house was in the making.

The Germans aboard (they were on their way home from Mexico and points South under a sort of flag of truce) were all either septuagenarians or cripples, but they leaped to their feet as one man, and began to *hoch* and howl in loud, exultant

tones. This, of course, brought forth hoots and hisses from the
English, Scotch, Canadians, French, Belgians, Russians, Japs,
Italians and Rumanians, with encouragement from most of the
Americans, Scandinavians, Hollanders and Latin Americans.
When the first beer glass smashed a window the waiters and
musicians took to flight, and in half a minute the master-at-
arms was on the job with a squad of sailors, and on his heels
came the captain. "Die Wacht am Rhein" having been played,
the captain now had to admit that, in common equity, all the
other national anthems should be played also, and when the
musicians were rounded up and brought back it was solemnly
done, with the master-at-arms and his goons mounting guard.
At the end of the ceremonial two Swedes sitting in a corner
rose up to protest that the anthem of Sweden had been forgotten. It was then that the enmity between the various Scandinavian nations became most painfully apparent, for the Danish
leader of the band, half sober after his scare, replied sneeringly
that Sweden *had* no anthem. The Norwegians and Danes
cheered this insult, whereupon the two Swedes climbed up on
their table and announced that they would *sing* their anthem,
band or no band. This they did in indifferent voices, while the
master-at-arms and his men kept order with drawn clubs and
knives.

The party lasted for three days and nights; in fact, it was still
going on, at least in spots, when we were hauled into Kirkwall
and the English came out to search the ship and investigate its
passengers. During this business, which went on intermittently
for two days and ended with a dozen passengers being taken
off for internment, the Danes denounced all the Swedes and
Norwegians as German spies, the Swedes denounced all the
Danes and Norwegians, and the Norwegians denounced all
the Danes and Swedes. The only Finn was jugged at Kirkwall,
and most of the Britons of various factions went ashore there,
but the Walrus and his adjutant remained aboard, and during
the trip across the North Sea to what was then Christiania, the
first stop on the final lap to Copenhagen, he gave one of his
most impressive exhibitions. The principal dish at lunch that
day was a so-called suckling pig large enough to have grandchildren: it was garnished with links of sausages, stuffed with
bread crumbs and fine herbs, and had in its maw an apple so

large that it seemed to have choked to death. The Walrus sawed off both its head and tail, and with the tail got its whole left hind leg, including the ham. This herculean helping he tamped down with a dozen sausages and about two quarts of the stuffing. While he was gobbling away a steward rushed in with the news that a German submarine was in sight, and we all ran on deck to get a look at it, and make our peace with our Maker. Somewhat to our disappointment it merely circled round us twice, and then made off politely. When we got back to the dining-room the Walrus was helping himself to the forequarters of the pig, and excavating another quart of stuffing.

We got to Christiania (now Oslo) the next evening immediately after dinner, and the three waiters at the doctor's table went ashore at once, leaving the Walrus only half way through his mountain of Danish pastry. The rest of us followed soon afterward, eager for a tilt at the night life of Henrik Ibsen's old home-town, but it turned out to be under four feet of snow, and pretty dismal. Worse, something on the order of Prohibition had been clamped down a week or so before, and the only spot we could find that was open and functioning was the main dining-room of the Grand Hotel, a huge chamber with a plush carpet and tarnished gilt lighting fixtures, about as cheering as the slumber-room of a mortician. After we had swallowed some bad beer and looked at the favorite chair of Ibsen we took to plodding about in the snow, hoping against hope that we would hear the sound of revelry somewhere else. We never did, but twice we caught sight of our three waiters and judged enviously that they must have been more lucky. They were crowded into a decrepit taxicab with three girls who had certainly not come from the Y.W.C.A., and as they passed us they gave us loud and boozy greetings, but did not invite us to join them. The next morning, when the ship cast off for Copenhagen and we came down for breakfast, we heard the story of their evening's adventures. This was before the German inflation, but Mexico, always forward-looking, had already gone off the gold standard, and in New York the boys had picked up a couple of hatsful of fifty-peso Mexican greenbacks at a quarter of a cent on the dollar. Two of these greenbacks, we learned, had paid for their whole entertainment in Christiania, though it included wine, women and song. The girls, not knowing about Mexico's forehandedness and assuming that a peso was still worth half a Norwegian crown, had provided all the drinks of the evening, the taxi hire, square meals for six, and the room rent—and even returned $3 change in sound crowns, then still worth 25 cents apiece.

This news got about before the three waiters themselves showed up. When they marched in with their trays, and the Walrus stretched out his mighty hooks to grab them, all the other men at the doctor's table leaped up and gave them three cheers, such being the natural hatred of men for women. And at lunch that day the three Danes and two Swedes at the table opened a couple of magnums of champagne in their honor, such being the natural hatred of all other Scandinavians for Norwegians.

XIII.

Gore in the Caribbees
[1917]

NO REPORTER of my generation, whatever his genius, ever really rated spats and a walking-stick until he had covered both a lynching and a revolution. The first, by the ill-favor of the gods, I always missed, usually by an inch. How often, alas, alas, did I strain and puff my way to some Christian hamlet of the Chesapeake Bay littoral, by buggy, farm-wagon or pack-mule, only to discover that an anti-social sheriff had spirited the blackamoor away, leaving nothing but a seething vacuum behind. Once, as I was on my travels, the same thing happened in the charming town of Springfield, Mo., the Paris and Gomorrah of the Ozarks. I was at dinner at the time with the late Edson K. Bixby, editor of the Springfield *Leader*, along with Paul Patterson and Henry M. Hyde, my colleagues of the Baltimore *Sunpapers*. When the alarm reached us we abandoned our victuals instantly, and leaped and galloped downtown to the jail. By the time we got there, though it was in less than three minutes, the cops had loaded the candidate—he was a white man—into their hurry-wagon and made off for Kansas City, and the lynching mob had been reduced to a hundred or so half-grown youths, a couple of pedlars selling hot-dogs and American flags, and a squawking herd of fascinated but disappointed children.

I had rather better luck with revolutions, though I covered only one, and that one I walked into by a sort of accident. The year was 1917 and I was returning from a whiff of World War I in a Spanish ship that had sailed from La Coruña, Spain, ten days before and was hoping, eventually, to get to Havana. It was, at the moment, somewhat in the maze of the Bahamas, but a wireless reached it nevertheless, and that wireless was directed to me and came from the *Sunpaper* office in Baltimore. It said, in brief, that a revolution had broken out in Cuba, that both sides were doing such rough lying that no one north of the Straits of Florida could make out what it was about, and that a series of succinct and illuminating dispatches describing its issues and personalities would be appreciated. I wirelessed back that the wishes of my superiors were commands, and then sent another wireless to a friend in Havana, Captain Asmus Leonhard, marine superintendent of the Munson Line, saying that I itched to see him the instant my ship made port. Captain Leonhard was a Dane of enormous knowledge but parsimonious speech, and I had a high opinion of his sagacity. He knew everyone worth knowing in Latin America, and thousands who were not, and his estimates of them seldom took more than three words. "A burglar," he would say, characterizing a general played up by all the North American newspapers as the greatest trans-Rio Grande hero since Bolívar, or "a goddam fraud," alluding to a new president of Colombia, San Salvador or Santo Domingo, and that was all. His reply to my wireless was in his usual manner. It said: "Sure."

When the Spanish ship, after groping about for two or three days in Exuma Sound, the North-East Providence Channel, the Tongue of Ocean and various other strangely-named Bahaman waterways, finally made Havana and passed the Morro, a smart young mulatto in Captain Leonhard's launch put out from shore, took me aboard his craft, and whisked me through the customs. The captain himself was waiting in front of the Pasaje Hotel in the Prado, eating a plate of Spanish bean-soup and simultaneously smoking a Romeo y Julietta cigar. "The issues in the revolution," he said, tackling the business in hand at once, "are simple. Menocal, who calls himself a Conservative, is president, and José Miguel Gomez, who used to be president and calls himself a Liberal, wants to make a comeback. That is the whole story. José Miguel says that when Menocal was reëlected last year the so-called Liberals were chased away from the so-called polls by the so-called army. On the other hand, Menocal says that José Miguel is a porch-climber and ought to be chased out of the island. Both are right."

It seemed clear enough, and I prepared to write a dispatch at once, but Captain Leonhard suggested that perhaps it might be a good idea for me to see Menocal first, and hear the official version in full. We were at the palace in three minutes, and found it swarming with dignitaries. Half of them were army

officers in uniform, with swords, and the other half were functionaries of the secretariat. They pranced and roared all over
the place, and at intervals of a few seconds more officers would
dash up in motor-cars and muscle and whoop their way into
the president's office. These last, explained Captain Leonhard,
were couriers from the front, for José Miguel, having taken to
the bush, was even now surrounded down in Santa Clara province, and there were high hopes that he would be nabbed
anon. Despite all the hurly-burly it took only ten minutes for
the captain to get me an audience with *el presidente.* I found
His Excellency calm and amiable. He spoke English fluently,
and was far from reticent. José Miguel, he said, was a fiend in
human form who hoped by his treasons to provoke American
intervention, and so upset the current freely-chosen and im-
peccably virtuous government. This foul plot would fail. The
gallant Cuban army, which had never lost either a battle or a
war, had the traitor cornered, and within a few days he would
be chained up among the lizards in the fortress of La Cabaña,
waiting for the firing-squad and trying in vain to make his
peace with God.

So saying, *el presidente* bowed me out, at the same time offering to put a motor-car and a secretary at my disposal. It
seemed a favorable time to write my dispatch, but Captain
Leonhard stayed me. "First," he said, "you had better hear
what the revolutionists have to say." "The revolutionists!" I
exclaimed. "I thought they were out in Santa Clara, surrounded
by the army." "Some are," said the captain, "but some ain't.
Let us take a hack." So we took a hack and were presently
worming our way down the narrow street called Obispo. The
captain called a halt in front of a bank, and we got out. "I'll
wait here in the bank," he said, "and you go upstairs to Room
309. Ask for Dr. ——" and he whispered a name. "Who is this
Dr. ——?" I whispered back. "He is the head of the revolutionary junta," replied the captain. "Mention my name, and he
will tell you all about it."

I followed orders, and was soon closeted with the doctor—a
very tall, very slim old man with a straggling beard and skin
the color of cement. While we gabbled various persons rushed
in and out of his office, most of them carrying papers which
they slapped upon his desk. In a corner a young Cuban girl of

considerable sightliness banged away at a typewriter. The doctor, like *el presidente*, spoke excellent English, and appeared to be in ebullient spirits. He had trustworthy agents, he gave me to understand, in the palace, some of them in high office. He knew what was going on in the American embassy. He got carbons of all official telegrams from the front. The progress of events there, he said, was extremely favorable to the cause of reform. José Miguel, though somewhat bulky for field service, was a military genius comparable to Joffre or Hindenburg, or even to Hannibal or Alexander, and would soon be making monkeys of the generals of the army. As for Menocal, he was a fiend in human form who hoped to provoke American intervention, and thereby make his corrupt and abominable régime secure.

All this naturally struck me as somewhat unusual, though as a newspaper reporter I was supposed to be incapable of surprise. Here, in the very heart and gizzard of Havana, within sight and hearing of thousands, the revolutionists were maintaining what amounted to open headquarters, and their boss wizard was talking freely, and indeed in a loud voice, to a stranger whose only introduction had been, so to speak, to ask for Joe. I ventured to inquire of the doctor if there were not some danger that his gold-fish globe of a hideaway would be discovered. "Not much," he said. "The army is hunting for us, but the army is so stupid as to be virtually idiotic. The police know where we are, but they believe we are going to win, and want to keep their jobs afterward." From this confidence the doctor proceeded to boasting. "In ten days," he said, "we'll have Menocal jugged in La Cabaña. Shoot him? No; it would be too expensive. The New York banks that run him have plenty of money. If we let him live they will come across."

When I rejoined the captain downstairs I suggested again that it was high time for me to begin composing my dispatch, and this time he agreed. More, he hauled me down to the cable office, only a block or two away, and there left me. "If you get into trouble," he said, "call me up at the Pasaje. I'll be taking my nap, but the clerk will wake me if you need me." I found the cable office very comfortable and even luxurious. There were plenty of desks and typewriters, and when I announced myself I was invited to make myself free of them. Moreover, as I sat down and began to unlimber my prose a large brass spittoon was wheeled up beside me, apparently as a friendly concession to my nationality. At other desks a number of other gentlemen were in labor, and I recognized them at once as colleagues, for a newspaper reporter can always spot another, just as a Freemason can spot a Freemason, or a detective a detective. But I didn't know any of them, and fell to work without speaking to them. When my dispatch was finished I took it to the window, and was informed politely that it would have to be submitted to the censor, who occupied, it appeared, a room in the rear.

The censor turned out to be a young Cuban whose English was quite as good as Menocal's or the doctor's, but unhappily he had rules to follow, and I soon found that they were very onerous. While I palavered with him several of the colleagues came up with copy in their hands, and in two minutes an enormous debate was in progress. He was sworn, I soon gathered, to cut out everything even remotely resembling a fact. No names. No dates. Worse, no conjectures, prognostications, divinations. The colleagues, thus robbed of their habitual provender and full of outrage, put up a dreadful uproar, but the censor stood his ground, and presently I slipped away and called up Captain Leonhard. My respect for his influence was higher than ever now, and it had occurred to me that the revolutionists up the street might have a private cable, and that if they had he would undoubtedly be free of it. But when, in response to his order, I met him in front of the Pasaje, he said nothing about a cable, but heaved me instead into a hack. In ten minutes we were aboard an American ship just about to cast off from a wharf down in the region of the customs-house, and he was introducing me to one of the mates. "Tell him what to do," he said, "and he will do it." I told the mate to file my dispatch the instant his ship docked at Key West, he nodded silently and put the copy into an inside pocket, and that was that. Then the siren sounded and the captain and I returned to the pier.

It all seemed so facile that I became somewhat uneasy. Could the mate be trusted? The captain assured me that he could. But what of the ship? Certainly it did not look fit for

wrestling with the notorious swells of the Straits of Florida. Its
lines suggested that it had started out in life as an excursion
boat on the Hudson, and it was plainly in the last stages of
decrepitude. I knew that the run to Key West was rather more
than a hundred miles, and my guess, imparted to the captain,
was that no such craft could make it in less than forty-eight
hours. But the captain only laughed. "That old hulk," he said,
"is the fastest ship in the Caribbean. If it doesn't hit a log or
break in two it will make Key West in five and a half hours." He
was right as usual, for that night, just as I was turning in at the
Pasaje I received a cable from the *Sunpaper* saying that my
treatise on the revolution had begun to run, and was very illuminating and high-toned stuff.

Thereafter, I unloaded all my dissertations in the same manner. Every afternoon I would divert attention by waiting on
the censor and filing a dispatch so full of contraband that I
knew he would never send it, and then I would go down to
the wharf and look up the mate. On the fourth day he was *non
est* and I was in a panic, for the captain had gone on a business
trip into Pinar del Rio and no one else could help me. But just
as the lines were being cast off I caught sight of a likely-looking
Americano standing at the gangway and decided to throw
myself upon his Christian charity. He responded readily, and
my dispatch went through as usual. Thereafter, though the
mate never showed up again—I heard later that he was sick in
Key West—I always managed to find an accommodating passenger. Meanwhile, the censor's copy-hook accumulated a fine
crop of my rejected cablegrams, and mixed with them were
scores by the colleagues. Every time I went to the cable office
I found the whole corps raising hell, and threatening all sorts
of reprisals and revenges. But they seldom got anything through
save the official communiqués that issued from the palace at
hourly intervals.

These communiqués were prepared by a large staff of press-
agents, and were not only couched in extremely florid words
but ran to great lengths. I had just come from Berlin, where all
that the German General Staff had to say every day, though
war was raging on two fronts, was commonly put into no more
than 300 words, so this Latin exuberance rather astonished
me. But the stuff made gaudy reading, and I sent a lot of it to

the *Sunpaper* by mail, for the entertainment and instruction of the gentlemen of the copy-desk. The Cuban mails, of course, were censored like the cable, but the same Americano who carried my afternoon dispatch to Key West was always willing to mail a few long envelopes at the same place. Meanwhile, I hung about the palace, and picked up enough off-record gossip to give my dispatches a pleasant air of verisimilitude, soothing to editors if not to readers. Also, I made daily visits to the headquarters of the revolutionists, and there got a lot of information, some of it sound, to the same end. In three days, such is the quick grasp of the reportorial mind, I knew all the ins and outs of the revolution, and in a week I was fit to write a history of Cuban politics from the days of Diego Velazquez. I was, of course, younger then than I am now, and reporters today are not what they used to be, but into that we need not go.

After a week it began to be plain, even on the evidence supplied by the revolutionists, that the uprising was making heavy weather of it, and when, a day or two later, the palace press-agents announced, in a communiqué running to 8,000 words, that José Miguel Gomez was about to be taken, I joined the colleagues in believing it. We all demanded, of course, to be let in on the final scene, and after a long series of conferences, with speeches by Menocal, half a dozen high army officers, all the press-agents and most of the correspondents, it was so ordered. According to both the palace and the revolutionists, the front was down at Placetas in Santa Clara, 180 miles away, but even in those days there were plenty of Fords in Havana, and it was arranged that a fleet of them should start out the next morning, loaded with correspondents, typewriters and bottled beer. Unhappily, the trip was never made, for at the precise moment the order for it was being issued a dashing colonel in Santa Clara was leading his men in a grand assault upon José Miguel, and after ten minutes of terrific fire and deafening yells the Cuban Hindenburg hoisted his shirt upon the tip of his sword and surrendered. He did not have to take his shirt off for the purpose: it was already hanging upon a guava bush, for he had been preparing for a siesta in his hammock. Why he did not know of the projected attack I could never find out, for he was held incommunicado in La Cabaña

until I left Cuba, and neither the palace nor the revolutionists
seemed willing to discuss the subject.

The palace press-agents, you may be sure, spit on their hands
when they heard the news, and turned out a series of communiqués perhaps unsurpassed in the history of war. Their hot,
lascivious rhetoric was still flowing three or four days later, long
after poor José Miguel was safely jugged among the lizards
and scorpions. I recall one canto of five or six thousand words
that included a minute autopsy on the strategy and tactics of
the final battle, written by a gifted military pathologist on the
staff of the victorious colonel. He described every move in the
stealthy approach to José Miguel in the minutest detail, and
pitched his analysis in highly graphic and even blood-curdling
terms. More than once, it appeared, the whole operation was
in dire peril, and a false step might have wrecked it, and thereby
delivered Cuba to the wolves. Indeed, it might have been baffled at its very apex and apogee if only José Miguel had had his
shirt on. As it was, he could not, according to Latin notions of
decorum, lead his men, and in consequence they skedaddled,
and he himself was forced to yield his sword to the agents of
the New York banks.

The night of the victory was a great night in Havana, and
especially at the palace. President Menocal kept open house in
the most literal sense: his office door was wide open and anyone was free to rush in and hug him. Thousands did so, including scores of officers arriving home from the front. Some
of these officers were indubitably Caucasians, but a great many
were of darker shades, including saddle-brown and coffin-
black. As they leaped out of their Fords in front of the palace
the bystanders fell upon them with patriotic gloats and gurgles,
and kissed them on both cheeks. Then they struggled up the
grand staircase to *el presidente*'s reception-room, and were kissed
again by the superior public there assembled. Finally, they
leaped into the inner office, and fell to kissing His Excellency
and to being kissed by him. It was an exhilarating show, but
full of strangeness to a Nordic. I observed two things especially. The first was that, for all the uproar, no one was drunk.
The other was that the cops beat up no one.

José Miguel was brought to Havana the next morning,
chained up in a hearse, and the palace press-agents announced

in a series of ten or fifteen communiqués that he would be tried during the afternoon, and shot at sunrise the day follow- ing. The colleagues, robbed of their chance to see his capture, now applied for permission to see him put to death, and some- what to their surprise it was granted readily. He was to be turned off, it appeared, at 6 A.M. promptly, so they were asked to be at the gate of La Cabaña an hour earlier. Most of them were on hand, but the sentry on watch refused to let them in, and after half an hour's wrangle a young officer came out and said that the execution had been postponed until the next day. But the next day it was put off again, and again the next, and after three or four days no more colleagues showed up at the gate. It was then announced by the palace literati that Presi- dent Menocal had commuted the sentence to solitary confine- ment for life in a dungeon on the Cayos de la Doce Leguas off the south coast, where the mosquitoes were as large as bull- frogs, along with confiscation of all the culprit's property, whether real, personal or mixed, and the perpetual loss of his civil rights, such us they were.

But even this turned out to be only tall talk, for President Menocal was a very humane man, and pretty soon he reduced José Miguel's sentence to fifty years, and then to fifteen, and then to six, and then to two. Soon after that he wiped out the jugging altogether, and substituted a fine—first of $1,000,000, then of $250,000, and then of $50,000. The common belief was that José Miguel was enormously rich, but this was found to be an exaggeration. When I left Cuba he was still protesting that the last and lowest fine was far beyond his means, and in the end, I believe, he was let off with the confiscation of his yacht, a small craft then laid up with engine trouble. When he died in 1921 he had resumed his old place among the acknowl- edged heroes of his country. Twenty years later Menocal joined him in Valhalla.

XIV.

Romantic Intermezzo

[1920]

TAKE WINE, women and song, add plenty of A-No. 1 victuals, the belch and bellow of oratory, a balmy but stimulating climate and a whiff of patriotism, and it must be obvious
that you have a dose with a very powerful kick in it. This, precisely, was the dose that made the Democratic national convention of 1920, holden in San Francisco, the most charming
in American annals. No one who was present at its sessions will
ever forget it. It made history for its voluptuous loveliness, just
as the Baltimore convention of 1912 made history for its infernal heat, and the New York convention of 1924 for its 103
ballots and its unparalleled din. Whenever I meet an old-timer
who took part in it we fall into maudlin reminiscences of it,
and tears drop off the ends of our noses. It came within an
inch of being perfect. It was San Francisco's brave answer to
the Nazi-inspired earthquake of April 18, 1906.

The whole population shared in the credit for it, and even
the powers and principalities of the air had a hand, for they
provided the magnificent weather, but chief praise went justly
* to the Hon. James Rolph, Jr., then and for eleven years afterward mayor of the town. In 1920, indeed, he had already been
mayor for nine years, and in 1931, after five terms of four years
each in that office, he was promoted to the dignity of Governor of California. He was a man of bold imagination and spacious ideas. More than anyone else he was responsible for the
superb hall in which the convention was held, and more than
any other he deserved thanks for the humane and enlightened
entertainment of the delegates and alternates. The heart of
that entertainment was a carload of Bourbon whiskey, old,
mellow and full of pungent but delicate tangs—in brief, the
best that money could buy.

The persons who go to Democratic national conventions
seldom see such wet goods; in truth, they had never seen any

before, and they have never seen any since. The general rule is to feed them the worst obtainable, and at the highest prices they can be cajoled and swindled into paying. Inasmuch as large numbers of them are Southerners, and most of the rest have Southern sympathies, it is assumed that they will drink anything, however revolting, provided only it have enough kick. In preparation for their quadrennial gathering to nominate a candidate for the Presidency the wholesale booze-sellers of the country ship in the dregs of their cellars—rye whiskey in which rats have drowned, Bourbon contaminated with arsenic and ptomaines, corn fresh from the still, gin that is three-fourths turpentine, and rum rejected as too corrosive by the West Indian embalmers. This stuff the Democrats put away with loud hosannas—but only for a few days. After that their livers give out, they lose their tempers, and the country is entertained with a rough-house in the grand manner. There has been such a rough-house at every Democratic national convention since Jackson's day, save only the *Ja*-convention at Chicago in 1940 and the incomparable gathering at San Francisco in 1920. The scene at the latter was one of universal peace and lovey-dovey, and every Democrat went home on his own legs, with his soul exultant and both his ears intact and functioning.

The beauty of this miracle was greatly enhanced by the fact that it was unexpected. Prohibition had gone into force only five months before the convention was scheduled to meet, and the Democrats arrived in San Francisco full of miserable forebodings. Judging by what they had already experienced at home, they assumed that the convention booze would be even worse than usual; indeed, most of them were so uneasy about it that they brought along supplies of their own. During the five months they had got used to hair oil, Jamaica ginger and sweet spirits of nitre, but they feared that the San Francisco booticians, abandoning all reason, would proceed to paint remover and sheep dip. What a surprise awaited them! What a deliverance was at hand! The moment they got to their hotels they were waited upon by small committees of refined and well-dressed ladies, and asked to state their desires. The majority, at the start, were so suspicious that they kicked the ladies out; they feared entrapment by what were then still called revenuers. But the bolder fellows took a chance—and a few hours later the glad word was everywhere. No matter what a delegate ordered he got Bourbon—but it was Bourbon of the very first chop, Bourbon aged in contented barrels of the finest white oak, Bourbon of really ultra and super quality. It came in quart bottles on the very heels of the committee of ladies—and there was no bill attached. It was offered to the visitors with the compliments of Mayor James Rolph, Jr.

The effects of that Bourbon were so wondrous that it is easy to exaggerate them in retrospect. There were, of course, other links in the chain of causation behind the phenomena I am about to describe. One, as I have hinted, was the weather—a series of days so sunshiny and caressing, so cool and exhilarating that living through them was like rolling on meads of asphodel. Another was the hall in which the convention was held—a new city auditorium so spacious, so clean, so luxurious in its comforts and so beautiful in its decorations that the assembled politicoes felt like sailors turned loose in the most gorgeous bordellos of Paris. I had just come from the Republican national convention in Chicago, and was thus keen to the contrast. The hall in Chicago was an old armory that had been used but lately for prize fights, dog shows and a third-rate circus, and it still smelled of pugs, kennels and elephants. Its walls and gallery railings were covered to the last inch with shabby flags and bunting that seemed to have come straight from a bankrupt street carnival. Down in the catacombs beneath it the victualling accommodations were of a grab-it-and-run, eat-it-if-you-can character, and the rooms marked "Gents" followed the primordial design of Sir John Harington as given in his "Metamorphosis of Ajax," published in 1596. To police this foul pen there was a mob of ward heelers from the Chicago slums, wearing huge badges, armed with clubs, and bent on packing both the gallery and the floor with their simian friends.

The contrast presented by the San Francisco hall was so vast as to be astounding. It was as clean as an operating room, or even a brewery, and its decorations were all of a chaste and restful character. The walls were hung, not with garish bunting, but with fabrics in low tones of gray and green, and in the whole place only one flag was visible. Downstairs, in the spacious basement, there were lunch-counters served by lovely young creatures in white uniforms, and offering the whole repertory of West Coast delicacies at cut-rate prices. The Johns were lined with mirrors, and each was staffed with shoe-shiners, suit-pressers and hat-cleaners, and outfitted with automatic weighing-machines, cigar-lighters, devices releasing a squirt of Jockey Club perfume for a cent, and recent files of all the principal newspapers of the United States. The police arrangements almost deserved the epithet of dainty. There were no ward heelers armed with clubs, and even the uniformed city police were confined to a few garrison posts, concealed behind marble pillars. All ordinary ushering and trouble-shooting was done by a force of cuties dressed like the waitresses in the basement, and each and every one of them was well worth a straining of the neck. They were armed with little white wands, and every wand was tied with a blue ribbon, signifying law and order. When one of these babies glided into a jam of delegates with her wand upraised they melted as if she had been a man-eating tiger, but with this difference: that instead of making off with screams of terror they yielded as if to soft music, their eyes rolling ecstatically and their hearts going pitter-pat.

But under it all, of course, lay the soothing pharmacological effect of Jim Rolph's incomparable Bourbon. Delegates who, at all previous Democratic conventions, had come down with stone in the liver on the second day were here in the full tide of health and optimism on the fifth. There was not a single case of mania à potu from end to end of the gathering, though the place swarmed with men who were subject to it. Not a delegate took home gastritis. The Bourbon was so pure that it not only did not etch and burn them out like the horrible hooches they were used to; it had a positively therapeutic effect, and cured them of whatever they were suffering from when they got to town. Day by day they swam in delight. The sessions of the convention, rid for once of the usual quarreling and caterwauling, went on like a conference of ambassadors, and in the evenings the delegates gave themselves over to amicable conversation and the orderly drinking of healths. The climax came on June 30, the day set apart for putting candidates for the Presidency in nomination. It was, in its way, the loveliest day of the whole fortnight, with a cloudless sky, the softest whisper of a breeze from the Pacific, and a sun that warmed without heating. As the delegates sat in their places listening to the speeches and the music they could look out of the open doors of the hall to the Golden Gate, and there see a fleet of warships that had been sent in by the Hon. Josephus Daniels, then Secretary of the Navy, to entertain them with salutes and manoeuvres.

There was an excellent band in the hall, and its leader had been instructed to dress in every speaker with appropriate music. If a gentleman from Kentucky arose, then the band played "My Old Kentucky Home"; if he was followed by one from Indiana, then it played "On the Banks of the Wabash." Only once during the memorable day did the leader make a slip, and that was when he greeted a Georgia delegate with "Marching Through Georgia," but even then he quickly recovered himself and slid into "At a Georgia Campmeeting." An entirely new problem confronted him as the morning wore on, for it was at San Francisco in 1920 that the first lady delegates appeared at a Democratic national convention. His test came when the earliest bird among these stateswomen got the chairman's eye. What she arose to say I do not recall, but I remember that she was a Mrs. FitzGerald of Massachusetts, a very handsome woman. As she appeared on the platform, the leader let go with "Oh, You Beautiful Doll!" The delegates and alternates, struck by the artful patness of the selection, leaped to their legs and cheered, and La FitzGerald's remarks, whatever they were, were received with almost delirious enthusiasm. The next female up was Mrs. Izetta Jewel Brown of West Virginia, a former actress who knew precisely how to walk across a stage and what clothes were for. When the delegates and alternates saw her they were stricken dumb with admiration, but when the band leader gave her "Oh, What a Pal Was Mary," they cut loose with yells that must have been heard half way to San José.

It was not these ladies, however, who made top score on that memorable day, but the Hon. Al Smith of New York. Al, in those days, was by no means the national celebrity that he was to become later. He had already, to be sure, served a year of his first term as Governor of New York, but not many people west of Erie, Pa., had ever heard of him, and to most of the delegates at San Francisco he was no more than a vague name. Thus there was little sign of interest when the Hon. W. Bourke Cockran arose to put him in nomination—the first of his three attempts upon the White House. Cockran made a good speech, but it fell flat, nor did the band leader help things when he played "Tammany" at its close, for Tammany Hall suggested only Romish villainies to the delegates from the Bible country. But when, as if seeing his error, the leader quickly swung into "The Sidewalks of New York" a murmur of appreciation ran through the hall, and by the time the band got to the second stanza someone in a gallery began to sing. The effect of that singing, as the old-time reporters used to say, was electrical. In ten seconds a hundred other voices had joined in, and in a minute the whole audience was bellowing the familiar words. The band played six or eight stanzas, and then switched to "Little Annie Rooney," and then to "The Bowery," and then to "A Bicycle Built For Two," and then to "Maggie Murphy's Home," and so on down the long line of ancient waltz-songs. Here the leader showed brilliantly his subtle mastery of his art. Not once did he change to four-four time: it would have broken the spell. But three-four time, the sempiternal measure of amour, caught them all where they were tenderest, and for a solid hour the delegates and alternates sang and danced.

The scene was unprecedented in national conventions and has never been repeated since, though many another band leader has tried to put it on: what he lacked was always the aid of Jim Rolph's Bourbon. The first delegate who grabbed a lady politico and began to prance up the aisle was full of it, and so, for all I know, was the lady politico. They were joined quickly by others, and in ten minutes Al was forgotten, the convention was in recess, and a ball was in progress. Not many of the delegates, of course, were equal to actual waltzing, but in next to no time a ground rule was evolved which admitted any kind of cavorting that would fit into the music, so the shindig gradually gathered force and momentum, and by the end of the first half hour the only persons on the floor who were not dancing were a few antisocial Hardshell Baptists from Mississippi, and a one-legged war veteran from Ohio. For a while the chairman, old Joe Robinson, made formal attempts to restore order, but

after that he let it run, and run it did until the last hoofer was
* exhausted. Then a young man named Franklin D. Roosevelt
got up to second Al's nomination. He made a long and earnest
speech on the heroic achievements of the Navy in the late war,
and killed Al's boom then and there.

That great and singular day was a Wednesday, and the bosses
of the convention made plans the next morning to bring its
proceedings to a close on Saturday. But the delegates and alternates simply refused to agree. The romantic tunes of "East
Side, West Side" and "A Bicycle Built For Two" were still
sounding in their ears, and their veins still bulged and glowed
with Jim Rolph's Bourbon. The supply of it seemed to be unlimited. Day by day, almost hour by hour, the ladies' committee produced more. Thus Thursday passed in happy abandon,
and then Friday. On Saturday someone proposed boldly that
the convention adjourn over the week-end, and the motion
was carried by a vote of 998 to 26. That afternoon the delegates and alternates, each packing a liberal supply of the Bourbon, entered into taxicabs and set out to see what was over the
horizon. San Francisco was perfect, but they sweated for new
worlds, new marvels, new adventures. On the Monday following some of them were roped by the police in places more than
a hundred miles away, and started back to their duties in charge
of trained nurses. One taxicab actually reached Carson City,
Nev., and another was reported, probably apocryphally, in San
Diego. I myself, though I am an abstemious man, awoke on
* Sunday morning on the beach at Half Moon Bay, which is as
far from San Francisco as Peekskill is from New York. But that
was caused, not by Jim Rolph's Bourbon, but by George Sterling's grappo, a kind of brandy distilled from California grape
skins, with the addition of strychnine.

After the delegates went home at last the Methodists of San
Francisco got wind of the Bourbon and started a noisy public
inquiry into its provenance. Jim Rolph, who was a very dignified man, let them roar on without deigning to notice them,
even when they alleged that it had been charged to the town
smallpox hospital, and offered to prove that there had not
been a case of smallpox there since 1897. In due time he came
up for reëlection, and they renewed their lying and unChris-
tian attack. As a result he was reëlected almost unanimously,

and remained in office, as I have noted, until 1931. In that year, as I have also noted, he was promoted by the appreciative people of all California to the highest place within their gift, and there he remained, to the satisfaction of the whole human race, until his lamented death in 1934.

XV.

Old Home Day
[*1922*]

IN THE Autumn of 1922, being at large in Europe, I was assigned by the Baltimore *Sunpaper* to go to the island of
Wieringen in the Zuider Zee to have a look at the German
Crown Prince, then interned there. I recall that I had a pleasant day with him, but what he had to say I forget. Indeed, my
only clear memory of the trip has to do with its difficulties, not
with its object. On the map Wieringen looks to be almost as
conveniently located as Staten Island, and its airline distance
from Amsterdam can't be more than forty miles, but it took
me two whole days and nights to get there and back, and I had
to use every common means of conveyance save wheelbarrows
and camels. Most of all, I remember that one of the two nights
en route was spent in a little town called Den Helder, at the
northernmost tip of the Holland mainland—the most depress-
* ing place, not excepting Waycross, Ga., and Elwood, Ind., that
I have ever encountered.

Den Helder lies just under the dike that keeps the North Sea
off the flat farmlands behind it, and serves in Summer as a
bathing place for the inferior bourgeoisie of the North Holland towns. How these customers manage to bathe there I do
not know and can't figure out, for the seaward side of the dike
slopes down at an angle of at least 40 degrees and is paved
with jagged and enormous cobblestones, brought in from Norway to turn the teeth of the sea. But that is neither here nor
there, for when I saw the place it was well along in September,
and all the Summer visitors had gone home. There was only
one hotel open, and in it I was given a room on the top floor,
just high enough in the air for me to see over the crest of the
dike. As I glanced out of my window to get my bearings a
wave was coming in from the northwest, which is to say, from
the very bowels of the North Sea. It looked, to my unpractised
eye, to be at least 200 feet high, and when it struck the dike
and was busted and baffled by the cobblestones it made a roar

like a whole herd of Niagaras. The hotel trembled so violently that I was knocked off my feet, and the ensuing reverberations must have shaken the villages as far south as Alkmaar.

Obviously, it would be impossible to sleep in that room without the use of drugs, and inasmuch as I had no opium or chloroform on me I returned downstairs to the coffee-room to find out what offered there. To my astonishment I found that none of the waiters on duty could speak English, nor, indeed, any other language that I was acquainted with, even by hear-say. I tried them with bad German, worse French, downright pathological Spanish, and even snatches of Danish, Russian, Czech, Turkish and Swahili, but they kept on spreading their hands and shaking their heads. Finally, I opened my mouth, pointed into it, made a show of swallowing, and indicated my stomach, whereupon they rushed off in a body—and returned anon with a cup of coffee! I must have lost consciousness momentarily, for by the time I found myself jawing them again there was a new man among them and he was addressing me in German so atrocious that I understood it perfectly. He was, he said, a waiter also, but he had been on duty since 6 A.M. and was preparing to go to bed when his colleagues called him. I thanked him for his kindness, asked him to bring me three large glasses of the best beer in the house, and when he returned with them invited him to sit down and drink one of them with me. He accepted politely, and turned out to be a very entertaining and even instructive fellow. We sat there together, in fact, for four hours, and during the first of them he gave me an account of his life in considerable detail. I forget most of it, but I recall that he said he was a native of a village that was half in Holland and half in Germany, and that he had had to clear out of it because of a difficulty with the German *Polizei*. At that very moment, he went on, there was a reward of fifty marks outstanding against him, dead or alive. He said he had come to Den Helder because it was the most remote spot in the settled parts of Europe, and a rival, almost, to Spitsbergen and Archangel. No stranger had been seen in it between the Napoleonic wars and the arrival of the Crown Prince at Wieringen.

From such matters he went on to consider larger affairs, and was presently discoursing upon a theme that has always

interested me—the differences between races. There was a
good deal of public talk at the time about Leagues of Nations,
international peace treaties, and such like hallucinations, and
on them he brought to bear a blistering scorn and what seemed
to me to be excellent sense. They would always and inevitably
run aground, he said, on the rocks of inter-racial enmity—a
thing as natural to mankind, and almost as hard to get rid of,
as thirst or lying. The Germans and the Dutch, he said, though
they had to live side by side, hated each other with a hatred
that was fathomless and implacable, and he himself, as a sort of
neutral or mongrel, hated both. This enmity, he continued,
had little basis in logic. It was simply a matter of taste, and its
springs lay in trifles—tones of voice, ways of trimming the hair,
the cut of clothes, table manners, and so on. Nor did it rage
only between definitely different races; it also split every race
into an endless series of hostile factions. "Holland," he said, "is
a small country, but the people of one part dislike those of
another almost as violently as a Bavarian dislikes a Prussian.
And when a Hollander goes abroad—say to the Dutch East
Indies or to America—and then comes home for a visit, he
finds that he dislikes them all." In witness whereof he told me
a curious story, substantially as follows.

There was living down in the *Polder* near Den Helder—the
Polder is the flat farmland, criss-crossed with tiny canals, that
lies below the dikes—an old farm-wife whose only son had long
ago emigrated to America, and there done very well by himself
in the Dutch colony of Michigan. He never forgot his old
mother, but sent her money constantly, and she lived very well
on the ancestral farm—a place of eight or ten acres—, with the
daughter of a neighbor to wait on her. Her house, indeed, was
a kind of show-place, for it was furnished with all the swellest
goods of the Amsterdam department-stores. She had a parlor
so jammed with marble-topped and mahoganized furniture
that it was impossible to get into it, and in her garret were
scores of feather-beds—still the touch-stones of wealth in all parts
of rural Europe north of the Alps. When she gave a coffee-party
to her buddies among the other farm wives of the neighborhood, there was so much on the table that fifty per cent. of the
guests were laid up the next day. She was Heaven's gift to the
pastor of the village church. Whenever he developed a brisk

appetite, which was often, she would set him a banquet that bulged him like a pouter-pigeon, and she kept him supplied with American Bull Durham for his pipe, sent to her by her loving and dutiful son.

This son, however, had not been home for years. For one thing, he had been busy building up a lime and cement business in a town near Grand Rapids, for another thing he had gone into politics, and for a third thing he had got married. His bride was a girl of Dutch ancestry, but born in Kalamazoo —a high-school graduate of aesthetic leanings, with some talent for interior decoration and the violoncello. Their affectionate coöperation had blessed them with a daughter, and the child was now four years old. The war having prospered both politics and the lime and cement business in Michigan, the son decided, in 1921, to make a long-overdue visit to his aged mother, and to take his wife and daughter along. They arrived at Rotterdam in November of that year, and early the next morning proceeded northward by train. It was a fast train, as such things go in Holland—in fact, it was known as the Kanonskogel, or Cannonball—but it took all day to make the trip from Rotterdam to the nose of North Holland, and by the time the pilgrims got to the farm it was pitch dark.

The old lady, of course, was ready with a big welcome, and had put on her best Sunday clothes for the purpose. Moreover, she and her slavey had prepared a stupendous meal to refresh the visitors after their long journey. Yet more, she had asked her friend, the pastor, to grace and bedizen the occasion, and he was present in his full ecclesiastical habiliments, with his beard beautifully curry-combed. As the visitors were set down at the door the old lady rushed out, grabbed her precious grandchild, and gave it a tremendous hug. Unhappily, the child was worn out by the long train-trip, and became alarmed by its grandma's strange costume, so it set up a shrill squawk, and by the time the party got into the house it was howling in a wild and deafening manner. Its father and mother combined to quiet it, first trying soothing and then clouting its bottom, but it took them ten minutes to shut off its caterwauling, and meanwhile the victuals had to wait.

When the party finally got to the table the pastor arose and let go with a prayer that was of truly appalling range and length. He not only prayed earnestly for all the persons present; he also prayed for the Dutch royal family, for Woodrow Wilson, for Clemenceau, for Lloyd-George, for the Dutch colonists in Michigan, for the lime and cement business, and for the heathen everywhere. And then, having got over all that ground, he prayed *against* the ex-Kaiser, the Crown Prince at Wieringen, Hindenburg, Ludendorff and all the other German generals, with occasional flings at the Austrians, the Bulgarians and the Turks. The bride from Kalamazoo, knowing little Dutch, could barely get the drift of it, so she devoted herself to a sly examination of the room they sat in. Unfortunately, there was only a single oil-lamp on the table, and in consequence the ceiling, upper walls and far corners were in shadow, but on the wall opposite she could see no less than five lithographs of Queen Wilhelmina—apparently a series showing her gradual increase in bulk from 175 pounds to 250.

The table itself was sufficiently lighted for a more minute survey. She counted six hams, a huge pile of black, red, gray and green sausages, a bowl containing at least 200 boiled eggs, a fish so large that it looked to be a dolphin, a loaf of rye bread two feet long and a foot thick, and no less than ten cheeses, some of them of the size of suitcases. She had been hungry when she arrived, but now her appetite oozed out of her. Her husband ate diligently, urged on by his loving old mother, but after he had sampled five of the cheeses he began to look faint, and begged for air. As for the child, it remained quiet enough until the old lady, having stoked the pastor, sawed off a slab of rye bread two inches thick, added a huge stratum of ham, and bade it eat. Its response was to resume its caterwauling, with the addition of loud demands for a plate of shredded wheat and prunes, its usual supper in Michigan.

The conversation at table, of course, was somewhat labored. The son tried to translate his mother's remarks, and the much longer observations of the pastor, but his wife's mind kept straying from the subjects they treated, and the child went on whining and whimpering. After the meal was got down at last and the pastor had prayed again—this time at less length, for he was pretty well gorged—the old lady suggested sensibly that the little girl must be tired out, and had better be put to bed. Its mother agreed joyfully, and a march to the upper re-

gions of the farmhouse began. It led up a stairway as dark as
the family entrance to an old-time Raines law hotel. The grandmother went ahead with a lamp fetched from the kitchen, but
its light was hidden by her body, and the child began yowling
again in a frantic manner, the while her mother tried to quiet
her, and her father, who brought up the rear, began swearing
dismally in English and Dutch. The yowling continued while
the undressing was going on, but the grand climax of the evening did not come until it was finished. Once the little girl was
in her nightie her poor grandmother claimed the privilege of
laying her in the bed awaiting her—the most sumptuous between Haarlem and the island of Texel. It was stuffed with at
least a hundred pounds of the finest goose feathers known to
science—not the common ones that go into ordinary feather-
beds, but fine pin-feathers from the most delicate and sanitary
areas of adolescent geese specially bred and fed for the service.
The old lady lifted the child fondly, and then let it drop ever so
gently. It gave a single blood-curdling yell—and straightway
disappeared!

    The waiter told me that such phenomena were not uncom-
mon in the feather-bed country. A really good bed, made of
the super-colossal feathers I have described, was as soft as a
powder-puff. Getting into it required a complicated technic,
and getting out was even more difficult. Why the old lady did
not remember this he did not say and I do not know: no doubt
she was somewhat addled by the sad failure of her party and
the general uproar. Whatever the fact, the child vanished like a
stone thrown into water, and at once both its father and its
mother leaped in after it, seeking to bring it to the surface and
drag it ashore. When it came up at last its little face was purple,
its psyche was aflame with complexes, and it was in the full tide
of hysterics. So, indeed, was its mother. Grasping her rescued
offspring to her breast, she shooed the heart-broken grandmother downstairs, and then sat down to calm it. She remained
at that labor, according to the waiter, until nearly 6 A.M. The
dawn was reddening when the child finally fell asleep, and the
mother fixed it a pallet on the floor. When she got to her own
bedroom, and found only the nose of her husband showing,
she broke into whoops of her own, and it took him another
half hour to get her to bed herself. Even so, she refused to

undress, but went into the feathers with all her clothes on, including her shoes.

The waiter said that the rest of the story was brief but melancholy. The poor old grandmother spent a miserable night
herself, wondering why her welcome to her son and his family
had been such a flop, and trying to puzzle out the strange ways
of American-born children. She determined to make amends by
setting a breakfast in the most lavish North Holland style—the
sort of thing that had brought her son down with grateful
bellyaches when he was a boy. To that end she got her slavey
out before dawn, and the two of them fell upon the job of
preparing it. When her guests came down at last the table was
spread even more royally than the evening before. On it stood
a jar of every kind of preserves or pickle in her storeroom, and
in the center of them was a huge platter covered with forty or
fifty fried eggs, sizzling. At one end was a ham to end all
hams—it apparently came from a hippopotamus—with a *Blutwurst* and a *Leberwurst* to flank it, and at the other end was a
cheese as big as *two* suitcases. The daughter-in-law took one
look, and then rushed out into the yard: something analogous
to *mal de mer* had fetched her. The child, seeing her flee, ran
after her, shrieking piteously, and the son made after the child.

At 9 A.M., continued the waiter, the three boarded the
south-bound Cannonball at the nearest flag-stop, with the child
still carrying on in a frenzied manner, and ten or twelve hours
later they were in Rotterdam. The next day they started back
for America—in the same ship that had brought them in only
three days before. "The poor old woman," he concluded,
"never got over it. She had been blowing about her rich son
and his family for months, and now they had walked out on
her. Whose fault was it? Nobody's. The pastor laid the whole
thing to God, and I believe he was right."

XVI.
The Noble Experiment
[1924]

PROHIBITION WENT into effect on January 16, 1920, and blew up at last on December 5, 1933—an elapsed time of twelve years, ten months and nineteen days. It seemed almost a geological epoch while it was going on, and the human suffering that it entailed must have been a fair match for that of the Black Death or the Thirty Years' War, but I should say at once that my own share of the blood, sweat and tears was extremely meagre. I was, so far as I have been able to discover, the first man south of the Mason and Dixon line to brew a drinkable home-brew, * and as a result my native Baltimore smelled powerfully of malt and hops during the whole horror, for I did not keep my art to myself, but imparted it to anyone who could be trusted— which meant anyone save a few abandoned Methodists, Baptists and Presbyterians, most of them already far gone in glycosuria, cholelithiasis or gastrohydrorrhea, and all of them soon so low in mind and body that they could be ignored.

My seminary was run on a sort of chain-letter plan. That is to say, I took ten pupils, and then each of the ten took ten, and so on *ad infinitum*. There were dull dogs in Baltimore who went through the course forty or fifty times, under as many different holders of my degrees, and even then never got beyond a nauseous *Malzsuppe*, fit only for policemen and Sunday-school superintendents. But there were others of a much more shining talent, and I put in a great deal of my time in 1921 and 1922 visiting their laboratories, to pass judgment on their brews. They received me with all the deference due to a master, and I was greatly bucked up by their attentions. In fact, those attentions probably saved me from melancholia, for during the whole of the twelve years, ten months and nineteen days I was a magazine editor, and a magazine editor is a man who lives on a sort of spiritual Bataan, with bombs of odium taking him incessantly from the front and torpedoes of obloquy harrying him astern.

But I would not have you think that I was anything like dependent, in that abominable time, upon home-brew, or that I got down any really formidable amount of it. To be sure, I had to apply my critical powers to many thousands of specimens, but I always took them in small doses, and was careful to blow away a good deal of the substance with the foam. This home-brew, when drinkable at all, was a striking proof of the indomitable spirit of man, but in the average case it was not much more. Whenever the mood to drink purely voluptuously was on me I preferred, of course, the product of professional brew-masters, and, having been born lucky, I usually found it. Its provenance, in those days, was kept a kind of military secret, but now that the nightmare is over and jails no longer yawn I do not hesitate to say that, in so far as my own supply went, most of it came from the two lowermost tiers of Pennsylvania counties. Dotted over that smiling pastoral landscape there were groups of small breweries that managed successfully, by means that we need not go into, to stall off the Prohibition agents, and I had the privilege and honor of getting down many a carboy of their excellent product both in Baltimore, where I lived, and in New York, where I had my office.

When I say New York I mean the city in its largest sense—the whole metropolitan region. As a matter of fact, the malt liquor on tap on the actual island of Manhattan was usually bad, and often downright poisonous. When I yearned for a quaff of the real stuff I went to Union Hill, N. J., and if not to Union Hill, then to Hoboken. Both of these great outposts radiated a bouquet of malt and hops almost as pungent as Baltimore's, and in Union Hill there was a beer-house that sticks in my memory as the most comfortable I have ever encountered on this earth. Its beers were perfect, its victuals were cheap and nourishing, its chairs were designed by osteological engineers specializing in the structure of the human pelvis, and its waiters, Axel, Otto, Julius and Raymond, were experts at their science.[1] This incom-

---

[1] Raymond, like Axel, was from upper Schleswig-Holstein, and hence technically a Dane. I naturally assumed that his baptismal name was an Americanized form of the old Teutonic name of Reimund, signifying a sagacious councilor. But one night he told me that his father, a *Stadtpfeiffer*, had named him after the "Raymond" overture by Ambrose Thomas, a work he greatly admired.

parable dump was discovered by the late Philip Goodman, then transiently a theatrical manager on Broadway and all his life a fervent beer-drinker, and he and I visited it every time I was in New York, which was pretty often. We would ease into our cannons' stalls in the early evening and continue in residence until Axel, Otto, Julius and Raymond began to snore in their corner and the colored maintenance engineer, Willie, turned his fire-hose into the washroom. Then back by taxi to Weehawken, from Weehawken to Forty-second street by the six-minute ferry, and from Forty-second street by taxi again to the quick, lordly sleep of quiet minds and pure hearts.

The fact that the brews on tap in that Elysium came from lower Pennsylvania naturally suggested an expedition to the place of their origin, and Goodman and I laid many plans for making the trip in his car. But every time we started out we dropped in on Axel, Otto, Julius and Raymond for stirrup cups, and that was as far as we ever got. Alone, however, I once visited Harrisburg on newspaper business, and there had the felicity of drinking close to the *Urquell.* That was in the primitive days when New York still bristled with peepholes and it was impossible to get into a strange place without a letter from a judge, but in Harrisburg there were no formalities. I simply approached a traffic cop and asked him where reliable stuff was to be had. "Do you see that kaif there?" he replied, pointing to the corner. "Well, just go in and lay down your money. If you don't like it, come back and I'll give you another one." I liked it well enough, and so did not trouble him further.

I should add, however, that I once came so near going dry in Pennsylvania, and in the very midst of a huge fleet of illicit breweries, that the memory of it still makes me shiver. This was at Bethlehem in the Lehigh Valley, in 1924. I had gone to the place with my publisher, Alfred Knopf, to hear the celebrated Bach Choir, and we were astounded after the first day's sessions to discover that not a drop of malt liquor was to be had in the local pubs. This seemed strange and unfriendly, for it is well known to every musicologist that the divine music of old Johann Sebastian cannot be digested without the aid of its natural solvent. But so far as we could make out there was absolutely none on tap in the Lehigh Valley, though we searched high and low, and threw ourselves upon the mercy of cops, taxi-drivers, hotel clerks, the Elks, the rev. clergy, and half the tenors and basses of the choir. All reported that Prohibition agents had been sighted in the mountains a few days before, and that as a result hundreds of kegs had been buried and every bartender was on the alert. How we got through the second day's sessions I don't know; the music was magnificent, but our tonsils became so parched that we could barely join in the final Amen. Half an hour before our train was scheduled to leave for New York we decided to go down to the Lehigh station and telegraph to a bootician in the big city, desiring him to start westward at once and meet us at Paterson, N. J. On the way to the station we discussed this madcap scheme dismally, and the taxi-driver overheard us. He was a compassionate man, and his heart bled for us.

"Gents," he said, "I hate to horn in on what ain't none of my business, but if you feel that bad about it I think I know where some stuff is to be had. The point is, can you get it?"

We at once offered him money to introduce us, but he waived us off.

"It wouldn't do you no good," he said. "These Pennsylvania Dutch never trust a hackman."

"But where is the place?" we breathed.

"I'm taking you to it," he replied, and in a moment we were there.

It was a huge, blank building that looked like a forsaken warehouse, but over a door that appeared to be tightly locked there was the telltale sign, "Sea Food"—the universal euphemism for beerhouse in Maryland and Pennsylvania throughout the thirteen awful years. We rapped on the door and presently it opened about half an inch, revealing an eye and part of a mouth. The ensuing dialogue was *sotto voce* but *staccato* and *appassionata*. The eye saw that we were famished, but the mouth hesitated.

"How do I know," it asked, "that you ain't two of them agents?"

The insinuation made us boil, but we had to be polite.

"*Agents!*" hissed Knopf. "What an idea! Can't you *see* us? Take a good look at us."

The eye looked, but the mouth made no reply.

"Can't you tell musicians when you see them?" I broke in.

"Where did you ever see a Prohibition agent who looked so innocent, so moony, so dumb? We are actually fanatics. We came here to hear Bach. Is this the way Bethlehem treats its guests? We came a thousand miles, and now—"

"*Three* thousand miles," corrected Knopf.

"*Five* thousand," I added, making it round numbers.

Suddenly I bethought me that the piano score of the B minor mass had been under my arm all the while. What better introduction? What more persuasive proof of our *bona fides*? I held up the score and pointed to the title on the cover. The eye read:

J. S. Bach
Mass in B Minor

The eye flicked for an instant or two, and then the mouth spoke. "Come in, gents," it said. As the door opened our natural momentum carried us into the bar in one leap, and there we were presently immersed in two immense *Humpen*. The quality we did not pause to observe; what we mainly recalled later was the astounding modesty of the bill, which was sixty-five cents for five *Humpen*—Knopf had two and I had three—and two sandwiches. We made our train just as it was pulling out.

It was a narrow escape from death in the desert, and we do not forget all these years afterward that we owed it to Johann Sebastian Bach, that highly talented and entirely respectable man, and especially to his mass in B minor. In the great city of Cleveland, Ohio, a few months later, I had much worse luck. I went there, in my capacity of newspaper reporter, to help cover the Republican national convention which nominated Calvin Coolidge, and I assumed like everyone else that the Prohibition agents would lay off while the job was put through, if only as a mark of respect to their commander-in-chief. This assumption turned out to be erroneous. The agents actually clamped down on Cleveland with the utmost ferocity, and produced a drought that was virtually complete. Even the local cops and newspaper reporters were dry, and many of the latter spent a large part of their time touring the quarters of the out-of-town *
correspondents, begging for succor. But the supplies brought in by the correspondents were gone in a few days, and by the

time the convention actually opened a glass of malt liquor was as hard to come by in Cleveland as an honest politician.

The news of this horror quickly got about, and one morning I received a dispatch in cipher from a Christian friend in Detroit, saying that he was loading a motor-launch with ten cases of bottled beer and ale, and sending it down the Detroit river and across Lake Erie in charge of two of his goons. They were instructed, he said, to notify me the instant they arrived off the Cleveland breakwater. Their notice reached me the next afternoon, but by that time the boys were nominating Cal, so I could not keep the rendezvous myself, but had to send an agent. This agent was Paul de Kruif, then a young man of thirty-four, studying the literary art under my counsel. Paul was a fellow of high principles and worthy of every confidence; moreover, he was dying of thirst himself. I started him out in a rowboat, and he was gone three hours. When he got back he was pale and trembling, and I could see at a glance that some calamity had befallen. When he got his breath he gasped out the story.

The two goons, it appeared, had broken into their cargo on the way down from Detroit, for the weather was extremely hot. By the time they anchored off the Cleveland breakwater they had got down three cases, and while they were waiting for de Kruif they knocked off two more. This left but five—and they figured that it was just enough to get them back to Detroit, for the way was uphill all the way, as a glance at a map will show. De Kruif, who was a huge and sturdy Dutchman with a neck like John L. Sullivan, protested violently and even undertook to throw them overboard and pirate the launch and cargo, but they pulled firearms on him, and the best he could do was to get six bottles. These he drank on his return in the rowboat, for the heat, as I have said, was extreme. As a result, I got nothing whatsoever; indeed, not a drop of malt touched my throat until the next night at 11.57, when the express for Washington and points East crossed the frontier of the Maryland Free State.

This was my worst adventure during Prohibition, and in many ways it remains the worst adventure of my whole life, though I have been shot at four times and my travels have taken me to Albania, Trans-Jordan and Arkansas. In Maryland there was always plenty, and when I was in New York Goodman and I made many voyages to Union Hill. One hot night in 1927, while we were lolling in the perfect beerhouse that I have mentioned, a small but excellent band was in attendance, and we learned on inquiry that it belonged to a trans-Atlantic liner of foreign registry, then berthed at one of the North river docks. Through Axel and Raymond we got acquainted with the leader, and he told us that if we cared to accompany him and his men back to the ship they would set up some real Pilsner. We naturally accepted, and at five o'clock the next morning we were still down in the stewards' dining-room on H-deck, pouring in *Seidel* after *Seidel* and victualing royally on black bread and *Leberwurst*. The stewards were scrupulous fellows and would not bootleg, but Goodman had some talent for mathematics, and it was not hard for him to figure out a tip that would cover what we had drunk of their rations, with a reasonable *Zuschlag* added.

Thereafter, we visited that lovely ship every time it was in port, which was about once every five weeks, and in a little while we began to add other ships of the same and allied lines, until in the end we had a whole fleet of them, and had access to Pilsner about three weeks out of four, and not only to Pilsner but also to Münchner, Dortmunder, Würzburger and Kulmbacher. It was a long hoof down the dark pier to the cargo port we had to use, and a long climb from the water-line down to H-deck, but we got used to the exertion and even came to welcome it, for we were both under medical advice to take more exercise. When we went aboard, usually at 10 or 11 P.M., there was no one on the dock save a customs watchman sitting on a stool at the street entrance, chewing tobacco, and when we debarked at 4 or 5 A.M. the same watchman was still there, usually sound asleep.

Gradually, such being the enticements of sin, we fell into the habit of sneaking a couple of jugs past the watchman—most often, of Germany brandy, or *Branntwein*. It was abominable stuff, but nevertheless it was the real McCoy, and Goodman and I found it very useful—he for drugging his actors and I for dishing out to the poets who infested my magazine office. One night there was some sort of celebration aboard ship—as I recall it, the birthday of Martin Luther—and the stewards put on a special spread. The *pièce de résistance* was a *Wurst* of some strange but very toothsome kind, and Goodman and I got down large rashers of it, and praised it in high, astounding terms. The stewards were so pleased by our appreciation that they gave us two whole ones as we left, and so we marched up the pier to the street, each with a bottle of *Branntwein* in one coat pocket and a large, globulous sausage in the other. To our surprise we found the customs watchman awake. More, he halted us.

"What have you got there in your pockets?" he demanded.

We turned them out, and he passed over the two bottles without a word, but the sausages set him off to an amazing snorting and baying.

"God damn me," he roared, "if I ever seen the like. Ain't you got *no* sense *whatever*? Here I try to be nice to you, and let you get something 100% safe into your system, and what do you hand me? What you hand me is that you try to do some *smuggling* on me. Yes, *smuggling*. I know the law and so do you. If I wanted to turn you in I could send you to Atlanta for the rest of your life. God damn if I ain't *ashamed* of you."

With that he grabbed the two sausages and hugged them to him. Goodman and I, conscious of guilt, stood silent, with flushed faces and downcast eyes. What was there to say? Nothing that we could think of. We had been taken red-handed in a deliberate violation of the just laws of this great Republic. We had tried with malice prepense to rob the Treasury of the duty on two valuable sausages—say, 67½ cents at 25% *ad valorem* on a valuation of $2.50 for the pair. The amount, to be sure, was small, but the principle was precious beyond price. In brief, we were common felons, dirt criminals, enemies to society, and as reprehensible, almost, as so many burglars, hijackers or Prohibition agents.

The watchman howled on for two or three minutes, seeking, apparently, to impress upon us the heinousness of our offense. We needed no such exposition. Our consciences were devouring us with red-hot fangs. There was no need for us to say a word, for we radiated repentance and regret. But finally, as the watchman dismissed us with a parting blast, Goodman ventured upon a question.

"Do you," he asked, "want the bottles too?"

"Hell, no," replied the watchman. "What *I* am trying to bust up is *smuggling*."

XVII.

Inquisition

[*1925*]

WHEN I was a *cand. jour.* in the infancy of the century, the old-timer reporters who entertained us youngsters with tales of their professional prodigies (at our expense, of course, for the drinks) always introduced anecdotes of the Johnstown Flood and the march of Coxey's Army. Those were the two great news stories of the last decades of the century just closed, and every reporter with any age and patina on him claimed to have covered them. Most of these caricatures of Richard Harding Davis, I suspect, were liars and no more, but in every considerable city, at least in the East, there must have been plenty who actually saw service on both occasions, for the Johnstown Flood (1889) attracted the largest swarm of journalists ever seen up to that time, and Coxey's Army (1894) had a camp following of them that was almost as large as the army itself. Their narratives, whether true or imaginary, were extremely amusing and instructive to their juniors in the trade, but it didn't take me long to notice that they differed radically in various details, some important and some not. For example, there was not the slightest agreement among them about the authorship of the most famous and enduring literary monument of the flood, to wit, the saying, "Don't spit; remember the Johnstown Flood"—now almost as firmly lodged among American maxims as "It will never get well if you pick it" or "Root, hog, or die." One Polonius laid it to James Creelman, another to Karl Decker, a third to a bartender in Altoona, Pa., a fourth to an office-boy on the New York *Sun*, a fifth to Lew Dockstader, and so on. Nor did they ever agree, even within wide limits, about the number of unfortunates washed into Heaven at Johnstown, or the number of hoboes, runaway boys, three-card monte operators, absconding debtors and other such advanced thinkers who marched with Coxey.

These discrepancies puzzled me at the time, for I was still young and tender, and had not yet learned that neither

543

journalism nor history is an exact science. Since then the fact
has been rammed into me by hard experience, and by nothing
more effectively than by the Scopes trial at Dayton, Tenn., in
1925, which, as I can prove by both witnesses and documents,
I assisted in covering myself. It was, in its way, the Twentieth
Century's effort to match the Nineteenth's flood and march.
As the reporters who had hands in it always agree when they
meet, it had everything—and when they say everything they do
not overlook its lack of what is called sex interest, for they know
as old hands (they are all fast oxidizing now) that sex interest is
not necessary to first-rate drama, as, indeed, the flood and the
march proved before them. In another respect, also, it closely
resembled those memorable events—that is, in the respect that
its saga was quickly embellished with many incidents that never
really happened. Before I got home from the scene I was already hearing details that I knew were not true, and more and
even less credible ones have been hatching ever since. On the
unveracity of one such detail, a small one, I can speak with
some authority, for I am a figure in it. It is to the effect that my
reports of the trial offended the resident yahoos so grievously
that they formed a posse and ran me out of town. This began
to get into print soon after the proceedings ended, and the
clipping bureaux continue to bring me in new and elaborate
forms of it at frequent intervals, even to this day. I have reason
to believe that many of the yahoos themselves now accept it as
true, and that there are heroes among them who claim to have
been members of the posse, and to have taken pot shots at me
as I ran screaming down the road.

Nothing of the sort ever happened. It is a fact that my dispatches from the courtroom were somewhat displeasing to
local susceptibilities, and that my attempts to describe the town
and its people were even more so, and it is also a fact that there
was talk among certain bolder spirits of asking me to retire
from the scene, but beyond that it did not go. So far as I can
recall, only one Daytonian ever went to the length of opening
the subject to me, and he was extremely polite. He was one of
the catchpolls of the court, and all he had to say was that there
was some murmuring against me, and that he thought it might
be a good idea if I met a few of the principal citizens and let

them tell me precisely what was complained of in my writings. I could see no objection to that, and accordingly offered to meet these notables at the drugstore—the Acropolis and Mars' Hill of the town—the same evening. I got there on time and so did the catchpoll, but a heavy thunderstorm was making up, and the rest of the committee failed to appear. So the catchpoll and I, after waiting half an hour, parted amicably, and that was the last I heard of the matter. I was in Dayton for at least four or five days longer, carrying on my work without the slightest molestation, and when I left at last—unhappily, before the butchery of Bryan by Clarence Darrow—it was at a time chosen before I came, and at my own sole volition. Some of the other reporters present, hearing of the murmuring aforesaid and eager to begaud the lily of the trial with gilding, professed to take the posse seriously, and let it be known that they were organizing a counter-posse of their own, with Lindsay Denison of the New York *World* as its commander. Inasmuch as there were nearly 200 reporters in the place, many of them veterans of riots, lynchings, torch murders and labor wars, it may be that the Daytonians took this counter-posse seriously and were induced thereby to cool off, but if so I certainly have no evidence of it. All I can report is that they treated me with *
great courtesy, despite the necessary unpleasantness of my reports, and that five years later, when the William Jennings Bryan Fundamentalist "University" was set up in a cow pasture adjoining the town, I was invited to attend its consecration, and it was even hinted that I might be allowed to make a speech.

The only strangers who actually suffered any menace to their lives and limbs during the progress of the trial were Clarence Darrow, the chief lawyer for Scopes; William K. Hutchinson of the Hearst papers; an unknown Y.M.C.A. secretary who wandered in from Cincinnati, and an itinerant atheist who came to town to exhibit a mangy chimpanzee. All four were threatened, not with assassination nor even with tarring-and-feathering, but simply with confinement in the town hoosegow; but inasmuch as the hoosegow was a one-room brick pillbox set in the middle of an open field, and the average noonday temperature in the valley of the Tennessee river during July, 1925 was at

least 100 degrees, this amounted virtually to capital punishment. Only the atheist and the Y.M.C.A. brother ever got into
that dreadful cooler, but the other two made narrow escapes.
Hutchinson, in fact, appeared to be doomed, but at the last
minute he was rescued by the magnificent forensic powers of
Richard J. Beamish, then of the Philadelphia *Inquirer* and now
a high dignitary in the Pennsylvania State government, with
the rank and pay of a lieutenant-general. The crime of Hutch,
a very competent and resourceful reporter, was that he had
outsmarted the learned judge on the bench, a village Hampden named Raulston. The lawyers for Scopes—Darrow, Arthur
Garfield Hays, Dudley Field Malone and John T. Neal—had
made the usual formal motion to quash the indictment, and
the judge, with a great show of judicial dog, announced that
he would ponder his decision. He kept on pondering it so long
that everyone ran out of patience, and various efforts were
made to pump him, but it remained for Hutch to do the trick.
He worked it by the simple device of asking the judge if, after
the decision was given, the court would adjourn until the next
day. The judge replied that it would, and Hutch had his secret,
for if the decision sustained the motion to quash, the trial
would be at an end and there would be no next day. Within
ten minutes the Hearst papers had a flash saying that the indictment would be sustained, and so they beat the country.
And within half an hour the representatives of all the super-
and infra-Hearst papers began to receive remonstrances from
their home offices, and were clustered around the judge like
bees in full fermentation, demanding to know why he had
given the beat to Hutch.

This upbraiding greatly upset His Honor, and also puzzled
him sorely. He realized in his dim, judicial way that he had
been had, but he couldn't make out how. He tried to solve the
problem by a two-headed device. First, he ordered the whole
corps of correspondents herded into his courtroom for an inquiry *en masse*, and second, he cited Hutch for contempt of
court. Many of the non-Hearst correspondents were inflamed
against Hutch for beating them so neatly, but when they began
to think of the possible consequences of the charge he faced—
say, thirty days in that red-hot coop of a can in the field behind
the courthouse—their sense of brotherhood overcame their

ire, and they tried to devise ways and means to save him. In this Christian work the leadership was soon taken by Dick Beamish. Rising in court in his most impressive manner, he made a speech saying that the matter at issue was full of vexation, and had given all the more seasoned correspondents great perturbation. Not only were grave questions of law involved, but also questions of journalistic ethics. It might very well be —who could say offhand?—that Hutch was guilty not only of violating the statutes of Tennessee but also of shaming the great profession he theoretically adorned. There was, in Maître Beamish's judgment, but one way to get to the bottom of the matter, and that was to appoint a committee of distinguished reporters to consider all its bearings and report upon them at length. The judge fell for this, and at once appointed a committee with Beamish as its chairman. The other members were Phil Kinsley of the Chicago *Tribune*, Forrest Davis of the New York *Herald Tribune*, Earl Shaub of the Universal Service, and Tony Muto, a free lance weighing 260 pounds.

This committee was in session all night in Beamish's quarters over the town hay, feed, lime and cement store. It appointed Lindsay Denison its sheriff, and from time to time he dragged in some elder correspondent to act as *amicus curiae*. I was the only reporter on hand who had any public standing as a moral theologian, but Beamish categorically forbade Denison to summon me—a lamentable evidence that the old feud between the civil and the canon law, running back to the Eleventh Century, was still running. The deliberations of the committee, of course, were secret, but with so many outsiders going in and coming out some notion of their drift reached the gallery. At the precise stroke of midnight, it appeared, Tony Muto drew a royal flush, and half an hour later Phil Kinsley, a great believer in bold experiment, drew four aces to a nine. As the laboring of legal and ethical points grew more and more animated even greater marvels were witnessed. There was, so we were told, one hand of five kings and another of six (some said seven) queens. Beamish was broke and in hock for $7 by 2.30 A.M., but toward dawn he made a glorious recovery, partly due to luck and partly to science, and when the committee, having finished its deliberations, rose at 6 A.M. he was solvent again. So, in fact, were all the others. Only one of them, Muto, was appreciably ahead of the game, and he was ahead to the extent of no more than $3 or $4. Their work done, the committee-men shaved with Beamish's razor, bathed in a washtub, and entered the hay for a brief snooze before reporting to Raul-ston, J. When His Honor rapped for order at 10 A.M. they were lined up respectfully before his bar, headed by their chairman and spokesman.

The whole course of the trial of Scopes was marked by gor-geous oratory, and I shall make note of another specimen of it anon, but from end to end I heard nothing more magnificent than Beamish's report. He was then at the height of his powers as a rhetorician, and in addition he was a very fine figure of a man, with broad shoulders, an attention-compelling but sym-metrical paunch, and a very cocky way of carrying his head. It was the fashion of the time to wear shirts of somewhat loud design, and he had the loudest in Dayton. They were of printed silk, and ran to all the colors of the rainbow, along with many aniline inventions that no rainbow since Noah's time had ever boasted. The public admired them and Beamish loved them so tenderly that he had affectionate names for some of them —the Garden of Allah, Who is Sylvia?, the Dark-Brown Taste, I'm Called Little Buttercup, the Apotheosis of the Rose, and so on. For his effort in behalf of poor Hutch he chose the queen of his sartorial harem—a superb polychrome creation called Everybody's Sweetheart. Nobody wore coats in Day-ton, so the crowd in the courtroom got a sizzling eyeful when he arose. But in half a minute the roll of his sonorous periods made everyone forget his splendors, and the whole audience, including the lawyers and the learned judge, was bedazzled and enchanted by the surge and thunder of his words.

So far as I know, no stenographic report of his speech was made, and I shall not attempt to recall it in any detail, for its effectiveness depended quite as much on manner as on con-tent. It included, I remember clearly enough, a review of the struggle for free speech in the Anglo-Saxon countries since Beowulf's time, with extracts from the Areopagitica, the evi-dence and arguments in the trial of John Peter Zenger, and the writings of John Stuart Mill. There were citations, first and last, of at least a hundred cases—some of them from the stan-

dard English and American reports, but a number dredged
up from obscure proceedings before county judges and police
magistrates in such States as Arkansas, Idaho and Vermont—
most of them unknown to the books and maybe also to history. The judge listened eagerly, and no wonder, for it is
highly improbable that any argument of the same scope,
punch and profundity had ever been offered in his court, or
indeed in any other court of Tennessee. At length the sough
of words ceased, and Beamish paused to mop his brow, hitch
up his pants, fleck a horse-fly off the left arm of Everybody's
Sweetheart, and intone the recommendation of the committee. His voice was now low and caressing, and as he came to
the end he took a statuesque stance, adjusted his Oxford
pince-nez on the end of his nose, threw back his head, and
looked *under* the horn-rimmed lenses at the judge. "And
therefore, Your Honor," he concluded, "your committee,
having considered all the facts in a fair and impartial spirit,
and given deep and prolonged thought to the questions of
journalistic ethics that appear to be involved, now recom-
mends most respectfully that no further proceedings be had."
"It is so ordered!" exclaimed the judge, with a loud bang of
his gavel, and thus Bill Hutchinson escaped the cooler, and *
the trial of the infidel Scopes was resumed.

Scopes himself, a modest and good-looking young man, was
quickly overshadowed by the eminent characters who heaved
and howled in the courtroom—Bryan, Darrow, Hays, Malone
and so on. Once, after he had been unseen and unheard for two
or three days, the judge stopped the proceedings to inquire
what had become of him. He was found—in his shirtsleeves
like everyone else—sitting in the middle of a dense mass of
lawyers, infidels, theologians, biologists and reporters, and
after he had risen and identified himself the uproar was resumed. Darrow, who wore wide firemen's suspenders and had
a trick of running his arms under them as he spoke, was threatened with the hoosegow out in the field for a chance remark
during one of his interminable arguments. The judge, sweating
under his logic, which was couched in somewhat bellicose
terms, stopped him and observed: "I hope counsel does not
intend any offense to this court." Darrow thereupon paused,
yawned ostentatiously, flapped his suspenders a couple of times,

and answered: "Your Honor is at least entitled to hope." This brought down the judicial gavel with a thwack that shook the courtroom, and ten seconds later the trial was suspended and Darrow was before the bar to answer a charge of contempt of court. He naturally asked for a chance to consult his associates, and there was a wait while they put their heads together. In the end they decided that the easiest way out was for him to apologize, and this he did in extremely grudging words, with his voice full of stealthy sneers. But the letter of the apology was there, and the judge accepted it without further ado.

The atheist who suffered in the town calaboose was a traveling showman who had wandered in with his chimpanzee to make propaganda for Darwin. He parked it at the railroad station, which was near the jail, and went through the town distributing inflammatory circulars. Their purport was that his chimpanzee proved to the eye, and with irrefutable force, that man and the higher apes were identical, and that a peek at it for the small sum of ten cents, along with the accompanying lecture by the atheist himself, would convince any reasonable customer, however pious. The days of Genesis, according to the circular, were pretty well over. As soon as every man, woman and child had seen the chimpanzee and noted its striking resemblance to a United States Senator, the American people would rise in a body and chase all their ordained pastors from their settlements. The atheist was a mild man, and his chimpanzee appeared to be at the point of death, but his selling talk aroused the local Fundamentalists, and in a little while he was clapped into jail. When Denison and I heard of this we went to the proper authorities, and demanded to see the chapter and verse of the Tennessee statute under which he was held. There was, of course, no such statute. The law that Scopes had run afoul of prohibited teaching Darwinism to children in the public schools, not to adults outside. But the authorities argued that they had general powers to put down any and every act in contempt of the revelation of God, and we had a dreadful time convincing them that caging the atheist in that furnace out in the field was cruel and unusual punishment. Finally, they compromised by agreeing to transfer him to a small hotel down at the railroad station, on condition that he would leave by the first outbound train, taking his obscene and sclerotic ape with him. There was a wait of three hours until the next train left, and the atheist gave them over to throwing copies of his circulars out of his second-floor window. A sort of vigilance committee was formed to gather up these circulars as they fluttered down, and burn them before they could fall into the hands of the young. But a number escaped, and they are still preserved, I hear, in the less pious sort of Tennessee Valley homes, in secret cupboards which also house jugs of forty-rod, pictures of naked women, and birth-control apparatus.

The Y.M.C.A. brother got into trouble as a result of an oafish pleasantry by my colleague, Henry M. Hyde, and my- * self, no doubt in bad taste. On our first day in Dayton we had gone about scraping acquaintance with the country evangelists who were swarming into town, and among them we were especially delighted by an old man named T. T. Martin, hailing from Blue Mountain, Miss. This Brother Martin, a white haired commissar of Yahweh in a clerical black coat and a collar so wide that he could pull his head through it, was a fellow full of Christian juices, and amiable to believer and infidel alike. He was one of the recognized stars of his profession, and had accumulated enough "plant," as he called it, to load two trucks. It consisted of a large stock of dog's-eared Bibles, another of hymn-books, a reed organ of powerful voice, a portable pulpit, and a set of knock-down bleachers like those used by a one-ring circus. These bleachers he set up on the courthouse lawn, and there he not only used them at his own services but also lent them freely to rival John Baptists. He made a gallant effort to save the abandoned souls of Hyde and me, and would take a hack at us every time he met us on the streets, which was ten or twenty times a day. Indeed, he continued these efforts by * mail long after the Scopes trial was over, and when he died at last, only a few years ago, he was full of friendly hopes that the seed he had jabbed into us would fructify soon or late, and that he would thus have the pleasure of meeting us in Heaven with his rings in our ears.

One morning, on meeting him in front of the town drugstore, we sought to get rid of his solicitations by hinting that important news was astir. What was it? We hemmed and hawed a bit, and then told him that it was a report from Cincinnati that a gang of Bolsheviki there were planning to come down to Dayton and butcher Bryan. At that time the Red scare following World War I was still in full blast, and in consequence Brother Martin was considerably perturbed. We warned him to keep his mouth shut, but when we left him he rushed off to the house where Bryan was staying and gave the alarm. The result was that the town constables got into a panic, and sent a hurry call for help to Chattanooga. An hour later thirty or forty Chattanooga cops got in, and the lieutenant in charge of them threw them in a cordon around Dayton, to challenge all suspicious persons as they approached. An extra heavy force was posted at the railroad station, where the afternoon express from Cincinnati was due in a little while. When it arrived only one passenger alighted—the Y.M.C.A. brother aforesaid. He looked innocent enough, God knows, for he wore a black cutaway coat and (despite the infernal heat) a high choker collar, and carried a Bible under his arm. But the Chattanooga cops were taking no chances, so they grabbed him as he alighted and rushed him to the hoosegow. There he sweated and bellowed for an hour while Hyde and I (whose consciences had begun to fever us) joined Brother Martin in trying to convince the cops that he was really what he said he was, and not a Russian trigger-man of democracy. In the end the cops let him go, but not until his choker collar was a ring of mush. He got another one somewhere, and that night he delivered a vociferous tirade against Bolshevism, boozing, atheism and their allied infamies from Brother Martin's collapsible tabernacle on the courthouse lawn. Brother Martin had forgotten where he got the tip about the attempt on Bryan even before he reached Bryan's quarters, panting and half scared to death. An hour later, in fact, when Hyde and I met him again, he imparted it to us as news, and we thanked him very politely.

*   Bryan, of course, was the star of the show, and when he appeared upon the streets, always in his shirtsleeves and wearing a curious deep-collared shirt made for him by his wife, he was followed by a large gallery of the local Bible searchers. Many tackled him with problems of exegesis that had floored them in their studies, but he never lacked a prompt and convincing answer. Now and then a Holy Roller, a Dunkard, a Unitarian or even a downright infidel had at him with a trick question, but he always turned them off facilely, for he was as thoroughly soaked in the Holy Scriptures as many another aspirant to the Presidency has been in alcohol. Bryan liked country people, and was at ease among them. Whenever he encountered a mountain family from the Pamirs behind Dayton, the husband and father in his go-to-meeting overalls, the wife and mother giving titty (as the local phrase had it) to her youngest child, and the rest peeking from behind her skirts, he would stop his parade long enough to greet them with the courtly deportment he had picked up from the Spanish ambassador during his days as Secretary of State. This ceremonious greeting always made a powerful impression upon the assembled hinds. There were many among them who believed that Bryan was no longer merely human, but had lifted himself to some level or other of the celestial angels, archangels, principalities, powers, virtues, dominations, thrones, cherubim and seraphim. It would have surprised no one if he had suddenly begun to perform miracles—say, curing a mule of heaves or a yokel of kidney weakness, or striking oil in the field behind the courthouse. I saw plenty of his customers approach him stealthily to touch his garments, to wit, his shirt and pants. Those with whom he shook hands were made men, and not a few of them, I daresay, are showing the marks on their palms to this day. If the Protestant theologies prevailing in Appalachia did not prohibit relics as heathenish, every church in the whole region would have some souvenir of him under its high altar, if only a lock of hair, a lead pencil or a page from one of his battery of Bibles.

That the Tennessee of 1925 was still in the Age of Miracles was proved to me by a curious personal experience. Before I left for the Scopes trial I had a session in New York with Edgar Lee Masters, a merry fellow who delights in poking fun at the common faiths and superstitions of the country, often by means of burlesque handbills. He told me that, if I would agree to distribute it at Dayton, he'd prepare such a handbill in the name of one of his favorite stooges, an imaginary evangelist named the Rev. Elmer Chubb, LL.D., D.D. I agreed of course, and a day or two before I set out I received about 1,000 copies of the following:

COMING!　　COMING!

To DAYTON, TENNESSEE

During the Trial of the Infidel Scopes

ELMER CHUBB, LL.D., D.D.

FUNDAMENTALIST AND MIRACLE WORKER

MIRACLES PERFORMED ON THE PUBLIC SQUARE!

Dr. Chubb will allow himself to be bitten by any poisonous snake, scorpion, gila monster, or other reptile. He will also drink any poison brought to him. . . . In demonstration of the words of our Lord and Saviour Jesus Christ, as found in the 16th Chapter of the Gospel of St. Mark:

"*And these signs shall follow them that believe: in my name shall they cast out devils, they shall speak with new tongues; they shall take up serpents, and if they drink any deadly thing it shall in no wise hurt them; they shall lay hands on the sick and they shall recover.*"

PUBLIC DEMONSTRATION of healing, casting out devils, and prophesying. Dr. Chubb will also preach in Aramaic, Hebrew, Greek, Latin, Coptic, Egyptian, and in the lost languages of the Etruscans and the Hittites.

TESTIMONIALS—*all favorable but one:*

With my own eyes I saw Dr. Chubb swallow cyanide of potassium. WILLIAM JENNINGS BRYAN, CHRISTIAN STATESMAN

Dr. Chubb simply believes the word of God, and his power follows. REV. J. FRANK NORRIS

I was possessed of devils, and Dr. Chubb cast them out of me. Glory to God. MAGDALENA RAYBACK, R.F.D. 3, DUNCAN GROVE, MICH.

When under the spell of divine inspiration Dr. Chubb speaks Coptic as fluently as if it were his mother tongue. As to Etruscan, I cannot say. PROF. ADDISON BLAKESLEY

Chubb is a fake. I can mix a cyanide cocktail that will make him turn up his toes in thirty seconds. H. L. MENCKEN

SPECIAL NOTICE: Dr. Chubb has never pretended that he had power to raise the dead. The Bible shows that only the Saviour and Twelve Apostles had that power.

Free will offering, dedicated to the enforcement of the anti-evolution laws.

When the trial got under way I hired a couple of boys to distribute these circulars, and that night Henry Hyde and I went to the courthouse green to see what would turn up. Precisely nothing turned up. Hundreds of copies of the circulars were flying about the grass, and dozens of yokels had them in their hands, but no one showed any interest in Dr. Elmer

Chubb. A few discreet inquiries told us why. It was that the miracles he offered were old stuff in upland Tennessee. Nearly every one of the evangelists roaring at that moment was ready to undertake at least some of them, and there were other evangelists back in the hills who offered to do them all. A few nights later we saw and heard some of the latter at a Holy Roller camp five or six miles from Dayton: it was patronized by yahoos who believed that Dayton itself was so full of sin that they refused to enter it, even to see Bryan. To be sure, the performers we saw confined themselves mainly to speaking in the tongues, and did not venture to drink poison or to let snakes bite them, but only a little while later they proceeded to both operations, and after half a dozen of them had been floored the State police closed in on them, Mark or no Mark. But they resisted stoutly, and their customers with them, and during the eight or ten years following the infidel Northern newspapers reported a great many unhappy failures of the magic, some of them fatal. The question whether the effort to put them down was or was not in contempt of Divine Revelation became a political issue in Tennessee, with all the principal statesmen of the State sweating to take up a safe middle position, as they had at the time of the Scopes trial.

So far as I can recall, Bryan never expressed any public opinion on the subject, but his frequent declaration that every word in the King James Bible was literally true, including the typographical errors, ranged him on the side of the wonder-workers, and they were all hot for him. For Darrow they naturally had no taste, not only because he derided the Good Book, but also and principally because they really believed in miracles, and were confident that Jahveh would fetch him soon or late. Thus they kept away from him, for they didn't want to be present when the lightnings from Heaven began to fall. Their customers shared this fear, and it went so far that whenever a thunderstorm blew up, which was very often in that tropical weather, everyone save a few atheists began to edge away from Darrow in the courtroom. On the street, when the skies were clear, he had followers like Bryan, but they were by no means so numerous and most of them kept at a prudent distance. Once a mule ran away on the main street, and the whole crowd took to its heels, convinced by the clatter that Darrow's time

had come. Bryan was gorged and stuffed at colossal country
meals by all the surrounding gentry and illuminati, but old
Clarence had to mess miserably with Hays and Malone. Both
of these juniors were also regarded as doomed, but it was
generally believed that Darrow would be knocked off first, so
the bolder spirits sometimes approached them quite closely,
especially when no thunderstorm was in prospect. Here
Malone's Irish blarney also came into effect, for he could talk
even a Tennessee Baptist into smiling on him. On one horrible
occasion, in fact, he came near talking the yokel jury into ac-
quitting Scopes.

This, of course, was not to the taste of Darrow, for he was
shrewd enough to see that if the prisoner in the box were acquitted the case would soon be forgotten, including even Bryan's part in it. Inasmuch as his main aim in defending Scopes
was to plaster Bryan before the country as a jackass, he hoped
that his ostensible client would be condemned to the hulks,
for that would enable him to appeal to the Supreme Court of
Tennessee, and maybe even to the Supreme Court of the
United States, and so keep the searing spotlight upon Bryan.
Thus he was dreadfully disconcerted one afternoon when
Malone launched into a speech so eloquent that in five minutes
the jurymen were visibly wobbling, and in ten minutes even
the learned judge was beginning to gulp, pant and scratch
himself. The subject of the speech was some formal motion of
no importance, and after sending in Malone to do the job
Darrow relaxed into his firemen's suspenders and prepared for
a quiet little snooze. But he got no snooze that day, for Malone
leaped into it with all the fervor of an Irishman pulling the
British lion's tail. As I have said, the Daytonians were (and, I
suppose, still are) great fans for rhetoric, and they were presently getting a horse-doctor's dose of it. Malone began no
louder than an auctioneer crying a sale, but in a few minutes
he let his larynx have the gas, and thereafter he produced such
blasts and hurricanes of sound that I never heard the like of
them until I encountered Gerald L. K. Smith eleven years later.
Let him come to the end of a sentence on an open vowel, and
it sounded like the roar of a thousand massed lions. Let him
stop upon a consonant, and the effect was that of smashing a
hundred tons of crockery. There was no loud-speaker in the

courtroom, but Dudley did not need it. With his own naked voice he filled the big room with so vast and terrifying a din that it seemed almost to bulge the walls. The yaps could not make out the drift of his remarks, but they were charmed by his execution. Sitting beside Darrow in the lawyers' pen, I watched them as the poison ran through them. First they sat up, then their eyes began to sparkle, and then they half rose from their chairs and fell to breathing heavily. In a little while they were breaking into cheers at the end of every sentence, and some of the more ebullient of them were leaping up and howling. The jurymen went the same way, and even the learned judge, as I have said, began to show signs of succumbing.

All this, of course, was very disturbing to Darrow. "Great God!" he whispered to me; "the scoundrel will hang the jury!" Thereupon he began to make frantic signals to Malone, commanding him to desist, but Malone, like any other orator, was so intoxicated by the exuberance of his own verbosity that he was deaf, dumb and blind. Indeed, if lightning had struck Darrow at that minute he'd have missed it. The one hope was that he would run out of breath soon or late, but for a while he seemed to be fetching up all that he needed, and more. But in the end, of course, his lungs began to creak and splatter, and finally, after a series of cyclonic gasps that first made his face a bright red and then left it dead white, he shut down at last and staggered out for air. One of his hearers had been his charming wife, Doris Stevens; she was standing in a corner of the courtroom surrounded by a group of Army officers who had come up from a nearby camp for the day's show. Dudley made for her with the sure instinct of any husband, and she proceeded to mop and soothe him as in wifely duty bound. I left Darrow and followed along, eager to offer my felicitations on what was undoubtedly the loudest speech ever delivered by mortal man since Apostolic times. The Army officers crowded up to be introduced to the orator and his wife, and it fell to me to present them. Doris, in those days, was a violent Lucy Stoner, and had been denouncing the reporters every time they addressed her or wrote of her as Mrs. Malone. But while the delighted anthropoids still roared their applause I bethought me of the first eight verses of Ecclesiastes III, so I approached the lady's ear and whispered: "What is it to be, Doris? Miss Stevens or Mrs.

Malone?" Stroking her husband's glistening bald head, she
* blushed prettily and answered: "Let it be Mrs. Malone—this
time." So when I presented the Army officers to her it was in
the character of a bourgeois wife. Her husband, under her
ministrations, recovered quickly, and that evening after dinner
he took Hays for $17 with four nines.

XVIII.

Vanishing Act
[1934]

TAKING ONE day with another I have but little hankering to
see ruins, but when, in the early part of 1934, I found myself aboard a ship approaching the French port of Tunis, in the
Mediterranean, and a Catholic bishop who was a fellow- *
passenger proposed that we go ashore the next day and have a
look at the remains of Carthage I agreed at once, for the Carthaginians have always fascinated me, if only because they made
so thorough a job of disappearing from the earth. His Excellency, it appeared, was but little interested in them himself, for
they were heathens as I was, and hence outside his ordinary
jurisdiction; what made him want to see their capital was simply the fact that the Roman city built upon its site had been
the stamping-ground of the celebrated Tertullian, who wrote
his "Apologeticus" there, and a frequent resort of the even
more renowned and much less dubious St. Augustine. The actual see of Augustine, however, was not Carthage but Hippo,
and the bishop and I put in a couple of hours trying to find
out where Hippo was, for if it was nearby we might very well
make a side trip to it. Unhappily, none of the guide-books in
the ship's library threw any light on the question, and we had
about given it up as unanswerable when we happened upon a
dog's-eared German encyclopedia and learned from it that
there were actually two Hippos, both of them to the west of
Carthage. The first, it appeared, was still carried on the books
of the Vatican as Hippo Diarrhytus and the second as Hippo
Regius, but now they were only the theoretical cathedral
towns of titular dioceses, without anything in them even remotely resembling cathedrals. If they actually had bishops
then those bishops had probably never seen them, nor made
any serious inquiries into their spiritual condition, but were
engaged instead upon paper work at Rome. Which Hippo was
Augustine's? The encyclopedia was not altogether clear on the
point, but we concluded after some speculation (as it turned

out, rightly) that it must be Hippo Regius, and dug up an atlas to find out where it lay. There was no such town in the
atlas, and it was not until we landed at Tunis the next day that
we learned that Hippo Regius had changed its name to Bône,
and was so far from Tunis that getting there and back would
take us three or four days. So we gave up the idea of visiting
the see of Augustine, and contented ourselves with taking a
look at Carthage.

What is left of it, we found, lies about ten miles northeast of
the city of Tunis, on the brow of a little hill now called Byrsa,
jutting out into the Gulf of Tunis, with the blue of the Mediterranean fading off into the distance beyond. The slope of the
hill is steep in front, and the pea-green inshore waters of the gulf
come quite close to the site, but on the landward side the descent is gradual, and vague farms that seem almost level show
themselves now and again through the dust of the Tunisian
plain. There is an automobile road up from Tunis, and also a
trolley line that stops at the foot of the hill. Down on the
beach a few fishermen haul in their nets, and in the other direction balls of denser dust show where some laborious hus-
bandman is plowing with donkey or camel. The landscape
looks almost as peaceful as that of Iowa. There is no quick
movement in it, not even from birds, and the ear catches no
sound. Yet it has seen some of the wildest fighting ever recorded, and the climaxes of that fighting were almost always
massacres. The earliest navigators of the Mediterranean, coming probably from Crete, fought for a toe-hold on the shore
against the primeval anthropophagi, and then against one another for the trade that, even in those remote days, flowed up
to the gulf from the black abysm of Africa. By the Ninth Century B.C. the Phoenicians, who were the English of the ancient
world, had driven out all the rest and built a handsome *cart
hadash*, or new town, on the bluff, and by the Third Century it
was greater than Tyre, their capital, and its sailors and traders
roved all the waters from Syria to the Pillars of Hercules, and
even beyond. There is, indeed, every reason to believe that
they circumnavigated Africa at least 1,800 years before Vasco
da Gama. The chief port of this Western trade was always
Carthage. From it radiated routes that reached to the farthest
frontiers of the known world. The Carthaginians controlled

the sea-borne carrying trade of that world, and were its greatest jobbers and bankers, and whenever they found a good harbor they set up a colony, and reached out from it for the business of the back country. One of those colonies, Tarshish in Spain, was so prosperous that it became, in Biblical times, a sort of common symbol of opulence. Also, it became a refuge for the broken and outlawed men of the whole Mediterranean littoral, and it was there that Jonah tried to hide himself when he got into trouble with Jahveh, as your pastor will tell you. But today Tarshish is only a measly fishing village at the mouth of the Guadalquiver, bearing about the same relation to Cádiz that Sagaponack, L. I., does to New York. As for Carthage itself, it is not even a village, but only a spot.

Certainly there must be few parallels in history to the completeness of its destruction. The Romans, like all the other Japs and Nazis of antiquity, threw their hearts into the job when they undertook to pull an enemy town to pieces, but there is no record that they ever went so far anywhere else as at Carthage. Consider, for example, the kindred case of Jerusalem, destroyed in the year 70 A.D. That was an earnest and comprehensive piece of work, as such things go, and the Jews still wail it as their worst disaster since the Babylonian Captivity; but let us not forget that the wall before which they do their wailing survived the Roman mortars and torpedo-bombs almost undamaged, and remains in excellent repair to this day. Nor is it the only healthy relic of the days before Jerusalem was hypothetically wiped out, to rise no more; the town, in fact, is full of odds and ends that are ascribed, at least by the guides, to the ages of Solomon, Moses, Abraham and even Adam. But at Carthage the Romans really spit on their hands, and in consequence the remains of the city, once so rich and so puissant, are no greater in bulk and hardly greater in significance than the remains of a barn struck by lightning. The French fathers settled in the place have raked up everything they could find and stored it in what they call a museum, but you could get the whole contents of that museum into a couple of boxcars, and most of them are mere scraps and potsherds, unidentified and unidentifiable. For when the Romans demolished Carthage they not only tore down and removed all its buildings, and plowed up its streets, and filled its wells, and emptied its

graves; they also devoured and annihilated all its records, so
that what is known about it today, save for the major outlines
of its history, is next to nothing. Of its people we have only a
few names—Hannibal, Hamilcar and so on, nearly all of them
of military men. The one Carthaginian author who is remembered is Sanchuniathon, and he is remembered only because a
fifth-rate Greek once mentioned him, and probably also invented him.

The bishop and I were through with the relics in half an
hour, and when we had finished we were no wiser than we had
been before. What use did the Carthaginians make of the little
stone boxes that were stretched out in a meagre row? The
prevailing theory is that they were coffins for the ashes of children sacrificed to the national god, who is assumed to have
been the Phoenician Moloch, but that is only a guess, and for
all anyone knows to the contrary the name of the god may
have been Goldberg or McGinnis, and the creatures sacrificed
to him may have been, not children at all, but dogs, cats or
goats. If he had a temple that temple is now less than dust, and
if it had priests then all the gold, silver, myrrh and frankincense
accumulated by those priests is now the same. Even the new
town that the Romans built on the site long after the old one
was destroyed is far along the road to annihilation and forgetfulness. Its best preserved relic is the shell of a theatre—now
greatly resembling a stone quarry in the last stages of bankruptcy and decay. While His Excellency and I contemplated
what is left of it, some boys who were passengers in our ship
recreated themselves by leaping up and down its moldering
tiers. Presently one of these boys missed his step and skinned
his shins, and under cover of his caterwauling we withdrew.
There was an Englishman nearby engaged upon a lecture to
such visitors as cared to hear him. We listened for a while and
found his patter far superior to that of the average guide, but
what he had to say was, after all, precisely nothing, and that
was what we already knew.

So we moved away to a quiet place overlooking the dusty
Tunisian plain, and fell into silent pondering, each on his own.
I can't tell you what form the bishop's meditations took, for
high ecclesiastics are not given to confidences in that field, but
my own, I recall, dwelt altogether on the complete oblitera-

tion, not only of Carthage the town, but also of its people. They were, I have no doubt, divided into groups and moieties as we are today, and showed all the sharp differences of fortune, virtue, capacity and opinion that have marked human societies at all times and everywhere. There must have been Carthaginians who were admired and envied by the rest, and other Carthaginians who were envied and disliked. Whenever a new source of cocoa-nuts, ivory or ebony was discovered along the African coast, or a new tin mine in Cornwall, or a new fishing bank in the waters to the North, there must have been a heavy inflow of fresh money, and a large part of that fresh money, you may be sure, was collared by individual Carthaginians of superior smartness, and laid out in ostentations of the sort that win public respect and lay the foundations of doggy families. It is not hard to imagine what followed, for the same thing is going on today, not only in all the great nations of Christendom, but also in the black kingdoms of the African jungle and the barbarisms of Inner Asia. Once Father had the money the rest followed almost automatically. If there were any daughters in the family the general estimation of their pulchritude went up by 200 or 300%, and all save the one who fell in love with a lieutenant in the army made elegant and even gaudy marriages—maybe with the sons of old families that traced their ancestry back to the motherland of Phoenicia and claimed descent from a Duke of Byblus or Zarephath; maybe even with some actual member of the Phoenician nobility, sent out to the colonies to recoup the failing fortunes of his house. As for the sons of the new plutocrat, they went through the Harvard of the time (first missing Groton, but making Lawrenceville), put in five or six years playing polo and keeping dancing women, and then married soberly and settled down to sitting on boards of directors, serving as vestrymen of the temple of Moloch (or Goldberg, or McGinnis), and waiting patiently for the exitus of their now venerable pa.

By the time he shuffled off at last, leaving doctors' bills to the amount of at least a ton of gold, they were fathers themselves, with wives growing bulky and pious, daughters who never had enough clothes, and sons who broke the legs of the family elephants playing polo and had to be ransomed ever and anon from the clutches of designing wenches from Crete,

Sicily and Spain. The grandchildren continued the sempiternal and inevitable round, familiar in Sumer and still familiar in this great free republic. Some of them, born idiots, became philosophers and refused to bathe. Others went in for gambling and were soon in hock to their brothers and cousins. Others succumbed to the evangelists of new religions who were constantly coming in from the eastward, and went about arguing that Moloch (or Goldberg, or McGinnis) was really not a god at all, but only the emanation of a god, and that his parent divinity was someone of the same name, or some other name, in Mesopotamia, the Hittite country, or elsewhere. Yet others laid out their heritage backing schemers who claimed to have discovered tin mines in Carthage itself, not twenty miles from the City Hall; or assembled vast collections of unintelligible papyri from the upper Nile, and employed Greeks with long whiskers to catalogue them; or bought large ranches in the hinterland and undertook to raise elephants, camels or giraffes; or organized gangs of gladiators and took them along the North African coast, challenging all comers; or drove chariots down the main street to the peril of the cops, street-sweeps, blind men and school children, and landed finally in the sanitarium on the mountain over behind what is now Tunis. The fourth generation produced a high percentage of whores and drunkards, and began to slip back to the primordial nonentity. Some of the cadets of the younger lines enlisted in the army, or in the Phoenician Foreign Legion, and were killed fighting Assyrians, Persians, Greeks or Romans. Others became policemen, bookkeepers, sailors, collectors for the orphans, *schochets* or *mohels* (for the Carthaginians were Semitic), school teachers, fortune tellers, barbers, priests, stone masons or horse doctors, or even garbage haulers, fish pedlars or jail wardens. But not infrequently there was at least one line that kept its money and held up its collective head, and after a century or two it came to be accepted as ancient and eminent, and began to look down its nose at the rest of the people. The gradual accumulation of such lines produced an aristocracy—an inevitable phenomenon in human society, then as now. That aristocracy had arisen from the trading class, but in the end it was clearly and admittedly superior to the trading class. Its members were regarded with deference by the commonalty, and had a long list of special opportunities and privileges. One of its constituent families, in the later days of Carthage, was that of Hannibal and Hamilcar.

But that it actually ruled the country is not very probable, for aristocracies, taking one century with another, are hardly more than false-faces. They sit in the parlor, so to speak, but down in the boiler-room quite different gangs are at work. Those gangs, whatever the form of government, are composed of professional governors, which is to say, of politicians, orators, intriguers, demagogues. They commonly occupy, in the hierarchy of caste, a place below the salt, and it is unusual for them to transmit their talents and power to their descendants, but while they last all real power is in their hands, whether the country they infest be a monarchy, an oligarchy or a free republic. As I have said, we know next to nothing of the internal history of Carthage, but the little we know indicates that it went through the same upheavals that periodically wrack all the great states of today. Every now and then the parliament, or grand council, or steering committee or whatever the governing body was called suffered a wholesale purging, and as the old gang took to the hills a new gang came in. We know nothing of the issues involved, or of the personalities participating, but it is not unreasonable to assume that what happened then was substantially what happens now. Let us not be deceived by recalling that in Carthage, so far as the meagre record shows, the proletariat had no voice in the government, and that demagogy in our sense was thus impossible. Let us recall, rather, that demagogues do not operate on the proletariat only, but also on aristocracies, plutocracies and even kings and emperors. Nay, I have seen them, with my own eyes, operating upon bishops, university presidents and newspaper editors. They are the most adept practical psychologists of the race, and when they rise to their full gifts it is impossible to prevail against them by any means whatsoever, save only by the sorry means of setting another and worse gang of demagogues upon them.

Thus Carthage lived and had its being for 668 glorious years, constantly reaching out for new trade, setting up new bridgeheads on ever remoter and remoter coasts, and piling up wealth as no other nation had ever piled it up before. Its liners and tramp freighters went everywhere, and its ships of war controlled all the seas. Now and then, to be sure, some other nation objected to this relentless penetration, and especially to the monopoly that usually followed it, and there were bloody wars, but the Carthaginians took such unpleasantnesses in their stride, for they were well aware that blood was the price of admiralty. One of their wars lasted a hundred years, but they drew profits out of it all the while it was going on, and came out of it richer than ever. Every savage tribe from the Congo to the Baltic got a taste of their steel, and they did not hesitate to tackle the greatest empires. Even mighty Rome, at the apex of its power, found them formidable antagonists, and on several occasions they came within an ace of sacking the Imperial City itself. Altogether, it took the Romans 119 years to knock them off, and when it was accomplished at last it was made possible only by the fact that the blackamoors of Africa, tired at last of Carthaginian rule, joined Rome against them. As I looked out over the scene of what must have been the decisive battle of the war, I could not help wondering what these blackamoors had got out of the victory. Perhaps the Romans let them carry off a few women, and maybe a share of the lesser bric-a-brac. Otherwise, they got nothing, for the Romans grabbed everything really valuable for themselves, and a little while later they were running the blackamoors precisely as prisoners are run in an efficient house of correction, which is to say, precisely as the Carthaginians had been running them before the war.

The descendants of those poor people were before me as I pondered—laboriously plodding the Tunisian plain behind their archaic plows and spavined donkeys and camels, each surrounded by his ball of dust. It seemed a bleak and miserable life that they were leading, but I couldn't help adding to myself that they had at least survived. Of their old masters, the Carthaginians, there was nothing left save a Valhalla of blurred and incredible ghosts. I tried, though cold sober, to conjure up some of them as I contemplated their jumping-off place, but it was a vain undertaking, for even conjuring needs materials, and I had next to none. Who was the chief poet of Carthage in, say, the year 500 B.C., and what sort of poetry did he write? I asked myself the question, but that is as far as I got, for I was not too

sure that Carthage had any poets, and if they existed no specimens of their work have come down to us. Well, then, what of
the executive secretary of the Carthage Chamber of Commerce
in the year 400? Here I got a little further, for a people as excessively commercial as the Carthaginians must have had a chamber of commerce, and it is impossible to imagine one without
an executive secretary. I therefore imagined him, but having
gone so far I was stalled again, for I could not figure out what
he must have looked like, or what sort of office he did his work
in, or how much of his time he devoted to port statistics and
how much to writing speeches for the shipping magnates,
grain exporters and bringers in of ivory, apes and peacocks
who were his employers.

It was easier, somehow, to contrive plausible phantoms of
lesser folk—for example, the stevedores down at the docks, the
rowers of galleys, the cops patrolling their beats, the wine-sellers
behind their bars, the hawkers of charms and images, the farmers in from the country with their loads of turnips and cabbages, the soldiers sparking the housemaids, the barbers with
their sharp razors and clattering tongues. But even the barbers,
when I got to them, hauled me up, for I was not sure that the
Carthaginians shaved. Did the other Semites of that era? The
portraits of Moses, Abraham and company in the art galleries
of the world seem to indicate that they didn't, and I recalled
that even the orthodox Jews of New York, up to the time they
moved to the Bronx, still wore their beards. In the end the old
gentry of Carthage gave me less trouble than any of the other
folks, for the gentry are much the same everywhere. As the
motorman of the Tunis trolley began to bang his gong and the
bishop and I climbed aboard his car I was thinking of the ancient families that saw at one stroke the ruin of their nation
and the annihilation of their own lines. Some of them, by 146
B.C., had been settled in Carthage for five or six hundred years,
and their position in its society must have been quite the equal
of that of the Percys in England. Whenever there was a public
procession they marched at its head. No one ever dared to
flout them, not even the politicoes in whose puppet-show they
served as glittering dummies. They were the living symbols of
half a millennium of Carthaginian power and glory, pomp and
circumstance, and each of them was a living repository of

honor, dignity, *noblesse oblige*. Not a few of them, I daresay, were so finely bred that they had lost the calves of their legs and were more or less hollow in the head, but they would not lie and they could not be bought. So they stood as the third Punic War came to its catastrophic end, and the ruffianly Romans closed in. By the time the burning and slaying, the raping and looting were over they had all vanished—and this is the first friendly mention that they have had in print, I suppose, for 2,088 years.

The bishop and I were silent as we were hauled back to Tunis, each sunk in his own thoughts. When the trolley-car finally stopped at the Tunis four corners we debarked from it and looked for a hack to haul us down to the wharf where a launch from our ship was waiting. At that moment a brisk and handsome young man, obviously an American, emerged from the assembled crowd, approached me politely, and asked me if I were not Mr. Mencken from Baltimore. When I replied that I was he introduced himself as a Baltimorean who had come out to the North African coast some years before, and was at present living in Tunis. I naturally asked him what he was doing there, and his reply was so astounding that I could only stare at him like an idiot. He was, he said, the manager of a baseball league stretching all along the coast, from Casablanca in the west to Cairo in the east, with a couple of outlying clubs in Syria and the Holy Land and another at Gibraltar. But where, I faltered, did he get his pitchers and catchers, his batters and fielders? What did the Moroccans, Berbers, Copts, Syrians, Arabs, Jews and the rest know about the national game of the United States? His reply was that they knew a lot, for he had taught them. They were young fellows with plenty of enthusiasm in them, and hence quick to learn. Baseball, he said, was now the favorite sport along the whole south shore of the Mediterranean, and when two good teams met for an important game a large crowd turned out and there was a great deal of loud rooting. There was to be one the next day, and if I were free he would be delighted to have me see it as his guest. He had lived in Tunis so long, he said, that he was now almost a native, but his thoughts still turned to old Baltimore, and whenever he heard that a Baltimorean was in town he looked him up.

There was no time to cross-examine this amazing stranger, for the bishop and I had to get back to our ship, but he was a very well-appearing fellow, so I swallowed his tale without too much resistance. When I got back to Baltimore I found that it had been true in every detail. There was, in fact, a thick envelope of clippings about him in the morgue of the Baltimore *Sunpapers*. I went through those clippings with great interest, and was not surprised to discover that not one of them mentioned the fact that the home grounds of his Tunis club were on the site of what had once been Carthage.

XIX.

Pilgrimage

[1934]

I WAS fifty-three years, five months and sixteen days old before ever I saw Jerusalem, and by that time, with Heaven
itself beginning to loom menacingly on the skyline, my itch to
sob at the holy places was naturally something less than frantic.
I had not, in fact, gone to Palestine for the purpose of touring
them, and had no intention of doing so; the only aim that I
formulated to myself, in so far as I had any at all, was to visit
and investigate the ruins of Gomorrah, the Hollywood of antiquity and the only rival of Sodom in the long and brilliant
chronicles of sin. What attracted me to it, of course, was simply
this almost unparalleled reputation for wickedness, for my experience of mankind had taught me that ill fame was commonly
very much exaggerated, just as good fame was exaggerated.
Hadn't I been to Hollywood itself, and found it to be almost if
not quite as respectable as Newport News, Va., or Natchez-
under-the-Hill? What if I should discover evidence, on turning
over the débris of Gomorrah, that it had been maligned by
history, and even by Divine Revelation? In all this, I confess,
there was a certain amount of attitudinizing, but I do not
apologize for it, for it was attitudinizing more than anything
else that led Columbus to discover America, as you will learn
by reading Dr. Samuel E. Morison's excellent work, "Admiral
of the Ocean Sea." In any case, I was willing to pay my own
way, which was a good deal more than could be said for Columbus. If it cost me $250 to establish my thesis I'd be glad to
meet the bills out of my own pocket and call it a day, and even
if it ran to $500 or $1,000 I'd not be importuning the Queen
of Spain for assistance or otherwise passing the hat.

Unhappily, I quickly learned, on inquiry in Jerusalem, that
the brimstone and fire described in Genesis XIX, 24 had been
so effective that nothing remained of Gomorrah save a name
to scare Sunday-schools. Even on the elementary question of

its site all the local authorities seemed to be at odds. One of Cook's agents, a young Welshman speaking five languages, told me that it was somewhere in a swamp south of the Dead Sea, and offered to get me there in a Buick, with a chauffeur, an interpreter and three meals a day included, at a flat rate of $18.75 *per diem*; but while I was negotiating with him a Syrian employed by the Palestine Exploration Fund, and speaking seven languages, horned in with a noisy declaration that the true location was fifty miles away, on the *north* shore of the sea. Leaving these experts snorting at each other, I returned to the King David Hotel outside the walls and there consulted the *portier*, an intelligent Swiss speaking nine languages. He told me that what remained of the town was really in the bed of the sea, and offered in proof the fact that the workmen of the English company engaged in dredging the bottom for potash often brought up bones, musical instruments and bogus jewelry. This shook me, and I devoted the next morning to looking into the matter more particularly. Before noon I had accumulated six more opinions, all of them positive and authoritative, but each differing from the rest. By that time I was in a considerable sweat, for it is warmish in Jerusalem even in Winter, so I finally adopted the escapist theory that Jahveh had made a really all-out job of Gomorrah, as the Romans had of Carthage, and abandoned my plan to explore its ruins.

My decision left me with some unexpected leisure on my hands, and I employed it in moseying about Jerusalem, the glory of Israel as Ireland is of God. It turned out to be a town of about the size of Savannah, Ga., or South Bend, Ind., but differing radically from both. There had been, a short while before, some gang fights between Jews and Arabs, and they were destined, a little while later, to fall upon one another in the grand manner, but at the time of my visit, which was in 1934, there was a hiatus in these hostilities and I was not molested, though I was warned by an English cop that some sassy Arab might have at me with a camel flop as an infidel or some super-orthodox Jew might hoot me as a *chazirfresser*. Most of the so-called streets I traversed were not more than ten feet wide and a good many of them ended in dead walls. Nearly all were lined with so-called *suks*, or bazaars—a series of holes in the wall not much larger than kitchenettes. In each *suk* lurked a merchant sitting cross-legged, and in front of each merchant were spread his wares—most often, only sleazy looking rugs, tarnished brass vessels full of dents, crude pottery of the thunder-mug species, and other such gimcrackery. Having just come from Cairo, where some of the *suks* approximate the glitter of Fifth avenue specialty shops, and Algiers, where many of them offer wines and liquors and there is a bawdy-house every block or so, I was not impressed by those of Jerusalem.

There was a good deal of crowding and jostling in the streets, but what made walking really unpleasant was the paving. It was kept in reasonable repair, but it consisted predominantly of cobbles, and they were made of a soft native limestone that became as smooth as glass under foot traffic, and quite as slippery. Having come down a couple of times, I paused in a little plaza to take stock of my injuries, and there saw a British soldier in full equipment land on his *tochos* with a fearful clatter. When I helped him to his feet he told me that he had served in H. M. Army for twelve years, in posts ranging from Gibraltar to Ceylon and including such hells as Aden and Rangoon, but that Jerusalem, in his judgment, was the bloodiest goddam place of them all. It was a lucky day, he said, when the cobbles fetched him less than five times, and there were bad days when he got back to barracks with his caboose as badly macerated as a pug's nose and ears. He spoke in favorable terms of the destruction of the city by the Romans in the year 70 A.D., though he apparently thought that the date of the job was as recent as Napoleonic times. A man of speculative mind, he tried to figure out how long it would take a smart battery of artillery posted on the Mount of Olives to knock the whole bloody settlement to pieces, and his guess was that it could be bloody well done in half an hour. He was, he said, bloody hot for trying it, and he hoped that it would be done in some bloody future war.

This soldier told me, somewhat to my surprise, that I was standing directly in front of the Church of the Holy Sepulchre, and advised me with a derisive wink to have a look at the interior. A few weeks before, he said, the walls had cracked and the building threatened to tumble in, but since then it had been shored up by the British authorities and was now reasonably safe. Entering by a small door at a cost of an American quarter, collected by an Armenian clergyman in long whiskers, I found myself in what appeared, at first glance, to be the midway of a small carnival. The whole roof was hung with shabby banners and streamers, and pendent from them were almost innumerable lamps and lanterns, some lighted and smoking but the majority out of service. The floor was divided by low railings into four or five sections, and I learned from a sort of map that had been handed to me at the door that each belonged to one or another branch of the Christian Church—the Roman, the Greek Orthodox, the Armenian, the Nestorian, and so on. Each section was manned by ecclesiastics of the branch in charge of it. The actual Sepulchre, it appeared, was in charge of the Copts—whether by a permanent arrangement or by some sort of rotation I was not informed. It cost me another quarter to see it, and the priest in charge threw a good deal of hocus-pocus into showing it. What he finally had to offer, after cautioning me in half a dozen languages to keep my hat off, was simply a hole probably ten feet wide, twenty feet long and twelve feet deep, hollowed out of the solid rock and reached by a stone stairway. Obviously enough, at least to anyone familiar with John XIX, 41, as I was, it was bogus; indeed it was bogus by the Synoptic Gospels also, for unless Joseph of Arimathea was a reincarnation of Samson no one could imagine him rolling a stone large enough to close it. But I kept my doubts to myself, bowed politely to the rev. Copt, and shoved off to see what the Jews and Moslems had to offer, for Jerusalem is a holy city to both of them just as it is to Christians.

The Moslems, I found, put on nothing describable as a first-rate attraction, and in fact discouraged visits to their sacred stands by unbelievers, and the best Jewish show currently playing was that at the famous Wailing Wall. A British cop showing me a short cut by way of the old city ramparts, I found the place without any difficulty. It was a huge excavation in the rock recalling those that laborious Italians used to make in the Archean underpinnings of Manhattan island in the days when men of vision were still building sky-scrapers. It was lined with masonry, and one of the walls was considerably higher than the others. At the bottom of this high wall was the wailing place, and as I came down the long stairway to the bottom of the great pit perhaps twenty-five Jews were lined up, all of them with their faces to the wall. I naturally expected to hear some hubbub, but save for an occasional mild shriek or groan the wailing was carried on *pianissimo*, and one had to come close to a given Jew to hear him at all. Their operations were apparently ritualistic in character, for each had a book in front of him, held up against the wall, and some of them followed the text with their forefingers. At one end of the pit stood a camp-stool and a little camp-table, and on the stool sat a British sergeant in his shirt-sleeves, intent upon a copy of the *News of the World* spread out upon the table. I assumed that he was there to protect the Jews against the Arabs, who might have bombarded them very easily from the tops of the walls, but when I tackled him he said not.

"I have my men up there," he explained, "and they keep all suspicious characters moving. Before an Arab could let go with a dead cat they would have nippers on him, and he would be on his way to three months hard. What I am down in this bloody hole for is to keep the peace among the Jews. They are all very religious fellows, and so they tend to hate each other. Suppose a Jew from Baghdad comes down in the morning and finds that the place he used yesterday has been grabbed by a Jew from Salonika. Does he say, 'Excuse me, Mister, but you have my pitch. Would you mind shoving over a bit?' Not at all. In the first place, the Baghdad lingo is as different from Salonikan as English is from French, and both speak Hebrew with thick accents, the one, let us say, like an Irishman and the other like a Welshman. So they simply screech at each other, and in two minutes, if I didn't jump into the ring and make them break, they would be pulling whiskers, and then their friends would join in, and we'd have a couple of jobs for the ambulance. But it's not hard to handle them if you know how. All I have to do is to let go with my fists, and it is all over. I have been sitting here for six months, and I know most of the steady customers. Some of them, I hear, have been at it off and on for years. It is a kind of trade with them. Nine out of ten are as peaceable as so many blind men. When a shindy is going on at one end of the wall the old fellows at the other end keep on wailing. I have been told that it has been going on since Adam's time. What they are wailing about I don't know, though I have heard two or three different stories. You can never believe anything you hear in Jerusalem. The place is full of liars."

Slipping the instructive sergeant a five-cent American cigar and wishing him many happy returns of the day, I went back to the King David Hotel, and there hired a car to take me to Bethlehem, five miles out of town. The driver, a Soudanese Negro who had been a dragoman in Cairo and spoke very fair English, pointed out the places of interest along the road. The only one that I remember was the Y.M.C.A., a huge structure not far from the King David, resembling in a way a country-club in Florida and in another way the General Motors building at a world's fair. I asked the driver how so large an establishment could be supported in Jerusalem, for Protestants are almost as rare there as in South Boston or the Bronx. He replied that the money came from America, and that the actual patrons were Moslems and Jews. The Moslems, he said, went in for track work in the gymnasium, and the Jews patronized the free classes in double-entry bookkeeping, foreign exchange and scientific salesmanship. On the common ground of their dislike of Christians they met amicably, and there had never been any rough stuff at the Y, even when riots were going on at its very door. I ventured to suggest that maybe this was due to the calming influence of the Y.M.C.A. secretaries, and asked the Soudanese if they had converted any of the Moslems or Jews to their Rotarian theology. His only reply was to laugh. He said that the Salvation Army, a much more powerful theological engine than the Y.M.C.A., had been banging away in Jerusalem for years, but that its only converts to date were a few soldiers drummed out of the British Army, a few drink-crazed Scandinavian sailors wandering in from Haifa and Jaffa, and a meagre haul of other such poor fish. It was just as unlikely for a Moslem to turn Methodist, he said, as it would be for a Methodist to turn Moslem. Protestantism had no more chance in Palestine, he went on, than cannibalism would have in England. Not only were the Moslems and Jews unanimously against it; the Latin, Greek, Abyssinian, Armenian, Coptic and other old-fashioned dirt Christians were even more against it, and spent a great deal of time talking against it. The Holy Land, he said, did not have any taste for novelty, and was

generally hostile to strangers. Nearly everything in sight was at
least ten thousand years old, and the people distrusted anything newer. The great majority of them, including most of
the Jews who were there before Zionism got afoot, preferred
Turkish rule to that of the English, who were constantly shor-
ing up tumbledown churches and mosques, arresting poor
folk for clubbing donkeys or committing nuisances up alleys,
issuing insane regulations for the disposal of garbage, and
otherwise making pests of themselves. The Turks believed in
living and letting live, and were thus esteemed. To be sure,
they had laid on heavy taxes, but it was always possible to get
out of paying more than a small part by seeing the right persons, and no tax they ever laid on was as heavy as those laid on
by the incorruptible English.

The Soudanese told me that the only thing worth seeing at
Bethlehem was the Church of the Nativity—for the rest, he
said, the town consisted only of souvenir shoppes full of relics
made in Japan—, so I proceeded to take a look at the sacred
edifice as soon as we got to the town. It was managed jointly,
the Soudanese explained, by monks of the Armenian, Greek
and Latin rites, and not infrequently they got into lamentable
disputes over nuances of dogma, and had been known, histori-
cally, to back up revelation with a certain amount of eye-gouging,
nose-biting and whiskers-yanking. I was amazed to discover,
when I got to the place, that its builders back in the Ages of
Faith had apparently forgotten to give it a front door, just as
Thomas Jefferson, centuries later, was to forget to provide a
stairway in his mansion at Monticello. The entrance, in fact,
was a mere hole in the wall, and in order to get through it I
had to bend almost double. Arriving inside, I was even more
amazed to discover that there was a large and even huge door
in the rear wall—one big enough, in fact, to let in a Fifth avenue bus. Why wasn't it used instead of the hole in front? I
asked the question of everyone I encountered in Bethlehem
who could speak English, but never got a satisfactory answer.
On my return to Jerusalem I renewed my inquiries, and was
told by the Swiss *portier* at the King David that the hole was
used simply because the monks believed that putting customers to a little discomfort threw them into a mortified frame of
mind, and so promoted their fear of God and made them

generous with contributions. They had read in some quackish forerunner of "How to Make Friends and Influence People" that it was sound psychology to make the pious sweat a bit, lest pride consume them. If that was actually their theory, then it certainly failed to work in my own case, for I emerged from the hole in the front wall, after a scant fifteen minutes inside, full of wayward doubts and cholers. I even began to suspect that the whole establishment was a fake, just as the Church of the Holy Sepulchre was a fake. How, indeed, could any rational person reconcile the elaborate marble grotto that the monks had shown me with the manger described in Luke II, 7, 12 and 16?

Back in Jerusalem, I took a walk that evening to work off my dubieties, and, on encountering a sort of information bureau run by the Jewish Agency, dropped in to pick up some of its literature. One of the young Jews in attendance asked me to sign the visitors' book and I did so. By the time I got back to the hotel a couple of smart agents of the Agency, both speaking fluent English, were waiting for me. It appeared that they had recognized my name as that of a man connected with the press, and had dropped in to say that if I cared to make a tour of the Jewish colonies to the north of Jerusalem they were at my service. This friendly invitation sounded so attractive that I accepted at once. As a result, one of the agents and I started out in a car very early the next morning, and by nightfall had accomplished one of the most charming trips I have ever made in this life. The day was fine, the roads were good, the car was fast, and the agent who steered me, Mr. A. L. Fellman, was an intelligent young man speaking English, Yiddish, Arabic and Hebrew, with family connections in my native Baltimore. Nearly everything worth seeing in Palestine, he told me, was north of Jerusalem, and we covered virtually all of it in the one day, for the distance from Jerusalem to the line of the Sea of Galilee, Nazareth and Mount Carmel is less than seventy-five miles. The road northward runs almost straight, but we debouched from it often, and at the end of the day our speedometer showed a run of 350 kilometers. At one time we ran along the Jordan for a dozen or more miles and made a foray across it into Trans-Jordan, which looked a good deal like the worst parts of Arizona. Stopping at noon for a hearty *kosher* lunch at Tiberias, on the Sea of Galilee—I recall that there were two * soups, three kinds of meat, and four kinds of pastry—, we struck westward over the Galilean highlands, and after seeing the place where the Gadarene swine were possessed by devils and leaped into the water, the birthplace of Mary Magdalene, the scene of the miracle at Cana—often mentioned favorably in the American newspapers of the days of Prohibition—, the town of Nazareth, and the ancient battlefield of Armageddon, we landed finally at Haifa on the sea coast. On the long way we stopped at half a dozen of the Jewish colonies, and had friendly palavers with their public relations agents, most of whom, I found, could speak either English or German, and often both.

These colonies interested me greatly, if only because of the startling contrast they presented to the adjacent Arab farms. The Arabs of the Holy Land, like those of the other Mediterranean countries, are probably the dirtiest, orneriest and most shiftless people who regularly make the first pages of the world's press. To find a match for them one must resort to the oakies now translated from Oklahoma to suffering California, or to the half-simian hill-billies of the Appalachian chain. Though they have been in contact with civilization for centuries, and are credited by many fantoddish professors with having introduced it into Europe, they still plow their miserable fields with the tool of Abraham, to wit, a bent stick. In the morning, as Fellman and I spun up the highroad to the north, I saw them going to work, each with his preposterous plow over his back, and in the evening, as we went westward across Galilee, I saw them returning home in the same way. Their draft animals consisted of anything and everything—a milch cow, a camel, a donkey, a wife, a stallion, a boy, an ox, a mule, or some combination thereof. Never, even in northwestern Arkansas or the high valleys of Tennessee, have I seen more abject and anemic farms. Nine-tenths of them were too poor even to grow weeds: they were simply reverting to the gray dust into which the land of Moab to the eastward has long since fallen. As for the towns in which the Arabs lived, they resembled nothing so much as cemeteries in an advanced state of ruin. The houses were built of fieldstone laid without mortar, and all the roofs were lopsided and full of holes. From these forlorn hovels ragged women peeped at us from behind their greasy veils, and naked children popped out to steal a scared look and then pop back.

Of edible fauna there was scarcely a trace. Now and then I saw a sad cow, transiently reprieved from the plow, and in one village there was a small flock of chickens, but the cows always seemed to be dying of pellagra or beri-beri, and the chickens were small, skinny and mangy.

These Arab villages were scattered all about, but most of them were on hilltops, as if the sites had been chosen for defense. Sweeping down from them into the valleys below were the lands of the immigrant Jews. The contrast was so striking as to be almost melodramatic. It was as if a series of Ozark corn-patches had been lifted out of their native wallows and set down amidst the lush plantations of the Pennsylvania Dutch. On one side of a staggering stone hedge were the bleak, miserable fields of the Arabs, and on the other side were the almost tropical demesnes of the Jews, with long straight rows of green field crops, neat orchards of oranges, lemons and pomegranates, and frequent wood-lots of young but flourishing eucalyptus. Fat cows grazed in the meadows, there were herds of goats eating weeds, and every barnyard swarmed with white Leghorn chickens. In place of the bent sticks of the Arabs, the Jews operated gang-plows drawn by tractors, and nearly every colony had a machine-shop, a saw-mill and a cannery. The contrast between the buildings on the two sides of the hedges was as remarkable as that between the fields. The Arabs, as I have said, lived in squalid huts letting in wind, rain and flying things, and their barns were hardly more than corrals, but the Jews lived in glistening new stucco houses recalling the more delirious suburbs of Los Angeles, and their animals were housed quite as elegantly as themselves. The architecture on display, I should add, caused me to cough sadly behind my hand, but it had at least some relevance to history and the terrain, for the general effect was genuinely oriental, as indeed it is in Los Angeles. The Jews appeared to be very proud of their habitations, for every time Fellman and I stopped at one and found the householder at home he insisted on showing us through it, and almost always pointed with swelling emotion to its tiled floors, its screened doors and its running water in the kitchen.

These Jews, however, appeared to spend but a small part of their time admiring their quarters: virtually all their waking hours were given to hard labor in the fields. In the larger colonies they did not even come in for meals, but were fed from a lunch-wagon working out of the central kitchen. Nor were their wives idle, for cooking was their job, and in addition they usually had to attend to the chickens and milk the cows. In some of the more advanced-thinking colonies the care of their children was taken from them to give them more time for these chores, and handed over to professionals, always including a trained nurse with a sharp eye for loose teeth and wormy tonsils. A mother, of course, could see her offspring in the intervals of her labors, but until they were six or seven years old they slept in dormitories attached to the schools, and she was not responsible for either their alimentation or their indoctrination. Fellman and I dropped in at several schools, and inspected the young inmates. They looked as healthy and happy as the prize babies whose pictures appear in the rotogravure advertisements of the milk companies.

It was pleasant roving about these luxuriant farms and palavering with the laborious and earnest men and women who ran them, but it didn't take long to discover that their passion for a constructive idealism was accompanied by the usual and apparently inevitable aches and pains. Much of the land they wrestled with was fertile enough, once the poisonous Arabs had been cleared off it, but there were other tracts that had suffered so badly by the misuse of centuries that getting them back to fecundity was an appallingly onerous business. They not only needed draining and grading and the repair of washouts; they also needed a long course of nursing, with heavy expenditures for fertilizers. Would this coddling ever really pay? Would the soil thus restored ever provide sufficient livings for the heavy work forces needed to restore it? On that point I found a certain amount of doubt, concealed only defectively by tall talk. So long as there was a steady flow of money from Zionists all over the earth the problem would not be pressing, but what if that flow were ever cut off? Also, what would happen if another world war interrupted overseas trade, and left Palestine to butter its own parsnips? One of the chief customers for the excellent oranges of the country, in 1934, was Germany. Could the Jews, with such markets closed, live on vitamins alone? I suspect that many a sweating colonist, his back bent in the field, occasionally let his mind play upon such unhappy questions, and if not in the field then in his scant hours of ease of an evening, with his radio blaring music from Berlin, Vienna and Rome, and an occasional whiff of jazz from points west.

But this fear of remote and still theoretical catastrophe was much less apparent than a fear of closer and even more unpleasant possibilities. The Arabs, who had been dispossessed of some of their best (as well as of some of their worst) lands, still hung about, and there was little reassurance in their dark and envious eyes. They blamed the *effendi* landlords in Cairo and Damascus for selling them out to the Jews, but they blamed the Jews even more for trading with the *effendis*, if only because the Jews were directly under their noses. It had been assumed by the pumpers up of Zionist enthusiasm, and in fact announced confidently, that the example of the colonists would lift these degraded step-brothers out of their ancient shiftlessness and imbecility, and make competent and successful farmers of them, but the event had proved that they were as incapable of competent farming as so many Florida crackers. Some of them had tried more or less earnestly, but all save an infinitesimal minority had failed. In plain view of the broad and smiling fields of the smart and diligent Jews they were still plowing idiotically with their bent sticks, and if Allah, by any chance, sent them more than eight bushels of wheat to an acre they hustled off to Mecca to give thanks. Like all such Chandala they ascribed their congenital unfitness to the villainy of their betters, and not infrequently they tried to cure it in the ancient Chandala manner. That is to say, they took to assassination. Already in 1934 it was becoming common for a Jew at work on the slopes making down to the Jordan to be knocked off by a shot from the other side of the river. The British had built concrete block-houses all through that lovely country and armed them with machine-guns, but those machine-guns offered no protection to Jews on outlying farms, and by the time a squad of soldiers got to the scene of a murder the Arab was lost in the wilds of Trans-Jordan. Nor could the poor Jews do anything effective in defense of themselves. I saw a number of them plowing with rifles strapped to their backs, but it was usually in the back that the brave Arabs shot them, and when that happened the rifle went down with the man. Altogether, there was an air of dread hanging over the border, and I was

582   HEATHEN DAYS

glad when we struck into the Galilean high country. As we
mounted the first hill we looked back at the Sea of Galilee and
saw a rainbow set prettily upon it, but if that rainbow was actually a promise, as recollections of Genesis IX, 16 suggested,
then it was only too obviously a false one. Only a few years
later the whole land was running with blood, and then came
the even greater calamity of World War II. I wonder as I write
what has been the fate of some of the hopeful and persevering
Jews I met on that beautiful Winter day. Most of them, I trust,
are still alive, but I am not too sure that those who are still
alive are more fortunate than those who are dead.

Perhaps appropriately, I made my exit from the Holy Land
by way of the battlefield of Armageddon, which began to soak
up gore in the remotest mists of the past, and had seen its last
battle so recently as 1918, when Allenby and the Turks rounded
out their little war by fighting all over it. No military geogra-
pher was needed to explain its immemorial popularity among
professional blood-letters. The great barrier of the Syrian mountains here ends in the promontory of Mount Carmel, and the
only way for an army to move northward or southward in any
comfort is by way of the narrow beach which separates Mount
Carmel from the sea. By that route all the hordes of antiquity
had moved or tried to move. Here the Hittites met the Egyptians, the Egyptians met the Persians, the Persians met the
Greeks, and the Jews were slaughtered by one and all. Below
the narrow pass the land widens out into a wide and almost flat
plain, and it was on it that the ancient battles joined. There is
probably no more likely battlefield on earth; it seems to have
been made for the marching and counter-marching of infantry,
and dashing cavalry charges. As we rolled over it I could not
help thinking of the hundreds of thousands of miserable John
Does who had watered it, over so many ages, with their
blood. More than one long forgotten captain won his bays
there, and more than one great empire came crashing down. If
it were in America it would be dotted with hideous monuments to the Fifth Pennsylvania and the Tenth Wisconsin, and
there would be guides to carry tourists over it, and plenty of
hot-dog and Coca-Cola stands to stoke them. But at Armageddon I couldn't find so much as a marker or a flag. Over the
dust of the immemorial and innumerable dead some Jewish

colonists were driving Ford tractors hitched to plows. It was much safer there than along the Jordan shore, and so they looked contented and even somewhat complacent. But I noticed that the earth their plowshares were turning up was redder than the red hills of Georgia. In the afternoon sunshine, in fact, it was precisely the color of blood.

XX.

Beaters of Breasts

[1936]

O N SEPTEMBER 1, in the presidential campaign year of 1936,
I received an office chit from Paul Patterson, publisher of
the Baltimore *Sunpapers*, proposing that I go to Boston to
cover the Harvard tercentenary orgies, then just getting under
way. On September 3, after a day given over, at least in theory,
to prayer and soul-searching, I replied as follows:

> The more I think over the Harvard project, the less it lifts me. I'd
> much prefer to join Alf Landon. I like politicoes much better than I
> like professors. They sweat more freely and are more amusing.

My prayer and soul-searching, of course, were purely bogus,
as such exercises only too often are. I had actually made up my
mind in favor of the politicians a great many years before, to
wit, in 1900 or thereabout, when I was still an infant at the
breast in journalism. They shocked me a little at my first intimate contact with them, for I had never suspected, up to then,
that frauds so bold and shameless could flourish in a society
presumably Christian, and under the eye of a putatively watchful God. But as I came to know them better and better I began
to develop a growing admiration, if not for their virtue, then at
least for their professional virtuosity, and at the same time I
discovered that many of them, in their private character, were
delightful fellows, whatever their infamies *ex officio*. This appreciation of them, in the years following, gradually extended
itself into a friendly interest in quacks of all sorts, whether
theological, economic, military, philanthropic, judicial, literary,
musical or sexual, and including even the professorial, and in
the end that interest made me a sort of expert on the science
of rooking the confiding, with a large acquaintance among
practitioners of every species. But though I thus threw a wide
net I never hauled in any fish who seemed to me to be the
peers of the quacks political—not, indeed, by many a glittering
inch. Even the Freudians when they dawned, and the chiro-

practors, and the penologists, and the social engineers, and the pedagogical wizards of Teachers College, Columbia, fell a good deal short of many Congressmen and Senators that I knew, not to mention Governors of sovereign American states. The Governors, in fact, were for long my favorites, for they constituted a class of extraordinarily protean rascals, and I remember a year when, of the forty-eight then in office, four were under indictment by grand juries, and one was actually in jail. Of the rest, seven were active Ku Kluxers, three were unreformed labor leaders, two were dipsomaniacs, five were bogus war heroes, and another was an astrologer.

My high opinion of political mountebanks remains unchanged to this day, and I suspect that when the history of our era is written at last it may turn out that they have been one of America's richest gifts to humanity. On only one point do I discover any doubt, and that is on the point whether those who really believe in their hocus-pocus—for example, Woodrow Wilson—are to be put higher or lower, in entertainment value, to those who are too smart—for example, Huey Long. Perhaps the question answers itself, for very few of the second class, in the long run, are able to resist their own buncombe, and I daresay that Huey, if the Japs had not cut him down prematurely, would have ended by believing more or less in his share-the-wealth apocalypse, though not, of course, to the extent of sharing his share. After the death of William Jennings Bryan, in 1926, I printed an estimate of his life and public services which dismissed him as a quack pure and unadulterated, but in the years since I have come to wonder if that was really just. When, under the prodding of Clarence Darrow, he made his immortal declaration that man is not a mammal, it seemed to me to be a mere bravura piece by a quack sure that his customers would take anything. But I am now more than half * convinced that Jennings really believed it, just as he believed that Jonah swallowed the whale. The same phenomenon is often visible in other fields of quackery, especially the theological. More than once I have seen a Baptist evangelist scare himself by his own alarming of sinners, and quite as often I have met social workers who actually swallowed at least a third of their sure-cures for all the sorrows of the world. Let us not forget that Lydia Pinkham, on her deathbed, chased out her doctors and sent for a carboy of her Vegetable Compound, and that Karl Marx (though not Engels) converted himself to Socialism in his declining years.

It amazes me that no one has ever undertaken a full-length psychological study of Bryan, in the manner of Gamaliel Bradford and Lytton Strachey, for his life was long and full of wonders. My own contacts with him, unhappily, were rather scanty, though I reported his performances, off and on, from 1904 to 1926, a period of nearly a quarter of a century. The first time I saw him show in the grand manner was at the Democratic national convention of 1904, in St. Louis. He had been the party candidate for the presidency in 1896 and 1900, and was to be the candidate again in 1908, but in 1904 the gold Democrats were on top and he was rejected in favor of Alton B. Parker, a neat and clean but bewildered judge from somewhere up the Hudson, now forgotten by all save political antiquarians. Jennings made a stupendous fight against Parker, and was beaten in the end only by a resort to gouging *a posteriori* and kneeing below the belt. On a hot, humid night, with the hall packed, he elbowed his way to the platform to deliver what he and everyone else thought would be his valedictory. He had prepared for it by announcing that he had come down with laryngitis and could scarcely speak, and as he began his speech it was in a ghostly whisper. That was long before the day of loud-speakers, so the gallery could not hear him, and in a minute it was howling to him to speak louder, and he was going through the motion of trying to do so. In his frayed alpaca coat and baggy pants he was a pathetic figure, and that, precisely, is what he wanted to appear.

But galleries are always brutal, and this one was worse than most. It kept on howling, and in a little while the proceedings had to be suspended while the sergeants-at-arms tried to restore order. How long the hiatus continued I forget, but I well remember how it ended. One of the dignitaries in attendance was the late J. Ham Lewis, then in the full splendor of his famous pink whiskers. He sat at a corner of the platform where everyone in the house could see him, and so sitting, with the fetid miasma from 15,000 Democrats rising about him, he presently became thirsty. Calling a page, he sent out for a couple of bottles of beer, and when they came in, sweating with cold, he removed the caps with a gold opener, parted his vibrissae with a lordly gesture, and proceeded to empty the beer down his esophagus. The galleries, forgetting poor Jennings, rose on their hind legs and gave Ham three loud cheers, and when they were over it was as if an electric spark had been discharged, for suddenly there was quiet, and Jennings could go on.

The uproar had nettled him, for he was a vain fellow, and when he uttered his first words it was plain that either his indignation had cured his laryngitis or he had forgotten it. His magnificent baritone voice rolled out clearly and sonorously, and in two minutes he had stilled the hostility of the crowd and was launched upon a piece of oratory of the very first chop. There were hundreds of politicians present who had heard his Cross of Gold speech in Chicago in 1896, and they were still more or less under its enchantment, but nine-tenths of them were saying the next day that this St. Louis speech was even more eloquent, even more gaudy, even more overpowering. Certainly I listened to it myself with my ears wide open, my eyes apop and my reportorial pencil palsied. It swept up on wave after wave of sound like the *finale* of the first movement of Beethoven's Eroica, and finally burst into such coruscations that the crowd first gasped and then screamed. "You *may* say," roared Jennings, "that I have not fought a good fight. [*A pause.*] You *may* say that I have not run a good race. [*A longer pause, with dead silence in the galleries.*] But *no* man [*crescendo*] shall say [*a catch in the baritone voice*] *that I have not kept the faith*!!!"

That was long, long ago, in a hot and boozy town, in the decadent days of an American era that is now as far off as the Würm Glaciation, but I remember it as clearly as if it were last night. What a speech, my masters! What a speech! Like all really great art, it was fundamentally simple. The argument in it, so far as I can recall it at all, was feeble, and the paraphrase of II Timothy IV, 7 was obvious. But how apt, how fit and meet, how tremendously effective! If the galleries had been free to vote, Bryan would have been nominated on the spot, and to the tune of ear-splitting hallelujahs. Even as it was, there was an ominous stirring among the delegates, boughten though most of them were, and the leaders, for ten minutes, were in a state of mind not far from the panicky. I well recall how they darted through the hall, slapping down heresy here and encouraging the true faith there. Bryan, always the perfect stage manager, did not wait for this painful afterglow. He knew that he was done for, and he was too smart to be on hand for the formal immolation. Instead, he climbed down from the platform and made his slow way out of the hall, his huge catfish mouth set in a hard line, his great eyes glittering, his black hair clumped in sweaty locks over his epicycloid dome. He looked poor and shabby and battered, but he was pathetic no more. The Money Power had downed him, but his soul was marching on. Some one in the galleries started to sing "John Brown's Body" in a voice of brass, but the band leader shut it off hastily by breaking into "The Washington *Post* March." Under cover of the banal strains the leaders managed to restore law and order in the ranks. The next morning Parker was nominated, and on the Tuesday following the first Monday of the ensuing November he was laid away forever by Roosevelt I.

I missed Bryan's come-back in 1908, but I saw him often after that, and was present, as I have recorded, at his Gethsemane among the Bible searchers at Dayton, Tenn., though I had left town before he actually ascended into Heaven. He was largely responsible for the nomination of Woodrow Wilson at Baltimore in 1912, and was rewarded for his services by being made Secretary of State. In New York, in 1924, after howling against Wall Street for nearly three weeks, he accepted the nomination of its agent and attorney, John W. Davis, of Piping Rock, W. Va., and took in payment the nomination of his low comedy brother, Charlie, to second place on the ticket. During the great war upon the Rum Demon he hung back until the triumph of Prohibition began to seem inevitable, and then leaped aboard the band-wagon with loud, exultant gloats. In brief, a fraud. But I find myself convinced, nevertheless, that his support of the Good Book against Darwin and company was quite sincere—that is, as sincerity runs among politicoes. When age began to fetch him the fear of Hell burgeoned out of his unconscious, and he died a true Christian of the Hookworm Belt, full of a malignant rage against the infidel.

Bryan was essentially and incurably a yap, and never had much of a following in the big cities. At the New York convention of 1924 the Tammany galleries razzed him from end to end of his battle against the Interests, and then razzed him again, and even more cruelly, when he sold out for the honor of the family. He made speeches nearly every day, but they were heard only in part, for the moment he appeared on the platform the Al Smith firemen in the galleries began setting off their sirens and the cops on the floor began shouting orders and pushing people about. Thus the setting was not favorable for his oratory, and he made a sorry showing. But when he had a friendly audience he was magnificent. I heard all the famous rhetoricians of his generation, from Chauncey M. Depew to W. Bourke Cockran, and it is my sober judgment, standing on the brink of eternity, that he was the greatest of them all. His voice had something of the caressing richness of Julia Marlowe's, and he could think upon his feet much better than at a desk. The average impromptu speech, taken down by a stenographer, is found to be a bedlam of puerile clichés, thumping non sequiturs and limping, unfinished sentences. But Jennings emitted English that was clear, flowing and sometimes not a little elegant, in the best sense of the word. Every sentence had a beginning, a middle and an end. The argument, three times out of four, was idiotic, but it at least hung together.

I never traveled with him on his tours of the cow country, but it was my good fortune to accompany various other would-be heirs to Washington and Lincoln on theirs, and I always enjoyed the experience, though it meant heavy work for a reporter, and a certain amount of hardship. No politician can ever resist a chance to make a speech, and sometimes, in the regions where oratory is still esteemed, that chance offers twenty or thirty times a day. What he has to say is seldom worth hearing, but he roars it as if it were gospel, and in the process of wearing out his vocal cords he also wears out the reporters. More than once, accompanying such a geyser, I have been hard at it for eighteen hours out of the twenty-four, and have got nothing properly describable as a meal until 11.30 P.M. Meanwhile, unless there is an occasional lay-over in some hotel, it is hard to keep clean, and in consequence after a couple of weeks of campaigning the entourage of a candidate for the highest secular office under God begins to smell like a strike meeting of longshoremen.

Of all the hopefuls I have thus accompanied on their missionary journeys—it is perhaps only a coincidence that each and every one of them was licked—the most amusing was Al Smith. By the time he made his campaign in 1928 he was very well known to the country, and so he attracted large crowds everywhere. Sometimes, of course, those crowds were a good deal more curious than cordial, for Al passed, in the pellagra and chigger latitudes, as no more than a secret agent of the Pope, and it was generally believed that he had machine-guns aboard his campaign train, and was ready to turn them loose at a word from Rome. But the only time he met with actual hostility was not in the tall grass but in the metropolis of Louisville, and the persons who tried to fetch him there were not credulous yokels but city slickers. His meeting was held in a large hall, and every inch of it was jammed. When Al and his party got to the place they found it uncomfortably warm, but that was hardly surprising, for big crowds always engender calories. But by the time the candidate rose to speak the heat was really extraordinary, and before he was half way through his speech he was sweating so copiously that he seemed half drowned. The dignitaries on the platform sweated too, and so did the vulgar on the floor and in the galleries. Minute by minute the temperature seemed to increase, until finally it became almost unbearable. When Al shut down at last, with his collar a rag and his shirt and pants sticking to his hide, the thermometer must have stood at 100 degrees at least, and there were plenty who guessed that it stood at 110. Not until the campaign party got back to its train did the truth reach it. There then appeared an apologetic committee with the news that the city administra-
* tion of Louisville, which was currently Republican, had had its goons fire up the boilers under the hall, deliberately and with malice prepense. The plan had been to wreck the meeting by frying it, but the plotters had underestimated the endurance of a politico with an audience in front of him, and also the endurance of an American crowd feasting its eyes upon a celebrated character. It took Al twenty-four hours to cool off, but I had noted no falling off in his oratorical amperage. He had, in fact, hollered even louder than usual, and his steaming customers had howled with delight. What his speech was about I can't tell you, and neither, I daresay, could anyone else who was present.

The truth is that some of his most effective harangues in that campaign were probably more or less unintelligible to himself. The common report was that he knew nothing about national issues, and that he had never, in fact, been across the North river before he was nominated, or even so much as looked across, so he carried a Brain Trust with him to help him prove that this report was all a lie, and its members prepared the first draft of every one of his set speeches. Its chief wizard was the famous Mrs. Belle Israels Moskowitz, but she did not travel with the candidate; instead, she remained at his G.H.Q. in New York, bossing a huge staff of experts in all the known departments of human knowledge, and leaving the field work to two trusties—the Hon. Joseph M. Proskauer, a justice of the Supreme Court of New York, and the Hon. Bernard L. Shientag, then a justice of the New York City court. The two learned judges and their secretaries sweated almost as hard every day as Al sweated in that hall in Louisville. They had a car to themselves, and it was filled with files, card indexes and miscellaneous memoranda supplied from time to time by Mrs. Moskowitz. Every morning they would turn out bright and early to concoct Al's evening speech—usually on some such unhappy and unfathomable subject (at least to the candidate himself) as the tariff, the League of Nations, Farm Relief, the Alaskan fisheries, or the crimes of the Chicago Board of Trade. They would work away at this discourse until noon, then stop for lunch, and then proceed to finish it. By three or four o'clock it was ready, and after a fair copy had been sent to Al it would be mimeographed for the use of the press.

Al's struggles with it were carried on *in camera*, so I can't report upon them in any detail, but there is reason to believe that he often made heavy weather of mastering his evening's argument. By the time he appeared on the platform he had reduced it to a series of notes on cards, and from these he spoke—often thunderously and always to the great delight of the assembled Democrats. But not infrequently his actual speech resembled the draft of the two judges only to the extent that the ritual of the Benevolent and Protective Order of Elks resembles the Book of Mormon and the poetry of John Donne. The general drift was there, but that was about all— and sometimes even the drift took a new course. The rest was

a gallimaufry of Al's recollections of the issues and arguments
in a dozen New York campaigns, with improvisations suggested by the time, the place and the crowd. It was commonly
swell stuff, but I'd certainly be exaggerating if I said it showed
any profound grasp of national issues. Al, always shrewd, knew
that a Chicago crowd, or a rural Missouri crowd, or a crowd in
Tennessee, Michigan or Pennsylvania did not differ by more
than four per cent. from a New York crowd, so he gave them
all the old stuff that he had tried with such success in his state
campaigns, and it went down again with a roar. Never in my
life have I heard louder yells than those that greeted him at
Sedalia, Mo., in the very heart of the no-more-scrub-bulls
country. His meeting was held in the vast cattle-shed of a
county fair, and among the 20,000 persons present there were
some who had come in by flivver from places as far away as
Nebraska, Oklahoma, and even New Mexico. The subject of
his remarks that night, as set by the two judges, was the tariff,
but he had forgotten it in five minutes, and so had his audience. There were stenographers present to take down what he
said, and transcripts of it were supplied to the press-stand sheet
by sheet, but only a few correspondents actually sent it out. The
rest coasted on the judges' draft, disseminated by the press associations during the late afternoon and released at 8 P.M., as
he arose to speak. Thus all the Americans who still depended
on the newspapers for their news—and there were plenty of
them left in 1928—were duped into accepting what the two
laborious jurisconsults had written for what Al had actually
said. I do not know, but the thought has often crossed my
mind, that Hoover's overwhelming victory in November may
have been due, at least in part, to that fact.

Al bore up pretty well under the rigors of the campaign, but
now and then he needed a rest, and it was provided by parking
his train on a side-track for a quiet night, usually in some
sparsely settled region where crowds could not congregate.
After his harrying of Tennessee, and just before he bore down
upon Louisville to be fried, there was such a hiatus in rural
Kentucky. When I turned out in the morning I found that the
train was laid up in a lovely little valley of the Blue Grass country, with nothing in sight save a few farmhouses and a water-
tank, the latter about a mile down the track. My colleague,

Henry M. Hyde, suggested that we go ashore to stretch our legs, and in a little while we were hanging over a fence some distance to the rear of the train, admiring a white-painted house set in a grove of trees. Presently two handsome young girls issued from the house, and asked us prettily to have breakfast with their mother, who was a widow, and themselves. We accepted at once, and were very charmingly entertained. In the course of the conversation it appeared that another daughter, not present, aspired to be the postmistress of the village behind the tank down the track, and Hyde, always gallant, promised at once that he would see Al, and get her a promise of the appointment come March 4, 1929.

When we got back to the train Hyde duly saw Al, and the promise was made instantly. Unhappily, Hoover won in November, and it seemed hopeless to ask his Postmaster-General to make good on Al's pledge. Four years of horror came and went, but the daughter down in the Blue Grass kept on hugging her ambition. When Roosevelt II was elected in 1932 her mother got into communication with Hyde, suggesting that the new administration should be proud and eager to make good on the promise of the Democratic standard-bearer four years before, even though that standard-bearer had since taken his famous walk. Hyde put the question up to Jim Farley, and Farley, a man very sensitive to points of honor, decided that Roosevelt was bound to carry out the official promises of his predecessor, however revolting they might be. An order was thereupon issued that the daughter be made postmistress at the water-tank at once, and Hyde went to bed that night feeling that few other Boy Scouts had done better during the day. But alas and alas, it turned out that the tank was a fourth-class post office, that appointments to such offices were under the Civil Service, and that candidates had to be examined. Farley so advised the widow's daughter and she took the examination, but some other candidate got a higher mark, and the scrupulous Jim decided that he could not appoint her. Hyde and I often recall the lamentable episode, and especially the agreeable first canto of it. Never in all my wanderings have I seen a more idyllic spot than that secluded little valley in the Blue Grass, or had the pleasure of being entertained by pleasanter people than the widow and her daughters. The place was really

Arcadian, and Hyde and I wallowed in its bucolic enchantments while Al caught up with lost sleep on his funeral train.

He was, in his day, the most attractive of all American politicoes, but it would be going too far to say that he was any great shakes as an orator. Compared to Bryan he was as a BB shot to a twelve-inch shell, and as he was passing out of public life there was arising a rhetorician who was even greater than Bryan, to wit, Gerald L. K. Smith. As I have said, I have heard all the really first-chop American breast-beaters since 1900, and included among them have been not only the statesmen but also the divines, for example, Sam Jones, Gipsy Smith, Father Coughlin and Billy Sunday, but among them all I have encountered none worthy of being put in the same species, or even in the same genus, as Gerald. His own early training was gained at the sacred desk but in maturity he switched to the hustings, so that he now has a double grip upon the diaphragms and short hairs of the *Anthropoidea*. Add to these advantages of nurture the natural gifts of an imposing person, a flashing eye, a hairy chest, a rubescent complexion, large fists, a voice both loud and mellow, terrifying and reassuring, *sforzando* and *pizzicato*, and finally, an unearthly capacity for distending the superficial blood-vessels of his temples and neck, as if they were biceps—and you have the makings of a boob-bumper worth going miles to see and hear, and then worth writing home about. When I first heard Gerald, at the convention of the Townsend old-age pension fans at Cleveland in 1936, I duly wrote home about him to the *Sunpaper*, and in the following fervent terms:

> His speech was a magnificent amalgam of each and every American species of rabble-rousing, with embellishments borrowed from the Algonquin Indians and the Cossacks of the Don. It ran the keyboard from the softest sobs and gurgles to the most ear-splitting whoops and howls, and when it was over the 9000 delegates simply lay back in their pews and yelled.

Never in my life, in truth, have I ever heard a more effective speech. In logical content, to be sure, it was somewhat vague and even murky, but Dr. Townsend's old folks were not looking for logical content: what they had come to Cleveland for was cheer, consolation, the sweet music of harps and psalteries.

Gerald had the harps and psalteries, and also a battery of trumpets, trombones and bass-drums. When he limned the delights of a civilization offering old-age pensions to all, with $200 cash a month for every gaffer and another $200 for the old woman, he lifted them up to the highest heaven, and when he excoriated the Wall Street bankers, millionaire steel magnates, Chicago wheat speculators and New Deal social engineers who sneered at the vision, he showed them the depths of the lowest hell. Nor was it only the believing and in fact already half dotty old folks who panted under his eloquence: he also fetched the minority of sophisticates in the hall, some of them porch-climbers in Dr. Townsend's entourage and the rest reporters in the press-stand. It is an ancient convention of American journalism, not yet quite outlawed by the Newspaper Guild, that the press-stand has no opinion—that its members, consecrated to fair reports, must keep their private feelings to themselves, and neither cheer nor hiss. But that convention went out of the window before Gerald had been hollering five minutes. One and all, the boys and gals of the press abandoned their jobs, leaped upon their rickety desks, and gave themselves up to the voluptuous enjoyment of his whooping. When the old folks yelled, so did the reporters yell, and just as loudly. And when Gerald, sweating like Al at Louisville, sat down at last, and the press resumed its business of reporting his remarks, no one could remember what he had said.

A few weeks later I saw him give an even more impressive exhibition of his powers. At the Townsend convention just described one of the guest speakers had been the Rev. Charles E. Coughlin, the radio priest, who, in return for Dr. Townsend's politeness in inviting him, invited the doctor and Gerald to speak at his own convention, scheduled to be held in Cleveland a few weeks later. But Gerald's immense success apparently sicklied him o'er with a green cast of envy, and when the time came he showed a considerable reluctance to make good. Finally, he hit upon the device of putting Gerald and the doctor off until the very end of his convention, by which time his assembled customers would be so worn out by his own rabble-rousing that nothing short of an earthquake could move them. On the last day, in fact, they were so worn out, for Coughlin kept banging away at them from 10 A.M. to 8 P.M., with no breaks for meals. The device was thus a smart one, but his reverence, for all his smartness, was not smart enough to realize that Gerald was actually an earthquake. First, old Townsend was put up, and the general somnolence was only increased, for he is one of the dullest speakers on earth. But then, with the poor morons hardly able to keep their eyes open, Gerald followed—and within five minutes the Coughlin faithful had forgotten all about their fatigues, and also all about Coughlin, and were leaping and howling like the Townsend old folks. It was a shorter speech than the other, for Coughlin, frowning, showed his itch to cut it off as soon as possible and Gerald was more or less uneasy, but it was even more remarkable. Once more the boys and gals in the press-stand forgot their Hippocratic oath and yielded themselves to pure enjoyment, and once more no one could recall, when it was over, what its drift had been, but that it was a masterpiece was agreed by all. When Gerald came to Cleveland it was in the humble rôle of a follower of the late Huey Long, jobless since Huey's murder on September 10, 1935. But when he cleared out after his two speeches it was in the lofty character of the greatest rabble-rouser since Peter the Hermit.

Coughlin, it seems to me, is a much inferior performer. He has a velvet voice, and is thus very effective on the radio, but like his great rival on the air, Roosevelt II, he is much less effective face to face. For one thing, he is almost totally lacking in dramatic gesture, for his long training at the mike taught him to stick firmly to one spot, lest the fans lose him in the midst of his howling. It is, of course, impossible for an orator with passion in him to remain really immovable, so Coughlin has developed a habit of enforcing his points by revolving his backside. This saves him from going off the air, but it is somewhat disconcerting, not to say indecent, in the presence of an audience. After the convention of his half-wits in Cleveland in 1936 a report was circulated that he was experimenting with a mike fixed to his shoulders by a stout framework, so that he could gesture normally without any risk of roaring futilely into space, but if he actually ever used it I was not present, and so cannot tell you about it.

DAYS REVISITED
MENCKEN'S UNPUBLISHED COMMENTARY

Notes on Happy Days

11 *fetched me into sentience*: My father and mother were married on November 11, 1879. It was the only marriage among his children that my grandfather Mencken did not have some hand in arranging, and even so he probably determined the place of the ceremony, for it was held in St. John the Baptist Protestant Episcopal Church and the officiating clergyman was the rector thereof, the Rev. J. Chipchase, one of his friends among the clergy.

My father, who was always a great one for keeping accounts, preserved among his papers a detailed memorandum of the costs of getting married and setting up housekeeping. It appears that his wedding suit cost $50, and that he bought a plug hat for the ceremony at $4.50.

Dr. Buddenbohn's [. . .] office in 1880 was at 166 south Paca street, between Fremont and Warner, then a quiet and even somewhat elegant residential neighborhood. I recall seeing him as a boy, but he was supplanted by Dr. Z. K. Wiley as our family doctor after we moved to Hollins street in 1883. He was a short, bustling German with mutton-chop whiskers, and had the reputation of being far from gentle in his handling of patients. My mother once told me that my birth had been a very hard one, but that was certainly not altogether Buddenbohn's fault, for I was a large baby and she was a small woman. In those days there were no trained nurses, but every doctor in obstetrical practice among the bourgeoisie sent a practical nurse to help him. All babies, of course, were born at home: it was rare for a solvent person to go to hospital for any purpose —even surgery was done in the house—and almost unheard of for a white woman above the level of a street-walker to go there for a confinement.

I recall vaguely the practical nurse who helped to bring my sister Gertrude and my brother August into the world, in 1886 and 1889, both times in Hollins street. She was a Mrs. Fordwell, and my mother had a very good opinion of her. While my mother was still in bed Mrs. Fordwell ran the house, and

Charlie and I had a grand time of it. The family doctors of those days were very hard-worked men. Buddenbohn's office-hours ran from 7 to 9 A.M., and from 1 to 3 and 7 to 9 P.M. The rest of his time he roved Southwest Baltimore in his buggy, visiting his patients. He died in 1909, worn out at fifty-eight.

I was born at 380 Lexington street, now (1943) no. 811 west. It was a small three-story house, and is still standing. A photograph of it, made by me in 1940, follows the title-page of "Souvenirs of Childhood and Schooldays / 1890–96." Lexington street in the vicinity of Fremont was a good residential section in 1880, chiefly inhabited by Germans, and in the block east of Fremont there were some fine houses, some of which survive today, though they are now infested by Jews. West of Fremont the street was taken over by Negroes, and my birthplace is now owned by a colored man of the thriftier sort. When I made the photograph I dropped in on him and found him hard at work renovating the house with the aid of a white helper.

He had a sad story to tell. For years, he said, he had owned and occupied a house on the north side of the street, directly opposite, and all of his savings had gone into its improvement and furnishing. But then the New Deal seized the whole block for a colored housing project, and he was forced to sell at what he considered a very poor price. "They said," he told me, "that my house wasn't worth much because it was in a slum, and I had to take what they offered me, though it was news to me that I was living in a slum. Then, when I looked about for another house—for I like this neighborhood—and found the one you are now standing in, I had to pay a stiff price for it for the ground that the housing project occupied had increased the value of all the property near it. Thus I have been rooked twice, and it will take every cent I can scrape up to make this house as good as the one they turned me out of." This worthy blackamoor told me that he hoped to install an oil-heater in the cellar, but had been unable to find one within his means. I was tempted to offer him one with my compliments, but he seemed so independent a fellow that I feared the offer might insult him, and while I was pondering this difficulty my good impulse vanished, as all my good impulses have a way of doing.

Mencken's birthplace on West Lexington Street. Photograph by
H. L. Mencken, 1940.

11 *the backyard in Hollins street*: In rainy weather, of course,
Charlie and I had to remain indoors. The house in Hollins
street seemed large to us, and we roved it in search of adventure. Before the cellar was cemented, which must have been in
1885 or thereabout, we were forbidden to play in it, for it was
often damp and sometimes flooded, but we sneaked downstairs whenever our mother was out. We also floated boats in

the old zinc bathtub and slid down the banisters of the front stairway and romped with the cat that was usually in the house: its name was invariably Pinkie. The folding doors between the front parlor and the sitting-room fascinated us, and we liked to whirl them along their metal tracks. Sometimes they jumped the tracks, and we had a dreadful time getting them back.

In our very early days we spent a great deal of time in a little room at the head of the kitchen stairs. It was called the play-room, and was papered in colored wallpaper showing characters from Mother Goose. I'd give something pretty for a roll of that paper today. When I was six years old or thereabout the play-room was handed over to the hired girl as her bedroom,

1524 Hollins Street. Photograph by H. L. Mencken and August Mencken, c. 1939–42.

and we thus lost it. After that most of our indoor playing was done either in the cellar, which had been cemented and was dry, or in the third floor back. In the third floor back there was an old framework on which blankets and feather beds were stored in Summer. In Winter Charlie and I used it to play store. We always sold books, which is to say, the colored books, often on linen, in our own library. One of us would stand up behind the framework and carry on negotiations with imaginary customers. When a sale was made the book sold would be dropped through the framework to the other brother, who always remained underneath. He would then quietly sneak it back into stock. For some unknown reason, we greatly enjoyed this silly game, and spent hours playing it in Winter.

12 *Union Square*: The square has changed very little since my childhood. The square was opened in 1847, and the spring that used to supply the drinking-fountain in its cast-iron Greek temple was walled in four years later. In 1939 the city laid out a large amount of money on an effort to revive the square's greenery, which had become sadly dilapidated. No less than 525 loads of worn-out soil were removed, and a like amount of new top-soil was brought in. This new top-soil was sodded and a great many shrubs were planted. The work occupied a gang of W.P.A. clients, white and black, for months, and for a

The Greek Temple and the Fishpond, Union Square. Photograph by H. L. Mencken, c. 1940.

couple of years the square looked charming. But then the rise of war plants brought a flood of new residents to the neighborhood, and by 1943 the new lawns were all trampled down and many of the shrubs had been torn up. These new residents came mainly from either the Appalachian chain or the poorer cotton-mill sections of the Carolinas, and were of the lowest order of white people. I have sat at my office-window and watched their little children digging great holes in the lawns: the poor brats had never heard of lawns and regarded every spot of grassland as a mere field. The depredations of these yahoos inspired a saying in Baltimore: "There are now only 45 states in the Union. West Virginia and South Carolina have moved to Maryland, and Maryland has gone to Hell."

13 *Grandfather Abhau*: My Grandfather Abhau was Carl Heinrich Abhau, born at Bebra in Hesse-Cassel on December 14, 1827. He was descended, according to the family tradition, from one of the French Huguenot families that fled to Hesse in the Seventeenth Century. His parents died when he was a child and he was brought up by a sister old enough to be his aunt. Farmed out in his teens to an uncle, who trained him as a cabinet-maker, he ran away from home at twenty and made several voyages to the West Indies as a ship's carpenter. He settled in Baltimore after that and on November 11, 1852, was married to Eva Barbara Gegner, who had been born in Lower Bavaria on May 21, 1828. His wife died on July 7, 1889, and he himself on April 17, 1905. I was summoned to his house when he came to his last hours, and he died, in fact, in my arms. My mother and Aunt Louise Caskey, with whom he lived, were present, and so was an old German whose name I forget—one of my grandfather's early friends. As he drew his last breath this old German, a pious fellow, dropped to his knees beside the bed and gave thanks that my grandfather's end had been so easy. I remember well the simple eloquence of his thanksgiving, and how greatly it impressed me.

My grandfather was very short of stature, and rather spare. He always went clean-shaven, which was rare indeed in a man of his generation. He showed no sign of baldness when he died at seventy-eight, though his hair was white. He was almost devoid of business capacity, and was poor all his life. In his later years, in fact, his sons had to support him. But he was an amiable fellow and my brother Charlie and I were very fond of him. He never came to Hollins street without bringing us a bag of candies.

13   *My mother was an active gardener*: In the days when my mother began gardening in Hollins street the backyard was a blaze of sunlight, and it was thus possible to grow almost anything. To be sure the soil was not good, for the site had been an open lot for years and was full of rubbish of all sorts, and the building that had been going on had added a store of brickbats and other debris. But this deficiency was remedied, at the advice of my grandfather Mencken, by having the surface layer skinned off and hauled away and replacing it with good top-soil. So much top-soil was brought in, in fact, that the level of the ground on both sides of the long brick walk was raised six or eight inches. In these rich beds my mother grew not only flowers, but also vegetables. I well recall the excellent radishes and scallions that used to come to the table every Spring, and likewise the parsley, carrots and tomatoes that followed. For several years my mother even grew strawberries. Her flowers were nearly all of the old-fashioned varieties. She loved phlox, zinnias, petunias, asters, geraniums, dahlias, sweet alyssum, portulaca (always called Mexican roses) and the like, and always had them in abundance. Along the fences there were sunflowers, and in the Autumn chrysanthemums. Her chrysanthemums (the small-buttoned sort) survived in the yard long after her death, and some of her bulb-plants still come up every Spring. She also grew roses, and experimented with various vines.

Unhappily, the growth of trees in the yard, and, worse, the rise of back-buildings in the yards of our neighbors, gradually cut off its sunlight, and so it became increasingly difficult to keep a garden. There was also, after 1892, the evil effect of abandoning Hollins street every Spring to go to the country. When we returned in the Autumn the yard would be a wilderness of weeds. From 1898 onward we remained in town during the Summer, and so the yard was rehabilitated, but it never recovered its original glories. My mother, in her later years, planted ivy, and it is now the principal ground-cover, with myrtle intermingled.

When I returned to Hollins street in 1936 my brother August and I tried to revive the yard, and for a couple of years we had prosperous beds of petunias, but after that they began to languish, and now we confine our gardening to ivy, ferns and morning-glories. The ferns flourish in the now wide shade of the old pear-tree. My mother started a wild-garden there many years ago, and after her death it was improved by my sister Gertrude. It is now the most successful part of the yard. There are not only ferns in it, but also May apples, mosses and other woodland plants.

The old pear-tree still flourishes, and for a week in Spring it is a blaze of white blossoms. But the pears never ripen. In the late Summer they begin to fall—a considerable hazard, for some of them weigh more than a pound. Sometimes, before Christmas, my mother would cut a few branches and bring them into the house. Put into bowls of water they would be in full blossom by Christmas Day. My brother and I still do this.

14 *Aunt Pauline*: Aunt Pauline was extremely amiable but not too bright. When, in 1899, I got a job as a cub reporter on the Baltimore *Morning Herald*, she alarmed my mother by telling her that all newspaper men were enormous boozers, and that large numbers of them died in the gutter.

15 *They taught one another*: In the same way the boys taught one another their own special games. Some of them were leap-frog (always called par), catty, shinny (a form of marbles), marbles proper, and various competitive top-games. We also, of course, played baseball, usually in an abbreviated form, with four or five boys to a side. It was still quite safe, in those days, to play it in the street, for a wagon or cart approaching over the cobblestones made so much noise that it could be heard a block away. Our mothers frowned upon catty, for sometimes a catty hit a passer-by and hurt him. Our favorite among all group games, in Hollins street, was Run a Mile, which consisted simply in galloping in a gang. It was also known as Run Sheep Run.

We spent most of our time playing in the back alleys, which were even safer than the streets. Moreover, they were full of cats, rats and other such fauna, all of which were hunted violently. But playing in the country in Summer was always much more pleasant than playing in the city. There was greater space, and a greater variety of interests. I spent one whole Summer at Mount Washington making rabbit-traps, but never caught a rabbit. I also set out lines every night in Jones Falls, and sometimes landed a miserable little fish. The life along the Falls was magnificent. There were all sorts of small animals and reptiles afoot, and the woods were full of birds. In the falls itself were a good many fish, including a couple of very old and large carp.

It was universally believed among the boys of my generation that the wheels of skates were made of blood from the stockyards. This was probably due to the fact that they had a somewhat pungent smell. They were very dark brown in color, with white spots, and the boys believed that the white spots were bits of bone. In all probability, the wheels were actually made of some sort of asphalt, and the spots were small fragments of limestone. I never was able to navigate on two skates—in fact, doing so in those days was regarded as somewhat effeminate. The boys employed only one skate. They would climb to the top of a high hill and then come down at high speed. In Union Square the hill running from the corner of Hollins and Gilmor streets to the fish pond was called the Big Hill. Several of the other paths in the Square had names. The one running along Gilmor street was uncemented in those days, and the boys called it the Sandy Path.

In Winter, when the gutters were frozen, the boys made sliding places. Some of these became extraordinarily slippery, and navigating them was a somewhat difficult art. I was clumsy as a boy, but I was always a good slider. When top season came around in Spring, I preferred the tops that were operated with a whip. Those that had to be set spinning by winding a cord around them were rather beyond my always poor skill with my hands. Every new top had to have a license burned into it. This license consisted of two shallow holes made with a red hot poker or nail. Any passing boy was free to pick up and carry away an unlicensed top, but if he took one that had been licensed he was regarded as a thief.

19 *who lived next door in Hollins street*: My uncle Henry bought the house at 1522 Hollins street in 1883, at the time my father bought 1524. In my boyhood there was a gate between the two backyards, and his two older children and my brother Charlie and I were constantly together. "The Menckens," as they were always called in our house, had a Shetland pony as we did, and it was housed in a small stable identical to ours, and adjoining it. My uncle Henry was born in Baltimore on August 22, 1857, and was married to Charlotte Roedel on October 6, 1878, when he was barely twenty-one years old. They had five children. Emma Pauline, the oldest, was born on August 21, 1879, and was thus my senior by nearly a year, but we went through F. Knapp's Institute in the same classes. John Henry was born on March 17, 1882, and was thus two months older than my brother Charlie. Anna Estelle, named after my mother but always called Stella, was born on February 19, 1884. Then came Arthur Burkhard, born on June 22, 1886, and finally Charlotte Harriet, born October 1, 1895.

My uncle Henry and his family moved out of Hollins street in the nineties to a new house that he bought at 2827 St. Paul street. The next tenants were the family of the Rev. Mr. Austin, pastor of a little Presbyterian church that had just been built at Hollins and Stricker streets. There were four children. Julia, the oldest, was just my age; years later she married one of my newspaper colleagues, J. Edwin Murphy. When Pastor Austin got a better church and moved away, the house at 1522 was taken by William Carroll, a Chesapeake Bay pilot, and his handsome blonde wife. They lasted only a short while, and soon afterward Carroll died. Then came William Deemer and his wife. Deemer ran a small cigar business, and built a two-story building at the end of his backyard to house his factory. In order to make room for it the Menckens' pony-stable had to be torn down. He and his wife were both very stupid, and their idiotic talk greatly entertained my mother. Deemer's business gradually ran downhill, and after the death of Mrs. Deemer, in 1925 or thereabout, he gave it up and moved to Washington, where he presently married again. In his last years he ran an elevator in the Capitol. He is now dead also (1943).

After the Deemers came a pleasant family whose name I forget —a grandmother and two small girls. One of the girls was a piano student, and I loved to listen to her practising on lazy Summer afternoons, with the windows open, for the uncertain, tinkling playing of a little girl has always delighted me.

When these tenants moved out the house was bought by William Stricker, a functionary in the city tax department. He and
his wife had two daughters and a son.

Stricker was a Catholic and his wife was a convert. Both
were very pious, and their son, William F., eventually became a
priest. He is a tall, handsome fellow, and not at all sacerdotal in
his manner. He is now serving in Washington as an assistant to
Monsignor Buckley, whom I met on my trip to the Holy Land
in 1934. The elder Stricker girl married a young man who had
a farm somewhere in Maryland, and became the mother of a
boy. The boy, by the time he was four years old, had acquired
an astonishing vocabulary of profanity, and his loud swearing
as he played in the yard entertained us immensely. He died at
the age of six. His father and mother, by this time, had separated, and soon afterward the mother scandalized her family
by getting a divorce and marrying another man. The younger
sister is still unmarried and still lives in the house. Mrs. Stricker
died in 1938 or thereabout, and Mr. Stricker in 1942. Whenever I think of 1522 I am reminded of the old superstition
about cancer houses. My Aunt Charlotte (always called Lottie)
died of cancer of the uterus in the twenties, though that was
after she had moved to St. Paul street, and her daughter Stella
died horribly of the same dreadful disease about 1938. Carroll
the pilot also died of cancer, and so did Mrs. Deemer and Mr.
Stricker.

My cousin Pauline has never married. After her mother's
death she was the chatelaine of her father's house in St. Paul
street. When the firm of Aug. Mencken & Bro. finally blew up
at the beginning of 1926, they lost the house and moved to a
small two-family house in Arlington. My uncle owned an equity in this house, but it was a small one and he presently lost
it. Simultaneously he developed glaucoma and became virtually blind. After that poor Pauline had to support him. She did
so by setting up a cosmetics business. In 1935 or thereabout she
and her father moved to Cleveland, Ohio, where her young
sister Charlotte was married to a man named Willson. They
lived with the Willsons in a remote suburb, and I visited them
there in 1936. Unhappily, Charlotte had five or six children and
her husband, a commercial photographer, was not too prosperous, so living with them was uncomfortable, and Pauline

soon took an apartment for herself and her father. There he died in 1940.

Pauline is still living in Cleveland. She has a job, but what it is I do not know, for I hear from her very seldom and she is not communicative. Her life has been a dreadful mess. She is rather too cocksure and bossy to have made a good wife, but I believe that she would have been a success as a trained nurse, for she is of more than average intelligence and has always been greatly interested in medicine. If she had trained in her youth she'd have become head nurse of some hospital long ago, and I believe she would have made a good one.

The second Mencken girl, Stella, married a man named Christopher Schaefer in 1908, and a year or so later became the mother of twin sons. Five or six years afterward Schaefer developed tuberculosis, and thereafter he was an invalid for ten years, confined in a sanitarium. When he died at last the boys were growing up. Stella kept the house going all the while her husband was ill, and put the boys through the Polytechnic. She was tart of speech and hence disliked in the family, but there was good stuff in her. How she managed to get on I do not know, for I seldom saw her, but at one time, I recall, she had a job in a department-store. By the time her two boys were self-supporting she developed a long and painful illness that turned out in the end to be cancer. Her last days, so her sons told me, were full of excruciating agony.

Her older brother, John Henry, was frail as a child and not too bright. Once in our early youth, when my brother Charlie and I were sky-larking with him at our front door on a Summer night, he fell off the marble steps and broke his arm. My father and his were summoned by our yells, and his father picked him up and felt of his arm. I can still hear the verdict: "It's broken." A little while later Dr. Z. K. Wiley drove up, and after that John Henry had his arm in a sling for six weeks. This was the only fracture in the Mencken family circle in my childhood, or indeed afterward. My brother Charlie and I, though we were frequently hurt in our games and explorations, never broke a bone.

John Henry, in 1906, married a young woman named Edna Pearl McCauley, and they had two daughters. Soon after these daughters were born Pearl became a convert to the theology of the Seventh Day Adventists, and began to afflict poor John Henry in a large and protean way. For one thing, she refused to serve any meat at her table, and for another thing she kept Saturday as a holiday instead of Sunday. Her meatless bills-of-fare reduced John Henry to a skeleton and after a while he came down with stomach ulcers and was very ill. I remember visiting him at the University of Maryland Hospital when he was laid up there. He was being fed through a duodenal tube and it had been in his throat for weeks. He could not speak and seemed to be at the point of death, but eventually he recovered more or less and is still alive today.

What he is doing for a living I don't know: at last accounts he was on the staff of the Maryland School for Boys at Loch Raven. When I left Aug. Mencken & Bro. in 1899 to become a newspaper reporter he succeeded me in the office, and there he sat with his father for twenty-seven years, until the old firm finally collapsed in 1926. He was a stupid and indolent fellow, and full of curious eccentricities. Though he spent all his days in a cigar factory and was a heavy smoker, he never smoked cigars, but stuck to all-tobacco cigarettes, always boughten. When the Maxim silencer was invented, he somehow acquired one, and thereafter spent his leisure shooting cats from a window of his suburban house. At one time he developed an interest in chemistry, and began mixing cigar flavors so bad that the cigars of Aug. Mencken & Bro. became unsmokable. Hitherto I had bought a box of them now and then, if only for the sake of family amity, but I had to give them up. When Prohibition came in John Henry began to make whiskey, and, what is worse, to press it on callers. My brother August and I, after a couple of shots of it, resolved to keep away from him.

His wife Pearl became a very ardent Seventh Day Adventist, and in the early stages of his stomach ulcers insisted on taking him to a hospital run by her co-religionists at Takoma Park, Md. Later one of her daughters trained as a nurse there. This daughter, after graduation, went to another Seventh Day Adventist hospital in California, and there married a doctor. What became of the other daughter I do not know. In all his years with Aug. Mencken & Bro. I never heard of John Henry leaving the office. He sat there gloomily day after day, smoking his all-tobacco cigarettes and keeping his father company.

They were then occupying the building at the northwest corner of Pratt and Greene streets, owned by my father's estate. In return for a very low rental they were supposed to keep it in repair, but they actually let it go to pot. For twenty years on end, to my certain knowledge, they never even had the windows washed.

My uncle's second son, Arthur, was born in 1886, and, like his father, was an assiduous hunter. He had a little shotgun when he was no more than ten years old. When he was twenty years old he developed tuberculosis and had to go to a sanitarium in the Blue Ridge mountains of Maryland. There he encountered a young woman named Eva Lillian Behrens, and on July 5, 1907, two weeks after his twenty-first birthday, he married her. She was older than he, and a dubious person. After his discharge from the sanitarium, his father, who had acquired an interest in an alleged silver mine in Idaho, sent him there to learn the mining business. He remained five years, and became the father of two sons. The day after Christmas, 1912, he went on a hunting expedition. A blizzard came up and he was separated from his companions, and when he failed to return the next day a party set out to find him. He was discovered in a hay-rick, frozen to death. He had tried to protect himself against the cold by burrowing into the hay, but in vain. His body was brought back to Baltimore, and buried from his father's house in St. Paul street. I well recall the funeral, which was conducted by the Freemasons. Their ritual required all of the lodge brothers to look at the corpse, but the looks they took were very brief, for the embalmers out in Idaho were bad workmen and poor Arthur's remains were in a sad state of dilapidation.

The youngest daughter, Charlotte, was the flower of the flock. She was a really pretty girl, with a blooming complexion and dark eyes and hair, and when I saw her at her father's funeral in 1940 she was still a good-looking woman, though she had five or six children behind her. Her husband, Willson, was a Catholic, and she had become a convert herself and brought up her children in the faith. I often wonder what my grandfather Mencken would have said if he could have been brought back from Hell and confronted with the family of his son Henry—Charlotte a Catholic, Pearl and her children

Seventh Day Adventists; even worse, poor Stella a Methodist, as she was in her later days. Pauline, I believe, remains the agnostic she was when we were young, and Arthur never showed any sign of piety. But Arthur probably offended the shade of the old man still more sorely than Charlotte and Stella—by naming one of his sons Calvin!

This poor boy still survives. He was named, not after the Presbyterian saint, but after one of his father's friends in Idaho —but Calvin is Calvin. Arthur's wife, Lillian, did not long survive him. She returned to Baltimore after his death, took to evil courses, and presently married again. My uncle Henry, convinced that she was unfit to bring up her two boys, kidnapped them from her. For a little while thereafter I was very uneasy, for she threatened to prosecute him, and kidnapping, by Maryland law, is a serious offense. But then Lillian relieved the situation by swallowing a lethal dose of carbolic acid. My uncle told me with some relish that her death was extremely painful.

Meanwhile, he had the boys, and they remained in his house in St. Paul street until Pauline revolted against caring for them, and they were farmed out. Where they were brought up I do not know. I met them at their grandfather's funeral in 1940. They seemed to be amiable fellows—one was then thirty-two and the other twenty-nine—but not too bright. They are the only male Menckens of their generation in America.

19 *Baltimore-street horse-car*: Coming westward, the Baltimore street cars picked up a hill-horse at Baltimore and Stricker streets. The boy who rode this horse was one of our heroes. As the westbound car approached at top speed, he galloped alongside, slipped an iron hook through a ring at the edge of the front platform, and then urged on his horse. Some of the cars had shafts between the horses, with rings at their forward ends. The hook was rigged to ropes like traces, which ran to the horse's collar. Once the car-horses felt the pull of the hill-horse, they relaxed in their harness, and let it do nine-tenths of the work. In Winter, when Baltimore street was covered with snow or slush, the Baltimore street cars were operated with four horses, for there was then no thought of snow removal. Very often, in clattering eastward up the hill toward Paca street, they ran off the track, and the four horses dragged them banging over the Belgian blocks. Inside, there was straw on the floor, to keep the passengers' feet warm. My cousin and I, in riding to and from school, always kneeled on the longitudinal seats, in order to see the unfolding panorama of Baltimore street.

20 *to feel the competition*: It was the so-called German-English public-schools that gave the professor his worst competition. They had been set up in the 70's as a means of corraling the German vote, then rapidly increasing. In them German was the basic language, not English, though many branches were taught in English, including, of course, the language itself. My father was bitterly opposed to these schools, and denounced them as an outrage upon the taxpayer. Germans who wanted their children instructed in their native tongue, he argued, should pay for it themselves. How many such schools there were in Baltimore I do not know—probably five or six. They came to grief in World War I. If my father had been alive then, he'd have been delighted.

20 *Otherwise, the professor*: I had paid the following tribute to the old professor in the *Smart Set*, March, 1923, pp. 55–57:

Of all the schoolmasters who belabored me in my nonage, I think most often in these later days of one Friedrich Knapp. He was the owner, principal and chief teacher of the first school I ever went to, and such was his professional confidence that he attempted instruction in all the known branches of knowledge. A Suabian who came to America in 1848, to the end of his life he wore the official uniform of a German schoolmaster, to wit, a black alpaca coat with long tails, a white string necktie, and a shiny plug hat. Among other accomplishments he had that of pulling teeth. When he noticed a boy laboring with a loose milk-tooth—and what boy ever had force of character enough to refrain from wobbling it with his tongue?—he would call the unfortunate up to the flogging arena beside his desk and there do execution upon him. That was before the days of aseptic surgery, but the old professor nevertheless seems to have had some notion of it. At all events, he would never tackle the tooth with his bare hands. Instead he would wrap the corner of one of his coattails around his thumb, and so have at the business. To this day I can see his peculiar expression: how he would screw up his face

as he operated. It was etiquette in that school for a boy to yell
under the bastinado; if he courageously refrained the professor
would simply keep on fanning him until he responded. But, for
some reason that I do not know, it was regarded as unmanly
to weep under dentistry. Sometimes it hurt, and the gush of
blood was always terrifying, but I can't recall ever hearing a victim make a sound. Even the girls stood it bravely. After it was
over, the patient was allowed to retire to the playground until
his hemorrhage ceased, and now and then, if he happened to
conduct himself in a particularly soldierly manner, the professor
would pull his ear amiably and call him a *Kerl.*

The professor, in the intervals of teaching music, bookkeeping, geography, spelling, long division and the elements of what
is now called civics, used to instruct deaf and dumb pupils in
lip reading. He was, I believe, the first man to teach this art in
America, and it was not uncommon for pedagogues from afar to
visit his school and study his method. After he had taught a deaf
and dumb boy to read by the lips, he would put him in a class
with normal boys. Such dummies, as we called them with the
innocent cruelty of youth, were usually older than the rest of us,
and more adept in sin. I learned the elements of profanity from
them, and one of them once offered to teach me how to pick
pockets. The professor not only taught them to read the lips; he
also taught them how to speak themselves. But they could not
hear their own words, and so their speech was often misgauged
as to pitch and volume, and they occasionally broke into unearthly falsetto shrieks. Once, seated on the last bench with such
a dummy, I observed with great satisfaction that the professor
was showing the familiar signs of having participated in a *Bierabend* the night before. That is, he was gradually falling asleep
at his little desk, his ancient spectacles perched on his forehead.
The dummy noticed it too, and when the professor emitted the
first *piano* snore he turned to me and said: "Look at that old
—— —— —— ——!"

The dummy thought he was whispering, but his words were
actually shrill enough to carry a block. The professor, without
moving a muscle, slowly opened his eyes and made a sweep
of the room. The poor dummy, guilt radiating from him like
heat from a stove, blanched, trembled and began to shrink. Instantly the professor detected him—and reached for his rattan.
The dummy needed no invitation. With an heroic shrug of his
shoulders, he arose, straightened his necktie, and marched up
the aisle. When he reached the arena of punishment he stood at

attention with the air of one of Napoleon's marshals. Without
moving from the desk the professor said *Eins*, and the dummy,
in accordance with the school code, hoisted his arms in air. Then
the professor, arising laboriously, said *Zwei*, and the dummy
brought his arms down to the level of his shoulders. Then the
professor, taking position, said *Drei*, and the dummy touched
his ankles with his hands. His person being thus conveniently
displayed, the professor brought down the rattan with a loud
swoosh, and a small cloud of dust arose from the dummy's pantaloons. Another swoosh, and then a third. Then the professor
shifted his rattan to his left arm and solemnly held out his right
hand. The dummy as solemnly shook it—and the two parted
with every appearance of mutual respect. It was a chaste and
decorous episode, with something of the grand manner in it.
Condign punishment for a most heinous offense—but no hard
feelings in it. Later in the day, for conjugating *ich liebe*, *du liebst*,
er liebt with no more than five or six errors, the professor gave
the dummy a "merit," which was a small card gaudily lithographed and bearing the dummy's name, the professor's initials
and the date. A pupil who accumulated 50 such cards in any one
year got a book on the last day of school.

The professor is dead these many years, and his old pupils are
so scattered that I haven't met one since before the war. I have
a feeling that modern pedagogy would look at him askance.
He taught grammar as if it were an abstract and disembodied
science, with no relation to actual language. To mistake an ad-
verb for an adjective was in his sight a far worse offense than to
burn down an orphan asylum. He taught music with the aid
of a violin that had no G-string and was always out of tune. In
teaching geography, he used maps without any names on them,
and forced his pupils to learn the towns and rivers by reciting
a maddening sing-song. The penmanship that he favored was
full of spidery hair-lines and lavish down-strokes. He loved to
test the spelling of his pupils by reading aloud from incomprehensible newspaper editorials, the while they wrote them down.
He had stool-pigeons, chiefly acidulous little girls with tight
pigtails, who reported boys who jumped on drays on their way
home from school, and he rattaned them magnificently the next
morning. He was not above yanking the ear of a boy who came
to school with his hair uncombed. There were days when he
seemed bilious, and it was impossible to convince him that nine
eights were seventy-two. He wore out at least a half dozen rattans a year.

Nevertheless, I remember the old man pleasantly. Even in the remote days I speak of, he was already a bit archaic. The new-fangled public schools were hurting his business. Every year saw fewer pupils on his benches. But he never slacked. If there was a pupil before him who found it difficult to achieve the capital X in penmanship, he flung himself upon the business of teaching it with almost military ferocity. He stormed and cajoled. He employed bribes and threats. He wore out rattans. And in the end he taught it. To this day I can bound Ohio and parse the word *cat* in "The cat caught the rat." Such accomplishments, perhaps, are useless, but nevertheless they give me some distinction in an ignorant world, and they are monuments to the old professor's competence. If I meet him on the heavenly shore, I'll be genuinely glad to see him. He was a good teacher and a kind man.

21 *they all managed to sing the songs*: Following the opening singing there were what were known in the vocabulary of the school as exercises. These were simple calisthenics, and were gone through at the desk. They consisted in doubling the fists and thrusting the arms at full length overhead, and then at full length forward. This routine was carried out to the loud counting of one of the teachers, usually Mr. Willie. It lasted but a few minutes.

23 *the student-body included German-Americans*: The German boys at Knapp's carried their books to and from school in knapsacks. This seemed outlandish and a shade ignominious to the other boys, and we always used straps. Every pupil had what was then called a scholar's companion—a wooden box with a sliding cover, filled with pencils, pens and other such supplies. They always included a sponge to wash slates, but we never used it. Instead we wet the slate by spitting on it, and used our coat or shirt sleeves for rubbing it. This was forbidden by the school statutes, but we always managed to evade the watchful eyes of the faculty. Only prissy little girls used sponges. Scholar's companions were favorite Christmas presents for the young. I recall that mine was made, not of wood, but of *papier mâché*, with a colored top, and that I regarded it proudly.

24 *One actually married a saloonkeeper*: The hired girl who married a saloonkeeper was Anna Waldman, a tall, husky and extremely homely Bavarian. Her husband's first name, I recall, was Veit, and his saloon was on Eastern avenue, nearly opposite the entrance to Bayview. He took to drink and was presently dead, and Anna carried on the place to support herself and her daughter. Finally she sold out, apparently at a good price, for thereafter she seemed to live a life of ease. About once a year, down to 1920 or thereabout, she made a call of state upon my mother. She was always elegantly dressed, as elegance was understood by saloonkeepers' wives, and she and my mother palavered amicably for an hour or two, with the current hired girl (by that time colored) serving them tea. Anna's wedding was a notable social event in the Highland-town region. Veit hired a hall for it, and laid in a keg of beer and a whole chicken for each guest, beside huge stores of other provisions. My brother Charlie and I went to it, and had a grand time. The marriage ceremony preceding the orgies in the hall was in a Lutheran church, and I recall the dreadful singing of a choir of young girls.

Rather curiously, I remember the names of very few of our early hired girls. One was Katie Rafferty, a strapping and handsome Irish girl from Texas, Md., where there was a settlement of her countrymen. Many a time did Charlie and I help her to get into her stays on her day off, and it was she who once fainted under the ordeal, as described on p. 78 of *Happy Days*. In the early 80's hired girls got $10 a month, beside their board and lodging. About 1890 the scale was raised to $12. When one had saved $100 she was ripe for matrimony, and there was usually a taker in waiting—sometimes an iceman, sometimes a plumber, sometimes a fellow-countryman of other occupation, encountered at a party. The comic papers of that era depicted every hired girl as having a policeman in attendance upon her, but though I remember an occasional cop in the kitchen at Hollins street, none of our girls ever married one. The Germans were snatched up the fastest, for they saved every penny of their wages and were commonly hard workers and good cooks.

After 1895 the supply of white girls began to run thin, and my mother had to resort more and more to blackamoors. Most of them were sloppy, dirty and incompetent, but I recall two exceptions. One was a tall, stately woman from Calvert county, Md., by name Harriet Gross. She had got her superb figure, so my mother said, by carrying weights on her head in her country girlhood. She dressed floridly, and whenever she quit work for the day and started home she put on a pair of *pince-nez* with gold frames. She did not need them to help her sight; she wore them simply because any colored woman wearing *pince-nez* was regarded with respect by other blacks; in fact, the men usually took off their hats when they encountered her on the street. Harriet survived in the house from the beginning of World War I to the advent of Prohibition.

She was married to a stevedore, who, when the war began and shipping boomed in the port of Baltimore, made very large wages. He was, rarely for a blackamoor, a thrifty fellow, and invested his money in Ford cars. In these he and a staff of assistants transported other colored folk to and from the country on Sundays—a very profitable business, for Negroes are great travelers, and like to show themselves back home when they are in funds. Not infrequently Harriet would take a couple of weeks off to visit her relatives in Calvert county. In the end she made so many such journeys that my mother became convinced that she had another husband there. Harriet was an excellent cook, but she had a failing, to wit, kleptomania. As a result everything of any value in the house had to be kept under lock and key. When Prohibition approached and I began accumulating wines and liquors in my father's old wine-room in the cellar, she discovered a way to break into it, and soon I was mourning the loss of a dozen bottles of precious stuff, including two of old brandy. I responded by putting a Seagall lock on the door, and by covering the wooden slats of the room with concrete. This baffled Harriet, but soon after she made off with a couple of tablecloths that my mother had received as a wedding present and had cherished ever since, and so she had to be fired.

Her successor was a short, squat colored woman named Zorah Savoy. Zorah was not as good a cook as Harriet, but she did not steal, so she survived until my mother's death in 1925. She was a diligent and thrifty woman, and I often encountered her depositing money at a branch savings bank in the neighborhood. But misfortune pursued her. Once her daughter, the

apple of her eye, shocked and humiliated her by presenting
her with what she called "a single child," *i.e.*, a child born out
of wedlock. Another time, going home by way of the alley
behind the house, she stepped into an open coal-hole behind
the Foos candy-factory and badly skinned her shin. I went to
see Fred Foos and demanded justice for her, and after some
negotiations his insurance company paid her $25. By that time
her skinned shin had healed and she was delighted.

The least intelligent but most faithful of all our white hired-
girls was Mary Spangenberg, the daughter of pious German
Catholics, but herself born in Baltimore. Hers was a large family, and the Spangenberg home in Christian street, near Carroll
Park, was badly overcrowded. What the father did for a living
I do not know, but his pay must have been small, for his wife,
Mary's mother, served us as laundress. Mary came to work
when she was still in her teens, and remained for three or four
years. Charlie and I liked her very much, for her stupidity was
such that it was easy for us to raid the kitchen under her very
eye. She took a childish interest in our enterprises, and especially in the games we played on Winter evenings. We put in
many such evenings playing parchesi with her.

She had a younger sister who was even more stupid. This
idiot believed that she had a religious vocation, and entered
the House of the Good Shepherd as a novice. But she was fit
for nothing save physical work, so the sisters put her into a
sub-sisterhood that ran the institution's kitchen and laundry.
For all I know, she may be there yet. Mary, at twenty-one or
thereabout, was married off by her parents to a confectioner
in Millington avenue. She was indifferent to her husband, and
had, in fact, no inclination toward marriage, but she went to
the altar docilely, and was presently installed in his little store.
There Charlie and I visited her frequently, for each call upon
her was good for a bag of candy. She had no children and in a
little while began to pine away. Before she was twenty-five she
was dead of tuberculosis.

24 *her father*: For my Grandfather Abhau see the note
to p. 13. One of his peculiarities was his frequent citing of
proverbs, usually in German. My mother borrowed the habit
from him, and among her favorites were several in the original

German, for example, "Morgen früh ist die Nacht herum." Her English répertoire was large and in frequent use. Of it I recall "A guilty conscience needs no accuser," "Curiosity killed the cat," "The better the day the better the deed," "There's no rest for the weary," "It's never too late to learn," "Lazy people take the most pains," "Early to bed and early to rise makes a man healthy, wealthy and wise," and "What is worth doing at all is worth doing well."

I have long thought of doing a reminiscent account of her speech, as characteristic of the Baltimore of her time. It had, so far as I can recall, but one personal peculiarity: she often voiced an unvoiced *s*. Thus she pronounced *assembly* as if it were *azzembly*. Rather curiously, my wife, Sara Haardt, born in Montgomery, Ala., had precisely the opposite difficulty: she unvoiced the voiced *s*, turning *zinc* into *sink* and *zoo* into *soo*.

My mother's speech was full of idioms that have almost vanished from Baltimore. She said of a girl who had gone into domestic service that she "lived out" and of one who had got a saleswoman's (then always a sales*lady's*) job that she "stood in a store." To her the marble steps in front of the Hollins street house were always the *front steps*, never the *stoop*. When Charlie and I went to play on the sidewalk or in Union Square we had "gone out front." The backyard was never the *garden* to her, but always the *yard*. She called a drunkard a *tope*—a noun borrowed from a verb that does not appear in the N.E.D., though the verb does and is traced back to 1654. To her a dealer in vegetables was always a *huckster*, though he had a regular stall in Hollins market. She shared the prudery of her time and never spoke of a *bitch*, a *bull*, a *sow*, or even a *mare*. When she had to refer to a lady of easy virtue she called her a *lewd woman*. Her English was clear and excellent, and she avoided even the more respectable sort of slang, for example, *cop*, *coon*, and *hayseed*.

My father's speech was much less decorous. He seldom swore in the presence of his children—his expletive of all work was the banal *darn*, which he pronounced *durn*—but he was very negligent of grammar. This last was partly due to the fact that he had grown up in a household where no one spoke really correct English, and partly to the fact that Baltimore, in his youth, was strongly Southern in its *Kultur*, and even educated Southerners, in those days as in these, were much less careful in their speech than Northerners. As I got on in school I was outraged by his occasional use of "I seen" and other similar barbarisms. But his répertoire of them, however shocking to a young grammarian, must have been very small, for I do not recall him ever using, for example, "I done."

His brother Henry was much more careless. But my mother always spoke precisely correct English. I suspect that her German, though quite fluent, was much inferior. In her later years, in fact, she often appealed to me for a German word that she could not fetch up. But though my vocabulary was thus larger than hers, chiefly because of my wider reading, she knew a great deal more about German grammar and idiom than I did. She was never at a loss in speaking to our German hired girls, and they seemed to regard her German as quite elegant.

34   *it was made of the ammoniacal liquor*: It was the Spring Garden beer, according to my father, that was made of ammoniacal liquor, mill-feed and picric acid. Some of the small breweries in West Baltimore, in his judgment, brewed rather more potable stuff, and he and his brother Henry would sometimes visit them on Sunday mornings, taking their older children along. While they sampled the beer we kids would drink sarsaparilla and munch pretzels. I recall one of these small breweries—it must have been either the Enterprise or John Sommerfeld's—as a very charming place, with a grove of trees beside it, plots of flowers, and a pleasant smell of malt and hops in the air.

The Von der Horsts, Harry and Herman, were friends of my father, for they were interested in baseball as he was, and later became owners of the Baltimore club, but he always insisted that their beer was virtually poisonous. He knew most of the brewers, but had a very low opinion of all save a few of them: the rest, he said, were next-door to idiotic. My brother Charlie and I greatly admired the workmen we encountered in the breweries we were taken to, mainly because we heard that they were allowed to drink 25 free beers a day. My Grandfather Mencken occasionally drank the *Weissbier* produced by Mrs. Berger—chiefly, I believe, to open his pores in Spring—but my father and uncle denounced it as dishwater and would have none of it.

40 *the beginning of the Summer vacation*: I left F. Knapp's Institute at the end of the school year 1890–91 and entered Baltimore Polytechnic Institute in September, 1892. Knapp's, early in the year, had moved from 201, 203 and 205 (formerly 29, 31 and 33) Holliday street to 851 and 853 Hollins street, at the corner of Parkin. This brought it very close to our home at 1524 Hollins street.

On the morning of May 23, 1891, my brother Charlie and I set off to school very early, for it was announced that the Druid Hill avenue cable-line, the first in Baltimore, was to open that day, and we wanted to see the new marvel. We made for the corner of Paca and Fayette streets, and had barely arrived when a car came thundering down Paca street, headed for the curve into Fayette street. We crowded up close, and I, alas, crowded up a bit *too* close, for I was as yet unaware of two facts: first, that a cable-car was much longer than a horse-car, and hence stuck out further on rounding a curve, and second, that once the gripman had thrown in his grip he could not release it until the curve was rounded. The result of my ignorance was that the starboard bow of the car hit me a heavy crack and knocked me down. Why my legs were not cut off by the front wheels I do not know to this day: all I can recall is that I somehow managed to get them away in time. Another thing I can recall is the scream of a woman on the sidewalk. She thought that I was done for, and let go with a will. I was, in fact, not hurt at all, but my clothes were pretty well messed up, and I assumed as a matter of course that when I got to school either the old Professor or Mr. Willie would do execution on me. But when I told of my miraculous escape, supported by the still alarmed Charlie, I was let off without even a jawing.

41 *The Baltimore of the Eighties*: I printed the following picture of life in Baltimore in the 80's in the *American Mercury*, April, 1931, pp. 415–16:

The Next Fifty Years

Sometimes I wonder what the Americans of 1981 will find in our civilization of today that will amuse, annoy and disgust them as much as some of the things we recall in the civilization of 1881. I was an infant in arms in that year, and hence could not make personal observations, but things were not much changed

six or seven years later, and I remember the United States of
1887–8 very vividly. There was a porcelain spittoon in every decent American parlor, and castors still lingered on dinner-tables.
The bathroom in the house I infested was floored with pine,
and had pink flowered paper on the walls, and the bathtub was
a long walnut chest lined with zinc. Under the washstand there
was a dark and damp cupboard, and a poor Irish servant-girl, at a
wage of $12 a month, spent a good deal of her time chasing and
slaying the cockroaches that issued from it. At night in Summer
I slept under a hot and dreadful mosquito-net, for there were no
fly-screens on the windows, and at mealtime the flies swarmed
over the dinner table. On the floors in Winter were heavy Brussels carpet, with designs suggesting the ravings of John Mc-
Cullough in the madhouse, and in Summer they were replaced
by brittle Chinese matting. Hair-cloth was going out, but the
velvets and brocades that replaced it were ten times worse. The
woodwork in all houses save the palaces for the rich was grained
in imitation of oak, and a crescent-shaped bone-dish stood beside every dinner place. I wore a polo cap to school and heavy
flannel underwear, and travelled on a horse-car. Every Winter I
had five or six bad colds.

There was a pony stable at the end of the backyard, and a
manure-pit in front of it. In all America there was not a single shower-bath. The schoolroom I frequented was heated by a
stove under the mantelpiece, and the boy who sat next to it fried
every day. In Winter I wore rubber boots to school, along with
ear-muffs and pulse-warmers. I carried my lunch with me, and it
was cold and soggy. Milk was supposed to cause intestinal stasis,
and was drunk as little as possible. The night air was blamed for
pneumonia, rheumatism and malaria. It was considered a good
thing for a child to get its measles and chickenpox as soon as
possible, and so have done with them. When the family doctor
was needed, some chance colored boy was sent for him, and he
not infrequently arrived in a state of liquor: he was thought to be
better drunk than any of his rivals sober. The milkman brought
his milk in a large can with a spigot, and the servant-girl went to
the curb with a pitcher to get the day's supply. Pullman cars were
decorated like bordellos, and the more advanced saloons had little galleries at one end, with telegraph operators in them, to take
the baseball scores. A woman who smoked cigarettes needed
no red light. Cuffs were detachable and neckties were ready-
tied. Paper collars and Congress gaiters were just going out. A
pleasant present to an elderly gentleman was a gold tooth-pick

with a ring on the handle, to attach it to his watch-chain. The first United States Senator that I ever saw also had a gold ear-pink, shaped like a small shovel. Thousands of American men crowded into theatres nightly to see women's legs. A business man's lunch, consisting of soup, a meat dish, two vegetables, a piece of pie and a cup of coffee, cost a quarter.

42 *she came home from Hollins market*: My mother went to Hollins market, while we were in the city, every Wednesday and Saturday morning. Her accumulated purchases were hauled home by Mr. Wedi, her vegetable man. When, for any reason, she could not go to market herself, I went for her. I recall relatively few of the dealers there in practise. One is Harris, the fish man. He was a stocky, ruffianly fellow who was often drunk, and was assisted at his labors by his wife. On cold Winter mornings she wore so many petticoats and jackets that she looked almost spherical. She also wore heavy woolen gloves, but in order that she might clean fish their finger-tips had to be cut off, and I remember watching her sympathetically as her fingers turned blue.

We got all our sausages from one Wetzler, whose daughter, a red-cheeked, bosomy girl, tended his stand. Our pork came from Poppy Lang, the Nestor of the market. He had been running his stand since the Civil War, and died eventually at a

Hollins Market. Photograph by H. L. Mencken and August Mencken, 1940.

great age. There was a cake-baker named Berger, and I always invested some of the change I snitched in his wares. I recall especially his little round cakes with cream on top and chocolate over the cream. I remember the name of Barranger, a beef butcher, but nothing more about him, save that, like Poppy Lang, he lived in Garrison lane, and had his slaughter-house behind his dwelling. Virtually all the Hollins market butchers lived in that vicinity, and were Germans. They belonged almost to a man to a Lutheran church that was always called the Butchers' church. It had (and still has) a golden rooster at the top of its steeple, instead of a cross. This fact delighted my father, who called attention to it frequently, and offered it as evidence that religion was dying out in the world.

43 *Oysters were not too much esteemed*: The oysters consumed in Hollins street were always bought of one of the colored vendors described on p. 43. They were, of course, shucked, and were sold by the quart. If there were any oyster-crabs in them, which was usually, my brother Charlie and I had the crabs as our perquisites. We always swallowed them alive, and loved to feel them scratching as they went down our throats. The oysters themselves were usually served fried, though occasionally we had an oyster pot-pie. My mother, who was an indifferent cook, never managed to teach our hired girls how to make a really good oyster-pie. When my sister Gertrude began to experiment with cookery, in 1900 or thereabout, they improved considerably, but I never tasted one that seemed to me to be genuinely worth eating until I encountered those served at the Rennert Hotel, noted on p. 44. This was in 1908 or thereabout.

44 *Rennert Hotel*: I began to lunch at the Rennert in 1908 or thereabout and continued to do so until I quit my "Free Lance" job on the *Evening Sun* in 1915. I almost always ate at the men's eating-bar downstairs, where the food was uniformly excellent and of moderate price. In all those years I don't recall ever being served a really bad dish. I seldom lunched alone, but almost always in company with either Albert Hildebrandt or H. E. Buchholz or both. Until my marriage in 1930 I did most of my evening entertaining in the private dining-rooms upstairs.

Some of the colored waiters of that era were town characters. One of them, Harvey by name, made calls upon all the regular patrons of the place in turn, alleging that his old mother had just died and borrowing $20 to bury her. Jeff Davis, the manager during most of my time, was an Eastern Shoreman whose actual given name was Edward. His wife was Anna Mahon, the daughter of John J. (Sonny) Mahon, the Democratic political boss of the town, who lived upstairs and had his office in the lobby. Another Mahon daughter was married to Joseph J. Kelly, one of the stars of the Baltimore Orioles in the nineties, who settled in Baltimore after his playing days were over, and spent a large part of his leisure hanging about the Rennert.

Davis was born at Snow Hill, Md., in 1876, and came to Baltimore at sixteen. Seven years later he was given the job of cashier of the Rennert by Robert Rennert, and soon afterward he was made chief clerk, which post he held for sixteen years. He married Anna Mahon in 1908, and two years later was made manager of the hotel, vice J.P.A. O'Conor, the father of a future Governor of Maryland. During the Summer months from 1910 to 1912 he was also manager of the Buena Vista Hotel, at Buena Vista, Pa. When Robert Rennert died in 1912 Davis organized a company to take over the hotel, but Mrs. Rennert stayed on as a sort of supervisor of the eating arrangements, and she was still in charge of them when I first began to lunch in the men's eating-bar. She gave special attention to the baking, and her breads and pies were magnificent.

Davis was made president of the hotel company on June 15, 1920, and also continued as manager. But the Rennert, despite its famous cuisine, had been going downhill since old Rennert's death, and on February 10, 1932, it was thrown into bankruptcy. The receivers put in a new manager named Paul Lake, also an Eastern Shoreman, and Davis, after thirty-seven years of service, was on the beach. He was offered a job by the Hotel New Yorker in New York, but preferred to remain in Baltimore, and so became assistant manager of the Southern Hotel in Light street. There he greatly improved the cuisine, but he had hardly got under way before his health began to fail, and on December 23, 1936, he died. His widow survived him, but there were no children.

Lake found it impossible to revive the Rennert, and after a

few years of vain effort resigned. The old hotel then fell into the hands of a syndicate operating a long chain of third-rate establishments, with headquarters in Tennessee. This syndicate put in a night-club, but it was a dismal failure, and meanwhile, the eating in the hotel degenerated to the Pullman diner level. This spectacle of deterioration greatly upset Davis, and he and I discussed it sadly every time we met. In 1940 or thereabout the Rennert was seized by the city for unpaid taxes and put up at auction. It was bought by speculators who proposed to tear it down and convert the site into a parking-lot, but there were violent objections to this by various residents and property-owners of the neighborhood, including the rector of Old St. Paul's Church, the ancient rectory of which was directly across Saratoga street.

In the end the hotel was torn down—just in time to miss the enormously profitable rooming business that came to all the Baltimore hotels and lodging-houses on the entrance of the United States into World War II, with the ensuing influx of hundreds of thousands of war workers. At the moment (1943) there seems to be a revival of the plan to turn the site into a parking-lot, but there are now insufficient automobiles on the streets to fill the parking-lots already in operation downtown.

Eddie Rennert, the son of old Robert, is still alive. He is now more than eighty years old and seems to be well provided with money. I encounter him occasionally in the Lord Baltimore Hotel, where he lives when he is in Baltimore. He lived at the Rennert so long as Jeff Davis and Lake managed it, but when the Tennessee chain took over he left in disgust, and ever afterward refused to enter its doors, or even to pass it on the street.

45 *he ducked into the cupboard*: The cupboard in which my father kept his whiskey had no lock, and Charlie and I, if we had been so inclined, might have burgled it with ease, but we never did so. This despite the fact that when a tablespoonful of rye was prescribed for an aching tooth we liked its taste. I was, in fact, at least sixteen before I ever tasted it, and it was not until I became a newspaper reporter that I began to drink it regularly. So with tobacco. There were cigars all over the place, but Charlie and I never went any further than an occasional experiment with a wicked cigarette.

49 *in reverse at the ides of September*: Another sign of the approach of Winter was the appearance of wooden covers for the white marble front-steps of all the Baltimore houses. These covers were so made that they could be removed in Spring and stored in the cellars. They served two purposes: first, they were thought to be less slippery than marble under snow and sleet; second, it was the theory that they protected the marble against frost, which would otherwise crack it. I was probably the first Baltimore householder to challenge their utility. This was in 1920 or thereabout, at the time I had the entrance to 1524 Hollins street rebuilt and installed a wrought-iron hand-railing on the front steps. The next Winter I omitted covering the steps—and nothing happened. The Winter following they began to disappear all along Hollins street, and in a few years they were gone all over town. I got some heavy exercise sawing up our covers for firewood.

56 *Guided by the Reus boys*: Charlie and I often tried going barefoot, as the Reus boys did, but our city feet were too tender for it. Once we made the experiment in the Darsch barnyard, where a thick coating of manure ameliorated the harshness of the Howard county terrain. But there was the head of an old rake concealed therein, and when Charlie came down upon it one of the rusty teeth went clear through his foot. The Reus boys stopped the bleeding with large gobs of cobweb from the

Marble Front Steps to 1524 Hollins St. Photograph by H. L. Mencken and August Mencken, September 24, 1939.

barn. The dangers of tetanus were unheard of in that simple age. Another time, while some country carpenters were underpinning the big house, I went into the cellar to watch them at work, and began to play with one of their adzes. In a moment I had cut a piece off the end of the second finger of my left hand. The carpenters stopped the bleeding with cobwebs from the rafters. The end of my finger showed a scar for nearly forty years, and was somewhat flattened. Of late it has grown out again, and the scar is reduced to a barely discernible ridge.

57   *its anthropophagus*: The anthropophagus was a youth named Knott, whose family farm adjoined the Vineyard to the northward, beyond the Sucker branch. We had heard nothing in those days of homosexuals, and were astounded and horrified when the Reus boys told us that if he captured us he would tear off our penises. So far as I know, there was no evidence that he had ever attempted anything of the sort. His evil reputation, in fact, was probably grounded upon nothing more substantial than country gossip, which is often as gratuitous as it is venomous.

64   *grandfather Mencken*: My grandfather was born at Laas in Saxony, between Leipzig and Dresden, on June 7, 1828, and died in Baltimore on February 26, 1891. His second wife, Caroline Belz Gernhardt, a widow at the time of their marriage, was born in Germany on July 9, 1829, and died in Baltimore on March 19, 1910. After my grandfather's death she lived with her own daughter, Emma, who was born in Baltimore on November 23, 1866, and is still living (1943). The old lady had sufficient income from my grandfather's estate to maintain her comfortably, but taking care of her was a heavy chore to her daughter, for she became a professional invalid and demanded a great deal of attention. When the automobile came in she developed a violent fondness for it and insisted upon being driven at the highest speeds then attainable.

She was a constant reader, but her literary tastes were hardly of the best. At my mother's suggestion my father gave her, on successive Christmases, the complete works of two fourth-rate German novelists, E. Marlitt and W. Heimburg (Bertha Behrens), each in six or eight volumes. She read them seriatim over and over again, starting with Vol. I of Marlitt and finishing with the last volume of Heimburg, and then beginning anew. In her last years she made elaborate efforts to deceive her doctor about her somewhat heavy eating, saying that he was paid to find out such things. All her property went to her daughter Emma. Soon after my grandfather's death she had falsely accused my father and Uncle Henry of trying to deprive her of part of her husband's property, and for some years they refused to have anything to do with her. But this feud was settled by the middle nineties. She was buried beside my grandfather in Loudon Park Cemetery.

64 *that age, which was immensely more hairy*: My father, until the end of the eighties, wore both a moustache and what were then called sideboards. By 1892 he had dispensed with the sideboards, and trimmed his moustache, once somewhat flowing, to toothbrush dimensions. This toothbrush he wore until the time of his death in 1899. His brother Henry wore a more flowing moustache until 1920 or thereabout, when he shaved it off and was smooth-shaven for the rest of his life. Until well into the Twentieth Century smooth-shaven men continued rare in the United States. Setting aside actors and the Roman Catholic clergy, very few of the New Yorkers whose portraits appear in *Notable New Yorkers of 1896–1899*, by Moses King, New York, 1899, were altogether free of facial foliage. Many still wore beards, sometimes of fantastic cut.

64 *inclined toward the ironically misnamed Democratic party*: Many other Baltimore Germans voted with the Democratic party, mainly because of their vivid memories of the wild doings of its opponents, the Knownothings, during the 1852–1860 era. In both 1856 and 1857 the Knownothings carried Maryland. Their chief animosity was to the Irish Catholics, but they also harassed other foreigners, and in the middle fifties my other grandfather, Abhau, was several times stoned on the streets of Baltimore.

66 *would have to be called August*: August was born at 1524 Hollins street on February 18, 1889. He has always been closer to me than either my brother Charlie or my sister. We not only think alike; we also look alike. Since I returned to Hollins street in 1936 he and I have kept bachelor hall together, for he has never married. He was floored by tuberculosis in 1906 and was thus unable to complete his studies at the Polytechnic, but he recovered later and has been practising as an engineer since 1908. He was a contributor to the *Scientific American* before he was twenty, and has since written three books, two of which, *First-Class Passenger* and *By the Neck*, have been published.

67   *the Eutaw House*: The Eutaw House survived until 1914, when it was pulled down to make room for the Hippodrome Theatre. The head clerk, in my days as a reporter, was Ned Herbert: I had frequent business with him and became well acquainted with him. He was an amiable fellow with a hawk nose and a bald head, and after the Eutaw House closed he transferred to the Emerson. There he remained in service until 1935 or thereabout, when he retired. A few years later he died. In the days before his marriage my father lived at the old hotel for a short while.

In my youth it was Baltimore's baseball headquarters, and the members of visiting clubs always stayed there. At about two o'clock in the afternoon, when there was a game in Baltimore, an old-time bus, drawn by six or eight horses and with seats for twenty or more persons, would pull up at the entrance in Eutaw street, and the visiting players would file out in uniform, and start for the ball-park. There was always a crowd of boys on hand to see them off.

The main dining-room of the Eutaw House was on the second floor, and was very large. In it an almost endless dinner, with at least fifty dishes on the bill-of-fare, was served for $1. The hotel was operated on the American plan, and a room and meals could be had for as little as $2.50 a day. Ned Herbert once told me of an old fellow who had eaten in the dining-room for several years without paying a cent. He did not live in the hotel, but spent much of his time in the lobby, which was a place of public resort. When he went to his meals the waiters in the dining-room assumed that he was a regular guest, and the clerks downstairs assumed that he paid the waiters.

69   *subscribed toward the Baltimore crematorium*: When my grandfather died in 1891 his two sons prepared to have him cremated, but their step-mother and their three sisters made such an uproar that they had to consent to his burial. When my father died in 1899 the same thing happened: it was then my mother who objected. I tried to persuade her that cremation was much more civilized than burial, but she could not overcome her horror of it. The first member of the family ever to be cremated was my wife, in 1935. She was strongly in favor of cremating the dead, and would have had my body cremated if I had pre-deceased her. My brother August and I have an iron-clad agreement whereby the survivor will make sure that the one who dies first goes to the crematory. My sister Gertrude knows of this agreement, and consents to it.

69 *the only example of overt social-mindedness*: Despite the fact that he was an unbeliever my grandfather had all of his children baptized in the Protestant Episcopal Church, apparently in sentimental compliment to his first wife, Harriet McClellan. My father was confirmed by the Right Rev. William Rollinson Whittingham, Bishop of Maryland, at the Church of St. John the Baptist on April 23, 1868, when he was just short of fourteen years old.

69 *aloof from the German societies*: My grandfather, so far as I know, never belonged to any German society. My father regarded them all with like disdain, but at various times he seems to have been a member of the Germania Männerchor, no doubt for purely business reasons. I never joined any of the German social organizations myself, save only the Germania Club, but I was made an honorary member of several of them during World War I, including the Germania Männerchor. I cleared out of them as soon after the war as I could do so decently.

71 *frequent trips to Pennsylvania*: My grandfather's trips to Pennsylvania to buy tobacco ceased after he retired from active business at the age of 60. Long before this my father and his brother Henry had made similar trips, and very frequently. They had a warehouse somewhere in Lancaster county, Pennsylvania, and another in the Wisconsin tobacco region. They also accumulated stocks in the vicinity of Dayton, Ohio, in northern New York, and in Connecticut.

My father made two or three trips to the tobacco-growing

regions every year, and my uncle did the same. They were full of strange tales about the Pennsylvania-Dutch. My father's favorite had to do with two Dutchmen who were in partnership as tobacco dealers. They kept no books and had no bank account. All expenses were paid in cash, and each contributed 50¢ in every dollar. When a check came in they cashed it at once and divided the money. This, according to my father, had gone on for years.

My uncle was full of stories about travel in the remoter parts of the Pennsylvania tobacco country. Once, he said, he was making a trip on a little branch railroad on a very hot day, and became extremely thirsty. When the train stopped at a small station he happened to see a beer sign back in the village, perhaps a block away from the station. He told the conductor that he wished there were time for him to get a couple of beers. "Why not?" answered the conductor. "We'll wait for you." So my uncle went to the saloon, laid in a sufficient supply, and then came back to the train.

73 *on Christmas morning*: Preparations for Christmas began in Hollins street immediately after Thanksgiving. The Christmas tree was trimmed not only with boughten balls of colored glass but also with home-made ornaments. My mother put in many December evenings on the making of them, with such help as Charlie and I could give her. Some of them, I remember, were made of gilded egg-shells and others of gilded pine-cones. The gilding came in a small bottle and had a pungent smell. It was always bought at the Newton toy-store, at Baltimore and Calhoun streets.

In my childhood the green flooring of the Christmas garden was provided by moss that farm-boys brought to the door; it was not until the nineties that dyed sawdust was invented. The chief adornment of the garden was a three-story house resembling our own home in Hollins street. The front was hinged, and when it was opened a series of rooms was revealed, all of them elegantly papered. In front of this house were arranged the usual gaily-painted effigies of the animals in Noah's Ark, along with various human figures, some biblical and the rest modern. The glaring incongruities and anachronisms were universal in that era, and no one noticed them.

74 *the Baltimore medical colleges*: There were six or eight medical colleges in Baltimore in the eighties, and all of them, including that of the University of Maryland, were third-, fourth- or fifth-rate. In fact, most were simply rackets run by small groups of practitioners who charged their students, chiefly from the South, high fees for indifferent lectures and gloried in the title of professor. In my youth a consultant was always introduced as "the professor." It took the impact of the Johns Hopkins, which opened its medical school in 1893, to clean up the University of Maryland, and shut down the rest of the colleges. One of them, the Maryland Medical, occupied a building in Baltimore street, just east of Carrollton avenue, that had been built years before for the Newton Academy, an old-time private school for boys. [. . .]

Rather curiously, the colored folk of our neighborhood did not fear the Maryland Medical College, though it was quite near; their terrors were reserved for the University of Maryland, nearly a mile away. Perhaps this was due to memories of the Emily Brown case. Emily Brown (who was white, not colored, as I say on p. 190, though she was murdered in the house of a colored woman) came to her death on December 10, 1886, at the hands of a Negro who sold her body to Anderson Perry, the colored dissecting-room *Diener* at the University of Maryland, for $15. The murderer, John Thomas Ross, was hanged on September 9, 1887.

75 *his standard treatment*: I suspect that Dr. Wiley's free and frequent mopping of my throat with ferric chloride may have done some permanent damage. It seems plain in retrospect that what set him to work was usually tonsillitis, but in those days the surgical removal of diseased tonsils was unheard of, and it was not until many years later that mine came out. Meanwhile, the ferric chloride, a very powerful astringent, probably laid the foundation for those troubles in the mucosa of the mouth and throat that have badgered me ever since. He used the standard solution, running to 13%, and so far as I can recall he never diluted it.

The household remedies in use in Hollins street in my childhood were few in number: most of the bottles that jammed the medicine cabinet in the bathroom were filled with Dr.

Wiley's prescriptions. My mother never laid in any of the favorite nostrums of the time—for example, Ayer's Cherry Pectoral, Hood's Sarsaparilla, and so on. My brother and I studied Dr. Ayer's Almanac diligently, but we never tasted any of his medicines. Most of the balms and elixirs that I remember were for external use—for example, camphorated oil for sore throats, turpentine and lard for the same, and Perry Davis's Pain-Killer. This last was also used internally—a few drops on a lump of sugar. The formula, or what purported to be the formula, was printed in the *Formulary and Druggists' Magazine* for November, 1889, p. 344, as follows:

Guaiacum resin	20 ounces
Camphor	2 ounces
Capsicum	6 ounces
Water of ammonia	1 ounce
Opium in powder	½ ounce
Alcohol	2 gallons

The amount of opium here was small, but nevertheless there was opium. This was long before the passage of the Harrison Act, and such preparations of opium as laudanum and paregoric was sold to all comers by the drug-stores and even by the grocery-stores.

The family medicine cabinet included bottles of both laudanum and paregoric, and one unhappy evening my mother, thinking that she had the latter in hand, gave my brother August, then about five years old, a dose out of the former. Discovering her mistake at once, she gave the alarm, and I was dispatched to the office of Dr. Wiley. He was out, and after finding other doctors also out, we at last got hold of Dr. Hood, a homeopath in Gilmor street—a stately man with a long beard. He gave August an emetic and my father and I walked him for hours. The patient was naturally alarmed by all the uproar, but no symptoms of opium poisoning appeared, and by the next morning he was quite well. I suppose that he had had a belly-ache, and that my mother had chosen paregoric to treat it, though her usual remedy for it was the Pain-Killer aforesaid. Other household medicines that I recall were licorice powder (for intestinal upsets too mild to call for castor oil), and tincture of myrrh. The latter was used for toothache, but Charlie and I preferred my father's remedy, which was a tablespoonful of whiskey held in the jaw.

My mother was on a course of codliver oil in the early eighties, for she had a chronic cough. It was probably asthmatic, but Drs. Buddenbohn and Wiley both suspected tuberculosis. She had recovered by 1888. In those days codliver oil was not given to children, for vitamins were unheard of. There was a bottle of tincture of iodine in the medicine cabinet, but it was used so little that it dried out. There was no roll of aseptic cotton, and no surgical tape. Cuts and bruises were dressed with Pain-Killer and wrapped in rags from the rag-bag in the kitchen. The favorite household hemostatic was cobwebs.

75 *by a milkman*: Our milkman, during most of my nonage, was a solemn and laborious fellow named Gherkin, who had his cow-house on Edmondson avenue, a bit beyond Gwynn's Falls. He was a man of somewhat elegant manners and reputed to be rich, and inasmuch as he was a bachelor more than one of our hired girls laid a caressing eye on him. He married, eventually, at the great age of forty or thereabout—a time of life that was regarded, in the nineties, as almost beyond the age of consent. His milk business blew up when the Baltimore health department began to lay down strict rules for the sanitation of dairies in the city milk-shed. This was at the turn of the century.

82 *Mr. Thiernau's store*: There should have been a chapter in *Happy Days* on the storekeepers of the Hollins street neighborhood in my nonage. Most of our household groceries were bought from either Thiernau or Philip Knatz, whose store was on the south side of Baltimore street, between Stricker and Calhoun. Another nearby grocery-store was that of Fuller Waters, at the southeast corner of Baltimore and Stricker streets, and yet another was that of William Cook, at the southeast corner of Baltimore and Calhoun. Waters was a fattish, solemn and somewhat pompous fellow who lived in Hollins street, in the block west of ours. At the turn of the century, when I was already a newspaper reporter, the Republican politicians induced him to run for City Comptroller on their municipal ticket, and it fell to me to report some of his speeches before ward clubs. He was defeated overwhelmingly, but the politicians got enough money out of him to ruin him. Soon afterward he sold his store, and what became of him I don't know. His son was a member of the Hollins street gang.

Cook was actually a German named Koch. His store was so filthy that my mother would not buy in it and forbade us to enter it. He had a daughter named Mamie who was the first lady embalmer in Baltimore. One of the Cook sons was William, who died in 1943 or thereabout as the richest undertaker ever seen in the town. He advertised regularly, and for years his $50 funerals were the butt of local wits, but they paid handsomely, and he eventually bought the old Winans mansion at St. Paul and Preston streets, and after a hard legal struggle with the neighbors, who contended that his presence would lower the value of their property, converted it into the William Cook Funeral Mansion, which still survives (1944). At his death he left $1,000,000. His sister Mamie was associated with him as lady embalmer for years, but finally left him, married a rival undertaker named Syfer, and is now, as Syfer's widow, established in business on her own at 1600 west North avenue.

Shortly before his death Cook bought the old Garrett home at 11 west Mt. Vernon place, and apparently toyed with the idea of making it an annex to the Cook Funeral Mansion. There was another neighborhood uproar, and soon afterward he sold the building to Boumi Temple, Ancient and Arabic Order of the Mystic Shrine, of which my father had been a member. He was the hero of "The Funeral King," a novelette by Robert B. Vale, published in the *Smart Set* for January, 1915.

Dr. Charles R. Pue, whose drugstore was at the northeast corner of Baltimore and Stricker streets, filled most of the prescriptions written for the Mencken family by Dr. Z. K. Wiley, though now and then we also resorted to that of Roe & Smith, at the northeast corner of Stricker and Lombard, or to that of Herbert G. Wilson, at the southwest corner of Gilmor street and Frederick avenue. Pue was later succeeded at Stricker street by Wilson, who married the sister of Hoggie Day. Roe & Smith, in the early 90's, moved their drugstore to Columbia avenue (now Washington boulevard) and Scott street, and their place at Stricker and Lombard streets became a candy-store. All Baltimore druggists, in those days, gave

L. H. Newton's store, near the corner of Baltimore and Calhoun
streets. Photograph by H. L. Mencken and August Mencken, c. 1940.

children who brought in prescriptions sticks of wood licorice
as *lagniappe*. In the same way bakers gave them biscuits.

There were three bakeries in our neighborhood. The first was
William Dankmeyer's, at the southwest corner of Baltimore and
Stricker streets; the second was the Vienna Bakery, in Baltimore
street next door to Pue's drug-store, and the third was Gustav
H. Carl's, at 1317 west Baltimore street, between Calhoun and
Carey. Dankmeyer also sold pastry, and early in the 80's he put
in an ice-cream parlor in his back room. [. . .] Boys in their
teens, who had acquired girls, patronized his place heavily, for
he was willing to serve a ten-cent plate of ice-cream with *two*
spoons. We young bucks disliked its air of amour, and most of
the ice-cream we consumed came from hokey-pokey men on
the street, who offered a big block for five cents.

My mother was convinced that the stock of the hokey-pokey
men was full of adulterations and contaminations, and in all
probability it really was, but we devoured it none the less. The
chief rivals to the hokey-pokey men were the waffle men. They
had gasoline stoves in their wagons, and prepared their waffles
on the spot. They always wore white clothes and announced
themselves by ringing a bell. Those who were most liberal with
their powdered sugar got our trade. They were followed by

gangs of ragamuffins who had no money to buy, but were in hopes that the more fortunate would offer them bites.

The bread offered by Dankmeyer was rather tasteless, and we seldom had it in the house. The Vienna Bakery offered something much better—long, crisp loaves baked in the French style. But the best bread of all came from Carl, who also offered the best biscuits as *lagniappe*. He had a young son who as a member of the boys' choir at St. Luke's Protestant Episcopal Church in Calhoun street, north of Lexington, as were three of the Dankmeyer boys.

This service inspired young Carl with an itch for the sacerdotal life, and in the course of time he was duly ordained. In my early reportorial days, when he was fresh to the cloth and I was specializing in hangings, we were both assigned to one at Annapolis. The condemned, as I recall, was a white youth named Wyatt, who had murdered the white captain and colored cook of an oyster pungy. I was already so blasé that I took the proceedings in my stride, but Carl had never seen a hanging before, and was very much flustered. I remember well how, after he had escorted the condemned up the gallows steps, he rushed down before the trap was sprung. His father's bakery was closed many years ago, and the Vienna Bakery disappeared even earlier. Dankmeyer's, also, is gone so long that West Baltimore has forgotten it. But its quarters have been occupied by other dealers in pastry and ice-cream ever since. [. . .]

The Dankmeyer daughter, always called Ida in my boyhood, was cashier at Thiernau's grocery-store, and I well remember how my brother Charlie and I marvelled at the speed with which she would make change. She inhabited a small cage in the store, and her hours apparently ran from 7.30 A.M. to 6 P.M. She was in those days a very thin and spinsterish woman, but her brother Clarence tells me that she has taken on bulk in recent years. She must be nearly 70, for she seemed a young lady to Charlie and me. Old Dankmeyer drank himself to death, and that was also the fate of one of his sons. Clarence, alarmed by this double family tragedy, has been a teetotaler all his life. He is also a practitioner and ardent advocate of the Hay diet. He seems to be making a living out of his advertising business, but it is apparently not too prosperous.

Our favorite candy-store in the 80's was that of John H.

Kunker, at 1402 west Baltimore street, next door to Newton's stationery and toy emporium. Kunker gave a large piece of taffy for a cent, and whenever he had a housecleaning offered the debris of his showcases in small bags at the same price. These were called grab-bags, and along with the fragments of taffy and other sweets he usually included a ring or stickpin. He also sold pickles—great favorites among the little girls. (It was unusual then for the young of *Homo baltimoriensis* to employ any money save copper. It was not until the hokey-pokey wagons appeared on the streets that nickels came into common use. Across the street from every school-house there was a shop that did nine-tenths of its business in pennies. A slate pencil was a cent, and so was a pickle.) This was long before the day of Pure Food laws, and both his pickles and his candies were very far from sanitary. In every pickle jar was a copper penny, to make the contents a bright green. Many a time, biting into one of his large, round candies, I have found it filled with clay. But his taffy was pretty good, and my brother Charlie and I got down many a cent's worth of it. When he died at last his old wife carried on alone for a while and then died too. His store is still given over (1944) to the candy trade, but the Greek who now operates it has added magazines and other such goods.

At 1419 west Baltimore street was the harness-shop of William Kemper, an elderly German. He raised canary birds on the side, and his store was a favorite resort of all the boys of the neighborhood. The old man and his wife were polite, but not too hospitable. His work-bench was in the rear of his store, and there he labored all day long preparing harnesses for the clients of Reveille's livery stable. My brother Charlie and I were free of the place because we often took the old man harnesses for repair. Also, we bought from him Castile soap and harness oil.

In the same block, at 1427, was the store (with living quarters upstairs) of Richard Carruthers, a plumber. Carruthers was the first storekeeper in West Baltimore to tear up the brick sidewalk in front of his place and put down a so-called improved pavement. What it was made of I don't know, but I remember that it was very rough. About midway down the block was the grocery store of Philip Knatz, already mentioned. His

boy Albert, always called Buck, was a member of the Hollins
street gang. A bit farther down, at 1411, was the drygoods and
notion store of Isaac Nordlinger. Nordlinger had begun business at 895 west Baltimore street, east of Fremont, but in the
early 90's he moved to 1411, for the Hollins street neighborhood was then looking up, and all of its store-keepers were
thriving. He was a Jew, but he married a beautiful *Shiksa* who
was one of his salesladies—a sensational event in that era. Another saleslady married one of the elder Knatz boys.

There was a primeval tea-store at the southwest corner of
Baltimore and Calhoun streets, and it gave a gaudy chromo
with every purchase, but my mother did not patronize it. To the
westward of it, at 1405, was what was then called an oyster-bay.
Clarence Dankmeyer writes to me that "it was famous for its
fried oysters, and used to send out fries in big nickle-plated
dishes that had spirit-stoves under them to keep the oysters
hot." We never had any truck with it, for all the oysters consumed in the Mencken house were bought raw at the door
from itinerant colored oyster men.

At 1407 west Baltimore street was the tobacconist's shop of
Henry Bingel, a one-legged Civil War veteran. He had a little
cage in the rear, and in it he rolled cigars. He was a surly fellow
and did not welcome visits by boys. All the other tobacconists
of West Baltimore, in those days, sold them cigarettes at the
rate of two for a cent, but he refused to do so. I well remember a huge and wicked-looking hinged knife, used for cutting
chewing-tobacco, that stood on his counter.

At 1403, between the oyster-bay and the tea-store, was a
china and tinware store kept by a Jew whose name I forget.
He was a hideous creature with sore eyes. One day a woman
customer ran out of his store crying that he had tried to kiss
her. He was arrested on a charge of assault, and the magistrate
at the watch-house at Pratt and Calhoun streets fined him $20.
Ever thereafter, until he finally moved away, he was known as
the $20 Jew in the neighborhood. My mother never spoke of
him in any other way. She refused to patronize him, and so did
most of the other housewives in Hollins street.

At 1415 west Baltimore street was the wine and liquor store of
William C. and Otto Schilling, which survived until Prohibition.
They had no bar, but gave prospective customers samples of

their wares at a little counter. I well recall their batteries of copper measures and the rows of barrels along their walls. William was a reserved and melancholy fellow whose wife had run off with another man. He sat at a table at the rear of the store, and spent all morning reading the *Sun* from its first page to its last, including the advertisements. Otto was the treasurer of Zion Church in the City Hall plaza and of a dozen German singing societies, orphan asylums, building associations and other such organizations. Whenever the Germans of Baltimore formed a new one they elected him its treasurer almost automatically. When Prohibition ruined the wine business he went into the selling of motorcycles, but apparently he did not prosper, and I suspect that his last years were difficult and unhappy ones.

At 1425 was the stove-store of F. Hildebrand & Sons—a healthy line of business in those days, for all cooking was done with coal stoves and most houses were still heated by Latrobe stoves, frequently out of order. When coal-stoves began to disappear John Hildebrand, the owner of the business, went to work for the Gas and Electric Company, and was one of the singers in the glee-club of its employees. At 1429 was a notion and fancy goods store kept by William F. Hendrickson. It was there, probably in 1888, that I bought my first bought-with-my-own money Christmas present for my mother. I remember that my Aunt Minnie, her sister, took me to the place, and helped me to select it. It was a small cloisonné vase that survived in the house for many years. As I recall it, I had saved up 60 cents to pay for it.

Next to Hendrickson's, at 1431, was the cobbler's shop of John Loechel. Loechel, a tall, sturdy, solemn fellow, built for blacksmithing rather than for shoemaking, had a wife of extraordinary plainness, and both of his children, a boy and a girl, were very homely too. In the early 90's the wife died, and I remember watching Loechel working away at his cobbling, sad and lonely. Some time before this the wife of a toy-dealer in the 1300 block, Wolf by name, had died, and I well recall my sympathy for his children, and my miserable thought that some day my own mother might die too. I have been unable to find Wolf in any of the city directories of the time. Perhaps I have got his name wrong. Soon after his wife's death he closed his toy-store and vanished.

He had heavy competition in the store of L. H. Newton, at the northwest corner of Baltimore and Calhoun streets—for many years the West Baltimore headquarters for toys, stationery, writing materials, and other such goods. It survived until 1940 or thereabout. Next to Fuller Waters's grocery-store, at the upper end of the block, was the jewelry-store of Louis Lemkul. He had a son and a daughter, but I recall them only dimly.

On September 5, 1927, I printed on the editorial page of the Baltimore *Evening Sun* an article on the old-time storekeepers

Caricatures of Baltimoreans of the 1880s drawn by Mencken as a schoolboy.

of the neighborhood which included the following about the Knatz grocery:

> I remember it very well as a boy, with its huge bins of coffee and its stock of mysterious jugs in the rear. Mr. Knatz, the proprietor, was a very dignified man with a long Admiral Tirpitz beard. He lived in Hollins street, just behind his store, and had a house with a charming garden beside it. The present occupant of the house keeps up that garden: it is one of the ornaments of West Baltimore. Some time ago, when I referred to Mr. Knatz in this place, I was made to spell his name Knitz. His son, now the head of the E. G. Knatz Sugar Company, wrote in to denounce me as a Bolshevik, and dared me to meet him on the lot behind the Greisenheim and fight him with stilettos. Alas, there is no longer any lot behind the Greisenheim. Moreover, the printer was to blame, not I. He makes fewer mistakes than I do, but now and then even a printer will drink out of the wrong bottle.

The son mentioned here was Edward G. Knatz, a bustling fellow with a bristling black beard who made a considerable fortune in the wholesale sugar business. He married a young woman named Becky Hoffman, and they had a large family of children—I believe ten or twelve. The original Knatz home was not the one I mentioned in my *Evening Sun* article, which stood (and still stands) in Hollins street between Stricker and Calhoun, but a house in our own block. The move down the street must have been made in the 80's, but the house in our block remained the property of Knatz the elder, and on his death it was taken over by his son Ed.

Ed had lived in it as a boy, and loved it so much, and the Hollins street neighborhood with it, that he would never sell it. Until his death in 1935 or thereabout he often came to Hollins street to look at it, and refresh his memories of the old neighborhood, and sometimes I encountered him. He had become rich by that time, and had a fine place at Reisterstown, but he told me that he still considered the Union Square region the most charming residential section of Baltimore, and if his family had not been so large I am sure that he'd have lived in the old house himself.

There were two Knatz daughters, Minnie and Lillie. Lillie, the elder, married a flour dealer named Charles Fangmeyer, and thereby came to grief, for Fangmeyer turned out to be a

sport and boozer and soon lost his business. When he finally
deserted her, leaving her with a child or two, she returned to
the parental home. The other Knatz daughter, Minnie, never
married. She lived on until 1940 or thereabout. Her brother
Buck (Albert F.) is still living but the other Knatz sons, Ed,
Elmer and Philip, are all dead.

On the north side of Baltimore street, in the 1400 block,
was the saloon of one Graham—a very respectable place, reputed to serve the best clam-chowder in West Baltimore. Graham
would not tolerate drunks; if one staggered in he was immediately kicked out. Mrs. Graham was the cook of the establishment.
I recall very few other tenants on that side of the block. One is
Andrew H. Lyeth, who operated a tombstone yard at 1418. It
was at the northeast corner of the alley leading up to the rear
of Reveille's livery-stable, and my brother Charlie and I often paused to watch the stone-cutters at their work. In Winter
they were housed in a crude shed, but in Summer they worked
in the front yard.

In the 1300 block were two shoe-stores—August Conrades's
at 1321 and Otto Schaub's, at 1325. Schaub and Conrades were
related by marriage. Despite the fact that they were rivals in
business they appeared to keep on good terms. My mother
always patronized Schaub, not Conrades. He sold a shoe for
boys called the Solar Tip, and I wore it all through my nonage.
It was extremely durable, but far from comfortable.

At the northwest corner of Baltimore and Carey streets, with
a long frontage on Baltimore street, was the wine and liquor
store of Leon Greenbaum. He was the only rival to the Schilling brothers in the West End. His store survived until Prohibition. At Christmas, 1919, I sold my first and last automobile,
and laid out all the money I got for it on wet goods against
the coming drought. I got some fine bargains in German and
French wines from Greenbaum, who complained sadly that he
could never sell them to West Baltimoreans. I remember that
I paid him a flat $1 a bottle for all the prizes on his top shelf.
They also included some capital Malaga.

In the block of Baltimore street directly behind our house
the Dankmeyer bakery stood at one end and the grocery
of Thiernau at the other. Between them were Frederick E.
Foos's candy factory (still standing) at 1507, the wallpaper

establishment of Asa Smith at 1509, the saloon of William J. Bitz at 1521, the grocery and feed store of Madison L. Day, the father of Hoggie Day, at 1523, the larger grocery and feed store (with a warehouse across Booth street from our back gate) of Roloson Bros. at 1525, and a saloon at 1529 that was kept at different times by various *Wirte*, including a German named Henry Freund and Jake Kilrain, the pugilist. Jake lasted only a short while, and we boys never came to grips with him. He was a stupid oaf who did not encourage advances, and he never offered to teach us any of the mysteries of his trade.

Asa Smith, who took contracts to paper whole rows of houses and was in a large way of business, was an old man in a long beard. He died many years ago and was succeeded by his son Albert, who survived, and the business with him, until 1925 or thereabout. All the paperhanging undertaken in Hollins street until the turn of the century was done by them.

The Foos candy factory was naturally an object of much interest to the boys of the neighborhood, but we were never permitted to enter it, and I can't recall ever wangling any candy out of it. It occupied an old house in Baltimore street, and there was a back building fronting on Booth street. This back building housed the engine and boiler which operated the machinery. Foos, the proprietor, devoted himself mainly to making round candies, so he had a large battery of revolving copper drums. We boys could stand in the alley and watch the candies churning and popping up in the drums, but as I have said, we were never offered any.

The engineer was Fred's father—an old German who sat in the alley smoking his pipe and keeping an eye on the boiler and engine. He was a morose and silent man and did not encourage us to hang about. During the 1920's Fred Foos tore down two houses in Baltimore street, and erected a modern factory. He died in 1943. He was a bachelor, and for years lived with his old-maid sister in Catonsville. She died in 1925 or thereabout. The Bitz saloon was a common doggery, but there was a Bitz boy who was tolerated as an occasional member of the Hollins street gang.

Directly behind our back gate was the feed warehouse of the Roloson brothers, Charles H. and J. Otis. Their father had for years operated a refrigerator factory in the triangle where the

Salvation Army headquarters now stands, between Frederick avenue and Baltimore street. It was said to be the first refrigerator factory in America. The elder Roloson was apparently a German, for his sons showed some interest in the German Red Cross during the first World War, and one of his grandsons is president of the old German (now Central) Insurance Company to this day. On his death his business was operated by his unmarried daughter. He and she made old-fashioned wooden refrigerators with zinc linings. She was finally driven out of business by the march of improvement.

William F. Lehnert, the barber, had his studio at 1613 Frederick avenue just west of Baltimore street. I remember well an old stove in the corner with a copper kettle of water bubbling on it all the time. On the walls were gorgeous landscapes, with pieces of mother-of-pearl set in to represent the moon. Lehnert afterward moved to the north side of Baltimore street, east of Gilmor, and there died. He never got more than ten cents for shaving and fifteen cents for cutting hair, but nevertheless he rolled up a considerable estate.

In Baltimore street just west of Gilmor there was a paint store run by an old man named Smith, and after his death by his two old-maid daughters. These ladies were afraid of fire, and never had any heat in their store in Winter. It was kept as neat as a pin, and they waited on their customers in heavy woolen petticoats and knitted jackets.

Pilson, an eccentric druggist, had his store on the south side of Baltimore street, east of Calhoun. He never went out, and was reported to own no hat. His place was a perfect chaos. When a box of supplies came in from the wholesale house he stood it on the floor and let it lie there. Nevertheless, he always knew how to find things, and he had a much larger stock than any other druggist in West Baltimore. His sedentary life had given him a peculiarly pale and puffy face, and he always looked ready to die, but he lived to a considerable age. After his death one of his daughters, a very pretty girl, undertook to run his store with the aid of a drug clerk. She couldn't make a go of it, and finally shut it down. I recall waking up Pilson in the middle of the night when my father was seized with his last illness, at New Year's, 1899. It was very cold weather, and I shivered outside until he came down.

The Nestor of the Hollins street neighborhood, down to his death in 1935 or thereabout, was L. A. Spelshouse, who had been running a hay, feed, cement and brick business at 1621 Frederick avenue, west of Gilmor street, since 1869. He and his old wife lived upstairs, and in my days as an amateur bricklayer I often dropped in on him. He was of an inventive turn, and among other things devised a mailbox that would not leak when it rained, and a scheme for casting small concrete garages. He spent years trying to induce the government to adopt his rain-proof mailbox and carried on an endless correspondence with the functionaries of the Postoffice and the Maryland members of Congress. [. . .]

The Knoop brothers were three melancholy Germans who kept a grocery-store at the northeast corner of Baltimore and Gilmor streets, opposite Thiernau's. It was a dirty place, and we never patronized it, but my brother Charlie and I often lifted apples, sweet potatoes, turnips, etc., from the baskets which stood outside. The Knoops made money, invested it in the coal business, and died rich. In my boyhood only one of them was married. When he died his widow married one of his brothers. Thiernau died in the early 90's, and was succeeded by his brother-in-law, William H. Lantz, but his widow, Lantz's sister, continued to live above the store. What became of Lantz I don't know, but he had disappeared by 1900. There was a Jew named Baer who kept a drygoods and notion store in the 1400 block of Baltimore street, but whether he preceded or followed Nordlinger or was his contemporary I do not remember.

My mother's small purchases were usually made from a strapping Irishwoman named Mary Daly, who kept a little store opposite Hollins Market. Despite the smallness of her place she made money, and presently moved to a larger store on the southwest corner of Baltimore street and Arlington avenue, where she remained until her death. She was an old maid and very pious. Clarence Dankmeyer, in some notes that he has sent me, mentions a tailor named Max Cohen and a dealer in notions named Clark, but I do not recall them.

Farther down Baltimore street were various stores that I remember well. Thomas & Messer, dealers in window-shades, were at 1015—and are still there. Next door to them, to the

eastward, was John Ward's coal-yard—also still in operation.
The Provident Savings Bank's West Baltimore branch was at
1007. My first savings went to it, and I remained a deposi-
tor until I was grown. It took ten-cent deposits, and recorded
them by pasting stamps in a book. Across the street was
Seim's pastry-shop, which survived until 1935 or thereabout.
Farther up the block was Helfrich's lumber-yard. Next to the
lumber-yard, *c.* 1900, a veterinarian named Spranklin built a
horse-hospital, with a horse's head carved in stone over the
front door. He did not prosper, and in a little while his place
became an ice-plant.

On the north side of Baltimore street, at 808 and 810, opposite Winans' wall, was the establishment of John Scherer &
Son, manufacturers of doors, sashes and blinds. The junior
partner in the firm, William C. Scherer, was our neighbor in
Hollins street—he lived at 1520—and his son Theodore was
a very active member of the Hollins street gang. The head
of the firm was William's father, John, who lived at 857 west
Fayette street. On the north side of Baltimore street, east
of Pine, was the toy- and novelty-store of one Spencer. My
grandmother Mencken always bought presents for us children
there. Another old-timer was J. J. Landragan, who kept a
stationery-store at the northeast corner of Baltimore and Paca
streets. He sold fireworks for the Fourth of July, and Charlie
and I bought many a Roman candle and many a package of
firecrackers from him. He survived to 1930 or thereabout.

The oldest of all the West Baltimore storekeepers was John
C. Nicolai, whose heirs operated a grimy and forbidding candy-
store at 755 west Baltimore street until 1942. The house in
which the business was carried on was built by the original
Nicolai in 1850. He had come to Baltimore from Hanover in
1834, and was one of the founders of the old Liederkrantz
Singing Society, launched on December 30, 1836. For a number of years he operated a shoe store in Market street (now
Baltimore street) near Holliday. But in 1850 he switched to the
candy business and moved to Baltimore street near Fremont,
and there his heirs and assigns continued after him.

89 *none, to my knowledge, ever got to the death-house*: No
member of the Hollins street gang ever reached any genuine

distinction in later life. Most of them, so far as I know, lived obscurely—for example, Harry Freedley, the son of a faro-dealer, who became a bartender; Willie Richardson, who became a pedagogue at the Polytechnic; Eddie Nitsch, who was half-witted and soon vanished; Wilbur Stubbs, who studied medicine and died as a member of the staff of the Baltimore Health Department; and Willie Koch, who, at last accounts, was working for the *Sun* as a commercial artist.

Freedley's father, a somewhat imposing man with goat whiskers, dealt faro in a downtown gambling-house—I think it was in Calvert street. There was a sister in the family, Minnie, who was afflicted: she was a huge, uncouth creature whose speech was almost unintelligible. Eddie Nitsch's father was the head of the old Baltimore cigar manufacturing firm of Nitsch and Kuhn, whose factory was at the northwest corner of Eutaw and German (now Redwood) streets. He and my own father were on friendly terms. There were other children in the family, but they were all extremely stupid. Wilbur Stubbs was a pleasant fellow, and gave promise of going far in medicine, but he suffered from some sort of kidney complaint, and it killed him in his early forties. Soon after graduating from the University of Maryland Medical School he joined the staff of Karl von Ruck, a German physician who operated a tuberculosis sanitarium at Asheville, N.C. There he helped von Ruck develop a tuberculosis vaccine that never came to anything.

Willie Koch was the son of Wilhelm Koch, head of the old toy importing firm of Rogge & Koch, whose establishment was in Baltimore street, just east of Eutaw. The elder Koch was a dignified old German in a round beard, and the two daughters of the family, Mamie and Dora, were leading figures in Baltimore's German society of the period. Their home was at 1530 Hollins street, next to the Newbold house at the corner. Willie married early and acquired four children, but never got on in the world.

Next to the Koch house was that of the Schlenses, their cousins: Mrs. Koch and Mrs. Schlens were sisters. Old Gustav Schlens, the head of the family, was in the shipping business, and at one time was very well-to-do. But he clung to sailing ships too long, and so died broke. His son, Freddie, was older than I. Freddie had an important job with the William Wilkins

Company, owners of the smelly hair factory out the Frederick road: in fact, the Wilkinses and Schlenses were somehow related. He lost his mind and began to loot the Wilkins strong-box, and before he was detected had got away with a large amount of money. He then shot himself—and managed to blow out both of his optic nerves without killing himself. But after lingering blind for several months he finally died.

95 *the House of the Good Shepherd*: The House of the Good Shepherd presented an extremely romantic aspect to the boys in Hollins street. Its high stone wall with glass along the top made it seem mysterious and remote. Looking down from the third story windows at 1524, we could see the nuns and their charges working in the garden. In those days nuns who died were buried in the northeast corner of the grounds, at Gilmor and Hollins streets. The funerals were often very impressive. Nuns acted as pallbearers and the only man present was a priest. In recent years this cemetery has been abandoned, and nuns who die are taken out for burial in a Catholic cemetery elsewhere.

The House of the Good Shepherd convent bell is so familiar that I long ago ceased to hear it. Years ago, when my mother was ill, she complained that its heavy jangling early in the morning disturbed her rest. I wrote a polite note to the

The House of the Good Shepherd. Photograph by H. L. Mencken, 1942.

Mother Superior, and she replied with equal politeness. She said that she'd try to have the nuisance abated but was not too hopeful. The business of ringing the bell, she explained, was always given to the youngest novice, and the youngest novice was always full of pious enthusiasm. She worked it off by ringing the bell for fifty or a hundred strokes.

Some time later the Mother Superior invited my mother and sister to the ceremonies attending the reception of a class of novices. These ceremonies were carried out in the chapel on a very hot day in Summer, and the officiating priest was Father Broderick, an old and picturesque Irishman, who was rector of St. Martin's parish. My mother used to tell with great amusement how, at the most solemn moment of the proceedings, when the nuns were lying on their faces in front of the high altar with black cloths over them, Father Broderick reached under his robes, produced an enormous red bandana handkerchief and proceeded to mop his bald head.

I was not invited to these ceremonies myself, for men are ordinarily barred—in fact, male visitors have to talk to the nuns through a grille—that is, to the nuns of the cloistered order in charge of the place. There are, I believe, two other orders within the compound. The lowest of them is devoted to menial drudgery and consists in the main of very ignorant women. One of them for many years was a sister of one of our old servant girls, Mary Spangenberg. Mary herself was pious and yearned to join the order, but for some reason her mother objected and proceeded to marry her off to a confectioner out Wilkens avenue way. Her younger sister then took her place, and for all I know may be still in the institution.

The wicked girls that the nuns cared for and tried to reform made frequent attempts in my early days to escape, and sometimes successfully. The stone wall around the place must be at least twelve feet high, and along the top of it is a formidable row of broken bottles set in cement. Nevertheless, an occasional girl managed to get over it. Now and then, in fact, some of the boys in the neighborhood saw one of them in the act. I never did so myself, but I frequently watched with joy the rushing up of cops from the old Southwestern station at Pratt and Calhoun streets, and the general turmoil in the neighborhood.

97 *yelling "Rats!"*: It was believed by every boy of that era that Chinamen ate rats and were all opium addicts. It was also believed that they were so frugal that they lived on eight cents a day. Most of the Chinese laundrymen in West Baltimore employed colored women to help them at their work, and not infrequently they entertained these wenches carnally when the work of the day was done. The result was a considerable emission of Sino-African bastards. It is not uncommon in Baltimore to this day to encounter a Negro showing strong traces of Mongolian blood.

104 *The first long story*: In 1945 Alfred Knopf set up a little periodical to promote his Juvenile books, by title the *Borzoi Battledore*. The editor asked me to write something for it and I sent her the following. She headed it "Early Days" and it was illustrated by Warren Chappell.

My first recollection of beautiful letters has to do with "The Story of Simple Simon," published, in full color, by the old firm of McLoughlin Brothers in the early eighties. My copy of it, still surviving though without the front cover, is elegantly inscribed "Harry Mencken, 1887 ¾." I was seven years old precisely in the year 1887 ¾, and could read for myself, but my mother had been reading it to me for several years before, and I recall very vividly sitting with her at an upstairs window in Hollins street, looking down upon a snow-storm in Union Square, and hearing:

> Simple Simon went a-fishing
>   For to catch a whale;
> All the water he had got
>   Was in his mother's pail.

At seven—or more likely it was only five—this seemed to me to be a perfect comic situation, and it retains that character to this day. Indeed, I sometimes suspect that my lifelong view of the American yokel was generated by poor Simon, though he was, I believe, a British subject. I still know half of his saga by heart, and the rest comes back by merely glancing at it.

Most of my other primordial literary recollections also derive from the excellent books of McLoughlin Brothers. In the late eighties my brother and I (he was twenty months my junior) studied the imprint with fascination, and spent a great deal of time debating the pronunciation of the name. We finally settled on MacLawflin, and so it remains to me, though maybe something else is correct. One of the curious things I discover, thumbing through my shelf of McLoughlin incunabula, is that all of the books linger in memory only as fragments. There is, for example, "A Peep at Buffalo Bill's Wild West," published in 1887 and acquired instantly. All the pictures save two strike me as new today, and all the stanzas of the text save this one about the cowboy's doxy, Madge:

> And Buckskin Joe and Hurricane Dick
>   Regard her doings with pride,
> For to them she owes whatever she knows;
>   They taught her to shoot and to ride.

Again there was a mysterious miscellany, apparently of English provenance, though part of it was American, which contributed a single distich:

> No fiddle nebber played a jig
> Wid de bow ten miles away.

I remember these lines as clearly as I remember "Now lay me," and alongside them in my memory floats the excellent colored picture by L. Hopkins that faced them, and further on in the book I recall with equal clarity a drawing by Gustave Doré showing a clown and his wife coddling a child that has fallen in the arena and is spattered with blood, but beyond that the contents are as new to me today as a volume just off the press. By what power or process is it decided what we are to recall and what we are to forget? I have never heard an answer. If one ever comes it will tell us a great deal more than we now know about the way in which the likes and dislikes, the ideas and feelings of mankind are hatched.

III *my Grandfather Mencken*: My grandfather, after the death of his father, Johann Christian August Mencken, in 1867, made a trip to his old home in Germany, and returned with a formidable collection of family documents. [. . .] After World War I, I began to take an active interest in them and had most of the documents translated. They are now in a series of volumes that will go to the Pratt Library, Baltimore, at my death, along with my collection of books by early Menckens. My father's view of the former glories of the family was always somewhat skeptical, and he showed his Philistinism by having the family coat-of-arms registered as a trade-mark for his business. An oval label bearing it was pasted on every box of cigars that issued from his factory. [. . .]

Despite his general attitude of indifference, my father showed some interest in the fact that Bismarck's mother was a Mencken. There were several books on Bismarck in the house, and so late as September 27, 1898, he bought another, *Bismarck Denkmal*, paying $10 for it.

112 *I had no more mechanical skill than a cow*: Despite my complete lack of mechanical skill I was fond, like any other boy, of watching workmen at their tasks, and whenever a new building was going up in the Hollins street neighborhood I spent a large part of my time in the assembled gallery. There was a tombstone-cutter in Baltimore street, at the northeast corner of the alley which made up behind Reveille's livery-stable, who especially fascinated me. I was also very partial to blacksmiths and wheelwrights. The blacksmith at Mt. Washington had an almost classical shop, with a spreading chestnut tree in front of it. There Charlie and I used to watch him shrinking tires on wheels and making farm wagons. In those days the Studebaker factory-made wagons were still rare, and the better sort of farmers looked on them with scorn. They were commonly blue in color and covered with gaudy decalcomania stamps advertising Studebaker. Custom-made farm wagons were made much more solidly. They were also commonly painted blue, usually a very pale shade.

I also liked to watch bakers at work. In those days they always occupied cellars, and began to roll their dough at about 8 P.M. Tinsmiths and carpenters were fascinating, too, and so were cobblestone pavers. The men who operated the cobblestone stomper were heroes to all the boys. So were electrical linemen, for it was the beginning of the electrical age, and their gymnastics on telephone and light poles were still novelties. It was a happy day for Charlie and me when the horse John or the pony Frank needed shoeing, for that meant a trip to Sam Morrison's shop at the northeast corner of German (now Redwood) and Greene streets.

Sam did a large business, for there were many stables nearby, including the livery establishment of Coblens. He was a sturdy Irishman who looked his trade, and none of his horseshoers could match him in getting at the hooves of a refractory mule. I have seen him tackle an animal that seemed to be frantic, and work his will upon it in half a minute. One of my father's office-boys, Jim Lee, was apprenticed to him at sixteen or thereabout, and remained with him long enough to become a journeyman. While Jim was there Charlie and I had the run of the place, and we seldom came home without pockets full of souvenirs of the sort esteemed by boys—old nails curiously twisted, shoes that had worn as thin as tin-cans, or pieces of pared hooves. Whenever the pony Frank was shod we recovered all four of his old shoes, and passed them out to our friends. One of them is still nailed over the door of the old pony-stable in Hollins street, and another, gold-plated, hangs in the hall of the house.

The horseshoers worked half-naked in Summer, but Morrison, as their boss, affected white boiled shirts on even the warmest days. In the 80's all men of condition wore such shirts at all times, and those who were careful of their appearance often also wore paper collars. Those paper collars came in boxes of a dozen and were thrown away after use. Using them was considered a shade more elegant than wearing linen, which had to be laundered and was thought to be unsanitary. My father wore Rubens Reversible Linene Collars, size 17, and always bought them of Mrs. Praeger, a widow who kept a small haberdashery in Baltimore street, east of Carey. Charlie and I were usually dispatched for them, and I can still hear Mrs. Praeger's friendly invitation when the purchase was completed: "Call again, please." My mother always called her Call Again Please. It was from her that I bought my neckties when the proliferation of my hormones turned my attention to my personal appearance. They were ready-tied four-in-hands and the price was 25 cents.

I was at least ten years old before I ever saw my father in a colored shirt. He then bought a couple experimentally, but wore them only in the country. I don't believe he ever put one on to go to his office in his whole life. When I was twelve or fourteen years old even boys of that age wore boiled white shirts when they were dressed up. It was the fashion to iron them in such a way that they had a brilliant shine and were very stiff. A little while later boiled shirts in colors came in, but men of over forty seldom wore them. For such a man to put one on was a public notice that he was on the loose.

In those days all working men doing really heavy work wore red flannel shirts, which were supposed to keep off rheumatism. They were the standard garb of the iron-molders at the Mount Clare shops of the Baltimore & Ohio Railroad, in Pratt street, not far from Hollins street. Charlie and I went down into that region relatively seldom, for it was infested by the boys of a tough gang that was always at war with the Hollins street gang, but now and then we took the chance in order to see the molders at work. Their shop was at the southeast corner of Pratt and Carey streets, and is still standing (1943). We had to climb up to the windows to get a good look, but it was worth it, for the stream of molten iron running out of the furnace into the molds fascinated us, and we often tried to imitate it by melting lead at home, usually at the cost of burns. All the street workmen of the time wore the red shirts aforesaid: indeed, such shirts were the hallmarks of their calling. At that time most of the hard labor in the streets of Baltimore was still done by Irish immigrants. The native Anglo-Saxons disdained such work; the Negroes were barred out by politics, for they were Republicans; and the Italians and other such anthropoid strangers had not yet arrived.

Most of the factories of West Baltimore were owned and operated by Germans, and they always lived close by. This was true, for example, of William Wilkins, who founded the big hair factory on the Frederick road, which continued to flourish for many years. It radiated a dreadful scent; nevertheless, Wilkins lived beside it. When he grew rich and built a better house farther out the Frederick road, he turned over his old quarters to his superintendent, who lived in them to the end.

Christian Lipps, who owned a soap factory, almost equally smelly, in Garrison road, lived in Baltimore street no more than a block away. He had an enormous red brick house, marble trimmed in the Baltimore manner and of very passable design. When he died he left within a few dollars of a million. It was divided among his eight or nine children, and most of them managed to get rid of their shares very promptly. One of his grandsons, Christian Wattenscheidt, served a term in the Maryland Penitentiary along about 1910. He was a lawyer and was ruined by a wicked woman. Her demands for money induced him to lift the cash of a client. He was a stupid fellow, and was caught very promptly. As I recall it, he served about three years. I believe that only one of Christian Lipps's heirs is still well-to-do today. The rest have spent their money and returned to the folk.

114 *a branch in Hollins street*: The branch library that I patronized is still standing unchanged (1943). I not only read hundreds of the books on its shelves; I was also a heavy patron of its magazine tables. My favorites were the *Scientific American* and its supplement, and I also read the *Popular Science Monthly*. Of the juvenile magazines it offered, the only one that ever interested me in the slightest was *Golden Days*. I looked through *Harper's Young People* and *St. Nicholas* occasionally, but they left me cold. *Golden Days* was a weekly published by James Elverson in Philadelphia; it began in 1880 and survived until 1907. *St. Nicholas*, which began in 1873, was

Enoch Pratt Free Library, No. 2 Branch, Hollins and Calhoun streets. Photograph by H. L. Mencken and August Mencken, c. 1940.

edited by Mary Mapes Dodge until 1905. It was abandoned
during the Depression of the 1930's, but was revived in 1943
by Juliet Lit Stern, wife of David Stern, publisher of the Philadelphia *Record*. *Harper's Young People* was set up in 1879 and
continued until 1895, when its name was changed to *Harper's
Round Table*. Not long afterward it was abandoned. The *Popular Science Monthly* began in 1872 and ran on until 1919.

114 *my father subscribed to* Once-a-Week: My father's subscription to *Once-a-Week* was still running at the end of 1892. [. . .]
My brother Charlie and I studied it diligently every week, and
I still recall a series of prose sketches called "Queer City Folk"
and one of brief notes headed "Purely Personal." I remember
also a double-spread illustration showing "the Atlantic liner of
the future"—1,000 feet long and with an open-house aboard.
Little did Charlie and I think that we'd live to see this nightmare substantially realized.

123 *finally escaped when I went into long pants*: On Palm Sunday, 1895, as a concession to my mother, I was confirmed at
Pastor Stall's church by his successor, the Rev. George W.
Miller, D.D. My mother could certainly not be described as
religious, but she was very conventional, and it was one of
her beliefs that there was something respectable about formal
membership in a church. Even my father, she would argue,
had been confirmed in his day, though I can recall him going to church no more than three or four times during all the
time I knew him, and then only for special reasons and under
heavy connubial pressure. I wore my first long pants at my
confirmation. Under the rules of the church I was required to
put myself down for a regular contribution every week, and
I subscribed ten cents. But I never paid it, and never entered
the church afterward. For a year or two the church collector
used to dun me for the money, but in the end he gave me up
as hopeless. My father advised me not to pay him a cent, and
described him as a leech and scoundrel.

I well recall the dreadful boredom of the catechetical class
conducted by Pastor Miller, who was a very dull fellow. I never
looked into the catechism until I arrived in the class, and then
my exploration was rapid and cursory. As a result, I was unable
to answer the pastor's questions, but inasmuch as all the other

boys and girls save two or three were in like case the fact did not prevent my graduation. To this day I am profoundly ignorant of the English Lutheran theology, though I believe that it has Wesleyan touches. Once, I recall, Pastor Miller was expounding some point of doctrine to the Sunday-school in the presence of a visiting clergyman. On concluding he turned to the visitor and said: "Well, I suppose that sounded like Arminianism to you." I don't recall ever meeting any of my fellow-catechumens afterward. The sixteen boys among them all failed to make the slightest noise in the world.

125   *a series of lady teachers*: My first female music teacher was Miss Lillie Mezger, who lived in Lombard street directly across the square from our house. Her father, Gustav, operated a small tomb-stone *Fabrik* in Baltimore street, opposite where Arlington avenue (then called Oregon street) makes in from the south. I say in the text that the uniform fee of such teachers was twenty-five cents a lesson, but Miss Lillie actually charged $8 for twenty-four lessons, which worked out to 33⅓ cents. In 1892 she married a man named Charles H. Dinkelman, and was succeeded by Miss Kate M. Jones, a tall, thin old maid with a weak chest, who eventually succumbed to tuberculosis. Miss Kate, as we called her, took on my brother Charlie as a second pupil, and charged $15 a quarter for the two of us. The music teachers of that era also supplied music to their pupils; they got a heavy discount from the dealers, but charged full list prices. Some of the compositions prescribed by Miss Lillie, beside instruction books, were:

"Gipsy Countess"	.40
"Echo Song"	.10
"Margaret"	.75
"Auld Lang Syne"	.10

Miss Kate's bills were larger, though her tastes were equally homely, as this list shows:

"La Eolien Harpe" and "La Chatelene [sic]," together	.60
Duett de Bravura	1.00
"Wang" waltzes	.75
"Stradella"	.60
"Nearer, My God, To Thee"	.75
"Orange Blossom" waltz	.50

"Oxen" waltz	.40
"Racing Down the Rapids"	.80
"High School Cadet"	.40
"Danse Ecossaise"	.60

Under one of Miss Kate's bills is written: "Three lessons due yet. I will make good in the Fall." This bill was for the quarter ending June 22, 1893, and she was already more or less disabled by ill health. After 1914 I received no more music lessons, and it was not until the end of my teens that my interest in music really began to revive. My brother Charlie never showed any interest in it at all. He managed, somehow, to master and memorize a showy piece called "The Chariot Race March," but that was as far as he got. In his later years, after he had left Baltimore, he would always sit down to the piano when he came home on a visit and play this dreadful composition with the loud pedal held down. He knew no other and could not read music. My sister Gertrude had some lessons from Miss Kate early in 1897, but soon after that the poor old woman died and was supplanted by Miss M. E. Maris. One of Miss Maris's bills, dated November 11, 1897, shows that the neighborhood music-teachers of Baltimore were still charging $8 for twenty-four lessons. Soon after this my sister transferred to the nuns at St. Martin's school in Fulton avenue. She never made much progress and cannot play today. Nor does she show any interest in music.

127 *kept me on the piano-stool at parties*: The singing at Ellicott City, mentioned on p. 61, was continued when we moved to Mt. Washington in 1892, for the Lürssen boys, who were our next-door neighbors, loved to roar of an evening. Their father had built an extension on their house which was mainly given over to a big music-room, and in it the second son, George, banged a sclerotic piano, and his older brother, Herman, and the two younger boys, John and Willie, sang. Herman had been a member of the Liederkranz, a German singing society of the time, and fancied his voice, which was a loud baritone. Whenever she heard him sing my mother always laughed, but the rest of us got used to him, and even esteemed him, for he was a very friendly fellow. George had a nasal tenor, and also sang *forte*. John could do little more than growl, but

Willie was somewhat tenorish like George. The Lürssens knew nothing about good music, and played and sang only bad. My brother Charlie and I often joined them, and thus became acquainted with their répertoire. It consisted for the one part of the popular vaudeville songs of the day, and for the other of the Sousa marches and such simple pieces as "Hearts and Flowers." When George wished to really exhibit his powers as a pianist he played the intermezzo from *Cavalleria Rusticana*.

In April, 1946, one Russell Cole, of Chouteau, Okla., sent me some printed lists of popular songs, prepared and dated by himself, which awoke many memories. It recalled to me that when Charlie and I first joined the Lürssens in their yowling they were singing "Annie Rooney," "Down Went McGinty," "Daisy Bell," "Maggie Murphy's Home," and "Ta-ra-ra Boom-de-aye." But in 1892 came "After the Ball," "The Bowery," "My Sweetheart's the Man in the Moon," and "He Never Cares to Wander From His Own Fireside," and in 1893 "The Cat Came Back," "Say Au Revoir but Not Good-bye," "Two Little Girls in Blue" and "Sweet Marie," along with two Sousa marches, "The Manhattan Beach" and "The Liberty Bell." From 1894 onward the big hits were:

1894
El Capitan March
Forgotten
I Don't Want to Play in Your Yard
A Little Bunch of Whiskers on His Chin
Louisiana Lou
She May Have Seen Better Days
The Sidewalks of New York
A Sweet Bunch of Daisies

1895
The Band Played On
The Belle of Avenue A
Just Tell Them That You Saw Me
The King Cotton March
Put Me Off at Buffalo
The Sunshine of Paradise Alley

1896
All Coons Look Alike to Me
In the Baggage Coach Ahead

A Hot Time in the Old Town
I Love You in the Same Old Way
Mr. Johnson, Turn Me Loose
My Gal's a High-Born Lady
Sweet Rosie O'Grady
You're Not the Only Pebble on the Beach

In 1896 I began going to the theatre, and became a steady patron of the old Monumental burlesque house in Baltimore street, at the Jones Falls bridge. I recall that the chief favorite at that time was "My Gal's a High-Born Lady." The hits of 1897 and 1898, according to the aforesaid Western historian, were:

1897
Asleep in the Deep
At a Georgia Camp-Meeting
Break the News to Mother
I Don't Care If You Never Come Back
On the Banks of the Wabash
The Stars and Stripes Forever March
The Wedding of the Winds Waltz

1898
I Guess I'll Have to Telegraph My Baby
Just As the Sun Went Down
Just One Girl
Mandy Lee
My Creole Sue
My Old New Hampshire Home
Oh, Listen to the Band
The Rosary
She's More To Be Pitied Than Censured
She Was Bred in Old Kentucky
When You Ain't Got No Money You Needn't Come Around
When You Were Sweet Sixteen

The Spanish-American War revived "A Hot Time in the Old Town" and greatly prospered "Just As the Sun Went Down," "The Blue and the Gray" and many another current song. Our last Summer at Mt. Washington was that of 1898. After that we never returned there, for my father died on January 13, 1899, and I rented and then sold the house. But meanwhile I had got the free entreé of the Baltimore theatres as a newspaper reporter, and heard all the new hits as they came out. This went on until about 1911, when I ceased to go to the theatre. [. . .]

Moreover, the new ragtime was displacing the old-time sentimental songs—and I had long since developed an eager interest in better music. [. . .] I recall only "It's a Long Way to Tipperary," which became popular in World War I; "When Irish Eyes Are Smiling"; "There's a Long, Long Trail," which I first heard at San Francisco in 1920, at the time of the Democratic National Convention; "Aloha Oe," an importation from Hawaii; the "Missouri" waltz, which became the State song; "Pack Up Your Troubles," a war song; "God Bless America," which did not become popular until 1940 or thereabout; "Over There," another war song; "Hinkey Dinkey, Parlee Voo" ("Mademoiselle From Armentières"), yet another; "I'm Forever Blowing Bubbles," and "Oh, What a Pal Was Mary."

129 *Joe Callahan*: Joe Callahan was my assistant when I was city editor of the Baltimore *Morning Herald*, and became city editor himself when I was made managing editor. It was through him that I met Albert Hildebrandt and many of the other musicians who were to be my constant associates in the years following. After the *Herald* blew up Joe established a weekly paper called the *Builders' Weekly Guide*, which still exists. His health began to fail in 1910, and symptoms of general paralysis presently developed. By September his mind was so far gone that he had to be sent to the Laurel Sanitarium at Laurel, Md., the head of which, Dr. Jesse C. Coggins, was a friend of his and mine. Salvarsan was then still a novelty, and the supply in the United States was controlled by the Public Health Service, but Coggins managed to procure a few doses, and they worked what seemed to be a miraculous improvement in poor Joe. He was, in fact, permitted to leave the sanitarium on February 24, 1911. But by January 27, 1912, he was back, and there he remained until his death in August of the same year.

One Sunday Hildebrandt and I drove out to see him, and found him in excellent spirits and apparently quite clear in mind. He told us that all of his symptoms had disappeared save one. "I eat well and sleep well," he said, "and I haven't a single ache or pain. The only thing that troubles me is that *my head is as hard as a brick.*" With that he dropped to all fours, and gave the radiator in the room a tremendous butt with his skull. Hildebrandt and I, horrified, fell upon him at once, and held him until help arrived. It turned out that he had cut his scalp a little, but done no other damage. Soon afterward he was dead.

He was a very pleasant fellow, and he and I were good friends. Often, after a hard night's work in the office, we would take a trolley-car to the Broadway Hotel, at Broadway and Orleans street, and have a little supper and a few beers before going home. This was before the Baltimore fire of 1904. When the fire drove the *Herald* to Washington and then to Philadelphia, and I went with it, Joe held the fort in Baltimore. He was a bachelor, and is now pretty well forgotten in Baltimore, even among newspaper men. Like Paul Armstrong, Percival Pollard, W. G. Owst and more than one other man that I have known intimately, he acquired the infection that killed him very early in life, and assumed for years that he had been cured of it.

140   *a passion for photography*: I must have received my first camera, a poor one, at Christmas, 1891. It used dry plates and made a picture $3\frac{1}{4} \times 4\frac{1}{2}$ inches in size. I got a better one the Christmas following. It also used dry plates, but its size was 4×5. My cameras were without shutters, but I designed and made a wooden shutter for the larger of them, and it enabled me to make instantaneous pictures.

My photographic supplies were all bought of Joseph Cummins, who had a shop upstairs in Charles street, between Fayette and Lexington, on the present site of the O'Neill Building. I remember driving in from Mt. Washington one hot Summer afternoon to lay in, among other things, a bottle of toning solution, which cost the better part of a dollar. Coming down Cummins's stairway, I slipped at the door and the bottle was smashed on the sidewalk. I had too little money on me to buy another, so I had to go back to Mt. Washington to save up another dollar. As has always been my habit when a subject has interested me, I read everything about photography that I could lay my hands on—much of it beyond my understanding. My grandmother Mencken always gave me a dollar at Christmas, and for several years running I laid it out on a subscription to the *Photo-American*, one of the earliest American

Young August Mencken misspelling his name. Photograph by H. L. Mencken, February 15, 1895.

photographic magazines. I answered all of the advertisements in it, and was thus in receipt of a constant stream of illustrated circulars. Every afternoon in Summer I would go to the post-office in Mt. Washington village to see if any more had arrived. I probably received more mail than any other of its patrons.

141 *in later life he took to engineering*: One Summer afternoon in 1897, as my father and I were driving home to Mt. Washington, he confided to me that it had been his boyhood ambition to study engineering. It was for this reason, he said, that he had been so greatly interested in mathematics. Unhappily, he had been unable to get the requisite training and so he had drifted into business. I had always believed that he liked business, but he said not: his thoughts at forty-three still played about engineering. This story astonished me greatly, but he never returned to it, and I said nothing about it, not even to my mother. Certainly my brother Charlie heard nothing of it. Yet when Charlie was graduated from the Baltimore Polytechnic, on June 9, 1899, five months after my father's death, he announced spontaneously and at once that he was resolved to become an engineer. I then told my mother what my father had told me in 1897, and she was as surprised as I had been, for it appeared that he had never mentioned the matter to her. Moreover, we marvelled at what seemed to be a case of atavism, otherwise unaccountable, for there were no engineers within our range of acquaintance. Charlie had his way and has been an engineer ever since. When my brother August, after being floored by tuberculosis in 1906, recovered his health, he went into engineering also. This also seemed curious to my mother and me, for Charlie had left home by this time and August was strongly under my influence. Yet he chose engineering, not journalism.

144 *who some years later returned home*: Abner must have returned to Germany at the end of the eighties, for there is a Christmas card from him, dated Cologne, December 19, 1890, on p. 17, Vol. I, of "August and Anna Mencken and Their Children / 1878–1920." He and my father carried on a correspondence until my father's death in 1899, and it went on afterward with my uncle Henry. When Abner got home he reported that he had two attractive chances to marry—one with a very beautiful but penniless young woman, and the other with a less beautiful but still sightly girl who had the *dot* mentioned in my text. I recall hearing my father and my uncle discussing this at great length in their Sunday morning palavers in our Summer-house. They also consulted my mother and my aunt Charlotte. The two women were in favor of the poor girl, but my father and my uncle represented, probably to tease their wives, that they were advising Abner to take the rich one. At all events he did so.

In April, 1899, he sent my uncle a long letter on the current state of relations between Germany and the United States, strained because of German sympathy with the Spaniards in the Spanish-American War, and my uncle turned it over to me and I made a story of it for the *Morning Herald* of April 20.

This story got me credit with Max Ways, but apparently embarrassed poor Abner, for when he heard of its publication he protested to my uncle. He was, as I recall him, an unusually imposing man—tall, stoutly built and very handsome, with a flowing blond moustache. After his return to Germany he sent my mother various presents that she greatly cherished—among them, a pair of opera glasses that are still preserved in the family.

While he was in the United States he imported a young brother with red hair—always referred to as "my red brudder." This brother, Ed by name, became the Washington agent of the Anheuser-Busch brewery, and my father and uncle bought bottled beer from him. He prospered, and after a while established a brewery of his own in partnership with a man named Drury. The Abner-Drury brewery, in the days before Prohibition, brewed a very excellent imitation of Pilsner, and I often drank it in Washington after the supply of authentic Pilsner was cut off by World War I. I believe the brewery still exists (1943). At all events, the first bottle of beer that I drank in Washington following Prohibition bore its name.

145 *Jake Kilrain opened a saloon*: Jake Kilrain's saloon was on the south side of Baltimore street, a door or two east of the corner of Gilmor street. Its back gate opened into Booth street, only a little distance from our own. Jake's tenancy must have begun in 1893 or thereabout. He had two small children, and they were entered at F. Knapp's Institute, then at Hollins and Parkin streets, but that was after I had moved to the Polytechnic. He did badly in his saloon, and ran up many bills, including one to Aug. Mencken & Bro. for cigars. In 1897, when my father served for four months on the Baltimore grand jury, he came home one day with the news that he had concocted a plan, as a grand juror, to put the heat on Jake. Boy as I was, I warned him that this was dangerous, and he apparently came to the same conclusion on reflection, for Jake got away without paying the bill. Just what my father's plan was I forget.

He served on the grand jury for the May term of 1897, and greatly enjoyed his experience, which took him on official visits to various penal institutions and made him privy to phrases of life in a large city that were new to him, and not a little shocking. He was the chairman of the jury's committee on the House of the Good Shepherd, which was half a block from our house in Hollins street, and a member of the committees on St. Mary's Industrial School, which he already knew very well, and the exits of public buildings.

One of his fellow members was an old man named Gustavus Ridgely, a member of a distinguished Maryland family. Ridgely, who was then well on toward seventy and wore a patriarchal beard, took a liking to my father, and often dropped in on him afterward at the office of Aug. Mencken & Bro., at Pratt and Greene streets. The old man was a devotee of Maryland rye, and I once heard him say that he bought a barrel for his own use every year. The one bought in a given year was not tapped until seven years afterward, and there were thus always seven in a row in his cellar. One day toward the end of 1898 he dropped in at a time when my father was out, but, catching sight of me, entrusted me with a message. He had come, he said, to say good-bye, for after more than sixty years of whiskey-drinking his stomach had at last given out. "I am completely raw," he said, pointing to his neck, "from here to here," pointing to his abdomen. He actually died within the next year, but not before my father, who became ill on the day before New Year, 1899, and died on January 13.

147   *they were getting $1500*: Some light upon the baseball salaries of those primeval days is to be found in *Billy Sunday: His Tabernacles and Sawdust Trails*, by Theodore Thomas Frankenberg; Columbus, O., 1917. Sunday became a member of the Chicago White Sox in 1883, and remained in professional baseball until 1887 or 1888. Frankenberg quotes him as saying that the once immortal Mike Kelly, who was sold to Boston by Chicago for $10,000, was paid $4,700 a year by Boston. Frank Flint, the Chicago catcher, was paid $3,200. When Sunday finally left baseball to become a Y.M.C.A. secretary he was offered a contract at $500 a month to continue. Frankenberg says (p. 70) that "a salary of $1,000 a month was possible for a top notch player of national acclaim," but he gives no example of any player ever actually getting it. Even down to the time of the Baltimore Orioles, in the early 90's, $5,000 a year was a large salary, and only a few pitchers got it.

148 *Sam Trott*: Sam Trott, unlike Kilroy, was a Marylander. He was born in Towson near Baltimore, but was taken to Washington at the age of a few months, and brought up there. He was called Babe as a boy and youth. After a gaudy career on the sand-lots of Washington he ran away from home to join the Philadelphia Athletics, and he played with the Nationals of Washington and the Detroit and Boston teams before coming to Baltimore. After he began to deteriorate the Baltimore Club farmed him out to Des Moines, Iowa: I recall that when this sad news was brought home by my father I heard of Des Moines for the first time, and at once looked it up on a map. When Sam married, at thirty-two, he retired finally from baseball and devoted the rest of his life to the cigar business. After he left Aug. Mencken & Bro., he became the Baltimore agent of Eisenlohr & Co., of Philadelphia, manufacturers of a once enormously popular five-center, the Cinco.

His wife was Emily J. MacCurry, of Washington, who is still living in Baltimore (1943) at 2220 Barclay street. I hear from her now and then, and she is apparently much pleased with the account of her husband given in *Happy Days*. She tells me that her family name was actually Curry, but that her father, whose given name was Isaac, added the Mac in order to avoid being mistaken for a Jew. When she was married to Sam she was but eighteen. They had two children—a son named after his father and a daughter named Dorothy. Sam, Jr., was a very promising lad, and finished his education at St. John's College, Annapolis, where he was graduated in 1922. He was captain of the college tennis team and an adept golfer. He was also a singer, and had a promising tenor voice. On August 27, 1922, he was killed in a smash-up of the family automobile, which he was driving. Old Sam was crushed by this disaster, for he had set all his hopes on his son. He died himself in 1925. The daughter, Dorothy, is now twenty-eight years old. She is in training as a nurse at the Hospital for the Women of Maryland. Mrs. Trott wrote to me on June 10, 1943:

> My parents objected greatly to our marriage, because in those days ball players were not, I guess, considered very swell, but Sam was always the gentleman and my family learned to love him. He was noted for his grooming and was always well dressed. No couple ever lived a happier married life than we did.

Sam was a lover to the very end. He died after much suffering with his heart. He and my son were both so sweet to me. Young Sam always called me his pretty mother and Big Sam would say he married the prettiest girl in Baltimore.

149   *we had games going on all the time*: Baseball was not the only game that we played. There was also cricket. Less than half a mile from our house, in the low valley of Jones Falls just south of Mt. Washington, were the grounds of the Baltimore Cricket Club, and we learned the game by watching its members at play. There were frequent matches with other clubs in Summer, and we saw them from the railroad embankment which ran along the west side of the field. Some of the players wore beards, which struck us as comic. On the other side of the field ran the Falls, and not infrequently the players batted balls into it. We recovered many of these balls at the rapids under Belvedere avenue bridge, and attempted cricket of our own with them. We whittled out our own bats. But the game, compared to baseball, seemed slow, clumsy and idiotic, and we never liked it. There were also tennis courts on the cricket club grounds, and they supplied us with tennis balls, recovered from the falls like the cricket balls. But we never played tennis. It was still regarded, in the nineties, as a rather effeminate game. We used the tennis balls for condescending games of one-two-three with the smaller children of the settlement.

Our chief recreation, next to baseball, was walking. We had a walking club headed by Otto Schoenrich, whose family spent the Summers at Melvale, less than a mile away, and it often went on long hikes. Its members were my brother Charlie and myself, John and Willie Lürssen, and Charlie Bartz, whose home was on the hill near ours. Sometimes George Siemers, a cousin of the Lürssens, joined us. We occasionally took to bicycles, but usually walked. One of our favorite routes was to the head of the Green Spring Valley, the lower end of which was about a mile above Mt. Washington. We also liked to walk to Towson, and then out the Cromwell's bridge road to Loch Raven. The dam of the city water works at Loch Raven had been built long before this—it was much smaller than the present one—but the region was still profoundly rural. There was a grocery-store below the dam that I still recall vividly:

we always took our noon-day rest there, and reinforced the lunches that we had brought along with chocolate-cakes from its stock. Nearby was an old grist-mill, still in operation after a century. We liked to lie on the mossy bank beside its mill-race and watch its clattering wheel. Once the club walked all the way to Washington, but I was not with it that day. Our ordinary hikes ran to at least twenty miles. I well recall how stiff and tired I would be the next day.

The woods just behind our house were largely primeval forest, and in them were all sorts of wonders—for example, a sassafras tree and several wild-grapevine swings. Down along the falls was an even wilder region, and we roved it almost every day. I was too impatient for fishing, but sometimes I set out lines at night, and now and then I found a few small fish on them in the morning. I never had any interest in botany, but I liked to collect minerals, and soon I had dozens of specimens. When the stable was built behind our house it was necessary to make room for it by cutting into the steep hillside, and this cut revealed a stratum of black, crumbly stuff that I suspected to be coal. I took a specimen to Hollins street in the Autumn and examined it in the chemical laboratory that I had set up. I was disappointed to find that it was not coal, but a kind of rock containing copper. There was copper all through the Mt. Washington region, and a mile or two up the Falls road was a mine that had been worked, off and on, since the Revolution. But I knew that the ore was poor in metal and very refractory, so there was no hope of working the vein revealed by the excavation of our stable. If it had been coal, we'd have been rich.

There were very few farms left in the Mt. Washington region in the nineties. Nearly all the country was already cut up into Summer places for city folk. But an old German named Sittig operated a small market-garden in the valley below our house and from it came our table supplies. His vegetables were of very fine quality and he grew an enormous amount of them in a small space. Beside his house was a grape-arbor, and from it, toward the end of Summer, hung huge bunches of magnificent grapes. When we boys from the hill were sent down to his place to buy tomatoes, peas or lima beans, one of us would engage him in his little field, and the rest would raid his grapes.

Twelve-year-old H. L. Mencken (far right) with parents and siblings at the family's summer house in Mount Washington. Photograph by James F. Hughes, 1892.

In the intervals of his labors on his own crops he served as gardener for the city people of the vicinity.

His son, Gus, was telegraph operator in the Northern Central tower half way between Belvedere avenue and Mt. Washington station. A telegraph operator, in those days, was a hero to all boys, but Gus was of a dour disposition and did not encourage us to visit him. In his later years he took to some sort of political or theological radicalism—I forget just what it was—and used to drop in on me at the *Herald* office, hoping to induce me to give it publicity in the paper.

What is now Roland Park was still, in the early nineties, a wild woodland. In one part of it there was a pond belonging, as I recall, to the Dushanes, and there we boys hunted turtles and bull-frogs. We caught the frogs by baiting a fishing-line with a piece of red flannel, and then cautiously swinging it before the frog as he sat on the bank. If we managed to avoid scaring him he would leap for it, and then the hook had him. There were turtles, too, in Jones Falls, and some of them were ferocious. One day my brother Charlie and I caught one, and, boy-like, proceeded to cut off his head. When, headless, it calmly walked away, we were so alarmed that we ran all the way home. We made long and laborious efforts to dam the Falls, but never with any success. We also made rafts for navigating its occasional pools, but inasmuch as they were built of water-soaked driftwood, they were usually too heavy and clumsy to carry us.

At the northeast corner of Belvedere avenue and Falls road, in a little grove on a sharp bluff, there was, in the nineties, an old-time one-room country schoolhouse. I was never a pupil there, but some of the other boys of the neighborhood had sat under its ma'm. At the southeast corner of the two roads was another steep bluff, and on top of it was a grove of chestnut-trees. There was then no trolley-line running out the Falls road, and as a result no city boys ever came to gather the nuts. We thus had them all to ourselves. All along Falls road were clusters of blackberries and raspberries, and more were along the edge of the woods which runs along the western border of what is now the Baltimore Country Club golf links. We gathered many large buckets of the berries, and had the hired girl stew them, and serve them on slabs of home-made bread. They stained our teeth beautifully, and we liked to exhibit ourselves with smears all over our faces. There were also huckleberries in the woods, and these were stewed and devoured in the same way. On the bank above the railroad just north of the Belvedere avenue bridge there were wild strawberries, but getting them was a laborious and even dangerous job. Once, while I was at work upon them, a long freight train lumbered past and I came near losing my hold on the steep bank.

The Roland avenue trolley line opened on April 23, 1893, and on July 2 it was extended to Lake Roland, but the Falls road line was not opened until October 17, 1897. During the interval we boys often went to town by the Roland Park trolley. This involved a walk of a mile or so through the woods. I recall how lovely they were on Summer mornings. The Roland Park spring had already been covered in, and we always stopped at it for a drink of its cool water, which bubbled up through a layer of large white gravel.

Along the edge of the Roland Park woods, on the Falls road side, was a long row of the most beautiful morning-glories I have ever seen. When the Falls road trolley line was built the rock for its ballast was taken from the southeast corner of the road and Belvedere avenue, and the blasting gradually gnawed into the grove of chestnuts that I have mentioned. One day, while four or five of us boys were watching the workmen getting out rock, a blast failed to go off, and the Italian foreman of the dynamite crew got down on his hands and knees to find out what was wrong. Suddenly the charge of dynamite exploded, and we saw him hurled in air. He bled freely and seemed to be badly hurt. His fellow workmen loaded him on a common dirt-cart and hauled him up Belvedere avenue to Roland avenue, where they transferred him to a trolley-car and took him to hospital. Two weeks later, to our astonishment, he was back at work. It was from his camp that we got the stick of dynamite which killed the old carp of Jones Falls. The burglary was committed by Charlie Bartz, and it was he who lighted the fuse and threw the stick.

Before the days of the trolley the Falls road was an extremely rough road and we never used it in driving to and from the city. My father, in the mornings, usually drove westward on Belvedere avenue to Green Spring avenue and then southward to and through Druid Hill Park. Coming out of an evening he would sometimes use the incredibly named Charles street avenue road to Belvedere avenue, and then proceed westward along Belvedere. The chief traffic of the Falls road was provided by huge horse-drawn trucks carrying bales of cotton from the Baltimore wharves to the mills at Mt. Washington and beyond. They were drawn by four, six or eight horses, and had wagon-tires at least six inches wide. It took them from early morning to late afternoon to get from the wharves to the mills south of Lake Roland; to reach those further out must have taken the better part of twenty-four hours.

The Falls road was metalled with broken stone. This stone was simply thrown on the surface: the only rolling it got was from the wheels of the cotton trucks. It was broken on the spot by men with long hammers. One of these men, Jim Leech by name, did laboring work for all the nearby residents in the intervals of his stone-breaking. He got $1.25 a day, and on it managed to raise a large family of children. He and they lived in a tenement on the Falls road, at the south end of Mt.

Washington village, which passed under the name of the Bee-hive. Four or five families lived in it, and it was one of the marvels of the vicinity.

I went to the village almost every day in Summer, some-times driving Frank in his cart along the Falls road but more often hoofing it along the North Central railway tracks. There was no rural mail delivery in those days, and we had to get our mail at the Mt. Washington postoffice, which was in Smith and Hamilton's grocery-store, and in charge of Miss Annie Smith. Most of our groceries came from Smith and Hamilton. There was another grocery-store in the village, operated by one Wie-dey, but for some reason that I forget we did not patronize it.

A third store, chiefly devoted to hay and feed, was on the Falls road. Its proprietor was Sylvester J. Roche, and from him we bought oats, mill-feed, corn, baled hay and bedding for our horse and pony. Roche was a gloomy fellow who dabbled in politics, and eventually he became a member of the Legisla-ture. He died horribly of cancer. Miss Annie Smith I remem-ber very well. She was a small, black-eyed and rather pretty woman, and was always most polite to Charlie and me. Just to the north of Mt. Washington village, on a high hill, was Mt. St. Agnes school for girls. The girls of our settlement—that is, those whose families lived there all the year round—were day scholars at this academy, though none of them were Catholics.

150 *their new prodigies, in 1894*: I was, like every other Balti-more boy of 1894, a violent fan for the Orioles, and went to their home games whenever I could raise the quarter that it cost for a seat on the bleachers. Their playing-ground, called Oriole Park, was then in Huntington avenue (now Twenty-fifth street), a little east of Charles. The games started at 4 P.M. and I always got there by three, to see the great stars of the team arrive in mufti and then watch them at their preliminary prac-tise. I had a camera by that time and made many copies of their portraits. I also drew them. When the Orioles won the pen-nant in 1894 the Lürssen boys, Charlie and I rode on top of a bus in the great street parade that celebrated their triumph.

Despite my early abandonment of baseball it left indelible marks upon me, and though I never go to see it played I still think that it is the best game ever invented. It calls for skill, it rewards hard practise, it offers quick action, its plays are nearly always clear and obvious, and it offers little opening for mere brute force. Compared to football, which suggests a combat of gorillas, it is a game for gentlemen. How great an impression it made on me in my boyhood is shown by the fact that when I am trying to aid sleep at night I never count the traditional sheep, but always pitch a baseball. The scene is Oriole Park, and I see the green sward, the packed grandstand, and the long shafts of the setting sun as clearly as if I were back in 1892. After half a dozen magnificent curves, all of which cause the batter to fan absurdly, I fall asleep.

158 *Mr. Eckhardt*: Mr. Eckhardt was William Eckhardt. He lived next door to us, at 1526 Hollins street, and his "art emporium," as he described it, was at 345 west Baltimore street, just east of Eutaw. [. . .]

Beside Walter, there were two other Eckhardt boys, Willie and Harry. Willie was older than Walter, and what became of him in later life I do not know. Harry, when grown up, moved to Chicago. One night he went to a theatre there, alone, and was never seen or heard of again. It is supposed that he was murdered by street bandits, and his body disposed of. There was also, I think, an Eckhardt daughter, but I forget her name. Mrs. Eckhardt was a very vixenish woman, and her tirades against her poor husband, a somewhat mousy fellow, were plainly audible in our house.

When the Eckhardts moved away they were succeeded by the Hancocks. Hancock was in charge of one of the Baltimore & Ohio warehouses down in the dock region of Baltimore, and now and then his son Seymour, a member of the Hollins street gang, invited Charlie and me to visit it with him. We had a grand time burgling prunes, nuts and other eatables from the bags in storage. One day, cavorting in the warehouse, Seymour broke his leg, and was laid up for months. When he emerged at last he had a limp, and thereafter he was known as Hop. Mrs. Hancock, like Mrs. Eckhardt, was a virago, and her bellowings entertained Charlie and me as pleasantly as those of her predecessor. There was also a Hancock daughter, Beatrice, whose stable-name was Beagie.

Hancock was a thin, deprecating fellow in sedate mutton-chops, and his wife's denunciations of him, so we gathered, had chiefly to do with his failure to bring home as much money as she wanted. These goadings eventually induced him to embezzle some of the B. & O.'s funds, and he was arrested and sent to prison. The family then moved away, and I have heard nothing of any of its members since.

It was followed by the Fortenbaugh family—Charles Fortenbaugh, a box manufacturer; his second wife; two daughters by his first wife; and a son and daughter by the second. The old man was an assiduous boozer and his wife often belabored him with shrill screams: thus the character of the house was maintained. He is now dead and so is his wife; also, one of the two elder daughters, Mamie by name, who succumbed to tuberculosis twenty years ago. The rest still live in the house.

160 *their competitors*: The principal cigar manufacturers of Baltimore in those days, as I recall them, were Elliott, Oppenheimer & Elliott, Freeman Bros., C. C. Isaacs, Nitsch & Kuhn, Charles R. Becker, and Aug. Mencken & Bro. It was the custom of the time for cigar factories to have names, and my father's was called the Metropolitan. An old salesbook showing the names of its drummers in the 1887–1902 era is in the Mencken collection at the Pratt Library, Baltimore, along with a letter-book of 1894–95, a stock book of 1883–92, and a ledger of 1878–80. Three of these books passed safely (but not unsinged) through the fire which destroyed the warehouse at 28 & 30 south Paca street on December 2, 1893. They were protected by a stout Miller safe, and after the fire the manufacturer, L. H. Miller, exhibited it in the show-window of his establishment in Baltimore street, opposite the head of Hanover street, which then stopped at Baltimore. When, at the end of 1925, the old firm blew up at last, I found that my numskull cousin, John Henry Mencken, was preparing to hand over all its surviving books to the junkman. I rescued those above mentioned because they all showed my father's handwriting, had them bound, and presented them to the Pratt Library. The rest, dating from the degenerate days after my father's death, I let go.

I had known for some time that the old firm was going downhill, for my uncle and his son were both too stupid and

Site of the factory of August Mencken & Bro., on 368 West Baltimore Street. Photograph by H. L. Mencken and August Mencken,
c. 1940.

lazy to breast the competition that was ruining all the old cigar firms of Baltimore, but I always supposed that my uncle
was well-off outside the business. But when he sent for me
on December 11, 1925, saying that he had important news, I
found that he had lost all his money in a mining venture in the
West and was virtually bankrupt. Indeed, his only remaining

property, very small in amount, was in the name of his daughter Pauline. He chose a bitterly bad day to give me his news, for my mother had just been taken to hospital and was to die two days later. I was incensed at him for not telling me of his situation sooner, and from that time until his death in 1940 I had little to do with him. In particular, I was incensed by the fact that I might have to tell my mother (there was still hope of her recovery), for I knew how proud she had always been of the high credit of Aug. Mencken & Bro., and how crushed she would be by its débâcle. In order to avoid the need of telling her at once I advanced some money for the immediate needs of the firm—I think the amount was about $500. After my mother's death I advised my uncle to admit his bankruptcy and make an assignment for his creditors, but he insisted that he could compromise with them without it, and in the end he managed to do so. But some of them were very indignant, and I had to help him placate them.

In my father's time the firm had a rating of $100,000 in Bradstreet, with the first grade of credit. In fact, it never asked for credit, but always discounted its bills. I should add that if my father had lived it would probably have been impossible for him to ward off the inevitable disaster. The cigar manufacturing industry of Baltimore was going downhill even in his time—first because its old field, the Southeast, was being occupied by local jobbers, and second because of the rise of large firms doing national advertising. If my father had survived as long as my uncle he might have gone broke too, but certainly he'd have shown more industry and resourcefulness in struggling against fate.

179 *the alley behind our house*: The alley behind Hollins street was known officially (and still is) as Booth street, but we always called it simply "the alley." In it, on the north side, was a row of four-room houses occupied by colored folk. These houses have no gas laid in, and no running water save what was supplied by open hydrants in their tiny backyards. Their sanitary facilities consisted of outdoor privies. A very narrow blind alley ran behind the row of houses, and we boys often explored it. It was full of fleas and after we emerged we had to spend some time delousing ourselves. Beside the personages described in

The alley (Booth Street) behind 1524 Hollins Street. Photograph by H. L. Mencken and August Mencken, 1940.

Chapters XVIII and XIX I recall very few of the old inhabitants of the alley, though I knew them all.

One was a coal-black fellow who had lost an eye, Scotty by name. He never did any work, but lived at ease at the expense of various laborious colored women, and it was believed by us boys that he had cohabited, at one time or another, with every woman in the alley, including those who had husbands and children. Indeed, it was believed that Scotty's veneries had even extended to the Alsatia of Vincent alley, which ran north from Baltimore street between Gilmor and Mount.

One of the families in the alley consisted of a hard-working colored woman, her worthless white lover, and their family of six or seven mulatto children. The white man was a low fellow who was often drunk, but otherwise he was peaceable enough, and I don't recall any particular indignation against him. He was forbidden by the Maryland anti-miscegenation law to marry his lady, but the cops did not bother him, for in those days fornication was not unlawful in the state and his lady never laid a complaint of bastardy against him. The children were known simply as the mulattoes. They were poor creatures with yellow, stupid faces, and began doing odd jobs at the age of eight or ten, just like black children. Long after they disappeared from the alley it was reported in the neighborhood that they had all come to bad ends—the girls taking to looseness and the boys to crime. Indeed, it was reported that one of the latter had been hanged. But this, I suspect, was only gossip.

It was the custom of colored parents in my youth to threaten their children with all sorts of dreadful penalties for misbehavior. A colored mother thought nothing of threatening her young son with flaying alive. Such talk went on constantly in the alley, but it was never accompanied, so far as I could observe, by anything properly describable as cruelty. As a matter of fact, the colored people, then as now, were extremely kind to their children, and devoted a great deal of their time to looking after them. A colored father thought nothing of devoting practically all his leisure to caring for the younger members of his family.

I recall much later witnessing a charming scene in the alley. One of the small houses there was then occupied by a gigantic Negro who appeared to have a job as a coal-heaver. At all events, he always arrived home in the evening covered with coal dust. One evening as he turned into the alley on his way home, his young daughter, perhaps eight years old, rushed to meet him. She had been rigged out by her mother in clean and highly colored clothes. She rushed up to her father as if to hug and kiss him, but then shrunk back shyly when she saw the state of his own clothes. He reached out for her very gingerly, and they marched down the alley separated by a distance of two feet. She looked up at him proudly, and it was obvious that there was great affection between them. For some reason or other, I have always remembered that scene.

During the era when the colored people of Baltimore were moving out of the alleys into streets formerly occupied by whites, *c.* 1915, the alley was pretty well deserted, and some of the four-room houses were pulled down. But four of them remained, and when the Depression came on in 1929 there began a new competition for them, for their rents were very low. They had been bought, by that time, by a retired Jewish shoemaker known to the neighborhood only as Benny, and he still owns them (1943). He collects his rents every Saturday night, and when the money is not forthcoming the tenant is set out

into the street at once—or was, at all events, until the war-time
rent laws were enacted. Benny never spends any money on the
houses, and as a result all of them save one are in a bad state
of disrepair.

The exception is occupied by a young colored couple of
aesthetic tastes. The husband lately outfitted the house with
shutters that had seen long service somewhere else: the fact
that they were six inches too short for the windows did not
seem to bother him. Simultaneously his wife fitted the door
with a screen-door, and painted it in bright colors, with what
was apparently intended to be a woodland scene on the screen.
The little front room is now papered in an arty blue paper,
and there is a luxurious couch in it, with a pile of gaudy sofa-
cushions. These aesthetes are the first the alley has ever seen.

In a book entitled "H. L. Mencken / Photographs and
Other Portraits / 1881–1936" are some group pictures of a typical alley family of 1929. Two of the pictures, numbered 224
and 225, show me in the alley with some of its members, and a
third, numbered 223, shows me in the Hollins street backyard
with seven of them. Their name was Johnson, and they were
the children of an honest and diligent rag-and-bone man. So
long as he and his immensely fat and fecund wife had no more
than four or five they got on fairly well, but when the number
increased to eight, to ten and finally to eleven it was a sheer impossibility for him to support them. They then became charges
on the white neighbors. Even before my mother's death, at the
end of 1925, they were in need of assistance.

The boys, according to the Aframerican scheme of things,
were expected to earn their own keep by the time they reached
twelve years, and the girls went to work even earlier—sweeping
yards and scrubbing front-steps—but despite this, and the
constant handouts from white back-gates, the family was always on short commons. The arrival of the Roosevelt dole, in
1934, was a godsend to the Johnsons. Of a sudden they were
well fed and even more or less well dressed, and soon they
moved out of the alley to a better house.

Two of the girls, Evelyn and Daisy, were on our auxiliary
domestic staff, one at a time. Evelyn was the first. She scrubbed
our front steps twice a week and swept the backyard every
Saturday. When she got married, in 1940 or thereabout, she

Mencken with children of the Johnson family in Booth Street, the alley behind the house. Unknown photographer, 1929.

recommended her younger sister Daisy, who duly succeeded her. But in 1942 Daisy landed a job in a munitions factory, and presently her attendance was so irregular that our colored housekeeper, Hester Denny, had to supplant her with a colored boy. When Daisy applied for her munitions job she gave me as a reference, and I received a long questionnaire from her prospective employer. One of the questions asked was how I rated her mentality. She was, in fact, a low-grade moron, but I certified that she was of unusual intelligence. Apparently the fact that she was very far from it was never discovered by her employer. She is still working in the munitions factory and looks prosperous. Like her mother, she is very fat, and by the time she is thirty she will probably be enormous. Her sister Evelyn also has a war job. Altogether, Hitler and the Japs have been even greater blessings to the Johnson family than Roosevelt.

180   *all these sermons*: The alley was a favorite preaching place for colored evangelists in my boyhood, and I heard hundreds of their sermons. I remember especially a female exhorter who wore a glaring purple costume of what was apparently intended to be clerical cut. She made such a hullabaloo on Sunday afternoons that the white residents of Hollins street had to call in the cops for relief. Most of the old-time Negro street preachers have now disappeared from Baltimore, but only a few months ago (1943) a group of gospel singers disturbed my Sunday afternoon nap. In the days when my brother August had an office in the Garrett Building, in the heart of Baltimore's financial section, he was visited regularly by an ancient survivor of the old order. This venerable brother, of course, called on white folks in the hope of getting contributions. He kept a book showing his benefactors and the amounts they had given him. One day August took a look at it, and found these entries:

Pennsylvania Railroad	5 cents
Standard Oil Company	10 cents

Both corporations had offices nearby, and the pastor visited them on his rounds. The contributions credited to them had been given to him by clerks eager to get rid of him.

197   *Mr. Landgrebe*: In 1939, while *Happy Days* was under way, I got word from my brother-in-law, T. M. McClellan, Jr. (the husband of Sara's sister Philippa), of Birmingham, Ala., that Karl Landgrebe was living in Birmingham, where he was vice-president of the Tennessee Coal, Iron and Railroad Company, a subsidiary of U.S. Steel. I wrote to him at once, and through his inquiries learned something about the fate of the Almroths mentioned on pp. 195, 198 and 199 of the text. Landgrebe told me that he was then 63 years old, which made him four years older than I. He mentioned a younger brother that I had forgotten, but this brother, who had been a medical man, was dead. There were another brother and a sister, both still living in Cleveland.

The village where the Almroths lived at the time my Grandfather Abhau and I visited them in 1891 was Elliston, in Ottawa county, Ohio, not far from Toledo. Landgrebe's inquiries developed the fact that one of their cousins, Reuben R. Stick, was now postmaster there. I must have met Stick during our visit, for the Almroth and Stick houses were close together. The two Almroths that I remembered best were a daughter a little older than I, Mary by name, and her elder brother Conrad. Conrad must have been in his late teens when I was a boy of ten, but we exchanged letters for some years after I returned home. Under date of October 23, 1939, Stick wrote to Landgrebe:

> Conrad Almroth died three years ago this Spring. He had two sons: Clarence lives in Elinore and Lester in Toledo. I do not know Lester's street address, but he works for the Jersey Bread Company. Conrad's brother Will died nine years ago, but there are still three brothers living—John, Henry and George, and they live in Toledo.
>
> My father's name was George. He passed away nine years ago and I am running the store and postoffice formerly conducted by him. Two of my father's brothers are still living—John at Graytown and Henry at Martin.

Landgrebe's inquiries of Stick were reported in the Toledo *Blade* of February 7, 1940, in a column called "Among the Folks," conducted by Chub de Wolfe, and thereby attracted the attention of Mary Almroth, who wrote to me from 918 Marmion avenue, Toledo, under date of February 9. She reported that she was married to a man named Hellwig and sent me the following news of her people:

> Conrad was my brother. Oh, how he suffered before he died! It will be five years the 25th day of May.
>
> Do you remember me? My name was Mary, and do you remember the taffy we made when you were at our house—you and your grandad?
>
> I have three children and one grandson. He will be four years old the 26th of this month. I was 64 last Sunday. There were six brothers and two sisters in our family when you were out home; now there are only two brothers left, and us two girls. We are all in Toledo.
>
> My husband has been sick. He did not work for one year. He was in Toledo Hospital, Ford's hospital, attended by Dr. Robacker, one of our best doctors in Toledo, and I don't know how many more.

I replied to this, asking for more news of the Almroths and Sticks, and during the two years following Mary wrote to me half a dozen times. It was only too obvious that her education had not gone beyond the village school-house, and I soon gathered that she had had a hard and dismal life. [. . .]

What had happened to the Almroths? The father of the flock, as I recall him in 1891, was a very prosperous and progressive farmer. He had a large farm of good land, and on it was a comfortable brick house. He was a leader in his community, and was regarded with obvious respect by the other farmers. His daughter Mary I remember as a really charming country girl, full of energy and by no means unintelligent. His son Conrad worked hard on the farm, and was a beau in the neighborhood. Was it the disabling of the wife and mother in 1912, followed by her death in 1915, that started the family downhill? Or did its fate simply offer one more example of the curious degeneration that has overtaken so many families of German immigrants in the United States? Certainly it would be impossible to imagine a sharper contrast than that between the competence, hopefulness and security that I saw in 1891, and the black despair visible in poor Mary in 1942. America, alas, is not always kind.

201 *No school tomorrow!*: In my original plan for *Happy Days* there were included sketches of various other familiar figures of the Hollins street neighborhood, white and black, but lack of space forced me to omit them. One that I had in mind would have dealt with Joe Gibney, who lived in Stricker street, opposite Union Square, with his sister Jennie. He was the only white man I ever knew who never did a stroke of work from end to end of his life. He had been left about $100,000 by his parents, and he devoted himself exclusively to loafing. Every morning at about 10 o'clock he marched down Baltimore street carrying an umbrella, and took his stand at the corner of Calhoun street. There he would stay until lunch, and then, after going home to eat, he would return for the afternoon. We boys all knew him well. So far as I can recall, no scandal about him was ever circulated in his lifetime. He was a completely unvicious man, and never even got drunk. After his death it began to be reported by the neighborhood gossips that he had lived in sin for years with a lady in Lombard street—in fact, they were said to have had several children. It was also reported that this lady did a quiet trade in abortions, but it was always added that Joe made her stop it. In his later days he suddenly married, and when he died he left his widow his $100,000.

His sister Jennie, a florid, handsome woman who was always very showily dressed, married E. Madison Mitchell, an undertaker. Mitchell was well-to-do, wore a black beard, and looked after his business in a very shiny buggy. Jennie rode around with him after their marriage. They never had any children. When he died he left her almost his whole estate, so she became a really rich woman. She is probably long dead, as her brother Joe is.

After *Happy Days* came out I received many letters from men (and also women) who told me that its picture of my childhood in Baltimore coincided precisely with their memories of childhoods in other American cities of the eighties.

Notes on Newspaper Days

213 *My father died*: The story of my father's last illness well illustrates the state of medicine in Baltimore at the turn of the century. He was taken ill after dinner on New Year's Eve, 1898. He and my mother were in the downstairs sitting-room in Hollins street, reading. She was in her chair at the table and he was stretched out, as usual, on the old walnut lounge in the room. She spoke to him casually and he replied incoherently, but she thought nothing of it, for she assumed that he was falling asleep. A little while later he began to breathe heavily, and almost at once had a brief convulsion and lost consciousness. I was in bed upstairs at the time, floored by influenza, but when she called to me I ran downstairs at once, and could see at a glance that he was seriously ill. I thereupon started out on foot to summon Dr. Z. K. Wiley, the family doctor, whose office was at 724 north Carey street, eleven blocks away. It was a cold and blustery night and I got thoroughly chilled, but Wiley was *non est*. I left word for him, and trudged home. When I got there I found that my mother had appealed for help to the Scherers, who lived at 1522 Hollins street, and that she had found that Dr. James Bosley, later the health commissioner of Baltimore, was visiting them.

Bosley was examining my father when I reached home. It was obvious that he was stumped: all he could say was that the situation seemed to be very serious. We put my father to bed, and after an hour or two Wiley showed up. He was far gone in liquor, but he seemed to be functioning more or less, and he soon dispatched me to Pilson's drug-store, in Baltimore street near Carey, for a prescription. When I got back with it, he had drawn a lounge to the foot of my father's bed, and there he spent the rest of the night, with one eye upon his patient. Wiley was then 55 years old, but he seemed almost ancient to me. He was suffering from a severe dermatitis of the scalp, and I recall how obscene he looked lying on the sofa, with his closely-cropped gray head covered with huge white patches. But my mother and I had confidence in him, and preferred him as he was to any other doctor in West Baltimore.

The Johns Hopkins Hospital's training school for nurses had turned out several classes before 1898, but it was still very unusual in Baltimore for a nurse to be employed in a private house, and no one suggested getting one for my father. He was nursed by his wife, his children and a few volunteer relatives and friends. My brother Charlie and I took turns watching him, and my mother was busy day and night. He recovered somewhat after a couple of days, and was quite rational, but after that his mind began to cloud again. Wiley made an apparently accurate diagnosis: acute nephritis. After a week or so, he decided to try an application of leeches over the kidneys. He came to this decision rather late one night, and I had to go down to Greene street and wake up a German barber who was a grower of leeches. They apparently did some good, for the next morning my father was clear in mind and showed other signs of recovery. Unhappily, he soon turned the other way, and Wiley asked for a consultation.

The consultant he chose was Dr. Samuel C. Chew, then one of the bigwigs of the University of Maryland—a stately old man in a round beard. But Chew had nothing to suggest, and all I remember of him is that his consultation fee was $5. My Uncle Henry paid it as he left the house. My father by that time was unconscious again, and there began a series of formidable convulsions. Charlie and I held him in bed during one of them, listening to his ravings. They were in large part incoherent. This nursing wore us out, and as the end of the second week approached the whole family was more or less disabled. I was asleep in the next room when he died. My mother's brother, William C. Abhau, finally woke me and told me that it was all over. My father was buried by the Freemasons, and they put on a considerable show. Just before their march into the house, a bugler at the corner of Hollins and Gilmor streets let go with a fanfare. What the meaning of this fanfare was I don't know.

I remember well how, as I was trotting to Wiley's house on that first night, I kept saying to myself that if my father died I'd be free at last. I was then eighteen years old. I had got along with him very well, but I detested business and was frantic to go into newspaper work. He knew this and he made no formal protest, but neither did he give his formal consent, and I feared that there would be a considerable family debate before I could be set free. My influenza somehow passed over during his illness, but it left me with a cough that persisted for years.

I had been working in my father's office during the last Summer vacation before my graduation from the Polytechnic in 1896, and immediately after I had my diploma I went to work there regularly. My starting wages were $3 a week. My duties, for a while, were vague and general. I helped Daniel T. Orem the bookkeeper, I ran errands, and I was janitor of the lower floor of the building. My father had brought me into the business in the hope that I would stay in it and follow him, for he had no confidence in his brother. I had not smoked as a boy, but when I went to work he suggested that I had better begin, for I could not learn anything about tobacco if I didn't. I soon developed a taste for its better and more expensive varieties, and used to sneak into the cellar, abstract a few leaves from an Havana bale, and make myself some smokes.

Once, when I had one of them going, my father got a whiff of it, and gave me a suspicious and searching look, and after that I had to be more careful. He put me to the bench to learn cigar-making, for he believed that it was necessary to begin at the bottom, as he had done himself. My bench, however, was not in the shop upstairs, but at a window on the first floor of the factory at Pratt and Greene streets, looking into Greene street. There I began on cheroots and was then promoted to mold-made cigars. I never became adept enough to be put on handmade cigars, though I made many of them for my own use. After I got to the bench I was paid the regular piece-work rate for apprentices, and my income soon shot up to $7 a week. In 1897 my father tried to launch me as a city salesman, but I hated the job and made a failure at it. I was by this time fully determined to leave the cigar business for newspaper work, but I knew that it would be difficult to break away, and I can recall a despairing moment when I contemplated suicide.

Soon afterward I revealed my desire to my mother, and was heartened by her approval, though she was well aware that my father's plans for the future were all grounded on the assumption that I would remain with him. Her support emboldened

August Mencken, Sr. Photograph by H. L. Mencken, January 1, 1895.

me to open the subject to my father himself. This must have been toward the end of the Summer of 1898. He was naturally pretty well dashed, but he did not protest with any rancor, and it was understood between us that we were to resume the discussion in a year or so. His unexpected death early in 1899 saved me from what must have been a painful unpleasantness, for even if he had consented to my leaving it would have been at the cost of his long-cherished plans. Looking back, indeed, I am convinced that his death was the luckiest thing that ever happened to me, though we were on good terms and I missed him sorely after he was gone.

He had told me, between 1896 and the end of 1898, a great

deal about the tobacco business, and about his own experiences in it. As we drove home to Mt. Washington on Summer afternoons he would launch into long lectures on the characteristics of different kinds of cigar tobacco, the management of labor, the vagaries of drummers, the elements of credit, and other such pertinent matters. To this day I remember a good deal of his teaching, though it has never been of any use to me. Moreover, he instilled into me something of his general view of the cosmos, and I still subscribe to his Chinese moral system.

There was never a time in my youth when I succumbed to the Socialist sentimentalities that so often fetch the young of the bourgeoisie. My attitude toward the world and its people is and always has been that of the self-sustaining and solvent class. It requires a conscious effort for me to pump up any genuine sympathy for the downtrodden, and in the end I usually conclude that they have their own follies and incapacities to thank for their troubles. I don't think it would be fair to call me heartless, but my feelings for others are certainly concentrated upon my own class, and I am a good deal less moved by the woes of other classes. In brief, my attitude in the latter case is substantially analogous to that of a Christian toward the sufferings of Jews, or that of an Englishman toward those of Germans, or that of a German toward those of Russians.

This is the common human way, but there is a hypocritical tendency to deny it. When I am aware of such prejudices I never deny them. In the present case my attitude has colored and conditioned my whole life. In so far as I have been free to choose my everyday associates I have chosen only men who knew how to do what seemed to me to be some useful thing in a workmanlike manner, and who got a respectable living out of it. Among newspaper men I have always dismissed the poor fish as mere ciphers, and among writers I have never had anything to do with the failures.

During my days in the factory of Aug. Mencken & Bro. my interest in chemistry continued, though it was fast yielding to my desire for newspaper work. The taste among smokers, at that time, was for cigar wrappers of spotted Sumatra, and it was often difficult to get leaf with enough spots. I accordingly made earnest efforts to invent a compound that would spot plain leaf, but unhappily all those that I devised damaged the texture, and so my labors came to nothing. I also tried to concoct a solution that would improve the flavor of domestic filler—most of it grown in Pennsylvania—, and here I had better success. In the Havana factories, as I learned from my father, a cheap Spanish wine was used instead of water for moistening the leaf before it went into work. I therefore proposed that wine be tried on the domestic fillers, and when my father agreed we experimented with various cheap American wines. We finally hit on scuppernong, and presently I improved it greatly by steeping Havana stems in it before using it. The first lot of Pennsylvania tobacco so cased—as the process of moistening was called—made cigars that had an aroma strongly suggesting genuine Havana, and thereafter my prescription was followed. When I left the firm and was succeeded by my cousin John Henry he tried to improve on my flavor by adding various artificial essences, but only succeeded in ruining it. The cigars that he produced, in fact, gradually became so bad that I had to stop smoking them.

One of my odd jobs was the pasting up of the paper envelopes in which cheroots were then packed—five to a package and 50 packages to a box. The work was then done by hand, and was unendurably tedious and monotonous. I therefore tried to design a machine to do it. Such machines already existed, but I did not know it. Unhappily, my mechanical skill was of the slightest, despite my schooling at the Polytechnic, and I never managed to design a machine that seemed worth making.

221 *a later period*: Max died on the morning of June 5, 1923. Hamilton Owens, then editor of the Baltimore *Evening Sun*, called me up with the news and asked me to write an article on him for that day's paper. I fell to at once, and the article appeared on the editorial page. It ran as follows:

> Max Ways, I dare say, will be remembered by most Baltimoreans as a politician, but to those of us who served with him on the old *Morning Herald*—now dead, alas, for 17 years!—he will always remain the perfect model of the city editor. City editing is surely no trade for indolent or for fussy men, as I can testify who have tried it to my sorrow. It is bad enough today, with a new

and vast mechanical equipment for the handling of news and a harsh, military discipline prevailing in daily journalism; it was far worse in the last years of the old century, with the telephone scarcely developed beyond a toy, and no taxicabs or aeroplanes for use in a pinch, and the whole corps of journalists infected by the delusion that they were literary gents and artists, and hence not amenable to the regulations governing messenger boys and counter-jumpers.

Max got himself together a staff of strange fish, indeed, and managed to manufacture with their aid—often, indeed, in spite of them and against their violent opposition—the liveliest morning newspaper ever seen in these parts. This was accomplished partly by the sheer magic of an extraordinarily charming personality; he had a way with him that could get honest work out of even the most bacchanalian old reporter. But more important than this charm was the force of his hard professional competence. He had been a reporter himself and a very good one, and he knew every dodge and backwater of the trade. No one could fool him; no one could leave a job half done and escape his withering denunciation. His vocabulary, in those days, had a florid effulgence, well suited to the exigencies of his office. I have seen him reduce a veteran court reporter almost to tears by a few ferocious blasts; more, I have seen him swear down and silence the foreman of the composing room, an achievement almost superhuman.

But it was not only by such assaults that he got his work done; it was far more often by shrewd advice and delicate flattery. When I was 20 years old I worked for him 12 hours a day, often seven days a week, for the wage of $14. Some weeks I averaged 5,000 words of copy a day—an inconceivable stint for a modern reporter. But it was not hard work; it was going to school—and in a school infinitely agreeable and romantic. He read every line of copy himself, and just as he never missed an inaccuracy, a banality, or a rubber-stamp phrase, so he never missed anything that had any merit in it. Nor was he silent about what he discovered. The whole office knew it instantly—sometimes with the effect of making a young reporter wither to the size of one of the office cockroaches, and sometimes with the effect of making him walk on air.

Max was the only city editor I ever heard of who had no enemies on his own staff. They slaved for him, often with violent murmurs, but they always loved him, and, what is much more, respected him. He knew his trade thoroughly, and every man under him was aware of it. He knew how to handle a big story economically and quickly; he knew how to detect and offset schemes to "work" the paper; above all, he knew and esteemed good journalistic writing. I well remember the first private palaver I ever had with him, a greenhorn just in from the street. "I don't expect you," he said, "to beat the *Sun* boys getting the bald news. The *Sunpaper* has the people of Baltimore in its pocket. If it doesn't send a man for the news, they send it in themselves. The best you can do in that department is to match them evenly. But if you can't beat them *writing* the news after you have got it, then all I can say is that you are a —— —— —— ——"

A pity that such a man ever left journalism. He gave it color and charm. When he threw away his editorial pencil and took to politics, something very genuine was lost. He was a thoroughly competent editor, and an incomparable likeable man.

224 *promoted to the Central*: One of my jobs as Central district reporter was covering the house of Cardinal Gibbons at Charles and Mulberry streets. I seldom saw His Eminence, but I got to know his staff of priests very well. I was expected, among other things, to report his monthly sermon in the Cathedral. This was an unpleasant job, for his voice was feeble and the place was so crowded when he preached that it was difficult to get a good seat. One of his steady hearers was Charles J. Bonaparte, then a professional reformer in Baltimore and later to be Secretary of the Navy and Attorney General under Roosevelt I. After I had struggled to hear and report His Eminence four or five times one of the priests in his house told me that all of his sermons were written out, and offered to get me access to the next one. After that my job was much easier, for the Cardinal usually stuck to his script. Unhappily, he departed from it one Sunday morning, and the priests neglected to tell me, and so I was beaten on some impromptu matter that was worth headlines in the newspapers. I found that the old man had only a few dozen sermons. These he preached and repreached in rotation.

225 *the victim was a lovely young gal*: I recall the name of this unfortunate young woman after forty-four years. It was Virgie Taylor, and she lived in Fulton avenue, in a row of houses (then new) just south of North avenue. If she were alive today she'd be a grandmother, with her conscience long since worn to a stump and her old age lighted by sentimental memories of her first love affair.

225   *my first autopsy*: My first autopsy was on one of the cadavers stolen and sold by the dissecting-room *Diener* mentioned on pp. 227 and 439 of *Heathen Days*. The body was that of a policeman's father; hence the diligence of the cops in tracking it down. It was brought back to Baltimore in a metal coffin and turned over to Hackman, the morgue superintendent mentioned on p. 230 of *Newspaper Days*. It was a stout coffin, and Hackman had at it with a cold chisel and a hammer. When he broke through there was an explosion, for the body was far gone in decay, and a stream of the dreadful contents hit James E. Hare, then a reporter for the Baltimore *World*. Some of the other persons present—reporters, doctors and policemen—were also spattered, but I escaped, for I arrived just too late. But the smell in the morgue was certainly enough to shake me. Hare, who was always known as Ned, had been on the *Herald* in his time, and was a good reporter. Later he became a press agent for animal shows and carnivals. He is long dead.

226   *my first hanging*: My first hanging made very little impression on me. Several of the older reporters were upset, and one fainted, but I was unperturbed. I recall clearly that I came much closer to being overcome when I saw my first dead workman, killed on the job. This was while the present south building of O'Neill's department-store, at Lexington and Charles streets, was being built. As I saw the poor man lying in the dirt of the cellar, in his shabby clothes and scuffed shoes, I was really greatly touched, and I have never forgotten him. The men I saw hanged had all done something to deserve it, but here was an honest and laborious fellow who had been struck down in the midst of his work. Later on I saw many other such workmen lying in their blood, and the spectacle became less poignant, but it always moved me more or less. It seemed so dreadful to see an honest man done for, with the marks of his toil upon him. I couldn't help thinking of the cruel disaster that his death may have been to his wife and children. In those days there was no safety-first movement in Baltimore, and the death-rate among workmen in the building trades was really appalling. Moreover, there was no

Workingmen's Compensation Act, and more often than not the widow got nothing. Seeing such things made me a strong advocate of that act. I believe that every industry should take care of its own dead and wounded.

226   *The sheriff of Baltimore*: I am not certain whether the sheriff who sprung the trap was E. M. Hoffman, who went out of office during 1899, or Dr. John B. Schwatka, a political doctor who succeeded him. Whoever he was, he was half seas over when he reached the jail, and by the time he departed for Atlantic City he was well advanced upon a glorious drunk. In those days all police captains and lieutenants, court officials and other such functionaries who had to step carefully at home went to Atlantic City when the mood to lush and howl came on them. All Maryland sheriffs got drunk in preparation for a hanging, and in the counties everyone else concerned was more or less under the influence too, including even the officiating clergyman and the condemned.

229   *before his judicial days*: The lawyers principally in practise before Grannan were A. Foley Butler and William Weissager. Butler was a somewhat pompous Irishman, and on Sundays he arrayed himself in a frock coat and a plug hat and took his wife and four children for airings in a dayton-wagon. He always drove through the downtown streets—to give the loafers who were regular clients a chance to see his glories, and also, I think, to impress the cops. He did so well with his police-station practise that he was eventually able to abandon it for the higher branches of Class D divorce, personal injuries, and habeas corpus.

Weissager stuck to petty criminal business, and went very far with it. Once I overheard him, in his early days, in conference with a potential client in the cells at the Central police-station. The prisoner was a colored youth from St. Mary's county, and had lost all his money in the course of the carouse that had got him behind the bars. But he had somehow managed to hang on to an eighth-hand banjo that a Jew in Harrison street had sold him, and this he offered to Weissager. Weissager appraised it with a practised eye, and declared that it was not worth fifty cents, but in the end he took it as his fee, and, what is more, got his client off, for Gene Grannan was always merciful to colored yokels who got into trouble in the big city.

There was in those days elaborate machinery for rooking them, operated by con-men of their own race. When one of them, after laboring in the Calvert county tobacco fields for two or three years, managed to save up $20 and decided to see the city, he was met at Light street wharf, where all the Chesapeake Bay packets disgorged, by a shiny swindler who hailed him as a cousin. When he disclaimed the relationship the swindler would exclaim, "Ain't you my cousin Sam Jackson's boy?" "No, sah," the come-on would reply. "Mah name ain't Jackson. I'se Will Johnson." "Well, I'll be goddam!" the swindler would then roar. "Johnson is my *own* name. Come on, Will, and let me show you your way about. You gotta be keerful of robbers in this town. The place is full of them." After a couple of drinks in a saloon across the street the yokel would entrust his money to the swindler for safekeeping, the swindler would retire to the lavatory, and ten seconds later he would be on his way out of a rear door, leaving the poor yokel to blubber to the bartender, who immediately threw him out. Now and then the cops brought in such a swindler, and Grannan sent him to the House of Correction, but nine times out of ten the yokel simply returned to the boat and went back to Calvert county, there to amass another $20 by the sweat of his brow.

Weissager did so well at the Central police-court bar that he soon bought a house in east Baltimore street, in the heart of what was then called the Ghetto, and a year or so later astounded the neighbors by having its brick front peeled off and substituting marble. This palace was one of the show-places of the Ghetto for half a dozen years. By that time Weissager had become so prosperous that he resolved to move to New York. There he quickly became the chief star of the Jefferson Market police-court bar, and when he died in 1935 or thereabout all the New York newspapers printed long obituaries of him. It appeared that he had once broken all the records of police-court practise, even for New York, by representing seventy-two clients in a single day. He had an office directly across the street from Jefferson Market, and employed a large staff of ambulance-chasers, straw bondsmen and professional witnesses. He died rich.

230   *John Weyler*: John Frederick Weyler was born in Montgomery county, Maryland, on February 8, 1844, but was brought to the city in 1852, and grew up in the old Seventeenth Ward of Baltimore. It was a tough region, and young Weyler was not the least tough of its denizens. As a follower of Jim Busey, the Democratic boss of the ward for many years, he took an active hand in the ruffianism that Busey always staged on Election Day. Opposition voters were jabbed with shoemakers' awls as they stood at the windows of the polling-places, or otherwise mauled and intimidated. A favorite device was to bespatter one of them with blood obtained from a slaughter-house and then chase him through the ward. Usually he was a Negro, which is to say, a Republican. The other Negroes, seeing him bloody and assuming that he had been stabbed and was about to be killed, kept away from the polls.

Weyler was a leader in all such social-minded exercises, and did not stop at mere simulation of bloodshed. It was generally believed in South Baltimore, in fact, that he had had a hand in more than one actual murder on Election Day. In 1867, as a reward for his services, he was appointed a police sergeant, and soon afterward he was made a detective. The Baltimore police force, in those days, was in full alliance with the gangs which ravaged the town, and Weyler was one of its worst members.

In 1879 Busey sent him to the Second Branch of the City Council and there he remained for nine years, oscillating between that branch and the First. At one time he was president of the First Branch, and as such officiated as mayor *pro tem* during the absences of Mayor Ferdinand C. Latrobe. As a city councilman he played the Busey game of politics just as assiduously as he had done as a cop, and when, on May 18, 1888, he was made warden of the State Penitentiary there was a genuine uproar in the town. Old Goldsborough S. Griffiths, a leading reformer of the time, voiced the general opinion among decent Baltimoreans when he said publicly that Weyler had been sent to the right place, but was on the wrong side of the cell bars.

This sneer somehow touched his pride, and he resolved to abandon his old ways and make a good record. No more striking example of an honest and permanent reformation has ever been seen. In a little while it became noised about that he was running the penitentiary honestly and efficiently, and by the time I first encountered him, in 1899, he had already become a sort of model public officer. He made no effort to conceal his lurid past; on the contrary, he seemed to enjoy references to it, and more than once I heard him tell tales, not without some show of satisfaction, of his former exploits. But he stuck to his new line resolutely, and when, on May 1, 1912, he was retired as warden and made warden emeritus there was an outburst of public regret and sincere praise. [. . .]

Weyler's life, in the days when I knew him, was confined strictly to his duties. He took no hand whatsoever in politics, and belonged to no fraternal organizations. As I say in the text, he never left the Penitentiary save on rainy days. Then he would take long solitary walks, and not infrequently I would meet him on the street, plodding along in his solemn, dogged way. He was very proud of the fact that he had made the Penitentiary self-sustaining, and provided a means for its inmates to earn money for themselves. His rule was just, but very strict, and he believed in the lockstep and flogged recalcitrant prisoners, himself wielding the lash. This flogging was urged against him by the uplifters who occasionally harassed him, but he defended it stoutly.

After his retirement the workshops that he had so laboriously organized were broken up by the passage of a Federal law forbidding the shipment of prison-made goods in interstate commerce, and the resultant idleness of the prisoners made for frequent disorders. Worse, a drunken Army colonel, by name Claude Sweezy, was appointed warden, and soon his idiot devices had the place in an uproar, and there were frequent escapes. One of those devices was the organization of a so-called Sweezy Club, for the social relaxation and moral improvement of the prisoners. Its chief effect, naturally enough, was to enable them to get together to plan not only escapes but also fresh crimes afterward. Weyler, by now approaching eighty, viewed these didoes with a bilious air, and was always glad to talk against them to newspaper reporters.

249 *the Boer leader*: I was against the Boers during the Boer War, mainly for the reason that Hesketh Pearson gives for the opposition of George Bernard Shaw—that he could not stomach the Bible-searching of Oom Paul. The old boy was a pious quack to me, and I could not think of a quack as a hero. The pull of Kipling also helped, but I inclined toward the English principally because of my disgust with the Boers.

256 *good writing*: Good writing did not become the rule on the *Herald* until my days as its city editor. Max knew it from the bad, but in his day there were very few men on the staff who could produce it. His two successors, W. Dwight Burroughs and Isidor Goodman, were both incompetent. On becoming city editor I made desperate efforts to improve the quality of the local copy, and to that end rewrote a lot of it. But it did not show any general improvement until I began to get rid of the survivors of the Colonel Cunningham era and substitute younger and better men.

263 *we palavered with the females*: The captain's palavering consisted in approaching a woman standing in front of one of the huts, holding up an American silver dollar, and pointing to her daughter, a wench of perhaps fourteen or fifteen. Mother and daughter were both willing, but just then the siren blew.

264 *a Dane*: This Dane was Captain Asmus Leonhard; he always thought of himself, in fact, as a German. He appears at some length in Chapter XIII of *Heathen Days*. He was a racy character, and his speech was studded with apothegms on the order of those recited by Al Goodman. One of his favorites was: "God help the rich; the poor can beg." A. H. McDannald and I met him aboard the North German Lloyd liner *Kronprinzessin Cecile* in 1912, on our first trip to Europe together. The cigars he smoked were actually Romeo et Julietas. He carried a large stock of them, and when we got to Bremen I saw him get them through the customs by boldly handing a German inspector three American silver dollars.

During the years after our first encounter he often dropped off in Baltimore to see McDannald and me. He once told us that the foundations of his fortune had been laid at the start of the Spanish-American War, when he found himself in the Cuban port of Banes, in command of a banana boat. Hundreds of Spaniards of the Oriente Province flocked down to the coast with their families and valuables, in fear that the invading Americans would loot them and maybe even murder them. The captain ferried these fugitives over to Cape Haitien, in Haiti, a very short trip, even for a nine-knot banana boat. They had their money in gold, and gave it to him for safe-keeping. Thus he learned the approximate cash capital of each fugitive, and charged a fixed percentage of each hoard for the passage. What that percentage was I forget, but I remember the captain saying: "I never robbed them. The most I ever charged was $1,000." This money he invested in Cuba after the war, and when he became marine superintendent of the Munson Line at Havana he put it into the common stock of the company. That common stock greatly appreciated in value, and at the time McDannald and I met him he was rich. Along toward 1930 the Munson Line got into difficulties and his wealth vanished, and in his last years he was very hard up. He died in 1935 or thereabout.

266 *his whole time was given over to his missionarying*: The amateur evangelist of Port Antonio was L. D. Baker, president and manager of the Boston Fruit Company, the largest of the banana shippers that later combined to form the United Fruit Company. He hailed from Barnstable, Mass., and the head office of the Boston Fruit Company was in Boston, but he insisted on living in Port Antonio. The Old Man Buckman mentioned on p. 260 of *Newspaper Days* was C. C. Buckman, president of the rival Buckman Fruit Company of Baltimore, the offices of which were on Bowley's Wharf, where its ships tied up. Buckman was also a pious fellow, not as passionate in the faith as Baker. He wore a round beard and was very stiff in manner. When he took his company into the United Fruit he became rich, and in his later days he and his wife lived in what was then great luxury at the Belvedere Hotel, Baltimore. Both he and Baker carried passengers in some of their ships, and tried to encourage tourist travel to Jamaica. To this end Buckman printed small advertisements in the Baltimore papers. His advertising man was Ralph D. Nolley, who had been in charge of the art department of the *Herald*, but was now launched in the advertising business. I wrote these Buckman ads for Nolley.

One day in 1902 or 1903 he approached me with a proposal from Buckman that I serve as conductor of a tour to Jamaica that the two had projected. I was offered no payment in cash, but only my transportation. I accepted and the tour party presently set off. It consisted of no more than a dozen persons, and

Mencken with his uncle Charles Abhau and Kemp Hennighausen en route to Jamaica. Photographer unknown, c. 1900.

the only ones I remember were a Mr. and Mrs. Lauten, of Baltimore. The husband's actual name was Lautenberger, but he had shortened it for convenience. He was a victim of hay fever and asthma, and a few years later his heart gave out during a severe asthmatic attack and he died. I recall little of the tour save that we were met at Port Antonio by a colored intellectual of the sort described on p. 264 of *Newspaper Days*, and that he made all the shore arrangements. They included a trip to Kingston by train. What Buckman charged the tourists I forget, but I think it was about $75. Our stay on the island had to be shortened a day because the bananas our ship was to carry were delivered at Port Antonio sooner than expected. On the return trip the tourists held a meeting and demanded a rebate. I approved this demand and it had to be granted, but as a consequence of my approval I was never asked to conduct another tour. I made two other trips to Jamaica in the early years of the century. On one of them two of my fellow passengers were my uncle, Charles H. Abhau, and my classmate at the Polytechnic, L. Kemp Hennighausen, whose sister Bertha my uncle later married.

278 *Theodore M. Leary*: Teddy Leary stuck to the theatrical business, and died eventually in Hollywood. He had married, meanwhile, a young woman in a stock company at the Auditorium Theatre, Baltimore, but this marriage soon blew up. When he came back to Baltimore on occasional visits he always stayed at Aunt Ellen Martin's theatrical boarding-house in Howard street, between Monument and Madison, a famous place in its day. Aunt Ellen, who was a pious Catholic with two daughters, ran a very respectable house, and would not tolerate fornication, though some of her guests, I am sure, cheated.

One day in the Summer of 1903 Teddy dropped into Baltimore from the road and was given a gorgeous party by his old colleagues of the *Herald*. When he got to Aunt Ellen's at 3 A.M. he was in an advanced state of liquor. The night being hot, he went to the bathroom on the second floor, stripped off his clothes and took a cold bath. Hearing no one astir, he then proceeded to his room stark naked, and took a leap into his bed. He landed squarely upon the leading woman of a Summer opera company, and her yells soon had the whole house at the door. Poor Teddy, in his befuddled condition, had forgotten that Aunt Ellen had assigned him to a new room, and that the one he had slept in so often was occupied by the strange lady. I heard the story when I got to the office at noon the next day, for Teddy was there waiting for me. What he wanted was a loan of $20 to buy conciliatory presents for Aunt Ellen and her two virtuous daughters, Sadie and Gertie. I lent him the money and he bought the presents and dispatched them by messenger. He was afraid to return to the house himself, for the low comedian of the opera company, a gorilla-like fellow, was in love with the leading woman, and refused to believe that Teddy had not tried to rape her.

Teddy did not prosper in the theatre, and at the time of his death in Hollywood was in a low state financially. The only Baltimore friend who attended his funeral was Percy Heath. On the way to the cemetery the automobile in which Percy was riding ran down and killed a Chinaman, thus adding a final note of tragedy to the futile career of a charming fellow who, in his day, had been full of promise.

278 *a third that played dollar shows*: The theatre playing dollar shows was the Auditorium in Howard street, now (1943) the Mayfair movie-house. The vaudeville house was the Maryland in Franklin street, around the corner. The stock company house was the Lyceum in north Charles street, now torn down. The home of melodrama was the Holliday Street, opposite the City Hall, destroyed in the great Baltimore fire of 1904. The burlesque houses were the Monumental, at the eastern end of the Baltimore street bridge over Jones Falls, and the Odeon in Frederick street. The Auditorium, Maryland and Monumental were owned by James L. Kernan. The Auditorium was a sort of mixture of theatre and assignation house: all the loose girls of the town patronized its matinées and scouted for men in its bar. The Odeon, like the Holliday Street, was destroyed in the fire of 1904, but the Monumental survived for some years afterward. In its later days its burlesque business went to two new theatres—the Palace in Fayette street opposite Ford's Opera House (now a garage) and the Gayety in Baltimore street, still open (1943). After that the Monumental was chiefly given over to boxing and wrestling matches.

284 *they were joined by a Baltimorean*: The Baltimorean who horned into the falsetto debate between Davies and Fitch was Dr. Frederick Taylor, then society editor of the *Evening News* and later of the *Sun*. He was known to all Baltimore newspaper men as Maud Taylor, and was a well-known figure in the town during the 1900–15 era. The *Sun* retired him on a pension in 1935 or thereabout, and he is still alive (1943). He was born in Virginia but liked to be thought an Englishman. "I was born in the United States," he once said to me, "but I was conceived in England." Despite his effeminate manner, he was never, so far as I am aware, accused of overtly homosexual practises. Like Alexander Woollcott, he was probably a nomo rather than a homo. That is to say, he had no sexual life at all, physically speaking.

285 *Stuffy Davis*: Stuffy Davis, whose actual given name was

Glenmore, was a salient figure along the Broadway of the first years of the century, but is now quite forgotten. He was a heavy boozer and his appearance was made notable by an extraordinarily large nose—not at all Jewish in cut, but rather Roman. He had drunk himself to death by 1915.

285   *George Fawcett*: Fawcett died at his Summer home on Nantucket island on June 6, 1939, aged seventy-seven. He was born in Virginia and educated at the University of Virginia. He made his début as an actor at the Manhattan Theatre, New York, in 1886, and later supported the two Salvinis, Nat Goodwin and Maude Adams. He never reached stardom, but he made a big success in London in 1908 in *The Squaw Man*, there called *A White Man*, and later appeared in the United States in various plays. He was what the actors call a bad study, and could never be trusted to know his lines. This made for many unpleasant situations when he essayed rôles with his stock company in his Baltimore days. In 1917 or thereabout he gave up the stage and went to Hollywood, where he made a considerable success in old men parts. But with the advent of the talkies his inability to remember his lines began to incommode him, and in 1932 he returned to New York. I used to meet him occasionally at the Algonquin Hotel, where he always stayed when he was in town. He was an agreeable fellow, and, as I say in the text, educated and intelligent. Two days after his death the Baltimore *Sun* published the following account of him:

> A popular actor who was "too intelligent" was the comment here yesterday by one of the many acquaintances of George Fawcett, who died Tuesday in Nantucket, Mass.
>
> Thirty-five years ago, in the heyday of the Old Lyceum Theatre, Fawcett came to town with the Percy Haswell Stock Company and remained for four or five years. He was a graduate of the University of Virginia, and Percy Haswell, his wife, was the daughter of a Texas Congressman.
>
> Fawcett prospered here, mingled in the literary and society circles, and then stepped to the rôle of matinée idol in London. He was embarrassed by friends from Baltimore who went to see him in London and all but inundated by women admirers.
>
> In London, he often spoke of Baltimore, its slowness in changing from old to new, Lexington Market, and that "terrible

fault of having too many good things to eat." He didn't come back until 1916, to play John Silver in *Treasure Island*.

Then Fawcett moved to Hollywood. He had a near corner on the character of a "gruff old man with a heart of gold," with his stern features and bulky figure. When the talkies arrived, his friends recall, the rôles stopped because he could not learn his lines.

"Often," a former intimate remarked, "in a Baltimore appearance he would butcher a whole scene by forgetting his lines. He was too intelligent to be able to sit down and just study them in humdrum fashion, and that was the only way open to him. He was sure he would be prompted."

In recent years, his heart was bad, forcing him to cancel a lecture tour last year. He remained at Nantucket with his wife and daughter, Mrs. Margaret Fawcett Wilson.

When I made my first trip abroad, in 1908, I met him in London, where he was playing in *A White Man*, and he showed me the sights of the Fleet street region. When, on going to the Lyric Theatre to meet him after a matinée, I found a gang of what were then called matinée girls gathering to greet and admire him, I was genuinely astonished, for George was surely not a beauty. In the *Sun* of April 12, 1908, I had the following unsigned report on the business, under date of London, March 21:

> A tall, pallid, unemotional policeman appeared at the stage door of the Lyric Theatre in Great Windmill street this afternoon just as the clocks down toward Piccadilly chimed five. A few moments afterward the curtain was rung down upon the matinée of *A White Man*, and about 150 gushing, buzzing matinée girls came trooping around the corner from the theatre exits in Shaftesbury avenue. The policeman held up his portentous finger and the girls fell into two long lines. The gabble of gossip and the crunching of caramels made a sweet, soft din.
>
> Suddenly the stage door opened and a thick-set, rather stern-looking man came out. The soft-sweet din rose to *fortissimo*, and there was a great craning of necks. "There he is!" whispered Maggie to Gwendolen. "There he goes!" whispered Eliza to Jane. The thick-set man settled his overcoat and plodded on between the lines of fair and admiring Londonese. He was George Fawcett, late of Baltimore, and now the theatrical idol of the hour in the British capital.
>
> The shop windows are filled with postcard portraits of Mr. Fawcett as Big Bill in *A White Man*, and his name stares at you from every second billboard.

As you no doubt know, *A White Man* is our old friend, *The Squaw Man*, renamed for London use. Mr. Fawcett has his old part, which he created in the United States, and the Londoners like him in it immensely. On the first night of the play, indeed, he was greeted in a manner almost alarming. Never since Sir Henry Irving's farewell, said one critic, has there been such a riotous outburst in a London theatre.

As a result, *A White Man* was an assured success, and there is little doubt that it will run until the Autumn. Just at present there is a lull in the demand for seats on account of Lent, but when the London season begins, after Easter, the standing-room-only sign will be brought forth again for nightly exercise. And those who know say that if there had been no George Fawcett there might have been no such joyful tale to tell.

Though he is thus a celebrity—and being a celebrity in London means being besieged by all sorts of persons—Mr. Fawcett is taking things very quietly. He lives at a retired hotel, not far from the Lyric Theatre, and spends most of his time wandering about the older parts of the city. He is a perambulating guidebook—not of the places starred by Baedeker, but of the half-forgotten, out-of-the-way shrines held dear by lovers of English history and English literature. After the matinée today he took the *Sun*'s correspondent for a walk in old London—to Garrick's house, to Goldsmith's grave, to the chambers of Pendennis and the haunts of Sheridan. He led the way up toward Charing Cross and Fleet street, and as night came on we strolled through the Temple, through Brick Court, Temple Court and all the other byways immortalized by the immortals of our English tongue, and then to Simpson's for a dinner of English mutton and greens and a pint of English beer.

286 *the play was put on*: Mary Shaw died in 1929, aged sixty-nine, and Lewis not long afterward. He had given over most of his later years to Shakespearean parts. Virginia Kline is still alive (1943). She has been living at the Astor Hotel in New York for many years, and busies herself writing plays that are never produced. She writes to me occasionally and always sends me a card at Christmas, but I haven't seen her for at least twenty-five years. She hailed from Cleveland, O., where her mother ran the Colonial Arts Rooms. After the long tour of "Ghosts" ended she had parts in various other plays, but never made any success. I recall seeing her in Baltimore in *The Red Kloof*, a South African play presented by Louis Mann. Her performance was very bad. In the same company was an English actor who appeared in one act only. Virginia told me that he had never seen the play as a whole, had no idea what it was about, and showed no interest in it whatever.

Under date of June 20, 1943, Virginia informed me that the other plays presented by the Mary Shaw company were *Hedda Gabler*, by Ibsen; *Mrs. Warren's Profession*, by George Bernard Shaw; and *Alice-Sit-by-the-Fire*, by James M. Barrie. La Shaw made an enormous sensation in 1920 or thereabout by appearing in a new play (I think the first night was in Newark) in which she played a whore-madam who had the line: "Go to hell, you goddam son-of-a-bitch." This was alarming stuff in that era, and the line had to be changed before the play was brought into New York. Today (1943) it would hardly cause a ripple. She was, in her day, the undisputed leader of the intellectual faction among American actresses. Even the admirers of Minnie Maddern Fiske acknowledged her preëminence. So far as I know, she never had a popular success. She was an Irishwoman of massive build, and was born in Boston. I saw her only a few times after she left Baltimore.

287 *Eugene Bertram Heath*: There is more about Percy Heath in Chapter XV of *Newspaper Days*. He and I became fast friends, and when I was made city editor he was appointed by Meekins to succeed me as Sunday editor, at my suggestion. He also took over the job of dramatic editor. In that capacity he presently began to receive offers to serve as press-agent for theatrical managers, and before long he succumbed. After spending some years ahead of road-shows, and as office press-agent in New York, he went to Hollywood, and there had a successful career as a writer of movies. I was best man at his wedding, and stood godfather for his only child, a son named Bertram. His bride was Marcia Dodge, the blonde step-daughter of the younger Peter Reveille, of Reveille's livery-stable. I recall that both Percy and I were somewhat in liquor at the wedding, and that he made a scandal by dropping the ring.

When, a year or two later, the time came to baptize the Heath baby the same Episcopal rector officiated. He remembered me and was plainly suspicious of me, for just as the ceremony was about to begin he gave me a long, searching look and demanded, "Young man, are you a Christian?" When I assured him that I was, he asked me the name of the clergyman who had baptized me. Here I was stumped, for I simply could not remember it. But I recalled suddenly the name of an old-time Episcopal clergyman who had been one of my Grandfather Mencken's companions in beer-drinking and theological disputation and so hazarded "Father Chipchase." This satisfied the rector, and the baptism went on.

Marcia was one of two tall, handsome, blonde sisters, the daughters of a doctor long dead at the time of her marriage. Reveille was her mother's third husband. They had been married only a short while when the advance of the automobile ruined his livery-stable and he got into serious money troubles. One day he went out to the bridge spanning Gwynn's Falls at Edmondson avenue, and jumped off, thus ending his woes. Percy and Marcia always seemed to get on very well, but I marvelled at the fact, for Percy was an intelligent fellow and Marcia was extraordinarily vain, shallow and stupid. When I was in Hollywood with Joseph Hergesheimer in 1926 I visited them. It was pleasant to see Percy again, though we had had but little communication for a long while, but Marcia was hard to bear, for as she gathered years her imbecility increased.

Percy died during the thirties, leaving her very well provided for. Their son, Bertram, turned out badly. When he was in his early twenties he was snared by a kept-woman who subsequently induced him to marry her. Then he fell ill, and Marcia had to support him. He died in 1942. In October, 1941, Marcia came to Baltimore for treatment at the Johns Hopkins Hospital, and I had to see her, but it was an extremely disagreeable duty. I gathered from her chatter that she was determined to marry again, and had her eye on several likely candidates. In fact, she gave me descriptions of two of them and asked my advice. Under date of Columbus, Ga., December 18, 1942, I received a letter from her announcing that she had married a captain in the army, Bert McKay, Jr., by name. After speaking of the death of her son she said:

> It was pretty bad for me, so I came to Ga. and married the guy. That dame that wrote "Live alone and like it" is a *liar*. I am very happy with my captain. He's lots younger than yours truly,

but I happen to be a "young old girl" while he's an "old young fellow." Time, they say, heals, but this Xmas will be the first I have ever had without Bertram and it's going to be hell. Drop a line and tell me you don't think me foolish to marry again.

I did not reply to this note. A few days later came a Christmas card in the names of Marcia and Bert McKay, Jr. On the envelope Marcia gave her name as Marcia Heath McKay and her address as 1337 Fourth avenue, Columbus.

Percy had some ability, but his marriage was a heavy handicap to him, though he probably didn't know it. It was impossible, in the constant presence of a hollow and trashy woman, to undertake any work of difficulty and importance; she shoved him along the easiest way, and so he became a fashioner of trade goods for the movies. More than once in this life I have seen the same melancholy story played out. The worst burden that a competent and ambitious young man can carry is a stupid wife. When, as in the case of Marcia, she is also egotistical and bossy, his case is almost hopeless.

288 *Charlie Ford*: There were four Ford brothers—Charles Elias, John Thompson, Jr., George T., and Harry E., and they were all the sons of the John T. Ford who built Ford's Opera House in 1871 and had been the proprietor of that Ford's Theatre in Washington in which John Wilkes Booth assassinated Abraham Lincoln on April 14, 1865. The old man was one of the salient town characters of Baltimore, but that was before my time, for he died on March 14, 1894. He had had fifteen children, but only the four sons aforesaid and five daughters were alive in 1900. They all grew up in the family home at 1536 north Gilmor street—a large, rambling house with a garden and orchard surrounding it. When the old man bought it in 1860 Gilmor street had not been cut through, and the entrance to the grounds was on the Liberty road. Harry Ford, a bachelor, still lived there with his mother and two unmarried sisters in my theatre days, but the other surviving brothers and sisters were married and had homes of their own. The mother died on October 22, 1922, aged ninety-one, and two years later the old home was put up at auction. It was bought by a real-estate operator named Robert Seff, and he cleared off the house, which was 150 years old, and built thirty two-story houses for Negroes on the site. The lot measured 167 by 267 feet.

Charlie was the oldest son, and apparently got a larger share than the others out of the revenues of the opera house. Born in 1852, he was a portly, handsome fellow with a somewhat pompous air. His wife, who died in 1920, had been Anna Hardcastle, a member of an Eastern Shore family of some pretensions, and Charlie himself had a yearning for fashionable society. Early in the century he built an Italianate villa on Park Heights avenue beyond the Pimlico race-track, and gave it the sonorous name of Carlford Manor. There he entertained upon a considerable scale and there his two daughters, Mabel and Edith, were launched upon social careers. He had no son. Edith, as a young woman, was very good-looking, and Charlie showed much pride in her. Every Monday evening she sat in the forefront of his box at the opera house. In 1905 or thereabout she married a man named Reese and was presently the mother of two sons. But her marriage turned out badly, and she was soon divorced. Later she married Walter R. Mitchell, of Norfolk, Va., and went there to live. The other sister, Mabel, married Walter Hopkins, and is still (1943) living in Baltimore.

Charlie had been educated at the University of Virginia, where he took his A.B. in 1870. After that he made a tour of Europe under the tutelage of Dr. Basil L. Gildersleeve, then professor of Greek at Charlottesville, and later, from 1876 to 1915, head of the classical department at the Johns Hopkins. When the Ford fortunes declined Charlie disposed of his manor-house and went to live at the Charles Apartments, 3333 north Charles street. There he died on January 10, 1928. He had served his apprenticeship in the theatre by managing traveling companies of his father, one of them (according to his own story) the first to play the Gilbert & Sullivan operettas on the road. When he died it was recalled that he had several times appeared as an amateur actor, and that he was the author of two plays—one of them, *Joan of Arc*, presented by the Paint and Powder Club of Baltimore.

The other Ford brothers were much less haughty and ostentatious than Charlie. George, the next older, was a solemn, stupid fellow who spent his whole life selling tickets at the opera house. He was invariably clad in black, and wore a boiled shirt, a low standing collar without wings, and a black bow tie. No one ever saw him smile, not even a patron stepping up to buy a whole row of seats. Indeed, he was so funereal in appearance and manner that he was generally known as the Undertaker. He died in 1912, after having served as treasurer of the opera house since it was opened on October 2, 1871. The third brother, John T., Jr., was as amiable as George was dour. His duties were to help Charlie in the lobby before performances. They took their stand abeam of the downstairs entrance where old Basil Moxley, of whom more anon, officiated as ticket-taker. Between them they knew all the regular theatre-goers of Baltimore, and at least two-thirds of the incoming patrons were greeted by name. Harry, who was the youngest brother, also had a station in the lobby, but he confined himself mainly to newspaper men, press-agents, visitors from other companies, and so on.

John was a short, thick-set fellow with a pronounced stoop, and looked countrified beside his elegant brother Charlie. He had no social aspirations, but lived modestly in Forest Park and there dabbled in politics. When I first knew him, in 1900, he was a member of the City Council from the Fifteenth Ward. He was an honest fellow but not too bright, and Major Richard M. Venable, then the boss of the council, found it easy to hold him in line. The newspapers whooped him up as the only city councilman who never made a speech: this was supposed to be a proof of a resolute virtue, but it was actually due to his excessive shyness. John was born in Baltimore in 1863, and was thus eleven years younger than Charlie. His first term in the City Council ran from 1899 to 1901. In 1911 he was appointed a member of the Baltimore Jail Board, but three years later he returned to the council, serving this time until 1927, when the politicians tired of him and dropped him. He became manager of the opera house on the death of Charlie in 1928, but functioned as such for only a short time, for the place was sold on June 5, 1929. John was educated in the Baltimore public schools. After a year or two at the City College he was put to work by his father at the age of seventeen. He served for some years as a manager of traveling companies but soon settled down at the opera house. In 1887 he was married to Elizabeth

Mitchell, a member of one of his father's operetta companies. They had three sons, all of whom turned out well.

Harry, the baby of the family, never married. He was, next to John, the most amiable of the brothers, and I saw a great deal of him in my days in the Baltimore theatres. When his brother Charlie tried to lure me into doing press-agent jobs it was easy for me to throw him off, but resisting John was harder, and putting off Harry was harder still. Nevertheless, I managed to do it. Harry had been a gay dog in his youth, and paid the penalty for his wickedness by dying of locomotor ataxia. In his last years his walking was seriously impeded, and he was a sad figure. He died some time before 1922. All four of the brothers lived in constant terror that there would be a fire in the opera house and a vast slaughter of customers, for they were well aware that it was a fire-trap.

Once, as I was standing just inside the downstairs door with Charlie, some idiot dropped a lighted cigar-stump behind the last row of seats, and almost instantly a woman following him picked it up with the hem of her long dress. A wisp of smoke curled up and she gave a scream—fortunately not loud. Charlie and I hustled her out into the lobby and beat out the fire. George, immersed in the box-office, saw nothing, but the other brothers were in a state of extreme jitters all the rest of the evening. In 1943, after the opera house had passed out of the hands of the family, a fire in a night-club in Boston induced the Baltimore building inspectors to give it a thorough examination. They were so appalled by what they discovered that they ordered the place closed until extensive reconstruction could be undertaken. Unhappily, it was impossible to get priorities for the needed material, and so Ford's was dark at last. The house has wooden joists and beams throughout, and directly under the orchestra floor are old store-rooms that would give a fire a magnificent start.

The Fords knew about this, but they also knew that an adequate reconstruction of the theatre would cost a great deal of money, and they simply didn't have it. For their lack of it there were two principal reasons. One was that the profits of the house had to support four brothers, their old mother and their maiden sister; moreover, four married sisters also had some shares in them. The second reason was that the theatre had been blacklisted by the so-called Theatrical Trust in 1900 or thereabout, and had had great difficulty, ever thereafter, in getting the better and more profitable sort of bookings. When the Theatrical Trust was formed by Marc Klaw and Abraham L. Erlanger, Charlie Ford opposed it violently, and as a result the bookings that Ford's used to get were diverted to the Academy of Music in Howard street, which was operated by Klaw and Erlanger's allies, Nixon and Zimmerman. For some years Charlie fought on, but as one traveling star and manager after another fell into the maw of the trust the competition of the Academy of Music became more and more serious, and in the end Ford's dropped to second place among the Baltimore theatres. Stars and managers who had been the associates and even employés of the elder John T. Ford were forced to play at the rival house.

Finally, Ford's sank to so low an estate that the brothers had to part with it. It was sold to their old enemy, Erlanger, in 1929, and Harry A. Henkel, formerly the manager of the Academy of Music, was sent in to operate it—a bitter pill, indeed. Henkel was a jackass and did not last long, but his successor, John D. Little, was also an old Academy man. Altogether, the Ford brothers had plenty of misery in their later years. After the death of Erlanger in 1930, the opera house, and with it the Academy, fell into the hands of a Philadelphia Jew who called himself Stanley: what his real name was I do not know. He rebuilt the Academy, turned it into a movie house, and renamed it the Stanley. The opera house continued to make heavy weather under his management, and some time after he died it was sold to a Baltimore Jew named Morris A. Mechanic, who was also manager of the Hippodrome in Eutaw street. Only a little while after he took possession of it the house was condemned.

The elder Ford was still remembered in the Baltimore of my first days as a reporter, for he had been dead but five years. In his time a group of his cronies gathered in the lobby of the opera house every Monday night, and this gathering came to be a Baltimore institution. Its original members were John S. Bullock, Thomas S. Wilkinson, Basil Fusselbaugh, Finley Burns, Thornton Rollins, Frank Krems, W. A. Boyd, William Murray, Robert A. Jones, and Jacob Frey, the latter marshal of police. By 1900 only Rollins was left. He appeared every Monday night, and was hospitably greeted by Charlie, John and Harry. He lived at 746 west Fayette street west of Pine. The neighborhood had been invaded by highly dubious residents in the early nineties, but Rollins stuck to his roomy old house until his death in January, 1935, aged ninety-four.

He had made his money in the Brazilian coffee trade in the last days of the Baltimore clipper ships, and the appraisal of his estate showed a value of $862,310.66. He was a childless widower and had lived in his old house alone for many years. Until he was beyond eighty he gave a terrapin party once a year in memory of the Lobby Club. His last party, I believe, was in January, 1924, when his guests were Mayor Howard W. Jackson, George M. Shriver (vice-president of the Baltimore & Ohio Railroad), William A. Marburg, John M. Marshall, August Ryan, F. C. Seeman, Dr. C. F. Davidson, Dr. J. Percy Wade, Louis Muller, Thomas Hildt, John M. Dennis, George F. Rudolph, George Cator, George Weems Williams, W. Harry Barnes, John J. Milligan, Joseph Di Giorgio and Samuel H. Harris, a visiting theatrical producer.

The elder John T. Ford, with a huge family to feed, did its marketing in person. According to the stories I heard, he would go to Lexington Market twice a week with a huge market basket and a pad of passes to the opera house and proceed to trade passes for victuals. "How much for that ham?" he would say, and the dealer would answer, "Four orchestra seats." "Not on your life!" old Ford would reply. "Two orchestra seats or four dress-circle seats." And so the bargaining would go on until he had his half-week's supplies.

The opera house, in my time, had a staff of employés who had served it, in most cases, for years. One of them, a shabby old man who was always called the Lithographer, spent his time distributing one-sheets to storekeepers who were given passes for displaying them. There were stagehands who had been in the service for twenty, twenty-five and even thirty years. Old Lazarus H. Fisher, the Jewish conductor of the orchestra, had lasted so long that no one recalled when he came. During the Summer, when the opera house was closed, he led a band at Electric Park, at the southeast corner of Belvedere avenue and the Reisterstown road. Fisher had a son, Louis, who was graduated from the Peabody Conservatory of Music, and seemed to be launched on a very promising career as a composer, but some mysterious paralysis seized him and he became a helpless invalid. He is still, I believe, alive, but Baltimore has forgotten him, as it has forgotten his father.

The show-piece of the opera house was Basil Moxley, the downstairs ticket-taker. He was, when I knew him, a tall, slim old man with a long gray beard. He sat on a stool just inside the door, and was reputed to have never seen a performance in the theatre, for a curtain above the backs of the last row of seats blocked his view of the stage, even when he was not busy with his duties. Moxley was working in Ford's Theatre, Washington, the night Lincoln was shot, and was jailed afterward along with the elder John T. Ford. He knew the Booth family intimately and was called in to identify the remains of John Wilkes when they were brought back to Baltimore. He pretended to be reluctant to talk of the Lincoln assassination, and was actually a very reticent and even surly old fellow, but the Baltimore newspapers printed stories about him at frequent intervals, and I believe that he enjoyed the publicity.

297   *Lew Schaefer*: Schaefer's real name was Julian K., but he was always called Lew. He was the son of an old-time Baltimore musician of some dignity, but never got beyond writing children's pieces himself. He would sell them for a few dollars to the music publishing firm of George Willig & Company, which flourished in Baltimore for more than half a century. He was the man mentioned on p. 224 of *Newspaper Days*, to whose post as Central District reporter I was promoted when he got drunk. For some time after this he resented me bitterly and refused to speak to me, but after a while he apparently concluded that his displacement was not my fault, and we became friends. It was Lew who introduced me to the Odeon Theatre, mentioned on p. 251, and he continued to frequent the place after I had succeeded him in the Central District, wherein it was located. I soon noticed that he was very attentive to one of the ladies of the ensemble, a girl whose name I forget. These ladies, in the intervals of their hoofing, were supposed to enter the boxes and drink with the patrons sitting there, but Lew told me that the object of his own devotions refused to do this. She was a short, somewhat squatty young woman, and certainly not very attractive, but he was mashed on her, and in 1903 or thereabout he married her, to the horror of his family and the amazement of all his colleagues on the *Herald*.

Soon afterward began a saga of misfortunes that continued until his death twelve or fifteen years afterward. First came a bout with pneumonia in 1904, following the great Baltimore fire. As he was recovering from it in the early Summer he came down with typhoid fever, then endemic in Baltimore. This illness lasted a long while, and when it was over it was discovered that he had developed tuberculosis. There was, at that time, no sanitarium for its treatment in Maryland, but the faculty already advised mountain air, so Lew and his wife moved to a small village in the Blue Ridge of Western Maryland, and there lived, Winter and Summer, for three years. The place must have been unutterably lonely, especially in Winter, but they stuck it out resolutely, and in the end Lew was permitted to return to Baltimore. He told me then that the only person of any intelligence whatsoever that he had found in the mountains was a Lutheran preacher—and this intellectual had never heard of Thackeray! His expenses were paid during the three years by his brother in Baltimore, for the *Herald* did not carry sick members of the staff for more than a week or two; moreover, it blew up in July, 1906, while he was still in the mountains. Toward the end of his exile he was able to write an occasional article for the *Sunday Sun*, of which I had become Sunday editor, but his output was small and the *Sun*'s rate of pay was meagre, so his income from this source was very scanty.

When he got back to Baltimore his brother set him up in a small grocery store in a working-class street making off from Eastern avenue, to the eastward of Patterson Park—and at once he celebrated the fact by breaking his leg. This threw upon his wife the triple burden of keeping house for him, nursing him, and attending to the store. I saw him there after his broken bone had begun to mend, and he was able to get about on crutches, but it was still impossible for him to give her any effective help. In the end, however, he got rid of the crutches—and began to develop mental symptoms. This fresh misfortune was a dreadful blow to his brother, who was of small means and had found his support for so many years a crushing weight.

Meanwhile, his faithful wife, the former Odeon chorus girl, had stuck to him faithfully. There were times when they had barely enough to eat, but what little there was went to the invalid, and the wife dragged on without complaint. In all my life, I have never encountered or heard of a more loyal help-meet, in the most conventional sense. She had no life whatsoever save the care of Lew. Old friends dropped off, and she had no chance to make new ones. Exiled for three years in the mountains, and then in that miserable by-street in Highlandtown, she was virtually forgotten.

Unhappily, Lew's mental illness, whatever it was, did not mend. On the contrary, it grew worse, and after a while it became apparent that he would have to be sent to a lunatic asylum. His brother did not want him to go as a charity patient, but was unable to pay anything beyond a small weekly sum for his keep, so it was arranged that the wife should get a job and contribute whatever she could to his support. She was too old by now to resume her old trade, but she found work somewhere —I think in a factory—and Lew was presently moved to the asylum, and she began sending in her meagre contribution. So far, not a word of complaint had ever been heard from her. She had accepted all her burdens with complete courage and genuine heroism. But now, of a sudden, her resolution snapped. Perhaps, with her patient off her immediate hands, she had begun to look ahead—and seen only blackness there, with abject poverty in her own old age. Perhaps there is a natural limit to wifely devotion, as there is to every other high virtue, and she had reached it.

Whatever the chain of causes, she sat down one day and wrote Lew a note running about as follows:

> I have come to the end of my rope. I can't go any further. Good-bye, Lew. You will never see or hear of me again.

I got the news of this note from an old *Herald* man who got it from Lew's brother. The woman had vanished before it was delivered, and when the brother rushed to her lodging place he found that not a trace of her was left. The old *Herald* man believed that she had gone West and tried to resume her life in burlesque shows. "No woman," he said, "ever believes that she is too old or too homely for that—and maybe they are right."

But that was only speculation. Four or five years later poor Lew died, and was buried by his long-suffering brother.

298 *Goodman had an elder brother named Al*: There were six Goodman brothers—Al, Isidor, Isaac, Gustav, Edgar and Bernhard. [. . .] Bernie, the youngest brother, was put through medical college by the others, but took to drink and for years his practice was confined to baseball players and the town whores. Now and then he did a little reporting, chiefly of sporting events, for the *Herald*, but after the advent of Meekins he was barred from the office. Once, dropping into a bawdy-house in Josephine street late at night, along with three or four other *Herald* men, I found that Bernie was upstairs delivering a young harlot who had neglected prophylaxis and become pregnant. The madame told us that Bernie himself was probably the father of the child. His poor patient made a considerable uproar, and we left before the accouchement was achieved.

299 *This went on for a minute or two*: I forget the rest of Al's soliloquy, but all of it was amusing and full of his acid cynicism. He believed in nothing and no one save politicians, and his favorites were usually the worst. When two newspaper reporters meet their common greeting is "What do you know?" for each always hopes to dredge some news from the other. Though Al was as thoroughly Hebraic in aspect as Israel Zangwill his invariable answer was "I know that my Redeemer liveth." One of his stories had to do with an ancient Confederate major who served the Baltimore *American* as editorial writer. This old fellow was a violent atheist but one of his duties was to write the long religious editorial which the *American* (like many other newspapers of the era) printed every Sunday morning. One Saturday afternoon Al, who was then on the *American*, met him in the city-room and said, "Well major, I hope you are striking a hard blow for piety tomorrow morning." "Yes," replied the major. "Once more I'll knock 'em over the head with the shit-bags of the Gospel."

305 *that goddam son-of-a-bitch*: The colonel's vocabulary, in his dealings with the staff, was that of an old cavalryman. Once a young reporter named Smith came to him diffidently

with the offer of a poem for the editorial page. The colonel
promised to read it, and the next day sent for the author. "Mr.
Smith," he said, "I like your poem very much and I'll be glad
to print it. But I have decided to change your signature. You
sign it 'W. Cecil Smith' but I prefer '*Bill* Smith.' That sounds
more like a man with *balls* hanging on him." This Smith later
studied law and became State's attorney in Baltimore and a
frequent candidate for other offices. He is long dead.

305   *Wesley M. Oler*: There is more about Oler on pp. 307–308
and 398 *ff* of *Newspaper Days.* He was born in Baltimore on
April 3, 1856, and was the son of William H. Oler, who organized the Cochran-Oler Ice Company and made a comfortable
fortune. After the death of Oler the elder, Wesley expanded the
business, and by 1904 took it into the newly formed American
Ice Company. He became president of the latter simultaneously,
and thereafter lived in New York until his death on January
26, 1927. He was also president of the Knickerbocker Ice Company. He was, for years, the chief butt of the campaigns against
the so-called Ice Trust that were launched by the Pulitzer and
Hearst papers in New York, and bore those afflictions with
Christian fortitude. I had but little contact with him during the
years of his ownership of the *Herald*, and in fact recall meeting
him only a few times. He left the management of the paper to
the preposterous Peard. He was a cold fellow, as befitted his
business, and I avoided him as much as possible. On the few
occasions when he had any advice to offer about the conduct of
the *Herald* what he suggested seemed to me to be idiotic.

    In his Baltimore days he was one of the chief Babbitts of
the town, and had a hand in many enterprises beside the ice
business. For a while he was president of the Citizens' National Bank, and he also had an interest in the Spring Garden Wharf and Land Company, which owned a large tract of
land along the Baltimore water-front. He was a trustee of the
Woman's College of Baltimore (later Goucher College), which
was in those days run by Methodists, and was the chairman
of its finance committee. He acquired an interest in the Baltimore *Herald* in 1880, and was the largest stockholder after
Alexander Bechhofer, the publisher from 1886 onward. When
Bechhofer died in 1897 he became the majority owner. On

the suspension of the *Herald* in 1906 he told his friends that the venture had cost him, first and last, about $250,000. His hopes of horning into politics never got him anywhere. The Republicans of Maryland always touched him for large campaign contributions, and in 1888 they made him a delegate to the national convention of their party, but they never ran him for any elective office, for it was only too obvious that his solemn, Methodist front and frigid manner would make him an easy mark for an opponent. He was a Freemason and after he moved to New York joined the Union League Club. He lived at Larchmont and belonged to golf and yacht clubs there. Some time after his death I received a friendly letter from his son, Wesley, Jr., a stockbroker in New York. Young Oler said that he knew I was no admirer of his father, but that he was nevertheless a reader of my books. [. . .]

Bechhofer, as a matter of fact, was a highly dubious fellow, and belonged to the worst type of pushing, unscrupulous Jew. Nearly all the stories I heard of him when I entered the *Herald* office were of his savage business methods. One of the favorites of the editorial rooms had to do with his bold blackmailing of his fellow Jews who operated stores in Howard street, at the time the Baltimore & Ohio tunnel under the street was being excavated. This work began in 1890 and at first proceeded rapidly, but then veins of quicksand were encountered and there were long delays and frequent difficulties. In 1892 or thereabout it was discovered that the walls of the new City College, in Howard street opposite the end of Center, were settling, and the building was evacuated. This gave Bechhofer his chance. He had a long and alarming article written, charging the B. & O. with imperiling the lives of the shoppers in the Howard street stores, and then sent proofs of it to the storekeepers. Most of them had refused hitherto to advertise in the *Herald*, but now they saw a great light, and a few days later the article was killed and their announcements were being printed. The tunnel was finished in 1895, and by that time the scare was over, but the Howard street Jews, having learned a valuable lesson, continued to advertise in the *Herald* until Bechhofer's death. After that they began to drop out, and the effort of Oler and Peard to get them back failed. That failure was the principal cause of the collapse of the paper in 1906. [. . .]

The name of the *Herald* did not appear in the Baltimore
Directory until the issue for 1878, when its address was given
as 122 west Baltimore street and the name of its manager as
J. B. Askew. In 1880 and 1881 it was still at the same address,
but F. A. Savin was its manager. The Directory for 1882 showed
that it had moved to Baltimore and Eutaw streets, with L. P. D.
Newman in charge, but it did not remain there long, for the
Directories for 1883, 1884 and 1885 put it at 6 south Calvert
street, with William J. Hooper as "proprietor." By 1895 it was
at Charles and Baltimore streets, and by 1896 the new building at Fayette and St. Paul streets was finished and occupied.
Bechhofer advertised in the Directory for 1890 that the *Herald* was "Baltimore's great penny paper." It then sold for a
cent on week-days and three cents on Sundays. The week-day
issues were delivered by carrier at six cents a week. There was a
Weekly Herald at fifty cents a year—in my time, its circulation
of 2,500 or thereabout went mainly to penitentiaries, the inmates of which were forbidden to take daily papers—but the
Evening Herald had been abandoned. How we revived it after
the great Baltimore fire of 1904 is told on pp. 397 *ff* of *Newspaper Days*. In the Baltimore Directory for 1894 Bechhofer
advertised that the morning issue had been "enlarged to eight
pages since December 2, 1893." When I joined its staff it had
gone to ten pages, with occasional spurts to 12, 14 and even
beyond.

309   *the satirical title of Bishop*: Stockbridge, a member of a
prominent Maryland family, got the title of Bishop of Sodom
and Gomorrah on account of his habit of wearing a Christian Endeavor pin on his frequent visits to bawdy-houses and
his equally strange habit of trying to convert the inmates to
Methodism. He was a solemn fellow, and not too bright. Once
he actually converted a girl, Lottie by name, and set her up
in a little cigar-store in Hanover street, somewhere below
Camden. One afternoon he asked me to accompany him on a
visit to her, for he was very proud of her reformation. During
that visit I heard him argue with her in all seriousness that she
ought to receive him as a free patient in consideration of his
salvation of her soul. Lottie was a low-grade moron, but this
argument was too much for her. She replied tartly that if she

were going to resume sin she might as well be paid for it, and soon afterward she gave up her cigar-store and returned to a life of shame.

When Stockbridge was married, in 1902 or thereabout, I was best man at his wedding, which took place with considerable pomp at Strawbridge Methodist Episcopal Church, at Park avenue and Wilson street. He married a small and foolish girl named Bowersox, the daughter of a bookkeeper. He was an assiduous husband, and they had a large family—I believe about ten children, if not more. He became more and more pious as he grew older, and in his later years was superintendent of a Methodist Sunday-school. He never got anywhere as a newspaper man, for his talents were extremely modest. When he died he was a copy-reader on the *Star*, the evening edition of the *American*. He had some private means, but they were dissipated by the expenses of his large family, and he left his wife and children virtually penniless. Some years later the widow applied to me for a loan. I let her have the money, which was never returned.

310   *fundamentally a somewhat prissy fellow*: Meekins's son, Lynn W., professed to like *Newspaper Days* very much, but he objected to my characterization of his father as "fundamentally a somewhat prissy fellow." On this point he wrote to me on February 7, 1942:

> He wasn't prissy, somewhat or at all! One of his chief qualities, probably his outstanding characteristic, was consideration for others. He was a kind man and he tried always to give everybody a break. You might have called him "somewhat proper," but "somewhat prissy" doesn't fit. Otherwise you have dealt very kindly with him. It means a great deal to me to see in print after so many years your splendid tribute to my father. I am deeply grateful to you for it.

I replied to this politely and reassuringly, but I am still convinced that the word "prissy" described Meekins pretty well. He never got over his early Methodist training, and it would sometimes crop up, in the midst of the turmoil of a newspaper, with an almost comic effect.

314   *primeval comic-strip artist*: The artist who photographed the $5 bill was W. R. Bradford, who served the *Morning*

Herald as cartoonist, but also did some work for the Sunday comic supplement. He was a wild man when drunk. Once his wife left Baltimore for a month or so, and he essayed to keep bachelor hall in their house along with an even wilder Irishman, one Peter Pry Shevlin, who then wrote a column in verse and prose for the *Herald*, not unlike my old "Knocks and Jollies" column. Finding that housekeeping was beyond their skill, they recruited two loose women to help them. Thereafter, until poor Mrs. Bradford returned, the quartette had a roaring time of it, and pretty well wrecked the house. In 1903 or 1904 Bradford left the *Herald* to become cartoonist for the Philadelphia *North American*, and there he was soon a fearsome figure in the local journalism.

Once he sailed from Philadelphia in a small sailing craft that he had bought, and was presently reported missing. The search for him went on for two weeks. He was found at last moored up a tidal creek making off from the lower Delaware, where he had been lying drunk all the while. The firm of Marshall, Beek & Gordon, which published my first book, *Ventures Into Verse*, in 1903, brought out, later in the same year, a paper-bound pamphlet of Bradford's cartoons, with a brief preface by me. This pamphlet was called "Bill Elk in Baltimore" and its contents consisted of cartoons that Bradford had drawn during the convention of the Elks in Baltimore, July 21–23, 1903. I had completely forgotten it when, on October 18, 1941, Charles S. Gordon sent me a copy of it from Portland, Ore. What has become of Bradford I do not know: he is probably dead.

315   *a Baptist clergyman*: I forget the name of the pastor mentioned here. He was a tall, clumsy fellow with a cross eye, and I had met him when he had a small Baptist church in Baltimore. He was the author of a book called *Homiletics and Preaching* and gave me a copy of it: I found it to be dreadful stuff indeed. His church was not in the Carolinas, but on the Eastern Shore of Virginia, a little way below the Maryland line. The farmers down there devoted themselves mainly to growing sweet-potatoes, and for years they had been robbed by the New York commission merchants. One day there arose in the community a native young man who had heard of the advantages of coöperation. He proposed to form a sweet-potato coöperative, and after some resistance by the older farmers he managed to launch it. It was an immediate success, and in a couple of years the whole peninsula was rolling in money. Scores of new brick dwellings went up, and also the new Baptist church that I mention. When the pastor above-mentioned dropped in to tell me that he was going there I was astonished, for Baltimoreans had long regarded the Eastern Shore of Virginia as a sink of poverty. But when he told about the coöperative and said that the members of the church proposed to provide him with a fine new house and give him $2,500 cash a year I understood. Unhappily, the New York commission men eventually discovered a way to bust the coöperative and the whole community returned to hard scrabble. One day the pastor came to Baltimore, took a room at the old Caswell Hotel (on the site of the present Lord Baltimore), and shot himself.

322 *the printers in the composing-room*: In those days there were still plenty of tramp printers afloat. The rule was that whenever one showed up in need of assistance (as they always needed it) he could come to the composing-room and hand his union card to the proof-press boy. The boy would then carry it about to all the printers at work, and those who were in a generous mood would lay small contributions upon it. The boy naturally tried to knock down something, but he was pretty closely watched. The total amount collected was then handed to the waiting tramp.

Sometimes, when one of the regular force was off on a drunk, the foreman would offer the tramp a job, and once in a great while it was accepted, and he hung on until fired, which was usually in a few days. But I recall one tramp who remained in the *Herald* composing-room for a year or more, and turned out to be an excellent make-up man. The International Typographical Union tried to put down this tramping by making a rule that a printer could not work in a strange town without getting the express permission of the local union. This rule discouraged the tramps, but a few persisted, for the *Wanderlust* was strong in them, and they bob up occasionally to this day. Under date of Victoria, B.C., January 11, 1943, I received the following letter from an old-time tramp, by name Arthur

Floyd, who is probably the all-time champion of his fraternity. In it he said:

> I have been a roaming printer for over 40 years, having crossed the Atlantic over 30 times and have set type on the linotype in nearly every State in the U.S.A., including Maryland. Also hit the keyboard in China & Japan, Australia, New Zealand, South Africa, Europe and lately here in Canada; also, being an incorrigible wanderer, I have loafed in such far-off places as Tahiti, Samoa & Fiji Islands in the South Pacific, Madagascar, Mauritius, Dutch East Indies, and it's been a great life.
>
> I liked your articles years ago in the *American Mercury*, and when I saw a book or two had been written by you I got it pronto. The one about your childhood & youth in Baltimore is a classic and some of your experiences reminded me of Mark Twain. Your newspaper life was absorbingly interesting & I liked your references to the pubs (saloons to you) and the good eats you enjoyed in the palmy days. And the prices made my mouth water—25¢ business lunch. I recall the free lunch of happy memory. They were the days!
>
> Being a printer I read fast, but I slowed down the tempo on your books so that I wouldn't miss anything. Your report of the Baltimore fire and the commuting between Baltimore and Philadelphia was a knockout & had me hanging on the ropes. You must have had abounding energy in those days! I recall an experience similar but not so exciting, my responsibility not being like yours. It was in 1906. I was a linotype operator on the Seattle *Times* & the earthquake in San Francisco resulted in an emergency call for operators, many having left in the confusion. I went to work on Willie Hearst's yellow sheet in San Francisco —36 linotypes erected temporarily in a livery stable. But you can't keep those cities down long, for both Baltimore and the city of the Golden Gate are now real places.

326 *One of the latter*: I forget the name of the glutton who lived at the Rennert. His story, as I tell it, is but little exaggerated. The eating-house he patronized was operated by a Scotsman named Tommy Gordon. It was at the southeast corner of Madison and Eutaw streets, with its entrance on Madison. Saloons with private dining-rooms upstairs were common in Baltimore in those days, and most of them were frequented by regular boards of lady visitors. There were no bedrooms, but save during a vice crusade it was all right to lock a dining-room door and serve a lady on the table. One of the most famous of such saloons was Logan and Schillinger's, on the east side of Calvert street, between Baltimore and Fayette.

It was the favorite resort, when he was in port, of Captain Corning of the *Ely*, who regarded it as very elegant. He was particularly impressed by the brass rods which secured the red carpet on the stairway leading up to the female department, and always called the place the Golden Stair. It was burned down in the great fire of 1904. When the ruins began to cool one of the lady frequenters visited them with the permission of the police, and began searching them for a souvenir. She finally trudged off with the cast-iron shell of a spittoon.

The glutton aforesaid never went above the ground floor at Tommy Gordon's, for, like most of the great trenchermen of that era, he disdained and avoided women. But the town had a considerable force of what were then called chippy-chasers, and if there had been more room in *Newspaper Days* I'd have devoted a chapter to them. The undisputed chiefs of the fraternity were Colonel Lucius Polk and Bill Levering. Where and how Polk got his military title I do not know: probably by service on a governor's staff. He was, at least in theory, a lawyer, and he had an office in Saratoga street between Courtland and Calvert, but it was used mainly for venery, and his revenues came from the Chesapeake Brewery in Highlandtown, which he owned and operated. He was a slim, somewhat elegant old fellow who affected the most extreme patterns of racetrack dress—loudly checked pantaloons, a gaudy waistcoat, a heavy watch-chain, a plug hat, and so on. But he always wore a black Prince Albert coat.

Every afternoon at about 2 o'clock he and his buddy, Bill Levering, took their places at the southwest corner of Charles and Lexington streets, and there gave their eyes to the passing procession of girls. Bill was stout and wore less flashy clothes, but he was almost as obscene an object as Lucius, and it seemed incredible that any girls, however moronic, should succumb to two such cadavers. But Lucius apparently roped a good many, first and last, for later in the afternoon he usually had one in his office in Saratoga street, and there, presumably, he worked his wicked will upon her. The other tenants of the building, which was an old dwelling, were full of tales about the voluptuous sounds emanating from his quarters.

Bill Levering was a brother to the twin leaders of moral endeavor in Baltimore, Joshua and Eugene Levering, and his evil courses naturally gave them great grief. But he threw off all their efforts, which must have been violent, to make a Christian of him. He was not a drunkard, but he drank very freely, and he chased women almost as ardently as Lucius. Where he took them when he got them I do not know. He and Lucius were already gray in the first years of the century, and they are now long dead.

Another amorist of the time was Joe Whyte, a brother to former Governor William Pinckney Whyte, though he was less public in his operations than Lucius and Bill. He lived in a large house at the northwest corner of Cathedral and Monument streets (still standing in 1943), and apparently had a competency, for, though he was a lawyer, his practise seemed to be negligible. He would issue from his residence every afternoon for a walk through the downtown streets, elegantly arrayed in a frock coat and a silk hat. It was the town report that he picked up girls on these tours, and took them back to his house for private conferences, but I never saw him with any such girl. In his later years, having retired from the stud and got too decrepit for walking, he spent every fair afternoon in a comfortable chair on the Monument street sidewalk of his house, taking the air and greeting passers-by.

330 *a rich old fellow*: The rich old fellow was William A. Marburg, whose wealth came from tobacco. He had a younger brother, Theodore, who was ambassador to Belgium before World War I, and a notorious jackass, but William was a fellow of some sense. He was a bachelor and lived alone in considerable state at 6 east Eager street, across the street from the Maryland Club. He was not actively engaged in business in his later years, but served as vice-president of the board of trustees of the Johns Hopkins Hospital and left the hospital the reversion of a possible $700,000 by his will. He died on January 10, 1931, aged eighty-two. [. . .]

I never met the old boy, greatly to my regret. Before the advent of Prohibition he laid in a large stock of wines and liquors, and during his last years he liked to have acquaintances drop in for a few drinks. Inasmuch as I did not know him, I missed these parties. His brother Theodore became a noisy Hun-baiter during World War I, but William remained a good German, and so did his two old-maid sisters. His brother Louis was the first of the brothers to die, and Charles was the second. The other members of the family erected the Marburg Building at the Johns Hopkins as a memorial to Charles. William was a constant benefactor of the Johns Hopkins, and, as I have noted, left it the reversion of a trust fund of $700,000 by his will. Unhappily, this legacy was subject to prior claims by his brother Theodore's children and grandchildren, and I suspect that the Johns Hopkins has got very little of it. In 1906 he presented the medical school with a collection of medical books which became the nucleus of the present Welch Library. This collection came from the Warrington Dispensary at Liverpool, England, and consisted of 944 works, many of them very rare. The gift was received at a meeting in the Physiological Building of the Johns Hopkins on January 2, 1907, with Dr. William Osler as the principal speaker. Osler said:

> One day a meek-looking young man came to me and said that there was for sale a notable collection of medical works. I asked him if he had a catalogue, and he said he had. I saw at once that the books were of great value and comprised a valuable collection. I at once thought of the Johns Hopkins Medical School and of the great benefit such an accession would be to its library. Such a collection, I thought, would supplement those works we had already.
>
> I wrote to Mr. Marburg and asked him if he would not purchase the collection for the Medical School. His reply was a prompt affirmative, and to that he added: "See that the bindings are put in good order, too."
>
> The books were collected with care and discretion by a remarkable body of men of the seventeenth century, some of whom rose to national distinction. The collection seems all the more remarkable when it is learned that 160 items in it are not found in the College of Surgeons Library, the largest library of the kind in Great Britain.

Marburg's personal estate was appraised at $1,978,768.81; in addition he left a considerable amount of real property. He was a quiet fellow, and never took any part in the orgies which followed his dinners at the Maryland Club.

337 *an old-time roundsman named Charlie*: Charlie was Charles M. Cole, a rotund and amiable fellow and a good policeman. He was born in 1861 in the jail at Alexandria, Va., where his father was sheriff. The Civil War drove the Cole family to Baltimore, and here young Cole, when he grew up, became a barber. Tiring of the razor and towel, he joined the force in 1891, was made a sergeant in 1897, and became a round-sergeant on March 18, 1899. In those days a round-sergeant worked on the street: the lieutenants stayed in the station-houses. Charlie was promoted lieutenant himself on January 30, 1900, and came indoors. On January 1, 1910, he was advanced to a captaincy and assigned to the Southern district, and there he remained until 1913, when he was transferred to the Western. He was a dirt policeman and liked to go with his men on dangerous missions. On May 18, 1913, just before he left the Southern, a Negro in south Charles street attempted to knife him during a raid, and he was saved only by two of his cops coming to his rescue. Characteristically, he refused to charge the Negro with assault, but let him escape with a fine of $5 for disorderly conduct.

But he had his fears like all of us, and one of them was of the water. He had the habit of sleeping with his arms stretched out above his head, and believed in the superstition that persons who follow it will die of drowning. Thus, though his district had a waterfront of five or six miles, he refused to venture on the police-boats which patrolled its waters, and never could be induced to go on a steamboat excursion. His forebodings turned out to be without ground, for when he came to die, on Christmas day of 1936, he was in bed at the Maryland General Hospital.

At the time he was sent to the Western district it included the largest of the Baltimore tenderloins. Within three blocks of the tomb of Edgar Allan Poe, in Westminster churchyard, at Fayette and Greene streets, there were at least a hundred undisguised whorehouses and probably a thousand dubious rooming-houses. A vice crusade was in progress at the time, and poor Charlie was expected to close all these places. Like all other cops, he was violently opposed to the crusade, but the Police Board of Baltimore, then headed by Morris A. Soper, later a Federal judge, had been fetched by the crusaders, and he couldn't help himself. I myself denounced the crusade and its backers with considerable heat in my Free Lance column in the *Evening Sun*, but the morning *Sun*, of which Frank R. Kent was then managing editor, took the buffoonery seriously, and on June 27 printed the following news story:

The Society for the Suppression of Vice is taking a lively interest in the changes in the police force, and it was stated yesterday by a member of that body that it was felt Captain Cole would be able to bring about a thorough cleaning up of the Western district's tenderloin.

It is recognized that the regular disorderly houses, which were formerly so numerous near the Western station house, will soon disappear. In one block there are only 16 left, the remainder being occupied by Negro families. The police have been ordered to see that no disorderly house, once closed, shall be opened for the same purpose again. This is being rigidly enforced.

"The appalling task," said a member of the society, "which is confronting Captain Cole is that of preventing the women who are leaving the district from inhabiting boarding or furnished room houses in the same vicinity. In three blocks in the district there are 455 furnished room dwellings. In a radius of three blocks from Fayette and Fremont streets there are 100 places selling liquor.

"Captain Cole's men will have to be wide awake. My suggestion is that they go to every person who conducts a boarding or furnished room house and explain the law regarding the protection of the morals of the community."

It is believed in many quarters that the recommendations of the society to the police commissioners had much to do with the reassignment of the officers, which was announced on Monday. The society has employed paid investigators, who have obtained information which the police have said they could not get. The board is of the opinion that the police can accomplish the same ends as the agents of the society if properly directed.

That disorderly houses are disappearing is shown from the report of the society, giving the results of the crusade since November 1, 1912. At that time there were, the report says, 192 houses in the city, having 572 inmates. On June 1 the number of houses had been reduced, according to the report, to 133 and the inmates to 440. In most of the places in the Western district where disorderly houses still exist the inmates who were young have gone elsewhere.

> Of 21 women who, the report declares, resolved to lead good
> lives within the last year only one is said to have gone back on
> her promise. Adherents of the society hold that segregation can
> be proved a failure by a fair trial.

I saw Charlie pretty often in those unhappy days, and had to
listen to his tales of woe. The vice crusade continued to harass
him for several years, but finally blew up when its chief promoter, one Samuel Pentz, was accused by a sixteen-year-old
girl of having lured her to his office in the Equitable Building
and there attempted to play with her private parts. This girl, I
have no doubt, was set upon Pentz by the police, just as they
set a Y.M.C.A. boy upon a Methodist pastor, Murray, who
was one of his most ardent supporters, but in both cases the
victims were ruined, and by 1916 the vice crusade was done for.

When Prohibition came on Charlie had more troubles, for
his district swarmed with drinking-places as it swarmed with
bawdy-houses, but he was relieved when the Attorney-General
of Maryland decided formally that the Baltimore police had
nothing to do with the enforcement of the Volstead Act. They
were bound, he said, to go to the aid of a Prohibition agent
who was being beaten up by bootleggers, but beyond that
they had no duty in the premises. Whenever there were com-
plaints from the drys that there were too many speakeasies in
the Western district, Charlie got rid of them by arresting a
few booticians on the charge of selling liquor without State licenses. Inasmuch as State licenses were unobtainable, this was
only sound and fury, signifying nothing, and two days later
the raided booticians were back in business. Some of the best
drinking-places of the Prohibition era were in his district. One
of them was Schellhase's, in Franklin street just west of Howard, which always had good beer. I went there two or three
times a week, and other regular customers were James H. Preston, former mayor of Baltimore, and the Rev. Arthur B. Kin-
solving, rector of Old St. Paul's Church.

One night, as I was sitting in the place with Sara, two
strangers came in and demanded drinks. The head waitress,
Anna, told them that nothing alcoholic was for sale, and they
settled down with two bottles of ginger-ale. But they had had
enough to drink before coming in to make them somewhat

noisy, and presently they were engaged in a loud and profane, though otherwise amicable, conversation. Anna warned them that such talk would not be tolerated, and they promised to pipe down, but in a few minutes they were roaring again. Then Mrs. Schellhase, who ran the cash register, warned them, and then Schellhase came out of his little bar in the rear to do the same. When they still continued to be noisy Schellhase sent out for the cop on the beat. The cop came in quietly, and took his place behind a high screen that stood within the front door. In a few minutes one of the men loosed another oath, and at once the cop collared both of them and threw them into the street. Thus Charlie saw to it that respectable speakeasies were protected from the annoyance of disorderly persons.

As he grew older he was often in the newspapers as a giver of Polonius-like counsel to young cops. On August 10, 1913, the *Sun* reported that he was advising them to marry early—he himself, he said, had married at sixteen, and never regretted it—and on March 30, 1921, the *Evening Sun* reported that he was urging them to avoid the gay life that had come in with Prohibition. These were his rules for the cop ambitious to rise in the profession:

> He should not stay on the streets late at night.
> He should spend more time at home.
> He should go to bed early.
> He should not take automobile trips out into the country without first asking the permission of his captain.
> He should pay more attention to business than to his own pleasure and thereby make a better policeman. [. . .]

Charlie's health began to decline in 1927, and he asked for permission to retire. The police commissioner at the time, General Charles D. Gaither, induced him to hang on until the coming into effect of a new law providing for the examination of candidates for captaincy: hitherto there had been examinations only for the grades up to lieutenant. He agreed, but on February 23, 1928, he was relieved of duty. He was by this time sixty-seven years old. He and his wife, Emma Weinreich, moved from 1612 east Lafayette avenue, where they had been living for years, to a new house at 1104 Bonaparte avenue, and he took things easy. They had three sons and a daughter, now all grown up and married. I saw him often during the years of his retirement, for he came downtown frequently, and, like any old cop, was eager to swap reminiscences with acquaintances of the days of his glory. But his health was not good, and he gradually went downhill. On December 14, 1936, he became so ill that he had to be taken to hospital, and on December 25 he died, aged seventy-five. There have been much worse cops, and plenty of much worse men.

339 *a man of the chastest integrity*: I printed the following note on Grannan in the Baltimore *News*, July 27, 1906, during the brief time when I was its news editor:

> Grannan, J. P., who smites the unjust with the rod of justice at the Central Police Station, is a man who, at first sight, seems to be slight in stature and build, but is, in reality, unusually stocky

H. L. Mencken. Portrait by Meredith Janvier, 1906.

and vigorous. He has a pair of shoulders that would be creditable to a stevedore, and, despite the fact that he is past 50,
he is so erect that he seems to curve backward. As chief of the
Baltimore and Ohio detective force and as police justice he has
dealt with wrongdoers all his life, and few men are keener connoisseurs of criminality. But if you take it from this that he is
case-hardened and cynical, you will go far wrong. On the contrary, he is a man of genuine sympathy and great liberality, and
the chief item of his private philosophy is a firm belief that most
criminals are good at heart and that most crimes are crimes only
in term. The wretches from the old "Space" who used to stand
at his bar each morning before the fire seldom failed to find him
merciful. In particular he tempered the justice he handed out
to victims of the insidious bowl. Once, for instance, a battered
specimen stood before him to answer a charge of obstructing
traffic by seeking sleep and forgetfulness in the middle of Baltimore street.

"Why did you get so drunk?" asked Grannan, J. P.

"It was my birthday," whispered the prisoner.

"Discharged," said the Court. "Some men celebrate their
birthdays by getting drunk and some by getting sober. He hurt
no one. Why send him to jail?"

341 *a certain toll from the pungy captains*: The storehouse
of the harbor cops was operated by Lieutenant Albert League,
then night commander of the police-boat *Lannan*. He was a
gay dog, and gave some loud parties on the police-boat, with
loose women among the guests. In the end there was a scandal
about this, and he was brought ashore for land duty. I knew
him well in his later years, and was very fond of him. He had
a large acquaintance among the whore-madams of the town,
and loved to drop in on them and listen to their gabble. Once
he took me to call on one who kept a surreptitious place in
Dolphin street near Linden avenue. The talk fell upon the devices used by harlots to prevent pregnancy, and the old madam
told us that all of them were ineffective—that a girl in active
practise had to have frequent abortions. She said that she herself, in her days as what the women always called a hustler,
had had no less than sixteen—all of them performed by herself
with a darning-needle. She said that she had suffered ill consequences on only one occasion, and that then her discomforts
cleared up quickly. Even League was astonished by this story,

but he professed to believe it, for he argued that the madam
was too stupid to have invented it.

He was born in 1863 and joined the force in 1886. He became a sergeant in 1891 and a lieutenant in 1892, and in 1914,
after the scandal aforesaid had been forgotten, was made a captain. He retired in 1924 and died in 1936.

341   *One actually married a banker*: The banker who married
a lady of the town existed in Baltimore legend, if not in actuality. He was the father of Alexander Brown, the present head
of the private banking firm of Alexander Brown & Sons, Baltimore and Calvert streets. I was told by the older cops and
reporters that he scandalized his family by marrying, as his second wife, at an advanced age, an eminent madam named Jessie
Hutchins, whose place was in Davis street, near Lexington,
not a block from the City Hall. They said that, on pleasant afternoons, he took her for airings in an open barouche through
the most fashionable streets of Baltimore.

342   *a coroner*: The coroner here mentioned was Dr. Frank
Germon. He was a son of Jane Germon, an old-time actress
who lived to be nearly ninety. She had been, in her time, a
famous soubrette and had played with all the American stars of
the pre-Civil War era. She and her son lived in Greene street,
near Franklin. In her later years she was frequently the subject
of articles in the Baltimore papers, but I can't find a single clipping about her in the morgue of the *Sunpapers*. Obviously, the
thick envelope that must have been devoted to her was thrown
out in one of the periodical house-cleanings.

Her son had a large acquaintance in Baltimore, and put it
to humorous account when he had to summon a coroner's
jury. He would walk down Baltimore street, spy a friend across
the street, beckon him earnestly to come across, and then lay
his hand on the poor fellow's arm and say: "I hereby summon you for service on a coroner's jury in the name of the
State of Maryland." As he accumulated victims he left them in
charge of a police sergeant trailing half a block behind him, so
that new prospects would not be alarmed. There was a belief
in Baltimore in those days that only citizens and voters could
be summoned for coroners' juries, and in consequence many
smarties claimed to be British subjects. But Germon knew that

under the ancient Maryland law even alien residents were eligible to serve, so long as they could speak English. Every member of a coroner's jury, in those days, was allowed fifty cents for his service, but very few of them knew this and Germon usually collared the honoraria of all twelve.

To men unaccustomed to violent death, service on a coroner's jury was sometimes very shocking, and more than once I have seen jurymen faint. Once, when there was an inquest on a man whose head had been crushed in an elevator accident, reducing it to a ghastly caricature at least two feet in diameter, the whole jury, after taking one look, fled. Many jurymen, having viewed the remains, failed to turn up for the actual inquest, which was usually held in the evening in a police station. To make sure of a quorum Germon would usually summon twenty or more, hoping that at least the statutory twelve would appear. In any case, he could collect the fees for twelve only. He was a gay fellow and took his gruesome duties lightly. He died soon after his ancient mother.

344 *Hank Schofield, the bull-fiddler*: Hank Schofield chewed tobacco all the while he played his bull-fiddle. When the Holliday Street Theatre was closed he took other engagements, and sometimes played at home weddings in high life. At such times his post was always in a corner. His first act, on taking his station, was to loosen and turn back the carpet in the corner. He then used the bare patch of floor as a spittoon, and when the wedding was over flapped back the carpet. Meanwhile, he was concealed by his colleagues and by the potted palms which, in those days, were always part of a wedding scheme or decoration.

Hank is dead many years. He had a brother who was a quack oculist, and from my earliest recollection down to 1935 or thereabout operated an establishment in west Baltimore street, opposite Winans' Wall. He lived upstairs, and on Summer evenings always sat on the sidewalk, smoking and ruminating. In his show-window was a case of glass eyes. Once, when my niece Virginia was a little girl, and I took her down Baltimore street, on one of her visits to Baltimore, on a shopping spree, she demanded one of these glass eyes. Inasmuch as I had promised to buy her anything she fancied I had to get it for her. I recall that

her other choices, that day, were a bottle of cheap perfumery
and a flat-iron.

349 *a minor labor leader*: My taste for labor leaders was always
slight, and the only one I ever got to know intimately was Ed
Hirsch, an *Evening News* linotype operator who became president of the Baltimore Typographical Union and then of the
Baltimore Federation of Labor. He afterward left Baltimore
and settled in Kansas City as an official of the Fraternal Order
of Eagles. All labor leaders, in those days, could be bought,
and Ed was no exception. His one peculiarity was that he always refused to take cash: the employers to whom he sold out
his lieges had to pay him in unmounted precious stones. In his
palmy days he carried a handful of these stones in a trousers
pocket and often took them out to play with them and admire
them. He made his largest haul when he settled a strike of
brewery workers—the first of the sort ever heard of in Baltimore. Part of his honorarium in this case was a ruby said to
be worth $1,500. He made no bones of his venality, but often
spoke of it, at least to me, in a quite matter of fact way. He
regarded all union men as idiots, and thought it was God's will
that smart fellows should rook them. He is now dead (1943).

353 *Miss Nellie d'Alembert*: The actual name of the woman
I call Nellie d'Alembert was Nellie Henderson, and her establishment was in Watson street. [. . .] After the vice crusade of
the second decade of the century forced her to close her place,
which was very high-toned, she took a shabby old house in
Saratoga street, just east of Gilmor, in a Negro neighborhood,
and operated it for some time as a bed-house.

A bed-house, in the vocabulary of Baltimore whoredom,
was a place which rented rooms to what were called loving
couples, but did not maintain a staff of boarders. It was not
etiquette for the madam to see her patrons. They were admitted and bowed out by a colored maid. The universal price for
the use of a room for an hour or two was $1. An establishment
whose madam, though she had no internes, was willing to send
for girls for lonely men was called a parlor- or call-house. The
girls who responded to calls were mainly saleswomen from the
lesser sort of stores, but there was also an admixture of married
women whose husbands served them badly or provided them

with less money than they craved. Some of the women went to a call-house on speculation, hoping that men would drop in and be fetched by their charms. Such regulars were said to sit for company.

There were no fixed honoraria in call-houses. The girl got what she could, usually from $3 to $5, and the man himself was supposed to pay the madam her fee, which was usually $2. In addition, she bootlegged drinks at high prices, and so eked out a living. Call-house madams moved pretty often, for soon or late a patron was bound to get drunk on the premises and make a disturbance, and then the neighbors, who were usually respectable people, complained to the cops. The cops needed only the bare complaint, for they knew all the madams. When they ordered one to move she had to do so within twenty-four hours. A round of beers in a call-house, as in an ordinary whorehouse, cost fifty cents. The glasses were very small, so two bottles sufficed for at least half a dozen men. The worst sort of domestic champagne was $5 a bottle.

A call-house, of course, had no music. Sometimes the married women who visited it had to be at home at night, and could thus come in only of an afternoon. This matinée business, as it was called, was considered especially desirable, for the patrons seldom got drunk and their visits were at hours which did not arouse the suspicions of the neighbors. It was the rule in all well-conducted call-houses that a woman and a man could not enter or leave together. There were such houses in all parts of Baltimore, especially after the vice crusade, but they were most numerous in decaying neighborhoods infiltrated by Negroes.

Another madam who favored me, like Nellie Henderson, with frequent news tips, was Cora Edwards, whose place was in Raborg street, near Pine. She was a fat, swarthy Jewess, and was commonly known as Jew Cora. When the vice crusade came on and she was ordered by the reluctant and sympathizing cops to close her house, she refused to move out of it on the sound ground that she owned it. This refusal upset the vice crusaders, but their lawyers advised them that she was within her rights. Cora had accumulated a considerable property, and was thus not forced, like most of the other old-time madams, to open a bed-house or call-house. Now and then I would meet her on the street, and we'd stop for a little gossip. She held out in Raborg street for two or three years, but when it began to be invaded by Negroes of the worst sort she sold her house and moved to a respectable neighborhood. Simultaneously her brother, a poor fish, died, leaving a widow and four children. Cora took the children and brought them up at her own cost. A little later her sister died, leaving one child, and she added that one to the other four. The cops had a high respect for her, and she was, in fact, an admirable woman.

One of the most eminent Baltimore madams of the 1900–1910 period was Aggie Sheldon, who had an almost luxurious place in St. James's street, a narrow thoroughfare in Northeast Baltimore, in the very shadow of a Catholic church. She was aided in its operation by her sister Gertie. One night I took a group of out-of-town newspaper men to the place, and launched them upon a booze party. Tiring of it after a while, I went to a sort of conservatory to the rear of the front parlors, and there sat down at the piano. I thought I was alone, and so began strumming some music that I liked, including a couple of German folksongs. Suddenly I was startled by a sob behind me. Turning 'round, I found Gertie Sheldon in tears.

Then she told me her story. She and Aggie were Germans from Würzburg, and their dream was to return there when they had accumulated a competence. She told me what their actual names were, but I have long forgotten them. Some time after this I was preparing to take a trip to Germany with A. H. McDannald of the *Sun*, and it occurred to both of us that it might be pleasant to see the native town of the two Sheldon ladies. We dropped in on them one Monday night—when business was always light—and told them of this idea, and they supported it with almost violent enthusiasm. Würzburg, they said, was the most heavenly town in all the world. If we would really stop off there, and send them a few postcards, they'd be in our debt forevermore.

In the Spring of 1912 McDannald and I duly made the trip, but we spent so much time in Munich that there was none left for seeing Würzburg. However, we found that, on our way northward, we could use a train that ran by way of the town, and in fact made a stop of ten minutes there. So we booked places on it, and when we came to Würzburg station we turned out on the platform, bought a guide-book, two dozen post-cards and some beer-mats, and arranged with the woman at the news-stand to send the cards to the Sheldon sisters at intervals of a couple of days. When we got back to Baltimore and dropped in to hand over the beer-mats, we found that all the cards had arrived, and that Aggie and Gertie were ecstatic. Indeed, if they had not been huge, horse-like women who had long outgrown sex appeal, and if McDannald and I had not been careful fellows, I believe we'd have ended in bed with them. We were, they said, the best and truest friends they had ever met with. On the way home I had studied the German guide-book and interpreted it for Mac, so we were able to tell them that we had spent a whole week in Würzburg and enjoyed every minute of it. Their one regret was that they had not asked us before we sailed to visit the *Friedhof* of the church where they were confirmed, and put wreaths upon the graves of their father and mother.

We promised to do so on our next visit to Germany, but on that trip we did not pass through Würzburg. Nor did they ever go home themselves, for soon after the vice crusade forced them to close World War I came on, and by the time it was over and travel to Germany was again feasible they were old women. They took a house in the suburb of Gardenville, and became members and benefactors of the Jerusalem Lutheran Church there, in the churchyard of which my Abhau grandparents and a number of uncles and aunts are buried.

Another worthy madam of those days was Ella Stuart, whose place was in Edward street, another narrow thoroughfare of Northeast Baltimore. She ran a call-house, but many of her regular girls spent all their leisure in her house, and it was a very pleasant drinking-place. Ella, like the Sheldon sisters, was a German, but she alleged that she had lawfully acquired the name of Stuart by marriage. She had a married daughter who occasionally visited her, bringing a couple of small children. It was understood by all her male friends that this daughter was to be treated with the utmost decorum.

One of the stars of her regular staff was the wife of a street-car conductor. This lady said that she had a good husband, but that it was simply impossible for him to satisfy her libido. She was, in fact, a true nymphomaniac, and old Ella told me some curious tales of her almost unbelievable feats of venery. Such women were very rare in the oldest profession. The average prostitute, in fact, at least after her first dizzy few months in the trade, tended to be cold rather than incandescent. What was done for money soon ceased to be romantic, and in the end it became tolerable rather than agreeable. To be sure, almost every girl had a lover, and with him she was supposed to dally for the joy of it on Sunday afternoons, but this was a concession to a pattern and a tradition, not a natural impulse. When such girls married, which was their normal end, it was almost unheard of for them to be taken in extra-marital carnality, or even accused of it. They made faithful but phlegmatic wives.

I recall the names of only a few other madams of the 1900 era. One is that of Mary Healy, a tall, slim, elderly, business-like woman who ran a place in Rogers avenue, much patronized by sporty printers. Another is that of Blanche Forbes, whose establishment was in Watson street, across the street from Nellie Henderson's. Blanche, a complete moron, had a protector in Charlie Forbes, a saloonkeeper in McMechan street, and used his name. Whenever he went on a drunk, which was often, he had himself hauled to Watson street by nighthack, and she put him to bed. One hot night Percy Heath and I dropped in at her place and found the parlor empty and nobody in sight save the Negro maid, whom we at once sent to the kitchen for a drink. She had barely left the room before there was a dreadful smash upstairs, followed by the sound of a great threshing about. In a little while the maid returned without the drink. "Miss Blanche says," she said, "please excuse her. Mr. Forbes is drinkin'." Then came another smash, and then a third. Percy and I thereupon withdrew. I recall the name of one other whore madam—Mamie Spradling—but no more. They have gone like the wind.

358 *Jean-Baptiste du Plessis de Savines*: The actual name of du Plessis de Savines was Thompson and he called himself Victor de Royallieux. Nobody believed that he was a Frenchman, but it was office etiquette to listen to him gravely. He was a slim, stoop-shouldered, shabby fellow who looked like a bookkeeper. Jacques de Corbigny laid claim to the name of Raoul

L. Clutier (pro. Cloo-*teer*), and alleged that he was a native
of Louisiana and the son of a Confederate general. He was
known to everyone as Clute. He was a tall, heavy, smooth-
faced fellow, and very amiable. He belonged to the Stevedores'
Club and was one of its merriest members, and also one of its
butts. When he came in drunk, which was almost every night,
the boys would greet him with a song running:

> Way down in old Creolio
> They never use Sapolio;
> Oli, oli, oli, oli, oli, oli, olio-
> Arse-hole-i-olio!

They spent a lot of time kidding him about the distinguished
ancestry he laid claim to, but most of them, I am sure, really
believed that he was a Louisianan and the son of a general, as
I did myself. A good deal of his talk was Confederate bragga-
docio, and I recall well his plan for solving the Negro problem
in the South. "On some day to be fixed," he proposed, "let
every white Southerner shoot at least one nigger. There will
be too many assassins to be put on trial—and the problem
will be solved at one crack." Clute, during 1900, became
so steeped in drink that the club appointed a committee to
make quiet inquiries about him, to find out if he was properly
housed and fed. The chairman of this committee was Shimek
Clarke. One night he came in with the report that he had followed Clute the night before, and found that he was living in
a cheap lodging-house in Calvert street above Franklin, with a
street-walker. This was the Battleship, mentioned on p. 362 of
the text as his savior when he was confined in St. Agnes hospital. Clarke reported that Clute and the Battleship had no bed,
but slept in two hammocks. She was well-known to all of us as
a street-walker: her beat was the sidewalk of the new Baltimore
Courthouse. Half a dozen other women worked the same
route, and all of them had nautical sobriquets—the Torpedo-
boat, the Destroyer, the Cruiser, and so on.

The theatrical manager who gave St. Agnes the *porte cochère*
mentioned on p. 362 was James L. Kernan. He went on a big
drunk twice a year, and always landed in St. Agnes. Also, on
being discharged as cured he always gave the nuns some expensive present. One of these presents was a hand-painted

oil-painting of Cardinal Gibbons. Kernan professed to be an art connoisseur, and had a large collection of atrocious paintings in the lobbies of his theatre building at Howard and Franklin streets, which included two theatres, the Maryland and the Auditorium, and a hotel, the Kernan (now the Congress). When the Maryland, which was a vaudeville house, was ready to open he went to New York and booked a splendiferous opening bill, headed by Adelina Patti, then sixty years old and making her tenth or twelfth farewell tour of the United States. Triumphant, he sent a telegram to the *Herald* beginning: "The star of the first $10,000 bill at my $1,000,000 Maryland Theatre will be the world-famous singer, Mme. Patti." Joe Callahan, then my assistant, wired back: "Which Patti, the white or the black?" The Black Patti was a colored woman named Sissieretta Jones who toured the country singing in a voice of brass. Kernan was violently offended, and threatened to take his advertising out of the *Herald* and to maul Callahan at sight.

Clute must have been fired for drunkenness in 1900, for he does not appear in the group photograph of the *Herald* staff on p. 7 of "Photographs and Other Portraits / H. L. Mencken / 1881–1936," taken just before Max Ways left the paper. The drink-cure which gave him a job as capper was at Towson and was run by an old quack named Springer. Clute died in a saloon at Hollins and Fremont streets, standing at the bar. This was probably in 1905. It is not true, as I say in the text, that he was a Philadelphian and that his true name was revealed by his death certificate. What really happened was this: One day in 1907, while I was Sunday editor of the *Sun*, a stranger dropped in at the office, introduced himself as a citizen of one of the small towns of the Shenandoah Valley—I think it was Harrisonburg —and asked me if I could tell him anything about the last days of a dead fellow-townsman, Bob Clutter. I said no, for I had never heard of Bob Clutter. "Maybe," said the stranger, "you knew him as Clutier. That is what he sometimes called himself." I replied that I had known Clutier very well, and the stranger then proceeded to tell me his history. He was the son of a man who had served in the Confederate Army, not as a general, but as a sergeant. The father, after the war, set up a small contracting business in his native town, and had survived

The staff of the Baltimore *Morning Herald* in 1900. Mencken is in the top row, third from right. Unknown photographer, 1900.

there until only a few years before. Bob (not Raoul) had been born there and was known to every old resident. He was not a graduate in law, as he pretended, but a product of the village public-school, and so far as the stranger knew he had never been in Louisiana in his life. I forget the name of this man, but I recall that he seemed quite honest and that I believed him. Why he wanted to track down poor old Clute I forget.

382 *We had a story*: The story, in fact, was big enough to bring in a swarm of reporters from other cities, and for ten days it fought with the Russian-Japanese War, which had begun at almost precisely the same moment, for space on the first pages of the newspapers. One of the reporters from New York was Herbert Bayard Swope, then of the *Herald*. I believe that this was my first meeting with him; later on I came to know him well and when he was married in Baltimore in 1912 I was best man at the wedding. After "Fire Alarm" appeared in the *New Yorker*, on July 6, 1941, I received a number of letters from old-timers who had covered the fire.

386   *Meekins had only $5*: Meekins's son, Lynn W., wrote to me on February 7, 1942:

> That he had as much as $5 on the night of February 7, 1904 was, and is, news.

It was certainly not common, in those days, for journalists to carry any considerable amount of cash in their jeans. For one thing, they seldom had it, and for another thing they all believed that having it would set up a temptation to spend it. But I dissented, and always went armed with at least $25. Maybe that was because I was beginning to pick up an appreciable income outside the office, and thus felt rich.

The new copy-reader here mentioned was C. C. Foss, a cherubic little fellow who was also a Methodist preacher. He was the office encyclopedia, and in recognition of his learning the boys gave him the nickname of the Reverend Professor Doctor. Foss occasionally supplied pulpits in Baltimore and its suburbs, to the derision of the *Herald* agnostics. For this service he arrayed himself in an old-fashioned frock coat with long skirts. He was not noticeably pious on week-days, and now and then he joined the boys of a Saturday night on what they called a sentimental journey, *i.e.*, a roving expedition through the downtown saloons, usually ending in a bawdy-house. He excused these unclerical doings by declaring that he was a student of sociology, and eager to investigate the life of the depressed classes.

Percy Heath, a merry fellow, specialized in leading the Reverend Professor Doctor astray and had a lot of fun with him. Once, when he was known to be booked for a sermon at a Methodist church on Sunday morning, Percy steered him on Saturday night to Schild's wine-room in Holliday street near Baltimore, and there filled him with so much California Rhine wine at five cents a glass that when he got into the pulpit the next day he was barely able to read his text. Another time, also on a Saturday night before a sermon day, Percy locked him in a room at Blanche Forbes's house of call in Watson street with a deaf-and-dumb girl, and there he remained all night, occasionally beating on the door but afraid to make too much noise, lest the cops rush in and his infamy be exposed. Blanche was in on the joke. She reported later that he had been liberated at last at 5 A.M. Cross-examined on Monday by Percy, Foss said that he had learned a lot about the life of the poor from the deaf-and-dumb girl and had thus been enabled to preach a very powerful sermon. After a year or so on the *Herald* he vanished, and I don't know what became of him.

391 *the magnificent Murray*: Murray has been forgotten in Baltimore, but deserves to be remembered. He kept a sort of harem at the Stafford, then a fashionable place, and it was considered fair sport for the young bucks of the town to use his girls. Born in Connecticut in 1847, he had a long railroad career before coming to the B. & O. in 1896. He died on March 14, 1917.

394 *the Mayor*: The mayor who committed suicide was Robert M. McLane. This was on May 30, 1904, nearly four months after the fire. It is the official legend in Baltimore, as I say in the text, that fears for the future of Baltimore induced him to take his life, but I have always had doubts of it. For the Baltimore papers his suicide was a story only less grand and gaudy than that of the fire itself, and for days the staffs of all of them sweated over the job of finding his true motive.

The most plausible of the tales that came in to the *Herald*, though we could not print it, was unearthed by a woman reporter named Edith M. Walbridge. She got it from women friends of the McLane family and it was to the following effect: McLane, only a little while before, had married a young widow—and made the disconcerting discovery that he was virtually impotent. On the day of his death he returned from the City Hall early in the afternoon and found his wife in the house. One thing led to another, and they were presently on a couch in his library. When, after he had brought her to a high state of incandescence, his manly powers again failed him, he rushed to a cupboard, took out a pistol (or maybe it was a gun), and shot himself in her presence. The poor woman was in a state of hysteria for days, but her friends wormed the story out of her, and one of them blabbed to La Walbridge. There was, in fact, no more uneasiness about the future of Baltimore at the time he killed himself. The town, after refusing

all assistance from outside the bounds of Maryland, had proceeded energetically to the work of clearing off the debris of
the fire, and plans to widen the streets of the burned district
and otherwise improve it were already under way.

403 *any responsibility for it*: Like all atheists, I am somewhat superstitious, and one of my pet superstitions has to do
with the number 13. On the family gravestone in Loudon Park
Cemetery there are (1943) four inscriptions. Three of the dead
died on the 13th and the fourth on the 31st. Also, two died on
Friday. I was thus somewhat upset when the page proofs of
Happy Days came through and I found that the book made
313 pages. I was even more upset when those of *Newspaper
Days* came through, and I found that it, too, made 313. When I
passed the final copy for *Heathen Days* my count indicated that
it would hit 313 also, but I miscalculated a bit and it actually
made 299.

Notes on Heathen Days

406: This photograph was made in my office in Hollins street on the day after Palm Sunday, 1942. The office is the second-story front room of the house, formerly occupied as a bedroom by my father and mother. The snow visible through the window in Union Square is quite real. There was a belated snowstorm on Palm Sunday. The photographer was H. George Aschaffenburg, a refugee from Vienna, sent to me by some Jewish friend, and it was made with a German Leica camera. I liked the picture (it was one of several that he made that day) and ordered some enlargements of it with the understanding that the right to reproduce them in print should go with them. Unhappily, I forgot to give Aschaffenburg credit when the copy for the book was sent in. He wrote to me on April 2, 1943, protesting politely, and I asked S. R. Jacobs, Knopf's manufacturing man, to remedy the oversight. Jacobs did so by adding a line of credit to the colophon of the second printing, then just going to press.

407 *the troubles of the teens*: The teens are at once too grotesque and too pathetic to be dealt with in the mood of the three *Days* books. They belong, intrinsically, to pathology, and it is no wonder that they offer a happy hunting ground to quack psychologists. The individual passing through them has lost the artlessness of childhood but is still far from the rationality of maturity. I ceased to be a child when I was graduated from the Baltimore Polytechnic in June, 1896, and I began to be a man when I went to work for the *Morning Herald* in June, 1899. Thus my adolescence was short, but while it lasted it was marked by the usual groping imbecility. There is some account of it in my record of my magazine days, but it is confined mainly to my literary beginnings. If I live a few years longer I may go back to the subject, but it will certainly not be in the manner of the *Days* trilogy.

421 *only too soon we learned*: The pony Frank was not the first quadruped to live in the yard. There had been, in my earlier

Mencken, age 12, holding the reins of the family's shetland pony Frank,
with brothers Charles and August and sister Gertrude. Photograph by
James F. Hughes, 1892.

infancy, guinea pigs, rabbits and a goat—all of them supplied,
I believe, by my grandfather Mencken. We also had cats and
an occasional dog, and in the house, from time to time, there
flourished a canary in a cage, though never a parrot. After the
turn of the century there were two dogs, both of them black-
and-tans and both named Tessie, that comforted us, between
them, for eighteen years. The first Tessie, in her second year,
was scalded fatally by an accident in the kitchen. Tessie No.
2, almost her duplicate but rather sturdier and courser, was
bought from a colored dog-stealer in Booth street a little while
afterward, and when she died in 1921 she was sixteen years
old. She is buried in the backyard and over her grave is a small
bronze tablet that cost me $10, which was $7 more than I had
paid for Tessie herself. Her death was such a calamity that my
mother decided that we should never have another dog, and
there has been none since. The yard is spotted with the graves
of other pets, but Tessie's is the only one that is marked. There
is also the grave of a magnificent blooded bulldog, Victoria by
name, that my sister Gertrude acquired in 1928 for her farm,
but it is likewise unmarked. I well recall what a dreadful time
my brother August and I had digging Vickie's grave in the
hard pan that underlies the yard's top-soil.

For many years my mother and sister, and after their time, my brother August and I kept land tortoises (*Terrapene carolina*) in the yard, and not only kept them but bred them. There were usually three or four in the flock at one time, and they all had eminent names. In 1921 my sister came upon one named General Sawyer (in honor of Harding's body-physician) in the act of laying eggs, and so General Sawyer was rebaptized Mary Baker G. Eddy. Another was named Josephus Daniels. Three of La Eddy's progeny survived. We kept them in a box in the kitchen during their first year, but after that they had a rat-proof pen in the yard. Rats often came in from the alley to fight their elders, and one night Josephus lost his tail and had a hole gnawed in his carapace. But when the rat came back the next night for another bite he was tackled by La Eddy, and in the morning his carcass lay in the garden walk, with a huge hole in the throat. When my sister moved to the country she took Eddy and Josephus with her and turned them loose, but soon afterward my brother and I put in three successors to them. These successors survived from 1936 to the Autumn of 1942, when they were all done to death by extra-ferocious rats. They had become so tame that they appeared at the kitchen door every morning, waiting for their breakfast. It consisted of anything, whether animal or vegetable, that happened to be handy, for they were completely omnivorous, but their favorite was pieces of buckwheat cake spread with molasses. They dug in every Autumn at the first hint of frost, and did not emerge from their burrows until the Spring sun was beginning to be warm.

432 *false alarms as secular law*: As a member of the West Branch of the Y.M.C.A., as it was called, I had the right to use certain of the facilities of the Central Y.M.C.A., then housed in the hideous building at the northwest corner of Charles and Saratoga streets. For example, I was free of its reading-room, and had a season ticket for its Star Course of lectures and concerts. There were half a dozen such affairs in the course of the Winter and I went to all of them. Of them, I recall only two. One was a concert by a male quartette whose basso was a short, bald-headed fellow who was the comedian of the outfit. The other was an author's reading by Ruth McEnery Stuart, the first I ever heard. This must have been in 1894 or 1895, and La Stuart was then at the height of her popularity. Born in 1849, she was less than forty years old, but she seemed an elderly woman to me. Of her reading, I remember but a single detail—that in one of the stories she read, dealing with a Negro funeral, there was the line: "The corpse is now ready to receive its friends." This struck the audience as excessively humorous. La Stuart must have been successful with it elsewhere, for when she read it she paused coyly to wait for the applause.

When I became a newspaper reporter in 1899 the Central Y.M.C.A. was one of my regular assignments, and I often dropped in to look through the magazines in its reading-room. Now and then I had to cover one of its Sunday afternoon religious meetings. They were always dull and gloomy. Once, I recall, the speaker was Dr. Bernard C. Steiner, librarian of the Enoch Pratt Library—a solemn, humorless, intensely pious fellow who, because of his shambling way of walking, was known to the reporters of the time as Gum-shoe Steiner. He delivered an harangue so inconceivably stupid and uninteresting that I remember it clearly to this day. Until he died in 1926 the main building of the Pratt Library, then in Mulberry street, west of Cathedral, was a morgue, and getting out a book was a tedious process. There was no card-index, but only a series of printed books with typewritten addenda, and the female attendants, mainly sour old maids, were far from helpful. Nevertheless, I patronized it assiduously, and whatever education I may be said to have came out of it. I used Branch No. 2, at Hollins and Calhoun streets, until 1894 or thereabout, but by that time I had pretty well exhausted its somewhat meagre stock of books, and after that I resorted to the main library. I had two cards—one a regular card, and the other what was called a student's card—and I kept both of them working steadily. In addition, I dropped into the reading-room at least twice a week.

In 1903 or thereabout, after I had become dramatic editor of the *Herald*, I went to the central library one day to draw out one of the plays of Pinero. I found that it was starred in the catalogue, which meant that it seemed lewd and lascivious to Gum-shoe Steiner and could be issued only with the express permission of a member of the staff. I applied for that permission, and was directed to one of the younger members.

Mencken at his desk in the city room of the *Baltimore Herald*. Unknown photographer, November 26, 1901.

In fact, she was a girl who seemed to be no more than eighteen or nineteen years old. There was I, a grown man and a professional dramatic critic, and there, across the desk, was that preposterous flapper, eyeing me critically and giving me a sharp examination. In the end she decided that I could be trusted to read the book without being seduced to sin, and it was accordingly handed to me, and I took it home. It turned out, when I read it, to be completely innocuous. Gum-shoe, I suppose, had picked up the notion, at the time of the uproar over *The Second Mrs. Tanqueray* in the nineties, that Pinero was an indecent dramatist, and so starred all of his plays. Gum-shoe himself never went to the theatre. His only recreation was Christian Endeavor.

434 *Of the former, there were two*: In the *Smart Set* for December, 1921, pp. 30–31, I hymned Kines and Blake as follows:

Some time ago I made casual mention in this place of two teachers of my youth, both drunken and disreputable men. One taught me to chew tobacco—an art that has done more, perhaps, to establish my evil repute in the world than even my Socinianism. The other introduced me to Rabelais, and so filled me with that taste for coarseness which now offends so many of my customers lay and clerical. Neither ever came to a dignified position in academic circles. One abandoned pedagogy for the law, became involved in cases of a dubious nature, and finally disappeared into the shades which clothe third-rate attorneys. The other went upon a fearful drunk one Christmastide, got himself shanghaied on the water-front, and is supposed to have fallen overboard from a British tramp, bound east for Cardiff. At all events, he has never been heard from since.

Two evil fellows—and yet I hold their memories in affection, and believe that they were the best teachers I ever had. For in both there was something a great deal more valuable than mere pedagogical skill and diligence, and even more valuable than correct demeanor, and that was a passionate love of sound literature. This love, given reasonably receptive soil, they knew how to communicate, as a man can always communicate whatever moves him profoundly. Neither ever made the slightest effort to "teach" literature, as the business is carried on by the usual idiot schoolmaster. Both had a vast contempt for the text-books that were official in their school, and used to entertain the boys by pointing out the errors in them. Both were full of derisory objections to the principal heroes of such books: Scott, Irving, Pope, Jane Austen, Dickens, Trollope, Tennyson. But both, discoursing in their disorderly way upon the heroes of their own, were magnificently eloquent and persuasive. The boy who could listen to one of them intoning Shakespeare and stand unmoved was a dull fellow indeed. The boy who could resist the other's enthusiasm for the old essayists was intellectually deaf, dumb and blind.

I often wonder if their expoundings of their passions and prejudices would have been half so charming if they had been wholly respectable men, like their colleagues of the school faculty. It is not likely. A healthy boy is in constant revolt against the sort of men who surround him at school. Their puerile pedantries, their Christian Endeavor respectability, their sedentary pallor, their curious preference for the dull and uninteresting, their general air of so many Y.M.C.A. secretaries—these things infallibly repel the youth who is above milksoppery. In every boys' school the favorite teacher is one who occasionally swears like a cavalryman, or is reputed to keep a jug in his room, or is known to receive a scented note every morning. Boys are good judges of men, as girls are good judges of women. It is not by accident that most of them, at some time or other, long to be cowboys or ice-wagon drivers, and that none of them, not obviously diseased in mind, ever longs to be a Sunday-school superintendent. Put that judgment to a simple test. What would become of a nation in which all of the men were, at heart, Sunday-school superintendents —or Y.M.C.A. secretaries, or pedagogues? Imagine it in conflict with a nation of cowboys and ice-wagon drivers. Which would be the stronger, and which would be the more honest, intelligent, resourceful, enterprising and courageous?

437 *gave great delight to his pupils by going crazy*: The gogue who went crazy was A. Newton Ebaugh, Ph. B., the head of the department of mathematics and vice-president of the school. He was a member of a Maryland family—originally, I think, from Carroll county—that had produced a great many teachers. He recovered somewhat toward the end of my senior year, but had to give up his vice-presidency and soon afterward had a relapse and was forced to retire. What became of the poor old fellow eventually I do not know. He was a reasonably competent teacher and a well-meaning man, but completely devoid of humor. Like old Professor Knapp, he wore the traditional uniform of his gloomy trade—a black alpaca coat and a white necktie.

439 *the* Diener *in the dissecting-room*: The dissecting-room *Diener* who did a trade in cadavers was one William Devine. His chief customer was the Sioux City Medical College of Sioux City, Iowa, where he did business with Dr. Maxwell E. Silver, the demonstrator in anatomy, who had formerly been an intern at the City Hospital. They seem to have gone undetected for a considerable time. Devine came to grief by shipping Silver the body of a policeman's father, killed on the street. The body had gone unidentified at the morgue, and had thus reached Devine's storehouse, but the dead man's son bestirred his colleagues to make a thorough search for his missing father, and they finally traced his remains. It turned out that selling a human body was not forbidden by the laws of Maryland, so Devine had to be indicted under Section 299, Chapter 123 of the Acts of 1899, forbidding the shipment of one without a permit from the health department. My recollection is that he escaped with nothing worse than sixty days in the House of Correction.

454 *A. Toxen Worm*: When, in preparation for these notes, I tried to find out something about the origin and career of

Worm, I discovered that there was next to nothing in the record. The *New York Times* must have missed his death in 1922, for there is no mention of his name in its index for that year. In *Variety*, the theatrical weekly, I found only the following brief and very sketchy obituary:

A. Toxen Worm, for over 20 years identified with the Shuberts in an executive capacity, died in Paris, France, Jan. 12, of apoplexy. Worm had been ill for about six months, having suffered a slight stroke in Boston, where he was acting as the general representative of the Shuberts. He came to New York and then went abroad for his health. Late advices from Paris were to the effect that he had decided to spend the rest of his life there. He was a native of Denmark, having been born there 55 years ago.

His full name was Conrad Henrik Aage Toxen Worm. As a boy he was a playmate of William Hohenzollern. In this country he made his mark as a theatrical publicity man and is credited with having hopped the famous Anna Held milk bath story and the tan bark in front of the Republic theatre on 42nd street while Mrs. Patrick Campbell was playing an engagement there so that the rumbling of the vehicles on the street would not annoy her during the performance.

Dudley Field Malone, who is in Paris, had charge of the funeral arrangements under cable instructions from Phelan Beale, Worm's attorney in New York.

The size of Worm's estate, according to Mr. Beale, is unknown. He said that the residue was left to Mr. Worm's niece in Copenhagen, with the exception of several personal articles distributed to other members of the family. There is also a clause in the will leaving $500 to an institution for the benefit of members of the theatrical profession and to an institution for indigent newspaper men.

The gaps in this notice are evident. It does not say where Worm was born in Denmark, or who his people were, or where he was educated, or when he came to the United States, or how he contrived to make his way into the front rank of Broadway press-agents. Moreover, it includes a number of incredible details, *e.g.*, the statement that he was a playmate of Kaiser Wilhelm II as a boy. If he was actually 55 years old when he died—and I believe that that was quite close to his actual age—then he was born in 1866 or 1867. Wilhelm was born in 1859, and was thus seventeen when Worm was a boy of ten. It is certainly most unusual for youths of seventeen and boys of ten to be playmates. The story probably originated in one of Worm's hoaxes.

The fact that he signed his name A. Toxen Worm naturally caused some wit to call him Antitoxen, but this nickname did not stick. He was usually referred to simply as Toxen, or Tox. He received a large salary from the Shuberts, and no doubt saved most of it, for all his parties were charged to his expense account. I was present at a number of them. He usually gave them at the Beaux Arts restaurant at Sixth avenue and 40th street, a favorite haunt of Nathan's and mine, and they always included women. These women, nine times out of ten, were chorus girls and he was fond of introducing them in a brutally sportive manner. One would be described as "the girl with round heels," another as "the girl who can't say no," and a third as the kept woman of some distinguished New Yorker, say Elihu Root or Nicholas Murray Butler. Worm was never known to have a steady girl of his own. He traded cynically among the ladies of the Broadway half-world, but kept clear of entanglements.

456 *Charlie Connolly*: Charlie Connolly, in his day, was one of the salient figures of Broadway, but he is now quite forgotten. He hailed from Buffalo and undertook the study of medicine. One night, as a senior student, he went out in an ambulance answering an accident call, and on the way passed his home, where his parents and sisters were sitting on the front porch. He waved to them as he passed. Two minutes later, arriving at the scene of the accident, he found that its victim was his only brother, who had been run over by a train. This shock so upset him that he abandoned medicine and took to journalism, and from the job of a reporter he passed to that of a theatrical press-agent. He was a very merry fellow, and had friends all over the country. He had something of a name as a sexual Sandow, and once, when he was in Baltimore, I saw him go to bed with three women seriatim between 11 P.M. and 1 A.M. He died many years ago.

458 *the music critic of the* Morning Herald: The music critic of the *Herald* was Wilberfoss George Owst, an Englishman. Born on June 1, 1861, he was destined for the law, and actually went through the three years of heavy eating and light study that constitute the training of an English barrister. But his heart was in music, and instead of entering upon practise he went to Stuttgart to study under Immanuel Faisst, Percy Goetschius, Paul Klengel and Karl Doppler. One of his fellow students was Victor Herbert. Owst chose the organ as his instrument and was brought out to Baltimore in 1893 to be organist of St. Michael and All Angels' Church. But he was too indolent a fellow to relish the routine work of a church organist, and after four years he threw up his job and became a teacher of theory in the Maryland College of Music, a private institution of the 1900 era. He also taught theory at the Washington College of Music. Once, at the turn of the century, he was induced to return to the console at St. John's Church, Waverly, but he lasted there only a short time. He had a small private income, and in the days when I first encountered him appeared to be reasonably prosperous, though his income as a teacher must have been very small. How he came to be appointed music critic of the *Morning Herald* I do not know. He knew a great deal about music, and had a very powerful influence upon my musical development. He directed me to the theoretical works of his master, Goetschius, and helped me on my blundering way through them.

A bachelor, he retained the Bohemian habits he had picked up in his student days in Stuttgart, and nearly all his evenings, save when he was exercising his critical art, were spent in beer-houses. His favorite among them was that of old Charlie Schneider in Fayette street east of Liberty—now (1943) Miller's restaurant. There he sat nearly every night, drinking beer and discoursing upon music. Like most other English musicians of that period, he cried down Brahms, but in all other directions his position was orthodox, and he had no patience with the experiments of the moderns. I was fond of him and enjoyed his talk, but unhappily he always had a current buddy who was a dreadful bore, and these bores tried me sorely. One I recall, an idiot named Salmon, knew no more about music than a cat, but insisted on horning into the conversation, and was patiently endured by Owst.

Owst's compositions were not bad, but he was so lazy that he wrote very little. Perhaps his best work was a setting of

Dante Gabriel Rossetti's "The White Ship," for spoken voice
and piano. Such melodramas, as they were called, were in favor
in the 1910 period, and this one was better than most, but the
fashion soon passed and it was forgotten. I well recall a performance of it at Owst's studio, then in Charles street, with
the composer at the piano and a man with a subterranean bass
voice reciting the words. Owst was a very bad pianist, and did
fearful execution upon his own score. He was (as I was) one
of the charter members of the Florestan Club in Baltimore,
and after it got under way spent a large amount of time in its
clubhouse in Charles street. He also became a member of the
Sunday Dinner Club which eight or ten of us organized. In
1912 or thereabout he produced another composition of some
merit—a sonata for flute and piano, written for Frederick H.
Gottlieb, a rich Baltimore brewer who was an amateur flutist
and a member of the Florestan. The rest of his work is quite
forgotten, even by me, who heard all of it.

When the *Herald* suspended in 1906 Owst transferred to
the *Sun*, and was its music critic, off and on, until his death on
January 17, 1928. His last years were very uncomfortable. His
pupils diminished in number—at one time the only one that I
knew of was a west Baltimore street paperhanger, Schlueter by
name, who aspired to write polyphonic church music—, his income from England was greatly reduced, and he was disabled
by illness. His fundamental trouble was lues, but he seems to
have suffered at the end mainly from arterio sclerosis, and in
December, 1924, one of his legs had to be amputated. He recovered from this operation more or less, and for three years
was able to get about on crutches, but toward the end of 1925
he began to break up. He had been afflicted all the while I
knew him by a nervous affection which caused him to wink his
left eye in a somewhat disconcerting manner, but his friends
had long since got used to it.

When he died it turned out that he had an adopted son,
one Grier Eubanks. This must have been a recent acquisition,
for I had never met Eubanks. Owst had a brother, Dr. Arthur
Owst, settled at the small town of Ilkley in Yorkshire, and an
unmarried sister, Miss E. E. Owst, living in London. In 1912 I
visited this sister on one of my trips abroad in company with
A. H. McDannald of the *Sun* staff. She turned out to be a

somewhat forbidding Englishwoman, though she received us politely. Down to the outbreak of World War I, Owst went home every year, and he and his mother, who was still living, spent a couple of months' holiday in France. The old lady died during the war, and after that, so far as I know, he never visited England again.

465 *a Baltimore brewer*: The brewer was Frederick H. Gottlieb, head of the Globe Brewery. He was an amateur flutist and a salient figure in the musical life of Baltimore for many years. Separated by an alley from his brewery in Hanover street was a three-story building ostensibly given over to the office of the establishment. In reality, only the first floor was occupied by its bookkeepers. The two upper floors were Gottlieb's private domain, and there he made merry according to his lights. He had a large music room, a billiard room, a kitchen, and a couple of pantries, beside his own quarters. He gave many musical parties in the music room and I went to dozens of them. Sometimes the guests would be distinguished visiting artists, sometimes they would be amateurs, sometimes they would be customers of the brewery, sometimes they would be cops and whores, and sometimes two or more of these classes would be mixed. I recall an evening when Antonio Scotti, the baritone, then at the height of his celebrity, was the guest of honor. Gottlieb put on a somewhat elaborate supper, and invited a number of women to entertain Scotti, who got mashed on one of them, went to bed with her, and was still there when Gottlieb came to work the next morning.

467 *William W. Woollcott*: Woollcott was one of my intimates for years. He was not only a listener-member of the Saturday Night Club, but also a member of the Sunday Dinner Club, and between 1908 or thereabout and 1930 I saw him constantly. He was a brother to Alexander Woollcott, but almost the complete antithesis of Alex in person, manner and ideas. Instead of being rotund he was rather spare, instead of being effeminate he was assertively masculine and the father of four children, and instead of being vain and waspish he was modest and amiable. I once tried to indicate the difference between the two brothers by saying that the Woollcott family had been allotted four gonads for the pair, and that Willie had got three

Members of the Saturday Night Club. Unknown photographer, 1925.
William Woolcott is in the center, in the bandleader's uniform.

and Alex only one. Willie was proud of Alex and professed to
admire him, and was quite convinced that he had no talent of
any kind himself, but he was actually the better man, and by far.

I met him soon after he had come to Baltimore as a minor functionary of the American Can Company. We took to
each other instantly, and have been excellent friends ever since;
indeed, I know of no one who has ever met Willie without
liking him. One night he went to a Boston Symphony Orchestra concert in Baltimore, and found himself seated beside a
red-haired young woman who took his eye. He picked her up
forthwith, and a year later they were married. She was Marie
Bloede, the daughter of Victor Bloede, a rich German of Catonsville, near Baltimore. The old man was shocked when he
first saw his prospective son-in-law, for Willie has always been
a very shabby dresser, and he seldom gets his hair cut until his
locks begin to curl. But in the end the two became fast friends.

Willie and Marie settled in a small house in the woods near
the old man's mansion, and were presently the parents of a
daughter. They wanted a boy, and kept on hoping for one,
but after four daughters had been born to them they gave up.
All four girls are now married (1943). Willie lost his job with
the American Can Company in 1925 or thereabout, and old
Bloede took him into the family business—the manufacture of

fine pastes and inks. He became superintendent of the plant, and continued as such until a heart attack early in 1943 forced him to retire. A dozen years before this he had been floored by stomach ulcers, but he survived two very serious operations, and was in reasonably good health until his heart began to fail. I have never known a man with less malice in him or more charm. He knew nothing of music, but he loved it, and until his stomach troubles forced him to reduce his intake of food and drink he was a faithful member of the Saturday Night Club. He had every good quality—intelligence, tolerance, humor, generosity, kindness—and no bad ones. He was truly a great soul in a small destiny.

470   *Al Herford*: Al was the son of a Jewish saloonkeeper in Canton avenue in East Baltimore, and operated the family business after his father's death. The place, under his management, became the sporting headquarters of the district, and it was thus that he became interested in boxing and made his first contact with Joe Gans. He began as a fight promoter by organizing the Eureka Athletic Club. On November 14, 1902, it staged a bout between Gans and Charlie Sieger (or Feiger), and Sieger got such a dreadful beating that the reformers of the time demanded that boxing be prohibited. In response to that demand laws were passed limiting fights to 15 rounds and providing that they must be before incorporated clubs, with only the members present.

It was in obedience to this legislation that Al organized the Eureka Athletic and Social Club, and began the mummery of reading its minutes at every so-called meeting. Its headquarters were at 115 west Fayette street, and there Al also carried on a bookmaking business. His chief aid was his younger brother, Maurice. Al, though he dressed gorgeously, was a somewhat rough diamond, and his English often showed defects, but Maurice was a very elegant fellow. In 1905 or thereabout Maurice married a highly respectable Irish girl, and they lived in great amity. After his death five or six years later she mourned him sincerely, and often called me up to tell me how vastly she missed him.

Al himself remained a bachelor until 1911, when he surprised Baltimore sportdom by marrying a damsel named Olive Fillingame. She was supposed to be from Cecil county, Maryland, but had gone on her travels early in life, and at one time, I believe, was a chorus girl. This union was not too placid, but it survived until Al's death on January 5, 1930, aged sixty-three. He had been failing for a year or more, and had spent several months at Sinai Hospital, but he died at his home at 1512 Wallis avenue. He was buried in Har Sinai Cemetery on January 7, with Rabbi Morris Lazaron officiating. All the Baltimore sports went to the funeral.

474 *Joe died in a low state*: Joe died in Baltimore on August 10, 1910, of tuberculosis. Some time before this he went to Arizona in the hope that the climate would benefit him, but he kept on going downhill, and early in August came home to die. He was accompanied by a Prescott doctor, Harry T. Southworth. The *Sun* reported on August 11 that Southworth had been paid $500 and his expenses for bringing his patient to Baltimore. The other costs of the return made the total bill $1,000.

Joe was born in Baltimore on November 25, 1874. His father is said to have been a colored baseball player named Joseph Butts, but who his mother was no one ever seemed to know. When he was four years old he was adopted by a colored woman named Maria Gant, and ever thereafter he regarded her as his mother. When he became prosperous he bought her a house at 1026 Argyle avenue, and transferred other property to her. It was in this house that he died.

In 1890, when he was sixteen, Joe fought his first battle before the Avon Club, a predecessor of the Eureka Athletic and Social Club. His opponent was another colored boy, and he got the usual $4 for winning. Thereafter he appeared frequently as a preliminary boy, and usually won. He called himself Joe Gant, but one day some primeval Al Herford of the time changed Gant to Gans, apparently influenced by the fact that a well-known Baltimore lawyer was Edgar H. Gans. Whatever the process, Joe was Gans thereafter.

He climbed the ladder slowly, and it was not until 1894 that his fights began to be recorded. In that year he fought twelve times, and won every time, eight times by knockouts. [. . .]

It will be noted that Joe was not once defeated until October 6, 1896, and that thereafter, until his historic fight with

Battling Nelson, he lost only four times. As champion, he naturally fought less than while he was making his way, but in 1907
he knocked out Kid Herman in the eighth round at Tonopah,
Nev., on January 1, and Jimmy Britt at San Francisco in six
rounds on September 9 (though he broke his wrist in the fourth
round), and got a decision over George Memsic at Los Angeles
after twenty rounds of hard fighting with his wrist yet unhealed.

He began 1908 by knocking out Bart Blackburn at Baltimore on January 8, in the third round, and by doing the same
in the same time for Spike Robson at Philadelphia on April 1.
On May 14, at San Francisco, he knocked out Rudy Unholtz
in the eleventh round, but that was the last of his triumphs.
Joe, by this time, was thirty-four years old, and beginning to
age. On July 4, at San Francisco, he gave Battling Nelson a
second chance at the championship, and Nelson knocked him
out in the seventeenth round. At Colma, Calif., on September
9, Nelson gave him his own second chance—and knocked him
out again, this time in the twenty-first round. That was the
end of poor Joe, though he kept on fighting for a little while
longer. In 1909 he went ten rounds to no decision with Jabez
White in New York, and during the same year I saw him fight
a pug whose name I forget at the Music Hall (now the Lyric
Theatre), Baltimore. This pug had an advantage in weight of
at least forty pounds, and Joe was plainly shattered in health;
nevertheless, he fought gamely for fifteen rounds, and gave a
really superb exhibition of boxing.

After his victory over Battling Nelson at Goldfield, Nev., in
1906, he invested his winnings in the first black-and-tan night-
club that Baltimore had ever seen. It was at the corner of Lexington and Chestnut streets, and he gave it the name of the
Goldfield Hotel. His investment in this place was $50,000, but
it was not much of a success. A little while before his death he
transferred the property to his second wife, a colored school
ma'm of Baltimore named Margaret, and she tried to revive it
after he was gone, but it began to lose money heavily and soon
it was closed. His first wife, Madge by name, was an actress. By
her he had two children, a boy and a girl. The boy, James, was
sixteen at the time of his father's death, and the girl, Julia, was
a year or two younger. What has become of them, or of the
widow Gans, I do not know.

Joe's funeral was the most spectacular and exciting event in the whole history of Baltimore colored society. It was actually carried on in three different churches, as I say in *Happy Days*, p. 189. Joe's body was planted in Mount Auburn Cemetery, a colored graveyard in Westport, a shabby suburb of Baltimore. There is a marker on his grave, and for a long while after his death the spot was visited almost daily by pious pilgrims. On August 4, 1931, the *Evening Sun* reported on the authority of James F. Halls, superintendent of the cemetery, that they then numbered between twenty and thirty a week, and included groups of white and black Gansistas arriving from far places by automobile. Since then they have fallen off, for Joe is beginning to be forgotten.

His earnings were never really large, for he lived before the days of $1,000,000 gates, and lightweights never earn as much as the big boys. After his death in 1910 Al Herford told the *Sun* that his net income from September, 1908, to September, 1909, was $84,000. This came mainly from shows and boxing exhibitions, for he did little fighting during the year. How much of the money was taken by Herford and how much remained to Gans did not appear.

After his death various projects for a memorial to him were launched, but they came to nothing. In February, 1922, Heywood Broun printed the following in the New York *World*:

> Joe Gans should not be allowed to drop out of the aesthetic tradition of America, all too slight as it is. He transcended the virtuosi of our day. With him the conservation of energy was developed to an extraordinary degree. In Gans the mechanism of movement was so sensitized that he could not endure the shock of a false movement. To hit at an opponent and miss jarred him more than to receive a blow. In order to protect himself against such shocks he did not miss. Sometimes he started a move which would have been unsuccessful, but he was quick enough to detect the lack of an opening before he had committed himself completely to the punch, and back would come his hand before it had betrayed him.
>
> There ought to be a statue of Gans in some public place in America. Greece had its discus thrower and appreciated him handsomely. His mastery of his medium undoubtedly was amazing, but, after all, his feats lacked the vitality of conquest. The discus never even tried to throw him.

482	*Preston would have given gold:* Preston gained nothing by his smartness. When the time came to put his name before the convention he chose a Maryland lawyer named Alonzo L. Miles as his spokesman. Unfortunately, Miles was drunk and the huge crowd in the Fifth Regiment Armory soon detected the fact. It was composed in large part of persons who did not like Preston, so Miles was presently the butt of such hoots and cat-calls that he had to be taken from the stage. Preston, of course, did not get the vice-presidential nomination, for his choice for head of the ticket, Champ Clark, was beaten by Woodrow Wilson. This was a bitter pill, for Wilson's victory was due at least in part to the ardent support of Charles H. Grasty. It was also helped by the fact that Clark himself, at a critical moment, got drunk too.

491	*W. Edwin Moffett*: Moffett was a member of the Sunday Dinner Club while it lasted, and has been, for ten years or more, a member of the Saturday Night Club. He is now (1943) more than seventy years old, but is still an ardent and assiduous double-bass player. He also plays with the Baltimore Symphony Orchestra, the Peabody Students' Orchestra and in fact with all the other orchestras of Baltimore, and devotes virtually all his time to music, for he is a man of independent means. His money came from a grocery business established by his father, a Union Soldier, directly after the Civil War. Its establishment was in Hillen street, and behind it was a large yard that the farmers of Baltimore county used, for many years, as an egg market. Next door was the old Farmers' and Planters' Hotel, the last of all the pre-Civil War inns of Baltimore to survive. It was still standing and in operation until 1935 or thereabout, when it was torn down to make way for some public improvement, and along with it the Moffett grocery store. Ed then retired from business, and has since given himself to music.

Even in his grocery days he played constantly at night, and also took part, as a trombonist, in many parades. In late years he has neglected the trombone and concentrated his efforts upon the double-bass. He was a bachelor until he was fifty-five or so, when he married the widow of Dr. H. H. Flood, a Norwegian who had also been a member of the Sunday Dinner

Club. He and his wife, Adelaide, live in great amity. She is the daughter of a farmer in Howard county, Maryland, and was brought up a Methodist, but living with two agnostics has pretty well purged her of her youthful faith. She came to Baltimore as a young girl to train as a nurse at the old Beidler and Sellman Sanitarium in north Charles street, and there met Flood.

Flood was a member of the Vagabonds Club and I met him when I joined it in 1905. He was an extremely racy and amusing character. His father had been a Norwegian ship-owner, and he was sent out to the East Indies as a youth to learn the shipping business. There ensued some years of wandering and he finally landed in Baltimore, where he decided to study medicine. The town, in those days, had six or eight medical colleges, most of them highly dubious, and Flood chose the worst for his training—mainly, I suppose, because its courses were easy. Even so, it is astonishing that he ever got his degree, for his knowledge of medicine was extremely slight. More than once I heard him argue that the germ theory of the cause of infectious diseases was nonsense. Nevertheless, he managed not only to graduate but also to get a license to practise, and when I first knew him he was doing very well.

He had an office in south Gay street, and confined himself to the medicating of sailors. In those days a great many small Scandinavian ships traded to Baltimore, chiefly in the banana trade, and Flood had contracts to take care of their crews and also to supply them with medical stores. By the laws of Norway, Denmark and Sweden every ship had to carry a medicine chest containing certain drugs: the captain was held responsible for this, and was supposed to know how to diagnose the commoner diseases and to suitably dose his men. The captains depended on Flood for advice, and his usual advice was that their drugs were stale and needed replenishing. His bill for such a replenishing sometimes ran to $75 or $100. Out of this he paid the captain a commission of 30 or 40%; the rest was his own, and it was nearly all profit, for the drugs he sent aboard seldom cost him more than a few dollars.

Flood was a gay grass widower when I first knew him: his first wife, a Dane, had left him. When he encountered Adelaide at the Beidler and Sellman Sanitarium, he became mashed on her at once, and began to take her to dinner and shows. In those days doctors were forbidden to pay attention to nurses, and he was presently called to the mat by the head nurse. He replied heatedly that if he couldn't see her under the rules, he would marry her and take her away, and this he did. She was, at that time, a very pretty girl, with large dark eyes, coal-black hair, a rosy complexion and a good figure. She is now somewhat dilapidated and has developed a considerable deafness, but Ed Moffett still finds her fair.

Flood's funeral was a grand event for the club, and four of us played Grieg's "Asa's Death" at the service. Flood's chief buddy was Holger A. Koppel, the Danish consul in Baltimore and an atheist like himself. Koppel engaged Julius Hofmann, pastor of Zion Church in Baltimore, to conduct the services, but Adelaide's kinfolks brought in two Methodist clergymen from their native wildwood. Hofmann, as usual, was half tight, but even so he was more than a match for the Methodists, and when they tried to horn into the service he elbowed them out. Flood's first wife came sailing in at the last minute and insisted on taking a front seat, greatly to the indignation of Adelaide and her people. The burial was in a Methodist cemetery far out in Howard county, directly beside a hideous Methodist church painted a staring yellow and set upon high stilts. At the grave Adelaide and the first wife contended for the privilege of throwing a final rose upon the coffin. I remember with a shudder how it went down into the soggy grave, for the day was rainy. It seemed really dreadful that so pleasant a fellow and so firm an infidel should be thrust into the mud of a Methodist graveyard so remote from civilization.

McDannald and I were not altogether content with Moffett as a traveling companion. He had never been abroad before and could not grasp the notion that the true aim of travel is to have a roaring time, regardless of cost. He complained constantly about tips and other such expenses, and kept a little red-bound memorandum-book to record his outlays. One night he brought it out in a bawdy-house in Rome to put down $4 that he had paid for a bottle of wine. He was also a drag on our pleasure in Munich, and by the time we got to Paris we were fed up on him. There we met Willard Wright and George Nathan, and they too were presently upset by his yappish ways.

Mencken (center) with A. H. McDannald (left) and W. Edwin Moffett (right) at the Forum in Rome. Unknown photographer, 1914.

In the end we got a cruel revenge on him by convincing him that the French police were after him, the charge being an attempt to swindle and a threat to kill one of the Jews who take American yahoos on tours of the Paris dirty shows. The joke was a huge success, but Moffett took it so seriously that he threatened to commit suicide, so we had to let up. He put the whole blame on Wright, and hated him ever thereafter, but the truth is that all of us had hands in the business.

500 *the Pope was passing before us*: As His Holiness entered the room where we were kneeling I glanced at Ed, who was beside me, and noted to my horror that the huge Masonic charm hanging from his (Ed's) watch-chain was plainly in view. I whispered a warning to him, and he thrust it into the fly of his trousers.

501 *a door which took us out*: We actually emerged into the same alleyway by which we had entered (*cf.* p. 500). As we made tracks toward the plaza of St. Peter's Ed noticed that there was a booth in the alleyway, offering rosaries and other such Catholic goods. During our audience with His Holiness most of the Austrian pilgrims had held up bunches of rosaries to be blessed. Ed now lamented that he had not had a supply himself, for they appeared to be very cheap and he was sure that some of his Catholic friends would greatly esteem strings blessed by the Pope. Mac and I thereupon suggested that it might be a good idea to buy a dozen or two now, for the Baltimore Catholics would undoubtedly take his word for it if he told them that the Pope had actually blessed them. Moreover, I added, Mac and I had been blessed ourselves so very recently that something of the papal grace probably still hung about us, and our blessing would be only a little less effective than the Pope's. Ed, agreeing, bought a pocketful of the beads, and Mac and I duly blessed them in the alleyway.

504 *At meals I sat at the doctor's table*: One of the passengers at my table was a dreadful ass named Ralph Dawson, a minor functionary of the Guaranty Trust Company. He was bound for Russia on business for the company, and I recall marvelling that any banking corporation operated by presumably rational men would entrust its affairs to such a fool. He swaggered and blustered in the classical manner of an American bounder away from home, and several times so greatly offended the Scandinavians at the table that they talked of giving him a beating. I encouraged them to do so, but they decided that he was not worth the risk of an international incident. Dawson is still alive (1943) and still in the service of the Guaranty Trust Company. He writes to me occasionally from his home at 116–26 82nd drive, Kew Gardens, L.I., and sometimes sends me philological items clipped from the newspapers, thinking to improve the next edition of *The American Language*. It is characteristic of him that he never dates these items, and often forgets to write on them the names of the papers from which they come. I have not encountered him in the flesh since our voyage together, and recall him only as a stout, shortish fellow who stammered.

507 *one of the Americans*: I was the passenger who palmed off "Die Wacht am Rhein" on the bull-fiddling band leader. I had been thumbing through his pile of music, and recognized the *potpourri* as one that the Saturday Night Club had in its library.

520 *James Rolph, Jr.*: Rolph was a native of San Francisco, born in 1869. He was the head of a firm of shipping merchants and also of an insurance firm. He was a Native Son, an Episcopalian and a Republican—in brief, an indubitable member of the local aristocracy. He made a considerable fortune in World War I, but lost it in the Depression of the thirties. He was a great handshaker and back-slapper, and was known in San Francisco as Sunny Jim. Said the Associated Press in its obituary on June 2, 1934:

> The Rolph smile was famous. He never appeared in public without a gardenia in his buttonhole. He was ever ready to crown a beauty queen, throw the first ball at the opening game of the national pastime, make a speech, meet an incoming dignitary or a visiting actor.

He first came into public notice at the time of the San Francisco earthquake of 1906. Many San Franciscans feared that it would be impossible to rebuild the city, but he was much more optimistic, and his loud, Rotarian exhortations to hope and vision made him a leader in the reconstruction of the city. He became mayor for the first time five years afterward. In 1919 he made his first attempt upon the governorship, but was defeated. In 1930 he tried again, and this time was elected by a large majority. He was mayor at the time of the famous Preparedness Day parade of 1916, when a bomb thrown at the marchers killed ten persons and injured forty. Sixteen years later he refused, as Governor, to grant clemency to Thomas J. Mooney, who had been charged with the crime, probably falsely.

Rolph, as a Native Son, was an outspoken advocate of the early California *Kultur*, and refused to be swayed by Eastern example or intimidated by Eastern disapproval. He wore the traditional boots of the 49ers until October, 1933, when rheumatism crippled his toes, and he was forced to resort to shoes. In November of the same year he made the front pages by issuing a statement approving a lynching in San José. The victims were two bandits named Thomas H. Thurmond and John M. Holmes, who had kidnapped and murdered a young man named Brooke Hart. His pronunciamento on the subject was thus reported by the Associated Press on November 27:

> "That was a fine lesson to the whole nation," Governor Rolph said. "There will be less kidnapping in the country now. They made a good job of it.

"If anyone is arrested for the good job, I'll pardon them all. I hope this lesson will serve in every State of the Union."

The Governor postponed his trip to Boise, Idaho, to attend a Governors' conference, not for the purpose of being on hand to call out troops, but to prevent it.

"If I had gone away some one would have called out the troops on me," the Governor said, "and I promised I would not do that. Why should I call out troops to protect those two fellows?

"The people make the laws, don't they?" he asked. "Well, if the people have confidence that troops will not be called out to mow them down when they seek to protect themselves against kidnappers, there is liable to be swifter justice and fewer kidnappings.

"I don't think they will arrest anyone for the lynchings," the Governor continued.

"With all the sorrows we have had why should we add the sorrows of kidnapping. It is about time the people should have comfort in their homes. This kidnapping business has become so bad that mothers and fathers are afraid to let their children out of their homes.

"Look at the Lindbergh case. Kidnappers have taken little children, killed them and then jockeyed for huge sums of money. Now they have taken to kidnapping men and women for the purpose of extracting money from distracted relatives."

Governor Rolph's attitude toward kidnappers was expressed further in his statement that he would like to parole to San José citizens all San Quentin and Folsom prison inmates convicted of kidnapping.

This statement naturally made an uproar, and Rolph was violently denounced by most of the newspapers of the country, and by a long list of assorted bigwigs, including Franklin D. Roosevelt, Herbert Hoover, Ray Lyman Wilbur, Rabbi Stephen S. Wise and scores of Governors, mayors, bishops and other dignitaries, but he stood firm. On November 28 the Associated Press reported that he was having a check made at San Quentin and Folsom to find out how many kidnappers were locked up, and then went on:

"No kidnapper will ever be turned loose or pardoned while I am Governor," was another statement by the Governor, who added that "kidnappers will learn they're not safe even in our penitentiaries.

"The aroused people of that fine city of San José were so enraged at the slaying and kidnapping from their midst of that fine youth it was only natural that, peaceful and law-abiding as they are, they should rise and mete out swift justice to these two murderers and kidnappers.

"They probably were reminded of the meting out of justice by the vigilantes in the early days of San Francisco's history. And the pioneer blood in their veins caused them in the height of their feeling to avenge the murder and kidnapping.

"The sheriff and law-enforcement officers of that community did all they could to preserve order and uphold due respect for the law. They did their duty as far as it was possible, but the might of the people was determined to serve notice to the world that kidnapping and murder will not be tolerated in California."

The Executive's attitude was first disclosed before the two men were lynched, when he said he would not send the National Guard troops "to protect those two guys.

"They made a good job of it and I hope this lesson will serve in every State of the Union," the Governor said emphatically. "I don't think they will arrest anyone for the lynchings. If they do I'll pardon them.

"It is about time the people should have comfort in their homes. This kidnapping business has become so bad that mothers and fathers are afraid to let their children out of their homes. Now they have taken to kidnapping men and women for the purpose of extracting money from distracted relatives."

The uproar over the lynching soon died down, and when Rolph died on June 3, 1934, many of his severest critics let it be known that they regretted his passing. Meanwhile, Evelyn Holmes, the widow of one of the lynched kidnappers, had entered suit against him for $1,050,000, alleging that he was primarily responsible for her late husband's butchery, but nothing ever came of this. When a public funeral service was held in the San Francisco City Hall, Hoover led the procession of mourners, and among the ecclesiastics who took part were the Most Rev. Edward J. Hanna, the Catholic archbishop of San Francisco; Dean J. Wilmer Gresham, of the Episcopal cathedral, and Rabbi Irving F. Reichert, all of whom had denounced the deceased at the time of the lynching. On September 14, 1934, the California Toll Bridge Authority passed a resolution dedicating the new San Francisco-Oakland bridge "as a lasting memorial to the memory of the late Governor James Rolph, Jr."

526 *a young man named Franklin D. Roosevelt*: This was Roosevelt's first appearance as an advocate of Al. He had yet to suffer the attack of poliomyelitis which soon crippled him, and was still a fine figure of a man. But his tenor voice, later so vast a success over the radio, made a poor impression upon the Democrats at San Francisco, and his speech was without question the worst failure of the convention. I mentioned that failure in my dispatch to the *Evening Sun*, only to find when I got back to Baltimore that I had unwittingly wounded Van Lear Black, who knew Roosevelt intimately and was very fond of him. Up to that time I knew nothing of this friendship. Roosevelt, despite his flop (or maybe because of it, for everyone present knew that Harding would be elected in November) was given second place on the ticket. He put Al into nomination at New York in 1924 and at Houston in 1928, and remained his partisan until 1930, when he began an effort to get the 1932 nomination for himself. This treason to his old leader and benefactor was typical of the man, and had fateful consequences in American history.

526 *Half Moon Bay*: My companion on the taxi trip to Half Moon Bay was Jane O'Roarke, then leading woman of a stock company in San Francisco. I saw a lot of her during the rest of

Mencken (typing) covering the 1936 Republican National Convention. Unknown photographer, June 1936.

my visit, and afterward in New York, where she took up her residence in 1921 or 1922. It was generally assumed by everyone who knew us, including George Sterling, that we were engaged in fornication, but, perhaps rather curiously, this was not true. Jane was a strange character, and very amusing. She lived in New York with her mother and a boy who passed as her nephew, but may have been her son. She had a large and beautiful apartment, and I naturally assumed that she had plenty of money. I was thus greatly surprised when newspapers reported that she had been jugged on a charge of getting her furnishings by various kinds of fraud. She was not only accused, but convicted, and for several years she was in prison. On her liberation she resumed her evil ways and this time was sent up for five or six years. She wrote to me several times in 1940, but I did not reply. In 1942 George Jean Nathan told me that she was back in New York, and apparently well supplied with money. She was a handsome creature, though somewhat too stout for my taste.

528 *not excepting Waycross, Ga., and Elwood, Ind.*: Sara and I were at Waycross, Ga., in 1933, stopping off on our way from Sea Island to Montgomery, Ala. The name of the place had been familiar to me since my boyhood, for many a shipment of cigars from the factory of Aug. Mencken & Bro. was addressed to it, and I often assisted in packing and addressing them. It turned out to be an almost incredibly dismal place, full of hideous Methodist and Baptist churches but showing no sign whatsoever of civilization. We had lunch in the principal hotel —a dreadful meal, indeed. The chicken, according to Sara, was cold-storage, and all the vegetables came out of cans. We drove to Waycross from Sea Island through the most desolate landscape I have ever seen—all gaunt pine woods. Nothing comestible was in sight save a few razor-back hogs—not even a chicken. The occasional farms were all small and miserable, and the yokels looked like savages.

I visited Elwood, Ind., in 1940. It was the native place of Wendell L. Willkie and he returned there to be notified of his nomination to the presidency by the Republicans. I found that it was a manufacturing town, once fairly prosperous, that had fallen upon evil days. The weather was very hot, and I subsisted mainly on Coca-cola. I tried to find iced tea, but there was only one stand in town that offered it, and there it was undrinkable. The food in the only restaurant, kept by a Greek, was almost uneatable. Yet the countryside, a few miles from Elwood, was smiling and prosperous. It had been ruined by the busted boom.

535 *to brew a drinkable home-brew*: I was taught to brew by Harry Rickel, of Detroit. He was a lawyer but his people had been in the malting business for years, and he knew all about brewing. He sent me not only detailed directions but also my first supplies, and after they ran out he found me a reliable *Lieferant* in Paul Weidner, of 350 Gratiot avenue, Detroit. By 1922 I was no longer dependent on Weidner, for a number of dealers in home-brewers' materials had sprung up in Baltimore. One of the best was a retired brewmaster named Brohmayer, who had set up a shop for the sale of home-brewers' supplies. He knew the chemistry and bacteriology of fermentation and gave me some very useful tips. Also, he supplied me with the best German and Bohemian hops and very good malt syrup.

At the start all home-brewers made their beer too strong. It took us a couple of years to learn that we should be sparing with the malt syrup, and especially with the corn sugar that we used to reinforce it. My first brew, put into quart bottles with old-time wire and rubber spring-caps (for the sale of crown corks had not yet begun) was bottled too soon, and as a result most of the bottles exploded. They were stored in the sideyard in Hollins street and the explosions greatly alarmed our neighbor, William Deemer. As soon as we had mastered the trick August and I made very good beer—or, rather, ale, for that is what it always was, technically speaking. When I was married in 1930 and moved to an apartment in Cathedral street, I set up a brewery there. I had kept a sort of cellar-book from the start, but the early years of it have been lost. Here are some entries for my last six months in Hollins street in 1930:

1. One can German light malt; one can German dark; one can Guilford; a pound and a half white sugar; two ounces American hops. Brewed March 9; bottled March 19.

2. Three cans German dark; a pound and a half corn sugar; two ounces Bohemian hops; corn sugar in bottles. Brewed April

20; bottled April 23. Bottled too soon. On opening the first bottle the beer boiled out, and I threw out the whole batch.

3. Five pounds Brohmeyer malt; five ounces German hops; a pound and a half corn sugar; one ounce hops in crock at the end of fermentation; Chattolanee water. Fleischmann's yeast. Brewed May 28; bottled June 1. A light, somewhat flabby brew.

4. Five pounds Brohmeyer malt; five ounces German hops; two pounds corn sugar; one ounce hops in crock; Chattolanee water; Fleischmann's yeast. Brewed June 1; bottled June 5. Good flavor. [. . .]

One of my early pupils was Max Brödel, professor of art as applied to medicine at the Johns Hopkins. He knew a great deal about bacteriology and became the best brewer within my range of acquaintance. Some of his brews, in fact, had a genuinely professional smack. He had a Summer place in Canada, and one Autumn, on returning in his car, he found after crossing the American border that there were three empty bottles of Labatt's ale in his baggage. There was some yeast sediment in them, and when he reached Baltimore he proceeded to cultivate this sediment at the Johns Hopkins. He soon had it free from contamination, and was presently brewing a really remarkable imitation of Labatt's ale, which has a peculiar (and very agreeable) flavor. Another time he cultivated a ferment from the wild yeast on grape-skins, and from it produced an ale that had a decidedly wine-like flavor. In 1921 Philip Goodman, who was also one of my pupils, brought home some dried yeast from the Löwenbräu brewery at Munich, and Brödel cultivated and purified it, and in 1925 Goodman brought home a test-tube of Hackerbräu yeast. Brödel labored long and hard over these bootlegged jewels, and finally produced pure strains. He gave me cultures of them and I tried them with success, but getting the cultures from him was some trouble, so I returned to the commercial yeasts, which had been perfected for brewing by 1925. In this humanitarian work Brödel had the aid of various Johns Hopkins colleagues, including Stanhope Bayne-Jones, who was associate professor of bacteriology in 1922 and 1923. The strains that he and they purified and cultivated survived at the Johns Hopkins until Prohibition finally blew up.

539 *the quarters of the out-of-town correspondents*: Young Dan Hanna, grandson of old Mark, was then general manager of one of the Cleveland papers. He installed a house of mirth for visiting journalists in the Hollenden Hotel, with a large stock of more or less potable whiskeys and gins and a staff of colored waiters. But this house of mirth was barred to his own staff and to all other Cleveland newspaper men save a few higher-ups. Thus the working journalists of the town suffered a severe drought, and Paul Patterson and I succored more than one of them out of the supplies we had brought from Baltimore.

545   *they treated me with great courtesy*: The story that I was run out of Dayton by the local Bible-searchers will probably go on until the Scopes trial is forgotten at last. Under date of December 27, 1925, I received the following from G. W. Rappleyea, manager of the Dayton mine of the Cumberland Coal & Iron Company:

> An hour after you left Dayton the defenders of the faith were looking for you to ride you out of town on a rail—yes, *after* you left. Before looking for you they made certain that you were on your way to New York.

This Rappleyea, a New Yorker who claimed to be a descendant of the first white child born on Manhattan Island, was probably primarily responsible for the Scopes trial. When Dayton was disturbed by reports that John F. Scopes was teaching evolution in the town high-school, it was Rappleyea who proposed, maliciously, that he be prosecuted. The yaps fell for it, believing that the case would give the place a lot of favorable publicity, and were greatly incensed when the publicity turned out to be blistering and ignominious, and Rappleyea began gloating over them. Along with the letter just quoted he sent me the following account of his adventures afterward:

> ### How It Feels to be the Only Evolutionist in Dayton
> #### By Dr. G. W. Rappleyea
>
> (I wrote this on request, but did not have nerve enough to let it go. They would kill me if it went out under my name.)
>
> Many interesting events have taken place in Dayton since the curtain dropped on the last act of the world's most famous trial last July.
>
> When I conceived the idea of testing the constitutionality of Tennessee's Anti-evolution Law last May, there were just four

evolutionists in Dayton—John F. Scopes, a high-school teacher, who later became the defendant; my pastor, Howard G. Byrd, a young Methodist preacher; my friend and attorney, Judge John L. Godsey; and myself. As soon as the trial was over, Scopes left for the University of Chicago to take a post-graduate course. Judge Godsey was quickly converted to the Fundamentalists' viewpoint and made his peace with the bar and community; Reverend Byrd was shamefully assaulted and driven out of town; thus I became the only "infidel" and like the eagle at sea—I was alone.

Immediately after the death of Mr. Bryan, and after all the reporters had departed, the 15,000 Fundamentalists which compose the population of Rhea County, of which Dayton is the county seat, proceeded to make their community safe for the Fundamentalists. Dayton had no resident newspaper correspondent and when Mr. Bryan died I promptly wired a brief telegram to Universal Service, who called me on long distance from New York, asking me to file a complete story as quickly as possible, and in the meantime they were sending their nearest representative from Nashville. I had written and dispatched 3500 words before the first newspaper men arrived from Chattanooga. The following morning I turned my notes and information over to the Universal representative and retired. Although I had asked and expected no pay, I received $200 for my services. Then the storm broke. Townspeople and attorneys in the Scopes prosecution denounced me for commercializing Mr. Bryan's death: "Why did he do it? Was it any of his business to notify the outside world? It would have been different if he had been a regular correspondent, but he had opposed Mr. Bryan and then had been the first to bring the news." Such were the comments to be heard on every hand.

Very soon afterwards Dayton held a memorial service in the courthouse in honor of Mr. Bryan, and efforts were made to organize an association to found the proposed Bryan Fundamentalist College. Like every Main Street town, there are two factions. For two hours these factions fought and wrangled over the appointment of the committee to handle all of the money that would come to Dayton from the outside world to build the college. Following this display of brotherly regard in memory of their departed leader, I met on the street one of the prosecutors of Scopes and remarked, "Looks to me as though you folks are trying to commercialize Bryan's death in a way that would make my little reporting stunt seem a trifle," to which the legal defender of the faith replied, "You are sacrilegious, and what's more, you have lost a lot of friends by insisting on holding to your views."

Soon another memorial meeting was held when Judge Raulston opened the regular term of court. The evangelical judge is a good Christian and supports the doctrine that "While the light holds out to burn the vilest sinner may return." Early in the proceedings I had engaged Judge Godsey as the first attorney to help defend Scopes. When arrangements were made he accepted a retainer through me from the American Civil Liberties Union, who were financing the case. No other Dayton lawyer would consent to have anything to do with the case on account of the state of public sentiment, and on the day the trial opened Judge Godsey announced his withdrawal from the case. After Judge Raulston completed the memorial session of court one of the State's attorneys arose and explained that Judge Godsey did not know what he was getting into when I retained him—that he did not anticipate the defense expected to make the trial an occasion for a general attack upon the Bible, and when he found out that he was going to have to be associated with Clarence Darrow he promptly withdrew. Judge Godsey himself then informed the court that everything the preceding speaker had said was true, and that he wished to be restored to the good opinion of the bar and community. The evangelical judge promptly forgave him and cleared the way for him to practise in Rhea county. Judge Godsey is now a member of the board of directors of the Bryan Fundamentalist School Association. I too would have found a welcome at the mourners' bench at the same time, but I remained stubbornly impenitent. Then followed insults; then came a series of arrests for violation of traffic rules, and still I refused to leave town or change my views.

On October 30, Dr. John Roach Straton was scheduled to speak in Dayton. In the eyes of Daytonians Dr. Straton has assumed the mantle of their fallen leader. The town was greatly honored by his visit, but horrors! what in the world would Dr. Straton say if he were to come in town and find an "infidel" among them! I was still in town like the fly in the ointment! Something would have to be done about it. The town commissioners met. The Chamber of Commerce had a meeting. The hour for Dr. Straton's arrival was rapidly approaching. The situation was becoming desperate. It was already three o'clock and the great Fundamentalist leader was to arrive at five o'clock. I was walking down Main street in a casual manner when one of the town's two policemen called me into a barber-shop, then asked me to sit down. I thought he was going to sit down by me and discuss a question of giving the city free road material, which practice I had stopped some several days before. The first thing I knew I was hit over the head—a rather bad gash was cut in the scalp. The policeman was pulled off by two friends of mine who fortunately happened to be in the barber-shop at the time. After having the scalp wound dressed by a physician I appealed to the City Recorder for protection. Instead of giving me protection that Recorder proceeded to explain the reason why the policeman had made the attack. This policeman, John Coleman, having discovered that he did not complete the job as he was expected to do, went out to finish it as soon as he could get away from those who were holding him. He proceeded to carry out his intentions while I was pleading with the City Recorder for protection. The other policeman of the town interfered and held him off. For this disturbance the policeman who made the attack was arrested—not for hitting me, but for disturbing the peace of the courtroom. A Fundamentalist leader paid the fine and told the other policeman who interfered that he should have been fined for interfering and prohibiting the ferocious cop to complete his job, but still I forgave them, because "They know not what they do."

The Liberal Church of Denver, Colorado, has ordained me Bishop of Dayton. I accepted with the reservation that I would not be expected to establish a Liberal Church in Dayton because I would be as successful as a lone Klansman in full regalia distributing Ku Klux literature from the steps of St. Patrick's Cathedral on the 17th of March, but perhaps the title of bishop will give me some protection in the future. It is a crime in this country to strike a minister, so perhaps they would even hesitate to insult a bishop.

The attitude of the community can be summed up in 22:20: "As they gather iron into the midst of the furnace to blow the fire upon and melt it, so will I gather you in my anger and leave you there to melt you."

As this document shows plainly, Rappleyea was something of a Pecksniff; indeed, he was an arrant fraud. He wrote to me a number of times after the Scopes trial, and was inviting me to revisit Dayton before the end of 1925. I must have replied (of course not seriously) that I had it in mind to do so, for in the letter already quoted he said:

I note with interest that you hope to come down to Dayton again. I always knew you to be a fearless man but if you should carry out your promise I will see that *Liberty* awards you their thousand dollar prize for bravery. . . .

Come on down. You can be my guest as long as you wish to stay. A few of my trusty miners will be your bodyguard. My car is equipped with bullet-proof glass. An army 45 is in the car at all times. You don't think this is necessary? Neither did I. After my friend, the Rev. Byrd, was knocked down and kicked around and chased out of town, I still did not think it was necessary; but after I had had my head split open and my blood spilled on Main street I found that so far as Dayton is concerned the Christian world after 1900 years does not yet understand the philosophy of Christ.

He then went on:

I dare say that the trial would have done some good for Dayton if hate had not so poisoned the system of Wm. J. Bryan that it killed him. This caused the Christian business men of Dayton to seek five million dollars for a Bryan Fundamentalist University.

They believe that to be successful with the university they must hate all unbelievers! That old moss-back Straton has been down here with his full line of bunk together with all the other fakers in the country, and they have talked so much that the poor morons have had no chance to reflect on the facts which were brought out at the trial.

I don't blame the yokels! They can't think for themselves. Half of the 300 miners that work for me cannot write their own names and the other half never went to school more than eighteen months. The ones I blame are the men who know better but who have in Dayton changed the cross of Christ into a dollar mark, and the high pressure dollar chasers who are here to get their percentage of the funds of the Bryan University.

I make it a rule never to engage in any verbal conflict with these fakers in Dayton, but a few nights ago I was seated in the drug-store reading a newspaper while waiting for my wife, who had gone to the movies. A few yokels were present gathered around the stove; also the faker in chief, who claims several college degrees and who has been engaged at something like seven hundred and fifty a month to raise the five million for the university.

Several remarks were passed for my benefit. The yokels gathered closer. Their leader who knew the Bible from cover to cover was like the bully of the block with a chip on his shoulder when a new kid arrives. Something was said about Darrow, Mencken and the rest of my friends being headed for Hell. "Well, Hell will be a better place when they arrive," I replied and the battle was on. "Do you believe that Hell is paved with infants?" I asked. "Of course I do," answered the faker in chief, drawing himself proudly erect. "To use John Wesley's words, 'Your God is my devil,'" I shot back at him and thus it went on for an hour. It does make them mad for me to quote John Wesley. That seems so sacrilegious to them. It is quite impossible for them to understand why I should defend the philosophy of Christ and not believe in the Virgin Birth or the divinity of Christ. [. . .]

Rappleyea made constant efforts to get something out of the notoriety that the Scopes trial and his subsequent troubles brought him. Among other things he undertook to go on a lecture tour. The Adams Lecture Bureau, 1480 Broadway, New York (operated by one Franz Josef Emmerich, who tried hard in those days to induce me to lecture under his management) got out a circular describing him as "the scientist who started the Scopes trial," and essayed to get engagements for him, but he wrote to me on January 8, 1926, that it had been able to book but two. This, of course, was not enough to cover expenses, so the proposed lecture tour blew up. [. . .]

I always suspected that Rappleyea's doctorate was imaginary. Dayton gradually became too hot for him, and before the end of January, 1926, he had quit his job with the Cumberland Coal & Iron Company and gone to Mobile, Ala., where he went to work for an outfit of realtors calling itself the Gulf Coast Investment Company. A few years later he was in Annapolis, Md., as manager of a small company building motorboats. He wrote to me from there, proposing to come to see me in Baltimore, but I put him off, and in fact never saw him. Since 1930 or thereabout I have not heard from him.

546 *The lawyers for Scopes*: Of the four lawyers for Scopes only Hays knew any law. Neal was a curious character who ran a small law-school in Knoxville, and was the only genuine Liberal in Tennessee. He was an earnest and worthy man, but highly impractical, and his frequent efforts to get public office always ended in ignominious defeat. He was one of the most filthy men, in his person, that I have ever encountered. Indeed, he looked more like a hobo than a publicist, and on his occasional visits to Washington his unkempt appearance always attracted attention.

I had never met Darrow until just before the Scopes trial began, but we became friendly at once, and I saw him often during the remaining years of his life, and heard from him even oftener. His letters to me, and those of his wife Ruby, are in my letter-file under his name, to go to the New York Public Library at my death. Darrow always dropped in on me when he was in Baltimore. On one such occasion, late in 1930, we had ourselves photographed contemplating sadly a huge lithograph of the Pabst Brewery at Milwaukee which hung in my dining-room on Cathedral street—a wedding present from my brother August. This photograph was published in many newspapers during the months following.

My opinion of Darrow was never very high. He was an orator, not a lawyer, and his frequent pronunciamentoes on legal and social questions were usually banal. Once I asked him why he spent so much time touring the country to engage in futile, puerile debates with Prohibitionists, Fundamentalists and other

Mencken with Clarence Darrow at Mencken's apartment, 704 Cathedral Street. Unknown photographer from the Baltimore *News*, November 17, 1930.

such idiots, many of them clergymen. His reply was: "Because I have never heard anything in this world that I like better than the sound of my own voice." I picked up a lot about him from his former law partner, Edgar Lee Masters, and what I picked up was generally unfavorable. Masters, in fact, said flatly that he was an unmitigated fraud, and offered plenty of evidence of it. His wife Ruby was really almost incredible—a woman much younger than her husband and showing some traces of former beauty, but extraordinarily silly. Her usual salutation on the postcards that she sent to Sara and me was "Dear Folks." Darrow had made a good deal of money in his time, but when he died in 1938 he was not far from broke. [. . .]

Darrow, in his later years, kept the soft pedal on the fact that he had been an eager supporter of Bryan during the Commoner's three campaigns for the presidency, and was also very reluctant to recall that he had been a violent Hun-hunter in World War I.

549   *Bill Hutchinson*: Hutchinson was a Pennsylvanian, born at Reading in 1896. He began work as a reporter in Reading at the age of seventeen and during the seven years following worked for papers in the East and Middle West. In 1920 he joined the International News Service (Hearst) and in 1921 was sent to its Washington bureau. On the death of George R. Holmes in 1939 he was made head of the bureau. He continued, however, as an active reporter, and in 1942 scored a notable beat on the electrocution of half a dozen German agents accused of landing explosives from a submarine. Roosevelt tried to throw an air of mystery about the execution, but Hutch kept watch at the jail, and so managed to discover that it had taken place some time before the reporters of the other press associations got wind of it. At some time or other during his very busy career he managed to study law, and is now (1943) a member of the bar of the District of Columbia, but he has never practised. He was, in 1925, a fine figure of a young journalist, and it was the trade gossip that when he got to a small town to cover a story his first step was to make love to the head operator in the local telephone exchange. In most cases, so it was said, he was soon entertaining this lady in his room, and after that he had access to all the news passing over her wires.

551 *Henry M. Hyde*: Hyde was nearly sixty years old at the time of the Scopes trial, but he was still a brisk reporter, and in fact remained in active service until 1941, when deafness forced him to retire. He was born at Freeport in Northern Illinois and was a congenital and incurable Republican, but he knew how to write objectively, and it was seldom that any hint of his private sentiments got into his reports for the *Evening Sun*. He began his newspaper career in Chicago in 1913, and for a while was London correspondent of the Chicago *Tribune*. By 1920 or thereabout he had amassed enough of a competence by writing books—none of them of any consequence, but nearly all of them very profitable—to enable him to shelve his typewriter and go to live on a farm that he had bought near Charlottesville, Va., not far from Thomas Jefferson's "Monticello."

When Paul Patterson became head of the Baltimore *Sunpapers* he induced Hyde, with whom he had worked in Chicago, to emerge from his retirement and join the staff of the *Evening Sun*, and thereafter, for nearly twenty years, he was one of its reliables. He knew news, he wrote well, and he was a completely honest man. In the days when I had contact with the young reporters of the staff I always advised them to model themselves upon him. Unhappily, his later years were full of trouble. His only son, Robert, came out of World War I a drunkard, and settled down in the character of a nuisance to his father. In 1940 or thereabout Robert married and presently had a child, but his wife soon left him, and after that he and the child were quartered on Hyde at Charlottesville. In addition, Hyde had to take care of his wife's old mother, a woman more than ninety years old, requiring the constant attention of a nurse.

Meanwhile, his deafness kept on increasing, and it became more and more difficult for him to do his work for the *Evening Sun*, which, after the advent of the New Deal, consisted mainly in reporting congressional hearings at Washington. He gave up at last because he began to fear that he would make some serious error in taking down testimony and so get the paper into a libel suit. He was retired on a pension of $5,000 a year. Early in 1943 Mrs. Hyde died suddenly, and the poor old fellow, now seventy-seven years old, was left in a dreadful mess.

"The real trouble with me," he wrote to me on May 23, 1943, "is that I am too damned old."

551 *he continued these efforts by mail*: To my great regret I did not preserve any of Pastor Martin's letters. They were extremely curious documents. After his death, in 1940 or thereabout, his daughter wrote to me that he had died in full hope of saving me soon or late. He was typical of the old-time Southern evangelists of the better sort. For years and years he had roved the Bible country warning the yokels to repent before it was too late, but he never indulged in the vituperations common to the gaudier sort of gospel-spreaders. Even on the subjects of Darwinism and Prohibition he was relatively moderate.

552 *Bryan, of course, was the star of the show*: When I first encountered Bryan at Dayton he was extremely polite to me, mainly because I had just printed an article in the *Nation* arguing that, whatever the truth about evolution, the Legislature of Tennessee had a clear right to prohibit its teaching in the public schools of the state, which were its creatures. But after my dispatches to the *Evening Sun*, reprinted daily in the Chattanooga *News*, began to reach him he frowned upon me, and by the end of the first week of the trial he was glaring ferociously every time he saw me.

558 *she blushed prettily and answered*: Harriet Beecher Stowe had long anticipated Doris's feelings. She said in *Dred*, 1856: "If ever a woman feels proud of her lover it is when she sees him as a successful public speaker."

559 *a Catholic bishop*: The bishop was the Most Rev. Francis Clement Kelley, D.D., of the Roman Catholic diocese of Oklahoma from 1924 to 1930, and after that of Oklahoma City and Tulsa. When Sara and I sailed for the Mediterranean in the *Columbus* in February, 1934, he was one of the other passengers. I had had some communication with him before then, and he introduced himself the first night out. After that I spent a great deal of time with him, for he was a very amusing fellow. He was in charge of a party of Catholic pilgrims bound for both Rome and the Holy Land, but he paid very little attention to them. One night, as we were sitting in the smokeroom he told me that he was much pestered by a Protestant woman aboard who insisted on consulting him about religion. She was, he said, one of those dismal females who shop from theologian to theologian. She had tried Christian Science, and was now eager for Catholic instruction. Kelley said that he had been seeking to avoid her, but that she cornered him at every opportunity. I thereupon volunteered to take her on—that is, I offered to give her instruction in Catholic doctrine, and so keep her away from His Excellency and the other clergy aboard. He rose to the idea eagerly, and when, a little later, the woman barged into the smoke-room, he turned her over to me but sat by to hear me perform. I must have done pretty well, for when we got rid of her an hour later she said that she believed she was almost ready to join the Church, and Kelley certified that I had not made a single mistake in my exposition of its doctrines. One of her stumbling blocks, it appeared, was the dogma of papal infallibility, and I managed to convince her that it was perfectly logical and obviously sound.

When the ship got to Haifa and its passengers swarmed down into Palestine Kelley got rid of his Catholic pilgrims by accepting an invitation to stay with the Patriarch of Jerusalem, an Italian. On rejoining the ship he told me that he had had an unpleasant time of it, for the weather was chilly and the Patriarch's house was unheated. One of the minor clerics on the ship, housed in the tourist cabin with the poorer pilgrims, was a German priest from North Dakota of the name of J. G. Sailer. After we got home he took to writing to me, and incidentally to grafting books from me. On May 17, 1943, after reading *Heathen Days*, he wrote as follows:

> My own impression of our trip to Jerusalem was minus. I could not muster the expected religious emotion. A mere corner of my church gives me more quiet reflection and moments of deep prayer than all the holy places combined. After expecting for decades to make this trip—such a disappointment!

Not only the holy places displeased Father Sailer, but also Bishop Kelley. Along with his letter came a pencilled sheet reading:

> That good bp. left us (in the tourist) to our own devices whilst he and his mgr. secretary toured the country in the pontifical car of the Patriarch of Jerusalem. He bothered very

little for his supposed pilgrims, but so do the politicians all over history.

Kelley, in fact, could hardly be called diligent in the labors of his ghostly office. He is seldom in his diocese, but devotes most of his time to traveling about the country. He has been to see me in Baltimore several times. Once he told me that there are very few Catholics worth knowing in Oklahoma. The poor, he said, are mainly idiots, and the rich try to stave off demands for money by setting up quarrels with their bishop.

577 *at Tiberias*: It was not until I got home that I learned that Tiberias is 680 feet below sea-level. This is probably the nearest I have ever got to the center of the earth. The lowest point in the Salton Sea region of Southern California, which I traversed by the Southern Pacific Railroad in 1926, is but 280 feet below sea-level. My highest leap into the air was made in 1920, when I crossed the Rockies by the Union Pacific. This was at Sherman, Wyoming, the elevation of which is 8,013 feet.

585 *I am now more than half convinced that Jennings really believed it*: That there was a touch of mental unsoundness in Bryan I always believed, just as I believe the same of F. D. Roosevelt. He had frequent moods of high exaltation, and his reasoning was seldom logical. Under date of San Francisco, May 5, 1943, I received the following curious letter from one P. P. Sewell, who described himself as having been "fourteen years in the Orient on land and at sea":

> Bryan travelled on the P & O SS. *Palethia* in 1901 from Singapore to Colombo. The *Palethia* and *Massilia* were sister flush-deck ships. The junior officers' quarters were in a deck-house just forward of the mainmast, quite near the forecastle head. Accompanying W.J.B. were his wife and his daughter Ruth. The night after leaving Singapore—after 7 P.M. dinner, about 8:30 P.M.—W.J.B. came to the forecastle head and hanging on to the anchor catfalls, started yelling: "I am the God!—the great God and only living God!" He kept this up until one of the junior watch-keeping officers requested him to go aft to the saloon deck, as the juniors had the 12 to 4 A.M. and 4 to 8 A.M. watches and needed sleep. Bryan complied with the officer's request and retired aft.
>
> The next morning he took a swipe at his cabin steward— Tommy Sutherland, a wee blond headed boy—with a heavy

hair-brush, knocked him out, and blood flowed. Bryan quieted
down. Ship's doctor was called, etc. Late that afternoon Bryan
started yelling in earnest and that night was transferred to the
second saloon cabin on the lower deck—there being no passengers there—with instructions to the second saloon steward
(or chief steward second saloon) that he was not to come on
deck. Next morning W.J.B. was dressed and coming up on deck.
Plodder White, the second saloon steward, stood at the top of
the stairs barring the gangway, telling him he must remain below. W.J.B. hauled off and caught Steward White one wallop in
the big bay window and down White went, gasping for breath.
W.J.B. was overpowered, and put in a cabin by the ship's doctor,
with handcuffs on and perhaps under opiates or chloral hydrate.

    We on the ship didn't know much about the U.S.A. and
political trends, so we decided he had been on a jag or had a
touch of the tropical sun. W.J.B. went ashore at Colombo with
his wife and daughter—Mrs. Bryan giving Steward Sutherland
two £5 notes as compensation for the poke on the head. W.J.B.
afterwards toured India and wrote a lot of tripe on the British
government. The only other time I have mentioned this was to
Alfred Holman, owner and editor of the San Francisco *Argo-
naut*, when Bryan was running for President in 1908. Holman
asked me to keep quiet on the subject, as Bryan was probably
sick and was a strict teetotaler.

Bryan's daughter Ruth, at the time of this voyage, was sixteen
years old. Soon after their return to the United States she was
married to an English artist. The artist was in the Bryan home
painting a portrait of her father, and one day the old man caught
the two together in a very compromising position. He sent for
a clergyman at once and had them married. The marriage begun so inauspiciously did not last, and in a little while the artist
returned to England and there was a divorce, but not, I think,
before a child was born. In her autobiography in *Who's Who in
America* Ruth does not give the name of this first husband. Her
second was Major Reginald Owen, of the Royal Engineers, British Army. They were married in 1910 and Owen died in 1927.
Once her husband and father were both dead Ruth began to
step out, and when she was elected to Congress from Florida
in 1928 her booze parties became famous in Washington. After
serving two terms she was appointed minister to Denmark by
Roosevelt, and proceeded to Copenhagen. There she snared

a Danish Junker named Borge Rohde, and they were married in 1936.

590 *Louisville*: The principal citizen of Louisville in those days was Robert W. Bingham, later ambassador to England. He was very rich, and owned, among other things, the Louisville *Courier-Journal*. He had got his money by marrying as his second wife the widow of Henry M. Flagler, the oil millionaire and Florida railroad magnate. There was something suspicious about the death of either Mrs. Flagler or the first wife, and for a while Bingham was under a cloud. The *Courier-Journal* was supporting Prohibition when Al Smith visited Louisville, but Bingham sent out invitations to the correspondents on the Smith train, and let it be known that there would be plenty to drink. Henry M. Hyde and I naturally refused to be the guests of so thumping a hypocrite, but many of the other correspondents went to the party, and it turned out to be extremely wet—in fact, so wet that a number of the younger reporters got drunk, and one of them missed the campaign train when it left, and lost his job in consequence. Bingham was a heavy contributor to the Roosevelt campaign fund in 1932, and was rewarded with the ambassadorship. He died at the Johns Hopkins Hospital, Baltimore, in 1937.

Chronology

1880   Born Henry Louis Mencken on September 12, at what was then 380 West Lexington Street, Baltimore, Maryland, now 811 West Lexington Street; eldest child of August Mencken and Anna Abhau Mencken. (Grandfather Burkhardt Ludwig Mencken, born 1828 in Laas, Germany, landed in Baltimore, November 1848; was naturalized October 1852, and set up a tobacco business. Father, born June 16, 1854, established August Mencken & Bro. between 1873 and 1875, managing it with his brother Henry, and building it into one of the most successful cigar manufacturers along the South Atlantic coast. An agnostic and a high-tariff Republican, August was a loyal member of the Masonic order, also part owner of the major-league baseball club of Washington, D.C. Mother, Anna Abhau, born June 11, 1858, was the daughter of Carl Heinrich Abhau from Hesse, Germany. August and Anna were married on November 11, 1879.)

1882   Brother, Charles Edward, born May 16.

1883   Family moves to 1524 Hollins Street, in a prosperous German-American neighborhood in West Baltimore, facing Union Square.

1886   Mencken enrolls at F. Knapp's Institute, a private school, in September. Sister Anna Gertrude born November 17.

1888   Begins piano lessons. Receives a self-inking printing press for Christmas.

1889   Brother, August, born February 18. Reads Mark Twain's *Huckleberry Finn*, which makes a huge impact on him. Family begins spending summers in Ellicott City, Howard County, west of Baltimore (1889–1892), and Mt. Washington (1892–1899), then a northwestern suburb.

1892   Mencken enters Baltimore Polytechnic Institute, a public high school, on September 5.

1893   Mencken keenly interested in chemistry, photography, journalism, and literature. Visits the Enoch Pratt Free Library, reads four or five books a week, mostly English literature (including Dickens, Chaucer, Shakespeare, Herrick, Pepys, Addison, Steele, Pope, Swift, Johnson, Boswell, Fielding, Smollett, Sterne, Arnold, Macaulay, George Eliot, Tennyson, Swinburne, Thackeray, Kipling). Mencken will later call the library "my school"; his brother August will recall that Mencken "read like an athlete." Fire engulfs August Mencken & Bro. Cigar factory, causing $25,000 worth of damage, December 2.

1895   Reads Stephen Crane's *The Red Badge of Courage*.

1896   Graduates at age 15 from the Baltimore Polytechnic Institute, with highest grade point average yet recorded, June 23. Publishes a poem ("Ode to the Pennant on the Centerfield Pole") anonymously in the Baltimore *American*, summer. Tells his father that he plans to become a newspaper reporter, but is strongly dissuaded. Starts full-time work as clerk and salesman at August Mencken & Bro.

1898   Subscribes to *The Criterion* (New York) and is influenced by the work of James Gibbons Huneker, Percival Pollard, Ambrose Bierce, Oscar Wilde, George Bernard Shaw, and Friedrich Nietzsche. Becomes an admirer of the prose style and ideas of Thomas Henry Huxley. Studies books on journalism; enrolls in a correspondence school, the Associated Newspaper Bureau School of Journalism in New York, and states his career goal is "to begin as a reporter & after that trust to hard work and luck for something better." Resolves to quit working at August Mencken & Bro.; his father asks him to postpone the decision for at least another year. In a moment of despair, Mencken contemplates suicide. August Mencken, Sr., collapses unconscious with acute kidney infection, December 31. (Mencken writes later: "I remember well how . . . I kept saying to myself that if my father died I'd be free at last . . . I had got along with him very well, but I detested business and was frantic to get into newspaper work.")

1899   Father dies on January 13 and is buried at Loudon Park Cemetery. Two weeks later Mencken visits the offices of the Baltimore *Herald* and asks for a job. First story published February 24. Hired at $7 a week, the youngest (and first) cub reporter on the *Herald* to get paid a salary, July 2. A poem addressed to Rudyard Kipling appears in December 1899 issue of *Bookman* magazine. Quits working part-time for his Uncle Henry at August Mencken & Bro.

to devote himself to journalism, which he later calls "the maddest, gladdest, damnedest existence ever enjoyed by mortal youth."

1900   Reads Edward Kingsbury's editorials in the New York *Sun*, George Ade's *Fables in Slang*, the work of Émile Zola. Discovers Theodore Dreiser's *Sister Carrie*. Works twelve hours a day, seven days a week reporting for the *Herald*, writing short stories, poetry, and articles for out-of-town newspapers. Suffers from chronic bronchitis. Travels to Jamaica to recover, June. Gets third raise in salary, to $14 a week, August. Assigned to cover presidential election between William Jennings Bryan and William McKinley, November.

1901   Salary increased to $18 a week, February 1. Covers fire that devastated Jacksonville, Florida, in May. Becomes drama critic of the *Herald*, September, and editor of *Sunday Herald*, October (holds both positions until October 1903). Becomes an advocate of the work of playwrights Shaw and Ibsen.

1903   Becomes city editor of the *Morning Herald* in October 1903. Publication of *Ventures Into Verse*, a book of poetry modeled on Kipling. Begins subscribing to a service that provides clippings mentioning him or his books. (The clippings will fill more than 100 volumes during his lifetime.)

1904   Fire destroys more than 140 acres and 1,500 buildings in downtown Baltimore, February 7–8. The *Herald* is printed in Washington and Philadelphia and does not miss a single issue. Mencken attends the Republican National Convention in Chicago, June 19–24, and the Democratic National Convention in St. Louis, July 5–11. Made city editor of the Baltimore *Evening Herald*, August 25. Saturday Night Club established, a group of musicians who meet regularly, with Mencken at the piano.

1905   Promoted to managing editor of the *Herald*. Publication of *George Bernard Shaw: His Plays*, first book-length study of Shaw.

1906   The *Herald* ceases publication, June 17. Becomes editor of the Baltimore *Sunday Sun*, July 25. Makes sweeping changes in typography and content; introduces poetry, music criticism by John Philip Sousa; runs a twenty-four-part report on the city's health concerns and serializes work by popular authors (such as George Ade's revised history of slang). Circulation climbs steadily.

1908   Publication of *The Philosophy of Friedrich Nietzsche*, first book in English on the philosopher. Meets Theodore Dreiser. First trip to Europe, March; he visits England and Germany. Meets George Jean Nathan, theater critic, in New York in May. Assumes additional duties as editorial writer for the *Sun* papers. Begins monthly book reviews for *The Smart Set*, November (to be continued until December 1923), and praises the work of James Branch Cabell, Twain, Joseph Conrad, and Dreiser among others.

1909   Works (in collaboration with Holger A. Koppel, Danish consul in Baltimore) on notes and introductions to a new edition of Ibsen's *A Doll's House* and *Little Eyolf*, to be published as part of *The Player's Ibsen*. The volumes are a commercial failure, and the series is discontinued.

1910   Baltimore *Evening Sun* established, April 18, with Mencken as an editor. Ghostwrites *What You Ought to Know About Your Baby* with Leonard Hirshberg. Publication of *The Gist of Nietzsche* and of *Men Versus the Man* (a debate in letters with socialist Robert Rives La Monte).

1911   Becomes close friends with Percival Pollard, American writer who widens Mencken's understanding of German culture. Begins "The Free Lance," a satirical daily column in the Baltimore *Evening Sun*, May 8, addressing issues of local public health, the plight of the city's African Americans, the women's movement, the American language, and the pretensions of moralists, and featuring humorous pieces including the kernel of what would become his fictitious history of the bathtub. "Before it had gone on a year," he later notes, "I knew precisely where I was heading."

1912   Travels to Europe in April, visiting England, France, Switzerland, and Germany. Covers the Democratic National Convention in Baltimore, June 28. Publication of *The Artist: A Drama Without Words*.

1913   Meets publisher Alfred A. Knopf. Covers suffragist parade in Washington, D.C., March 3.

1914   Meets and becomes close friends with James Gibbons Huneker, influential American critic. Sails to Europe with George Jean Nathan and Willard Huntington Wright,

April. Publication of *Europe After 8:15* with Nathan and Wright. First World War begins, July 28–August 4. Mencken and Nathan become coeditors of *The Smart Set*, September. Publishes material from writers including F. Scott Fitzgerald, Edgar Lee Masters, Sherwood Anderson, Willa Cather, Ben Hecht, Eugene O'Neill, and Ezra Pound, as well as British and European writers such as Alexei Tolstoy, Anatole France, D. H. Lawrence, and James Joyce. The book reviews by Mencken, as well as the theater criticism by Nathan, attract wide attention.

1915   German sinking of the British liner *Lusitania* on May 7 increases anti-German sentiment in the United States. First issue of *Parisienne* magazine, edited anonymously with Nathan, is launched (last issue under their editorship will be October 1916). Mencken's pro-German stance becomes dominant in his increasingly controversial "Free Lance" column, as he scrutinizes the role of the press and examines stories of deliberate propaganda. "The Free Lance" ends abruptly, without explanation, on October 23.

1916   Dreiser's novel *The "Genius"* is suppressed when passages are deemed obscene by the New York Society for the Prevention of Vice. Mencken solicits the support of the Author's League of America for a petition in defense of the book (the novel remains out of circulation until 1922). Launches *Saucy Stories*, which (from August to October) he edits anonymously with Nathan. Publication of *A Book of Burlesques* and *A Little Book in C Major*. Resigns editorship at the *Sun*. Sails to England, December 28; travels to Germany to report on World War I.

1917   Germany commences unrestricted submarine warfare against neutral shipping on February 1. Mencken departs Germany to cover the Liberal revolt in Cuba against the U.S.-supported government of President García Menocal. Arrives in Havana, March 5, and returns to the U.S. on March 14. Stops writing for the *Sun* with publication of last dispatch, March 29. The United States declares war on Germany, April 6. Espionage Act goes into effect June 15. Writes for the New York *Evening Mail* from June 18 to July 8, 1918. Mencken meets James Weldon Johnson, begins to focus attention on African American and cultural issues. "The Sahara of the Bozart," an indictment of southern culture, published in the New York *Evening*

Mail, November 13. "A Neglected Anniversary," Mencken's invented history of the bathtub, published in the New York *Evening Mail*, December 28. Publication of *A Book of Prefaces*, and of *Pistols for Two*, written with Nathan under the joint pseudonym "Owen Hatteras."

1918   The editor of the New York *Evening Mail*, Edward Rumley, is arrested July 8 over allegations that the paper received secret German government funding; control then passes to pro-war individuals and Mencken stops writing for it. (Mencken later reflects, "I stopped writing and believed I was done with newspaper work forever.") German language eliminated from Baltimore public elementary schools, July; anti-German feeling rampant. The Bureau of Investigation (later the FBI) opens a case file on Mencken; his mail is opened and he is watched by agents. Mencken's *Damn! A Book of Calumny* is published by his close friend, Broadway producer Philip Goodman, who also publishes *In Defense of Women* (later editions published by Knopf beginning in 1919). Germany signs armistice, November 11.

1919   Publication of *The American Language* (first edition quickly sells out) and *Prejudices: First Series*, which also proves successful. With *Sun* publishers Paul Patterson and Harry Black, Mencken helps develop plan for expanded national coverage and an independent approach. Attorney General Mitchell Palmer orders mass arrests of radicals and foreigners. Mencken becomes increasingly frustrated by his work at *The Smart Set*, telling a friend: "We live, not in a literary age, but in a fiercely political age."

1920   Begins series of regular Monday columns in the Baltimore *Evening Sun* (they continue until January 31, 1938), regularly denouncing interference with free speech and calling for civil rights for all Americans. Reads manuscript of *Main Street* by Sinclair Lewis and encourages its publication. With Nathan, launches *Black Mask*, a mystery magazine, April. Publication of *Prejudices: Second Series*. Publication of *Heliogabalus* and *The American Credo*, both written with Nathan. Publication of *The Anti-Christ* by Nietzsche, translated with an introduction by Mencken.

1921   Becomes contributing editor of *The Nation*, May (until December 1932). Covers the naval disarmament conference in Washington, D.C., November–December. Publication of the second edition of *The American Language*.

1922 Travels to England and Germany, August–October. Publication of *Prejudices: Third Series*.

1923 On May 8, while lecturing at Baltimore's Goucher College, he meets Sara Powell Haardt (born March 1, 1898, in Montgomery, Alabama), a fiction writer and member of the English faculty. Mencken solicits manuscripts from American writers for a new magazine focusing exclusively on American cultural and political themes, summer. Mencken and Nathan resign as coeditors of *The Smart Set*, December. Publication of the third edition of *The American Language*.

1924 First issue of *The American Mercury* is published in January with Mencken and Nathan as coeditors. Contributors will include Countee Cullen, James Weldon Johnson, W.E.B. Du Bois, Dorothy Parker, Sherwood Anderson, George Schuyler, as well as bricklayers, hoboes, bishops, senators, lawyers, American Indians, prisoners. Its layout, typeface, buoyant tone, and sections "Americana" (items culled from newspapers and magazines across the country) and "Profiles" (portraits written by well-known writers about well-known subjects) are widely imitated. Covers Republican National Convention in Cleveland, June 9–13, and Democratic National Convention in New York City, June 23–29. Writes columns for the Chicago *Tribune* (until January 29, 1928). Publication of *Prejudices: Fourth Series*.

1925 Tension between Nathan and Mencken increases, with Mencken insisting on more social and political commentary in *The American Mercury* and Nathan favoring an equal emphasis on literature. Nathan withdraws as coeditor of *The American Mercury* in July. Mencken travels to Dayton, Tennessee, in July to cover trial of John Scopes, high school teacher arrested for teaching theory of evolution in contravention of newly passed state law. Mother, Anna Abhau Mencken, dies 6 P.M. December 13 and is buried at Loudon Park Cemetery. Publication of *Americana 1925*. The first two books about Mencken are published (*H. L. Mencken* by Ernest Boyd and *The Man Mencken: A Biographical and Critical Survey* by Isaac Goldberg). Breaks friendship with Dreiser because of a series of misunderstandings, among them Dreiser's seeming lack of sympathy concerning the death of Mencken's mother and Dreiser's callous treatment of women.

1926   Walter Lippmann calls Mencken "the most powerful per-
            sonal influence on this whole generation of educated peo-
            ple." Through the influence of the New England Watch and
            Ward Society, the April issue of *The American Mercury* is
            banned in Boston because of Herbert Asbury's short story
            "Hatrack"; Mencken courts arrest by personally selling a
            copy to the Society's secretary; a judge declares the story
            not obscene and dismisses the complaint. Mencken tours
            the American South and arrives in California, October. Fa-
            ther's cigar firm, August Mencken & Bro., managed by
            Uncle Henry, goes bankrupt. Publication of *Notes on De-
            mocracy*, *Prejudices: Fifth Series*, and *Americana, 1926*.

1927   Publication of *Prejudices: Sixth Series* and *Selected Prejudices*.

1928   Travels to Havana, Cuba, to cover Pan American Confer-
            ence, January. Covers Republican National Convention,
            Kansas City, June 11–16, and Democratic National Con-
            vention, Houston, June 23–29. Travels with Al Smith on
            campaign tour, October 12–30. Publication of *Menckeni-
            ana: A Schimpflexicon*, a humorous collection of anti-
            Mencken invective that had appeared in newspapers and
            magazines across the country. Circulation of *The American
            Mercury* reaches its height of 84,000. Begins courting
            Sara Powell Haardt on a steadier basis.

1929   Sara Powell Haardt undergoes surgery for the removal of a
            tubercular kidney, July 6.

1930   Covers London Naval Conference, January–February. An-
            nounces secret engagement to Sara Powell Haardt to
            family members, April. Marries Sara Powell Haardt August
            27 at St. Stephen the Martyr Episcopal Church, Baltimore;
            they travel to Canada on their honeymoon. Moves to new
            residence, 704 Cathedral Street, Baltimore. Publication of
            Treatise on the Gods. Book sells well, but stirs controversy
            because of passage in which Mencken describes Jews as
            "plausibly the most unpleasant race ever heard of." (Pas-
            sage is deleted in later editions.) In newspaper interview
            he denies he is an anti-Semite: "I don't like religious Jews.
            I don't like religious Catholics and Protestants." Begins
            writing a diary.

1931   Writes a series of controversial columns against lynching of
            Matthew Williams in Salisbury, Maryland, on December
            4, causing a boycott of Baltimore businesses and the *Sun*

papers by residents of the Eastern Shore. *The Nation* recognizes Mencken for "distinguished journalism in the face of personal danger," December.

1932   Mencken sails to the West Indies with Sara, January 9. Covers Republican National Convention in Chicago, June 13–18, and Democratic National Convention in Chicago, June 26–July 2. Franklin D. Roosevelt elected President, November. Publication of *Making a President*. Continues suggesting authors and ideas for books to his publisher, Alfred Knopf; elected board member of Knopf, Inc.

1933   Mencken becomes increasingly critical of the New Deal, directing most of his criticism against the "quacks" of the Brain Trust rather than the President himself. Writes controversial columns against lynching of George Arnwood in Princess Anne on Maryland's Eastern Shore, October 18 (last lynching in Maryland). With Mencken's popularity at a low ebb, circulation of *The American Mercury* sinks to 28,329; Mencken resigns as editor with the December issue.

1934   Travels on a two-month cruise to the Mediterranean with Sara, January–March, and is fascinated by his visit with Jewish colonists in Palestine; his writing on the subject for the *Evening Sun* is privately printed in a book entitled *Eretz Israel*. Writes series of articles on American English for the New York *American*, July 9–May 20, 1935. Joins Board of Directors of the A. S. Abell Company, October 15. Resumes friendship with Theodore Dreiser. Speaks before the Gridiron Club in Washington, D.C., December 8; his address is mildly critical of the New Deal, but when it is Roosevelt's turn to speak, he turns Mencken's commentary on journalists against him by quoting a passage from *Prejudices: Sixth Series*. Publication of *Treatise on Right and Wrong*. Last article for *The Nation*, December 12.

1935   Testifies in favor of the Costigan-Wagner Anti-Lynching Bill at Senate hearing, February 14. (Bill is later blocked by Senate filibuster.) Wife Sara Haardt Mencken dies of tubercular meningitis, May 31. Edits a compilation of her work, *Southern Album*; travels to England with his brother August, June 15.

1936   Returns to his family home at 1524 Hollins Street, which he calls "as much a part of me as my two hands." Begins to organize his papers and family archives. Publishes "Three Years of Dr. Roosevelt," a scathing attack on the president, whom he compares to "a snake-oil vendor at a village carnival," in *The American Mercury*, March. Publication of "The Ordeal of a Philosopher" in *The New Yorker*, April 11, which is later used as a chapter in *Happy Days*. Covers Republican National Convention, Cleveland, June 8–13, and Democratic National Convention, Philadelphia, June 22–28, as well as convention in support of the Townsend Plan (Cleveland, July 14–20) and Union Party convention organized by Father Charles Coughlin (Cleveland, August 13–18). Travels with Republican nominee Alf Landon on his campaign tour, August–October. Publication of the fourth edition of *The American Language*.

1937   Vacations in Daytona Beach, Florida, with his brother August, January. Publication of *The Sunpapers of Baltimore*, written with Frank R. Kent, Gerald W. Johnson, and Hamilton Owens. Publication of *The Charlatanry of the Learned*, edited by Mencken and translated from the Latin by Francis Litz; the book is a satirical attack on academic pretension, written by Mencken's ancestor, Leipzig scholar Johann Burkhard Mencke (1674–1732).

1938   Alarmed by what he sees as the Roosevelt administration's mastery at setting the agenda with the press, Mencken writes publisher Paul Patterson that "we confront a high development of government propaganda," and at Patterson's request becomes temporary editor of the Baltimore *Evening Sun*, January 24–May 9. Writes "Sunday Articles" for the Baltimore *Sun*, May 16–February 2, 1941. Appointed chairman of the *Sunpapers'* committee to negotiate with the Newspaper Guild, summer. Travels to Germany, June–July; refrains from reporting on any of his observations. Writes column, "Help for the Jews," proposing the United States open its doors to German Jewish refugees fleeing Nazi persecution, November 27, 1938.

1939   Convinced that America's security would depend on its abstention from European conflict, Mencken becomes increasingly isolationist. In a speech given before the American Society of Newspaper Editors, on April 20, Mencken reminds his audience of government censorship in 1917 and warns that war will once again pose a threat to freedom of the press. Suffers a minor stroke, "generalized arteriosclerosis," July 31. Hitler invades Poland, September 1. England declares war on Germany, September 3. With his brother August, begins taking photographs of West Baltimore. Completes *Happy Days*, September 18.

1940   Covers Republican National Convention in Philadelphia, June 22–29, and Democratic National Convention in Chicago, July 13–19. Travels with Wendell Wilkie on his campaign tour, August 16–November 3. Publication of *Happy Days: 1880–1892*, first of a series of memoirs, January 22. Death of best friend, Raymond Pearl, biometrician at the Johns Hopkins University School of Medicine.

1941   Resigns from the *Sun* papers, January 16, because of publishers' unease with his anti-Roosevelt and anti-war views. Begins writing memoir on his journalism career, "Thirty-Five Years of Newspaper Work" (published in 1994). Publication of *Newspaper Days: 1899–1906*, October 20, 1941. From 1941 to 1943 *The New Yorker* publishes Mencken's series "Days of Innocence," later revised and published as chapters in *Newspaper Days* and *Heathen Days*. Travels to Havana, April. Helps several Jewish refugees find asylum in the United States; pleads their case in person to the United States State Department, August 26. Japanese attack on Pearl Harbor brings the United States into war, December 7.

1942   Begins writing memoir that focuses on his literary career, "My Life as Author and Editor"; works on it periodically until 1948 (published 1993). Publication of *A New Dictionary of Quotations*.

1943   Testifies in October on behalf of *Esquire* magazine, which had lost its mailing privileges on charges of obscenity. Publication of *Heathen Days: 1890–1936*, March 1, published as an Armed Services Edition in September. Begins compiling lengthy typescripts of "Additions, Corrections, and Explanatory Notes" for each of the *Days* books.

1944   Publication of Armed Services Edition of *Happy Days*, February, which becomes a GI favorite. "That is the difference between a soldier and a civilian," remarks Mencken. "The letters you get from civilians are from those who don't like your books."

1945   Publication of *The American Language: Supplement I*. The end of World War II officially declared September 2. In the aftermath of Allied bombing, which had appalled him,

Mencken sends packages of food, shoes, and other necessities to friends in Berlin, copies of his books to correspondents in Japan. Theodore Dreiser dies, December 28.

1946   Publication of *Christmas Story*, a satirical account of a holiday feast among the homeless of Baltimore, and how the organizers impose their Puritanical morality among the crowd.

1947   Buoyed by news of Truman's plans to help the economic recovery of Europe, March; argues for immediate economic rehabilitation of Germany. In August suffers a minor stroke but recovers after a few days. The autobiographical trilogy is published in one volume as *The Days of H. L. Mencken*. Interviewed by Edgar Kemler and William Manchester, who are separately writing biographies of Mencken.

1948   Vacations in Florida with brother August, February. Rejoins *Sun* staff to cover Republican Party Convention, June 19–22; covers Democratic National Convention, July 10–15, and Progressive Party Convention, July 23–26, all held in Philadelphia. Revival of interest in Mencken's life and work demonstrated by cover story in *Newsweek* magazine, April 5. Records an interview for the Library of Congress, June 30. Publication of *The American Language, Supplement II*. Last public appearance, speaking before the American Philosophical Society, November 4. Writes series of articles for the *Sun*, August 1–November 9. Publication of last column, arguing against segregation, November 9. Suffers a massive stroke that prevents any further reading or writing for the remainder of his life, November 23. (In his remaining years he is cared for largely by his younger brother August.)

1949   Publication of *A Mencken Chrestomathy*, Mencken's selection from his writings. Spends remaining years helping his secretary organize his papers for posterity, well over 100,000 letters, as well as original manuscripts, memoirs, and books, dedicating the bulk of the collection to the Enoch Pratt Free Library, as well as to the New York Public Library and Dartmouth.

1950   Suffers heart attack, October 12. Members of the Saturday Night Club agree in December to disband permanently.

Spends five months in hospital, before he is discharged in March 1951.

1955   *Inherit the Wind*, play about the Scopes Trial by Jerome Lawrence and Robert E. Lee, featuring a character based on Mencken, opens in April. On Mencken's 75th birthday, Alistair Cooke's edition of *The Vintage Mencken* is published, selling out in two days. Secretary Rosalind Lohrfinck comes across an unpublished manuscript written by Mencken before his 1948 stroke (published posthumously the following year as *Minority Report: H. L. Mencken's Notebooks*).

1956   Dies in his sleep from a coronary occlusion, between 4 and 5 A.M. on January 29, leaving an estate valued at $300,000. Three-fourths of his estate is willed to the Enoch Pratt Free Library. He is cremated, and his ashes are interred at Loudon Park Cemetery, in West Baltimore, January 31.

Note on the Texts

This volume contains three books of autobiography by H. L. Mencken: *Happy Days* (1940), *Newspaper Days* (1941), and *Heathen Days* (1943). The texts of these books have been taken from their first editions, all published in New York by Alfred A. Knopf. Also included is "Days Revisited," made up of excerpts from Mencken's typescripts of commentary, notes, and corrections for each of the *Days* books. The text has been taken from Mencken's three hand-corrected typescripts, corresponding respectively to each of the published books, which are currently part of the H. L. Mencken Collection at the central branch of the Enoch Pratt Free Library in Baltimore. It is accompanied by twenty-four illustrations (twenty-three photographs and a reproduction of caricatures Mencken drew during his childhood). In October 1939, and again throughout the 1940s, Mencken and his younger brother August took photographs of the West Baltimore neighborhood around the Mencken house at 1524 Hollins Street. These photographs are also from the Mencken Collection at the Pratt Library; many were taken by Mencken himself, who had been an amateur photographer since childhood (see pp. 666–67).

Mencken had written about his childhood on occasion for the Baltimore *Evening Sun*. But the primary inspiration for the autobiographical *Days* volumes came after the death of the writer Sara Haardt, Mencken's wife, which prompted him to leave his apartment at 704 Cathedral Street during the spring of 1936 and move back to the Mencken home at 1524 Hollins Street. During this period he began to organize his papers and family archives. In January 1936 he sent "The Ordeal of a Philosopher" (entitled "The Career of a Philosopher" in *Happy Days*) to *The New Yorker*, which published it on April 11, 1936; the following year the magazine published a second reminiscence, "Innocence in a Wicked World" (February 20, 1937), and encouraged Mencken to continue submitting autobiographical essays. Mencken began planning an entire book and soon settled on the title *Happy Days*, but he put aside working on the project until 1939.

Mencken later recalled that writing *Happy Days* gave him "genuine pleasure." For more than a year and a half after Sara's death, as he admitted in a letter to a friend, the author Joseph Hergesheimer, he was depressed and had "floundered." During the interim, however, he had worked with Baltimore journalists Gerald Johnson, Frank

Kent, and Hamilton Owens to write and edit the history *The Sun-papers of Baltimore, 1837–1937* (New York: Alfred A. Knopf, 1937), and he oversaw the publication of *The Charlatanry of the Learned* (New York: Alfred A. Knopf, 1937), a translation of a 1715 Latin work written by his ancestor, Johann Burkhard Mencke (1674–1732). But it was not until 1939 that Mencken began "to feel alive again," as he remarked to Hergesheimer; writing in his diary on September 18, 1939, the night he completed the final chapter of *Happy Days*, he noted that "it is always agreeable to ponder upon the adventures of childhood." Most of *Happy Days* was written in 1939, either in Baltimore or at the home of his friends Frederic and Elizabeth Hanes in Roaring Gap, NC; many of its individual chapters were first published in *The New Yorker*. (For Mencken's own account of the writing of *Happy Days* and *Newspaper Days*, see his preface to *Heathen Days*, pp. 407–10 in this volume.)

Published in 1940, *Happy Days* was an immediate critical and popular success, selling nearly ten thousand copies in five months. At the urging of Harold Ross of *The New Yorker*, Mencken continued writing autobiographical essays, which were published in the magazine from February 15, 1941, to September 25, 1943; many of these were revised and collected in *Newspaper Days*, Mencken's account of the beginnings of his journalistic career, with the remainder forming the basis of *Heathen Days*, a collection of miscellaneous essays spanning the period 1890–1936.

Mencken's relationship with the publishing house of Alfred A. Knopf, whose eponymous founder had been his friend since 1913, was congenial. Blanche Knopf provided Mencken with such steady encouragement that he remarked to her, "I should really call it 'Blanche's Days.'" When each of the *Days* books was about to be published, Mencken contacted the firm with ideas for publicity. For instance, noting how *Heathen Days* dealt with theater, music, and even his Shetland pony Frank, he urged the publisher to send review copies to *Variety, Musical Courier,* and "the editors of horse magazines." Although *Happy Days* was the most popular of the three volumes, all three sold well, and they contributed to a revival of Mencken's reputation among critics and the wider public. During World War II, the Council of Books in Wartime published undated, paperbound Armed Services editions of *Happy Days* and *Heathen Days* for American soldiers (not revised by Mencken), which became GI favorites; Kegan Paul, Trench, Trubner and Co. in London published *Happy Days* and *Newspaper Days* in 1940 and 1942, respectively, using the Knopf typesetting in both cases. The original Knopf typesettings for the three *Days* books were also used for the one-volume edition *The Days of*

H. L. Mencken (New York: Alfred A. Knopf, 1947), which included an Author's Note by Mencken, printed here in the Notes.

"Days Revisited"

After the *Days* books were published, Mencken added material to each of them in typescripts corresponding to each volume, subtitled "Additions, Corrections and Explanatory Notes." He stipulated that these three typescripts were to be given to the Enoch Pratt Free Library and were to be inaccessible until twenty-five years after his death. In 1981, they were duly made available to the public. Apart from quotations used in biographies of Mencken, and the texts of short, previously published pieces copied out in these typescripts, this material has not been published. Asterisks in the margins of the *Days* books in this volume denote that additional material can be found in "Days Revisited."

The complete length of the three typescripts rivals that of the *Days* books, but a considerable amount of the material is strictly documentary and not by Mencken: for example, in his added commentary about Baltimore boxer Joe Gans, he includes a copied-out record of the boxer's fights that runs to several pages. There are also indications of corrections to be made, though as a careful proofreader of his own work, Mencken congratulated himself that the *Days* books had so few errors. Many of the errors acknowledged in the typescripts were corrected in later printings of the Knopf editions of the *Days* books in the 1940s. In two instances, the text here has been corrected in accordance with Mencken's notes in the typescripts: in *Happy Days*, at 111.34, "down to 1910" has been emended to "down to 1908"; and in *Newspaper Days*, 383.35, in the description of the aftermath of the Baltimore fire of 1904, "got out one" has been corrected to "got out two." If the correction of an error would require too intrusive an editorial intervention in the text, the error is explained in the Notes: see, for example, the note keyed to 767.29, where Mencken clarifies the precise fee paid to the winners and losers of boxing matches.

In "Days Revisited," bracketed ellipses have been used to indicate cuts within Mencken's text (often due to the interpolation of material written by others). Cuts at the beginning or end of an entry are not indicated by such ellipses, nor are cross-references to documents in Mencken's archive or his other writings, or his occasional footnotes (salient footnotes to "Days Revisited" are given in this volume's Notes). In certain instances, paragraph breaks have been added. In general, the text presented here follows the editorial conventions of the *Days* books, including forms of usage such as the capitalization of seasons and the use of lowercase to designate thoroughfares in proper nouns (Hollins street, Falls road, etc.).

This volume presents the texts of the original printings and type-scripts chosen for inclusion here, but it does not attempt to repro-duce nontextual features of their typographic design. The texts of the books are presented without change, except for the correction of typographical errors. Spelling, punctuation, and capitalization are often expressive features and are not altered, even when inconsistent or irregular. The following is a list of typographical errors corrected, cited by page and line number: 12.22, Chick; 26.26, *Kölnischeswas-ser*; 51.30, noiser; 58.10, in few; 68.20, *Curcurbitaceae*; 89.35, father's; 118.18, I.W.W.'s; 127.14, cogeners.; 132.13 (and *passim*), Ayers'; 206.37, five several; 208.36, (1940) this; 231.20, worthy the; 231.28, onery; 259.25, weeks vacation; 365.31, Deutschland's; 447.7, seeemd; 461.8, emiinent.; 463.20, appelation; 498.36, a a few; 534.31, Who's fault; 589.32, chords; 593.8, another,; 636.21, were sold; 657.26, Reuben's; 660.1, Maples Dodge; 662.4, Eccosaise; 682.23, odds; 701.4, the see the; 776.34, Roy Lyman Wilbur,; 778.3, polyomielitis; 785.34, the mist of.

Note on the Illustrations

Listed below are expanded captions for the twenty-four illustrations that accompany "Days Revisited." All illustrations have been provided courtesy of the Enoch Pratt Free Library, Baltimore, H. L. Mencken Collection.

p. 601: Mencken's birthplace, numbered 380 West Lexington Street in 1880, renumbered 811 West Lexington Street by 1940, when Mencken took this photograph. H. L. Mencken Collection, Enoch Pratt Free Library, scrapbook "Souvenirs of Childhood and Schooldays 1880–1896," p. 1 (unnumbered).

p. 602: 1524 Hollins Street. The street was most likely named for John Smith Hollins (c. 1786–1856), an officer who served in the War of 1812 and was mayor of Baltimore, 1852–1854, or possibly his father, prominent Baltimorean and City Council member John Hollins, who died in 1827. Hollins Street faces Union Square, a 2.5 acre park donated by the John Donnell family from their estate to the city of Baltimore in 1847. Photograph by H. L. Mencken and August Mencken Jr., c. 1940. H. L. Mencken Collection, Enoch Pratt Free Library, "Photographs of the Mencken House, 1524 Hollins Street, Baltimore, 1939–1942," p. 49.

p. 603: Union Square. The fountain shown here was removed in 1941, probably so that its iron could be melted down and used in the war effort. A replica was dedicated to Mencken in 1971. Photograph by H. L. Mencken and August Mencken Jr., c. 1940. H. L. Mencken Collection, Enoch Pratt Free Library, "Happy Days: Fair Copy, Corrected, With Illustrations, vol. II," p. 9, with typed caption by Mencken: "The Greek temple and the fishpond."

p. 625: Hollins Market in West Baltimore. The block-long shed and two-story front was built in 1877 and renovated in 1977, and still looks much as it did in Mencken's day. Photograph by H. L. Mencken and August Mencken Jr., 1940. H. L. Mencken Collection, Enoch Pratt Free Library, "Happy Days: Fair Copy, Corrected, With Illustrations, vol. II," p. 50, with Mencken's typed caption: "Hollins Market (1940). The old market-house has been little changed in 50 years."

p. 629: The marble front steps and iron railing at 1524 Hollins Street. Photograph by H. L. Mencken and August Mencken Jr., September 24, 1939. H. L. Mencken Collection, Enoch Pratt Free Library, "Happy Days: Fair Copy, Corrected, With Illustrations, vol. II," p. 15, with Mencken's typed caption: "Looking westward along Hollins Street. The entrance to No. 1524 is at the right. In the left distance is the high stone wall of the House of Good Shepherd." Another print of this image in the Mencken Collection contains

Mencken's handwritten caption, "Iron railing at the door of 1524 Hollins street, designed by Edward L. Palmer, *c.* 1920."

p. 639: The site of L. H. Newton's store at 1400 West Baltimore Street. Photograph by H. L. Mencken and August Mencken Jr., c. 1940. H. L. Mencken Collection, Enoch Pratt Free Library, "Happy Days: Fair Copy, Corrected, With Illustrations, vol. II," p. 18, with typed caption by Mencken: "L. H. Newton's old toy-store at the northwest corner of Baltimore and Calhoun streets, now (1940) a drug-store. The building next door was occupied for many years by Kunker's candy-store."

p. 644: Caricatures of Baltimoreans of the 1880s drawn by Mencken as a boy. H. L. Mencken Collection, Enoch Pratt Free Library, scrapbook "Souvenirs of Childhood and Schooldays, 1880–1896," p. 22.

p. 652: The House of the Good Shepherd. The building was torn down in 1965 so that the Steuart Hill Elementary School could be built on the site. Photograph by H. L. Mencken, 1942. H. L. Mencken Collection, Enoch Pratt Free Library, "Photographs of the Mencken House at 1524 Hollins Street, Baltimore, 1939–1942," p. 91. From a series headed by Mencken's handwritten caption: "The following were made by H. L. M. after the heavy snow of March 30, 1942."

p. 659: Enoch Pratt Free Library No. 2 Branch, 1401 Hollins St. This building is now home to the Maryland Library Association. Photograph by H. L. Mencken and August Mencken Jr., c. 1940. H. L. Mencken Collection, Enoch Pratt Free Library, "Happy Days: Fair Copy, Corrected, With Illustrations, vol. II," p. 52, with typed caption by Mencken: "No. 2 branch of the Enoch Pratt Free Library, at Hollins and Calhoun streets, a block and a half east of No. 1524."

p. 667: Young August Mencken misspelling his name. Photograph by H. L. Mencken, c. 1894. H. L. Mencken Collection, Enoch Pratt Free Library, scrapbook "August [Mencken] and Anna Margaret Abhau and Their Family, 1865–1936," p. 9.

p. 674: Members of H. L. Mencken's family at their summer house in Mount Washington. From left to right: Charles (brother), Anna (mother), Anna (sister), August (brother), August (father), and H. L. Mencken, age 12. Photograph by James F. Hughes, c. 1894. H. L. Mencken Collection, Enoch Pratt Free Library, scrapbook "August [Mencken] and Anna Margaret Abhau and Their Family, 1865–1936," p. 5.

p. 680: Site of the factory of August Mencken & Bro., 414 West Baltimore St. (formerly 368). Photograph by H. L. Mencken and August Mencken Jr., c. 1940, with hand-drawn arrow (presumably by Mencken) to indicate the building. H. L. Mencken Collection, Enoch Pratt Free Library, "Happy Days: Fair Copy, Corrected, With Illustrations, vol. II," p. 67.

p. 682: Booth Street, the alley behind the Mencken home at 1524 Hollins Street. Photograph by H. L. Mencken and August Mencken Jr., 1940. H. L. Mencken Collection, Enoch Pratt Free Library, "Happy Days: Fair Copy, Corrected, With Illustrations, vol. II," p. 63, with typed caption by Mencken: "The house occupied by Old Wesley [see pp. 179–187] is almost in the center of this photograph. The sidewalk and part of the front wall have been white-washed by the present occupant (1940)."

p. 685: H. L. Mencken with children of the Johnson family in Booth Street. Unknown photographer, 1929. H. L. Mencken Collection, Enoch Pratt Free Library, "H. L. Mencken, Photographs and Other Portraits, 1881–1936," photograph no. 223.

p. 694: August Mencken Sr. Photograph by H. L. Mencken, January 1, 1895. H. L. Mencken Collection, Enoch Pratt Free Library, scrapbook F12, p. 2. A print of the photograph is also included in "Happy Days: Fair Copy, Corrected, With Illustrations, vol. II," p. 17, with Mencken's typed caption: "The old Summer-house in the backyard at 1524 Hollins street (*c.* 1896). The figure is that of my father. I made the picture. The Summer-house was finally pulled down in 1936."

p. 705: Mencken with his uncle Charles Abhau and fellow Baltimorean Kemp Hennighausen en route to Jamaica. Unknown photographer, c. 1900. H. L. Mencken Collection, Enoch Pratt Free Library, main photographic scrapbook, p. 3.

p. 738: H. L. Mencken. Photograph by Meredith Janvier, 1906. H. L. Mencken Collection, Enoch Pratt Free Library, main photographic scrapbook, p. 7.

p. 749: Members of the Baltimore *Morning Herald* staff in 1900. *Top row:* un-identified man, Jason Stockbridge, Theodore Leary, H. L. Mencken, Arthur W. Hawks, unidentified man. *Middle row:* Charles M. Cole, Julian Schaefer, unidentified man, D. Watson Fletcher, Max Ways, W. Dwight Burroughs, O. Harry Smith, Howard I. Harman, Frederick Strelan. *Seated:* Dan Scully, John H. Anderson, Raleigh C. Smith, Samuel Wilmer, and Albert Goodman. Two office boys are sitting on the floor. Unknown photographer, c. 1900. H. L. Mencken Collection, Enoch Pratt Free Library, main photographic scrap-book, p. 7.

p. 754: Mencken, age 12, holding the reins of the family's Shetland pony Frank, with brothers Charles and August and sister Anna. Photograph by James F. Hughes, 1892. H. L. Mencken Collection, Enoch Pratt Free Library, main photographic scrapbook, p. 9.

p. 757: H. L. Mencken at his desk in the city room during his tenure as dra-matic editor of the Baltimore *Herald.* Unknown photographer, November 26, 1901. H. L. Mencken Collection, Enoch Pratt Free Library, main photo-graphic scrapbook, p. 3.

p. 765: Members of the Saturday Night Club in 1925, at a gathering at Folger

McKinsey's, near Severna Park, Maryland. *From left to right*: unidentified boy, Hamilton Owens, Franklin Hazlehurst, Henry M. Hyde, Adolph Torovsky Jr., Edmund Duffy, Raymond Pearl, William W. Woollcott, Theodor Hemberger, Max Brödel, Adolph Torovsky Sr., Maxwell Cathcart, W. Edwin Moffett, Gustav Strube, Max Kahn. Unknown photographer, 1925. H. L. Mencken Collection, Enoch Pratt Free Library, main photographic scrapbook, p. 57.

p. 773: A. H. McDannald, H. L. Mencken, and W. Edwin Moffett at the Forum in Rome. Unknown photographer, 1914. H. L. Mencken Collection, Enoch Pratt Free Library, main photographic scrapbook, p. 19.

p. 778: Mencken at his typewriter, covering the 1936 Republican National Convention in Cleveland. Seated in the same row as Mencken, from left to right, are his colleagues Fred Essary (with bow tie), James Bone, and Frank R. Kent. Henry Hyde is standing next to Mencken. Unknown photographer, 1936. H. L. Mencken Collection, Enoch Pratt Free Library, main photographic scrapbook, p. 145.

p. 788: Mencken with Clarence Darrow at Mencken's apartment, 704 Cathedral Street. Unknown photographer from the Baltimore *News*, November 17, 1930. H. L. Mencken Collection, Enoch Pratt Free Library, main photographic scrapbook, p. 107.

Notes

In the notes below, the reference numbers denote page and line of this volume (the line count includes headings). No note is made for material included in standard desk-reference books. Quotations from Shakespeare are keyed to *The Riverside Shakespeare*, ed. G. Blakemore Evans (Boston: Houghton Mifflin, 1974). Biographical information beyond that included in the Chronology may be found in Charles A. Fecher, *Mencken: A Study of His Thought* (New York: Alfred A. Knopf, 1978); Vincent Fitzpatrick, *H. L. Mencken* (Macon, GA: Mercer University Press, 2004); Fred Hobson, *Mencken: A Life* (New York: Random House, 1994); Gerald W. Johnson, Frank R. Kent, H. L. Mencken, and Hamilton Owens, *The Sunpapers of Baltimore* (New York: Alfred A. Knopf, 1937); S. T. Joshi, *Mencken: An Annotated Bibliography* (Lanham, MD: Scarecrow Press, 2009); William Manchester, *Disturber of the Peace: The Life of H. L. Mencken* (Amherst: University of Massachusetts Press, 1986); H. L. Mencken, *The Diary of H. L. Mencken*, ed. Charles Fecher (New York: Alfred A. Knopf, 1989); H. L. Mencken, *The Impossible H. L. Mencken: A Selection of His Best Newspaper Stories*, ed. Marion Elizabeth Rogers (New York: Anchor/Doubleday, 1991); *Mencken on Mencken*, ed. S. T. Joshi (Baton Rouge: Louisiana State University Press, 2010); H. L. Mencken, *My Life as Author and Editor*, ed. Jonathan Yardley (New York: Alfred A. Knopf, 1993); H. L. Mencken, *Thirty-Five Years of Newspaper Work*, ed. Fred Hobson, Vincent Fitzpatrick, and Bradford Jacobs (Baltimore: Johns Hopkins University Press, 1994); *Dreiser-Mencken Letters: The Correspondence of Theodore Dreiser and H. L. Mencken*, ed. Thomas D. Riggio (Philadelphia: University of Pennsylvania Press, 1986); Marion Elizabeth Rodgers, *Mencken: The American Iconoclast* (Oxford: Oxford University Press, 2005); Marion Elizabeth Rodgers, *Mencken and Sara: A Life in Letters* (New York: McGraw-Hill, 1987); Richard J. Schrader, *H. L. Mencken: A Descriptive Bibliography* (Pittsburgh: University of Pittsburgh Press, 1998); and Terry Teachout, *The Skeptic: A Life of H. L. Mencken* (New York: HarperCollins, 2002).

v.2   THE DAYS TRILOGY] When *Happy Days*, *Newspaper Days*, and *Heathen Days* were collected in *The Days of H. L. Mencken* (New York: Alfred A. Knopf, 1947), Mencken contributed the following Author's Note:

> The history of the three books here brought together is told in their prefaces, and there is little to add save the hope that putting them

into one volume will be as convenient to the reader as it has been to the printer, the binder and the publisher. The volume is issued at a time when printing costs have risen so dizzily that every separate book is a furious headache to all concerned in its production. The amalgamation abates that headache by nearly two-thirds, and can be offered at a price considerably less than the price that would have to be asked for separate reprints of the original volumes. All of them have been published since I reached the perhaps indelicate age of sixty, and I am naturally glad to be able to report that they have sold very well, and brought me a great many agreeable letters from readers. Indeed they have sold better than any of my books save "The American Language" and its supplement, and the letters that have come in have been far more friendly than those that the others ever produced. Nearly everyone seems to be pleased, and it follows without saying that I am pleased myself.

One of the things that has most interested me in this correspondence is the fact that many letters have come from women, and that most of them, especially those relating to "Happy Days," have said, in substance, "I had precisely the same experience." It never occurred to me in my youth, or to any other normal American boy of the time, that creatures in skirts and pigtails saw the world as we did. Yet it seems to have been the case, and I am glad of it, for it means that many grandmothers of today, like their husbands and brothers, cherish memories of an era when the world was a great deal more comfortable and amusing than it is today. We were lucky to have been born so soon. As the shadows close in we can at least recall that there was a time when people could spend weeks, months and even years without being badgered, bilked or alarmed. Much of the tang we sensed, of course, was a mere function of youth, but there was also a good deal, I believe, in things themselves. The human race had not yet succumbed to the political and other scoundrels who have been undertaking of late to save it, to its infinite cost and degradation. It had a better time in the days when I was a boy, and also in the days when I was a young newspaper reporter, and some of that better time even slopped into the first half of the space between the two World Wars. I enjoyed myself immensely, and all I try to do here is to convey some of my joy to the nobility and gentry of this once great and happy Republic, now only a dismal burlesque of its former self.

HAPPY DAYS

4.4   *Tonkünstler*] German: musician, literally "tone artist."

5.2   Kallikuks] A reference to the pseudonymous family in *The Kallikak Family: A Study in the Heredity of Feeble-Mindedness* (1912) by eugenicist Henry H. Goddard (1866–1957).

5.29   with the Psalmist] At Psalms 16:6.

9.12   adjourned *sine die*] Indefinitely, without planning to resume (from Latin, "without day").

10.30–31   my brother Charlie] Charles Edward Mencken (1882–1956), the second oldest of the three Mencken brothers, grew up in Baltimore but lived for more than fifty years in western Pennsylvania, where he worked as an engineer for the Pennsylvania Railroad.

11.5   Kate Greenaway] English artist (1846–1901), painter and illustrator of children's books such as *Mother Goose* (1881).

12.10   since the Würm Glaciation] Late Pleistocene glaciation (named for a river in Germany), which began seventy thousand years ago.

12.21–22   small enough to have been designed by Chic Sale] As small as an outhouse. American actor and vaudevillian Charles "Chic" Sale (1885–1936) was the author of *The Specialist* (1929), a play about an outhouse builder.

13.23   grandfather Abhau] See Mencken's note on p. 604. His daughter Anna (1858–1925) married August Mencken Sr. in 1879.

13.30   his brother Henry] Henry M. Mencken (1857–1939).

14.33   Aunt Pauline] E. Pauline Hensel (née Mencken, 1879–1973).

17.21   Joe Hergesheimer and Paul Patterson] Mencken's close friend Joseph Hergesheimer (1880–1954), novelist whose many books included *The Three Black Pennys* (1917), *Java Head* (1919), and *Cytherea* (1922); Paul Chenery Patterson (1878–1952), president and publisher of the Baltimore *Sunpapers*.

18.9   *Märchen*] German: fairy tales.

19.24–25   Back Basin . . . the Basin] What is now known as Baltimore's Inner Harbor was formerly called "The Basin"; the Back Basin was the tidal area at the end of the canal that channeled the Jones Falls stream and much of the city's waste into the harbor.

22.4   Polytechnic] Vocational high school founded in 1883 (called until 1893 the Baltimore Manual Training School), which Mencken attended at 311–327 Courtland Street in downtown Baltimore between Saratoga and Pleasant streets, the first of its three sites; located since 1967 at Falls Road and Cold Spring Lane.

22.28   *Fibel*] German: primary school textbook.

22.34   were unanimously *Chazirfresser*] Ate pork, did not keep kosher.

22.36   Demerarans] From Demerara, South American colonial region that is now part of Guyana.

23.20   in its heyday] After more than seventy-five years as a private school, Knapp's English and German Institute closed in 1916.

23.24   Lateinisch] German: Latin.

24.3   Norddeutscher-Lloyd pier at Locust Point] The North German Lloyd shipping company made weekly crossings between Baltimore and Bremen; its terminal was at Locust Point, in the southern part of the city.

26.7   *Gartenlaube*] Popular German illustrated weekly magazine.

26.26   *Kölnischwasser*] Cologne water.

29.1   Admiral Winfield Scott Schley] American naval officer (1839–1911), commander of an 1884 mission to rescue the surviving members of the Arctic expedition led by Lt. Adolphus Greely; he later served as commander at the battle of Santiago de Cuba, July 3, 1898.

30.33   a Guelph and a Ghibelline] Members of warring factions in medieval Florence.

31.28   before even Muggsy McGraw had come to town] Hall of Fame base-ball player and manager John J. McGraw (1873–1934) played for the Baltimore Orioles, 1891–99.

32.17   Darley park] Park off Harford Road near 25th Street, with a beer gar-den and amusement rides for children operated by a nearby brewery of the same name.

35.15–16   "The Wreck of the Hesperus"] Poem (1842) by Henry Wadsworth Longfellow (1807–1882).

38.21   Tiglath-pileser] King of Assyria during the eighth century B.C.E.

38.33   McGuffey Readers] Series of six widely used *Eclectic Readers* (1836–57), the first five of which were edited by American educator William Holmes Mc-Guffey (1800–1873). (The sixth was compiled by McGuffey's brother Alexan-der.)

43.23   Kelly's] Kelley's Hotel and Restaurant, at 3–9 Eutaw Street above Bal-timore Street, popular oyster house established in 1880; because of the advent of Prohibition and high rent, it closed in 1920.

44.2–3   Rennert Hotel] The Hotel Rennert, opened in 1885 by Robert Rennert (1837–1898) at the corner of Saratoga and Liberty streets, quickly became Baltimore's leading hotel, and was nationally famous for its raw bar and for serving such Maryland delicacies as terrapin and duck. It was also a favorite meeting place among politicians, serving as headquarters of the local Democratic Party. The building was demolished in 1941; in 1950 the property became the site of a parking garage (since 1996 a parking lot).

44.23–25   Tom McNulty] Thomas Francis McNulty (1858 or 1859–1932), sheriff of Baltimore, 1913–23, known as "the singing sheriff" for his tenor voice; he sang at campaign events for various politicians.

46.29–30   Latrobe stoves, the invention of a Baltimore engineer] Popular home stove that was installed in a fireplace, also known as the "Baltimore Heater," the 1846 invention of John H. Latrobe (1803–1891).

49.20   Brussels carpets] Multicolored patterned woolen carpets with a sturdy back made up of linen thread.

49.23   Rogers group] Small-scale statuary of genre scenes by American sculptor John Rogers (1829–1904), widely available in affordable plaster reproductions.

49.25   Steuart's Hill] Part of the property located east of Mencken's Union Square neighborhood in West Baltimore that once belonged to General George Hume Steuart (1828–1903). It was confiscated by the U.S. government and used as the site of a hospital during the Civil War when Steuart sided with the Confederacy. After the war the estate was restored to Steuart, who sold it in 1867; his mansion was used as a boys' school and as a convent before it was demolished in 1884.

52.10–11   Washington Monument] The first large monument to George Washington built in the United States, dedicated in 1829 and designed by American architect Robert Mills (1781–1855), with a sculpture of Washington created by Italian artist Enrico Causici (1790–1835).

54.25   Loudon Park Cemetery] Created from Loudon Farms, the estate of shipbuilder, financier, and politician James Carey (1751–1834), the 365-acre tract of sloping hills, mature oaks, and winding lanes was incorporated as Loudon Park Cemetery in 1853.

55.25   *Bauer*] German: farmer.

61.34–35   at Mt. Washington, to the north of Baltimore] Suburban community (but since 1919 part of the city of Baltimore) developed in the mid-nineteenth century for families to escape the oppressive summer heat of the city. August Mencken Sr. bought the house at what is today 1307 Northern Parkway from Otto M. Mattfeldt in 1892 for $3,000, adding $1,500 for improvements. H. L. Mencken sold the house in 1902.

62.3–4   Roland Park] Planned suburban community (1897–1914) developed on two large estates then north of Baltimore; early phases of its extensive and innovative planning of land use and restrictions were designed by developer Edward Bouton (1858–1941) and landscape architect Frederick Law Olmsted Jr. (1870–1957). Roland Park was incorporated as part of the city of Baltimore in 1918.

66.24   *Stammhalter*] German term for the male who continues the family name.

68.31   "Halte im Gedächtniss Jesum Christum!"] German: hold in remembrance of Jesus Christ.

69.8   *Turnerei*] German: sports activities or acrobatics.

69.10   Hansa towns] Municipalities mostly in northern Germany that belonged to the Hanseatic League, trade organization linking independent sovereign cities to enlarge and protect their commerce.

69.11   *Plattdeutschen*] Literally "Low Germans," northern Germans who speak the dialect known as Plattdeutsch.

69.24   St. Mary's Industrial School] Catholic boys' orphanage and boarding school (1866–1950); its most famous alumnus was Babe Ruth, who learned to play baseball there.

72.4–5   *Pfeffernüsse, Springele, Lebkuchen*] Traditional German cookies and baked treats usually seen at Christmas: *Pfeffernüsse* are spice cookies; *Springele* traditionally have an embossed design; *Lebkuchen* resembles gingerbread.

72.14   "Chatterbox"] Children's magazine founded by the Rev. John Erskine Clarke (1827–1920), first published in England in 1866.

73.11   *oleum ricini*] Castor oil.

74.29   no Anatomy Act] Maryland passed a law regulating the procurement of cadavers by medical schools in 1882, stipulating that the body of anyone buried at public expense could be used for scientific research within the state.

78.9   *Fireside Companion*] Popular weekly family magazine.

78.14   designed for Marguerite Gautier] Tubercular heroine of *The Lady of the Camellias* (1848), novel by Alexandre Dumas fils (1824–1895).

80.2   *Cervelatwurst*] Sausage made of finely ground beef and pork, delicate and mild in taste.

81.11–19   Once a mob . . . never the same again] James McCubbin Lingan (1751–1812) was an officer in the Maryland line of the Continental Army during the Revolutionary War, much of which he spent on a British prison ship after being captured at Fort Washington on November 16, 1776. After the war he was a senior officer in the Maryland Militia. On June 22, 1812, four days after the United States declared war against Great Britain, the building housing the offices of Baltimore's *Federal Republican and Commercial Gazette* was attacked and demolished by a mob angered by its antiwar editorials. With Lingan's support, the newspaper's editor, Alexander Hanson (1786–1819), resumed printing from Georgetown, then a suburb of Washington, D.C. On the night of July 28–29, after the newspaper had set up new offices in a house in Baltimore, the building was attacked in a standoff that led to the surrender of the twenty-three men inside, Lingan among them. They were taken to the city's jail, which was stormed the following evening by another mob. Though he pleaded for mercy, citing his war service, advanced age, and the needs of his large family, Lingan was stabbed in the chest and died several hours later. The attackers also crippled and partially blinded General Henry "Light-Horse Harry" Lee (1756–1818), a cavalry commander during the Revolutionary War, governor of Virginia, 1791–94, and U.S. representative, 1799–1801.

82.5–6   "rushed the can"] Went to a saloon with a container to be filled with beer.

90.32   *Koseformen*] German: familiar shortenings of names.

100.28   Killer Williams of New York] Alexander S. Williams (1839–1917), police captain in New York City during the 1880s and 1890s, also known as "Clubber" Williams.

106.37–38   Oliver Optic, Horatio Alger, Harry Castlemon] Prolific authors of popular adventure novels for boys: Oliver Optic, pseudonym of William Taylor Adams (1822–1897); Horatio Alger (1832–1899), whose novels included *Ragged Dick* (1868) and *Luck and Pluck* (1869); Harry Castlemon, pseudonym of Charles Austin Fosdick (1842–1915), whose more than fifty novels included many about a boy protagonist named Frank.

107.20   Will Levington Comfort] American journalist and novelist (1878–1932), a war correspondent in the Philippines, China, Russia, and Japan and the author of *Routledge Rides Alone* (1910), *Fate Knocks at the Door* (1912), *Midstream* (1914), and other books.

107.21–22   Martin Tupper] English writer and poet (1810–1889), author of *Proverbial Philosophy* (1837).

107.29–30   "Ten Thousand Leagues Under the Sea"] I.e., Jules Verne's novel *Twenty Thousand Leagues Under the Sea* (1870).

108.27–28   "Looking Backward" . . . "Life Among the Mormons"] *Looking Backward: 2000–1887* (1888), utopian novel imagining America in the year 2000 by Boston lawyer Edward Bellamy (1850–1898); *If Christ Came to Chicago* (1894), an exposé of Chicago's underbelly by English journalist and editor William Thomas Stead (1849–1912); *Life Among the Mormons, and a March to Their Zion* (1868) by U.S. Army surgeon William Elkanah Waters (1833–1903).

108.35   Chambers's Encyclopedia] Encyclopedia originally published in ten volumes in 1859–68 in Edinburgh by the Scottish brothers Robert Chambers (1802–1871) and William Chambers (1800–1883); a new edition was published in 1888–92.

108.37   Ignatius Donnelly] Farmer, editor, populist author, orator, and politician (1831–1901) who served as lieutenant governor of Minnesota, 1860–63, and as U.S. congressman, 1863–69; his book *Atlantis: The Antediluvian World* (1882) argued for the existence of the legendary island of Atlantis cited in Plato's Dialogues.

108.37–38   "Around the World in the Yacht *Sunbeam*"] *A Voyage in the 'Sunbeam': Our Home on the Ocean for Eleven Months* (1878), by English travel writer Anna Brassey (1839–1887).

109.6–7   William Carleton's Irish novels] The novels of Irish writer William

Carleton (1794–1869) include *Fardorougha, the Miser* (1837–38), *Valentine McClutchy* (1845), and *The Emigrants of Ahadarra* (1848).

109.7–8 "Our Living World," by Rev. J. G. Wood] *Our Living World: An Artistic Edition of the Rev. J. G. Wood's Natural History of Animate Creation. Revised and Adapted to American Zoology* (1885) by Joseph B. Holder. Clergyman John George Wood (1827–1889) was a science writer and popularizer.

109.8–9 "A History of the War for the Union," by E. A. Duyckinck] Three-volume history (1861–65) by editor, publisher, and writer Evert Augustus Duyckinck (1816–1878).

109.9 "Our Country," by Benson J. Lossing] Popular history (1876–78) by Benson John Lossing (1813–1891), best known for his illustrated books on the American Revolution and Civil War.

109.10–12 "A Pictorial History . . . Yonge] Juvenile history (1882) of Greece, Rome, Germany, France, England, and the United States by English writer Charlotte Yonge (1823–1901), the author of many popular novels, including *The Heir of Redclyffe* (1853) and *The Daisy Chain* (1856).

109.15–16 "Peculiarities of American Cities," by Captain Willard Glazier] Book (1886) by soldier, explorer, and trapper Willard Glazier (1841–1905); the fifth chapter is devoted to a description of Baltimore.

109.16–17 "Our Native Land," by George T. Ferris] *Our Native Land: Glances at American Scenery and Places with Sketches of Life and Adventure* (1882) by George Titus Ferris.

109.17 "A Compendium of Forms," by one Glaskell] Reference book (1880, rev. ed. 1889) including a course on penmanship by American professor and handwriting authority George A. Gaskell (1844–1885).

109.19 "Uncle Remus,"] *Uncle Remus, His Songs and Sayings: The Folklore of the Old Plantation* (1880) by Joel Chandler Harris (1848–1908).

109.20 "Ben Hur,"] *Ben-Hur: A Tale of the Christ* (1880), enormously popular novel by American writer Lew Wallace (1827–1905).

109.20 "Peck's Bad Boy"] Stories and novels by American humorist and politician George Wilbur Peck (1840–1916), including *Peck's Bad Boy and His Pa* (1883) and *The Grocery Man and Peck's Bad Boy* (1883).

109.20–21 "The Adventures of Baron Münchhausen,"] Karl Friedrich von Münchhausen (1720–1797) was a German soldier and traveler known for his tales of fantastic adventures, which inspired the German librarian and political exile Rudolf Erich Raspe (1736–1794) to publish *The Surprising Adventures of Baron Munchhausen* anonymously in London in 1785. Later versions of the Münchhausen tales were further embellished and contained additional stories.

109.21–22 "One Thousand Proofs . . . Carpenter] *One Hundred Proofs that the Earth Is Not a Globe* (1885), pamphlet by English writer William Carpenter (1830–1896), who had moved to Baltimore in 1880.

110.40 the woodcut by W. F. Brown] A wood engraving after the drawing by American artist Walter Francis Brown (1853–1929) was one of 328 illustrations in the 1880 edition of the book, which also included those of other artists.

111.16 Haymarket anarchists] On May 4, 1886, a crowd assembled in Chicago's Haymarket Square to protest the police shooting of several striking laborers the previous day. A bomb was thrown, shooting ensued, and seven policemen and at least four workers were killed. Although the actual bomb-thrower was not identified, eight anarchists were convicted of conspiracy to commit murder. Four of the defendants were hanged, one committed suicide in prison, and the remaining three were pardoned in 1893 by the newly elected governor, John P. Altgeld, who called their trial unjust.

111.21–24 Mencken family . . . German universities] The Mencke family (the name was modernized during the eighteenth century, a shortened form of the Latin Menckenius) originated in Oldenburg, near Bremen. Eilard Mencke (1614–1657), archpresbyter of Marienwerder Cathedral, was its first prominent member. H. L. Mencken's direct line of ancestry can be traced to Eilard's cousin Helmrich Mencke, whose son Luder (1658–1726) taught law at the University of Leipzig and then became its rector; later his son Gottfried Ludwig (1683–1744) became a law professor at Wittenberg. Otto Mencke (1644–1707), the son of Helmrich's brother, founded the journal *Acta Eruditorum* in 1682. Otto's son, Johann Burkhard Mencke (1674–1732), became a member of the British Royal Society at age twenty-four, and returned to Leipzig as a professor. A translation of his satire against fake erudition, *De Charlataneria Eruditorum* (*The Charlatanry of the Learned*, 1715), was edited by H. L. Mencken and published by Knopf in 1937. For two centuries the family flourished in Leipzig; "Menckestrasse" is a major road leading to the city center. After several generations of scholars had attended university, Johann Christian August Mencken (1797–1867) did not; nor did his son, H. L. Mencken's grandfather Burkhardt Ludwig Mencken (1828–1891), who was born in Laas and immigrated to Baltimore in 1848.

114.3 Gog and Magog] See Revelation 20:7–8: "And when the thousand years are expired, Satan shall be loosed out of his prison, and shall go out to deceive the nations which are in the four quarters of the earth, Gog and Magog, to gather them together to battle."

114.21 Enoch Pratt . . . branch] The municipal free library system founded by businessman Enoch Pratt (1808–1896) opened its central library on January 6, 1886, and four inaugural branches in February and March of that year, including one not far from the Mencken residence in West Baltimore, at Calhoun and Hollins streets.

114.25–26 *Once-a-Week*, the predecessor of *Collier's*] *Once a Week*, an American weekly magazine of fiction, humor, and news founded in 1888 by

Irish-born book and magazine publisher Peter Fenelon Collier (1849–1909), was renamed *Collier's* in 1895.

114.28–29   Justin M'Carthy's "History of Our Own Times"] Four-volume history (1879–80) by Irish historian, novelist, and politician Justin McCarthy (1830–1912), later supplemented by three additional volumes (1897–1905).

114.31   Herbert Spencer] English writer (1820–1903) on philosophy, sociology, and evolution.

116.4–10   Mr. Garrigues . . . Methodist chapel] Henry Hill Garrigues (1840–1888), born in Philadelphia, fought for the Confederacy during the Civil War and then moved to Baltimore; it was largely through his efforts that the mission chapel of St. Paul's Southern Methodist Church was organized.

117.35   "Sweet Adeline."] Popular song (1903), with words by Richard H. Gerard (pseudonym of Richard Gerard Husch, 1876–1948), music by Harry Armstrong (1879–1951).

118.3   Paul Patterson] See note 17.21.

118.18   I.W.W.] Industrial Workers of the World, popularly known as the "Wobblies."

118.18–19   converted into proletarian ribaldry] The workers' song "Hallelujah, I'm a Bum" is based on the hymn "Revive Us Again."

123.11   Golden Text] Biblical verse that is supposed to encapsulate the central idea of the Sunday School lesson, to be memorized by pupils.

124.3–4   Stieff square] Affordable square piano sometimes called "the poor man's Steinway," designed by Baltimore piano manufacturer Charles M. Stieff (1834–1899).

124.34   Burnsides, Dundrearys, Galways] Colloquial terms for bushy sideburns such as those sported by U.S. Army general and politician Ambrose Everett Burnside (1824–1881) or by Lord Dundreary, a character in *Our American Cousin* (1858) by English playwright Tom Taylor (1817–1880). Galways were ear-to-chin whiskers, popular in County Galway, Ireland, sometimes known as "Galway sluggers," frequently worn by Irish comedians.

125.10–12   Beyer's Preliminary School . . . School of Velocity] Instructional pieces for the piano designed by German pianist and composer Ferdinand Beyer (1803–1863) and Austrian pianist and composer Karl Czerny (1791–1857), respectively.

125.26–126.1   A. Leduc] French composer and music publisher Alphonse Leduc (1804–1868).

126.3–4   "Monastery Bells"] "Cloches du Monastère" (1857) by French organist and composer Louis James Alfred Lefébure-Wély (1817–1869).

126.4 Leybach's Fifth Nocturne] The composition (1862) for which Alsatian pianist and composer Ignace Xavier Joseph Leybach (1817–1891) is best known.

126.4 the "Black Key" polka] "The Black Key Polka Mazurka" (1871) by August Herzog.

126.5 the "Chopsticks" waltz] "The Celebrated Chop Waltz" (1877) by English composer Euphemia Allen (1861–1949).

126.31–32 Jacques-Féréol Mazas's] French composer, violinist, and teacher (1782–1849).

127.13 Moszkowski] Moritz Moszkowski (1854–1925), German composer and pianist.

127.14–15 Paderewski's minuet in G] Solo piano composition (1887) by Polish pianist, composer, diplomat, and statesman Jan Paderewski (1860–1941).

127.25 Leschetizkys] Theodor Leschetizky (1830–1915) was a Polish pianist, composer, and celebrated teacher.

128.3–4 "*Im tiefen Keller sitz' ich hier*"] "Deep within the cellar, here I sit": drinking song (1802) for basso profundo, composed by German opera singer Ludwig Fischer (1745–1825).

128.7 *Harmonielehre*] German: study of harmony.

131.1 *Jugendwerk*] German: piece of juvenilia.

132.13 Dr. Ayer's Almanac] Patent medicine catalogue published annually in the late nineteenth and early twentieth centuries by J. C. Ayer & Co. of Lowell, Massachusetts.

134.20 *cartes de visite*] French: calling cards.

135.3 the Bodleian] The Bodleian Library at the University of Oxford.

143.23 Terence V. Powderly] Labor leader (1849–1924) who led the American Knights of Labor, 1879–93.

144.8 Delmonico's] Group of prestigious New York restaurants in the nineteenth and early twentieth centuries, the first of which was located in lower Manhattan.

145.27 Jake Kilrain] Bare-knuckles boxer born John Joseph Killion (1859–1937), best known for the seventy-five-round heavyweight championship bout with defending champion John L. Sullivan held in New Orleans on July 7, 1889, which Sullivan won.

146.19 Oriole Park] Wooden baseball stadium that opened on May 11, 1891, also known as Union Park.

147.9 Washington club] Washington's first club in Major League Baseball (which began with the formation of the National League in 1876) dates to

1884. The Washington club in the National League disbanded after the 1889 season, but under new management another major-league entry was organized in late 1890. That year, August Mencken Sr. was elected its Vice President and the club was admitted to the American Association as the Washington Base Ball Club, sometimes called the Statesmen. He held the office until 1892, when the Washington Statesmen transitioned to the National League and were renamed the Senators.

147.19   Barnie] William "Bald Billy" Barnie (1853–1900), manager of the Baltimore Orioles, 1883–91; in 1892 he managed the Washington Senators.

147.36–37   Matt Kilroy] Matthew Kilroy (1866–1940), pitcher for the Baltimore Orioles from 1886 to 1889, who led the American Association in strikeouts in 1886 and in wins the following year.

147.38   Amos Rusie] Pitcher (1871–1942) known as the Hoosier Thunderbolt, who played most of his major-league career for the New York Giants.

149.13   Frank Foreman] Left-handed pitcher (1863–1957) nicknamed "Monkey," who played for the Orioles in 1885, 1889, 1892, and 1901–2.

149.22   an inshoot] Pitch that breaks toward the batter.

150.8–9   Baltimore Orioles started out to astound mankind . . . 1894] The Orioles won the first of three consecutive National League pennants in 1894.

153.26   *Kartoffelsalat*] German: potato salad.

154.1   restauranteurs] Mencken's preferred spelling; see p. 343.

156.5   Thurn und Taxis] Aristocratic family that was given a postal monopoly in the Holy Roman Empire in the seventeenth century. It continued operating its postal services into the nineteenth century, and began issuing its own stamps in 1852.

158.23–24   engraving . . . Masonic significance] "The Iron Worker and King Solomon," engraving by American engraver John Sartain (1808–1897) after an 1860 painting by Christian Schussele (1824–1879), Alsatian-born artist who settled in Philadelphia. The image shows King Solomon allowing an ironworker to occupy a seat of honor at a banquet for craftsmen who had helped build the temple in Jerusalem. The engraving was displayed in some Masonic lodges.

158.26   Rogers group] See note 49.23.

158.32–33   "Rosen aus dem Süden"] Waltz ("Roses from the South," 1880) by Austrian composer Johann Strauss II (1825–1899).

158.33–34   "Boccaccio," . . . "The Tales of Hoffmann"] Operas or operettas by Austrian composer Franz von Suppé (1819–1895), French composer Edmond Audran (1840–1901), and French composer Jacques Offenbach (1819–1880), which premiered in 1879, 1880, and 1881, respectively.

159.15–16   the North river] Hudson River estuary between southeastern New York and northeastern New Jersey.

162.4   Cheyne-Stokes snores] An abnormal pattern of breathing marked by a cyclic crescendo-decrescendo pattern, named for the Scottish physician John Cheyne (1777–1836) and the Irish physician William Stokes (1804–1878).

162.11   big Bradstreet book] Book of credit ratings issued by the John M. Bradstreet Company, established in 1849 and named for its founder (1815–1863); it merged with a competitor to become Dun & Bradstreet in 1933.

163.9–10   Breckinridge-Pollard breach of promise case] In the summer of 1893, William C. P. Breckinridge (1837–1904), a fifth-term U.S. congressman from Kentucky, was sued for $50,000 for breach of promise by his lover, Madeleine Pollard, who claimed that they had been having an affair since 1884, when she was seventeen, and that Breckinridge had promised to marry her upon the death of his wife. Instead, in 1893, the recently widowed Breckinridge married someone else. Breckinridge admitted to the affair but denied promising to marry Pollard. The court found in her favor, awarding her $15,000 in damages. Breckinridge was defeated in his bid for reelection to Congress and his political career came to an end.

164.22–23   Cardinal Gibbons had joined the A.P.A.] Cardinal James Gibbons (1834–1921), archbishop of Baltimore, 1877–1921. The American Protective Association was an anti-Catholic secret society established in Iowa in 1887 by Baltimore-born Henry F. Bowers (1837–1911).

164.28   William Ruth] His actual name was George Herman Ruth Sr. (1871–1918), owner of several Baltimore saloons.

165.37   *Schafskopf*] Sheepshead, a popular German card game.

166.17   *mania à potu*] French: madness from drinking; delirium tremens.

167.15–16   his career as Münchhausen and Joe Cook] Münchhausen, see note 109.20–21; vaudeville actor and clown Joe Cook (1890–1959).

173.8   Glauber's salts] Sodium sulfate, named for the German chemist Johann Rudolph Glauber (1604–1670), who spent much of his life in Amsterdam.

179.7   *madura*] Spanish: middle-aged.

180.4   General George H. Thomas] U.S. Army officer (1816–1870), a Virginian who fought for the Union during the Civil War.

183.26   *quod ab omnibus, quod ubique, quod semper*] Latin: by all persons, in all places, and at all times.

195.32   Maud S.] Harness-racing champion of the 1880s owned by railroad magnate William H. Vanderbilt (1821–1885), a filly known as the "trotting queen."

199.27–28   "St. Elmo," by Mrs. Augusta Jane Evans Wilson] Novel (1867), the most popular of the domestic romances written by American novelist Augusta Jane Evans Wilson (1835–1909).

NEWSPAPER DAYS

207.8–11   Sir Thomas Overbury's sneer . . . familiarly,"] From the posthumously published "An Affectate Traveller" in *Characters* (1614) by English courtier Sir Thomas Overbury (1581–1613), who was involved in intrigues that led to his murder while imprisoned in the Tower of London.

217.37   a picture-play by Alexander Black] Black (1859–1940), a journalist and novelist, became known for his presentations of "picture plays" such as *Miss Jerry* (1894), in which projected lantern slides that dissolved from one to the next to suggest movement were accompanied by live narration.

217.39   Frank Beard] Illustrator and cartoonist (1842–1905) known for his "chalk talks," monologues accompanied by a succession of chalk illustrations.

218.5   Raff's Cavatina] Cavatina for Violin and Piano, op. 85, no. 3 (1859), by Swiss-born German composer and pedagogue Joseph Joachim Raff (1822–1882).

218.6–7   W. G. Owst] See Mencken's lengthy biographical portrait of Owst, pp. 761–64.

218.10   Mendelssohn's "Elijah"] Oratorio, op. 70 (1846) by German composer Felix Mendelssohn (1809–1847).

218.11   Baltimore Oratorio Society] A society of musicians organized in 1880 by Otto Sutro that performed three concerts per year. Within five years the Society grew to nearly eight hundred active members. It continued its activities until 1924, under the direction of German-born Joseph Pache (1861–1926).

218.30–31   Richard Harding Davis's "Gallegher and Other Stories"] Davis (1864–1916) was renowned as a war correspondent who covered the Second Boer War and Theodore Roosevelt's Rough Riders campaign in the Spanish-American War. *Gallegher, and Other Stories* was published in 1891.

218.31–32   Jesse Lynch Williams's "The Stolen Story and Other Stories"] Williams (1871–1929), in addition to *The Stolen Story and Other Newspaper Stories* (1899), was the author of *New York Sketches* (1902) and the Pulitzer Prize–winning comedy *Why Marry?* (1917).

218.32–33   Elizabeth G. Jordan's "Tales of the City Room"] Jordan (1865–1947), the editor of *Harper's Bazaar* (1900–13), published her first book, *Tales of the City Room*, a collection of stories about female journalists, in 1898. She also was the author of *May Iverson, Her Book* (1904), *Miss Blake's Husband* (1925), *The Life of the Party* (1935), and an autobiography, *Three Rousing Cheers* (1938).

220.1   Dorsey Guy] Dan Dorsey Guy (1870–1930), correspondent for the

New York Herald in Cuba during the Spanish-American War; he worked for various newspapers during his forty-year career, notably as telegraph editor, sports editor, and assistant city editor at the Baltimore *Sun*.

220.1   Harry West] Harold E. West (1866–1948) was a member of the staff of the Baltimore *Sunpapers* for forty-one years, working in various capacities, including as Sunday editor in 1910 and city editor in 1916 of the *Evening Sun*.

220.21   Rose Sydell's London Blondes] The burlesque company Rose Sydell's London Belles.

220.24–25   "full of strange oaths"] Shakespeare, *As You Like It*, II.vii.150.

222.27   bulldogs] Morning editions of a daily newspaper.

222.38   Nachman] George W. Nachman (1861–1950), business manager of the *Herald*, who moved to New York in 1915 to work for a diamond firm.

223.5–6   Colonel Cunningham] Albert B. Cunningham (1846–1915), managing editor of the *Baltimore Herald*, 1881–1901; see pp. 301–6.

225.2   Gene Grannan] Eugene E. Grannan (1852–1926), formerly chief of the detective service of the B & O Railroad, was appointed Baltimore's police magistrate in 1896 and served, with some interruptions, until 1911.

226.11   Keirle] Nathaniel Garland Kierle (1833–1919), professor of Pathology and Medical Jurisprudence at the College of Physicians and Surgeons of Baltimore, served for more than thirty years as the city's medical examiner.

226.24–25   four poor blackamoors were stretched at once] Executed for the assault of thirteen-year-old Annie Bailey were John Myers, Charles James, and Cornelius Gardner; also hanged was Joseph Bryan, convicted of murdering his common-law wife.

227.37   *Diener*] Morgue worker, from German for "servant."

229.32   yeggmen] Slang for "safecrackers."

229.34   Bertillon system] System to classify criminals based on bodily measurements and other physical characteristics developed by French criminologist Alphonse Bertillon (1853–1914).

230.17–18   Hackman, the superintendent] William H. Hackman (1841–1910), Keeper of the Morgue, 1891–1900.

230.36–37   Frank R. Kent] Journalist (1877–1958) on the staff of the *Sun* from 1898; managing editor, 1911–21; named vice president, 1921.

236.37   Charles J. Bonaparte . . . Napoleon I] American lawyer and reformer Charles J. Bonaparte (1851–1921), a grandson of Jérôme-Napoléon Bonaparte, king of Westphalia, and Elizabeth Patterson of Baltimore; secretary of the navy, 1905–6, and U.S. attorney general, 1906–9.

240.30–37   character named McCuen . . . lighting] Robert Johnston McCuen

(1855–1914), popular City Hall official nicknamed "Uncle Bob"; Superintendent of Lamps and Lighting, 1900–1914.

241.23 McKee Barclay] Cartoonist and political writer (1870–1947) who came to Baltimore in 1891; worked for the *Evening World* and *Herald* before joining the *Sun* in 1908, where he spent the rest of his career.

246.10 Isaac Goldberg] Author and critic (1887–1938) who contributed articles on theater and music to *The American Mercury* and other publications. In addition to *The Man Mencken: A Biographical and Critical Survey* (1925), he was the author of *George Gershwin: A Study in American Music* (1931) and *Havelock Ellis: A Biographical and Critical Survey* (1926).

247.8 Butler's "Hudibras," . . . "The Temple,"] *Hudibras* (1663–78) by English writer Samuel Butler (1613–1680); "The Temple," series of devotional poems by English poet and clergyman George Herbert (1593–1633) published posthumously in 1633.

247.8–9 contributions to the *Spectator* by Eustace Budgell] The London daily periodical *The Spectator* was published by the English essayists Joseph Addison (1672–1719) and Richard Steele (1672–1729) in 1711–12 (Addison briefly revived it in 1714); English essayist Eustace Budgell (1686–1737) was a frequent contributor.

247.9–10 Colley Cibber's Apology] *Apology for the Life of Colley Cibber, Comedian* (1740) by the English actor, playwright, and poet (1671–1757).

247.14 *cacoethes scribendi*] Latin: incurable itch to write.

247.16 Arthur W. Hawks, who had a brother] Arthur Worthington Hawks Jr. (1878–1949) was a childhood friend of Mencken who worked with him at the Baltimore *Morning Herald* before becoming city editor of the *News*. His brother Wells Hawks (1870–1941) worked for various newspapers, but was best known for his short stories about the circus, notably *Red Wagon Stories, or Tales Told Under the Tent* (1904).

248.11 The *Chap-Book*] American biweekly magazine (1894–98); its contributors included Henry James, H. G. Wells, Hamlin Garland, and Max Beerbohm.

248.11 the *Lark*] Literary magazine (1895–97) founded in San Francisco by Frank Gelett Burgess (1866–1951).

248.13 *M'lle New York*] Periodical (1895–99) by Vance Thompson (1863–1925) that helped introduce American readers to symbolist poetry, Nietzsche, and other modern European intellectual and artistic currents.

248.14 James G. Huneker] James Gibbons Huneker (1857–1921), American critic of literature, music, and art whose books include *Chopin: The Man and His Music* (1900), *Iconoclasts: A Book of Dramatists* (1905), *Egoists: A Book of Supermen* (1909), *Ivory Apes and Peacocks* (1915), the memoirs *Old Fogy* (1913) and *Steeplejack* (1920), and the novel *Painted Veils* (1920).

248.33   G. Alden Peirson] The Baltimore artist Golden Alden Peirson (1874–1921).

249.12   Edward Abram Uffington Valentine] Poet and novelist (b. 1870), author of *The Ship of Silence and Other Poems* (1901), *Hecla Sandwith* (1905), and *The Labyrinth of Life* (1912).

249.22   Austin Dobson] English poet (1840–1921), author of *Vignettes in Rhyme* (1873) and *At the Sign of the Lyre* (1885).

249.22   Andrew Lang] Scottish poet and scholar (1844–1912), translator of Homer's *Odyssey* (1879), author of *Myth, Ritual and Religion* (1887), and compiler of numerous compilations of fairy tales, beginning with *The Blue Fairy Book* (1889).

249.30–31   piece lately published by Edmond Rostand] "To Kruger" (1900) by French playwright Edmond Rostand (1868–1918), best known for *Cyrano de Bergerac* (1897).

250.13–14   Marshall and Beek . . . Gordon] Mencken's *Ventures Into Verse* (1903) was the first book published by the firm established by James H. Beek (1880–1942), the lithographer Charles Gordon (1878–1965), and the printer John H. Marshall in the Telegram building on North Guilford and Baltimore Street. The 1904 Baltimore Fire destroyed the building and any remaining copies of the book were lost.

250.19   John Siegel] John Frank Siegel (1878–1942), artist for the Baltimore *Herald*, 1899–1906; he joined the *Sunpapers* in 1910 and was staff artist for thirty-two years.

250.20   à la Roycroft] In 1895, Elbert Green Hubbard (1856–1915) founded the Roycroft Press, named after the seventeenth-century bookbinders Samuel and Thomas Roycroft. Inspired by the Arts and Crafts movement, the Roycrofters created books printed on handmade paper, with superior design and binding.

251.2   Harry Thursten Peck] American classical scholar (1856–1914) and first editor-in-chief, 1895–1906, of the literary journal *The Bookman* (1895–1933).

251.21   James Madison] Theater manager (1870–1943) who wrote sketches for Weber and Fields, Al Jolson, and others. His monthly *Madison's Budget* featured thousands of jokes and was widely consulted by stage comedians.

252.15   Juliet Wilbor Tompkins] American novelist (1871–1956), whose books include *Dr. Ellen* (1908), *Mothers and Fathers* (1910), and *A Girl Named Mary* (1918); editor of *Munsey's Magazine*, 1897–1901.

253.34   M. M. III age of Crete] The Middle Minoan III period, 1700–1600 B.C.E.

255.2   Lew Dockstader] Stage name of George Alfred Clapp (1856–1924), American vaudeville and minstrel entertainer and manager.

255.7   Ford's Opera House] Theater on the corner of Eutaw and Fayette streets, opened in October 1871 under the ownership of John T. Ford (1829–1894), theater owner and manager who had run Ford's Theatre in Washington, D.C., the site of President Lincoln's assassination, before it was seized by the federal government.

255.35–36   the Boston lemon-squeezer, Richard G. Badger] Publisher (1878–1937), founder of a vanity press in Boston, the Gorham Press.

256.9–10   Socialist named La Monte] Richard Rives La Monte (b. 1867), an editor at the Baltimore *News* and at the New York *Call*, a Socialist newspaper.

256.38–257.1   newspaper man . . . Harding] Harding bought the Marion, Ohio, *Star* in 1884 and was its longtime editor.

257.3   the thirteen years of horror] Prohibition.

260.6   Bowley's wharf] Wharf at the foot of South Street (near current site of the National Aquarium) named for Baltimore civic leader and lawyer Daniel Bowley (1744–1807); it was the center of the city's fruit-importing business until it was destroyed in the Baltimore Fire of 1904.

260.9   River Rouge] Site of enormous manufacturing complex for Ford automobiles in Dearborn, Michigan.

265.25–26   Mulvaney, Learoyd, and Ortheris . . . "Soldiers Three"] Fictional British army privates who appear in stories in Rudyard Kipling's *Plain Tales from the Hills* (1888) and *Soldiers Three* (1899).

267.28   "The Warriors at Helgeland"] Or *The Vikings at Helgeland* (1858), Henrik Ibsen's play based on Norwegian folklore and history.

269.36   Mayor of Jacksonville] James Edward Theodore Bowden (1858–1930), mayor of Jacksonville, 1899–1901, 1915–17. Mencken's story, published in the Baltimore *Herald* on May 12, 1901, was headlined "Good Things In the Car Greeted With Cries of Joy—Words of Gratitude from the High Officials."

274.5   a part in *Tobacco Road*] Long-running play (1933) by Jack Kirkland (1902–1969), based on the novel (1932) about Georgia sharecroppers by Erskine Caldwell (1903–1987).

277.4–5   Martinique volcano . . . first blow-off] The eruption on May 8, 1902, of Mount Pelée, a volcano located on the northern end of Martinique, ravaged the city of Saint-Pierre and killed most of its residents. The volcano erupted with equal force twelve days later.

277.16–17   lawsuit relating to my father's estate] To prevent the construction of a house adjacent to his property in Mount Washington, August Mencken Sr. bought an extra strip of land, fifteen feet wide and running down the lot, from the previous owner, Otto M. Mattfeldt, in 1892. Mattfeldt neglected to make the transfer, so that after August's death H. L. Mencken was obliged to lodge a friendly suit against his mother, leading to the incorrect public assumption that they had quarreled over the estate.

279.13   "Floradora"] Musical (1899) famous for its double sextet and chorus line of "Florodora Girls."

279.37   Daniel Frohman] Theatrical impresario (1851–1940), author of *Memories of a Manager* (1911) and *Daniel Frohman Presents* (1935).

279.37–38   Victor Herbert] American composer (1859–1924) of operettas, including *The Fortune Teller* (1898), *Babes in Toyland* (1903), *Mlle. Modiste* (1905), and *The Red Mill* (1906).

279.38   Clyde Fitch] Playwright (1865–1909) whose plays included *Barbara Frietchie* (1899), *The Climbers* (1901), and *Captain Jinks of the Horse Marines* (1901).

279.38   Paul Armstrong] Playwright (1869–1915), author of *Salomy Jane* (1905), *Alias Jimmy Valentine* (1909), *A Romance of the Underworld* (1911), and other works.

279.38   Augustus Thomas] Playwright (1857–1934) whose successes included *Alabama* (1891), *Arizona* (1900), *The Earl of Pawtucket* (1903), *The Witching Hour* (1907), and *The Copperhead* (1918).

279.39   Charles Klein] Playwright (1867–1915) known for *Heartsease* (1897), *The Auctioneer* (1901), *The Music Master* (1904), *The Lion and the Mouse* (1905), and *The Third Degree* (1909). He died in the sinking of the *Lusitania* in 1915.

279.39   A. M. Palmer] Albert Marshall Palmer (1838–1905), manager of the Madison Square Theatre and producer of such successes as *Alabama* (1891), *Lady Windermere's Fan* (1893), and *Trilby* (1895).

279.39   Charles Frohman] Frohman (1856–1915) organized the Theatrical Syndicate, which exercised monopolistic dominance in the 1890s. He oversaw the first American productions of works by Wilde, Barrie, Shaw, and Maugham. He died in the sinking of the *Lusitania*.

280.21–22   Anna Marble] Anna Marble Pollock (1871–1946), theatrical press agent, the daughter of Edward Marble, actor and member of one of the oldest theatrical families in the United States.

280.23–24   Paul Wilstach, who whooped up Richard Mansfield] Paul Wilstach (1870–1952) was the author of *Richard Mansfield: The Man and the Actor* (1908), biography of the American actor (1857–1907), educated in England, who had his first major American success in A. M. Palmer's production *A Parisian Romance* (1883).

280.25   James Forbes] Canadian-born playwright (1871–1938), author of *The Chorus Lady* (1906), *The Traveling Salesman* (1908), and *The Famous Mrs. Fair* (1919).

280.26   Robert Edeson] Actor (1868–1931) who starred in *Soldiers of Fortune* (1902) before going to Hollywood in 1921.

280.26–27   Eugene Walter] Playwright and theatrical manager (1874–1941); his dramas included *Paid in Full* (1908) and *The Easiest Way* (1909), both plays about prostitution.

280.27–28   Bayard Veiller] Playwright (1869–1943) known for such success-ful melodramas as *Within the Law* (1918), *The Thirteenth Chair* (1916), and *The Trial of Mary Dugan* (1928).

280.29   Margaret Wycherly] Actor (1881–1956) who made her name in classic revivals and in plays by Yeats and Shaw.

280.31   De Wolf Hopper] Actor (1858–1935) known mainly for his comic roles.

280.31   E. H. Sothern] Actor (1859–1933) celebrated for his Shakespearean roles, often costarring with his wife Julia Marlowe (1866–1950).

280.31–32   Viola Allen] Actor (1867–1948) who starred in Bronson Howard's *Shenandoah* (1888), the stage version of Frances Hodgson Burnett's novel *Little Lord Fauntleroy* (1886), Hall Caine's *The Christian* (1898), and many other plays and films.

280.32   William Faversham] Actor (1868–1940), leading man in Charles Frohman's company. He played Algernon in the first American production of Oscar Wilde's *The Importance of Being Earnest* (1895) and Captain James Wyngate in *The Squaw Man* (1905), a part written for him.

280.32   Mrs. Leslie Carter] Caroline Louise Dudley (1857?– 1937), actor who appeared in *The Heart of Maryland* (1895) and *Du Barry* (1901) by playwright, actor, and manager David Belasco (1859–1931), and many other plays.

281.16   Druid Hill Park] Large municipal park, Baltimore's first, which opened to the public on October 19, 1860.

282.1   *réchauffé*] French: meal of warmed-over leftovers.

282.1   Sardou, Pinero and Augustus Thomas] Popular dramatists: the French playwright Victorien Sardou (1831–1908), whose plays included *La Perle Noire* (*The Black Pearl*, 1862), *Fédora* (1882), and *La Tosca* (1887); English play-wright Sir Arthur Wing Pinero (1855–1934), author of *The Magistrate* (1885) and *The Second Mrs. Tanqueray* (1893); Augustus Thomas, see note 279.38.

282.32   Osler] Canadian physician Sir William Osler (1849–1919), author of the influential textbook *Principles and Practice of Medicine* (1892); physician-in-chief of Johns Hopkins Hospital, 1889–1905, and professor of medicine at Johns Hopkins University.

283.26   Reginald De Koven] Reginald DeKoven (1859–1920), American composer whose many operettas included *Robin Hood* (1890), *The Fencing Master* (1892), and *Rob Roy* (1894).

284.13 "Erminie" and "Fra Diavolo"] Comic opera (1885) by English composer Edward Jakobowski (1856–1929); comic opera (1830) by French composer Daniel Auber (1782–1871).

284.33 William Winter] American drama critic (1836–1917), reviewer for the *New York Tribune*, 1865–1909. His writings were collected in *Other Days* (1908), *Old Friends* (1909), *Shakespeare on the Stage* (1911–13), and *The Wallet of Time* (1913).

284.38 Hauptmann] German playwright Gerhart Hauptmann (1862–1946), author of naturalistic plays such as *Vor Sonnenaufgang* (*Before Dawn*, 1889) and *Die Weber* (*The Weavers*, 1893).

285.10–11 Brown's Chop-house] Browne's Chop House, restaurant exclusively for men (until 1911) at 1424 Broadway, across from the Metropolitan Opera House, the last of several locations; founded in 1856 by actor George F. Browne (1819–1885).

285.20–22 1919 . . . full-length play in collaboration with George Jean Nathan] *Heliogabalus: A Buffoonery in Three Acts.* George Jean Nathan (1882–1958) was the preeminent theater critic of his era; with Mencken he coedited *The Smart Set,* 1914–24, and cofounded *The American Mercury* in 1924, serving as coeditor until 1930. His many books included *Another Book on the Theater* (1915), *Mr. George Jean Nathan Presents* (1917), *Bottoms Up: An Appreciation of the Slapstick to Satire* (1917), *The Popular Theatre* (1918), and *The Critic and the Drama* (1922).

286.14–15 Mary Shaw] American actor and activist (1854–1929) and early advocate for the works of Ibsen and Shaw. Her appearance on Broadway in the title role of Shaw's *Mrs. Warren's Profession* (1893) in 1905 led to her arrest and acquittal on charges of indecency.

287.4 "Blue Jeans."] Popular play (1890) by Joseph Arthur (pseudonym of Arthur Smith, 1848–1906), best known for a scene where the unconscious hero is placed on a conveyor belt moving toward a spinning buzz saw.

287.14 American book of "Sari,"] Adaptation that premiered in 1914 of an operetta (1912) by the Hungarian composer Emmerich Kálmán (1882–1953).

287.21–22 "The Two Orphans,"] Play (1874) by French writers Adolphe d'Ennery (1811–1899) and Eugène Cormon (1810–1903).

288.23 Klaw and Erlanger] Theatrical agency founded by Marc Klaw (1858–1936) and Abraham Lincoln Erlanger (1859–1930), later merged into the Theatrical Syndicate.

290.20 *infra dig.*] Latin: beneath one's dignity.

290.26 *non est*] Latin: absent.

291.2–3 Simon Simple . . . Spiegelburgers] Comic strips from the first decade of the twentieth century: "Simon Simple," by Ed Carey (1870–1928), featuring a pointy-headed prankster; "Billy Bounce," about a messenger boy in a rubber suit, created by William Wallace Denslow (1856–1915) and continued by Charles William Kahles (1878–1931), creator of "The Teasers"; and "Herr Spiegelburger, the Amateur Cracksman" by Carl Thomas Anderson (1865–1948).

291.4   Foxy Grandpa] Comic strip (1900–18) by Carl Edward "Bunny" Schultze (1866–1939), later adapted for stage and screen.

291.23–24   George Ade and Finley Peter Dunne . . . Chicago] Chicago journalist and humorist George Ade (1866–1944) was the author of the column "Stories of the Streets and of the Town," as well as *Fables in Slang* (1900), *The Girl Proposition* (1902), *Breaking Into Society* (1903), and many other books and plays; Chicago journalist Peter Finley Dunne (1867–1936) created "Mr. Dooley," an Irish immigrant saloonkeeper who commented on the news of the day, featured in his columns and books such as *Mr. Dooley in Peace and War* (1898), *Mr. Dooley's Philosophy* (1900), and *Dissertations by Mr. Dooley* (1906).

292.22   Louis Brownlow] Journalist and political scientist (1879–1963) who served as a commissioner of Washington, D.C., 1915–20, and as a member of the Committee of Administrative Management, 1935–36, which recommended a reorganization of the federal government's Executive Branch.

292.23   Harvey Fergusson] Novelist (1890–1971), author of *The Blood of the Conquerors* (1921), *Women and Wives* (1924), *Rio Grande* (1933), and *The Life of Riley* (1937).

295.9–10   Tom Dempsey, an old-time police lieutenant] Thomas F. Dempsey (1856–1931), twenty-seven-year veteran of the Baltimore police force, 1888–1915.

295.23–24   What would now be called an Open Forum] Progressive movement founded in 1908 by publisher and Baptist leader George W. Coleman (1867–1950), who established a series of lectures followed by discussion on religion and on topical issues at Ford Hall in Boston.

298.17–18   exists to the present day . . . Saturday night sessions] New members were admitted until 1945 into the Saturday Night Club (which was not a formal club, lacking a constitution, dues, or officers); after Mencken's debilitating stroke in 1948, it was disbanded on December 2, 1950.

299.26   "Barbara Frietchie"] Poem (1863) by American poet John Greenleaf Whittier (1807–1892).

302.5   those of Jeb Stuart . . . Wheeler] Prominent Confederate officers J.E.B. Stuart (1833–1864), cavalry commander of the Army of Northern Virginia, 1862–64; John Singleton Mosby (1833–1916), commander of cavalry raiding unit known as Mosby's Rangers; Joseph Wheeler (1836–1906), cavalry commander of the Army of Mississippi, 1862–65.

302.9–10   the celebrated John Albert Cockerill] American newspaper editor (1845–1896) of various publications, including the *Washington Post*; at the St. Louis *Post Dispatch*, 1879–83, he was chief aide to Joseph Pulitzer, who brought him to the New York *World* in 1883.

302.27   McNelly's Scouts] Unit led by Leander Harvey McNelly (1844–1877) for the Confederate Army in Louisiana and Texas.

305.10   window of the Athenaeum Club] In the Greek Revival building (1830–1910) at the northeast corner of Charles and Franklin streets, a Baltimore landmark; home to a social club, 1877–1908.

305.12   *Rittmeister*] German: cavalry captain.

307.36–37   Canadian named Peard . . . no more capacity for the job] Frank Furnival Peard (1868–1925), business manager of the *Herald*, 1899–1903 (later its general manager and publisher), had come to Baltimore as representative of the Remington Typewriter Company in the early 1890s. He had been business manager of the Baltimore *News*, 1893–99.

308.12   Baltimore *American*, a rival] Newspaper with a storied history, including the first publication of "The Star-Spangled Banner" (1814).

311.35   his only son] American diplomatic official Lynn Webster Meekins (1893–1969); commercial attaché to the U.S. Embassy in London, 1933–39.

314.9–10   Hulls . . . Lewises] Cordell Hull (1871–1955), U.S. secretary of state, 1933–44; Frances Perkins (1880–1965), U.S. secretary of labor, 1933–45; William Thomas Manning (1866–1949), bishop of the Episcopal Diocese of New York, 1921–49; John L. Lewis (1880–1969), president of the United Mine Workers of America and a founder of the Congress of Industrial Organizations.

318.4   Stephen H. Horgan] Stephen Henry Horgan (1854–1941) invented the halftone engraving process, which made possible the reproduction of photographs in newspapers.

322.26–27   Felix Agnus . . . hero of the Civil War] French-born newspaper publisher (1839–1925), soldier, and sculptor who took over the leadership of the *American* after the death of his father-in-law, Charles Fulton, in 1883. Agnus's career as a soldier began in Europe, where he fought at the Battle of Montebello (1859) and with Garibaldi. Fighting on the Union side during the Civil War, he was decorated for his bravery, was twice wounded, and rose to the rank of brigadier general, awarded in 1865. He convalesced from the wounds he suffered in 1862 in Baltimore, where he met his wife, Annie E. Fulton.

324.40   Dunkard] A member of the German Baptist Brethren.

325.39   Maryland Club] Formed in 1857, a club whose membership has included many of Baltimore's civic and business leaders.

330.39 Tammany leaders] The Tammany Society (1789–1961), known as Tammany Hall after its headquarters on 14th Street, was the political machine that controlled Democratic Party politics in New York City through the 1930s, when its influence waned due to the reforms of Mayor Fiorello La Guardia and its loss of federal patronage.

337.27 a white-wings] A street cleaner, member of a workforce named for its white canvas uniforms first organized in New York City in 1896; four years later, a similar group was established in Baltimore.

339.25 *Goy Schul*] Yiddish: Gentile school.

341.13 *octroi*] French: tax collected on goods entering a given area.

342.17 Scribe] Eugène Scribe (1791–1861), French playwright, author of hundreds of plays alone or in collaboration, noted for his mastery of stagecraft and plot construction.

342.18 Russell Sages] Financier and U.S. congressman Russell Sage (1816–1906).

343.20 Frank Junker] Businessman (1859–1910), proprietor of the Hotel Junker at 20–22 East Fayette Street, which began as a small establishment in 1884. The five-story building housing the hotel and restaurant was destroyed in the 1904 Baltimore Fire; within a year he had built a new, fireproof seven-story building.

344.11–12 Theodore Kremer and Charles E. Blaney melodramas] Plays of German-born American actor and playwright Theodore Kremer (1871?–1923), the most successful of which was *Bertha, the Sewing Machine Girl* (1906), and of actor, theatrical manager, and playwright Charles Edward Blaney (1866–1944), "King of the Melodramas," whose numerous plays included *King of the Opium Ring* (1899), *For His Brother's Crime* (1905), *The Hired Girl's Millions* (1907), and *Kidnapped for Revenge* (1907).

344.26 *col arco*] Italian: with the bow.

345.38 Ned Schleigh] Edward Schleigh (1849–1912), veteran policeman nicknamed "Captain Ned"; captain of Baltimore's Central police district, 1901–8.

347.8–10 Weber and Fields . . . two comedians] The vaudeville team of Joe Weber (1867–1942) and Lew Fields (1867–1941).

348.35–36 and in a little while he vanished from the place] When McGraw left Baltimore in 1902 to manage the New York Giants, he sold his interest in the Diamond Café at 519 North Howard Street to Robinson, his former Oriole teammate and partner in the lucrative restaurant, which contained a bowling alley, pool tables, and a reading room.

348.40 *Schwartenmagen*] A variety of head cheese.

349.32–33 Mike Ganzhorn, who kept a small stag hotel in Baltimore street]

Ganzhorn's City Hotel, 226 East Baltimore Street, destroyed in the Baltimore Fire of 1904.

351.28   Union Station] Baltimore's primary train station, since 1928 named Pennsylvania Station.

356.12–13   out of date as Joe Miller's Jest-book] The name of English comic actor Joe Miller (1684–1738) is a byword for a stale joke; the first of several collections of jokes bearing his name was published shortly after his death.

358.13–14   Sam Gompers or Gene Debs] American union leaders Samuel Gompers (1850–1924), founder of the American Federation of Labor (AFL), and Eugene Debs (1855–1926), five-time Socialist Party candidate for president.

358.15   James Creelman, who had interviewed the Pope] Canadian-born writer James Creelman (1859–1915) scored the journalistic coup of a rare interview with Pope Leo XIII in 1890.

359.10   M. de Blowitz] Bohemian-born French journalist Henri Georges Stephane Adolphe Opper de Blowitz (1825–1903).

359.16   James Gordon Bennett] American publisher and financier James Gordon Bennett Jr. (1841–1918), flamboyant editor of the New York *Herald*.

361.14   Li Hung Chang] Chinese statesman, soldier, and diplomat (1823–1901).

364.25   Ward McAllister . . . 400] Ward McAllister (1827–1895) was a wealthy attorney who helped Caroline Schermerhorn Astor select the members of the New York social elite known as "the Four Hundred."

364.26   the *Deutsche Correspondent*] German-language newspaper published in Baltimore, 1841–1918.

365.20–21   song by the celebrated Viktor von Scheffel] German student song (1875) with music by Ludwig Teichgräber (1840–1904) based on "Die Schlacht im Teutoburger Wald" ("The Battle in Teutoburger Forest," 1847) by German poet and novelist Joseph Viktor von Scheffel (1826–1886). An anonymous translation of its opening lines reads: "When the Romans, rashly roving / Into Germany were moving."

365.33   *Liederbücher*] German: songbooks.

365.37   *Polizeistunden*] German: closing times.

366.30   *Häringsalat*] Herring salad.

368.19   *Rinderbrust mit Meerrettig*] Rinderbrust mit Meerrettich, breast of beef with horseradish sauce.

368.25   *Bohnensalat*] Bean salad.

371.5–6   Leander J. de Bekker] American journalist, editor, and author (1872–1931), on the staff of the Baltimore *American*, 1899–1901; his books include

The Serio-Comic Profession (1915), on journalism, reviewed by Mencken in *The Smart Set*, April 1916.

371.34   York street, Hughsie street and Elbow Lane] York Street ran from the harbor west to the vicinity of Camden Yards, and Hughes Street bordered the northern portion of Federal Hill in the southern part of the city; both streets exist today in altered and diminished form. Elbow Lane, which no longer exists, ran from South Paca Street to Sterrett Street in the area now known as Ridgley's Delight, west of Camden Yards.

373.24–25   Frank Kent . . . Alexander] Frank Kent, see note 230.36–37; Walter Alexander (1869–1934), longtime City Hall reporter for the *American* and, from 1911 until his death, the *Sun*.

378.18–19   my bogus history of the bathtub] "A Neglected Anniversary," published in the *New York Evening Mail* on December 28, 1917, claimed that the bathtub had been introduced to the United States in 1842 and had become broadly acceptable when President Millard Fillmore had one installed in the White House in 1850. Mencken's hoax gained widespread acceptance and was subsequently quoted as fact in medical journals and reference books.

378.40   George Worsham] Journalist (1875–1937) who joined the *Herald* staff in 1900 and succeeded Mencken as police headquarters reporter when he was moved to City Hall.

380.2–3   nearly two weeks . . . authentic details] An exaggeration; details of the battle began to appear in American newspapers on June 2, two days after Mencken published his story.

382.12–21   Joseph Conrad . . . youth!"] From Conrad's "Youth: A Narrative" (1898), collected in *Youth: A Narrative and Two Other Stories* (1902).

383.9–10   Horton . . . was in hospital] George W. Horton (1846–1920), chief of Baltimore's fire department, 1901–12, was injured by a live trolley wire that fell and burned him on the Sunday of the fire. He left his post but returned to work the next day.

389.39–41   The face in which this line is set . . . Scotch Modern] Referring to the 1941 Knopf edition of *Newspaper Days*.

398.34–35   Oler, the iceman who owned the paper] See Mencken's account of Oler, pp. 724–25.

401.23   E. F. Dakin book on Ma Eddy] *Mrs. Eddy: The Biography of a Virginal Mind* (1929) by editor and writer Edwin Franden Dakin (1898–1976), reviewed by Mencken in November 1929.

HEATHEN DAYS

407.4   Dr. and Mrs. Frederic M. Hanes] Frederic Moir Hanes (1883–1946) and Elizabeth ("Betty") Peck Hanes (1883–1958) were close friends of both

Mencken and his wife, Sara Haardt. Frederic Hanes, a pathologist and neurologist, was chair of the Department of Medicine at Duke University, and author of *Ashford's Bibliography of Sprue* (1938) and *A Study of Mental Health in North Carolina* (1938).

407.19–20 "New Dictionary of Quotations,"] *A New Dictionary of Quotations on Historical Principles from Ancient and Modern Sources* (New York: Alfred A. Knopf, 1942).

408.13 *Erinnerungen aus dem fröhlichen Bubenleben*] German: recollections of early boyhood, perhaps a reference to the title of a 1929 memoir by the American humorist Hermann Zagel (1859–1936), who wrote in German.

409.39 George Jean Nathan] See note 285.20–22.

409.40 A. H. McDannald] Journalist and editor Alexander H. McDannald (1877–1957), who worked for the Baltimore *News* and *Evening Sun* and served as editor-in-chief of the *Encyclopedia Americana*; his books include *Across Germany* (1914), *Costs of the World War* (1920), and *The Storied Hudson* (1927). Mencken traveled with McDannald to Europe in 1912 and 1914.

410.1 Paul de Kruif] Bacteriologist (1890–1971), author of many books of popular science, including the best-selling *Microbe Hunters* (1926).

410.2 Richard J. Beamish] Journalist (1890–1945) who served as directing editor of *The Philadelphia Press*, 1911–20; secretary of the Commonwealth of Pennsylvania, 1931.

424.2 Cross Keys, a nearby village] African American community south of Mt. Washington, now the site of an upscale commercial and residential development.

424.13 Herman Ellis] Cigarette and cigar manufacturer (1856–1927), owner of H. Ellis & Co., established in 1870, at 211 N. Sharp Street, Baltimore. His business was absorbed by the American Tobacco Company of New York in 1895.

428.35 *Hylobates*] Genus of gibbons.

429.28–29 certain eminent politician . . . radio crooning] Franklin D. Roosevelt. In the 1936 presidential race the Republican campaign of Alf Landon (1887–1987) ridiculed Roosevelt's use of radio to speak to the nation; at an event in Minneapolis, U.S. congressman and former Minnesota governor Theodore Christianson (1883–1948) introduced Landon as the candidate who was "no radio crooner."

431.17 jitney Dwight L. Moody] American evangelist Dwight Lyman Moody (1837–1899), who, with evangelist, composer, and singer Ira David Sankey (1840–1908), held revival meetings throughout the United States and Great Britain.

431.38 Dr. Orison Swett Marden] American author (1850–1924) of self-help books including *The Secret of Achievement* (1898), *Cheerfulness as a Life Power* (1899), *The Hour of Opportunity* (1900), and *Masterful Personality* (1921).

431.38–39   Dr. Frank Crane] American Methodist clergyman (1861–1928) who wrote a popular syndicated newspaper column of short inspirational homilies.

435.4   Bernoullis] Daniel Bernoulli (1700–1782), Swiss mathematician and physicist.

439.3   medical school attached to the hospital] The College of Physicians and Surgeons, later incorporated into the medical school of the University of Maryland.

439.11   *attentat*] German: assassination attempt.

441.6   president of the Polytechnic] William R. King (1852–1923), the school's principal, 1899–1921; for Schley (441.8), see note 29.1.

442.3–4   Lydia Pinkham] American businesswoman (1819–1883) whose popular "Vegetable Compound," a patented herbal medicine, was used especially for the alleviation of menstrual and menopausal pain.

442.20   wowsers] In *The American Language* Mencken writes: "It is a pity that American has not borrowed the Australian invention *wowser*. Says a writer in the Manchester *Guardian*: 'Wowser, whether used as an adjective or a substantive, covers everyone and everything that is out of sympathy with what some people consider *la joie de vivre* [. . . ']. In the United States fully 99 per cent of all the world's *wowsers* rage and roar, and yet we have no simple word to designate them."

445.6   *Geschäft*] German: business.

451   Eugene Walter . . . Swope] For Walter, see note 280.26–27; for Pollock, see note 280.21–22; for the Wilstach brothers, see note 280.23–24 on Paul (his older brother Frank was a theatrical manager); Charles Emerson Cook (1869–1941), originally an associate of David Belasco, was a producer, playwright, press agent, and founder of the Friars Club, a private club organized in 1904 for press agents but later including comedians and other show business personalities; for Veiller, see note 280.27–28; for Swope, see p. 280.12–18.

451.31–32   all talk was about Lotta . . . old-timers] Comic actor, dancer, and entertainer Charlotte Crabtree (1847–1924), known as Lotta, who retired in 1891; American comic actor Maggie Mitchell (Margaret Julia Mitchell, 1832–1918), best known for her starring role in *Fanchon the Cricket* (1860), based on George Sand's novel *La Petite Fadette* (1849); American Shakespearean actor Charlotte Cushman (1816–1876); American actor Mary Anderson (1859–1940), who starred in Shakespearean and other roles before her retirement in 1890.

451.34–35   Mauch Chunk, Pa.] Since 1954 called Jim Thorpe, Pennsylvania.

452.24–25 Foxy Quiller in the musical comedy of the same name] Operetta (1900) by Reginald DeKoven (see note 283.26) about the character created by Sykes in DeKoven's *The Highwayman* (1897), a constable.

452.31–32 the local Frohman] The local theatrical producer (for the Frohman brothers; see notes 279.37 and 279.39).

452.33 "The Chimes of Normandy"] English title of popular operetta *Les cloches de Cornville* (1877) by French composer Robert Planquette (1848–1903).

452.38 "The Mascot"] See note 158.33–34.

458.17 Cheyne-Stokes] See note 162.4.

459.11 anvils . . . celebrated Patrick Sarsfield Gilmore] The Irish-born bandmaster and composer (1829–1892) led concert spectacles featuring music ensembles and music punctuated by cannon shots and anvil blows as percussion.

460.27 Black Hander] Member of the criminal organization the Black Hand.

462.23–24 "La Paloma"] "The Dove," popular song (1859) written by Spanish composer Sebastian de Yradier (1809–1865).

463.10 "Funiculi-Funicula"] Popular song (1880) by Italian composer Luigi Denza (1846–1922), incorporated into Richard Strauss's tone poem for orchestra "Aus Italien" (1886).

463.39 Mann Act] The White-Slave Traffic Act of 1910 addressed human trafficking for prostitution and prohibited the transportation of women and girls across state lines for "immoral purposes." It was named after its sponsor, James Robert Mann (1856–1922), Republican U.S. congressman from Illinois.

464.14 *Deserto sulla terra*] "All alone on earth," from Giuseppe Verdi's opera *Il Trovatore* (1853), a serenade sung offstage.

466.29 *Geheimrat*] German court title equivalent to privy councillor.

470.23 Perkins Square] Small city park in West Baltimore, home to a spring of reputed medicinal value.

472.19 Young Terry McGovern] Named for American champion bantamweight and featherweight boxer Terry McGovern (1880–1918).

473.2 John F. Kieran] Sportswriter (1892–1981) for the *New York Times*, 1915–43.

473.2 Grantland Rice] Sportswriter (1880–1954) whose columns were nationally syndicated.

473.27 Young Jeffries] Named for the heavyweight champion boxer Jim Jeffries (1875–1953).

473.28 Young Fitzsimmons, of Yale] American boxer Robert Fitzsimmons Jr., the son of English-born heavyweight champion Bob Fitzsimmons (1863–1917).

474.21 *in petto*] Italian: in private.

475.7 Young Peter Jackson] Sim Tompkins (1877–1923), named for Peter Jackson (1861–1901), originally from the West Indies, who moved to Australia and won the Australian heavyweight championship in 1886.

477.33–34 Champ Clark] James Beauchamp Clark (1850–1921), U.S. congressman from Missouri, 1893–95, 1897–1921; speaker of the House, 1911–19.

478.16 those of Tweed] William Magear Tweed (1823–1878), New York City Democratic politician and leader of Tammany Hall (see note 330.39). With others, Boss Tweed swindled millions of dollars from the city treasury and was convicted on charges related to his corrupt activities in 1873.

484.34 "The Two Orphans,"] See note 287.21–22.

485.19 "The Fatal Wedding"] Melodrama (1901) by Theodore Kremer (see note 344.11–12).

487.24 "Rigoletto" . . . women were mobile] A play on "La donna è mobile" ("Woman is fickle"), the most famous aria of Verdi's 1851 opera.

490.6 than *dolce far niente*] Italian: the sweetness of doing nothing.

492.36 W.C.T.U.] Woman's Christian Temperance Union, organized in 1873.

494.11 Ehrlich, Metchnikoff] German bacteriologist Paul Ehrlich (1854–1915) and Ilya Ilyich Mechnikov (1845–1916), who were jointly awarded the 1908 Nobel Prize in Physiology or Medicine for their work on immunology.

495.23 John Adams Thayer, then the proprietor of the magazine] American publisher John Adams Thayer (1861–1936), publisher and owner of *The Smart Set*, 1911–14.

496.5 *Humpen*] German: tankards, beer mugs.

499.11 Billy Watson's Beef Trust] Watson (born Isaac Levie, 1866–1945) was a well-known burlesque performer who appeared with a "beef trust" of chorus girls, each weighing as much as two hundred pounds.

505.15 *frokost*] Word meaning "breakfast" in Norwegian and "lunch" in Danish.

507.33–34 "Die Wacht am Rhein"] "Watch on the Rhine," patriotic German song with words by Max Schneckenburger (1819–1849) and music by Karl Wilhelm (1815–1873); the first line of its refrain, "Dear Fatherland, be tranquil," is quoted at 507.35.

512.5–6 Munson Line] Steamship company that operated between Atlantic seaports from the United States, Cuba, and South America, from 1899 to 1937.

517.13 days of Diego Velazquez] The Spanish conquistador Diego Velázquez de Cuéllar (1465–c. 1524), first governor of Cuba.

520.13 New York convention of 1924] The Democratic convention met in Madison Square Garden in New York, June 24–July 9, amid a heat wave and a spirit of dissension. Sixty candidates were nominated for the presidency; it took thirteen days and 103 ballots before the delegates nominated John W. Davis (1873–1955) and Charles W. Bryan (1867–1945).

521.18 *Ja*-convention at Chicago in 1940] Mencken lamented that Roosevelt's nomination at the 1940 Democratic convention, which he attended as a reporter, marked the end of the two-term tradition among American presidents, "held almost sacred in American politics for nearly a century and a half." Roosevelt's nomination, he wrote in August 1940, was managed "precisely like the Reichstag sessions that Hitler calls at long intervals"; the convention's delegates could only "vote *Ja* or they could be damned."

524.21 Mrs. FitzGerald] Susan Walker FitzGerald (1871–1943), social worker, advocate for women's suffrage, and member of the Massachusetts House of Representatives, 1923–25; at the 1920 Democratic convention she served as Alternate Delegate-at-Large.

524.27 Izetta Jewel Brown] Stage actor, advocate for women's suffrage, and politician (1883–1978) who had been married to William Gay Brown Jr., U.S. congressman from West Virginia, from 1914 to his death in 1916.

525.2–3 Hon. W. Bourke Cockran] Irish-born American politician William Bourke Cockran (1854–1923), U.S. congressman from New York, who served several terms in office between 1887 and 1923.

525.38 Hardshell Baptists] Members of the fundamentalist Primitive Baptist Church.

525.40 old Joe Robinson] American Democratic politician Joseph Taylor Robinson (1872–1937), U.S. congressman, 1903–13, and U.S. senator from Arkansas, 1913–37, as well as vice presidential candidate in 1928.

526.29–30 George Sterling's] American poet George Sterling (1869–1926), Mencken's close friend and the leader of a literary circle in Carmel, California. His books included *A Wine of Wizardry* (1909), *The House of Orchids* (1911), and *The Caged Eagle* (1916).

528.6–7 German Crown Prince] Friedrich Wilhelm Victor August Ernst (1882–1951), the last Crown Prince of Prussia and the German Empire.

533.2 family entrance to an old-time Raines law hotel] A law passed in New York State in 1896 allowed an exemption to the prohibition of liquor sales on Sunday for guests taking meals in a hotel, an establishment defined as having ten or more furnished rooms. To qualify for the exemption many saloons rented rooms in their buildings, which, often used for gambling and prostitution, became known as "Raines law hotels."

534.21   *mal de mer*] French: seasickness.

535.2   *Noble Experiment*] Phrase for Prohibition popularized by its detractors, derived from Herbert Hoover's speech accepting the Republican nomination for president, August 11, 1928, in which he referred to Prohibition as "a great social and economic experiment, noble in motive and far-reaching in purpose."

535.25   *Malzsuppe*] Spicy beef soup.

536.26   Union Hill, N.J.] Since 1925 a part of Union City; home to many beer houses because of its German American population. The establishment Mencken praises was the Alt Heidelberg.

536.38   *Stadtpfeiffer*] *Stadtpfeifer*, "town piper" in German, a municipal musician.

536.39   "Raymond" overture by Ambrose Thomas] Overture to *Raymond* (1851), opera by French composer Ambroise Thomas (1811–1896).

537.1   Philip Goodman] Broadway producer (1885–1940) who promoted the careers of Madge Kennedy and W. C. Fields; his hit shows included *Poppy* (1923) and *The Five O'Clock Girl* (1927). In 1918, Goodman published Mencken's *Damn! A Book of Calumny* and *In Defense of Women*.

537.19   *Urquell*] German: original source.

537.32   my publisher, Alfred Knopf] American publisher (1892–1984) of the firm that bears his name and of *The American Mercury* magazine, 1924–34. Mencken's lifelong friendship and partnership with Knopf began when they met in 1913.

537.32–33   celebrated Bach choir] The Bach Choir of Bethlehem, founded in 1898, inaugurated its annual festival in May 1900, which included the first complete American performance of Bach's Mass in B Minor.

540.2–3   friend in Detroit] Harry Rickel (1876–1965), lawyer who taught Mencken how to brew his own beer.

540.26–27   John L. Sullivan] American bare-knuckles boxer (1858–1918), world heavyweight champion, 1882–92.

541.10   *Seidel*] German: a large glass for beer.

541.11   *Leberwurst*] German: liver sausage.

541.15   *Zuschlag*] German: surcharge, premium.

543.8   Coxey's Army] Protest march of unemployed men, led by Ohio Populist politician Jacob Coxey (1854–1951), that headed to Washington, D.C., during the economic depression of March 1894 to demand job creation.

543.27–30   James Creelman . . . Dockstader] For Creelman, see note 358.15; Karl Decker (1868–1941), journalist for the New York *Journal* known for organizing, on behalf of publisher William Randolph Hearst, a jailbreak in Cuba in 1897 to free political prisoner Evangelina Cisneros; for Lew Dockstader, see note 255.2.

545.24–25 five years later, . . . set up in a cow pasture] Before the building of its campus was completed, the school (now Bryan College) began offering classes in 1930 in the high school building where John Scopes had taught evolution; it had broken ground for its campus in 1926.

546.10–11 village Hampden named Raulston] John T. Raulston (1868–1956), judge who presided over the trial of John Scopes. "Village Hampden" refers to Thomas Gray's "Elegy Written in a Country Churchyard" (1751), line 57. John Hampden (1594–1643) was a leader of the parliamentary opposition to Charles I.

546.11–12 Arthur Garfield Hays] Lawyer and author (1881–1954), a founder of the American Civil Liberties Union in 1920, serving as its general counsel until his death, and author of *Let Freedom Ring* (1925), *Trial by Prejudice* (1933), and *City Lawyer* (1942).

546.12 Dudley Field Malone] Lawyer (1882–1950) who was active in progressive political causes, including women's suffrage and the repeal of Prohibition, as well as being a well-known divorce lawyer.

546.12 John T. Neal] Law professor John R. Neal Jr. (1876–1959), who as dean of the University of Tennessee was one of seven faculty members dismissed by the university in 1923 for, among other reasons, support for the teaching of evolution.

548.37 the Areopagitica] *Areopagitica: A Speech of Mr. John Milton for the Liberty of Unlicensed Printing to the Parliament of England* (1644).

548.38 the trial of John Peter Zenger] Printer John Peter Zenger (1697–1746) emigrated from his native Germany to New York in 1710 and in 1733 founded the *New York Weekly Journal*, an antigovernment newspaper. The central figure in a libel trial, 1734–35, he was acquitted in a decision that set an important precedent for freedom of the press in the United States.

551.16 T. T. Martin] Southern Baptist minister Thomas Theodore Martin (1862–1939), dean of the School of Evangelism at Union University, 1910–30; author of *God's Plan with Men* (1912) and *Hell in the High Schools* (1923).

553.32–33 Edgar Lee Masters] Lawyer and poet (1868–1950), law partner with Clarence Darrow, 1903–1912; best known for his book *Spoon River Anthology* (1915). Mencken met Masters in 1913 but they did not become good friends until 1924.

555.6–7 we saw . . . Holy Roller camp] See "The Hills of Zion" in Mencken's *Prejudices: Fifth Series* (1926).

556.36 Gerald L. K. Smith] Gerald Lyman Kenneth Smith (1898–1976), Christian fundamentalist preacher and supporter of extreme right-wing organizations.

557.26   Doris Stevens] American social activist (1892–1963), an advocate for women's suffrage and member of the executive committee of the National Women's Party.

557.35   Lucy Stoner] A feminist, after Lucy Stone (1818–1893), leader of the women's rights movement, abolitionist, and orator.

563.25   Byblus or Zarephath] Byblos, Greek name for ancient Phoenician port of Gebal in present-day Lebanon, north of Beirut; Zarephath, Phoenician town on the Mediterranean coast south of Sidon.

564.28   *schochets* or *mohels*] Hebrew: *shochet*, ritual slaughterer; *mohel*, man who performs the rite of circumcision.

567.35   the Percys in England] Powerful aristocratic families from Northumberland.

568.15   handsome young man] Methodist missionary Caleb Guyer Kelly (1887–1960).

573.22   John xix, 41] "Now in the place where he was crucified there was a garden; and in the garden a new sepulchre, wherein was never man yet laid."

577.2   "How to Make Friends and Influence People"] Best-selling self-help book (1936) by writer and public speaker Dale Carnegie (1888–1955).

578.3   the Gadarene swine were possessed by devils] See Matthew 8:28–34, Mark 5:1–20, and Luke 8:26–39.

578.5–6   miracle at Cana . . . Prohibition] According to the gospel of John, Jesus's first miracle was to turn water into wine at a wedding at Cana. See John 2:1–11.

581.24–25   Chandala] One of the lowest Hindu castes.

582.4   rainbow . . . recollections of Genesis IX, 16] In the story of the flood in Genesis 6–9, God tells Noah in the flood's aftermath that the rainbow is a sign of his promise that "the waters shall no more become a flood to destroy all flesh."

582.15–16   Allenby . . . war] Edmund H. H. Allenby (1861–1936) commanded the British expeditionary force that won a decisive battle against the Turks in September 1918 on the plains of Megiddo, site of the battle of Armageddon prophesied in Revelations 16:14–19.

585.40   Lydia Pinkham] See note 442.3–4.

586.5–6   Gamaliel Bradford and Lytton Strachey] American biographer Gamaliel Bradford (1863–1932), author of *Confederate Portraits* (1914), *Union Portraits* (1916), *A Naturalist of Souls: Studies in Psychography* (1917), and other books; English writer and critic Giles Lytton Strachey (1880–1932), founding member of the Bloomsbury group whose books included *Eminent Victorians* (1918) and *Queen Victoria* (1921).

586.35–36 J. Ham Lewis . . . famous pink whiskers] American Democratic politician James Hamilton "Ham" Lewis (1863–1939), who served terms in Congress representing Washington state and Illinois, including six years, 1913–19, as Majority Whip in the Senate; also a lawyer and diplomat, he was known for his elegance, his red hair, and his fastidiously parted whiskers.

587.35 II Timothy iv, 7] "I have fought a good fight, I have finished my course, I have kept the faith."

589.11 rhetoricians . . . Chauncey M. Depew] American lawyer and politician (1834–1928), president of the New York Central Railroad, 1885–99, and a Republican U.S. senator from New York, 1899–1911; he was well-known as an orator, speaking at such events as the unveiling of the Statue of Liberty in New York Harbor and the opening of the Chicago Exposition of 1893. For W. Bourke Cockran (589.12), see note 525.2–3.

589.14–15 Julia Marlowe's] Julia Marlowe (1866–1950), English-born American Shakespearean actor.

592.12 no-more-scrub-bulls country] In western stock raising, breeders consider the mongrelizing influence of strays, or scrub-bulls, that have grazed and wandered on the land as wreaking havoc on herds in which care had been taken to produce thoroughbred or purebred breeds.

593.22–23 taken his famous walk] Withdrew his support. The phrase "take a walk" associated with Smith comes from a later speech, given in January 1936, when he castigated Roosevelt for betraying Democratic principles and, regarding the upcoming presidential campaign, declared that for "us millions of Democrats . . . there is only one of two things we can do, we can either take on the mantle of hypocrisy or we can take a walk, and we will probably do the latter."

593.23 Jim Farley] Democratic political operative James Farley (1888–1976), who ran Roosevelt's presidential campaigns in 1932 and 1936, and served as Postmaster General, 1933–40.

594.11–12 the divines . . . Billy Sunday] Samuel Porter Jones (1847–1906), American Methodist evangelist; Rodney "Gipsy" Smith (1860–1947), English evangelist who made frequent preaching tours of the United States; Charles Coughlin (1891–1979), Catholic priest and popular radio broadcaster during the 1930s who made anti-Semitic and pro-fascist statements in his broadcasts; Billy Sunday (1862–1935), American evangelist who gave up a career as a major-league baseball player to become one of the most influential preachers of the early twentieth century.

594.26 convention of the Townsend old-age pension fans] Francis Everett Townsend (1867–1960) was an American physician who in 1933 proposed the Old Age Revolving Pension Plan, also known as the Townsend Recovery Plan, which would dispense monthly pensions of $200 to U.S. citizens over 60 years of age, to be raised by a 2 percent tax on every business transaction.

His ideas soon gave rise to a social movement, sustained by thousands of local Townsend Clubs across the United States. Bitterly opposed to Franklin D.
Roosevelt, Townsend continued to attack the president's policies even after
the passage of the Social Security Act in 1935, and aligned himself with right-
wing figures such as Gerald L. K. Smith and Father Coughlin. Mencken attended the convention of Townsend's supporters in Cleveland in July 1936.

595.29–31   Coughlin . . . his own convention] The August 1936 convention of National Union for Social Justice, organization founded in 1934 by
Coughlin.

596.18–19   the late Huey Long . . . murder on September 10, 1935] American lawyer and populist Democratic politician Huey Long (1893–1935), known
as "The Kingfish," was governor of Louisiana, 1928–32, and U.S. senator,
1932–35. He was planning a run for the presidency in 1936 when he was shot
on September 8, 1935, and died two days later. Smith had been hired in 1934
as the national organizer of the Share-Our-Wealth Society, a network of clubs
supporting Long's plan for a national redistribution of wealth.

596.20–21   greatest rabble-rouser since Peter the Hermit] The French priest
and military officer known as Peter the Hermit (1050–1115) drummed up support for the First Crusade, raising an army that was defeated by the Turks.

DAYS REVISITED

600.9   "Souvenirs of Childhood and Schooldays / 1890–96."] One of the
scrapbooks given by Mencken to the Enoch Pratt Free Library in Baltimore.

615.11   *Kerl*] German: fellow.

615.29–30   *Bierabend*] German: night of beer-drinking.

621.1   "Morgen früh ist die Nacht herum."] German: tomorrow morning the
night is over.

624.11–12   ravings of John McCullough in the madhouse] Irish-born American actor (1832–1885), who in 1884 broke down during a performance in Chicago and was hospitalized in an asylum; after the incident, his "ravings" were
widely imitated.

630.38   E. Marlitt] Pseudonym of German novelist Eugenie John (1825–1887).

633.24   *Männerchor*] German: men's choir.

636.19–20   the Harrison Act] The Harrison Narcotics Tax Act of 1914 regu-
lated the use of opiates and cocaine.

640.37   Hay diet] Nutrition plan developed by American physician William
Howard Hay (1866–1940), advising the separation of food into different cat-
egories, such as alkaline and acidic, which were not to be consumed together.

647.6   *Wirte*] German: proprietors.

655.21 L. Hopkins] American illustrator Livingston Hopkins (1846–1927), who spent much of his career in Australia.

661.14 *Fabrik*] German: factory.

684.15–16 "H. L. Mencken / Photographs and Other Portraits / 1881–1936"] One of the books of photographs and personal effects that Mencken gave to the Pratt Library.

703.36 Hesketh Pearson] English popular biographer (1887–1964), author of *Bernard Shaw: His Life and Personality* (1942, published in the United States as *G. B. S.: A Full Length Portrait*).

709.10–11 the two Salvinis . . . Adams] Italian actor Tomasso Salvini (1829–1915) and his son Alessandro Salvini (1860–1896), who toured the United States; American actor Nathaniel Carll Goodwin (1857–1919), known mostly for his comedic roles; American actor Maude Adams (1872–1953), best known for her performance in *Peter Pan* (1905).

711.5–6 Sir Henry Irving's] English actor-manager (1838–1905) who dominated the London stage for many decades.

711.24–25 chambers of Pendennis] Fictional lodgings in London of the young writer Arthur Pendennis, eponymous hero of the novel (1848–50) by English writer William Makepeace Thackeray (1811–1863).

712.17 Minnie Maddern Fiske] Leading American stage actor (1865–1932) who promoted realism and Ibsen's plays on the New York stage.

713.28 That dame that wrote "Live alone and like it"] *Live Alone and Like It: A Guide for the Extra Woman* (1936) by Marjorie Hillis (1889–1971).

717.25 a fire in a night-club in Boston] At the Cocoanut Grove nightclub, November 28, 1942, in which 492 people were killed.

745.19 *Friedhof*] German: cemetery.

755.8 Josephus Daniels] American journalist (1862–1948) and secretary of the navy, 1913–21.

756.5 one of the stories she read] "The Widder Johnsing" (1893).

757.9–10 uproar over *The Second Mrs. Tanqueray*] Pinero's 1893 drama was a problem play about a wealthy widower's marriage to a woman with an immoral past.

760.17 the famous Anna Held milk bath story] The story spread about Polish-born French American actor Anna Held (c. 1870–1918) claimed that her skin was too delicate for her to bathe in anything but fresh milk.

760.19 Mrs. Patrick Campbell] English actor (born Beatrice Tanner, 1865–1940), renowned in particular for her roles in plays of Shaw and Pinero; the publicity story claimed that her nerves were so sensitive that she could not perform without a soundproofing of tan bark on surrounding streets and buildings.

761.17   Elihu Root or Nicholas Murray Butler] Elihu Root (1845–1937), American lawyer and statesman, secretary of war, 1899–1904, secretary of state, 1905–9; Nicholas Murray Butler (1862–1947), American educator and diplomat, president of Columbia University, 1902–45, president of Carnegie Endowment for International Peace, 1925–45.

761.34   Sandow] Eugen Sandow (born Friedrich Wilhem Müller, 1867–1925), Prussian-born bodybuilder and physical-culture proponent.

762.4–5   Immanuel Faisst . . . Doppler] Immanuel Faisst (1823–1894), German organist, conductor, composer, and teacher; Percy Goetschius (1853–1943), American music theorist who studied with Faisst and taught with him at the Stuttgart Royal Conservatory; Paul Klengel (1854–1935), German composer, conductor, and instrumentalist; Karl Doppler (1825–1900), Hungarian composer, conductor, and flutist.

767.29   the usual $4 for winning] "I say in the text that the standard fee was $4, win or lose, but it was actually $4 win and $1 lose" (Mencken's note).

769.23–24   Heywood Broun] American journalist (1888–1939), sportswriter, drama critic, and author of the syndicated column "It Seems to Me."

769.38   Greece had its discus thrower] The sculpture known as the Discobolus (Greek, "discus thrower"), by fifth-century B.C.E. sculptor Myron, shows an athlete about to hurl the discus.

775.23–24   refused, as Governor, to grant clemency to Thomas J. Mooney] The American labor leader Thomas Mooney (1882–1942) was convicted and sentenced to death for the bombing that killed ten and wounded more than forty during the San Francisco Preparedness Parade on July 22, 1916. Mooney's trial was marked by perjury by witnesses and other irregularities, and the case became a cause célèbre; his death sentence was commuted to life imprisonment in 1918. (Another man accused of the crime, Warren Billings, was tried separately.) Mooney was pardoned by California governor Culbert Olson in 1939.

776.33   Ray Lyman Wilbur] American physician (1875–1949), president of Stanford University, 1916–42, U.S. secretary of the interior, 1929–33.

776.34   Stephen S. Wise] Prominent American Reform rabbi (1874–1949).

778.9–10   Van Lear Black] American publisher (1875–1930), owner of the Baltimore Sunpapers.

781.5   Chattolanee water] "This water came from a spring in the Green Spring Valley near Baltimore. I got it in five gallon carboys costing $1" (Mencken's note).

784.6–7   "While the light . . . return."] Cf. hymn beginning "Life is the time to serve the Lord" from Hymns and Spiritual Songs by the English

hymnist Isaac Watts (1674–1748): "And while the lamp holds out to burn /
The vilest sinner may return."

785.23   The Liberal Church of Denver, Colorado] "The Liberal Church of
Denver was a racket. It offered bishoprics to all sorts of preposterous persons.
It got a lot of space in the newspapers by deciding to eliminate wine from its
communion service use and substitute a popular soft-drink. This soft-drink
was not Coca-Cola; I forget its name" (Mencken's note).

785.33   22.20] Cf. Ezekiel 22:20.

785.38   a Pecksniff] Villain who makes a show of piety in Charles Dickens's
novel *Martin Chuzzlewit* (1843–44).

789.26   the electrocution of half a dozen German agents] In June 1942, two
teams of saboteurs of four men each were landed by German submarines on
American soil, on Long Island and on the Florida coast near Jacksonville. The
Long Island group was spotted by a U.S. Coast Guardsman, who, fearing for
his safety, accepted a bribe to keep silent but reported the incident to his
superiors. Feeling misgivings about the mission shortly thereafter, one of the
saboteurs, George John Dasch (1903–1992), turned himself in to federal authorities. The information provided by Dasch led to the apprehension of all
the saboteurs. Six of the men were executed on August 8, 1942; the death sentences of Dasch and another man were commuted to lesser sentences because
of their cooperation with the FBI, and in 1948 they were released and sent to
West Germany.

Index

859

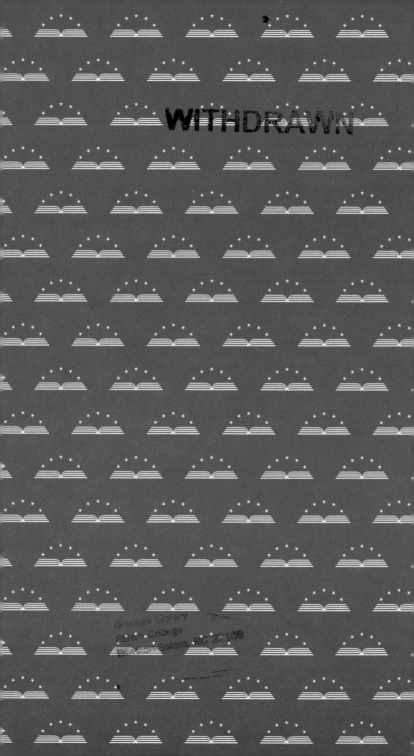